MARKETING MANAGEMENT

MARKETING MANAGEMENT
Strategy and Action

Henry Assael
New York University

KENT PUBLISHING COMPANY

Boston, Massachusetts

A Division of Wadsworth, Inc.

Kent Publishing Company
A Division of Wadsworth, Inc.

Editor: David Anthony
Production Editor: Pamela Rockwell
Text Designer: Catherine Johnson Dorin
Cover Designer: Trisha Hanlon
Production Coordinator: Linda Siegrist

Printed in the United States of America

2 3 4 5 6 7 8 9 — 88 87 86

Library of Congress Cataloging in Publication Data

Assael, Henry.
  Marketing management.

  Bibliography: p.
  Includes index.
  1. Marketing — Management.   I. Title.
HF5415.13.A87 1985   658.8   84-23534
ISBN 0-534-04788-2

Cover photo © Daniel Quat/Phototake

To Alyce

About the Author

Henry Assael is a Professor of Marketing and Chairman of the Marketing Department at New York University's Graduate School of Business Administration. He has led in the application of research and analytical techniques to marketing problems, particularly in the areas of market segmentation, product positioning, survey research methods, and evaluation of advertising. He has consulted to such diverse companies as AT&T, American Can, Nestlé, the New York Stock Exchange, and GTE.

Professor Assael is the author of *Consumer Behavior and Marketing Action.* He has published widely in the *Journal of Marketing, Journal of Marketing Research, Journal of Advertising Research*, and *Administrative Science Quarterly.* He has edited a thirty-three volume series on the history of marketing.

Professor Assael received a BA from Harvard University in 1957, graduating with honors, an MBA from the Wharton School in 1959, and a Ph.D. from the Columbia Graduate School of Business in 1965. He is listed in *Who's Who in America.*

Preface

Marketing management should be taught in a dynamic, applications-oriented framework. The course should deal with the marketing decisions managers make, the strategies they implement, and the consequences of these strategies. Yet many marketing management textbooks deal with the subject in a static, descriptive way, focusing more on marketing processes, functions, and institutions than on marketing strategies and action.

The motivation for writing this book was to demonstrate to the student the strategic environment of marketing, its dynamism and excitement. The strategic perspective of the book is offered with a firm conceptual foundation. Basic marketing concepts are linked to strategic applications. As a result, the book will enable the marketing student to better understand the development of marketing strategies in key areas such as product development, advertising, distribution, and pricing.

Since the book frequently cites the need to position products to meet customer needs, it might be wise to cite how it is positioned. The book offers three unique advantages that set it apart from others:

1. *Integration of product marketing planning and strategic marketing planning:* Product marketing planning develops strategies at the middle-management level, strategic marketing planning develops strategies at the top-management (corporate) level. Most marketing management books tend to emphasize one or the other, with a consequent lack of integration. As a result, product, price, promotional, and distribution strategies at the product level are not linked to broader issues of corporate growth and the firm's overall product mix. In *Marketing Management: Strategy and Action*, the strategic orientation is clearly established at both the product and the corporate level. The traditional emphasis on product marketing planning is linked to the more recent concerns with strategic marketing planning.

2. *An up-to-date strategic focus:* The depth of strategic applications set this book apart from others. Frequent examples of marketing strategies at both the corporate and the product level are used to illustrate marketing concepts, processes, and actions in response to a changing environment. Most of the strategic examples are taken from major American companies known to students. The strategic orientation should increase students' interest and motivate them to understand basic concepts. It should make it easier to generate classroom discussion based on the examples in the book.

3. *An integrated conceptual framework:* A conceptual structure is present in Part I based on three essential tasks of marketing managers: (1) identify marketing opportunities, (2) develop marketing plans to exploit these opportunities, and (3) implement these plans by introducing marketing strategies.

Marketing Management: Strategy and Action is organized around this conceptual framework. Part I describes the process of defining marketing opportunities and developing marketing plans. Three core sections of the book then extend this strategic perspective. Part II considers the identification of marketing opportunity by focusing on consumer and environmental factors that affect strategic decisions and by describing the informational needs for marketing planning. Part III is concerned with developing and implementing marketing strategies at the product level. This section first describes the identification of market segments and the development of new products to meet the needs of these segments. The basic components of marketing strategy are then described — product, promotion, price, and distribution. Each of these chapters presents a model of the planning process by which strategies are developed. Part IV considers marketing planning and strategy at the corporate level. Here, the concern is with evaluating longer-term marketing opportunities to ensure growth and with evaluating and controlling the firm's overall product mix.

The final section of the book presents applications of marketing planning and strategy in special sectors of marketing — international, service, and not-for-profit marketing. Special attention is given to these chapters since they are becoming increasingly important. Students are more interested in international marketing because of the preponderance of multinational companies. Services now represent a greater proportion of GNP than products, and service firms (particularly financial institutions) are recognizing the need for a more marketing-oriented approach. Nonprofit institutions such as museums, charitable organizations, and colleges are also recognizing the need to market their offerings. There is no separate chapter on industrial marketing because the strategic focus throughout the book is presented for both consumer and industrial goods.

The end-of-chapter questions are fairly comprehensive and should provide the basis for lively classroom discussion. They are not a simple rehash of the materials in the text but require integration of concepts and application of concepts to case situations. Many of the questions are actually mini-cases that serve as a basis for considering strategic applications. Utilizing these discussion questions should increase student involvement. A glossary of terms at the back of the book should also be of assistance to students.

Writing *Marketing Management: Strategy and Action* has been a rewarding task for the author. It has reinforced a basic belief that marketing is an applied field, albeit with a firm conceptual foundation, that must be taught in a strategic manner. Teaching it in this way brings concepts to life for students and facilitates the task of communicating these concepts.

Acknowledgments

The author owes thanks to many people who have helped in the preparation of this text. Special thanks are due to two colleagues, Mark Alpert at the University of Texas at Austin and Roger Kerin at Southern Methodist University. Their careful review of the manuscript and detailed comments proved invaluable. The following reviewers also provided valuable feedback at various points in manuscript preparation: James Nelson, University of Colorado; William Locander, University of Tennessee; Sharon Beatty, University of Oregon; Gary McKinnon, Brigham Young University; Bruce Stern and Robert Harmon, Portland State University; John Czepiel, John Keon, and Avijit Ghosh, New York University; Mary Joyce, University of Central Florida; Donald Norris, The American University; and Marlene Kahla, Stephen F. Austin State University.

Thanks are also due to the many people at Kent Publishing who assisted with sound advice and editorial support. David Anthony, marketing editor at Kent, provided guidance on various key issues involving organization, direction, and positioning of the book. His editorial assistance was most helpful. David McEttrick, formerly at Kent, first gave the author the idea of writing a book on marketing management. Pam Rockwell proved to be a faithful and devoted production editor. Her efforts ensured an accurate rendering of the book. As always, Tina Samaha pulled off a few miracles in overseeing production and ensuring schedules were met.

A number of secretaries at New York University spent many hours preparing the manuscript — Iantha Coleman, Marie Palumbo, and Willa Powell. Their faithful assistance is acknowledged. Special thanks go to Suzanne Diaz for her devotion to the necessary details required in final manuscript preparation. The author's research assistants — Susan Bechtel, Varda Haendel, and Julie Koeppel — were also very helpful in collecting and organizing information. Christine Eccleston also provided valuable help in the final stages of manuscript preparation. Thanks are due to Deanna Taylor at the NYU Library at the Graduate School of Business Administration for the many searches for references used in the book.

Finally and perhaps most importantly, thanks to my wife, friend, and colleague, Alyce Assael, for being a true partner in this effort. The long hours she spent collecting material for the manuscript was a necessary prerequisite to its writing. Her careful reading of each chapter and her many suggestions proved invaluable.

Contents

CHAPTER **3**

Opportunity and the Changing Marketing Environment

CHAPTER **4**

Marketing Planning and Strategy

PART **II**

Defining and Measuring Marketing Opportunity

CHAPTER **5** B.M ✓

Consumer and Organizational Buyer Behavior

CHAPTER 6 *B. M.* ✓

Marketing Strategies Based on Individual and Environmental Buyer Influences 148

CHAPTER 7

Marketing Information Systems and Marketing Research 186

PART III

Marketing Strategy and the Marketing Mix

CHAPTER 8 *B. M.*

Identifying the Target Market: Market Segmentation 223

PART **IV**
Strategic Marketing Planning

CHAPTER **18**   4/14

Strategic Marketing Planning and
Corporate Growth Strategies

Strategic Marketing Planning and Corporate Growth Strategies **565**

CHAPTER **19**   4/14

Evaluating the Company's Product Mix

Evaluating the Company's Product Mix **593**

CHAPTER **20**

Marketing Evaluation and Control

Marketing Evaluation and Control **623**

MARKETING MANAGEMENT

PART **1**

Marketing Planning and Strategy

The focus of this book is on marketing strategies; that is, the activities of firms to identify customer needs and influence customers to buy the firm's offerings. The development of marketing strategies requires (1) identifying marketing opportunities and (2) a planning process to formulate and implement strategies. This process is the subject of Part 1 of the book as follows:

- Identify Marketing — Chapters 2 and 3
  Opportunity
- Develop Marketing — Chapter 4
  Plans
- Implement Marketing — Chapter 4
  Strategies

Chapter 1 provides an overview and introduction by describing marketing.

The Nature of Marketing

FOCUS OF CHAPTER

Marketing is central to all business functions. This statement is true because marketing is defined as *all activities directed to identifying and satisfying customer needs and wants.* The marketing function is illustrated in Figure 1-1. Business organizations develop marketing strategies that are directed to customer needs. Organizations try to influence customers to buy their products through marketing strategies; that is, the *product* offerings to meet consumer needs, *advertising* to communicate product benefits, *distribution* to ensure product availability, and *price* to permit a reasonable exchange between buyer and seller at a profit to the firm. The customer will purchase according to his or her needs. Information on the customer's actions and on other aspects of the marketing environment is fed back to the business organization to provide a basis for developing future marketing strategies.

The focus of this book is on marketing strategy because strategies influence customer actions and customer actions determine sales and profits. Consider the following examples of marketing activities:

- Sony met the need for portable music in a faster-paced society by introducing the Walkman, a portable stereo recorder. The company gambled on a low price and intensive advertising to introduce one of the most successful electronic products in years.[1]

- In another electronic gamble that did not pay off, RCA lost about $575 million in its attempt to introduce videodisc players to the mass market.[2] The company felt there was a need for greater in-home entertainment and saw videodiscs as a means of providing variety. It did not foresee that lack of a recording capability would seriously inhibit sales, placing the product at a competitive disadvantage to videotape recorders. In 1984 it finally pulled its videodisc entry, SelectaVision, off the market.

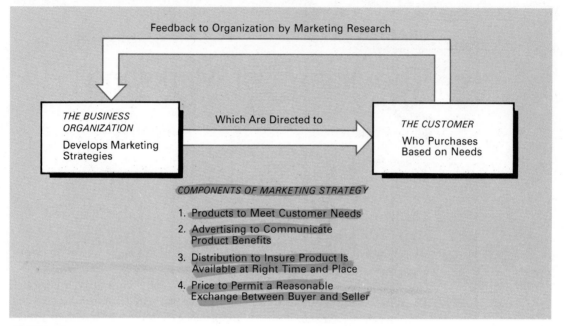

FIGURE 1-1
**Marketing encompasses all activities designed to identify and satisfy
customer needs**

■ Gillette has successfully transferred its expertise from men's to wom-
en's toiletries and cosmetics. In the late 1970s and early 1980s it introduced several products directed to well-defined needs. For example, it
introduced Dry Idea in 1978 to meet the need for a roll-on deodorant
that was not sticky; it introduced Mink Difference, a hair spray with
mink oil that leaves hair shinier and softer, in 1981; in 1982 it introduced Aapri, the first economically priced facial scrub for women. Gillette's formula for success is (1) identifying a consumer need, (2) developing new products, (3) backing them with heavy advertising, and
(4) distributing intensively through drug stores and supermarkets.[3]

■ Colgate-Palmolive did not fare as well as Gillette in the early 1980s. A
new management team found it necessary to divest the company of
many acquisitions because they were draining profits from the company's traditional toiletry products. Part of the problem was a failure to
develop any new products to satisfy changing consumer needs.[4]

■ Philip Morris, owner of Miller Beer, appealed to a calorie-conscious
market by being the first company to market a light beer successfully.[5]

■ Schlitz did not have the same ability to recognize marketing opportunity. Formerly number two in the industry, it dropped to fifth and was

recently acquired by a smaller company. The reason was a series of disastrous diversifications into nonrelated lines and a failure to develop new products to meet consumer needs in core markets the company was experienced in serving.[6]

The success stories just cited involved companies that could identify customer needs. They developed integrated marketing strategies — product development, advertising, distribution and pricing — directed to these needs. The failures involved companies that either misread customer needs or lost sight of corporate objectives in the marketplace.

In this introductory chapter we will first describe marketing and then discuss the development of marketing strategies by managers. Developing marketing strategies requires a planning process within the firm and an adjustment to forces outside the firm (such as competition, social and cultural norms, the economy, legal and political forces). Marketing planning is within the marketing manager's control and reflects *micromarketing* considerations. The marketing environment is outside the marketing manager's control and reflects *macromarketing* considerations. The primary focus of this book is on micromarketing activities: identifying marketing opportunity, planning marketing strategies and implementing them. This chapter concludes with a consideration of the external (macro) marketing environment to provide a more complete picture of the marketing process.

What Is Marketing?

Marketing involves a set of well-integrated activities in which the firm's resources are directed to opportunities identified by such environmental conditions as changing customer needs, competitive failures, and technological breakthroughs. The best way to bring this statement to life is to cite a company that has effectively directed its resources to the marketplace.

One of the most profitable marketing-oriented companies is Procter and Gamble (P&G). It has introduced some of the most successful consumer packaged goods: Crest toothpaste, Scope mouthwash, Folgers coffee, Charmin toilet tissues, Head & Shoulders shampoo. Procter and Gamble's successes provide a good example of what marketing is.

MARKETING IS IDENTIFYING CUSTOMER NEEDS

The customer bases new product introductions on known customer needs. One former executive states the philosophy succinctly:

> I don't think there's much secret to it. The company simply is tuned in to what consumers want, and it does a good job of making products to satisfy those wants.[7]

The development of marketing strategies based on consumer needs requires a research capability. P&G has a comprehensive marketing research capability. It is one of the few companies that maintains its own survey research staff capable of conducting interviews with a nationwide sample of consumers. Most other companies rely on outside marketing research firms. It conducts ongoing consumer research to obtain feedback on its product offerings and on its marketing strategies.[8]

MARKETING IS NEW PRODUCT DEVELOPMENT

P&G's growth is based largely on consistent new product introductions. It is testing a disposable diaper with a stripe that changes color when a baby wets, a shampoo in dry flake form, a paper-and-fabric sponge, and a sodium-free salt substitute without the usual bitter flavor.[9] It is also extending existing product lines by testing a liquid version of Tide and a new Ivory shampoo.[10]

P&G's success in new product introductions is not only attributable to identifying consumer needs, it is also a function of:

- long and patient basic laboratory research,

- a rigorous process of product development and consumer testing, and

- a selective process of external acquisition to obtain needed resources when they are not available internally.[11]

The result of the emphasis on new product development has been a doubling of the company's earnings on an average of every ten years.

MARKETING IS MAINTENANCE OF EXISTING PRODUCTS

The emphasis on new products at P&G does not diminish the need to nurture existing brands. Existing products are reinforced by high levels of advertising expenditures to maintain their cash-producing potential. For example, the company spent more than $100 million in advertising over two years to expand Folgers from a regional to a national brand.[12]

MARKETING IS TARGETING AND POSITIONING BRANDS TO CONSUMER SEGMENTS

Marketing strategies must be directed to specific segments of the market. (A **market segment*** is a group of customers with similar needs.) Products must be positioned to meet the needs of these segments. P&G is segmenting the toothpaste market by extending its leading brand, Crest. The toothpaste market can be divided into three distinct segments on the basis of consumers' emphasis on: (1) cavity prevention, (2) taste, or (3) white teeth. Crest was originally targeted to the cavity-prevention segment. But as fluorides began to be introduced

---

*All terms in bold type are defined in the glossary in the back of the book.

into more brands, P&G sought to maintain a competitive edge by introducing a new, improved version of the traditional Crest formula to appeal to the cavity-prevention segment,[13] and by introducing Crest in gel form to appeal to the taste segment.[14] The new-formula Crest is being positioned as providing twice the cavity protection of the original brand, whereas Crest in gel form is being positioned as a means of obtaining good taste while preventing cavities.

MARKETING IS DEVELOPING A MIX OF STRATEGIES TO INFLUENCE CONSUMERS

Companies must develop a ***marketing mix*** to influence consumers to buy their offerings. The marketing mix is frequently described as composed of *the four P's*: product, promotion (including advertising, personal selling, and sales promotions), place (distribution), and price. These elements must work together in a single marketing plan. For example, when P&G decided to expand Folgers coffee from its base on the West coast, it developed a well-integrated marketing mix that:

- ensured distribution through a strong sales force and trade discounts to retailers;

- followed up with an intensive advertising campaign to create brand awareness;

- offered price incentives initially through coupons and in-store discounts to influence consumers to try the brand; and

- maintained the product, once it was introduced, by widespread distribution, continuous advertising, and occasional sales promotions (coupons and discounts).

MARKETING IS EVALUATING THE ENVIRONMENT

So far, marketing has been defined in the context of strategies developed by the marketing organization. But in developing strategies, the organization must look to environmental forces beyond its control: competition, the economy, technology, government regulation, and changing consumer needs. P&G's chairman describes the need to constantly evaluate the **marketing environment:**

We study the ever-changing consumer and try to identify new trends in tastes, needs, environment and living habits. We study changes in the marketplace and try to assess their likely impact on our brands. We study our competition. Competitive brands are continually offering new benefits and new ideas to the consumer, and we must stay ahead of this.[15]

P&G has kept pace with changing societal and cultural norms such as the greater emphasis on convenience, a focus on self-enhancement, and consumer concerns with nutrition and weight control. The increasing proportion of working women has led the company to shift the emphasis in its advertising of household products from pride in homemaking to saving time. The greater proportion of single-person households has led the company to emphasize smaller sizes for many of its products.

The uncontrollability of environmental forces is illustrated by P&G's withdrawal of Rely tampons in 1981 after the product was linked to toxic shock syndrome in women. The company was held accountable for the product in several suits. But the greatest loss was to the company's good will and reputation as a result of the publicity.

MARKETING IS COMPETITION

Competition is one of the most important components of the marketing environment and is a pervasive element in the development of marketing strategies. Marketers must develop strategies based on the anticipated reactions of competitors. Information is required to enable the marketing organization to project competitive reactions. When P&G introduced Folgers in the East, it knew General Foods would protect Maxwell House, its leading coffee brand, by intensifying competition. P&G tried to preempt GF's moves by mailing millions of coupons to consumers offering forty-five cents off each purchase and providing retailers with a 15 percent discount from list price.[16] General Foods then matched many of these strategies. The Folgers example illustrates the marketing actions and competitive reactions that typify marketing strategy.

MARKETING IS SUCCESS AND FAILURE

Like any other business activity, marketing strategies involve risk and the possibility of failure. P&G has had its share of failures: Hidden Magic hair spray, Extend mouthwash, Tell toothpaste, and most costly of all, Pringle's potato chips.[17]

Pringle's illustrates the vulnerability of even the largest companies when they fail to gauge marketing opportunity correctly. P&G spent an estimated $300 million in developing Pringle's. Losses by the early 1980s were over $200 million.[18] The concept behind the brand was a potato chip that would stay fresh longer, break less often, and store more conveniently through improved packaging. The chips were a uniform size and stacked in packages similar to tennis ball cans. Within eighteen months of national distribution in 1975 it was apparent the brand was in trouble. Consumers found Pringle's had a bland, processed taste. One former executive said, "Pringle's tasted more like a tennis ball than a potato chip."[19] The company has since reintroduced the brand in a better tasting version.

How could a marketing-oriented company like P&G fail to evaluate correctly such a basic element as taste? "It got carried away with its own technological capabilities and lost sight of consumer needs."[20] The Pringle's experience demonstrates the importance of assessing consumer needs and the fact that even marketing-oriented companies are likely to misread the market on occasion.

What Was Marketing? A Historical Perspective

The philosophy that marketing strategies must be based on known consumer needs has come to be known as the ***marketing concept***.[21] This view, which began to win wide acceptance in the mid-1950s, seems so logical today that one wonders why marketers did not turn to it sooner. There are two reasons. First, marketing institutions were not sufficiently developed before 1950 to accept the marketing concept. Products were distributed and advertised on a mass-market basis; few were targeted to defined consumer segments according to their needs. The marketing concept requires a diversity of facilities for promoting and distributing products to smaller and more fragmented market segments. This diversity in marketing institutions did not exist before 1950, when the emphasis was on economies of scale in production and marketing.

The second reason the marketing concept was not widely accepted until the 1950s is that before that time there was no economic necessity to do so. There was little purchasing power during the Depression to spur an interest in identifying customer needs. During World War II and immediately thereafter, scarcities were prevalent. There was no competitive pressure to adjust product offerings to customer needs. Manufacturers sold what they made; they did not have to worry about making only what they could sell.

MARKETING WAS A PRODUCTION ORIENTATION

What was marketing like before 1950? When marketing was first recognized as a business activity at the turn of the century, it was essentially an adjunct of production and agriculture. It was seen as a means of exchanging standardized farm commodities and of bringing manufactured products to market. Management concentrated on increasing output and reducing manufacturing costs. Selling was secondary because, in most cases, high-quality products were scarce and could sell themselves. The former chairman of the Pillsbury Company summarized the earlier **production orientation** at the company as follows:

> We are professional flour millers. Blessed with a supply of the finest North American wheat, plenty of water power, and excellent milling machinery, we produce flour of the highest quality. Our basic function is to mill high quality flour, and of course (and almost incidentally) we must hire salesmen to sell it just as we hire accountants to keep our books.[22]

A good example of a company that was manufacturing oriented until recently is Polaroid. The company operated on the "love-it-or-leave-it" attitude of its founder, Edwin H. Land. Land developed products based on technological innovations and assumed there would be a demand. Generally he was right. But business began to turn downward in the 1970s with the increasing popularity of 35 millimeter cameras (spurned by Land). An attempt to introduce instant home movies also hurt the company. Research had shown there was little interest in home movies, but the company moved ahead at Land's urging and sustained huge losses.[23] Land resigned in 1979, and the company is now seeking to diversify to avoid overreliance on instant cameras.

MARKETING WAS A SALES ORIENTATION

Many companies shifted from a production to a **sales orientation** during the Great Depression of the 1930s because of a change from a shortage of products to a shortage of purchasing power. A sales orientation is fostered when consumers are unlikely to buy unless the company makes a substantial effort to influence them. The focus is not on the consumer's needs but on the company's selling effort.

Reliance on a sales orientation continued into the 1950s and is illustrated by General Electric's approach to marketing:

> What we could produce we could sell. Everybody wanted a home and needed a washer, so anyone who could build them could sell them. Mass thinking could prevail since everyone wanted what the neighbors had. Mass production could work because markets were homogeneous . . . forgiving . . . accepting minor differences in products. It was a decade of growth, of suburban tract houses, and the appliances inside . . . of cars and television sets. But it was basically selling, not marketing.[24]

DEVELOPMENT OF THE MARKETING CONCEPT

Many companies progressed from a sales to a marketing orientation in the mid-1950s as a result of the post–Korean War buyers' market. After the Korean War consumers were reluctant to buy durable goods. Many consumers had foreseen scarcities and purchased products at the onset of the war. Others had become more selective in their purchasing habits. As a result, supply exceeded demand in the face of consumer purchasing power. The economy experienced its first true buyers' market; consumers had the money but were not buying.

Some marketers reacted by continuing to be sales oriented — pushing the existing line, heightening selling efforts, repeating selling themes, unloading excess inventories. Others reacted with more foresight by recognizing the need to develop a greater diversity of products to meet customer needs. Minor differences in products were no longer acceptable.

One of the first companies to recognize the need for a marketing orientation was General Electric. The marketing concept that emerged from this period was stated clearly by one GE executive:

> The principal task of the marketing function . . . is not so much to be skillful in making the customer do what suits the interests of the business as to be skillful in conceiving and then making the business do what suits the interests of the customer.[25]

GE further elaborated on the marketing concept in its 1952 annual report:

> The marketing concept ... integrates marketing into each phase of the business. Thus marketing, through its studies and research, will establish for the engineer, the design and manufacturing person, what the customer wants in a given product, what price he or she is willing to pay, and where and when it will be wanted.[26]

The development of the marketing concept changed the nature of marketing activities by:

- *spurring new product development.* A greater diversity of products were required to meet customer needs.

- *emphasizing market segmentation.* Consumers with similar needs were identified (e.g., separate taste, convenience, and decaffeinated segments in the coffee market), and strategies were directed to these segments.

- *focusing on marketing communications.* Product benefits now had to be communicated to consumer segments. Whereas in a sales orientation advertising tended to be repetitive and simple, under the marketing concept advertising was more diverse and more likely to inform consumers about product benefits.

- *creating greater selectivity in personal selling.* Sales personnel first had to determine customer needs and develop their sales approach accordingly. Standardized sales approaches were no longer as effective.

- *creating more selective media and distributive outlets.* There are now more specialized magazines, greater uses of direct mail, and more specialty wholesalers and retailers.

- *encouraging marketing research.* Information on consumer needs was required. Consumer surveys were used more frequently to identify opportunity, and new products underwent more rigorous consumer testing.

The shift from a sales to a marketing orientation did not occur overnight. Some companies such as General Electric were quick to recognize the changes in marketing strategy required by the acceptance of the marketing concept. Other companies are still operating on the basis of a production or sales orientation. A recent convert to the marketing concept is Swift & Company, a leading meat producer. Until the mid 1970s, the company had "a purely manufacturing mentality of moving the highest possible volume of meat out the back door and worrying later about how to sell it."[27] A change of management resulted in an emphasis on new products geared to defined consumer needs and an expanded advertising budget to communicate product benefits. The head of consumer products at Swift reflects the change to a marketing orientation:

You find out what the consumer needs, develop a product, and give it a good trial before making a huge commitment. . . . I really want to know what we're going to do with the product after it's produced.[28]

Marketing Is Not Just Consumer Goods

The examples used to explain the nature of marketing might leave the erroneous impression that marketing activities primarily involve consumer products (products for final consumption). Marketing strategies are also required to market *industrial* goods (goods used to make products) and to market *services* for both the consumer and industry. To make matters more complicated, marketing is also required in *international* as well as domestic markets. If marketing activities are classified by type of market, then there are eight possibilities as illustrated in Figure 1-2: products or services marketed in either the consumer or industrial spheres in either international or domestic markets.

Most of the examples in this book deal with products in the consumer and industrial sectors. The basic principles of marketing are the same for industrial and consumer goods, but the applications differ. The principles for developing and implementing marketing strategies also apply to other boxes in Figure 1-2. Customer needs must be determined, target markets identified, products or services positioned to meet the needs of the target segment, and promotion, distribution, and pricing strategies developed. These steps are necessary for services as well as for products and in international as well as in domestic markets.

FIGURE 1-2
Types of marketing application

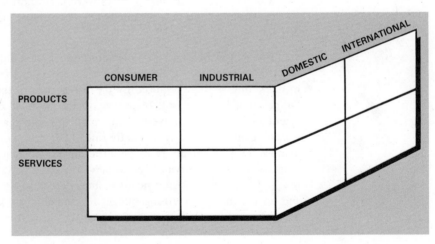

INDUSTRIAL MARKETING

Since industrial products are used in manufacturing or processing other products, they are purchased by **organizational buyers.** Compared to consumer buyers, industrial (organizational) buyers deal with products that are more technically complex. They are more likely to negotiate price and service with industrial sellers and are more likely to specify a product's characteristics.

Industrial sellers must develop marketing strategies to accommodate the needs of industrial buyers. Personal selling is likely to be the most important means of informing and influencing buyers in industrial markets, whereas advertising is likely to dominate in consumer markets. The new product development process is also likely to differ. Technological development is likely to be more important in industrial markets than in consumer markets. Service and maintenance are a more important part of the product offering and prices are more likely to be negotiated.

In general, the industrial sector has lagged behind consumer markets in adopting the marketing concept, applying principles of target marketing and product positioning, and using marketing research to identify consumer needs. But many industrial companies are currently adopting the methods, if not the strategies, developed in consumer marketing.

One formerly conservative industrial producer adopting a marketing orientation is Dun and Bradstreet. For almost 140 years the company operated by developing information services and selling them with little regard for customer needs. This approach was profitable until the computer and electronic revolution created competition. The company began to change its focus to develop new services geared to the needs of industrial users. By 1981 it had produced nearly 150 new offerings. It expanded its staff to include computer experts and marketing researchers. Formerly it was dominated by salespeople. The new philosophy is summarized by D&B's chairman: "Instead of concentrating on new ways to package and sell information we happen to have on hand, we are beginning to look at the changing needs of the marketplace and to devise ways to fill those needs."[29]

INTERNATIONAL MARKETING

Many American firms such as Coca-Cola and IBM have multinational operations and do over half their business abroad. Foreign firms such as Unilever and Nestlé have substantial operations in the United States. These firms are concerned with differences in marketing to countries outside their home base.

International marketing is riskier and more complicated than domestic marketing since marketers must deal with different cultures, economic systems, political regulations, and most important, a different set of consumer needs when marketing abroad. Marketing strategies for international markets differ significantly from those for the United States market because of:

■ *Cultural differences.* American marketers cannot assume marketing strategies developed in the United States can be transferred abroad because of different cultural norms.

■ *Language Differences.* The same themes cannot be used in different countries. Attempts at translation sometimes result in problems. For example, "Body by Fisher" translated in French into "Corpse by Fisher."[30]

■ *Differences in media.* American advertising strategies cannot be used abroad because of differences in media availability (e.g., fewer TV stations, not as many specialized magazines.)

■ *Differences in distribution.* Most countries do not have the well-developed distribution system characteristic of the United States.

■ *Differences in marketing research.* Marketers in the United States have come to rely on consumer surveys and consumer product tests in developing marketing strategies. Sophisticated research facilities do not exist in most foreign countries. For example, in many countries the majority of homes do not have telephones, precluding phone surveys.

■ *Differences in methods of doing business.* The American way of doing business is very different from that of other countries. For example, being late for business appointments is a prescribed ritual in many South American countries.[31]

SERVICES MARKETING

Services marketing is inherently different from product marketing. Banks, brokerage houses, restaurants, airlines, hotels, museums, and movie theaters all provide intangible services rather than tangible products. Services are not distributed as products are; they cannot be stocked. There is no transfer from a manufacturer to a wholesaler to a retailer and then to the consumer. Generally, the service transfer is direct from the seller to the buyer. In addition services are much more variable than products. Consumer products tend to be fairly standardized. Yet the services offered by a bank or a restaurant can vary significantly.

Much of the attention devoted to service marketing is due to the increased awareness of the marketing function among banks and other financial service establishments. Banks and brokerage houses have both become more marketing oriented because of deregulation of their activities, resulting in increased competition from nontraditional institutions. Banks have found companies such as Sears, J. C. Penney, and American Express offering financial services. As a result they have had to compete by identifying customer needs and positioning services more effectively — marketing requirements they had not known before. One bank executive said, "The seat of the pants approach simply doesn't work anymore. In this environment, a broad range of superior marketing skills may well be the key to survival."[32] Several large banks (Citibank, the Bank of New York) have begun to hire product managers from such staunch consumer goods companies as General Foods and Procter and Gamble to apply product marketing skills to banking services. In fact, one bank is "moving to a product management setup that is similar to the operation of consumer-goods companies."[33]

NOT-FOR-PROFIT MARKETING

One additional area of marketing deserves special attention, **not-for-profit marketing** (i.e., marketing by nonprofit institutions). Hospitals, museums, charities, educational institutions, and political associations are nonprofit institutions that have begun to recognize the importance of marketing their services. Marketing by nonprofit organizations has also come to be known as *social marketing* because these institutions generally market social services. Educational institutions are beginning to view their programs as products that must be sold to students, especially as they struggle with decreasing enrollments and greater competition for restricted funds. Charitable organizations are developing more personalized means to collect funds through direct mail campaigns by recognizing the different motives of donors. Hospitals are beginning to demonstrate more concern for the needs of their patients.

Several differences between profit and not-for-profit marketing highlight the importance of studying marketing in nonprofit firms. These firms:

- deal with public issues (health services, ecology, political action),
- are therefore more likely to be under closer public scrutiny,
- must appeal to both fund raisers and their own clients, and
- must pursue a greater diversity of potentially conflicting objectives to meet their goals.[34]

Marketing Planning: The Micro View

A description of marketing does not suggest the dynamic process required to formulate and implement marketing strategies. Marketing managers engage in a marketing planning process to identify opportunities and translate these opportunities into marketing strategies.

Marketing planning takes place at two levels, the product level and the corporate level. At the product level it identifies opportunities for new products or for revitalizing existing products and formulates strategies to take advantage of these opportunities. At this level it is the responsibility of product and marketing managers (middle management). At the corporate level marketing planning evaluates the firm's total mix of products. The corporate marketing plan is meant to examine alternative investment opportunities (new products, possible acquisitions, reformulating existing products) for long-term profit maximization. The corporate plan allocates resources to product managers to permit marketing planning at the product level. Corporate marketing planning is the responsibility of top management.

In this section we will first consider marketing planning at the product level (to be described in Part III of the book) and then at the corporate level (to be described in Part IV). Marketing planning provides a focus on marketing activities within the firm (the micro view). We will conclude by considering the institutions and systems needed to implement marketing strategies outside the firm (the macro view).

MARKETING PLANNING AT THE PRODUCT LEVEL

An outline of the marketing planning process is presented in Figure 1-3. The process is best illustrated by an example.

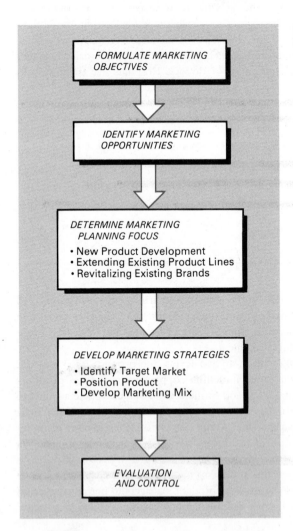

FIGURE 1-3
Marketing planning at the product level

Marketing Objectives

Marketing objectives are specific guidelines set by management for formulating marketing strategies. In 1982 Block Drug Company, a medium-sized producer of such pharmaceuticals as Nytol sleep aid tablets, Tegrin medicated shampoo, and Romilar cough syrup, identified an important area of opportunity — an acne preparation for the adult market.[35] This identification was based on a particular marketing objective: to search for opportunities in which the company can develop a distinct benefit compared to competition, but in relatively small markets. The company developed this objective because success in mass markets would attract larger and better-funded competitors, and the company did not have the funds to compete with the giants in the industry.

Opportunity Identification

This objective led the company to examine the acne preparation market. Existing products were positioned to teenagers. Marketing research showed that adults, particularly women, had acne problems and found teen acne remedies unsuitable because they left the skin dry and flaky. An area of opportunity was identified on the basis of an unmet need — an acne remedy for adult women that would leave moisture in the skin.

The Marketing Planning Focus

Management must determine the marketing planning focus — that is, whether marketing opportunity involves new or existing products, and if existing products, whether the focus is on product lines or individual brands.

New product development

The area of opportunity identified by Block Drugs required developing and testing a new product. By 1982 the company had developed an acne preparation without the drying agent in teen preparations and with a moisturizer. It was actively testing the product. Figure 1-3 shows that marketing planning might also be designed to extend existing product lines and revitalize existing brands.

Extending existing product lines

Many companies build on successful new product introductions by introducing extensions of the original brand. If Block's adult acne product is successful, it could expand the line to include face and skin moisturizers, cold creams, and hand lotions. The basis for any such expansion would be the success and good will established with consumers because of the moisturized acne preparation.

Revitalizing existing brands

Marketing planning is also required when attempting to revitalize an existing brand. Should competition enter the adult acne market and reduce Block Drug's market share, the company might revitalize its brand by introducing a new and improved formulation, reducing price, or intensifying advertising.

Developing Marketing Strategies

Marketing strategies must be the outcome of planning, whether one is dealing with new or existing products. Developing marketing strategies requires identifying the target segment, positioning the product, and formulating the marketing mix.

Target market identification

The market for Block Drug's acne preparation was well defined: working women between eighteen and forty-nine who have an acne problem and are dissatisfied with their current acne preparation. Marketing research estimated 10.6 percent of all women between eighteen and forty-nine, or 5.5 million women, are in this segment. Market tests of the product projected one-fourth of the target would try the product.

Positioning

A product's position represents the consumer benefits it seeks to convey and becomes the basis for developing the marketing mix. The acne product was to be positioned as a remedy that heals adult blemishes without the flaking and irritation caused by existing acne preparations.

Marketing mix

The marketing mix was composed of a well-integrated plan for advertising, pricing, and distributing the product. It involved a heavy advertising campaign to create awareness. The estimated advertising budget of $5 million was to be split, with 70 percent on network TV and 30 percent in women's magazines such as *Working Women, Working Mother* and *Self.* The product's retail price was to be $3.00 for a one-ounce tube, which was below the price of most other popular acne preparations. On introduction consumers would obtain discounts through coupons and price specials to encourage trial. Block planned to distribute directly to large drug chains and to use wholesalers to reach medium-sized and smaller drugstores. Block's sales force was instructed to visit retail stores to ensure the new brand had shelf visibility. Wholesalers and retailers would be offered trade discounts to ensure they stocked the brand.

Evaluation and Control

The process of evaluation and control requires tracking sales and marketing costs. Revenues and costs are compared to those projected in the marketing plan. If sales are below expectations, the product may have to be withdrawn or adjustments made in product characteristics or the marketing mix. Advertising, sales or distribution costs that are above expectation may also require corrective action.

MARKETING PLANNING AT THE CORPORATE LEVEL

An outline of the marketing planning process at the corporate level is presented in Figure 1-4. A corporate planning process was undertaken at Block Drug to evaluate the new acne preparation on the bases of corporate goals, alternative investment opportunities, and the "fit" of the new product with the company's overall **product mix.**

Corporate Objectives

Block Drug has several criteria for judging the performance of all new and existing products at the corporate level. The company expects to recoup its original investment within three years. In the first year of introduction, advertising expenditures should not exceed $5 million and total losses should not exceed $3 million. It expects a net return on investment of 15 percent within five years. A new products committee meets during the final phases of testing a new product to determine whether it is likely to meet these criteria. Market tests suggested that the new acne preparation would meet corporate objectives.

FIGURE 1-4
Marketing planning at the corporate level

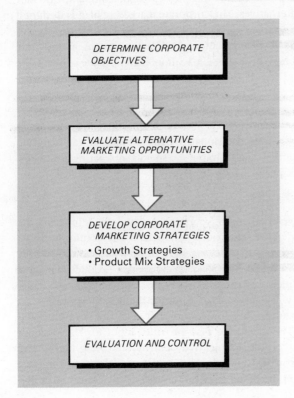

Evaluate Alternative Market Opportunities

The corporate marketing plan is also designed to evaluate alternative marketing opportunities. Block was considering two other new products, a tabular denture cleaner and an in-shower moisturizer. The new products committee will evaluate each alternative according to corporate objectives and determine whether one or more of the products should be introduced. Part of the review process is evaluating the company resources required to introduce each alternative (financial resources, technology, sales force, fit with other products). The acne preparation scored higher on these criteria than other new product opportunities.

Top management will also evaluate alternative investment opportunities. It will consider internal development versus external acquisition of companies. Block stresses internal development, but other companies such as Quaker Oats and Olin Chemical stress external acquisition as a means of introducing new products.

Develop Corporate Marketing Strategies

The corporate marketing plan is also meant as a planning document to ensure future growth. Companies can follow several growth strategies depending on their emphasis on revitalizing existing products, internal development of new products, or external acquisition of new businesses. Most companies do not rely on only one of these alternatives. The corporate marketing plan is designed to develop the optimum mix of existing and new products and existing and new markets to ensure future growth. Block Drug's investment in the new acne preparation would not have been possible without the existence of profitable products such as Tegrin and Nytol. The corporate plan must allocate the firm's limited financial resources to its leading brands to maintain their position, to other existing products to encourage growth, and to new products to further their development. Such allocation decisions are among top management's most important and difficult. These decisions are central to marketing planning since they determine the funds available to pursue specific marketing strategies, and thus influence product performance.

Evaluate and Control

The growth strategies developed in the corporate plan will determine the amount of funds to be expended on various products in the coming year. At the end of the planning period, top management will compare actual product performance to expectations for all the firm's product lines. Product managers will be asked the reasons for any deviations from original sales and cost estimates. Past product performance will then serve as input for the next corporate plan.

Marketing planning requires close integration between the corporate and product marketing plans. The corporate plan provides input for the product plan by specifying overall corporate objectives and by allocating funds. The product marketing plan provides input for the corporate plan by submitting sales and cost information on the brand to permit more effective future planning.

The Macromarketing System

In developing marketing plans, marketing management must consider the environmental forces that shape demand and influence the resources available to the firm. These environmental forces are part of a broader macromarketing system illustrated in Figure 1-5. At the center of the **macromarketing system** is the consumer, in keeping with the marketing concept. The next element is made up of the components of marketing strategy. These are directly within the control of the firm. The third element in the total marketing system is made up of facilitating institutions. These are systems required to implement marketing strategy — retailers and wholesalers for distribution functions, advertising agencies and media for communications, and marketing research

FIGURE 1-5
The macromarketing system

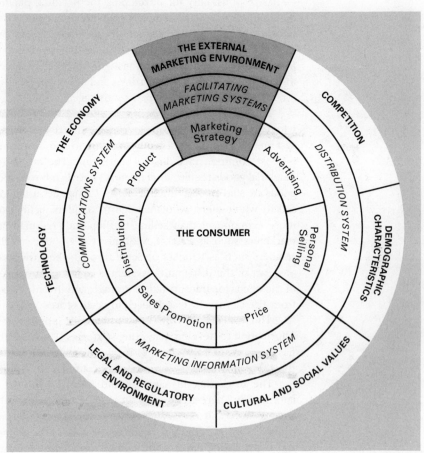

companies for marketing information. These facilitating systems are partially within the control of marketing management. Finally, the external marketing environment is made up of those forces which are not within management's control — the economy, technology, the legal and regulatory environment, social and cultural norms, the demographic makeup of the American consumer, and competition.

FACILITATING MARKETING SYSTEMS

Figure 1-5 depicts three marketing systems required to implement marketing strategies — a communications system, a distribution system, and an information system. The purposes of the *marketing communications system* are (1) to inform the consumer of the product's benefits and (2) to influence the consumer to buy. Three types of organization are involved in the marketing communications process: the marketing organization, advertising agencies, and media. The marketing organization — that is, the manufacturer of the brand being advertised — has responsibility for developing the product, positioning it, and financing communications. The company's advertising agency develops a campaign to inform and influence consumers. It also develops an overall communications mix composed not only of advertising, but of direct mail, in-store displays, free samples, and public relations. And the agency develops a media plan that might involve TV, radio, magazines, and newspapers. The media are responsible for running the ads developed by the agency.

The *marketing distribution system* delivers what the consumer wants, when and where the consumer wants it. There are various types of distribution system. The simplest is selling directly to the customer. This form of selling is most common in industrial marketing. The cost and complexity of many industrial goods require direct contact between buyer and seller. Most consumer goods are sold through intermediaries. Companies using intermediaries frequently sell to wholesalers, who then sell to retailers. Selling to a few wholesalers is more economical than selling to thousands of small retailers. Some national marketers such as P&G, Levi-Strauss, or Goodyear will sell directly to large retailers such as Krogers or Sears through their own sales staff.

Part of the distribution system is logistical support. It is required because of the needs for transportation, storage, and inventory control in moving goods from the factory to warehouses to retail stores and to the consumer's home.

The *marketing information system* supplies management with reliable information to develop marketing strategies. The marketing information system has three responsibilities: (1) to identify marketing opportunities, (2) to test the components of marketing strategy, and (3) to evaluate marketing strategy.

The marketing manager should be aware of the sources of marketing information. There are three basic sources: environmental sources, the marketing organization, and marketing research agencies. Environmental information is provided by government, trade associations, the company's sales personnel and distributors, and by the competition (through their actions and annual reports). The marketing organization also provides important information for planning such as sales data, cost information, return on investment, and cash flow.

The third source of information in the marketing information system is marketing research agencies. Marketing organizations frequently rely on research firms to evaluate marketing opportunities and marketing strategies. These firms conduct surveys to provide information on the consumer and run experiments to test components of the marketing mix.

THE MARKETING ENVIRONMENT

The environmental components in Figure 1-5 are the most difficult to evaluate because they are the most unpredictable and uncontrollable. Yet managers must try to assess future economic, technological, competitive, cultural, demographic, and regulatory trends.

Table 1-1 summarizes the changes that are occurring and are likely to occur into the 1990s in each of these components of the marketing environment. The changes in Table 1-1 will affect the development of marketing strategies. For example, Kellogg has begun to shift resources from children's cereals to adult cereals and to international markets largely as a result of environmental factors. The company realized that demographic changes were working against it. A long-term decline in the birth rate caused an industry-wide decrease in demand for cereals. Competition has also been a factor in the company's search for growth in international markets. Companies such as General Mills and Quaker Oats have shown "greater aggressiveness ... in bringing out new products during the past few years."[36] The economy has also influenced Kellogg's strategy. The sluggish economy in the early 1980s caused many consumers to buy low-priced private labels, cutting into the sales of the company's leading brand, Corn Flakes. The company's ability to search for new growth areas has also been affected by the legal and regulatory environment. A decrease in regulatory activity under the Reagan administration was a factor in causing the Federal Trade Commission to dismiss a monopoly suit against Kellogg.[37] The company could now focus on future growth. In Chapter 3 we consider the six factors listed in Table 1-1 and their role in defining marketing opportunity.

A Guide to the Organization of This Book

Considering marketing from the standpoint of marketing strategy and the marketing environment provides a basis for describing the organization of this book. The major focus is on planning and development of strategy by marketing managers. Figure 1-6 shows that these considerations are covered in Part I of the book.

Planning and strategy are then considered at the two basic levels in the marketing firm: the product level and the corporate level. Part II of the book

TABLE 1-1
Current Changes in the Macromarketing Environment

The Economy
Limited growth in real income
High interest rates
Increase in consumer credit
High cost of energy
Shortages of basic raw materials

Technology
Higher research and development budgets for product development
Improved communications capabilities
Greater importance of video technologies
Expansion of technologies for transmitting information
Increased capabilities for in-home shopping
Increased capabilities for transfer of funds
Improved facilities for data analysis

Legal and Regulatory Environment
Continued rigorous enforcement of anti-trust laws
Weakening of Federal Trade Commission's regulatory authority over
   advertising
Weakening of Environmental Protection Agency's regulatory authority over pol-
   lution and emission controls
Reduction in enforcement powers of Consumer Products Safety Commission to
   recall defective and unsafe products

Cultural and Social Values
Increased emphasis on self-fulfillment
Trend toward "voluntary simplicity" in life styles
Increased emphasis on immediate gratification
Greater ecological concerns

Demographic Characteristics
Increased proportion of singles
Increased proportion of working women
Aging of United States population
Later marriages and fewer children in families
Increased level of education

Competition
Increased levels of competition
Greater emphasis on price competition
Greater competition from nontraditional sources (e.g., Sears competing with
   banks for financial services)
Greater need for new product introductions to maintain profits
Greater competition from abroad

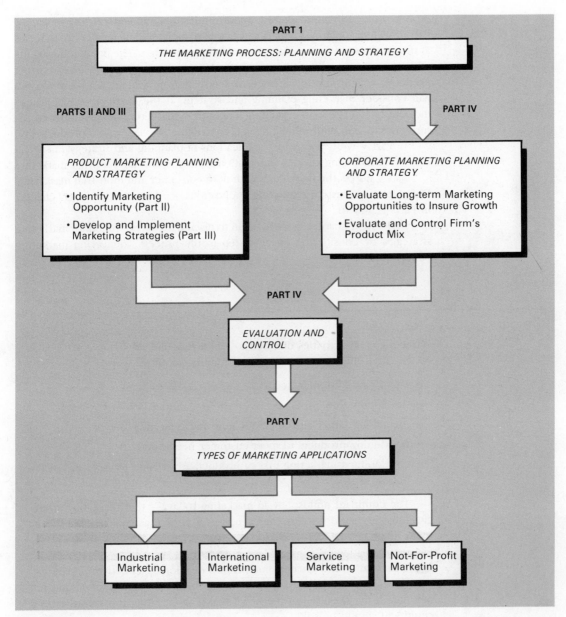

PART 1

THE MARKETING PROCESS: PLANNING AND STRATEGY

PARTS II AND III

PART IV

PRODUCT MARKETING PLANNING AND STRATEGY

- Identify Marketing Opportunity (Part II)

- Develop and Implement Marketing Strategies (Part III)

CORPORATE MARKETING PLANNING AND STRATEGY

- Evaluate Long-term Marketing Opportunities to Insure Growth

- Evaluate and Control Firm's Product Mix

PART IV

EVALUATION AND CONTROL

PART V

TYPES OF MARKETING APPLICATIONS

| Industrial Marketing | International Marketing | Service Marketing | Not-For-Profit Marketing |

FIGURE 1-6
A guide to the organization of this book

deals with identifying marketing opportunities for new and existing products. Part III will be concerned with developing and implementing marketing strategies at the product level to exploit marketing opportunities. The basic components of the marketing mix will be described — strategies for new and existing products, and promotional, price, and distribution strategies. In Part IV, we will consider marketing planning and strategy at the corporate level. There the concern will be with evaluating longer-term marketing opportunities to ensure growth, and with evaluating and controlling the firm's total product mix.

In Part V we will consider applications of planning and strategy in special sectors of marketing effort — international, service, and not-for-profit marketing.

As we noted, the book deals with both consumer and industrial marketing. Examples of industrial marketing applications are presented in each chapter in Parts II and III.

In the next chapter, we will begin to discuss the development of marketing strategies by considering the first step in the process, identifying marketing opportunities.

Summary

Marketing is all activities directed to identifying and satisfying customer needs. According to this definition, marketing requires:

- identifying customer needs,
- developing new products,
- identifying target customers for new and existing products,
- positioning products to meet customer needs, and
- developing a marketing mix of product, advertising, selling, and distribution strategies.

The dominant philosophy in marketing today — that marketing strategies must be based on customer needs — is known as the marketing concept. This concept became dominant in the mid 1950s because of tighter economic conditions, increased competition, and greater selectivity in buying. The result was a greater emphasis on developing effective marketing strategies. Prior to the marketing concept, there was a production and sales orientation that resulted in the belief that whatever the firm manufactured could and should be sold.

The marketing concept was developed primarily by companies producing consumer goods. But marketing strategies are also required to market industrial goods and to market consumer and industrial services. In addition, marketing is required in international as well as in domestic markets. The basic principles in developing and implementing marketing strategies apply equally to consumer, industrial, service, and international marketing. Differences do exist. For example, industrial marketing is more likely to stress personal selling, service and maintenance, and technological change. International marketing is riskier and more complicated because of the need to account for differences in media, distribution, business customs, and language across markets. These differences must be considered in developing marketing strategy.

The diverse activities of marketing must be brought together in a marketing plan. Marketing planning is required to identify opportunities and translate them into marketing strategies. Marketing planning takes place at two levels — the product level and the corporate level. At the product level it identifies opportunities to develop new products and to revitalize existing ones. The product plan will provide for the development of the product and the advertising, pricing and distribution strategies required to market it. The corporate marketing plan evaluates the firm's total mix of products in the context of longer-term marketing opportunities.

The emphasis on marketing planning and strategy provides a focus on marketing activities within the firm. This focus represents a micromarketing view. Marketing management also operates in a broader marketing environment (the macro view). The macromarketing environment includes additional institutions needed for implementing marketing strategy — advertising agencies, marketing research firms, distribution outlets. These outside institutions are represented in three types of systems in the marketing environment: communications, distribution, and information systems. The macromarketing environment also includes environmental forces marketing management must consider in developing marketing strategies: the economy, technology, the legal and regulatory environment, social and cultural norms, and competition. In the next chapter, we will introduce marketing planning and strategy by considering the identification of marketing opportunity.

Questions

1. What characteristics of Procter and Gamble make it one of the country's most successful marketing firms?

2. Assume you are at a meeting of the executive committee of a food company that is considering diversifying into higher-growth areas by acquiring companies in electronics and microcomputers. You argue that without marketing expertise, such acquisitions are risky and dangerous. You say that marketing is central to all business activities, and the company does not have the marketing know-how in these areas.

   □ Support your argument with some of the factors cited in this chapter.

     □ What arguments could be presented to refute the notion that marketing is central to all business activities?

3. In what ways did the introduction of Folgers by P&G into the eastern market represent an *integrated* marketing effort?

     Why is such an integrated effort important in developing marketing strategies?

4. Consider the statement "Marketing strategies must be based on known consumer needs."

     Why did the acceptance of this statement in the 1950s represent a marked departure from the past?

     What are the implications of the statement for:

     □ advertising strategies,

     □ product strategies,

     □ market segmentation,

     □ marketing research, and

     □ strategies to gain competitive advantage?

5. Assume the chairman of the board of a large oil company states, "The marketing concept is fine for companies providing packaged goods. These are differentiated products in highly competitive industries that need to advertise to stimulate demand. But we are producing standardized products in a situation of scarcity. Our main concern is not satisfying consumer needs, but trying to discover and exploit scarce resources."

     □ As executive vice president for marketing, you take exception to the chairman's statement. On what grounds?

     □ Under what environmental conditions might the chairman become more concerned with satisfying consumer needs?

6. In this chapter we noted the switch by Dun and Bradstreet from a sales to a marketing orientation. In the past the company emphasized its electronic capabilities rather than customer needs. But now the company's president recognizes that "introducing technology to a business for its own sake is a dangerous and costly mistake."[38]

     □ What did the president mean by this last statement? What are the implications for marketing strategy?

     □ What examples can you cite from this chapter of companies that "introduced technology for its own sake."

7. Assume a bank is developing a marketing strategy to introduce a new electronic funds transfer (EFT) service. It assigns a former product manager at Procter and Gamble the responsibility for developing the

marketing plan for the new service. The product manager can probably transfer certain experiences in marketing products at P&G to the development of a marketing plan for the EFT service, but not all experiences.

☐ What areas of product marketing might apply to the marketing of the new banking service?

☐ What areas of product marketing cannot be transferred to the marketing of the new service?

8. A fund raiser for a charitable organization is considering applying principles of market segmentation in order to (1) better understand donors' decisions and (2) target advertising appeals to nondonors who can be influenced to give.

☐ What information would be required to segment the market?

☐ How could such information be applied in developing marketing strategies?

9. What differences in the product marketing planning process in Figure 1-3 might occur:

☐ in developing a new product compared to repositioning an existing product?

☐ in developing a new product line compared to extending an existing product line?

10. How might the corporate marketing planning process in Figure 1-4 for developing a new product internally differ from that for acquiring the same product through the purchase of another company?

11. What would be the role of the three facilitating systems — communications, distribution, and information — in Block Drug's (1) evaluation of the adult acne preparation and (2) development of marketing strategy for the proposed brand?

12. Consider the changes in the macromarketing environment listed in Table 1-1. How might any of these changes have affected:

☐ Pepsi Cola's decision to buy Pizza Hut?

☐ Campbell Soup's decision to introduce Soup-For-One?

☐ Sears' decision to acquire Coldwell Banker, the largest real estate firm in the country?

☐ AT&T's decision to enter a joint venture with Knight-Ridder newspapers to test market in-home video technologies?

☐ Stroh's decision to acquire Schlitz, a direct competitor?

☐ Kellogg's decision to seek growth by introducing adult cereals and by expanding into foreign markets?

Notes

1. "The Selling of the 'Walkman,' " *Advertising Age,* March 22, 1982, pp. M2–M4, M37.

2. "Losses Lead RCA to Cancel Videodisk Player Production," *The New York Times,* April 5, 1984, pp. A1 and D25.

3. "New Products Program Really Cutting it at Gillette," *Advertising Age,* March 1, 1982, pp. 4, 67.

4. "Colgate Works Hard to Become the Firm it Was a Decade Ago," *The Wall Street Journal,* November 23, 1981, pp. 1, 8.

5. "Anheuser Tries Light Beer Again," *Business Week,* June 29, 1981, p. 136.

6. "What Went Wrong," *Advertising Age Magazine,* reprinted from April 13, 1981 and April 20, 1981 issues.

7. "At Procter & Gamble, Success Is Largely Due to Heeding Consumer," *Wall Street Journal,* April 29, 1980, p. 1.

8. *Wall Street Journal,* April 29, 1980, p. 35.

9. "Some Big Ideas from P&G," *The Wall Street Journal,* June 18, 1981, p. 29.

10. "Personality Change for P&G," *The New York Times,* March 23, 1984, pp. D1, D3.

11. "P&G: Past Is Prolog," *Advertising Age,* January 11, 1982, p. 48.

12. *Business Week,* October 1, 1979, p. 82.

13. "Colgate One-Ups Crest," *Advertising Age,* March 23, 1981, p. 102.

14. "Warring Toothpaste Makers Spend Millions Luring Buyers to Slightly Altered Products," *The Wall Street Journal,* September 21, 1981, p. 37.

15. *Wall Street Journal,* April 29, 1980, p. 35.

16. "Why Folger's Is Getting Creamed Back East," *Fortune,* July 17, 1978, pp. 68–9.

17. "P&G's New Product Onslaught," *Business Week,* October 1, 1979, p. 77.

18. "In Spite of Huge Losses, Procter & Gamble Tries Once More to Revive Pringle's Chips," *Wall Street Journal,* October 7, 1981, p. 29.

19. Ibid., p. 42.

20. Ibid., p. 29.

21. For a fuller description of the marketing concept, see Robert F. Keith, "The Marketing Revolution," *Journal of Marketing* 24 (January 1960): 35–8; and J. B. McKitterick, "What is the Marketing Management Concept?" in *The Frontiers of Marketing Thought and Science,* Frank M. Bass, ed. (Chicago: American Marketing Association, 1957).

22. Keith, "The Marketing Revolution," pp. 35–8.

23. "Polaroid Seeks Business Focus," *Industrial Marketing,* October 1981, pp. 8, 29.

24. John F. Welch, Jr., "Where is Marketing Now That We Really Need It," General Electric Speech, Reprint of address to the Conference Board Marketing Conference, October 28, 1981.

25. McKitterick, "What is the Marketing Management Concept?" p. 78.

26. General Electric Company, *1952 Annual Report,* New York, 1952, p. 21.

27. "A Meatpacker Discovers Consumer Marketing," *Business Week,* May 28, 1979, p. 164.

28. Ibid., p. 170.

29. "How D&B Organizes for a New-Product Blitz," *Business Week,* November 16, 1981, p. 87.

30. J. Douglas McConnell, "The Economics of Behavioral Factors on the Multi-National Corporation," in Fred C. Allvine, ed., *Combined Proceedings of the American Marketing Association,* Series No. 33 (1971), p. 264.

31. Roger Ricklefs, "For a Businessman Headed Abroad Some Basic Lessons," *Wall Street Journal,* January 16, 1978, p. 2.

32. "Now Bankers Turn to a Hard Sales Pitch," *Business Week,* September 21, 1981, p. 62.

33. Ibid., p. 67.

34. Philip Kotler, *Marketing Management* (Englewood Cliffs, N.J.: Prentice-Hall, 1980), p. 681.

35. The example of the adult acne preparation is cited by permission of Block Drug Co. Thanks are due to Mr. James Iseman, product manager at Block Drug, for providing the information reported in this section.

36. "Outlook Brightens for Profitable Kellogg," *The New York Times,* March 25, 1982, p. D1.

37. Ibid., p. D6.

38. *Business Week,* November 16, 1981, p. 90.

CHAPTER 2

Identifying Marketing Opportunity

FOCUS OF CHAPTER

The development of marketing strategies has two prerequisites: (1) the identifying of marketing opportunities and (2) the development of marketing plans to formulate and implement strategies. In this chapter and the next we will deal with identifying opportunities in the marketplace; Chapter 4 describes marketing planning and the development of marketing strategies.

The identification of marketing opportunities is essential to the firm because it is closely linked to growth and profitability. Opportunities can be identified on the basis of many factors, for example:

- identifying unmet consumer needs,
- identifying new markets from demographic or social changes,
- determining new uses for existing products,
- increasing use of existing products,
- developing new technologies or improving existing ones, and
- recognizing the vulnerability of competition to new or improved product entries, price promotions, advertising campaigns, or other marketing strategies.

This list shows why opportunity identification is so closely tied to profitability; it is generally associated with new product introductions or market expansion for existing products.

Three basic factors determine opportunity: the consumer, the marketing environment, and the firm's resources. In this chapter we will look at these three factors. Because of the importance and diversity of the environmental component in defining opportunity, we will consider the marketing environment in more detail in the next chapter.

The Process of Identifying Marketing Opportunity

Figure 2-1 depicts the process of identifying marketing opportunity. Formulating *corporate guidelines* provides the initial focus for opportunity identification. The firm's position on such issues as research and development, risk, diversification, return on investment (ROI), and market leadership will determine which opportunities it should pursue and which it should discard. An important corporate objective for Kodak, as stated by its chairman, was to ensure the company's leadership in amateur photography for the rest of the century. This objective required Kodak to stay in the forefront of new products and was instrumental in the decision to introduce the disc camera.

The next step in Figure 2-1 is *defining the market.* Is it a market the firm has not entered before, or is it an existing market the firm wishes to expand? In either case the market must be defined and evaluated using criteria such as potential growth, risk, and investment requirements.

The definition of the broad market area leads to the simultaneous consideration of the three cornerstones of opportunity identification in Figure 2-1: the consumer, the marketing environment, and corporate resources. *Consumer*

FIGURE 2-1
Identifying marketing opportunity

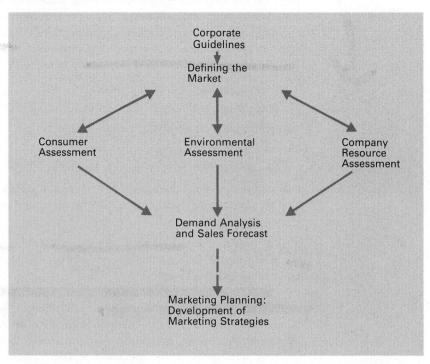

assessment first requires need identification. Regarding Kodak's disc camera, the key question is whether consumers need the flexibility and convenience provided by disc, and whether they are willing to trade up from the less expensive and popular Instamatic cameras. A favorable consumer assessment would prompt a company to test the product, identify a target market, and then introduce the product.

The disc camera is an example of a new product introduction. It is important to remember that opportunity analysis also applies to existing products and markets: for example, Procter and Gamble's strategy of market expansion for Folgers coffee into the Eastern market.[1] Such a strategy required prior evaluation of reactions of Eastern coffee drinkers to a Western coffee, especially since Easterners like their coffee stronger and Folgers is known as a mild coffee.

Evaluation of opportunity also requires an *assessment of the marketing environment*. Most important is the competitive environment. In developing the disc camera Kodak knew that competition would soon enter. The question is whether these companies are likely to drive the price of the camera down, causing Kodak to rely primarily on the film for profits. Technology is another aspect of the marketing environment. Technological risk is great when capital investment is high and the rate of technological change is rapid, as is the case for pollution-control equipment or personal computers. The legal and political environment of marketing must also be considered in assessing opportunity. Firms considering entry into the nutritional food market have become aware of more stringent labeling requirements.

Assessment of the marketing environment demonstrates that for every marketing opportunity there is a parallel risk and threat. In Kodak's case the risks are competitive entry, misestimation of customer needs, technological obsolescence, or a change in economic conditions that might affect discretionary purchases.

Concurrent with consumer and environmental assessment is *assessment of corporate resources*. Any firm, large or small, must consider whether its know-how, manufacturing facilities, marketing capabilities, and financial resources warrant market entry or expansion. Quaker Oats' acquisition of toy companies, restaurants, and chemical operations was an attempt to enter high-growth areas. But the company did not have the know-how to run these operations and only deflected its resources from its more profitable core business, food.[2] When RCA introduced SelectaVision it clearly had the marketing and technological know-how. But the subsequent withdrawal of the product was the result of a failure to recognize an important customer benefit that videodiscs do not have, the ability to prerecord TV programs.

The combination of consumer, environmental, and corporate assessment in Figure 2-1 permits the firms to make a preliminary estimate of market potential. Early forecasts of consumer demand and market potential give management a basis for gauging marketing opportunity. If the assessment is positive, the firm will pursue one of three broad strategic directions:

1. new product introduction,
2. market expansion for an existing product, or
3. refinement of marketing plans for an existing product.

Once it has identified the area of opportunity, the firm will go through a planning phase in which it develops marketing strategies. The marketing opportunity for Kodak's disc camera was defined when research showed that amateur photographers wanted to be able to take photos that were beyond their perceived competence. As a result, the positioning strategy utilized the theme "you'll be able to take pictures you may have been missing before," and advertising emphasized specific features such as automatic film advance, rapid flash recycling, and the technology of disc film.[3] The strategy clearly emerged from the definition of opportunity.

In the rest of this chapter we will consider each of the steps in Figure 2-1 in more detail. (Sales forecasting and marketing planning will be considered in later chapters.)

Corporate Guidelines

Corporate guidelines provide the initial direction for identifying opportunities and developing marketing strategies. Corporate guidelines progress from the broadest (and vaguest) sense of purpose to more specific performance targets. These guidelines are described on three levels in Figure 2-2: (1) the corporate mission, (2) corporate objectives, and (3) performance goals.

CORPORATE MISSION

Top management should provide the corporation with a sense of purpose — a corporate mission. If one accepts the marketing concept as stated in Chapter 1, then this sense of purpose must be directed to satisfying consumer needs. In an early article Theodore Levitt stated that management was sometimes plagued with "marketing myopia" — that is, a shortsighted view of the company's mission that is based on production and engineering criteria rather than marketing criteria.[4] When Levitt wrote (1960), many companies were still saddled with the idea that their resources should determine marketing opportunity rather than the reverse. Well-engineered products would sell themselves. As a result the corporate mission was defined in product terms. After 1960 economic necessity, competition, and greater consumer sophistication caused management to define their corporate mission in marketing terms.

General Electric has long recognized the need to state its corporate mission in consumer rather than product terms. The manager of consumer marketing for GE said that the "We bring good things to life" campaign reflects his company's efforts to reorient its planning focus "off the product and on to people and their values."[5] Because of this statement of corporate mission GE insists on bringing its marketing people and product engineers into close

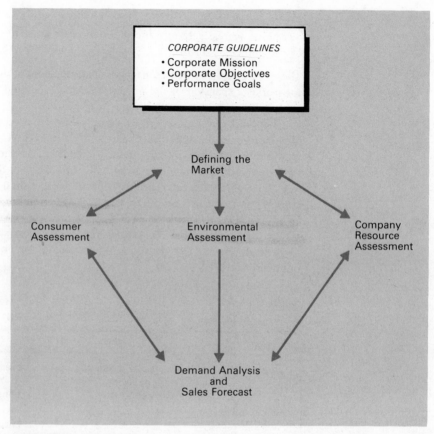

FIGURE 2-2
Corporate guidelines

cooperation to ensure that products will be directed to consumer needs. As a result GE's home products division talks of "home comfort systems, not air conditioners, of garment care, not iron and washing machines."[6]

Environmental changes require changes in the definition of corporate mission. For example, over the years AT&T has evolved its corporate mission from developing the demand for telephone services to telecommunications to communications in general. The 1984 divestiture of the operating companies allowed AT&T to compete in broader areas, expanding the corporate mission beyond telecommunications to information transmission and processing.

CORPORATE OBJECTIVES

Corporate objectives are more specific guidelines than corporate mission for opportunity identification and strategy development. PepsiCo's drive to beat out Coca-Cola for industry leadership led to two specific corporate objectives:

1. Attack markets in the U.S. heavily dominated by Coke, and

2. Move aggressively into the international market to cut out Coke's two-to-one edge abroad.[7]

These objectives give Pepsi's management guidelines for identifying opportunities for market expansion of the product. Clearly, it should allocate resources to compete with Coca-Cola head-on.

The link between corporate mission, corporate objectives, and opportunity identification is illustrated in Table 2-1 by the example of Standard Dairy (a fictitious name representing an actual company). In the mid-1960s Standard Dairy began diversifying away from its traditional dairy line because of a well-founded fear that greater health consciousness would cause a decrease in consumption of dairy products. By 1975 its corporate mission had evolved from providing the highest-quality dairy products to providing nutritional food products to consumers. This change reflected a clear shift (1) from dairy to food products and (2) from a product orientation to a consumer-benefits orientation.

TABLE 2-1
Corporate Guidelines for Standard Dairy; 1965 versus 1985

	1965	1985
Corporate Mission	Maintain a leadership position in selling existing dairy products.	Develop food products that have distinctive nutritional benefits.
Low Calorie Division's Mission	*	Develop food products that provide weight control benefits yet taste good.
Corporate Objectives	Utilize existing manufacturing and distribution facilities.	Use state-of-the-art technology, but be ready to acquire new managerial, marketing, manufacturing, and financial resources.
	Consider new markets only if they represent extension of existing markets.	Enter new markets when (1) unmet consumer needs, and (2) competitive vulnerability have been demonstrated.
	Consider new product entries and market expansion only if the product will not draw significant resources from existing products.	Support new entries and market expansion on the basis of long-term profitability, not short-term cash flow.

* The Low Calorie Division did not exist in 1965.

Standard Dairy's top management formulated corporate objectives to give more specific guidelines for opportunity identification. New or existing markets should be considered that:

1. can be entered with existing state-of-the-art technologies,
2. have few entrenched competitors,
3. represent an opportunity to satisfy unmet consumer needs, and
4. provide a learning experience as a basis for long-term growth.

From the statements of corporate mission and goals, management of the company's Low Calorie Division decided to investigate the opportunity to introduce a new line of low-calorie desserts, since these products would fit well into the division's weight control mission (see Table 2-1), and the new line would fulfill its corporate objectives.

PERFORMANCE GOALS

Many companies provide corporatewide **performance goals** to evaluate new product entries or existing products. Minimum performance levels may be established on the basis of sales volume, market share, return on investment (ROI), and payback period. Standard Dairy established such performance goals in the early 1970s when it began to emphasize new products in food lines. The following corporate guidelines were in operation in 1985:

Criterion	Performance
ROI	Not less than 20 percent
Payback on investment	Not more than four years
Earnings as a percentage of net revenue before taxes	Not less than 25 percent
Average sales volume per year over the first five years	Not less than $20 million per year

Defining the Market

Before undertaking a formal opportunity analysis, the firm must define the market category it wishes to investigate. This requirement involves three steps as illustrated in Figure 2-3: (1) the firm must determine the market's boundaries; (2) it must consider the market's characteristics; and (3) it must estimate the size of the total market.

DEFINING MARKET BOUNDARIES

The purpose of identifying a market's boundaries is to determine the relevant scope of the market and the product categories that fall within this market definition. The delineation of the relevant market then permits a firm to identify competition and estimate market size.

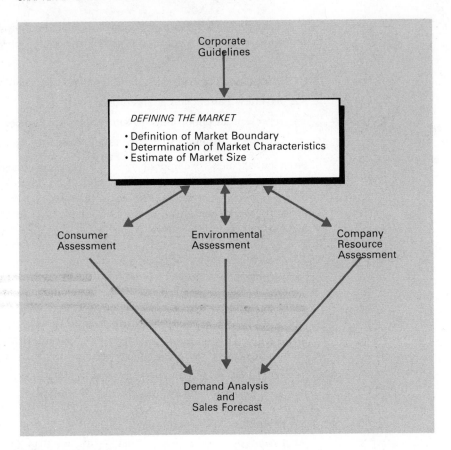

FIGURE 2-3
Defining the market

We will consider two methods for defining market boundaries: (1) establishing product categories by markets (that is, develop a **product/market matrix**), and (2) delineating markets on the basis of a hierarchical process of market definition.

The Product/Market Matrix

One approach to defining a market's boundary is to identify product categories by market type. GTE uses this approach in identifying the markets for its lighting products. It develops a product by market matrix (see Figure 2-4). The four basic lighting product categories are listed down the side. Three types of markets are identified: consumer, industrial, and private label. This produces twelve markets. The shaded boxes represent markets in which GTE has representation. The crossed-out boxes represent areas that are not relevant for entry. The white boxes represent markets that could be considered for

PRODUCT   MARKET

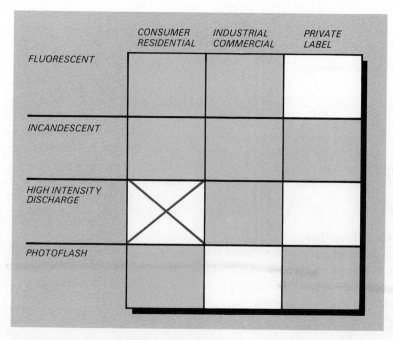

FIGURE 2-4
A product/market matrix for
GTE's lighting products
division*

*Shaded Areas Are Served Markets
X'd-Out Box Is Not a Relevant Market

entry. Of particular interest is the possibility of entering the industrial photoflash market. Identification of this potential area of opportunity would lead GTE to research industrial photoflash use, competition in that area, and the size of the market.

Hierarchical Market Definitions

A market's boundary can be defined hierarchically by starting with the broadest definition of the market and then progressively narrowing it until the market is defined at the brand level. For example, at the broadest level a consumer might consider the alternatives of buying a new car, going on a more extensive vacation, or remodeling the house. Automobile manufacturers do not consider themselves competitive with the travel industry or furniture manufacturers, but they must evaluate economic conditions and the likelihood that consumers will consider alternative expenditures. Having decided to purchase a car, a consumer might now consider product types (sedan, sports car, or station wagon) and then the specific category (luxury, intermediate, standard, compact, subcompact in either a domestic or foreign make). Assume a consumer decides to buy an imported compact sedan. The next step is to evaluate various brands in the chosen category. These steps are summarized on the next page.

Generic Category	Automobile
↓	
Product Type	Sedan
↓	
Product Category	Imported Compact
↓	
Brands	Toyota/Celica/Honda

Although the sequence may vary depending on the consumer, these steps can be used to define the specific markets for automobiles. Thirty submarkets can be identified from this sequence, three product types by five product categories for imports and domestic makes. An auto manufacturer would then investigate opportunities in one or more of the categories defined by this market structure.

DETERMINING MARKET CHARACTERISTICS

Market structure analysis identifies the relevant market for product entry or market expansion. The next step in market identification is evaluating the characteristics of that market. Urban and Hauser cite six desirable characteristics of any market targeted for entry or expansion:[8]

1. good potential for market growth,
2. ease of entry and competitive vulnerability,
3. stability in market demand,
4. no need for significant capital investment,
5. an increasing share of market for the brand, and
6. a high likelihood of a profitable return on investment.

In combination, these criteria represent an ideal situation. However, some criteria may actually deter profitability. The firm that restricts market entry to those markets requiring low capital investments may be robbing itself of the best opportunities for growth. The firm that considers only growth industries may fail to see lucrative opportunities to position existing brands to specific submarkets in stable industries (e.g., the market for light beer in the general beer market). Overall, however, these six criteria represent a reasonable basis by which to evaluate corporate resources.

SIZE OF THE MARKET

The total size of the relevant market must be estimated early in opportunity analysis. Management must have some preliminary idea of market potential in order to develop sales forecasts for the company's brands. Using Standard Dairy's possible entry into the low-calorie dessert market as an example, preliminary estimates for this market are given in Table 2-2. Dollar estimates of the total diet food market are approximately $1.5 billion. Standard Dairy estimates

TABLE 2-2
Estimating the Size of the Low-Calorie Dessert Market

Total market for low-calorie foods (excluding diet soft drinks)	$1.5 billion
Market for low-calorie desserts (30% of total market for low-calorie foods)	$450 million
Market for low-calorie gelatins/puddings (18% of total for low-calorie desserts)	$ 80 million
Market for low-calorie ice cream/frozen yogurt (27% of total for low-calorie desserts)	$120 million
Primary market addressed by Standard Dairy	$200 million
Remainder of low-calorie dessert market	$250 million

the current market for low-calorie desserts to be $450 million or 30 percent of the diet food market. The two submarkets representing Standard Dairy's area of opportunity are low-calorie puddings and ice cream. These submarkets are estimated at $200 million or about 45 percent of low-calorie desserts. Once it has defined the market, a company can analyze marketing opportunity by assessing consumer needs, the marketing environment, and corporate resources.

Consumer Assessment

Evaluating consumer needs and reacting to new or existing company offerings are central to the identification of marketing opportunity. Marketing research plays a key role in obtaining valid and reliable consumer information to permit management to decide whether sufficient opportunity exists, and if so, how much investment is warranted.

IDENTIFYING CONSUMER NEEDS

The consumer assessment phase has several steps (see Figure 2-5). First, the company must identify consumer needs and determine whether these are being met by current offerings. Marketing research is generally required to define unmet needs. Consumers are asked to rate the importance of certain product benefits (coffee flavor, strength, richness, economy, convenience, no caffeine, and so forth). If certain needs are not met by existing brands, there is a "gap" in the market, representing opportunity for a new product.

Standard Dairy identified an unmet need for good-tasting diet products, particularly diet desserts. A study it conducted found that dieters rated diet desserts or artificially sweetened snacks inferior in taste to regular products. Management saw that a basic need among dieters was not being met — the need for low-calorie desserts and sweet snacks that would provide adequate taste benefits.

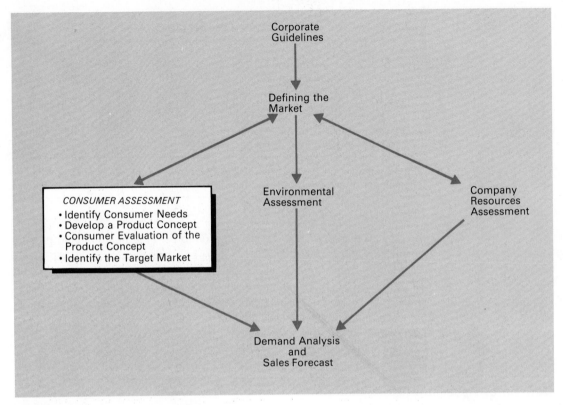

FIGURE 2-5
Consumer assessment

Evaluating consumer needs may prompt companies to reexamine existing products as well as introduce new ones. Both Colgate and Procter and Gamble determined that appeals to cavity prevention through fluoridated toothpastes have become so commonplace that consumers no longer consider this need as important as they used to. Consumers are now emphasizing flavor and mouth-freshening properties. This change in the priority of consumer needs has prompted both companies to come out with a line extension of their Colgate and Crest brands in gel form.[9]

DEVELOPING A PRODUCT CONCEPT

The second step in consumer assessment is developing a product description or *concept* designed to meet consumer needs. Three types of concept are most likely to be tested in evaluating marketing opportunity: (1) a description of a new product (Taster's Choice freeze-dried decaffeinated), (2) a description of a reformulated product (Crest in gel form), (3) a description of a repositioned product with no change in its physical characteristics (Anheuser-Busch's Light beer). In each of these cases a description of the concept is developed and presented to the consumer for testing. For example, Anheuser-Busch sought to reposition its natural Light beer by changing the advertising from a male-oriented barroom setting to a more female-oriented home setting in which the beer is associated with good food. It identified an opportunity to direct advertising to a neglected segment of the light beer market — women.[10] Before undertaking such a basic change in strategy, Anheuser-Busch would wish to test consumer reactions to the shift in positioning.

An Example of a Product Concept

At Standard Dairy marketing management and Research and Development jointly formulated specifications for a low-calorie dessert line on the basis of technology available to the firm. A **product concept** description was prepared to obtain dieters' reactions. The description pictured several flavors with the following statement:

> Good 'n Lite [the proposed name for the product line] is the good-tasting dessert that lets you enjoy sweets while still watching your weight. It's a soft pudding that comes in six delicious flavors. Each cup contains 40 calories. Just stick it in the freezer and eat it when you want. No defrosting necessary. Now you don't have to be frustrated when you crave an in-between meal or after-dinner treat.

The Product Concept as a Means of Positioning the Product

The product concept is meant to convey the positioning of the product. The term *product positioning* is used frequently in this book. A product's position is the set of product benefits that management wants to convey to a defined target segment to meet its needs.

Marketers have used various approaches to position a product. For example, a product can be positioned by:

1. *its attributes and features* (Subaru advertises Turbo Traction and four-wheel drive);
2. *problems the product can solve* (Crest prevents tooth decay);
3. *the feelings and emotions attached to the product* (Lincoln-Mercury advertises the luxury of the Mark VII Continental);
4. *use or application* (Campbell advertises soup for lunch on noontime radio);
5. *price and value* (Volkswagen originally positioned itself as a car that provided more value and economy for the dollar than the larger domestic makes);
6. *focusing on the consumer* (Nice 'n Easy hair coloring advertises "It lets me be me"); or

7. *focusing on a competitive product* (Avis advertises "We're number 2" relative to Hertz).

CONSUMER EVALUATION OF THE PRODUCT CONCEPT

The third step in consumer assessment requires determining consumer reactions to the product concept and developing an initial positioning strategy. Companies will test the concept on consumers before committing themselves to producing the product. If a specified proportion of the target group say they intend to buy, the company will then produce prototypes and ask consumers to use them to determine consumer reactions to the actual product.

IDENTIFYING THE TARGET MARKET

A target market (also called a market segment) is a group of consumers with similar needs that can be identified by marketing management and targeted for marketing effort. Marketing effort may require developing new products to meet the needs of the target market, directing advertising communications to the target, and distributing the product to this group. The allocation of marketing resources must be based on the different needs of various target segments. For example, Nestlé cannot introduce one instant coffee to meet the needs of a decaffeinated segment, a flavor segment, and an economy segment. Therefore, it introduces separate brands to appeal to each. Further, a marketing firm must be selective in its application of limited resources. It cannot be all things to all people. Thus Nestlé has limited its definition of the coffee market to instant coffee and has chosen not to compete with General Foods in the ground roast market.

Market segments must first be identified by their needs. For example, Nestlé determined that the target market for its Taster's Choice freeze-dried decaffeinated brand was decaffeinated coffee drinkers who were dissatisfied with the taste of their current brand. The common needs of this segment were for a coffee that was (1) good tasting and (2) decaffeinated. Having identified a segment of consumers by common needs, the marketer must then determine the characteristics, life styles, and attitudes of the target segment. These characteristics will guide management in developing marketing strategies. From the product concept and product use tests, Nestlé might have found that consumers who emphasize a good-tasting decaffeinated coffee are older urban dwellers without children. This demographic profile will help management select the magazines and TV programs most likely to reach the target group. Having identified the target group, Nestlé then positioned Taster's Choice decaffeinated, using the claim that the freeze drying process retains the coffee flavor.

Consumer evaluation of the product and definition of the target market gives management a sounder basis for estimating sales of the product. But the firm must assess the environment in which it will be operating and evaluate its resources before it can develop marketing plans to introduce a product.

Environmental Assessment

Success in identifying profitable marketing opportunities depends to a great extent on management's ability to evaluate and track a changing environment. The key word is *change.* Competitive, economic, technological, and demand conditions are likely to change. Management must track current environmental change and attempt to predict future change. One author points out that assessing environmental change is a basic weakness of marketing planning. He presents the following situation:[11]

Environment	Corporate & Marketing Objectives	Marketing Strategy	Organizational Structure	Company Resources
1984	1982	1980	1975	1970

Here we see a company that is operating with objectives appropriate for the environment two years ago. Marketing strategy lags behind objectives. Organizational structure and the company's resources lag even further behind. Although this situation does not apply to all companies, it does suggest that many organizations cannot adapt rapidly enough to take advantage of current opportunities. There is too much vested interest in outdated organizational structures and resources.

Figure 2-6 lists the environmental factors that management must assess to identify opportunity. Each deserves close attention and will be considered in detail in the next chapter.

Evaluating Corporate Resources

In evaluating marketing opportunity a company must consider external forces (the consumer and the marketing environment) and internal forces (the internal resources in the company's control — namely, its managerial, marketing, production and financial facilities). Identifying lucrative opportunities is pointless if the firm does not have the resources to exploit these opportunities. A firm is more likely to pursue an opportunity if resources are in place to exploit it. For example, Nestlé had the production, distribution and sales resources, and the marketing know-how to develop Taster's Choice freeze-dried decaffeinated coffee.

THE STRATEGIC WINDOW

Management's desire to pursue opportunities with existing corporate resources represents an objective of convergence — that is, a desire for a match between marketing opportunity and company resources. A company is more likely to pursue defined opportunities if it has the required resources listed in Figure 2-7.

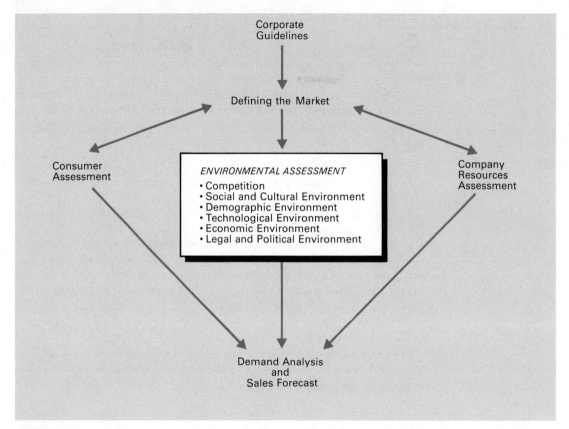

FIGURE 2-6
Environmental assessment

But there are times when criteria of divergence might be more appropriate than criteria of convergence. If the firm does not have the resources to pursue marketing opportunities, sometimes it should acquire them. One writer states the problem by formulating the idea of a **"strategic window."**[12] If the firm's strategic window is "open," this means that the firm's competencies are at an optimum to meet marketing opportunities. This situation does not occur frequently, because opportunities created by environmental change are dynamic, whereas the firm's organization and resources are more static. Corporate organization and resources tend to lag behind marketing opportunities. If the firm has the resources to meet opportunity, well and good. But a strategic window may be open even if the firm does not have the resources. Being tied to criteria of convergence might inhibit pursuing the best opportunities.

New resources are most frequently obtained through acquisition and diversification. In the early 1970s Philip Morris recognized the risks of relying

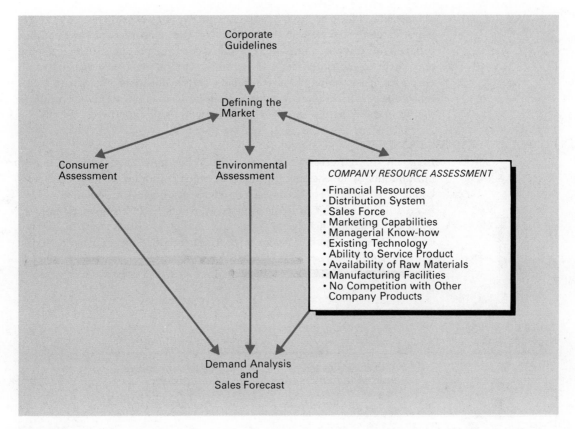

FIGURE 2-7
Evaluation of company resources

only on its cigarette brands. It decided to take action when cigarette advertising was banned from TV and radio, and diversified by acquiring Miller beer. The company quickly changed Miller's positioning from a beer for the upper class to one for blue-collar consumers, a much heavier beer-drinking group. It then recognized the opportunity for a light beer and successfully introduced Miller Lite. In both cases the "strategic window" for Philip Morris was opened by using the firm's resources to exploit opportunities. But Philip Morris acquired the resources to do so.

Management must carefully assess the risks in a policy of acquisition to obtain new resources. Such strategies can backfire if (1) basic managerial competence in the new business area does not exist or (2) marketing opportunity is not carefully assessed. In the early 1970s Olin embarked on an ambitious program of diversification, aggressively marketing products from camping equipment to industrial film and chlorides. The problem was that it had no corporate or marketing rationale for many of its acquisitions. By the late 1970s it had divested itself of many of these acquisitions to concentrate on "products that fit in much better with its established corporate expertise."[13]

CORPORATE RESOURCE ASSESSMENT

Generally, the criteria of convergence listed in Figure 2-7 are the ones used most frequently in assessing the match between corporate resources and marketing opportunity. For example, consider Coca-Cola's introduction of Diet Coke. It is likely that Coca-Cola assessed its resources in a systematic fashion, possibly by having management rate the extent to which each of the ten criteria listed in Figure 2-7 were met. The procedure it might have used is illustrated in Table 2-3. Management first evaluates the importance of each criterion based on corporate objectives. Each criterion is rated on a ten-point

TABLE 2-3
Hypothetical Example of Evaluating Company Resources for Introducing Diet Coke

	IMPORTANCE BASED ON CORPORATE OBJECTIVES (10 = MOST IMPORTANT 1 = LEAST IMPORTANT)	×	MATCH WITH COMPANY RESOURCES (10 = PERFECT MATCH 1 = POOREST MATCH)	=	EXPECTED UTILITY
1. Required Financial Resources	8	×	3	=	24
2. Utilize Existing Distribution System	3	×	9	=	27
3. Utilize Existing Sales Force	3	×	9	=	27
4. Match Existing Marketing Capabilities	8	×	9	=	72
5. Managerial Know-How	10	×	9	=	90
6. Existing Technology	4	×	10	=	40
7. Ability to Service Product	2	×	9	=	18
8. Availability of Raw Materials	2	×	10	=	20
9. Manufacturing Facilities	4	×	10	=	40
10. No Competition with Other Company Product	9	×	2	=	18
			Overall Resource Utility Score	=	376
		Corporate Norms for New Products Based on Past Experience		=	300

scale with 10 being most important and 1 being least important. In this example Coca-Cola rates four factors as most important; managerial know-how, required finances, marketing capabilities, and no competition with other company products. Other factors such as utilization of the same channels of distribution and the same sales force were not nearly as important.

The next step would be to rate the match between a company's resources and the resources required for entry into the area of opportunity. Again each criterion is rated 1–10 on convergence. The match was excellent for Diet Coke on all criteria but two; financial resources and possible competition with other products produced by the company. Coca-Cola might have been concerned about the huge advertising outlays required to introduce the brand nationally and the risk of using the Coke name for the first time for a product other than the company's flagship brand. Further, the company was probably concerned that Diet Coke might compete with its other major entry in the diet cola market, Tab, and thus yield less revenue than expected.

After rating each factor in Table 2-3, management multiplies the importance rating (column 1) by the convergence rating (column 2), producing a utility score for each of the ten criteria (column 3). The managerial ratings in Table 2-3 resulted in an overall resource convergence score of 376. If we assume that the average score for other products introduced by Coca-Cola was 300, we can see from the score for Diet Coke that the company has the resources to exploit the marketing opportunity for the brand.

Demand Analysis and Sales Forecasting

The final step in identifying marketing opportunity is developing a preliminary sales forecast. On this basis management can decide if it should develop marketing strategies for possible market entry or market expansion.

One simple method of obtaining a sales forecast is to calculate demand for the product category, estimate the probable market share for the company's brand, and multiply the two. Table 2-4 provides an illustration using the example

TABLE 2-4
Preliminary Sales Forecasts for Good 'n Lite

1: ESTIMATED SHARE OF COMPONENTS OF LOW-CALORIE DESSERT MARKET		
Size of low-calorie pudding market		$80 million
Estimated share of low-calorie pudding market; 20 percent of total =	$16.0 million	
Size of low-calorie ice cream market		$120 million
Estimated share of low-calorie ice cream market; 10 percent of total =	$12.0 million	
Size of remainder of low-calorie dessert market		$250 million
Estimated share of remainder of low-calorie dessert market; 5 percent of total =	$12.5 million	
Total Good 'n Lite Sales =	$40.5 million	

of Standard Dairy. The company had estimated total sales for the low-calorie pudding category at $80 million, the low-calorie ice cream category at $120 million, and all other low-calorie desserts at $250 million (see Table 2-2). Using results of the product use tests and its assessment of competitive strategies, the company estimates that it will get 20 percent of the pudding market, 10 percent of the ice cream market, and 5 percent of sales from all other low-calorie desserts. On this basis it estimates total sales in the first year at $40.5 million.

Several more sophisticated approaches to sales forecasting exist based on (1) time series sales analysis, (2) statistical modeling of demand, and (3) the analysis of consumer purchase records. These will be reviewed in Chapter 20.

Summary

In this chapter we described the process of identifying marketing opportunity as a lead in to developing marketing plans and strategies. Management must have a corporate framework to guide its assessments of marketing opportunity. Such a framework is provided by the development of specific corporate objectives and performance goals based on standards for sales, market share, and return on investment. The market in which opportunities are being analyzed must then be defined.

Once the market has been identified, a formal opportunity analysis can take place. Such an analysis requires (1) an assessment of the consumer in the relevant market, (2) an analysis of the marketing environment, and (3) an evaluation of the adequacy of corporate resources to pursue an opportunity. The basis for *consumer assessment* is evaluating consumer needs and determining if competitive offerings are meeting these needs. If they are not, there may be grounds for market entry (new product introduction) or market expansion (revising strategies for existing products to increase demand). Next, the company will develop a product concept to meet consumer needs and test it on the consumer. The company will then identify a target market for the brand composed of those who have reacted most favorably to the product (e.g., those who say they will definitely buy it).

Environmental assessment requires an evaluation of factors outside the company's control such as competition, social trends, and the economy. *Corporate resource assessment* requires determining the match between the firm's managerial, marketing, financial and production resources and the resources required to exploit opportunities. Such a match must not be restricted to existing resources. The firm must always be ready to consider acquiring new resources when warranted by the marketing opportunity.

The final steps in identifying marketing opportunity are analyzing demand in the market and developing a sales forecast based on the factors evaluated in the previous steps.

In the next chapter we will consider in more detail the central requirement in opportunity identification — assessing changes in the marketing environment.

Questions

1. Consider opportunity identification for an innovation such as personal computers versus a modification of an existing product such as freeze-dried decaffeinated coffee. What differences might occur in:

   ☐ defining the market,

   ☐ identifying consumer needs,

   ☐ developing and testing a product concept,

   ☐ evaluating changes in the environment, and

   ☐ forecasting demand?

2. Now consider the differences in opportunity identification for a product such as a decaffeinated cola versus a service such as guaranteed over-night mail delivery. What differences might occur in each of the five steps listed in question 1?

3. In this chapter we suggested that corporate mission should be defined based on consumer needs rather than product characteristics. Assume that in the process of evaluating the opportunity for videodiscs, RCA was debating whether to define its mission as (a) techological leader-ship or (b) supplying the best in in-home entertainment. What might have been the implications of these definitions of corporate mission for:

   ☐ product development,

   ☐ advertising strategy, and

   ☐ pricing?

4. Assume that management at Kodak is debating whether to define its corporate mission as (a) satisfying picture-taking needs or (b) satisfying imaging needs. What are the implications of these different definitions of corporate mission for:

   ☐ identifying new product opportunities,

   ☐ defining market boundaries, and

   ☐ acquiring corporate resources?

5. Develop a product/market matrix for a product line marketed by a par-ticular company (e.g., Nestlé's coffee products or Gillette's toiletry products). Define the markets broadly (e.g., consumer, industrial, insti-tutional, and international markets). Then indicate in which product markets the company has offerings. Which product markets represent areas of possibly entry? Why?

6. Define the market boundary for a product or service (e.g., Diet Coke,

IBM's Peanut personal computer, Express Mail service) using a hierarchical process of market definition. What are the strategic implications of your definition?

7. Consider the six characteristics cited by Urban and Hauser that are desirable for market entry (p. 40). Under what conditions might each of these criteria be legitimately ignored in a pursuit of marketing opportunity?

8. A company is considering introducing a diet food to appeal to three separate segments; frustrated dieters, social dieters, and self-disciplined dieters. What would be the arguments for positioning the product differently to each of the three segments, versus introducing one advertising campaign to appeal to all three?

9. A consumer survey identified four benefit segments in the toothpaste market; cavity prevention, flavor, social, and economy segments. What are the strategic implications of introducing a new product to appeal to each segment? Be sure to consider the implications for:

   □ product characteristics,

   □ advertising appeals, and

   □ price.

10. The chapter suggests the need to segment consumers by similarity in needs in order to identify marketing opportunity.

   □ Under what conditions might a company decide to appeal to the total market rather than segment the market by needs?

   □ What are the dangers of segmenting a market too narrowly?

11. What are the limitations of using the managerial rating system described in Table 2-3 as a basis for evaluating the adequacy of corporate resources to exploit marketing opportunities?

12. What is meant by the reference in the chapter to a "strategic window?" Why was the strategic window for Philip Morris "open" when it acquired Miller Beer?
Can you cite any examples of a company that faced a strategic window that was closed?

Notes

1. "Why Folgers Is Getting Creamed Back East," *Fortune,* July 17, 1978, pp. 68–70.
2. "Quaker Oats Retreating to its Food Lines," *Business Week,* February 20, 1980, pp. 153–54.
3. "Credit Success of Kodak Disc Camera to Re-search," *Marketing News,* January 21, 1983, Section 1. p. 9.
4. Theodore Levitt, "Marketing Myopia," *Harvard Business Review* 38 (July–August 1960): 45–56.
5. "Innovation GE's Good Thing," *Advertising*

Age, August 17, 1981, p. 72.

6. Ibid.

7. "Pepsi Takes on the Champ," *Business Week,* June 12, 1978, p. 89.

8. Glen L. Urban and John R. Hauser, *Design and Marketing of New Products* (Englewood Cliffs, N.J.: Prentice-Hall, 1980), pp. 80–84.

9. "Warring Toothpaste Makers Spend Millions Luring Buyers to Slightly Altered Products,"

The Wall Street Journal, December 7, 1981.

10. "A-B's Natural Exits Macho Fray," *Advertising Age,* October 19, 1981, p. 116.

11. Philip Kotler, *Marketing Management* (Englewood Cliffs, N.J.: Prentice-Hall, 1980), p. 96.

12. Derek F. Abell, "Strategic Windows," *Journal of Marketing* 43 (July 1978): 21–26.

13. "Olin's Shift to Strategy Planning," *Business Week,* March 27, 1978, p. 102.

CHAPTER 3

Opportunity and the Changing Marketing Environment

Opportunities in the marketplace are constantly changing as a result of changes in consumer characteristics, life styles, and values. In addition, changes in competition, technology, the economy, and the legal environment create new profit opportunities. The marketer must be aware of changes in the consumer and marketing environment if strategies are to exploit marketing opportunities fully. For example, the increasing proportion of working women represents a profound demographic change in American society and a consequent change in family life styles. The result has been greater opportunity for fast-food restaurants and more emphasis on time-saving convenience in household appliances. The 1970s saw a significant change in consumer values toward a *me* orientation represented by greater concern for self-enhancement, meaningful work, physical well-being, and privacy. This trend has created greater potential for products related to sports, leisure, health foods, and entertainment.

Technological change has been substantial. For example, the microprocessor has represented a significant technological advance that has resulted in new video technologies. This advance has led to the development of electronic mail delivery, in-home access to store catalogs, home computers, and the prediction of widespread ownership of complete home information video systems by 1990. Changes in the economic and regulatory climate also affect marketing opportunity. The trend toward deregulation in the Reagan administration resulted in less emphasis on pollution control, product safety regulations, and nutritional labeling requirements. Recession coupled with inflation in the early 1980s resulted in greater consumer price sensitivity and a significant boost for generic products, even during the economic recovery in the mid-1980s.

Marketing managers must identify these changes in the environment as a basis for marketing opportunity. The increase in the proportion of working women might be regarded as a threat by food companies since it means that a smaller percentage of the consumer's dollar is going to foods for home consumption. But the potential threat can also be turned into an opportunity by the food company that is creative enough to emphasize easily prepared yet tasty foods for the working woman. Similarly, the decrease in the birth rate might represent a threat to a company selling baby products. But the threat can be turned into an opportunity by the baby products company that begins to direct baby powders and lotions to the adult market.

This chapter describes changes in the marketing environment as a means of identifying marketing opportunity. But the potential for change as a threat rather than as an opportunity cannot be ignored. In the first part of the chapter we will review changes in the consumer environment, namely (1) changes in demographics and life styles, and (2) cultural trends. In the rest of the chapter we will consider the broader marketing environment, namely (1) competition, (2) technology, (3) the legal and regulatory climate, and (4) the economy. In all cases environmental changes will be considered as they affect marketing opportunities and the consequent development of marketing strategies.

Demographic and Life-style Trends

Changes in the **demographic** composition of the market and in **life styles** may define new market segments and identify new product opportunities, thus requiring a redirection of marketing strategies. Some of the most important changes affecting marketing strategies in the 1980s are:

1. the increasing proportion of working women;
2. changes in purchasing roles within the family;
3. changes in family composition — namely the increasing number of divorces, greater proportion of singles and unmarried households, and decreases in the birthrate;
4. changes in the age composition of the American market — namely, the increasing importance of the baby boom generation (30–40) and of the 65+ group; and
5. the changing life styles and purchasing behavior of the youth market (those 13–21).

INCREASING PROPORTION OF WORKING WOMEN

One of the most far-reaching changes in American society in the 1970s and 1980s has been the increasing proportion of working women. Figure 3-1 shows

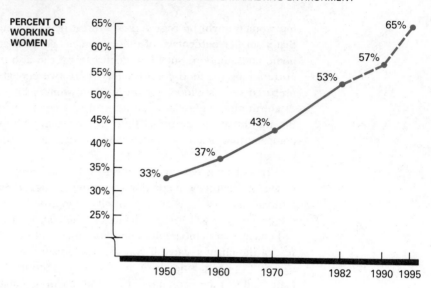

FIGURE 3-1
Percentage of women in the labor force
Source: "Employed Persons with Single and Multiple Jobs by Sex," *Monthly Labor Review,*
May 1982, p. 48, Table 1. Projections to 1990, Bureau of Labor Statistics, Department of Labor.
Projections to 1995, "Societal Shift," *The Wall Street Journal,* June 29, 1982, p. 1.

that the proportion of women in the labor force increased from 33 percent
in 1950 to 53 percent in 1982.[1]

Having more women in the work force means less time for shopping and
greater emphasis on product benefits such as speed and convenience. Household
products that previously focused on the pride of a job well done (e.g., shinier
floors) now focus on the time saved by the product (quicker-drying floors).
One advertising executive said, "Women are no longer finding their identities
and self-esteem in brighter-than-bright dishes and glasses without spots."[2] As
a Bureau of Labor Statistics report noted, working mothers "tend to purchase
more convenience items and services that reduce the time the wife must
devote to food preparation, laundry, and child care."[3]

There are numerous marketing opportunities (and threats) associated with
the greater number of working women. Consider the following:

1. Less involvement in homemaking and food preparation may be seen as
a threat by some marketers that insist on maintaining their traditional product
positionings. But other companies see an opportunity to adapt. For example:

☐ Avon has scheduled its door-to-door sales representatives to make sales
   calls at night, on weekends, and at offices.[4] It has also repositioned some
   of its fragrances to younger, more affluent working women.

☐ Food companies have adapted to the increasing number of working women by emphasizing easy-to-prepare foods. Campbell's Chunky soups are advertised as the perfect light meal that even a husband can fix for his working wife.[5] Food companies have further hedged their bets by buying fast food outlets. General Mills, General Foods, Quaker Oats, CPC International, and Pepsi Cola have all acquired fast-food chains. Fast-food outlets are a natural beneficiary of the greater numbers of working women. There has been a marked increase in meals eaten away from home, with working wives averaging 7.4 meals out per week.[6] The result has been increased sales at fast-food establishments such as McDonald's, Burger King, and Pizza hut.

2. Companies that have repositioned products to reflect changes in the working woman's self-awareness and confidence have generally been more successful. One fragrance company repositioned its line to reflect a "shift in emphasis from perfume used to support confidence to perfume demonstrating confidence."[7] The reason was that a study it sponsored found greater independence, freedom, and self-assurance among working women.

3. Companies have also had to adjust media strategies. Working women are more likely to read magazines and listen to radio than nonworking women, making these media more effective vehicles for reaching working women.[8] Magazines such as *Working Woman* (started in 1976), *Working Mother* (1978), and *Enterprising Woman* (1979) have been introduced to reach different segments of working women (See Figure 3-2).

CHANGES IN FAMILY ROLES

One of the most important marketing implications of the greater proportion of working women has been a change in family purchasing roles. The woman of the house may no longer be the purchasing agent for most family household needs. She may not even be the prime homemaker. A 1981 study found that one-third of husbands shopped for groceries, about one-half cooked, and 40 percent did housework.[9] Since these husbands are users of cooking and household products, they are also likely to be buyers. The days when advertisers could assume that Shake 'n Bake, Tide, or Easy Off oven cleaner commercials should be directed to women only are gone.

The increase in number of working women has also resulted in more liberated views of male-female roles. The traditional view of a husband at work and a wife taking care of the children applies to only one out of five married households. In 1960 it applied to about one out of every two.[10] An employed wife results in a more equal distribution of family power and will lead to more joint decision making.[11] It is now recognized that the husband can no longer be considered the major decision maker for many decisions traditionally in his realm such as cars, stocks and bonds, and credit. In fact, in 1980 about 40 percent of all new car purchases were made by women.[12] The trend toward joint decision making is also resulting in the husband's greater involvement

 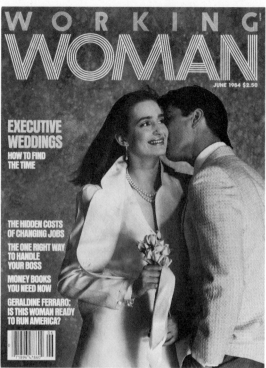

FIGURE 3-2
Magazines directed to working women
© *Working Mother Magazine,* January 1984. Photographer: Mark Kozlowski.
Used by permission.

in traditionally female-oriented decisions regarding appliances, furniture, and carpeting.

The blurring of traditional family roles is likely to continue into the 1980s. It has also affected the purchasing role of children. The fact that women are spending less time in the home means that teenagers are assuming increasing responsibility for shopping, meal preparation, and other domestic chores. As a result, "they are growing up a lot earlier. They play a more active role in household responsibilities."[13] This means that teenagers are educated as consumers more quickly by introducing them to a host of formerly unfamiliar household products. It is not surprising that college students have the self-confidence to buy laundry detergents, soaps, and washing machines, since they are the consumers of these products in the home.[14]

CHANGES IN FAMILY COMPOSITION

Significant changes in the composition of American households have direct implications for marketers. The divorce rate almost doubled between 1960 and 1980, while the number of marriages has decreased. In 1976 there was one divorce for every two marriages.[15] The birthrate is also decreasing. Fewer marriages and births and more divorces have resulted in a greater proportion of single- and two-person households. During the 1970s single-person households grew two and one-half times faster than multiple-person households.[16] It is estimated that by 1990 there will be as many single-person households as married households in the United States.[17]

The greater proportions of single-person households and households without children have direct implications for marketers. The trend to smaller families frees more discretionary income for expenditures on travel, leisure products, and investments. The reduction in the size of households and the decreasing birth rate have led some companies to translate the threat of lower sales of foods and toiletries into opportunities in new markets. For example:

■ Some companies have seen an opportunity to emphasize foods and toiletries in smaller sizes and to introduce kitchen appliances and furnishings in smaller models. Campbell's Soup-for-One and Miller's introduction of pony-sized beer bottles are examples.

■ Companies have expanded youth-oriented product lines to appeal to adult markets. Kellogg reacted to the threat of cereal sales tied to a declining birth rate by introducing adult cereals and by expanding into international markets.

■ Other companies have attempted to diversify into new lines. Gerber has shifted away from baby foods into life insurance. At one time it advertised its baby foods with the slogan "Babies are our business — our only business." Now it advertises life insurance with the theme "Gerber now babies the over 50s."[18]

CHANGES IN AGE COMPOSITION

Two age groups represent the greatest growth in the American population: The thirty- to forty-year-old group (the baby boom generation) has increased by 31 percent from 1974 to 1982 compared to an overall population increase of only 5 percent.[19] This growth is the result of higher birth rates from 1946 to 1957 (the post–World War II baby boom). The sixty-five and over segment increased by 22 percent from 1974 to 1982. It is expected to increase by another 20 percent by 1990.[20] (See Figure 3-3).

The Baby Boom Generation

The baby boom generation represents an important target for marketers because of its size and its disproportionate purchasing power. Because that generation is better educated and more upwardly mobile, purchasing power is likely to grow. *Advertising Age* describes this group as one that:

tends to buy with more regard to what it wants than to cost, and buys its

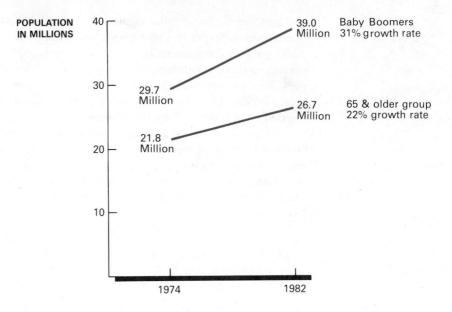

FIGURE 3-3
Two age groups representing greatest growth rate

Source: 1974 figures from U.S. Department of Commerce. 1982 figures from *Users Guide to Sales and Marketing Management, Survey of Buying Power, Data Services,* U.S. Department of Commerce, 1982, p. 23.

food the day it's eaten. It's also a group that doesn't want to spend more than half an hour on the average in preparing a meal. Not surprisingly this is the segment of the population most inclined to eat out."[21]

As a result of this trend, Pepsi-Cola bought Pizza Hut. *Business Week* reports that Pepsi felt that Pizza Hut was "positioned to catch the members of the post-World War II baby boom as they enter their 30s and 40s." This is the hamburger and coke generation that finds fast foods more acceptable.[22] Yet marketers realize that as this group grows older, purchasing patterns must adjust. Consider two examples of such adjustment:

- Levi Strauss, the jeans maker whose ads with psychedelic and sexual overtones were the commercial embodiment of the youthful culture of the 1960s, has made subtle changes in its pitch. The company now promotes sportswear with a fuller cut, for that 1965 college boy who can no longer squeeze into his size 30 Levis.[23]

- The FM rock radio stations that emerged in the 1960s are still thriving, but the sponsors are selling condominium apartments and suburban homes as well as phonograph records and acne remedies.[24]

The Elderly Market

The sixty-five and over segment will become more important to marketers. The income of this segment is rising because of better pension and retirement plans and is likely to continue to increase despite the limits of a fixed income. Purchasing power of this group is close to $100 billion.

This group is less willing to shop at discount stores, despite greater price sensitivity, and more willing to travel to downtown shopping districts. They are willing to pay higher prices if they perceive special attention being paid to the elderly.[25] They spend more on public transportation, household maintenance, and foods consumed at home.[26] They are also heavier TV watchers, possibly because, as one writer notes, TV provides an escape from loneliness and is a substitute for social interaction.[27]

Because of the purchasing power of this segment, it is surprising marketers have not paid more attention to it. The neglect is probably due to the orientation toward youth in American society and to the mistaken belief the elderly represent limited purchasing potential. Some marketers have seen the opportunity to design products for this group. Bulova recognized the need for larger numbers on watches by introducing easy-to-read dials. Pfizer has introduced New Season, a shampoo conditioner for older consumers.[28] Wrigley introduced a nonstick gum called Freedent for denture wearers. Marketers should also be aware of the need for easier to open jars and packages and easier-to-read labels. It is likely that the 1980s and 1990s will see more products positioned to the "gray market."

THE YOUTH MARKET

Another age group that represents changing life styles and values is the youth market (thirteen to twenty-one years old). This group is important to marketers because of its size, its purchasing power (estimated at $40 billion),[29] and the fact that most of this purchasing power is discretionary.

Whereas the youth market of the 1960s and early 1970s was described by *Ad Age* as "the unwashed, uncombed, anti-establishment activists," the youth market of the 1980s is seen as "much more conservative ... materialistic, ambitious and goal oriented."[30] This more conservative trend provides important directions for marketers. For one thing, the youth market is much more style and fashion conscious than its predecessors. The editorial director of *Co-Ed* magazine says, "Kids today are very sensitive about the way they look. This wasn't true in the 60's and 70's."[31] As a result they spend more on clothing and grooming products.

The youth market's greater discretionary income makes it the prime market for products such as records, tapes, video equipment, electronic games, and movies. Another important trend in the youth market is the emphasis on health and fitness, making this group prime prospects for bicycles, sports equipment, and running shoes. Companies such as Schick, Clairol, Revlon, Ford, and Coppertone sponsor sports events for the youth market.[32]

Although quality oriented, this group is also price conscious and much less likely to be brand loyal. A marketing research survey of teenagers concluded that advertisers:

> must concentrate more effort than perhaps in the past on the teen market in order to instill a sense of brand loyalty in these consumers while they are still young — so that perhaps some of that brand loyalty will remain when they grow older[33]

The media behavior of this segment also provides important implications for marketers. The youth market tends to watch less television and is much more skeptical of advertising.[34] The young are also more likely to read magazines and listen to radio. A host of magazines has been created to meet their needs. For example, *Ampersand* is geared to the college student's entertainment and cultural interests; *Circus* is a rock publication; *Graduate* deals with career prospects, job interviews, and adjusting to life after college; and *Rolling Stone* has feature articles from all areas of contemporary culture (see Figure 3-4).[35]

FIGURE 3-4
Magazines targeted to the youth market

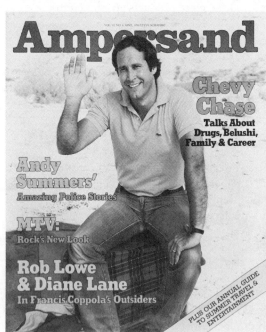

Used by permission.

Cultural Trends

Cultural trends in the 1980s have led to changes in consumer values that have had a profound effect on consumer purchasing behavior and marketing strategy. **Consumer values** are standards of behavior that are shaped by society and important groups such as the family. Values such as achievement, prestige, social acceptance, and self-fulfillment provide marketers with guidelines in developing products and advertising themes. The 1980s and 1990s are likely to see continued changes that began in the post–Vietnam and Watergate period, namely:

1. *me* orientation,
2. a return to a *we* orientation,
3. greater emphasis on personal self-fulfillment,
4. a trend toward a simpler life and reduced consumption referred to as "voluntary simplicity", and
5. a skepticism of public institutions.

A *ME* ORIENTATION

The *me* orientation reflects a need to live life "my way," a fierce desire to live for today without concern for the more restrictive values that might be imposed by society or family. The *me* orientation gained momentum in the mid-1970s and is likely to continue into the 1990s. In a sense it is a reaction to the self-sacrifice imposed on Americans by the Vietnam War. In the 1960s many of America's youths were willing to "put themselves on the line" for social and political causes — civil rights, Vietnam, Watergate. The youth of the 1970s became more inward looking; they strove for self-interest rather than self-sacrifice. Their parents followed the trend. In a period marked by high inflation and frequent recessions, why delay purchases? Buy now because the dollar may not be worth as much later.

The trend toward a *me* orientation has received a great deal of attention from marketers because of its effect on purchasing. Me-oriented consumers will select brands whose image they see as similar to their own. They will buy on the basis of ego-involvement. As a result consumers will examine products more carefully, read labels, examine ingredients, and seek information to make sure the product "is for me." On the other side of the coin, products that are not related to self are likely to be purchased on the basis of price. Generics and private brands are likely to become more important in these low-involvement categories.

The marketing opportunities resulting from a growing segment of me-oriented consumers are fairly direct, for example:

■ Firms that provide greater variety in product lines to meet the specific needs of me-oriented consumers stand to benefit.

- Marketers that emphasize quality and status will find a receptive target in me-oriented consumers.

- Marketers that develop low-priced alternatives in categories not oriented to self (e.g., paper towels, detergents) may find a receptive audience among a value-oriented *me* segment.

- Advertisers that emphasize self-oriented themes for involving products such as cosmetics and insurance are more likely to succeed. The following themes are examples:

  □ "I need me" (Prudential Insurance),

  □ "It lets me be me" (Nice 'n Easy), and

  □ "This I do for me" (Miss Clairol).

A RETURN TO A *WE* ORIENTATION

The *me* orientation has extended into the 1980s and is identified primarily with the youth market. There is a current debate among marketers as to whether the 1990s will see a return to a *we* orientation. Some feel that a self-indulgent, individualistic orientation among the young is fairly enduring.[36] Others feel that a return to more traditional values of family, country, and the work ethic is already occurring and is particularly evident among the baby boom generation.

The identification of a trend toward a *me* or *we* orientation is somewhat of an oversimplification. More realistically, *me* and *we* identify two broad segments of the American public with different values and purchasing habits. One study identified the *we* segment as consumers who buy with an eye to appearances and to what other people think.[37] They are family oriented, accept a work ethic, and seek to be upwardly mobile. The *me* segment buys to meet inner wants rather than the norms of others. Its members are likely to be young, single, and well educated.

The rising tide of political and economic conservatism has led some marketing analysts to predict that there will be a "slow trip back to more traditional values [so that] by the end of the '80s an age of WE will emerge."[38] The trend to conservatism is being reinforced as the baby boom generation grows older. The generation that reacted against traditional values and material possessions in the 1960s and 1970s is now made up of heads of households with responsible positions in mainstream America. The greater conservatism of this generation was described by a magazine editor as follows:

> In the 80s priorities changed. [The baby boom generation] became more involved in the establishment. They worked harder, dressed differently, had more money. They started wearing silk dresses and three-piece suits instead of Frye boots and jeans. And they became concerned with equity, tax investments, and deciding where they should live.[39]

EMPHASIS ON SELF-FULFILLMENT

Another significant trend primarily among younger consumers is the emphasis on self-fulfillment.[40] Some of these consumers redefined their priorities, reducing the importance of money and increasing the importance of personal self-enhancement and meaningful work. They sought:

- work that is challenging and meaningful over and above how well it pays;

- physical fitness and well being;

- personal creativity as expressed through a wide variety of activities, hobbies, and other personal expressions of fulfillment; and

- cultural self-expression — that is, the wish to acquire more cultivation, knowledge, and appreciation of cultural topics.[41]

A 1982 study by a large advertising agency forecast increasing demand for products and services that offer a sense of personal achievement such as sports equipment, home electronics, and educational products.[42] Further, products that enhance the consumer's health and well-being are receiving greater emphasis. One study noted, "Liquor is giving way to wine, medical articles for the layman flood the market, and consumers are displaying a new wariness and vigilance in health-related areas."[43] Arthur D. Little, a large consulting firm, sees an "increasing emphasis on activities that can be mastered easily, provide high rewards in a short time period, and can be accomplished at or near the home. As a result, such things as home computers, cable TV, videodiscs, and exercisers will be high on consumer shopping lists."[44]

The change to a more self-oriented life style is particularly evident among women. One survey found that women are more likely to choose products that "meet their personal needs and not simply the needs of their family."[45] The primary emphasis is on products related to physical fitness and personal grooming.

THE TREND TO VOLUNTARY SIMPLICITY

The energy crisis of the 1970s coupled with an ailing economy in the early 1980s caused many consumers to question the assumption of an economy of abundance. A prolonged period of stagflation (defined as a combination of recession and inflation) created a middle class with stagnant real incomes due to inflation.[46] Many of these consumers have reacted by changing both their values and life styles. They have shifted from a material "more is better" orientation to one based on simplicity, self-determination, and a do-it-yourself life style.[47] This trend has become known as *voluntary simplicity*. It is characterized by self-sufficiency, a return to the land, a greater concern for the environment, and more frugal consumption patterns. The reason for the choice of simpler life styles is not only economic; this group also expresses a concern for personal enrichment, a preference for smallness and a desire to live in as natural an environment as possible. As a result, the trend to voluntary simplicity has continued into the economic recovery of the mid-1980s.

One study projects the voluntary simplicity segment to be the fastest-growing segment into the 1990s. It represented 5 percent of the population in 1978, and has been projected to reach 10 percent in 1987 and 25 percent by 2000.[48] This segment tends to be younger, single, urban, and politically independent.[49] Consumers in this segment prefer small, simple, functional products. They are price conscious but emphasize quality, and are likely to shop in small, personal stores, flea markets, or cooperatives.[50] They are likely to buy private brands and generic products.

The profile of this fast-growing segment provides some important opportunities for marketers. For example, they should develop products that are simple, efficient, and value oriented such as:[51]

- first-class durable products such as solid wood furniture, top-grade hand tools, geared bicycles, etc.;
- sturdy cotton and wool clothing that deemphasizes fashion;
- do-it-yourself products;
- ecologically oriented products;
- easy-to-fix autos and appliances; and
- healthy, natural, unprocessed foods.[52]

Advertising should be based on information rather than imagery, because the consumer is interested in the function of the product, not its symbolism. Messages should stress value, quality, and simplicity, and rely on specialized print media rather than television.[53] Prices should reflect value.[54] Price promotions, specials, and coupons are likely to be less effective because the consumer will buy on the basis of product features. Marketers should also consider distribution through no-frill stores, since consumers in this segment are not interested in services that may increase cost. Some of the national brands that are beginning to target products to the emerging voluntary simplicity segment are General Motors trucks, AMC jeeps, Sears products, and Time-Life books.[55]

SKEPTICISM OF PUBLIC INSTITUTIONS

Deeper skepticism of public institutions was largely a result of the Watergate scandals and continues in the 1980s. This skepticism was further encouraged by the Iranian hostage crisis and the deep recession in the early 1980s. As a result consumers are more likely to question the motives of big business today than they were in the 1960s and early 1970s. Advertisers' claims and their credibility are more likely to be questioned. One study found that almost all consumers disagree with the statement that "the biggest most popular brands are the best."[56] As a result, consumers are:

- relying less on brand name and reputation,
- more likely to search for information on products that are important to them, and
- more likely to buy value-oriented items, particularly generics and private brands.

This trend means that national brand manufacturers will have greater difficulty in convincing consumers of product claims and product quality. Marketing management must be more aware of this general skepticism. It will have to be more attuned to convincing consumers of the credibility of advertising claims. Puffery is less likely to be effective, and benefit-oriented advertising is more likely to be used.

The Competitive Environment

Competition is a key factor in defining marketing opportunities. A company must carefully evaluate competition before it considers entering new markets or increasing investment in existing markets.

RECENT COMPETITIVE TRENDS

Some of the general trends in evaluating competition in the last ten years have been:

- *Greater intensity of price competition.* Although prices were being driven up in the 1970s and early 1980s by inflation and energy shortages, there were strong competitive counterpressures to reduce prices as a means of gaining competitive advantage. These trends were manifested in:

  - the introduction and widespread acceptance of **generic** (no brand name) **products** such as paper towels, pet foods, household cleaners, drugs, and even cigarettes in the late 1970s;
  - greater acceptance of lower-priced **private brands;** and
  - expansion of certain product lines to include lower-priced alternatives (a strategy known as price lining).

- *Entry of foreign competition with higher levels of productivity.* Foreign producers with lower labor costs and greater efficiency have created more intense price competition for American companies in industries such as steel, automobiles, home appliances, and electronics.

- *The widening of competitive boundaries.* Many companies have shown a willingness to diversify from their core markets, thus expanding the number and diversity of competitors faced by "traditional" companies. Nowhere is this expanded competition more apparent than in financial services. Banks have faced competition from brokerage houses and insurance companies for checking, credit, and fund transfer services. Insurance companies are facing competition in the development of insurance and annuity services from banks and brokerage houses. Retail institutions such as Sears have diversified into insurance, real estate, and brokerage services.

■ *Establishing new competitive areas.* Companies have sought to establish a competitive advantage by creating new product areas for competitive advantage. The introduction of light beer by Miller and the shift by 7-Up to a no-caffeine positioning represented two attempts by Philip Morris to create new areas of competition. The purpose was to outflank the leaders in each market (Anheuser-Busch in beer, Coca-Cola and Pepsi-Cola in soft drinks), thus putting new competitive pressures on them. The trend to developing new areas of competition has accelerated as marketing-oriented companies have improved their ability to identify segments with unmet needs.

■ *Greater concentration of sales in the hands of the market leaders.* A countertrend to the attempt to challenge market leaders has been the increasingly precarious position of many secondary brands. Many markets have been split down the middle between price brands (private brands, generics, and lower-priced national brands), and national brands that are market leaders. The deep recession in the early 1980s caused many consumers to gravitate to price brands or to minimize their risks by buying leading national brands. Products caught in the middle — the second-level brands in a market — have suffered. The result of this greater concentration of sales has been to make entry into certain markets more difficult.

COMPETITIVE INFORMATION

The trends we have just described are fairly general but do not apply to all industries. A company seeking to identify marketing opportunity should try to anticipate competitive strategies. Such a *proactive* approach to competition requires information on specific competitors in an industry, their characteristics, past actions, and anticipated future strategies.

GTE has developed an information system to monitor competition in its various product categories. The purpose of the system is to answer the following questions:

1. What are our competition's current strategies?

2. How are they performing (sales, ROI, market share)?

3. What are their strengths and weaknesses relative to GTE?

4. What action might they take in the future that would affect the company?

GTE's Competitive Information System attempts to collect the following information for major competitors:

competitor's plans	distribution facilities and strategy
competitor's organization	pricing strategy
product strategy	regulatory strategy

production strategy   major events

new product development   product-line strategy

investment strategy

The four questions asked by GTE are central to any evaluation of competition. Information on strategy is most important, for it provides management with a basis for evaluating the strengths and weaknesses of competitors. It is possible to obtain information on a competitor's marketing strategies from public and industry sources. Competitive advertising and pricing information is in the public domain. Competitive products can be purchased and tested. Sales and market share data can be obtained from **syndicated research services.** Annual reports frequently describe corporate objectives.

GTE's last question — a competitor's future actions — is harder to assess. But reasonable predictions can be made by studying the competitor's resources, investments, and marketing strategies.

COMPETITIVE STRATEGIES

Marketing management's evaluation of the competitive environment leads to the development of marketing strategies that either anticipate or react to competitive actions. Anticipatory **(proactive) strategies** are more in tune with the exploitation of marketing opportunities because they attempt to predict competitive actions in future environments. **Reactive strategies** leave the development of new markets and new technologies to competition. But such strategies are safer, because they do not risk a company's valuable resources on ventures that may not pay off.

In this section we will consider marketing strategies on two dimensions as illustrated in Figure 3-5. First is a brand's strategic thrust in relation to competition — namely, whether it tends to follow a proactive or a reactive strategy. Second is the brand's market position. A brand will belong to one of these three categories:

1. market leaders,

2. middle-level brands that have the option of following or challenging the leader, or

3. brands that seek to avoid competition by either (a) establishing a market niche or (b) maintaining the status quo (a "don't rock the boat" strategy).

These categories produce the six competitive strategies in Figure 3-5.

Market Leadership

A company can maintain and protect a position of market leadership by a proactive strategy of market growth in anticipation of competitive actions, or by a strategy of reacting to competitive challenges.

MARKET POSITION   **COMPETITIVE THRUST**

	PROACTIVE	REACTIVE
MARKET LEADER	Market Growth	React to Competition
MARKET CHALLENGER/FOLLOWER	Market Challenge	Follow the Leader
AVOID COMPETITION	Market Niche	Status Quo

FIGURE 3-5
Competitive marketing strategies

Market growth

Kellogg has established market leadership in cereals over the years, and its strategy is to "attempt to expand its already commanding 42% share of market."[57] The company has four of the five leading brands of cereal on the market and has supported these brands by advertising and periodic couponing to induce users of competitive brands to switch. A policy of market growth has paid off: Kellogg is the food industry's profit leader. The company has followed a policy of market growth in international as well as in domestic markets by attempting to increase the demand for cereals abroad. It has also attempted to expand domestic demand for cereals by introducing adult-oriented brands. Its objective is to increase cereal demand 5 percent annually.

Reaction to competition

A market leader might follow a reactive strategy of responding to competitive strategies rather than a proactive strategy of anticipating competitive action. The problem with a reactive strategy is that it leaves the initiative to the competitor. A sound marketing planning process would encourage contingency planning to anticipate competitive moves in the effort to exploit marketing opportunity.

A good example of a reactive strategy was General Foods' strategy for maintaining market share leadership for its Maxwell House brand of coffee in the face of Procter and Gamble's introduction of Folgers into the Eastern market. The competitive battle between General Foods and Folgers was described by *Fortune* as follows:

As the aggressor, P&G's coffee division is making most of the moves. But [General Foods'] troops countered quickly. When Folgers mailed millions of coupons offering consumers 45 cents off on a one-pound can of coffee, General Foods countered with newspaper coupons of its own. When Folgers gave retailers 15 percent discounts from the list price, General Foods met them head on. [General Foods] let Folgers lead off with a TV blitz that introduced tidy Mrs. Olson to all those Eastern housewives. . . . Then it saturated the airwaves with [television advertising][58].

The initial moves by Folgers and countermoves by General Foods are apparent. The result of GF's reactive strategy was a loss of market leadership to Folgers.

Market Challenger/Follower

Companies that seek to compete with the leader have two choices; either challenge or follow the leader.

Challenger

Companies with sufficient resources may wish to challenge the market leader. Folgers challenges Maxwell House coffee; Pepsi challenges Coke; Miller challenges Budweiser; Colgate challenges Crest. Such companies can directly challenge the leader through aggressive price and advertising policies. An example of a direct challenge to a market leader is Bic's challenge to Gillette's leadership in the blades and razors market. Bic's purpose is to "hit at the heart of Gillette's profit-making center — razors and blades."[59] It started a multimillion-dollar ad campaign in which it challenged the claim that Gillette's double-edged Trac II shaves closer than Bic's single-edged razor. (See the Bic ad in Figure 3-6.) *The New York Times* summarizes the competition between Bic and Gillette in the words of warfare: "Like two alley cats, the companies won't stop, having battled steadily for six years."[60]

Companies can also provide an indirect challenge to a market leader by:

- *introducing **flanker brands*** (different sizes, flavors, types — for example, Colgate's introduction of gel toothpaste to challenge Crest);

- *using different channels of distribution* (When Procter and Gamble introduced toiletries into supermarkets because of its strong distribution network in household cleaning products, it outflanked some of the leading toiletry brands that continued to be distributed in drugstores); and

- *creating new markets through product innovation* (when Miller's challenge to Anheuser-Busch in the premium beer market was faltering, it outflanked its chief competitor by introducing light beer).

Follower

A company may not have the resources to challenge the market leader; or it may not wish to risk the resources required for an intensive advertising battle, necessary price cuts, and reduced profits. Following leaders into a market but skirting a direct challenge is a way to avoid these risks. Such a "me-too" strategy does not involve introducing carbon copies of leading brands. A market

FIGURE 3-6
An example of Bic's challenge to Trac II

Used by permission.

follower must provide some distinctive advantage to the consumer — whether in service, location, convenience, or price.

Several well-known companies have used a follow-the-leader strategy to avoid risk. Philip Morris has adopted a follower strategy in cigarettes: "It is not an innovator. PM has not pioneered in a single cigarette category. It waits patiently for competitors to establish a category, and then it moves to capitalize on others' mistakes and successes."[61] The potential for success of a "me-too" strategy is illustrated by the fact that Philip Morris's brands have the second largest market share in the cigarette industry.

A follower strategy tends to be characteristic of industries such as steel, aluminum, and fertilizers, which are capital intensive and produce standardized items. The standardized nature of product offerings limits competition to price and service. Price competition tends to be unprofitable since a price cut will generally be followed, leaving everyone with lower profits. Therefore the typical strategy in these industries is to follow the leader in pricing and attempt to obtain a competitive advantage in service and delivery.

Avoid Competition

Companies can try to establish a niche in the market independent of other competitors. Companies may also seek to avoid competition by maintaining the competitive status quo.

Market niche

A **market niche** can be established in several ways. First, a company could serve a specialized market. For example, 3M Company successfully introduced a new abrasive designed to grind metal to a select niche — large manufacturers requiring metal-abrasive processes.[62] Second, a company might establish a geographic niche in the market. Pabst beer is cutting back operations to a geographic niche as a result of intense competition from the market leaders, Budweiser and Miller. The company is restricting sales to the Northern states and is cutting back on the number of brands offered.[63] Third, a company might offer a narrowly focused product line. For example, American Motors' sales of cars have decreased to such an extent that the company is beginning to concentrate solely on its jeep line.[64] Carving out a niche in jeep sales in the automobile market could make the company profitable once again. Fourth, a company could direct its products to the low- or high-priced segment of the market. Hewlett-Packard specializes in the high-quality, high-priced end of the hand-calculator market, thus avoiding direct competition with leaders such as Texas Instruments.[65] Fifth, a company could direct its appeals to a specific segment of the market. Chapstick's introduction of Lip Quencher and subsequent expansion to Skin and Face Quencher established leadership in the lucrative moisturizer niche of the skin-care market. The subsequent entry of many competitors illustrates one problem with a niche strategy: if the niche is too large and lucrative, it might invite competition, thus requiring the firm to consider the alternatives of market growth or competitive reaction.

Status quo

A company in a leadership position may try to maintain the status quo rather than seek further growth for several reasons. First, further growth might lead to antitrust action. Second, the cost of making further gains in market share after obtaining a dominant share may be too costly. Users of competitive brands may be reluctant to switch to the leader's brand. Such users could be "bought" only through excessively high advertising levels or unprofitable price cuts and couponing. Third, further growth might encourage competitors to start chipping away at a company's flanks by following a market niche strategy. Such strategies might begin to weaken the market leader's position.

A status quo strategy may be more subtle than a market leader's conscious seeking of competitive stability. Companies may implicitly agree on a "don't-rock-the-boat" approach. This strategy requires an implicit understanding that head-on confrontations are to be avoided. Gillette and Schick seem to be following a peaceful coexistence strategy. One industry analyst noted that they seem to have a pricing truce in razors across the board. "It's like, 'Hey, let's both do business and make a good buck and not bother each other.' "[66]

The Technological Environment

New technologies produce opportunities by providing the means to create new products and, in some cases, new industries. The pace of technological change has been increasing in recent years, resulting in greater pressures to invest in product development and maintain adequate research and development facilities. Today, expenditures on R&D for new and improved technologies represent close to 3 percent of total gross national product.

New technologies create opportunity, but they also create problems for the marketing firm. At times new technologies are pursued to fulfill internal corporate interests rather than legitimate marketing needs. A company whose actions become too technologically driven risks ignoring consumer needs. Investment in technology may result in trying to "find a market for this contraption." The solution to an engineering orientation is to ensure close coordination between marketing and R&D. Some companies have done this by developing committees for product development that would represent the perspectives of both marketing and R&D.

Another aspect of technological development is the importance of assuming a leadership position in the industry. Some companies invest more heavily in R&D in an attempt to maintain technological leadership. RCA's $200 million investment in the development of videodisc technology is an example. The subsequent failure of the product illustrates the risks associated with apparent technological opportunities.

These risks plus the high capital expenditures required to develop new technologies have led many firms to pursue minor product improvements rather than major product breakthroughs. Other companies avoid the risks of heavy initial development costs by following the leaders in technological improvements. Such companies prefer the potential opportunity loss of not being the first in the market to the loss resulting from a possible failure in new technology.

NEW MARKETING TECHNOLOGIES

Perhaps the most dramatic change in the technological environment in recent years has been the development of new marketing technologies. Technological innovations have occurred in four basic areas: (1) in-home information and entertainment, (2) media, (3) industrial information, and (4) research.

In-Home Information and Entertainment Technologies

One of the most profound changes in technology has been the development of integrated in-home information and entertainment systems. The television set of the future is likely to serve as a central control unit for a complete home information and entertainment system. As a result the consumer will have access to much more information and will be able to place direct orders based on this information. The consumer will also have a wider range of in-home video entertainment as part of the overall system.

Consider the following scenario in the year 2000 for a "typical" consumer with a complete home information system:

- It is Saturday. Our consumer (a suburban home owner) gets up, has breakfast, and turns on the television to one of 125 cable television stations for the latest weather forecast. He switches to another station that provides twenty-four-hour news.

- The consumer decides to do the wash and finds the dryer is not working properly for the third week in a row. The home information system includes a small terminal that can access outside information. In this case the consumer calls for the Sears catalog and the section on washing machines and dryers. Several other catalogs are also accessed to compare price. The consumer then accesses the Yellow Pages to call a local repair shop for an estimate.

- It is about 11 A.M., time for the mail. The consumer receives the mail on the video screen from other consumers and businesses with home information systems. Regular mail is also delivered from the post office.

- After lunch our consumer decides it is time for his third lesson in tapestry weaving (a hobby he finds very relaxing). He inserts a tape into the videotape machine, takes out his loom, and proceeds to follow instructions.

■ After an hour our consumer gets bored. He asks his son (an eighth-grader) if he would like some help with algebra. They then instruct the home computer to provide some algebra problems. His daughter comes by and reminds him his alma mater is about to play football on one of the cable channels. He is too involved with his son and tells her to tape it so he can watch it in half an hour.

■ After the game he decides to take the family out for dinner. He accesses the menus and prices of several restaurants in the area and then makes a choice. He also decides to take the family to a good old-fashioned movie after dinner.

Although the foregoing description of a home information system may raise questions about dependence on automated systems and computers, it does reflect current technology and future capabilities. An illustration of the components of the home information system is presented in Figure 3-7. It is composed of:

■ an interactive videotext system (a small keyboard permits the consumer to access and transmit information),

■ a home computer,

■ a videotape recorder, and

■ cable TV.

Interactive videotext systems

Interactive **videotext systems** are two-way cable TV systems that allow consumers to access information from a central computer by a small in-home terminal. The information is accessed over TV cables and transmitted on the TV screen. Consumers can also transmit information (answer questions, respond to surveys, or place orders with retail stores). Videotext systems differ from home computers in that a home computer is a self-contained system (not tied in to a central computer) and frequently has its own printer and console independent of the TV set.

The first videotext system, known as Qube, was introduced by Warner-Amex in test market in Columbus, Ohio, in 1977. It is now in four or five cities with plans for further expansion. Other videotext systems are in the testing stages. AT&T and Knight-Ridder Newspapers are jointly testing a new system known as Viewtron in Florida that will provide news, information, and in-home shopping capabilities. It also includes an in-home banking service, and last-minute information on entertainment and travel accommodations.[67] IBM, CBS, and Sears announced plans in 1984 to test a videotext system that is designed to hook into a consumer's home computer.[68]

FIGURE 3-7
Components of an in-home video system

Source: "The Dazzling Business of Home Video," *The New York Times,* February 17, 1980, Section 3, page 1. Copyright © 1980 by the New York Times Company. Reprinted by permission.

Home computers

Home computers can store information (past bills, check payments, data for business or school, and so forth) and allow the user to write special programs (for example, to budget monthly expenditures for entertainment and travel). Some computers are beginning to be priced within the range of the consumer market (under $500).

Videotape

Videotape systems have been used almost exclusively to tape TV programs off the air, primarily network movies. The first videotape system was the Betamax introduced by Sony in 1976. Matsushita quickly followed with its

VHS (Video Home System) recorder. By 1982 only 3 percent of American households owned a videotape system.[69] But prices for videotape machines started coming down, and by late 1983 10 percent of all households had videotape.[70]

New Media Technologies

The primary development in media technologies has been the advent of cable TV, a fast-growing medium. Almost 30 percent of households had cable in 1982.[71] Advertising over cable TV stations is still limited; total expenditures on cable are only 2.5 percent of advertising expenditures on network TV, and some stations do not even allow advertising.[72] Yet advertising expenditures are growing. Adding to this growth is the national coverage now provided by many cable TV companies. At one time these companies had to rely on local cables, and coverage was limited to their immediate area. Now the larger ones transmit programming to RCA's Satcom satellite, which in turn sends signals down to 2500 earth stations across the country. These stations then transmit the signal to the television set in the home via local cable.

Modern cable converters allow these companies to offer many stations, from 36 to 125. As a result, *The New York Times* has called cable TV "an electronic magazine rack with separate channels devoted entirely to sports, news, movies, culture, education, religion, business, public affairs, and pro-gramming specifically for children, the elderly, blacks and Hispanics.[73]

Industrial Information Technologies

Industrial information systems have been in use longer than home information systems. The basic difference between the two is that the video component for the home system is the television set, whereas that for industrial systems is the screen on the computer terminal. Both systems rely on terminals that hook into a central computer.

Industrial information technologies provide the facility to display sales trends, cost data, competitive analysis, historical trends, and statistical analysis on the console. Information is stored in the central computer and can be called up. This facility parallels the videotext system in the home, but the scope of usage is much wider. Industrial systems can also link up to other systems to provide electronic mail delivery, electronic funds transfers, news, or stock quotes. GTE's electronic mail system (Telemail) is being offered to business firms before the company considers offering it through the home video market.

Industrial firms have been using videotapes for sales training, demonstrations, and seminars. They are also beginning to use videodisc systems for the same purpose.[74] As an example, Chevrolet has distributed videodiscs to its dealerships to permit auto salespeople to show customers the functions and advantages of various models.[75] One element that is likely to spur the use of tapes for training and executive seminars is the high cost of travel. As transportation and hotel costs mount, companies are more likely to consider purchasing disc or tape systems for individual branch offices and distributing training and seminar material. If it is too expensive for the individual to go to the company, video technologies allow the company to go to the individual.

New Research Technologies

Technological advances have also occurred in the way marketers can obtain consumer data. Three advances stand out: use of videotext, cable TV, and scanner data.

Videotext systems

Videotext systems provide a means of asking consumers survey questions on the video screen. Consumers can then respond by the in-home terminal to each question. For example, a detergent manufacturer might have introduced a new advertising campaign and want immediate information on advertising recall. Consumers can be asked to recall advertising copy using videotext and respond directly, providing the manufacturer with day-after information. Such use assumes videotext systems will eventually be in most homes.

Cable TV

Cable TV allows marketers to test alternative advertisements on a controlled basis. A split cable facility permits a marketer to introduce two or three alternative brand advertisements to different homes on the same channel at the same time. Since different homes can be exposed to different ad campaigns, marketers can then attempt to determine which campaign is most effective by tracking consumer purchases. The marketer can never be sure that advertising caused sales results. But if two or three groups of consumers receiving the different advertisements are matched by purchasing behavior and demographic characteristics, it is likely that differences in sales between the groups is being caused by the different advertising strategies.

Supermarket scanner systems

A new in-store technology, scanner systems, is significantly improving the marketer's ability to obtain quick and reliable data on consumer purchases. **Scanner systems** rely on the **Universal Product Code** (UPC), the postage-stamp-size set of numbered vertical lines that appear on most packaged goods. In stores with scanner systems the clerk at the checkout counter rotates purchased items over a small window through which a scanner emits laser beams. The code on the package is read, the sale is recorded automatically, and the consumer is charged for the items. The purchase information is then fed into a computer that records the brand, size of the item, price paid, and coupons redeemed. Thus the marketer can obtain quick information on weekly or even daily sales for brands by type, size, and price.

By 1983 supermarkets with scanners represented 25 percent of grocery-store sales, a sufficient number to provide an accurate projection of nationwide sales.[76] Supermarkets' rapid adoption of scanner data means that scanner facilities will revolutionize data-collection capabilities.

STRATEGIC IMPLICATIONS OF NEW MARKETING TECHNOLOGIES

The development of new marketing technologies is likely to have a significant effect on media and promotional strategies into the 1990s. Consider the following:

1. *Exposure to television advertising is likely to decrease.* Before the advent of in-home video systems the television set was used almost exclusively to watch network TV programming. As more homes acquire new video technologies, exposure to television commercials will decrease dramatically. Already it has been found that among households with cable TV the viewing of network TV shows is 20 percent less than among household without cable.[77]

2. *Television stations will become more specialized.* Just as magazines shifted from general-circulation publications to specialty magazines in the 1960s and 1970s, television will shift from general-audience network shows to specialized channels in the 1980s and 1990s. Advertisers will begin to seek more specialized TV media to keep pace with a shift to more specialized viewing by consumers. The trend has already begun. General Foods is sponsoring Lead-In on cable TV, a series of ten-minute interviews for the Black Entertainment Television network. Hallmark is funding Kaleidoscope, a group of five-minute children's programs for the USA Cable Network.[78]

3. *Advertising will be targeted to more specific groups.* The shift toward cable TV will allow advertisers to target products to well-defined consumer segments. Consumers who tend to watch special-interest channels can be identified; for example, cooking enthusiasts, joggers, opera buffs. Specific product categories can then be identified to meet the interests of each of these groups within the context of specialized cable TV shows — (advertising kichen utensils on a cooking show, clothing on a fashion show).

4. *Consumers will have more information and become more aware of price and brand alternatives.* Videotext systems will allow consumers to call up information on price and brand alternatives from catalogs and other sources. Newspaper advertising will also be available on some videotext systems. One system, CompuServe, provides electronics delivery of seven newspapers to subscribers and is considered the forerunner of the home-delivered electronic newspaper.[79] The capability for receiving additional information may make the consumer a more efficient and price-conscious shopper.

5. *In-Home purchasing will increase.* Two-way interactive videotext systems permit the consumer to order goods directly from information supplied on the TV screen. The increasing numbers of retailers who are computerizing their catalogs suggests an expectation that in-home purchasing will increase.

The Legal and Regulatory Environment

Another set of changes that affect marketing opportunity occurs in the legal and regulatory environment. Marketers must be aware of the limits that government legislation and regulation impose on the definition of opportunity. For example:

- *The Sherman Antitrust Act* limits a firm's ability to acquire other companies if such acquisitions are likely to restrain trade.

- *The Clayton Act* prohibits price discrimination and contracts that tie the sale of a particular good to the sale of other goods.

- *The Federal Trade Commission* regulates trade practices to ensure they are not deceptive and unfair. It has broad power over advertising claims and disclosure of product content on packages.

- *The Food and Drug Administration* has authority to ban foods and drugs and to regulate their contents.

- *The Consumer Products Safety Commission* is empowered to set safety standards for products and ban the sale of dangerous products. It also has the power to recall them.

THE DECADE OF REGULATION

The basic issue in regulation is whether the major responsibility for ensuring product safety, truthful advertising, unrestricted competition, and other such safeguards should rest with government through regulatory agencies or with industry through self-regulatory codes. The 1970s came to be known as the decade of regulation because of "an outpouring of federal rules and standards, as well as the creation of new bureaucracies."[80] From 1974 to 1978 federal expenditures on consumer safety, job safety, and other industry-specific regulation increased by 85 percent.[81] New regulatory agencies such as the Environmental Protection Agency (created in 1970), and the Consumer Products Safety Commission (created in 1972) began to affect marketing decisions. The Consumer Products Safety Commission was particularly important to marketers, because it required manufacturers to perform safety tests and could ban or recall unsafe products. The commission played a role in over 1200 product recalls from 1973 to 1979.[82] The Environmental Protection Agency also recalled cars in the 1970s for failure to meet emission standards for pollution control.

Older regulatory agencies also played an important part in controlling marketing practices in the 1970s. The two most important were the Food and Drug Administration and the Federal Trade Commission. The Food and Drug Administration has the authority to ban or seize food and drug products it regards as a menace to public health. Its more activist stance in the 1970s is illustrated by rules it formulated in 1975 requiring more information on nutritional content on food labels. The Federal Trade Commission established a set of clear guidelines in the 1970s defining deceptive advertising. It took a more activist stand during this period in (1) investigating the effect of television advertising on children, (2) asking some major firms such as Ocean Spray and Listerine to cease making misleading advertising claims and/or to take action to correct these claims, and (3) requiring full disclosure of potentially harmful product features such as tar and nicotine content in cigarettes.

THE DECADE OF DEREGULATION

The scope and action of regulatory agencies under the Reagan administration has been much more limited than in the 1980s. As a result the 1980s will come to be known as the decade of deregulation. The Reagan administration's antifederalist philosophy provided the basis thrust toward deregulation. This philosophy is stated in the president's 1982 economic report: "While regulation is necessary to protect such vital areas as food, health and safety, too much unnecessary regulation simply adds to the costs to businesses and consumers alike without commensurate benefits."[83]

Actually, the trend toward deregulation started in the administration of President Jimmy Carter with deregulation of the airline, truck, and railroad industries, and certain financial institutions. But the Reagan administration's belief that the majority of regulatory agencies' activities represented an intrusion on the private sector accelerated this trend. An executive order by President Reagan on taking office in 1981 stated that regulation was justifiable only if it (1) produced benefits that outweigh the costs and (2) was the least expensive solution to the problem.[84] A central procedure was established by the executive branch to ensure enforcement of these guidelines.[85] As a result, regulatory agencies were required to justify the values of regulation. The burden of proof fell on the agencies, whereas in the 1970s it fell on industry. The Reagan administration made it clear to industry that it favored self-regulation rather than government regulation. (See Figure 3-8 for a cartoonist's rendition of the Reagan move to deregulation.)

One of the most important effects of deregulation for marketers has been limiting the activities of the Federal Trade Commission. On taking office, Reagan planned to cut back the FTC's activities in advertising regulation. In the 1970s there was no need for the FTC to prove deceptive advertising actually occurred in order to bring a judgment against a company. Advertising only had to have the capability to deceive. Today the commission is concerned with advertising that is clearly deceptive to most consumers.[86] As a result of this policy the FTC eliminated the following in the early 1980s:

- a proposed rule to ban certain advertising to children,
- industrywide guidelines for advertising claims in the over-the-counter drug market,

FIGURE 3-8
A cartoonist's rendition of Reagan's move to deregulation
Source: AEI Journal on Government and Society, January/February, 1982, pp. 15–18. Reprinted by permission of United Feature Syndicate.

- rules that would have required manufacturers to disclose nutritional information,

- a rule that would have extended to advertising warnings now required on labels of antacid products, and

- rules requiring disclosures within food ads making health and nutrition claims.[87]

The result of the FTC's current stance is that advertisers are less concerned about substantiating advertising claims. Critics of the FTC's trend to deregulation feel that "the commission's less-than-vigorous pursuit of new advertising violations are effectively changing the way the agency enforces the law by requiring less proof to back advertising claims."[88] Many advertisers feel that self-regulation is adequate for accurate and nondeceptive information. The advertising industry has a National Advertising Review Board that handled almost two thousand complaints in the 1970s. Generally when the board finds a claim substantiated, the advertiser voluntarily corrects it.[89]

Other actions toward deregulation taken by the Reagan administration were:

- cutbacks in the Environmental Protection Agency (by 1982, the Reagan administration cut the agency's staff by almost 50%);[90]

- a substantial reduction in the enforcement and recall powers of the Consumer Product Safety Commission;

- decontrol of oil and natural gas prices; and

- a rollback of automobile emission and pollution control and safety standards.[91]

The Economic Environment

Economic conditions have a direct effect on the evaluation of marketing opportunities. Most recently two periods have affected the definition of marketing opportunity: the recession of the early 1980s and the subsequent recovery in the mid-1980s.

EFFECTS OF THE RECESSION IN THE EARLY 1980s

The rapid inflation of the 1970s coupled with the deep recession in the early 1980s had a sobering effect on many companies in their drive to exploit marketing opportunities. A result of this period of stagnation was less willingness among marketing organizations to consider diversifying into unrelated areas. After an enthusiastic splurge of diversification in the late 1960s and early 1970s, many companies began to be wary of diversifying away from their core markets. As a result of the last recession companies such as Colgate-Palmolive, Olin, and Nestlé divested themselves of acquisitions in unrelated areas. Marketing management in these companies limited their definition of opportunity to areas of traditional competence: food products for Nestlé, toiletries for Colgate-Palmolive, chemicals for Olin.

Economic stagnation also had an effect on consumers. Not surprisingly, decreases in disposable income in this period made consumers more price sensitive. As a result, consumers were more likely to:

- buy low-priced private brands and generic products,

- engage in comparison shopping,

- hunt for price specials and bargains, and

- buy larger packages to economize.[92]

Greater price sensitivity did not result in substantial cutbacks in consumption. At the height of the recession in 1981 most consumers were not cutting back on expenditures for most items; the only exception was expensive items such as cars and houses. This meant that consumers were becoming more value oriented. Management implications for opportunity identification during this period were direct:

- exploit opportunities for introducing lower-priced products,

- couple price benefits with perceived value in product features, and

■ give a value-conscious public more information on price and quality benefits.

THE RECOVERY IN THE MID-1980s

The recovery in the mid-1980s has increased per capita disposable income. But the shifts in management and consumer psychology we have described and their effect on opportunity identification remain. Marketing management continues to be wary of diversifying into unrelated areas. The emphasis into the recovery is still on exploiting core markets. On the consumer side several trends are emerging. On the one hand price sensitivity and a value orientation endure. Some marketers believe that consumers will look to save money when buying. They forecast a trend to more standardized products because consumers will not desire additional frills. As a result sales of private brands and generics are likely to increase. But on the other hand consumers have demonstrated a willingness to spend more on products that are important to them. In such cases marketers will have an opportunity to identify specific segments willing to pay to get what they want. Opportunities into the 1980s are likely to focus on:

■ services (financial, travel, entertainment, sports),

■ electronics (home computers, videotape),

■ time-saving products,

■ nutritionally oriented products, and

■ self-actualizing products.

Summary

Identification of marketing opportunity requires an understanding of the changing consumer, competitive, technological, and economic environment of marketing. Changes in the consumer environment deal with demographic and life-style trends, and shifts in consumer values. Among the most significant demographic trends in the 1980s are: (1) the increasing proportion of working women, (2) the growth in single-person households, (3) the growing effect of the baby boom generation on consumer purchases, and (4) the effect of the teenage market on life styles and purchasing behavior.

Changing consumer values have paralleled changes in demographics. The 1980s are likely to see:

■ a *me* orientation reflecting a desire to live for today and a lack of concern for the values imposed by family and society;

■ a countertrend reflecting a *we* orientation, a return to more traditional values of family, country and the work ethic;

■ self-fulfillment as reflected in meaningful work, physical fitness, and personal creativity; and

■ voluntary simplicity leading to reduced purchases and an emphasis on simpler and more durable products.

Competition will directly affect a company's definition of marketing opportunity. More intense competition on many fronts has heightened management's awareness of the risks inherent in attempting to exploit marketing opportunities. Management must develop an information system capable of anticipating future competitive actions in an attempt to minimize competitive threats. Strategies can be developed to anticipate or to react to competition. Anticipatory (proactive) strategies are more likely to be successful in exploiting marketing opportunities.

Changes in technology will have an equally important effect on marketing strategy. The most important changes in technology have been the development of in-home information systems and new media, primarily cable TV. The effects of these technologies on marketing are likely to be profound. For example:

■ exposure to network television advertising is likely to decrease,

■ television stations will become more specialized, and

■ in-home purchasing will increase.

Regulatory and economic trends in the 1980s will also affect marketing decisions. The 1980s are likely to see a continuation of deregulation initiated in the Reagan administration. The emphasis is likely to be on self-regulation in advertising and information disclosure. The government will probably continue to be active in areas such as product safety and antitrust, however.

On the economic front the recession in the early 1980s resulted in greater price sensitivity, more comparison shopping, and greater concern for value for each dollar spent. In the economic recovery in the mid-1980s consumers are likely to show continued price sensitivity coupled with a willingness to spend more on products of importance to them. In this period marketing management is also likely to be more conservative in defining marketing opportunities.

The forces that influence marketing opportunity serve as input to the development of marketing plans and strategies. In the next chapter we will consider the marketing planning process as a means of developing marketing strategies.

Questions

1. A manufacturer of home cleaning products is considering expanding its line to include a new dishwashing detergent. It is considering introduc-

ing the product with an appeal to pride in cleanliness and the fact that a homemaker can rest easy in serving clean dishes, glasses, and cutlery when entertaining friends. The advertising appeal is "Why not take pride when you serve friends and family?"

☐ What are the potential problems in the company's positioning strategy?

☐ Could the company use this positioning to appeal to a particular segment of the market? If so, what segment?

2. One of the points made in this chapter is the blurring of traditional male and female roles, especially their responsibilities for shopping, homemaking, child care, and purchasing decisions. What are the implications of this trend for an advertiser considering introducing a new floor wax with a primary benefit of time saving? Specifically, what are the implications for:

☐ advertising,

☐ media selection, and

☐ marketing research to determine the potential for the new product?

3. A manufacturer of cereal products sees the decline in the birth rate as a long-term threat. The manufacturer recognizes the limits to company growth if it continues to gear its product line to cereal consumption by children. The chief executive officer of the company calls a high-level meeting to assess future directions for growth.

☐ What are the company's alternative growth opportunities?

☐ Of those options which would you choose and why? (Make any valid assumptions you wish in justifying your course of action.)

4. Assume a manufacturer of personal hair care appliances (hair dryers, setters, etc.) wants to introduce two lines, one directed to a *me*-oriented segment and the other to a *we*-oriented segment.

☐ What differences would you suggest in product features?

☐ What would be the differences in promoting and advertising the lines to the two segments?

☐ What are the pricing implications?

5. What are the implications of the emphasis on self-fulfillment for positioning (a) a new line of perfumes and (b) a line of exercise machines, both directed to the working woman?

6. A manufacturer of furniture wants to position a new line to appeal to a voluntary simplicity segment. What are the implications for:

☐ product features,

☐ advertising appeals, and

☐ price?

7. What have been the results of more intensive price competition in many markets in the late 1970s and early 1980s?

8. What are the risks of a reactive competitive strategy? Can you cite any examples?

   How can a company collect sufficient information to institute a proactive strategy in an attempt to anticipate competitive actions?

9. Campbell is clearly the market leader in the canned soup category. Under what circumstances is the company likely to follow a proactive market growth strategy, and under what circumstances is it likely to follow a reactive, status quo strategy?

10. What are the implications of the new marketing technologies cited in this chapter for:

    ☐ a consumer's search for information,

    ☐ consumers' shopping behavior,

    ☐ marketers' ability to direct advertising to specific segments,

    ☐ the nature and content of advertising directed to specific segments, and

    ☐ marketers' ability to obtain reliable sales data?

11. What are the implications of the recent trend toward deregulation for:

    ☐ advertising strategy,

    ☐ product development, and

    ☐ packaging?

12. Some of the effects of the recession in the early 1980s on consumers and marketing managers continued into the subsequent recovery in the mid 1980s.

    ☐ What recessionary effects continued into the subsequent recovery?

    ☐ What marketing opportunities might be produced by the effects you cited?

Notes

1. "Employed Persons with Single and Multiple Jobs by Sex," *Monthly Labor Review,* Department of Labor, May 1982, p. 48, Table 1.

2. "Societal Shift," *The Wall Street Journal,* June 29, 1982, p. 1.

3. "Dual-Earner Families: Doubling Marketers' Pleasure," *Sales and Marketing Management,* October 26, 1981, p. 43.

4. "Avon Seeks Diversity in Tiffany Merger Bid," *Advertising Age,* November 27, 1978, p. 94.

5. "Eating Habits Force Changes in Marketing," *Advertising Age,* October 30, 1978, pp. 30, 34.

6. Ibid., p. 65.

7. "Marketing Emphasis," *Product Marketing,* December 1977, p. 43.

8. "Working Women Now More Attractive — Y&R," *Advertising Age,* January 11, 1982, p. 76.

9. "Large Numbers of Husbands Buy Household Products, Do Housework," *Marketing News,* 14, October 3, 1980, pp. 1, 3.

10. Donald L. Lunda, "Personal Management: What's Ahead," *Personnel Administrator* (April 1981): 52.

11. Harriet Holter, "Sex Roles and Social Change," *Acta Sociologica* 14 (Winter 1971): 2–12.

12. "A Long Drive for Recognition," *Advertising Age,* June 22, 1981, p. S-24.

13. "Youth Media Market Diverse," *Advertising Age,* April 28, 1980, p. S-1.

14. Ibid.

15. *The Nielsen Researcher,* No. 2, 1978.

16. "Live-Alones: Fastest-Growing Consumer Unit," *Sales & Marketing Management,* October 26, 1981, p. 36.

17. "Kellogg Still the Cereal People," *Business Week,* November 26, 1979, p. 82.

18. Philip Kotler, *Marketing Management* (Englewood Cliffs, N.J.: Prentice-Hall, 1984), p. 89.

19. *Users Guide to Sales and Marketing Management, Survey of Buying Power, Data Services,* U.S. Department of Commerce, 1982, p. 2/3.

20. Ibid.

21. *Advertising Age,* October 30, 1978, p. 27.

22. "Pepsi Takes on the Champ," *Business Week,* June 12, 1978, p. 97.

23. "New Population Trends Transforming U.S.," *The New York Times,* February 6, 1977, p. 1.

24. Ibid., p. 42.

25. Betsy D. Gelb, "Exploring the Gray Market Segment," *MSU Business Topics* (Spring 1978); 41–46.

26. "You Can Sell to the Older Set if You Watch These Trends," *Advertising Age,* August 22, 1977, pp. 33, 42.

27. Lawrence Wenner, "Functional Analysis of TV Viewing for Older Adults," *Journal of Broadcasting* 20 (Winter 1976): 77–88.

28. *Advertising Age,* August 22, 1977, pp. 33, 42.

29. "Youth Media Market Diverse," *Advertising Age,* April 28, 1980, p. S-2.

30. "Conservative Consumer Typifies a New Generation," *Advertising Age,* April 28, 1980, p. S-1.

31. "Reaching Teens: Less Emphasis on the Product," *Advertising Age,* April 28, 1980, p. S-1.

32. "Conservative Consumer," p. S-1.

33. "Studying the Teen Market," *The New York Times,* August 31, 1981, p. D9.

34. Ibid.

35. *Advertising Age,* April 28, 1980, pp. S-2, S-16, S-22.

36. "Analyze Lifestyle Trends to Predict Future Product/Market Opportunities," *Marketing News,* July 10, 1981. p. 8.

37. Arnold Mitchell, *Changing Values and Lifestyles* (Menlo Park, Calif.: SRI International, 1981), p. 3.

38. "What Comes After the Age of ME," *Marketing & Media Decisions,* December, 1979, p. 108.

39. "New Elegance, New Needs," *Advertising Age,* October 19, 1981, p. S-30.

40. Paul Shay, "The New Consumer Values," *Advertising Quarterly* 56 (Summer 1978): 16.

41. *Social Trends Measured in Monitor No. 3,* from The Yankelovich Monitor; Yankelovich, Skelly and White, New York, 1981.

42. "DDB Study: More Driving for Success," *Advertising Age,* January 25, 1982, p. 10.

43. "Smith Outlines Eight Trends to Watch," *Advertising Age,* August 24, 1981, p. 22.

44. "Tomorrow's New Rich: Postwar Babies are Grown Up," *Sales and Marketing Management,* October 6, 1981, p. 29.

45. *Advertising Age,* August 24, 1981, p. 22.

46. Avraham Shama, "Coping with Stagflation: Voluntary Simplicity," *Journal of Marketing* 45 (Summer 1981): 120–34.

47. "Conspicuous Consumption Out, Voluntary Simplicity In," *Marketing News,* February 8, 1980, p. 8.

48. Shay, "The New Consumer Values," p. 18; and "Give Them the Simple Life," *Marketing & Media Decisions,* January 1980, p. 75.

49. Shama, "Coping with Stagflation," p. 127.

50. Ibid., p. 128.

51. Ibid.

52. *Marketing & Media Decisions,* January 1980, p. 75.

53. Shama, "Coping with Stagflation," p. 130.

54. *Marketing & Media Decisions,* January, 1980, p. 75.

55. Ibid.

56. "The Changing Role of the Consumer in the 1980s," *Marketing Review,* October–November 1980, p. 23.

57. "Kellogg Still the Cereal People," *Business Week,* November 26, 1979, p. 80.

58. "Why Folgers Is Getting Creamed Back East," *Fortune,* July 17, 1978, pp. 68–69.

59. "How Bic Lost the Edge to Gillette," *The New York Times,* April 11, 1982, p. F7.

60. Ibid.

61. "Philip Morris: The Hot Hands in Cigarettes," *Business Week,* December 6, 1976, p. 62.

62. "3M's Search for Strategic Identity," *Industrial Marketing,* February 1983, pp. 82, 86.

63. "Smaller Pabst Brewing Considers its Options," *Advertising Age,* January 17, 1983, p. 4.

64. "American Motors is About to Blot Itself Out to Build New Image Around Jeep, Renault," *The Wall Street Journal,* April 16, 1982, p. 35.

65. Philip Kotler, *Marketing Management,* 4th ed. (Englewood Cliffs, N.J.: Prentice-Hall, 1980), p. 286.

66. *The New York Times,* April 11, 1982, p. F7.

67. "AT&T, Knight-Ridder Test Electronic Home Info System," Marketing Abstracts, *Journal of Marketing,* 45 (Spring 1981): 146.

68. "IBM, CBS and Sears Plan a Joint Venture In At-Home Marketing Through Videotex," *The Wall Street Journal,* February 15, 1984, p. 8.

69. *Changing Media,* Ogilvy & Mather, Inc., New York, September 18, 1981, p. 2.

70. "How the VCR Spree Has New Technology On Hold," *Business Week,* October 17, 1983, pp. 184H, J, L.

71. "Media and a Changing America," *Advertising Age,* March 29, 1982, pp. M-52–M-55.

72. "Still Fighting for Advertisers' Respect," *Advertising Age,* November 7, 1983, pp. M-44, M-45.

73. "From the Air: Programs by Satellite and Cable," *The New York Times,* February 17, 1980, Section 3, p. 1.

74. "Videodiscs and Computers: A Dynamic Duo," *Business Week,* February 7, 1983, pp. 109–11.

75. *Advertising Age,* September 29, 1980, p. S-46.

76. "Scanning for Dollars," *Chain Store Age Executive,* July 1983, p. 80.

77. *Advertising Age,* November 7, 1983, pp. M-44, M-45.

78. "Why Advertisers are Rushing to Cable TV," *Business Week,* November 2, 1981, p. 96.

79. "Meet Technology with Technology to Survive Electronic Blizzard," *Marketing News,* November 27, 1981, p. 9; and "CompuServe Extends its Reach," *Business Week,* December 7, 1981, p. 88.

80. "A Decade of Deregulation?" *Industry Week,* January 7, 1980, p. 17.

81. George A. Steiner, "New Patterns in Government Regulation of Business," *MSU Business Topics* 26 (Autumn 1978): 53–61.

82. Walter Guzzardi, Jr., "The Mindless Pursuit of Safety," *Fortune,* April 9, 1979, pp. 54–60.

83. "The Consumer Movement: Whatever Happened?," *The New York Times,* January 23, 1983, p. A16.

84. "Deregulation, A Fast Start for the Reagan Strategy," *Business Week,* March 9, 1981, p. 62.

85. Christopher C. DeMuth, "A Strong Beginning on Reform," *AEI Journal on Government and Society* (January/February 1982): 15–18.

86. "Advertising as Usual Despite the FTC's Shift," *Business Week,* November 9, 1981, p. 40.

87. "Despite Antiregulatory Sentiment, Advertisers Still Must Battle Washington 'Policy Shapers,'" *Marketing News,* April 30, 1982, p. 1.

88. "FTC Easing Rules Requiring Firms to Support Ad Claims," *The Wall Street Journal,* July 21, 1983, p. 29.

89. *Business Week,* November 9, 1981, p. 41.

90. "U.S. Environmental Agency Making Deep Staffing Cuts," *The New York Times,* January 3, 1982, p. 20.

91. "Auto-Safety Agency Stalls in Deregulation After Setting Fast Pace," *The Wall Street Journal,* December 9, 1983, pp. 1, 29.

92. *Supermarket Shoppers in a Period of Economic Uncertainty* (New York: Yankelovich, Skelly, and White, 1982), p. 15.

CHAPTER **4**

Marketing Planning and Strategy

FOCUS OF CHAPTER

Marketing opportunities determine marketing strategies. The link between them is marketing planning. Marketing planning is of central concern because it determines strategies (1) at the individual product level and (2) at the corporate level. Marketing planning at the product level is the main concern of the product manager. It deals with developing a product, defining its target segment, and formulating advertising, distribution, and pricing strategies to market it to the consumer. Marketing planning and strategies at the product level will be described in Part III. Corporate planning is concerned with broader issues: the corporate mission, the firm's total product offerings, the allocation of resources across the firm's various business units. These considerations are also central to the marketing function and will be described in Part IV.

In this chapter we will consider the process of marketing planning and the types of strategy that result from the planning process. We will first distinguish between corporate and marketing planning. We will look at the organizational and managerial requirements for corporate and marketing planning, and then focus on the marketing planning process. We will conclude by considering various types of strategy likely to be formulated by management at both the corporate and the product level.

Nature of Corporate and Product Marketing Planning

Before considering the process of planning in developing marketing strategies, we must recognize the two types of plan that affect strategy development: the corporate plan and the product marketing plan.

CORPORATE PLANNING

A corporate plan (also called the **strategic marketing plan**) should (1) provide a blueprint for corporate growth; (2) guide the development of the firm's overall **product mix** (product offerings); and (3) allocate resources to each of the firm's business units. The corporate plan deals with the following questions:

- *What is the scope of the company's mission?* For example, should Kodak enter the photocopier market on the basis of a corporate mission of meeting the broad range of consumer *imaging* needs?

- *What are the strengths and weaknesses of the company's existing lines?* Will entry into the photocopier market weaken Kodak's position in cameras and films?

- *What are the alternative investment opportunities for growth?* Are there more profitable investment opportunities for Kodak than entry into the photocopier market?

- *How should the company allocate its resources* (financial, manufacturing, marketing, managerial) among its various business units to best exploit marketing opportunities? Will development of a photocopier line divert resources from other Kodak divisions? What is the optimal allocation across business units to maximize corporate profits?

- *How should the company exploit marketing opportunity?*
  - ☐ To what extent should the company stick to its core businesses (in Kodak's case cameras and film) or diversify away from them?
  - ☐ Should the company emphasize development of new products or market expansion of existing products?
  - ☐ Should it emphasize internal product development or external acquisition of resources?

- *Does the proposed corporate resource allocation plan provide a rational mix of product offerings?*
  - ☐ Will the addition of new products or businesses take away from other company brands?
  - ☐ Will they support existing brands by providing a more complete offering?
  - ☐ Will they provide an infusion of cash to support an expansion of offerings into related lines?

- *What likely environmental changes might substantially alter the com-*

pany's mission, definition of opportunity, resource allocation, or product mix?

☐ Do any cultural or demographic trends suggest a change in the demand for the company's offerings? For example, does the cultural trend to self-fulfillment suggest an increase in demand for cameras and film? If so, perhaps Kodak should limit resources to developing new camera lines rather than diverting resources to totally new markets.

☐ Are competitive, technological, or economic changes likely to occur that may require a substantial revision in allocations across business units (e.g., the development of the disc camera market)?

MARKETING PLANNING

It is apparent from the preceding questions that the corporate plan focuses on broad, long-term issues of opportunity and resource allocation that affect the total firm. In contrast, the marketing plan focuses on a particular brand or product line. Marketing planning deals with the following questions:

■ *What are the appropriate marketing objectives for the brand in terms of:*

☐ market share,

☐ return on investment,

☐ sales,

☐ distribution coverage,

☐ advertising awareness, and

☐ payout period?

■ *What is the positioning strategy for a brand?* What specific benefits should the brand be positioned to fulfill?

■ *Does the brand fill a gap in the market unfilled by competition?* Is it unique? Does it offer distinctive product benefits?

■ *What target segments is the brand positioned to?* Are they large enough to make the venture profitable? Can the segments be reached by specific media? Are their needs sufficiently well defined? How do they react to the firm's offerings?

■ *What marketing mix will best influence consumers to buy?* What strategies should be developed for advertising, media selection, sales promotion, pricing, product-line development, and distribution? What should be the allocation of dollars to each of these components of the marketing mix?

■ *What are the likely competitive actions and how will they affect the brand?* If the company is considering a new product, will competition enter the market shortly after introduction and thus decrease the firm's competitive advantage? If the company is developing marketing plans for an existing product, is competition likely to increase advertising spending, decrease price, expand the geographic distribution of the product, and so forth?

■ *How will alternative brand strategies affect spending levels and predicted performance?* What would be the effect of high, medium, and low advertising budgets on return on investment and market share? What would be the effect of an immediate national introduction versus a slower region-by-region rollout? How would various price levels affect sales and competitive reaction?

The Organizational and Managerial Framework for Marketing Planning

In recent years the organizational framework for planning has centered on the establishment of **strategic business units** (SBUs). These units are autonomous profit centers responsible for establishing marketing plans and reporting to top management. SBUs are generally defined on the basis of consumer markets and needs.

The rationale for organizing around SBUs is well illustrated by General Foods (GF). In the early 1970s General Foods' corporate performance began declining because of a lack of new product successes. At that time the company had a traditional divisional structure that was "the legacy of a generations-old policy of acquisition."[1] GF's major food divisions were Birds Eye, Jell-O, Post, and Kool-Aid. These divisions were organized around processing technologies rather than similarity of consumer needs. As a result new product development was inhibited. For example, gaps between divisions permitted competitors to come in with new products. Products were fragmented across divisions. Beverages were marketed by three of the four divisions. Irrational product groupings existed (cereals and pet foods were marketed by the same division). The divisional structure resulted in a lack of planning flexibility and rigid adherence to corporate norms for product performance.

The lack of success in new product development caused GF to reevaluate its organizational structure. Managers realized that products should be grouped by consumer needs rather than technology. Further, they saw that different business units could grow at different rates and achieve different earnings and profitability objectives. As a result General Foods organized into six strategic business units: (1) breakfast foods, (2) beverages, (3) main-meal products, (4) coffees, (5) desserts, and (6) pet foods. This organization permitted the grouping of products by marketing requirements. The business units could share manufacturing, research, engineering, and distribution resources. But each unit was accountable for its own profitability and acted as a minicorporation within the firm.

THREE PLANNING LEVELS

The strategic business unit is one of three main levels in a multiproduct firm. Table 4-1 lists the three levels, the planning framework in terms of the firm's offerings, and the type of plan enacted. Corporate planning is the responsibility of top management. The planning framework is the development of the firm's total set of product offerings across SBUs and the resource allocations required to market this product mix. Planning at the SBU level is the responsibility of business managers within these units. The planning framework is development of the product mix within each SBU and the resource allocations required for the individual product lines and brands that represent this product mix. Planning at both the corporate and the SBU levels is called *strategic marketing planning* because the focus is on long-term strategic issues dealing with the firm's or SBU's purpose, their approach to exploiting marketing opportunity, and the development of resources to permit the pursuit of such opportunities.

The third level of planning involves the product market unit. **Product Market Units** (PMUs) are product groupings aimed at broad markets (detergents, instant coffee, or frozen vegetables would be PMUs). Individual brands within PMUs are headed by product or brand managers. The planning framework for the product manager is the individual product line or brand he or she is responsible for. Strategies are developed through a process of marketing planning that establishes the product, promotion, price, and distribution strategies for products and brands.

Figure 4-1 presents a reasonable organizational framework for General Foods based on SBU and PMU organizational entities. GF's six SBUs are shown. The Product Market Units for the coffee SBU are used as an illustration. The coffee PMUs are ground roast, instant, freeze-dried, and international flavors. Each of these PMUs is split into a caffeinated and decaffeinated product line with the exception of the international line. GF brands within each product line are listed as the most discrete level in the organizational structure.

The planning focus for each level in Table 4-1 is represented by the level just below it. Top management is concerned with the activities of various

TABLE 4-1
Three Levels of Marketing Planning

PLANNING LEVEL	MANAGEMENT	PLANNING FRAMEWORK	TYPE OF PLANNING
Corporate	Top Management	SBU Mix	Strategic Marketing Planning
Strategic Business Unit (SBU)	Business Managers	Product Mix (Within SBUs)	Strategic Marketing Planning
Product Market Unit (PMU)	Product (Brand) Managers	Product Lines and Brands	Marketing Planning

LEVEL   ORGANIZATIONAL UNITS

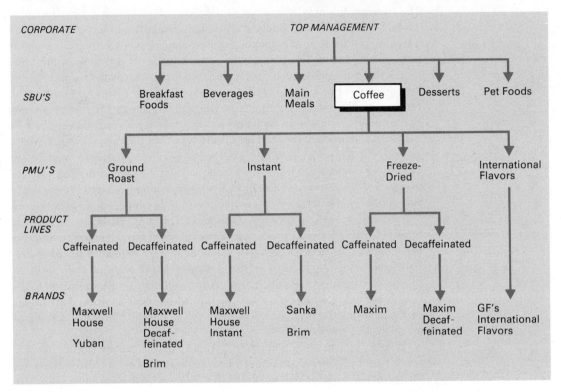

FIGURE 4-1
Example of an organizational structure for marketing planning: General Foods

business units. The business managers that run the SBUs are concerned with their offerings as represented by the various PMUs. Product managers are concerned with the marketing strategies for the product lines and individual brands in PMUs. The planning framework for each of these three levels will be considered in more detail.

THE CORPORATE LEVEL

The basic concept of the new organizational framework for planning is that products within business and product market units should be grouped according to consumer needs and marketing requirements, not technology. Top management must view the business units in this light. Figure 4-2 presents an SBU/Market framework for planning. The vertical axis presents the SBUs portrayed in Figure 4-1, the horizontal axis the broad market categories each SBU could address. The low-calorie SBU in Figure 4-2 is a hypothetical division that GF might

MARKETS

SBU'S	CONSUMER	INSTITUTIONAL	INTERNATIONAL	PRIVATE BRAND
Breakfast Foods				X
Beverages				X
Main Meals				X
Coffee				X
Desserts				X
Pet Foods				?
(Low Calorie)*	?	?	?	X

*The Low-Calorie SBU is hypothetical. Therefore, each market for this SBU is designated as under consideration, even though GF has low-calorie brands that are marketed by its existing SBU's.

FIGURE 4-2
The SBU market matrix at General Foods

eventually add to bring all diet foods under the same roof. All the cells together represent General Foods' potential product mix. The light cells represent categories in which GF has offerings — its actual product mix. Cells with question marks are areas that might be considered for entry. Cells with an X are areas that are unlikely to be considered. Figure 4-2 presents two important planning concepts: (1) planning for total markets rather than served markets, and (2) planning for the overall product mix (or portfolio) of the firm's offerings.

Total versus Served Markets

A basic purpose of the corporate plan is to consider market areas not currently being served as possible candidates for entry. Consideration of an SBU/market area for entry is based on the factors described in the previous chapter — consumer, environmental, and corporate resource assessment, market definition, and evaluation of profit potential. It is on this basis that GF will decide whether to form a separate low-calorie SBU.

Another important consideration in comparing total to served markets is product deletions. Top management may decide that an SBU's offerings in a particular market are not sufficiently profitable. The product lines may be draining cash from other areas and growth prospects may be dim. A candidate for deletion might be some pet food offerings because of a projected long-term decline in this category. GF might also consider producing pet foods for private brands (under a retailer's label) to utilize excess production capacity (see Figure 4-2).

Product Portfolio Analysis

Management's analysis of the firm's overall product mix in Figure 4-2 represents an evaluation of alternative investment opportunities for the firm. The problems in deciding on alternative investments are similar to those of the individual investor, namely to determine additions to or deletions from the portfolio (i.e. the product mix) in order to provide balance between objectives of growth and stability.[2]

One approach to **product portfolio analysis** (developed by the Boston Consulting Group) emphasizes two criteria for evaluating the firm's product mix; industry growth potential and the product category's market share compared to that of leading competitors. On the basis of these two criteria, products are classified as **stars** (high growth potential and relative market share), **cash cows** (low growth potential but high relative market share), **problem children** (high growth potential but low relative market share), and **dogs** (low growth potential and relative market share).

This and other approaches to product portfolio analysis will be described in Chapter 19, at which point its purpose and applications will be clarified. For now, it is important to recognize that product portfolio analysis provides management with guidelines for allocating resources to new and existing products with growth potential and withholding resources from weak products.

THE STRATEGIC BUSINESS UNIT (SBU) LEVEL

The second major planning level in the firm is the strategic business unit. Since the SBU operates as a minicorporation within the larger corporation, corporate (strategic marketing) planning can be applied directly to its operation.

Top management views the company's mix in terms of business units. SBU management views its product mix in terms of PMUs. Further, just as top management uses product portfolio analysis to evaluate the SBU mix, an SBU's management uses product portfolio analysis to evaluate the product mix within its business unit.

Figure 4-3 assumes that a large food company brings all its low-calorie products into one SBU. The classification in Figure 4-3 is known as a **product/ market matrix** because the product categories that are or might be offered by the SBU are listed down the side and the various market segments these products are directed to are listed across the top. Notice that instead of just dividing markets into consumer, institutional, international, and private brands as was done in Figure 4-2 at the corporate level, SBU management divides consumers into four market segments. These segments were determined by a survey of consumers' needs for diet foods. Frustrated dieters find it desirable but difficult to diet; self-confident dieters do not; and special dieters (e.g., diabetics) have health-related dieting needs. Social dieters are those who diet to gain social attention.

As in the SBU analysis in Figure 4-2, management will identify segments they are currently marketing to, segments they are considering (designated by a question mark), and segments they are not considering for entry (designated by an X). This matrix thus provides a basis for showing the total market (all boxes), the served market (light boxes only), and the potential future market (light boxes plus question marks).

THE PRODUCT MARKET UNIT (PMU) LEVEL

The third major planning level in the firm is the product market unit. At this level, the product mix is viewed as the individual brands within each product market unit; for example, specific brands in the low-calorie breakfast foods PMU or in the low-calorie beverage PMU. As a result the planning focus is product marketing rather than strategic planning, and the focal points for the marketing effort are the brand and product line (see Table 4-1).

In the next section we will look more deeply into product marketing planning at the PMU level. Chapter 18 describes strategic planning at the SBU and corporate level. (Product marketing planning will hereafter be called simply *marketing planning* in contrast to strategic planning.)

PRODUCT UNITS

MARKET SEGMENTS

PRODUCT UNITS	FRUSTRATED DIETERS	SELF-CONFIDENT DIETERS	SPECIAL DIETERS	SOCIAL DIETERS	INSTITUTIONAL	INTERNATIONAL	PRIVATE BRAND
MAIN MEAL					?		X
BREAKFAST					?		X
DESSERT					?		X
SNACKS	?	X	X	?	?		X
BEVERAGES	?	?	X	?	?		X

Light Boxes—Addressed Markets
?—Under Consideration
X—No Offerings and Not Under Consideration.

FIGURE 4-3
Product/market matrix for a low calorie unit of a food company

The Marketing Planning Process

Marketing planning at the product level is the responsibility of the product manager. It has two basic purposes: (1) to develop marketing strategies for a particular brand and (2) to estimate brand sales. Marketing strategies are required to market the company's product offerings and to influence consumers to buy the company's brands. Sales estimates are necessary to determine the level of marketing effort required and to provide business units and top management with profit estimates that can be integrated into the corporate plan.

The steps involved in marketing planning are presented in Figure 4-4. First, objectives and goals must be established. Second, marketing opportunity must be analyzed using the criteria described in Chapter 2. Third, the product must be positioned to meet consumer needs identified in the opportunity phase. Fourth, a mix of marketing strategies (advertising, price, distribution, product) must be formulated to influence the consumer to buy. Marketing strategy must not only determine the components of the marketing mix; it must also define the level of marketing expenditures and how expenditures are to be allocated to each component of the marketing mix (advertising, sales promotion, personal selling, distribution, and product development.)

If the product is already on the market, an implementation plan is required to ensure that advertising, sales promotion, and pricing strategies are followed. If the product is new, a plan for test marketing is frequently required. The test market phase permits the new product to be introduced into several cities to determine acceptance. It can also be the first step in a national introduction. The marketing mix can then be revised to reflect sales results in test markets.

From preliminary consumer surveys, product use tests, and test market results, a profit and loss statement is formulated for the brand. At this point fairly detailed cost estimates can be provided, since the marketing mix has been defined. The profit and loss statement is submitted to SBU management for approval, and allocations are provided for implementation. Marketing management oversees the operation of the plan and attempts to control costs and marketing performance.

MARKETING GUIDELINES

The first step in marketing planning is establishing marketing guidelines. These parallel the corporate guidelines discussed in Chapter 2, except that they are directed to a brand or product line. Marketing guidelines should be detailed enough to help management develop marketing strategies. These guidelines can be divided into marketing objectives and product performance goals. Specific objectives at the PMU level might be (1) to appeal to a broad spectrum of market segments, (2) by developing a full product line, (3) through internal development, (4) by using existing technologies. Performance goals for a particular brand might be stated in terms of:

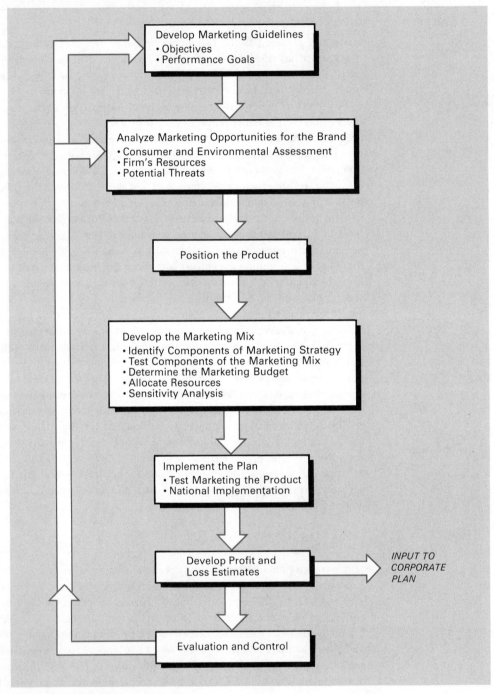

FIGURE 4-4
The marketing planning process

- sales revenue expected over the next five years,

- brand awareness (e.g., ensure brand awareness among 80 percent of the target market),

- return on investment, and

- distribution (e.g., maintain distribution in 90 percent of all supermarkets).

ANALYZE MARKETING OPPORTUNITIES FOR THE BRAND

The marketing plan incorporates the steps in identifying marketing opportunities described in Chapter 2, namely, evaluate customer needs, identify a target segment, analyze environmental factors that might influence product demand, and assess corporate resources. These considerations do not have to be repeated. At the product market level, management must ensure that opportunity identification results in targeting brands to defined consumer needs.

PRODUCT POSITIONING

Once a company has identified an area of opportunity and defined a product idea, it must use the marketing plan to develop a positioning for the product. Various product positioning alternatives were discussed in Chapter 3. In the context of marketing planning, product positioning must precede strategy formulation. Once management defines the product's position, advertising and promotional strategies follow.

If a brand is not clearly positioned, marketing strategy is ill defined and the brand is likely to fail. As an example, Aziza eye makeup had used a shotgun approach to marketing by introducing hundreds of product variations in the hope a few would catch on. It did so with little advertising and distribution support. By the mid-1970s, "there was a crying need for brand positioning. Aziza had to stand for something in the marketplace if it was going to go anywhere."[3] Marketing research uncovered a basic consumer need; to know how to apply eye makeup. The high-fashion image advertised by Revlon and others was glamorous, but consumers could not duplicate the effects they saw on TV. As a result, the company repositioned the line using a "how to" campaign. (See Figure 4-5.) The idea was to tell the consumer how to achieve the desired effect by using Aziza.[4] The campaign was successful in developing a unique positioning for the product that made it competitive with Revlon.

Aziza was positioned to meet a specific set of consumer needs. But as we noted in Chapter 2, products can be positioned by other criteria — feelings and emotions, price, the consumer's self-image, and competitive products. Positioning relative to competitive products has become a more frequently used strategy in recent years as companies have sought to demonstrate their products' advantages through more direct comparisons. For example, 7-Up was positioned as the "UnCola" in the mid-1970s to establish it as an alternative to Coke and Pepsi. There were "no product features, no customer benefits," only the association to other colas through the fact that 7-Up was an "UnCola"[5]

AZIZA DEMONSTRATES HOW TO GET THE WIDE-EYED LOOK.

Besides being easy to work with (or should we say play?) these silky powder shadows are noted for their smooth coverage and lasting color.

After all, what good is a wide-eyed look if it's going to crease or fade?

Send for our free booklet "Aziza Demonstrates All About Eyes." Enclose 40¢ for postage and handling. Write Aziza, P.O. Box 4054A, Jefferson City, Missouri 65102.

Every one of our 21 Aziza trios gives you eyecolor in a light, a medium and a deep tone. That's what makes these shadows blend together perfectly— which is the secret of the wide-eyed look.

To achieve this sensational look, just pick any Aziza trio, then apply all three tones just the way we do in our diagrams.

Your eyes will look soft, luminous, more opened up and wider-set. In short, you'll look wide-eyed.

THE WIDE-EYED LOOK.

1. The palest tone on inner half of eye from brow to lashline.

2. Medium tone on outer half of eye, browbone to lashline. Extend color beyond eye.

3. Outline eye with darkest tone from center to beyond outer corner, bring color around and under.

4. Model is wearing Heather Rose Trio.

FIGURE 4-5
Positioning Aziza with a "how to" strategy

Used by permission of Chesebrough-Pond's, Inc.

The advantage of competitive positioning is that the marketer links the product to what is already known to the consumer, generally a leading product or well-known product category. New ground does not have to be broken. In contrast, positioning by consumer benefits must sometimes establish a new frame of reference for the consumer. When Philip Morris bought 7-Up in the late 1970s, it eventually shifted the positioning from competition to a specific benefit claim, no caffeine. This was a risky strategy, because 7-Up had to establish itself with a new benefit in the soft-drink market. Consumers might not care that much about caffeine content in soft drinks.

There was another risk in Philip Morris's shift to a no-caffeine claim, the fact it was repositioning an existing product. Repositioning an existing product might be more difficult than positioning a new one, because the consumer's image of a familiar product may be hard to change. Consider the risk Cadillac faced when it had to reposition itself as a luxury mid-sized car during the energy crisis. Most consumers had a well-established image of Cadillac as a large, top-of-the-line model.

DEVELOPING THE MARKETING MIX

The next step in the marketing plan is to establish marketing strategy to introduce the product. The strategic components of the plan are known as the **marketing mix** because they represent the combination or mix of marketing elements required for product introduction or market expansion.

Figure 4-4 listed the five steps required to develop the marketing mix: (1) identify the components of marketing strategy; (2) test these components on the consumer; (3) determine the level of marketing effort; (4) allocate resources to each component of the marketing mix; and (5) undertake a sensitivity analysis to determine the effect of strategic alternatives on sales, market share, and ROI.

Components of the Marketing Mix

The components of the marketing mix are presented in Table 4-2. For example, advertising strategies specify the content of advertising themes, frequency of insertions, expected reach of the message, and type of media used. A company will consider alternative strategies in each of these seven areas. In addition, the marketing plan must ensure integration of all components. For example, it would be pointless to provide national distribution without a national advertising campaign, or to try to convey a high-price, high-quality image in advertising while using magazines and newspapers that are not directed to consumers in a high socioeconomic bracket.

Testing Marketing Mix Components

The marketing plan must also provide for testing alternative strategies. Alternative print and TV advertisements will be tested to determine consumer reactions. Alternative price levels will also be tested to determine their effect on sales.

TABLE 4-2
Components of the Marketing Mix

MARKETING MIX ELEMENT	FEATURES
1. Product	Product characteristics
	The package
	Brand name
	Service and maintenance
2. Product line	Position of brands within the product line
	Additional models, flavors, sizes, types within the product line
3. Advertising	Nature and content of advertising themes
	Frequency of messages
	Expected circulation and outreach of messages to target audience
	Media selected to communicate message (TV, radio, newspapers, magazines)
	Specific media to be used (specific magazines, thirty- versus sixty-second spots, TV and radio programs)
4. Sales promotion	Coupons (in newspapers, through direct mail, on package)
	Price promotions
	Product samples
5. Price	Price levels
	Changes in price based on competitive entry, projected changes in demand, and so forth
6. Distribution	Nature and type of wholesale and retail outlets
	Geographical coverage
	Markup to wholesalers and retailers
	Trade support offered to these outlets (advertising allowances, rebates, trade promotions)
	Physical distribution requirements (transportation, storage, inventory)
7. Sales force	Size of sales force
	Personal selling effort
	Sales territories and sales quotas

Coca-Cola must have undertaken rigorous testing to determine reactions to the name Diet Coke, since that was the first time the company was willing to use the Coke name on a brand other than its leading best seller. Various packaging alternatives must also have been tested before it settled on the red and white can.

Developing a Marketing Budget

Marketing mix components must be tested as part of an overall marketing strategy. Therefore, the firm must establish a marketing budget based on the required marketing effort to influence consumers. It must also allocate marketing expenditures to the components of the marketing mix. For example, the firm must establish an advertising budget as part of the marketing budget and allocate expenditure to various types of advertising media — television, newspapers, magazines. It must also determine a sales promotion budget and allocate money for coupons, product samples, and trade promotions. Similarly, it must set budgets for personal selling, distribution, and product development.

Evaluating sales responses

Developing a marketing budget requires estimating sales responses to the firm's marketing mix. A firm can estimate sales responses in three general ways. First, if past data exist, the firm can relate marketing expenditures to sales and attempt to assess the effect of the marketing mix on consumer responses by *statistical analysis.* Second, the firm can test various marketing strategies under controlled conditions and determine the effects on sales volume. Such an *experimental approach* might involve introducing a brand in two matched markets. Advertising expenditures or price might be high in one market and low in another. Sales results would be tracked. Since the markets are well matched, differences in sales results should be due to the different advertising and price strategies.

A third approach in evaluating sales response to the marketing mix is *managerial judgment.* Managers evaluate alternative strategies and estimate the likelihood of attaining a certain sales level. For example, managers might be asked to evaluate the likelihood of attaining $10 million in sales in the first year under various strategies — high advertising effect and low price, high advertising effect and higher price, and so forth. They would then develop a consensus as to what sales results would be most likely for a given strategy under specified environmental conditions. Managerial judgment is the weakest basis for evaluating the effect of the marketing mix. If historical data are available, the firm should conduct a statistical analysis. If not, it should consider test markets for evaluating alternative strategies.

Developing a marketing budget from the top down

The relationship between marketing effort and sales is known as a **sales response function.** Once this relationship is established, the firm is on a sounder footing to establish a marketing budget. The marketing budget can be determined in one of two ways: from the top down or from the bottom up.

A top-down budget establishes a total marketing expenditure figure and then allocates resources to each component of the marketing mix. A procedure for determining marketing expenditures on a top-down basis is illustrated in Figure 4-6, which shows estimated sales revenue and net profits at various marketing expenditure levels. The net profit curve is revenue minus marketing and nonmarketing costs. The point of profit maximization defines the optimal marketing expenditure level. In Figure 4-6 the firm should set the marketing budget at point M_1, where incremental sales dollars equal incremental marketing expenditures. If incremental sales dollars are greater than incremental marketing expenditures (a point below M_1), expenditures should increase; if incremental sales dollars are less (a point above M_1), expenditures should decrease.

There are three problems with the approach in Figure 4-6. First, it assumes sales response is strictly a function of marketing strategy. Many other factors might affect consumer responses — competition, a shift in consumer tastes, and so forth. Thus associations between sales and marketing expenditures are likely to change with shifts in the environment. Second, firms introducing new products would have trouble establishing a sales response function. Sales responses must be estimated from results of product tests and test markets. But such results may not accurately predict response when the product is introduced nationally. Third, the estimated marketing budget is only as good as the sales response on which it is based. If the association between marketing expenditure levels and sales is not accurate, the marketing budget will be equally inaccurate.

Developing a marketing budget from the bottom up

A marketing budget can also be developed by first determining the effort required from each of the marketing mix components to achieve marketing objectives. Advertising, sales promotion, personal selling, and distribution budgets would be established. Such an approach would require developing some association between each of the marketing mix components and consumer responses — for example, the association between advertising expenditure and sales. The marketing budget would then be the total of the individual budgets. This approach will probably produce a higher figure than a top-down approach, because product managers can more easily justify higher expenditures for individual pieces of the marketing plan. As a result, once the marketing budget

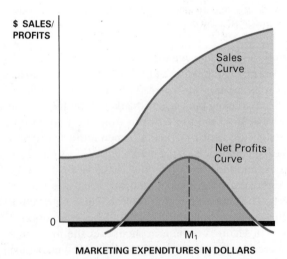

FIGURE 4-6
Determining the optimal marketing expenditure level

has been established, SBU management is likely to adjust it on the basis of an assessment of marketing strategy's overall effect on consumer responses.

Allocating Resources to Marketing Mix Components

If marketing expenditures are determined from the top down, the firm must have some reasonable basis for allocating resources to advertising, sales promotion, distribution, and personal selling. Let us take two components, advertising and sales promotion, as examples. For a fixed budget, the combinations of advertising and sales promotion expenditures are illustrated in Figure 4-7 on the straight line from $A_{100\%}$ to $S_{100\%}$, the former representing all advertising and no sales promotion, and the latter representing the reverse. The firm cannot test all the alternatives on the line, so it chooses to test five: a 75/25 split in favor of advertising or sales promotion, a 60/40 split in favor of one or the other, and equal allocations, as represented in Figure 4-7. It uses five test markets and,

FIGURE 4-7
Alternative allocations of advertising and sales promotion

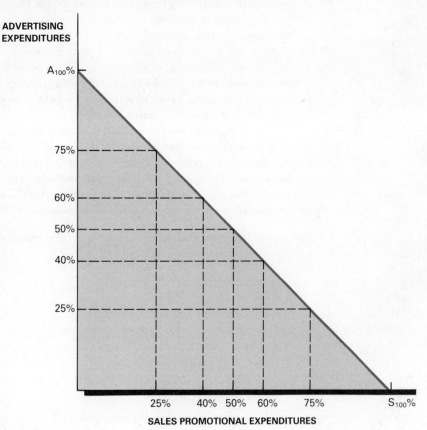

from sales results, develops a rough association between sales and the two marketing mix components. The association projected to the national level, is:

$$\text{Sales} = \$20 \text{ million} + 2.2\,(\text{advertising expenditures}) \\ + 1.8\,(\text{sales promotion expenditures})$$

The ratio between advertising's effect on sales and sales promotion's effect is 2.2 to 1.8 or 55/45. Therefore, marketing expenditures are allocated in this ratio on the basis of test market results.

More complicated procedures must be used to assess the effect of all marketing components simultaneously. Such procedures might rely on marketing models that establish a functional relationship between the components of the marketing mix and sales. An advertising agency developed one such model from the history of many new products in test market.[6]

Sensitivity Analysis

At this point the firm has selected the components of the marketing mix, established a marketing budget, and allocated the budget to these components. As a final check of the effect of the marketing mix on the consumer, management should undertake a sensitivity analysis to evaluate alternative marketing strategies. Perhaps the firm did not consider a price reduction in combination with an increase in advertising expenditures, or the possibility of introducing free product samples followed by an intensive coupon campaign. Management should consider expanding its set of strategic alternatives before making a final commitment to a particular strategy.

As an example, assume a brand is to be introduced at forty cents per unit with an advertising budget for the first year of $7 million and a $2 million budget for sales promotion. The company decides to test several alternatives in test market: higher advertising expenditures, higher sales promotion expenditures, and a lower price. Using test market results, management then assesses each alternative against the baseline strategy. The results are as follows:

Strategic Alternative	Estimated Effect on ROI
Baseline strategy: $7 million advertising, $2 million sales promotion, forty-cent price	0
Increase in advertising expenditures of $2 million with a one-cent increase in price	−1.0%
Decrease in advertising expenditures of $2 million with a three-cent decrease in price	−3.0%
Increase of $300,000: for coupons and trade promotions	+1.0%

Test market results thus show that a change in advertising expenditures accompanied by a change in price will not increase profitability. But an increase in coupon activity is a cost-effective way of increasing sales.

THE IMPLEMENTATION PLAN

After establishing the marketing mix the firm should formulate a procedure to ensure implementation of the marketing plan. There are two steps to implementation: (1) providing for a test market to evaluate the product in an actual market setting, and (2) providing for national introduction. Both test marketing and a national introduction are reviewed in Chapter 9 as part of the new product development process.

FINAL PROFIT AND LOSS ESTIMATES

After completing a test market, the product manager will be in a better position to estimate national sales and marketing and manufacturing costs, because the firm will have at least six months of operating history in several trade areas. Estimated marketing costs will be divided into advertising, distribution, consumer promotions, and trade promotions. (Table 4-3 shows the projected profit and loss for a new hair conditioner in the first year after introduction). Estimates are also made for manufacturing costs (including labor and raw material) and for overhead allocations (administration and research). Earnings before taxes are computed as revenue less total costs. Earnings in Table 4-3 are also presented as a percentage of revenue.

The profit and loss statement for a brand is given to management of the business unit. SBU management will combine this estimate with those of other

TABLE 4-3
Final Profit and Loss Estimates for a New Hair Conditioner

Revenue		$40.1 Million
Advertising and promotion		13.4 Million
Advertising	$7.0 Million	
Sales & distribution	2.5 Million	
Consumer promotions	2.0 Million	
Trade promotions	1.0 Million	
Other promotions	.9 Million	
Overhead allocations		2.3 Million
Research & development	1.5 Million	
Marketing research	.5 Million	
Administration	.3 Million	
Manufacturing costs		13.2 Million
Fixed	5.0 Million	
Variable	8.2 Million	
Earnings before taxes		$11.2 Million
Earnings as a percentage of revenues		27.9%

brands and provide top management with an integrated profit and loss statement for the entire business unit.

EVALUATION AND CONTROL

The product manager submits the marketing plan to business unit management for approval. If management approves, resources will be allocated in accordance with the estimated profit and loss statement.

Business unit management will compare actual to estimated sales performance and actual to estimated costs for each brand. The product manager will be asked to evaluate the brand's performance, particularly the effectiveness of the marketing mix. If sales are below estimate, the product manager will recommend changes in advertising, promotional, price, or distribution strategies. Such recommendations would have to be supported by data to indicate that planned changes in the marketing mix would improve sales performance.

Evaluation of sales performance leads to another planning cycle for the brand. This is represented by a feedback loop in Figure 4-4 from evaluation and control to marketing objectives. Failure to meet sales goals usually requires adjustments in the marketing mix. But management may occasionally realize that it miscalculated consumer needs or competitive reaction. Basic changes in the positioning of the brand might be required. Management must also consider withdrawing the product even after national introduction, difficult as this action may be.

Control will require SBU management to monitor marketing and manufacturing costs closely to ensure they are within budget. Some flexibility is provided the product manager to increase advertising and promotional costs. Competitive activity may require an increase in coupons; trade promotion expenditures might have to be increased to ensure acceptance of a new product by the trade; or adjustments in the advertising budget might be warranted. But business unit management would want to ensure that marketing costs are not excessive, especially since the product manager has a vested interest in increasing sales. Sales increases would occur at the expense of profits if there are excessive increases in advertising and promotional costs.

Marketing Strategies

The central responsibility of marketing management is to develop marketing strategies. Marketing strategies are of central concern to marketing managers for three reasons: (1) they represent the means by which the firm attempts to influence consumers; (2) their implementation requires major cost allocations; and (3) they determine the competitive position of the firm and affect growth potential. In short, the effectiveness of marketing strategies for the firm largely determines its product position and growth potential.

Marketing strategies are the result of the marketing planning process at each of the three planning levels cited earlier: the corporate, SBU, and product levels. Figure 4-8 links marketing strategies with the planning process at each of these three levels as follows:

1. growth strategies at the corporate level,

2. product mix strategies at the SBU level, and

3. marketing strategies at the individual product level.

Marketing strategies are further categorized as:

1. product positioning strategies,

FIGURE 4-8
Types of marketing strategies

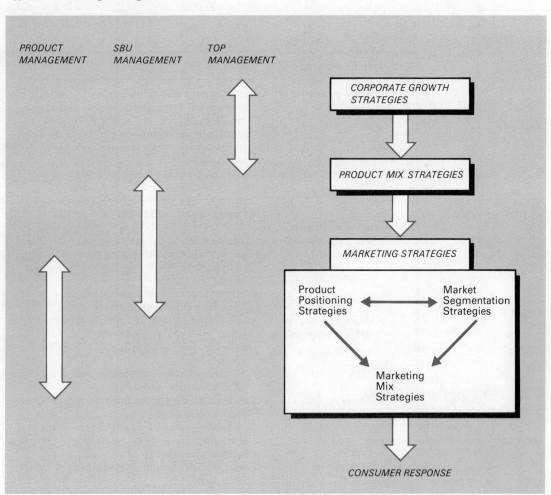

2. market segmentation strategies, and

3. marketing mix strategies.

Table 4-4 shows the purpose of each type of strategy.

    This section introduces the three basic types of strategies in Figure 4-8. In Part III we will review marketing strategies and in Part IV corporate growth and product mix strategies in more detail.

CORPORATE GROWTH STRATEGIES

Corporate growth strategies are designed for the firm's overall corporate mission. They provide a blueprint for the future by specifying the relative emphasis on (1) market expansion for *existing products*, (2) internal development of *new*

TABLE 4-4
Purposes of Marketing Strategies

TYPE OF STRATEGY	PURPOSE
1. Corporate growth strategies	Define corporate mission
	Identify relative importance of new versus existing products
	Identify relative importance of internal development versus external acquisition for new product growth
2. Product mix strategies	Determine product mix across SBUs
	Allocate resources to SBUs accordingly
	Determine product mix within SBUs
	Allocate resources to PMUs
3. Marketing strategies	
a. Product positioning strategies	Establish the brand's position relative to (1) consumer needs, and (2) competition
	Determine the need for repositioning existing brands
	Establish product positioning strategies as a basis for the marketing mix
b. Marketing segmentation strategies	Use needs to identify the primary target to which the brand is positioned
	Determine whether additional segments will be appealed to
	Determine whether additional brands will be offered to specific segments
c. Marketing mix strategies	Define advertising, sales promotion, distribution, and price strategies
	Determine spending levels for advertising and promotion
	Establish price level
	Ensure coordination of all elements of the marketing mix

products, and (3) acquisition of *new businesses.* For example, Polaroid is embarking on an active campaign to acquire new industrial companies to hedge against the fact that its resources have been concentrated primarily in photographic equipment.[7] In contrast, Colgate is divesting itself of many recent new product acquisitions because these acquisitions were sapping profits from the company's traditional soap and toiletry lines.[8] Colgate's product mission in the early 1970s of "increasing emphasis on developing new product categories distinct from our traditional product lines," resulted in a series of disastrous acquisitions.[9] A poorly formulated corporate mission and the resultant corporate growth strategies led the company down the wrong path. By the early 1980s traditional soap and toiletry products were reemphasized.

In defining its corporate mission, top management also determines the relative emphasis on new and existing products. Gillette found many of its traditionally male-oriented lines such as Right Guard in a stagnant position. It began to emphasize new products in the female market to ensure future growth.[10] As a result, it introduced six new women's products in three years.

PRODUCT MIX STRATEGIES

Figure 4-8 demonstrates that corporate growth strategies are developed by top management. The next set of strategies, product mix strategies, are developed both by top management and by management at the SBU level. Product mix strategies are developed by top management across SBUs; they are developed by SBU management within their business unit. In both cases the process is one of strategic marketing planning.

Product mix strategies determine the product offerings of the firm and its business units (see Table 4-4). They also determine changes in resource allocations designed to improve the firm's profit position. The firm might wish to "build" certain products into leading brands through an infusion of cash, to "hold" well-established brands in their present position, to "harvest" weaker brands in low-growth markets for their cash potential or to divest itself of unprofitable lines. Thus, Gillette used the resources from some of its entrenched brands such as Right Guard to finance the introduction of its Silkience shampoo for women.

MARKETING STRATEGIES

Corporate growth and product mix strategies provide the framework for marketing strategies for a particular brand. Figure 4-8 shows that marketing strategies are based on three closely interrelated components. Product positioning and market segmentation strategies are usually determined jointly because a product is frequently positioned to a well-defined market segment, and the needs of that market segment should determine the nature of the product positioning strategy. The characteristics of the market segment and the positioning of the product will then determine the marketing mix strategy (advertising, sales promotion, pricing, distribution, packaging, and product-line strategies) for a brand. For example, if a detergent brand is going to be positioned to the younger working woman with children with an appeal of time-saving and convenience, then the central theme of advertising must be this key benefit. The campaign might show a working mother able to spend more time with her children because of the time saved by using the product. Media would be selected to reach younger working mothers.

Product Positioning and Market Segmentation Strategies

Product positioning was cited as the basis for developing the brand's marketing mix. Table 4-4 specifies two criteria for defining a **product's positioning strategy:** (1) the set of consumer needs the product is targeted to meet, and (2) its uniqueness. The positioning strategy must recognize the market segment to which the brand is positioned. For example, Land O Lakes cheese was repositioned from an emphasis on good taste to an emphasis on freshness. This positioning was determined by the brand's segmentation strategy, since the brand was redirected from a smaller, gourmet taste segment to a broader-use group that emphasized freshness.[11]

Market segmentation strategies are designed to identify the nature and size of the target group. They also specify the potential for appealing to additional segments by expanding the target market. For example, a large food company positioned a low-calorie breakfast strip to meet the needs of a health-oriented segment that was somewhat older and used the product as a means of avoiding excessive cholesterol. The positioning was then expanded to include a nutrition-oriented segment that was younger and saw the primary benefit as low calories. As a result, the brand was advertised as a lean product that helped to keep weight down.

Another issue in market segmentation strategy is whether the firm should introduce additional products to meet the needs of segments the company is not now reaching. For example, when Philip Morris bought Miller beer, it moved from a one-product strategy to a full line directed to specific segments. In the words of *Business Week*:

> Miller's new managers borrowed the classic consumer marketing techniques that had brought Philip Morris success in the cigarette business and produced the nation's leading tobacco brand — Marlboro. The approach calls for dividing up the U.S. beer market into demand segments, producing new products and packages specifically for those segments.[12]

The result was repositioning the basic brand to the heavy beer drinker and introducing the first successful light beer, Miller Lite, in 1975. Miller also attempted to appeal to the premium beer segment by purchasing domestic rights to Lowenbrau and introducing Special Reserve beer. And it has a malt liquor entry, Miller's Magnum. Finally, Miller has segmented the market by size — introducing "pony" sizes to appeal to the light user. Miller became a full-product-line company by introducing offerings to every major market segment.

Marketing Mix Strategies

Product positioning and market segmentation strategies directly influence the development of the brand's marketing mix. **Marketing mix strategies** are the means by which the company attempts to influence consumers to buy. The components of the strategies that make up the marketing mix were listed in Table 4-2. It is apparent from Table 4-2 that the orientation of the marketing mix is tactical (specific implementation), whereas positioning and segmentation strategies are more strategic (broader guidelines to influence consumers). Because of the tactical orientation of the marketing mix, responsibility for its development is with the product manager.

In Part III we will deal with each component of the marketing mix in a separate chapter. Details of planning and strategy development will be considered at that point.

Summary

Marketing planning is the means of developing marketing strategies. It involves developing both a corporate plan and a plan to market a product. The corporate plan is a broader and a longer-term document that shows a growth strategy for the firm as a whole. It allocates resources across the firm's business units and provides guidance in developing the firm's offerings. The marketing plan includes only the strategies for a particular brand. As such it is a more specific and shorter-term document. Its main purpose is to develop the mix of marketing strategies for a brand and to specify the level of marketing effort for advertising, sales promotion, personal selling, and distribution activities.

The process of marketing planning requires an organizational and a managerial framework. There are three planning levels in the corporate hierarchy: (1) the corporate level (represented by top management), (2) the strategic business unit (represented by business managers), and (3) product market units (represented by product managers).

Top management is interested in the firm's product mix: the product offerings of all business units. The second level in the firm, the strategic business unit, operates as an autonomous profit center with independent planning responsibilities. It is concerned with the product offerings for its specific activities. The third planning level, the product market unit, is responsible for developing marketing plans for individual brands. The marketing planning process at the product market level requires:

1. developing marketing objectives based on corporate goals;
2. evaluating marketing opportunities for the introduction of new products or the market expansion of existing products;

3. positioning a product to convey its benefits to the consumer and to differentiate it from competitors;

4. developing a set of marketing strategies (a mix of advertising, sales promotion, personal selling, distribution, and pricing strategies) to market the brand;

5. establishing a budget for marketing activities and allocating it to the components of the marketing mix;

6. ensuring implementation of the marketing plan for national delivery of the marketing mix;

7. developing sales forecasts and cost estimates for the brand; and

8. evaluating sales performance and controlling costs.

We concluded the chapter by considering the basic output of the marketing planning process, marketing strategies. Marketing strategies are a central consideration of this book because they are the means by which the firm influences the consumer to buy. We considered three types of strategies: (1) growth strategies at the corporate level, (2) product mix strategies at the SBU level, and (3) marketing strategies at the individual brand or product level.

Marketing strategies are made up of (1) product positioning strategies, (2) market segmentation strategies, and (3) marketing mix strategies. These marketing strategies will be described in Part III, whereas corporate growth and product mix strategies will be described in Part IV.

In Part II we will consider the first element in strategy development, the identification and exploitation of marketing opportunity, which is based primarily on fulfilling consumer needs.

Questions

1. What are the (a) corporate planning issues and (b) marketing planning issues in:

   ☐ Kodak's decision to introduce disc cameras, and

   ☐ Coca-Cola's decision to introduce Diet Coke?

2. Why did General Foods shift from a traditional divisional organization to an organization based on strategic business units?

3. What are the distinctions between strategic marketing planning and product marketing planning? Focus on one example of a company entering a new business (e.g., IBM's entry into personal computers) and cite the strategic planning issues and the market planning issues that might have arisen.

4. Consider Philip Morris's acquisition of Miller Beer in the early 1970s.

   □ What strategic planning issues might have arisen in considering the acquisition?

   □ What product marketing planning issues?

5. What are the distinctions between strategic marketing planning at the corporate and at the SBU level? Focus on the same example you cited in question 3 in considering these distinctions.

6. Develop a product/market matrix for a particular SBU within a company by listing the products down the side and the markets across the top. Indicate the served markets, the markets that might be considered for entry, and the unserved markets (see Figures 4-2 and 4-3).

   □ Describe areas of marketing opportunity in your matrix.

   □ Describe areas of potential risk.

7. What are the risks of repositioning a brand? Can you cite any examples?

8. Why is it so difficult to establish a relationship between expenditure levels and sales responses? What are the advantages and disadvantages of the three methods cited in the text for establishing sales responses (statistical analysis, experiments, and managerial judgment)?

9. Figure 4-6 illustrates a basis for determining a marketing budget in an attempt to maximize profits. What is the profit maximization principle illustrated in Figure 4-6?

10. What are the relative merits of top-down and bottom-up methods of determining a marketing budget?

11. In what ways do corporate growth and product mix strategies influence development of marketing strategies?

12. What is the relationship between market segmentation and product positioning? Is the firm more likely to identify a target segment first and then define a product's position or the reverse?

Notes

1. Mack Hanan, "Reorganize Your Company Around Its Markets," *Harvard Business Review* 52 (November–December 1974): 69.

2. David S. Hopkins, "New Emphases in Product Planning and Strategy Development," *Industrial Marketing Management* 6 (1977): 416.

3. " 'How-to' Turns Aziza Toward Growth," *Advertising Age,* February 26, 1979, p. S-34.

4. Ibid.

5. Jack Trout, "Marketing in the 70's: Product Positioning," *The Conference Board Record* (January 1976): 42.

6. Henry J. Claycamp and Lucien E. Liddy, "Prediction of New Product Performance: An Analytical Approach," *Journal of Marketing Research* 6 (November 1969): 414–20.

7. "Polaroid Seeks Business Focus," *Industrial Marketing,* October 1981, pp. 8–29, 33.

8. "Colgate Works Hard to Become the Firm it was a Decade ago," *The Wall Street Journal,* November 23, 1981, pp. 1, 8.

9. *The Wall Street Journal,* November 23, 1981, p. 1.

10. "Gillette Makes Tricky Switch to Selling Women's Products," *The Wall Street Journal,* November 5, 1981, p. 31.

11. "Marketing Flows at Land O Lakes," *Advertising Age,* February 23, 1981, p. 80.

12. "Miller's Fast Growth Upsets the Beer Industry," *Business Week,* November 8, 1976, p. 60.

Defining and Measuring Marketing Opportunity

The marketer's first consideration in developing strategy is identifying marketing opportunities. Central to opportunity identification is the consumer — both the final consumer and the industrial buyer.

Part II focuses on the consumer. In Chapter 5 we will develop an understanding of consumer and organizational buyer behavior. The chapter shows how such an understanding aids the marketer in developing strategies. In Chapter 6 we will consider the internal and external factors that influence consumer choices, and how these factors affect the development of segmentation, positioning, and marketing mix strategies. The internal influences on marketing strategies are consumer needs, attitudes, and characteristics. The external (environmental) influences are culture, social class, and groups.

In Chapter 7 we will shift the focus from understanding consumer influences to measuring them through marketing research. That chapter describes existing sources of marketing information and techniques to define and collect consumer information.

CHAPTER 5

Consumer and Organizational Buyer Behavior

FOCUS OF CHAPTER

The development of marketing strategies requires an understanding of buyer behavior. Consider the following examples of companies that did not adequately research consumer needs, attitudes, and characteristics in shaping marketing strategies:

- A pharmaceutical company introduces an aspirin product that can be taken without water, failing to realize that consumers like the salutary effect of water when they swallow an aspirin

- A food company introduces a quick-cooking sausage strip in the eastern market, assuming its success in the Midwest will carry over. It fails to realize that eastern consumers will cook the product longer for fear of bacteria in pork. The result was a shrunken sausage after seven or eight minutes of cooking.

- A producer of condensed soup exports its product to England, failing to realize that English consumers are likely to react negatively to the product because of the smaller can. They are used to heftier home-made soups and prepared soups in larger cans.

- A manufacturer of industrial fastening products maintains a standardized line of products thinking that fasteners are bought on a routinized basis and there is little profit in producing them on specification. It fails to identify key segments of the industrial market that have specialized fastening needs and represent profit potential.

This chapter deals with the nature of buyer decisions for brands and products. The next chapter considers more specific buyer influences that affect strategy. Two types of buyers will be considered, the final consumer and buyers in organizations. The bulk of **organizational buying** is for industrial products (purchases of products directly or indirectly related to

123

production of other goods), but organizational buying also includes purchases by service institutions (schools and hospitals) and intermediaries (retailers and wholesalers). The importance of industrial purchases is reflected in the fact that they represent a larger proportion of total expenditures than purchases of consumer goods.[1] As a result, differences between consumer and industrial buying behavior will be emphasized.

In this chapter we will consider the consumer buyer and then the organizational buyer. For each case three types of purchasing behavior will be described: complex decision making, habit, and low-involvement decisions. Some decisions, such as those for an automobile or an industrial generator, involve a lot of deliberation, information search, and evaluation of alternatives. These processes make up *complex decision making*. Other decisions may involve minimal deliberation based on past satisfaction. A consumer may be happy with a certain brand of beer; an organizational buyer may be perfectly satisfied to keep rebuying from the current vendor. These decisions are governed by *habit* and result in brand or vendor loyalty. A third type of decision takes place when the buyer is not involved in the product or decision. The purchaser of canned peas may keep buying the same brand because it is not worth the time and effort to consider alternatives. The industrial buyer may decide that industrial tape is so inconsequential that it should always be purchased from the same vendor. These decisions are not governed by brand or vendor loyalty but by *inertia*.

The focus of the chapter is strategic. We will consider the marketing implications of complex decision making, habit, and low-involvement decisions. Further, we will look at the strategic differences arising from consumer versus organizational buyer behavior.

Types of Buyer Decisions

Buyers make several types of decisions. Most of marketing's focus is on decisions for alternative brands. This is because marketing strategies are generally developed for a specific brand. But as Chapter 2 noted, consumers go through a hierarchical process in which they also make decisions regarding the product category, product type, store, and in some cases brand options. This sequence is illustrated in Figure 5-1 for an automobile decision.

In the process of making these choices, a consumer will also select various information sources on which to base these decisions (dealers, friends, family, advertising, impartial testing agencies, and so on.)

Organizational buyers may also make several types of decisions. For example, in the purchase of a computer system, they must decide on the type of system

TYPE OF DECISION	ALTERNATIVES

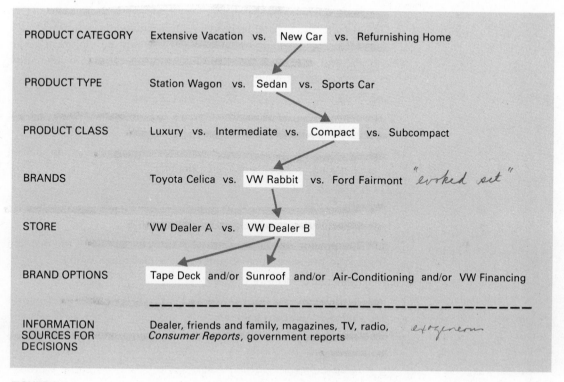

FIGURE 5-1
A sequence of consumer decision making (a family decision for a new car)

(configuration, output format, core, etc.) before deciding on a vendor. Specific decisions must also be made on information sources for the system. The importance of recognizing that consumers make different types of decisions is not so much in demonstrating the sequence of decisions but in suggesting strategic implications at each stage. For example:

1. Product category decisions:

   ☐ provide a broader framework for understanding the competitive boundaries of a product (e.g., do auto purchases compete with vacations?);

   ☐ indicate industry demand trends that have corporatewide implications as opposed to demand for an individual brand (e.g., increased gas prices resulting in a downturn in auto purchases); and

   ☐ might indicate the need for industrywide cooperative advertising to combat decreasing demand trends (e.g., the auto companies cooperating in advertising greater fuel efficiency of automobiles).

2. Product type and product class decisions:

☐ provide guidelines for the proper boundaries of a product line (e.g., Should Mercedes expand its product line to include a station wagon?); suggest opportunities for new technologies (the development of an electric car); and suggest new product opportunities (smaller, more economical station wagons).

3. Brand decisions:

☐ give management a basis for comparing the strengths and weaknesses of their brands to those of the competition; and

☐ suggest new product opportunities based on unmet needs (e.g., introducing a good-tasting, decaffeinated coffee brand).

4. Store decisions:

☐ provide retailers with a basis for comparing the strengths and weaknesses of their store to those of their competition; and

☐ indicate the importance of in-store promotional stimuli (if the decision is made in the store, such stimuli become more important).

5. Information source decisions:

☐ suggest the sources of information the marketer should rely on to inform and influence the consumer; and

☐ provide guidelines for more effectively directing messages to defined target groups.

A Classification of Buyer Decisions

A classification of buyer decisions is presented in Figure 5-2 that applies to both consumers and buyers in organizations.

CONSUMER BUYER BEHAVIOR

The example of an automobile purchase in the previous section might give the impression that consumer buying decisions involve extensive brand evaluation and information search. Yet many purchase decisions involve little prior deliberation. The classification in Figure 5-2 is based on two dimensions. The first dimension distinguishes between decision making and habit. An automobile purchase represents conscious decision making, but little or no decision making may be involved when one repeatedly buys the same brand of deodorant or toothpaste. The second dimension distinguishes between high- and low-involvement purchases. High-involvement purchases are important to the consumer and are tied to his or her self-image. The automobile is a high-involvement product. But deodorants and toothpaste can also be high-involvement products, even though they are purchased repeatedly and at times with little thought,

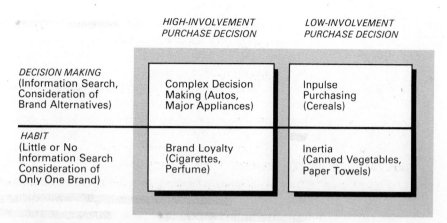

FIGURE 5-2
A classification of consumer decisions

because they are tied to the consumer's ego and social needs. Low-involvement purchases are less important to the consumer. For most consumers purchases of canned vegetables, salt, paper towels, and cereal are not related to self-image.

The two dimensions in Figure 5-2 produce four types of consumer decisions. The first, *complex decision making,* occurs when involvement is high and a decision process takes place. As in the automobile example, complex decision making involves extensive search for information and a complex process of brand evaluation. The second process, *brand loyalty,* occurs when involvement is high but little decision making takes place. Deodorants, toothpaste, perfume, cigarettes are all high-involvement products. They are also purchased regularly. At first a consumer must go through a decision process (frequently complex) to select a brand. But over time, the frequency of purchase of these items leads the consumer to judge one brand to be the best available and to continue buying that brand.

Figure 5-2 also illustrates two types of low-involvement purchase process. First, *impulse purchasing* is characterized by decision making with low-involvement. Since involvement for the product is low, consumers do not search for information and make prior judgments. Yet brands differ enough to warrant some comparison. As a result, decisions are generally made within the store impulsively or on the basis of immediate comparisons. Cereals and cookies have enough brand differences to warrant comparisons, but consumers are not involved enough to make a prior decision with extensive information search. For such items consumers are unlikely to stay with the same brand over time. Since involvement is low, purchase risks are low. Consumers may have little to lose by switching brands in the search for variety.[2]

Second, low involvement may lead the consumer to buy the same brand, not because of brand loyalty, but because of *inertia*.[3] When purchasing by inertia, consumers select a brand that is satisfactory but not optimal because they do not want to spend the time and effort to search for alternatives. They may not even spend the effort to go through a process of decision making in the store. Brands purchased by inertia (bleach, salt, canned vegetables) typically have few distinguishing characteristics. The consumer is not buying the same brand because of brand loyalty but because of a desire to avoid a decision process.

ORGANIZATIONAL BUYER BEHAVIOR

The classification in Figure 5-2 applies to organizations as well as to consumers. Writers have distinguished between organizational purchases that occur once only ("new task decisions"), and frequently recurring purchases ("straight rebuys"). The purchase of a telecommunications system or pollution control equipment would be a new task decision. Such decisions clearly require complex decision making since there is little past evidence to rely on. Extensive information search is required to identify alternative suppliers and develop proper product specifications. Straight rebuys occur frequently and can be handled routinely with little information search. Examples would be the purchase of industrial tape, piping, or fasteners. Such cases could be characterized as habitual purchases in which vendor loyalties develop over time because of satisfaction with the product, service, and price (lower left-hand box in Figure 5-2). Of course many situations fall in between a new task and a straight rebuy. These may be recurring purchasing decisions, but alternative vendors are considered and new information is required.

Traditionally, organizational buying is assumed to be high involvement. Buying is assumed to be riskier than for the consumer. Purchasing expenditures are significantly higher and, at times, a buyer's job may be on the line. But low-involvement conditions do operate in organizational purchasing at times. One study found that the most frequent reason for using the same vendor in industrial purchasing is not good service or better prices but a desire to avoid change.[4] This means that the distinction between brand loyalty and inertia in Figure 5-2 also applies to organizational buying. In some cases, organizational buyers will use the same vendor because the regular vendor is the best available. But at times, such vendors are repeatedly chosen because of inertia. It may not be worth the potential risk for an organizational buyer to switch to a new vendor. If delivery dates or product specifications are not met, the buyer will be blamed for switching. As a result, organizational buyers are more likely to use the same vendor.

Strategic Implications of Consumer Behavior

Marketing strategy depends largely on the buyer decision process. This section describes *consumer* behavior and explains the strategic implications of such behavior, depending on whether the consumer is engaged in complex decision making, habit, or low-involvement decisions. In the next section, we will consider *organizational* buyer behavior.

COMPLEX DECISION MAKING

The consumer generally goes through five steps in complex decision making as illustrated in Figure 5-3:

1. *Need arousal.* The consumer becomes aware of a need because of his or her demographic characteristics, life style, social and family environment, and economic condition. For example, a recent MBA graduate decides she can afford to buy a good 35-millimeter camera because she just got a job. In so doing, she decides to emphasize certain features — quality of the lens, ease in handling, speed and aperture settings, and price.

2. *Consumer information processing.* Once a need is aroused, a consumer becomes more aware of stimuli related to that need — advertising, friends using the product, recommendations of salespeople, and so forth. If the consumer is to be influenced by a marketing stimulus, he or she must first be aware of it, comprehend it, and retain it in memory. Such information may cause consumers to change their priority of needs (additional information causes our prospective camera purchaser to emphasize aperture setting over ease of handling). New information may also cause consumers to change their attitude toward certain brands (ads for a Canon result in a more favorable image of the camera), or to become aware of new brands (a friend tells our consumer about a new, lower-priced Nikon model).

3. *Brand evaluation.* As the consumer collects more information, he or she comes closer to a decision. The consumer will evaluate alternative brands in light of new information. Brands are evaluated on the criteria defined in need evaluation. For our camera purchaser, the most important features are quality of lens, speed and aperture settings, ease of operation, and price, in that order. She will evaluate various brands and select the one that best satisfies

FIGURE 5-3
The process of complex decision making

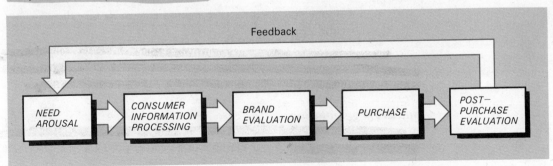

the most important criteria. For example, even if a Canon is least expensive and easiest to operate, she is unlikely to select it if it does not also score well on the most important criterion, quality of lens. Our consumer decides to buy a Nikon because she scores it highest on quality of lens and reasonably high on the other criteria except price. But price was not sufficiently high to outweigh the positive rating on the other criteria. If she had computed a score for each brand on the basis of the evaluative criteria weighted by importance, Nikon would have scored highest.

4. *Purchase.* The outcome of brand evaluation is an intention to buy the chosen brand. Purchasing in the process of complex decision making may not be immediate. Consumers may intend to buy a car, but may not do so immediately. In the meantime new information may change purchasing plans, or unforeseen financial contingencies may arise. If the product is purchased, the consumer then begins postpurchase evaluation.

5. *Postpurchase evaluation.* Consumers evaluate a product while consuming it. In the process they learn more about the brand. There are three possible outcomes of postpurchase evaluation: satisfaction, dissatisfaction, and dissonance. When consumption is repetitive, satisfaction increases the chances the same brand will be purchased (for example, a consumer buys a new brand of coffee, likes the taste, and buys again). Each time the brand is repurchased, the probability of buying again increases. Dissatisfaction will reduce the chances of buying again, sometimes almost to zero. **Dissonance** is the receipt of negative or contradictory information about a chosen brand.[5] It causes the consumer to have postpurchase doubts. Assume a consumer buys a car. Shortly after, a friend with the same model describes serious problems with his engine. In such a situation, the consumer is naturally concerned that she made the wrong choice. Many consumers reduce dissonance by either ignoring the information or by selectively interpreting it so it does not conflict with the purchase decision (saying the friend's car was probably a lemon).[6]

An important function of marketing strategy is to reduce dissonance by reinforcing recent purchases. What can the marketer do to reduce dissonance?[7]

☐ Provide a good warranty and ensure good service.

☐ Advertise reliable product quality to reassure recent purchasers.

☐ Follow up the purchase with direct contacts to make sure the customer understands product use.

The five steps of complex decision making have important implications for marketing strategy, particularly for market segmentation, product development, product positioning, and each component of the marketing mix.

Market Segmentation

A study of complex decision making should indicate the characteristics of a product's target market. In our example of a camera purchase we described only one consumer. The marketer will probably obtain data on a sample of consumers through marketing research. Information on needs might indicate that the market for high-quality cameras can be divided into two benefit segments, a features-oriented segment and a self-confident, quality-oriented segment. Different camera models could be developed for each segment, and advertising and pricing would have to differ accordingly. Research might also show that the quality-oriented segment is upscale (has a high income and education), older, and in professional-managerial occupations. Such information would guide marketers in developing advertising themes and in selecting media.

Product Development

The preceding example demonstrates that the definition of consumer needs will influence product development. The product for consumers in the features-oriented camera segment will contain more options to assist them in picture-taking. The model directed to the self-confident, quality segment will have a better-quality lens but fewer features. A third model might contain both features and a high-quality lens to appeal to members of the features-oriented group who are willing to spend more on quality.

The definition of consumer needs may also assist product development by identifying gaps in the market. For example, a segment of the paper towel market wanted a paper towel that was both absorbent and strong enough to permit reuse. The result was the introduction of several brands of heavy-duty paper towels to fill the needs of this segment (e.g., Teri, Bolt).

Product Positioning

The positioning of a product also depends heavily on how consumers define their needs in complex decision making. Needs for quality, features, ease of operation, and price define four possible positionings for a new camera. A camera could be positioned to compete at the top of the line in terms of quality. Its position could be based on the introduction of new features such as automatic setting. It could be based on ease of handling. Or the camera could be positioned as a lower-priced brand with sufficient quality to appeal to the serious photographer.

Advertising

Consumer decision making will also influence advertising strategies. A target segment's needs will provide direction for an ad campaign. Advertising to the serious photographer should be based on an informational rather than an image-oriented campaign, one that emphasizes quality and performance, not price, convenience, or ease of handling.

Brand evaluations will help answer a key question in assessing the effectiveness of advertising: Do consumers associate the brand with the advertising theme? One study for a major bank found that although the bank had a high level of name recognition and was rated high on service, few people associated the name of the bank with its primary advertising theme. This finding suggested a failure in communication and a need for redirecting the advertising strategy.

If purchasing a product involves financial, social, or performance risks, then an important role of advertising is to alleviate concern about the product. Advertising for autos or cameras might reduce performance risk by emphasizing service and warranties. Advertising for toothpaste or deodorants might reduce social risk by emphasizing group acceptance. It is also important to reduce dissonance after the purchase is made. Advertising has an important role in "keeping the customer sold" by stressing that current owners made the right decision. Yet historically the advertising industry has been more concerned with inducing trial than with maintaining existing customers.

Media Planning

Stimulus exposure among decision makers will provide guidelines for media selection. If *Modern Photography* is read by many Nikon owners, it would be a logical medium in which to advertise. The demographic characteristics of the target group should also be considered. If the target group is defined as high-income, well-educated urban dwellers, then magazines that reach such readers (e.g., *Business Week, The New Yorker*) should be selected.

Distribution

Products characterized by complex decision making are likely to be distributed selectively rather than intensively because they are more likely to be specialty items requiring personal selling or service at the retail level. Selective distribution permits the marketer to establish a high-quality image and to maintain some control over marketing at the retail level.

Pricing

Consumers are less likely to be price sensitive when evalutating brands by complex decision making. Because of the time and trouble in searching for information and in evaluating alternative brands, consumers are unlikely to decide on the basis of price alone. In contrast, when purchasing a less involving product, consumers generally demonstrate more price sensitivity. A consumer may use price as the primary criterion to avoid information processing and brand evaluation.

Less price sensitivity for products that require complex decision making suggests that marketers are more likely to establish a competitive advantage through product and promotional rather than pricing strategies. Deals, coupons, and price specials are less likely to be effective. Although certain brands may maintain a niche in the market as lower-priced brands, intensive price competition will be less likely. Most marketers will be wary of substantial price reductions because consumers may assume that lower price connotes lower quality.

HABIT AND BRAND LOYALTY

Prior satisfaction with a brand may lead to repurchasing and eventually to buying by habit. **Habit** is a consumer's way of ensuring satisfaction on the basis of experience and of avoiding decision making by reducing or eliminating information search and brand evaluation.

Habit sometimes leads to brand loyalty. As Figure 5-2 shows, **brand loyalty** is buying by habit when the consumer is highly involved with the brand (lower left-hand box). This is because the consumer has a high commitment to the brand as a result of past satisfaction.

When a consumer buys by habit, he or she has settled on a brand and has become a regular purchaser. Figure 5-4 shows that need arousal may lead to an immediate purchase (e.g., a consumer is out of paper towels and buys some the same day). Information processing is not necessary because the consumer had decided to purchase the same brand. Brand evaluation is also unnecessary.

Postpurchase evaluation may have two possible results. The consumer may be as satisfied with the brand as in previous purchases. This reinforcement will increase the probability of repurchasing. The high level of standardization for packaged goods makes the same level of satisfaction likely in repeat purchases.

FIGURE 5-4
The process of buying by habit

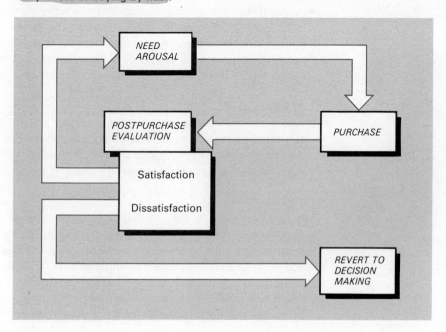

If the consumer is dissatisfied with the brand, a more active search for information and brand evaluation will occur. This causes the consumer to revert from habit to active decision making. The introduction of a new brand or of new product features may also cause the consumer to move from habit to a decision-making process. When consumers buy primarily by habit, strategic implications are totally different than those for complex decision-making.

Advertising and In-Store Promotions

Products bought by habit tend to be purchased frequently. These products are high-turnover consumer packaged goods. Frequent purchases require repetitive advertising to act as a reminder. Therefore frequency of advertising is more important than variation of message. In contrast, products that require complex decision making are more likely to use advertising to convey information. Advertising objectives center on associating product benefits with consumer needs.

In-store stimuli are important for products purchased by habit. Displays and shelf position remind consumers to buy once they are in the store. In complex decision making, consumers are less likely to make the decision in the store. They rely on advertising and personal sources to obtain product information before entering the store.

Product

Products purchased by habit are generally packaged goods with straightforward characteristics. Service requirements and warranties are rare. Products purchased by complex decision making are more likely to be durables. They are technically more complex, requiring information on product characteristics and performance. After-sales support such as service and warranties is more important. Personal selling is also more likely to be a means of communication and influence.

Pricing

Frequently the only way a competitior can get a brand-loyal consumer to try an alternative brand is to introduce a price deal or special sale. Another method is to provide free samples. Deals and free samples are less effective in complex decision making because the risks of buying by price alone are too great.

Distribution

Brands purchased by habit should be distributed intensively because they are frequently purchased items that do not require much shopping. The loyal purchaser of a brand of toothpaste, deodorant, or analgesic would expect to find it in most pharmacies and supermarkets. In addition to convenience, intensive distribution has an important reminder effect. Until recently, Hershey relied on intensive distribution rather than advertising to promote its chocolate products. The Hershey bar advertised itself. Products purchased by complex decision making are more likely to require selective distribution because of the need for personal selling and the importance of service.

LOW-INVOLVEMENT CONSUMER BEHAVIOR

Complex decision making and brand loyalty assume the consumer is involved in the purchase. Figure 5-2 provides for another decision process — low-involvement decision making.[8] In a **low-involvement** purchase, the consumer does not consider the product important enough to identify with it.

Most purchase decisions are low in consumer involvement. Kassarjian makes this point effectively: "[Consumers] just do not care much about products: they are unimportant to them. Although issues such as racial equality, wars and the draft may stir them up, products do not."[9]

When consumers are not involved with a product, they receive brand information passively; they will not actively search for information. They may receive brand information by watching TV or talking to friends, but they will not interpret and evaluate it. They just notice it. An ad for Green Giant frozen vegetables may be seen and stored in memory with very little cognitive processing. When the consumer is in the store, seeing the product on the shelf provides a link to the advertising. The consumer buys because of the familiarity of the brand name, not because of any process of need-association. Having bought, the consumer uses the product and decides it is reasonably good. Brand evaluation does not occur before the purchase because it is not worth the time and effort. Therefore, in low-involvement purchasing, the consumer acts first and might evaluate the brand later. In complex decision making, the consumer evaluates the brand first and then acts on this basis.

Figure 5-2 suggests that there are two types of low-involvement purchase: inertia and impulse purchase. In **inertia** there is no decision process. The consumer will either buy a brand at random (choosing the first brand of canned vegetables encountered) or will buy the same brand repetitively to avoid choice. Even though the consumer buys the same brand, this action does not represent brand loyalty since there is no commitment to the brand or strongly favorable attitude. The same brand is purchased to avoid the time and effort involved in a decision process.

The second type of low-involvement purchase process in Figure 5-2 is *impulse purchasing*. It differs from inertia since a more active decision process occurs. When there are enough differences between brands, a decision process is warranted, even though consumer involvement is low.

Consumers react to brand differences in low-involvement conditions by buying a diversity of brands on impulse. A consumer sees a different brand on the store shelf and buys it. The motivation for switching from the regular brand is not dissatisfaction as in the case of high-involvement products; it is a desire for change, a search for novelty. Because low-involvement products are mundane, impulse purchasing is a logical expression of consumer boredom.

The lack of consumer involvement in purchasing will result in marketing strategies totally different from those for high-involvement conditions. Once again, every facet of marketing strategy will be affected by the nature of the consumer decision process.

Advertising and In-Store Promotions

The consumer pays much less attention to advertising in low-involvement conditions than in high. The role of advertising in low involvement is to create familiarity and establish positive brand associations. As a result, advertising should:

1. *Emphasize repetition* to gain exposure and foster familiarity[10]
2. *Focus on a few key points in short messages* since there is little product interest and limited willingness to process information.[11]
3. *Keep the product visually in front of the consumer* since consumers learn passively and forget quickly.[12]
4. *Use symbols and imagery* to develop strong association with the brand and encourage learning fostered by repetition.[13]
5. *Use in-store displays and emphasize package design* since decisions for low-involvement products are frequently made in the store.

Media Strategy

Television rather than print media should be the primary vehicle for advertising low-involvement products. Television is a low-involvement medium that encourages passive learning because the viewer is relaxed and does not have to evaluate the content of the message.[14] Unlike newspapers or magazines, television gives viewers no control over pace and little opportunity for reflection or making connections. Print media are more suitable if the audience is involved with the message and actively seeking information. The pace of exposure is within the reader's control and the reader has more opportunity to reflect on the advertising.

Pricing

Low-involvement products are frequently purchased on the basis of price alone. A decrease in price or a coupon offer may be sufficient to induce the consumer to try the brand. Attempts at inducing trial are particularly important for low-involvement products since consumers frequently decide to continue buying the same brand to save time and energy. The marketer should therefore try to encourage trial in low-involvement conditions by price promotion and coupons.[15]

Product Positioning

Involved consumers will try to select brands that satisfy specific benefits in an attempt to maximize satisfaction. Less-involved consumers will probably purchase brands that are least likely to give them problems. In selecting plastic wrap, the uninvolved consumer may be motivated to select the wrap that is least likely to shred, stick together, or come apart, not the wrap that is strongest, provides the most protection, or is clearest. The importance of problem minimization also suggests some revision in the marketing concept. Marketing strategies should be directed to known consumer wants for high-involvement products and to known consumer problems for low-involvement products.

Market Segmentation

The definition of low-involvement decision making suggests that some consumers may be less involved than others with the same product. Although most consumers may not be very involved with paper towels, some consumers may be more highly involved. As a result, marketing strategies for the same product can be differentiated so that one set of strategies is directed to involved consumers and another set to less-involved consumers.[16]

Marketers are more likely to develop separate lines for high- and low-involvement segments rather than to try to appeal to both with the same brand. For example, in the cereal market a brand directed to the involved segment would have a higher nutritional content, a higher price, and a more informational advertising campaign with a greater reliance on print ads. A brand directed to the less-involved segment would be priced lower, use an image-oriented rather than an informational campaign, and rely on frequent advertising.

Using Marketing Strategy to Increase Consumer Involvement

It would make sense for marketers to try to get consumers involved with a product since involvement means commitment and a greater likelihood of brand loyalty. They can use these strategies:

1. *Link the product to some involving issue.*[17] Producers of household products such as floor cleaners link these uninvolving products to an involving issue such as peer group acceptance (e.g., praise for a clean floor from friends and neighbors).

2. *Link the product to an involving personal situation.*[18] A coffee commercial in the early morning or sleep aid commercials on late-night TV might increase product involvement because of the relevance of the situation.

3. *Link the product to involving advertising.*[19] An advertisement for a low-involvement product that expresses the consumers' values and identity might increase involvement (Pepsi drinkers think young).

4. *Introduce an important characteristic in the product.*[20] The introduction of a new characteristic to an uninvolving product might increase involvement. The introduction of fluoride into toothpaste increased involvement with the product by linking it to an important need — cavity prevention.

Organizational Buyer Behavior

Because industrial goods are so important in the American economy, it is appropriate to consider the processes that characterize organizational buying behavior. Organizational buying behavior has certain similarities to consumer buyer behavior, but it is different enough to require differences in marketing planning and strategies. In this section we will first consider these similarities and differences. Then we will look at the three basic decision processes — complex decision making, habit and low-involvement decisions — in the organizational setting.

SIMILARITIES TO CONSUMER BEHAVIOR

Buyers in organizations have generally been regarded as operating by rational criteria of cost, product quality, and service. As far back as 1924 Paul Converse stated, "The [industrial] buyers are generally experts. ... Buying tends to become scientific. Quality, price and delivery are the controlling factors."[21] Over thirty years later Shoaf studied 137 managers engaged in industrial buying and found that emotional factors such as subjective attitudes, desire to avoid risk, and longevity of supplier relations frequently come into play.[22]

If an industrial buyer does operate on personal rather than organizational motives, many of the characteristics of consumer behavior apply equally well to buyers in organizations. For example, the industrial buyer develops attitudes toward vendors on the basis of experience and the buyer's predispositions. The result may be vendor loyalty because of favoritism or longevity rather than rational criteria of price, service, and quality. Several studies have also shown that interpersonal influences may operate in organizational buyer behavior as they do in consumer buyer behavior.[23] Clearly, industrial buying cannot be understood by economic criteria alone.

DIFFERENCES FROM CONSUMER BEHAVIOR

Despite its similarities, industrial buyer behavior is substantially different from consumer behavior. Consider the following:

1. Industrial buying is frequently a *group decision process.* Several people playing different roles may be involved — the purchasing agent, the engineer, the production manager. These individuals represent a decision-making unit in the organization referred to as a ***buying center.***

2. There is a greater *technical complexity* in industrial buying. One authority states, "Consumer buying behavior never reaches the complexity of industrial buying."[24]

3. The *interdependence between buyer and seller* is likely to be greater in industrial buying. The buyer may have fewer alternatives for a given item, and the seller may be seriously affected by losing a larger industrial account.

4. The *postpurchase process* is likely to be more important in industrial buying because of the necessity for installation, service calls, and warranties.

5. Because of the greater need for interaction between industrial buyer and seller, a *negotiation* is more likely. As a result, personal selling assumes more importance than in consumer buying.

6. Industrial buyers are more likely to have individual needs requiring sellers to design products to meet *specifications*. As a result, they are less likely to be presold on the basis of advertising than are consumers.

7. Industrial buying requires two major decisions, *choice of a vendor and choice of a product*. Frequently the two are intertwined, but different criteria are used to select vendors (delivery, sales personnel, reliability) and products (price, quality, engineering specifications). Rational economic criteria suggest that product specifications should determine vendor selection. But frequently it is the other way around: loyalty to a certain vendor determines product choice.

8. Industrial buying is based on **derived demand**. That is, demand for industrial products is determined by the demand for other goods. As a result, the industrial buyer must be concerned with demand for related goods when deciding on the quantity to purchase. Consumer buying represents direct demand.

TYPES OF ORGANIZATIONAL BUYER BEHAVIOR

Earlier in the chapter we described three types of organizational decision: (1) the straight rebuy (recurring purchases requiring little information); (2) the modified rebuy (recurring purchases requiring information and evaluation of alternatives) and (3) the new task (new purchase decisions requiring extensive information search and vendor evaluation). New tasks and modified rebuy decisions generally require complex decision making; straight rebuys can be characterized by habit.

Complex Decision Making

Figure 5-5 presents a model of complex decision making in organizational buying behavior. The key components of the model are the same five steps as in consumer decision making. The organizational buying process differs as follows:

1. *Informational sources* will differ. Organizational buyers rely more on information from salespeople, from industry and trade sources, and by word-of-mouth from people within their organization and experts outside the organization.

2. *Evaluation* occurs at two levels, vendor and brand. Vendor criteria might be on-time delivery, installation, service capabilities, experience of the

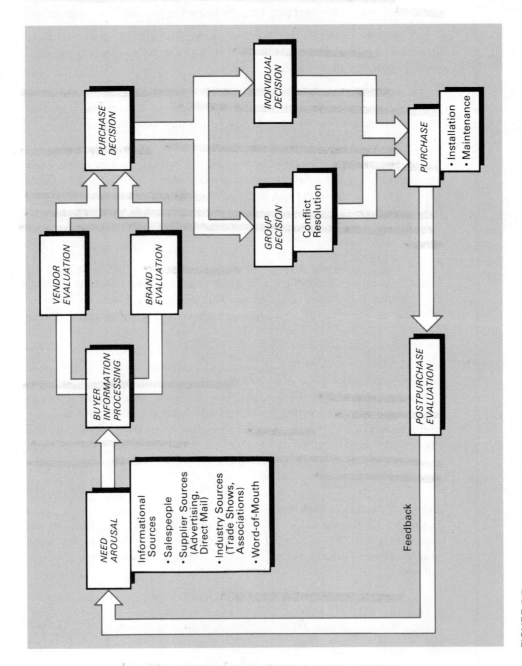

FIGURE 5-5
Complex decision making in organizational buying

sales force, and company reputation. Brand or product criteria would be price, reliability, product performance, and specific product features.

3. *The purchase decision* is frequently made on a group basis. A group decision is more likely if:

- ☐ the cost is high,
- ☐ it is a new product,
- ☐ the product is technologically complex, and
- ☐ the organization is large and decentralized.

A buying group is generally composed of a purchasing agent, production manager, and sales manager. It can also include an equipment engineer, a design engineer, and a corporate lawyer. Any group decision is likely to result in some conflict over the criteria members use to evaluate vendors and products. Typically the purchasing agent emphasizes price, the engineer product quality, the production manager delivery, and the sales manager a full product line.

4. *The purchase* generally requires product installation and maintenance in complex decisions. *Postpurchase evaluation* will be conducted by the buying group and involves evaluation of the operation and efficiency of the vendor and the product. Satisfaction increases the likelihood of vendor loyalty for future purchases. Dissatisfaction will result in open bidding the next time the product is ordered.

As an example, a manufacturer who wishes to buy an industrial pollution control systems forms a buying center. The buying center decides to emphasize the quality and reliability of the system. Cost and delivery would be secondary to quality because of the recognition that there could be no cost shortcuts to a reasonably efficient system. The emphasis on technical specifications means that the engineers in the buying group would have more influence than the purchasing agent.

The buying center forms a vendor list and evaluates each vendor on the basis of the criteria it has established. Three sets of factors will influence choice of a vendor: (1) product-specific factors (the nature and characteristics of the pollution control system offered by the vendor), (2) the vendor itself (technological expertise, reputation for product quality, service and delivery), and (3) environmental factors (competitors' selection of pollution control systems, government emission standards, economic projections).

The primary conflict in the buying center is between the purchasing agent and the design engineer. The purchasing agent plays down the engineer's emphasis on technical specifications. The design engineer feels the purchasing agent is too price oriented in favoring low-priced vendors at an unnecessary sacrifice of quality. Because of the emphasis on quality, the conflict in this case will probably be resolved in favor of the design engineer.

Since the most important criteria are product quality, reliability, service and maintenance, the vendor who rates highest on these criteria will probably be asked to develop the system. At this point, the terms of sale, installation, service, and maintenance are finalized and a contract is signed. The system is installed. Over time the buying center will evaluate the operation and efficiency of the system. Their satisfaction will determine whether they ask the same vendor to install pollution control systems for plants at other locations or to give specifications on other types of environmental control products.

Habit and Vendor Loyalty

Like brand loyalty, vendor loyalty is a natural outgrowth of past satisfaction. An industrial buyer who is satisfied with its present supplier may forego active decision making and buy certain products routinely. Such loyalty is more likely to exist for low-priced, frequently purchased products (straight rebuys). If the product is purchased regularly enough, purchases could be made automatically on the basis of prespecified stock levels.

Vendor loyalty fulfills an important organizational objective: it reduces the need for decision making and the unnecessary use of corporate resources. If a satisfactory vendor can be found for inexpensive low-risk items, then vendor loyalty is an efficient basis for purchasing.

Inertia

Vendor loyalty is not always cost efficient. Organizational buyers sometimes continue to buy from a particular supplier even when a search for alternative vendors might result in cost savings or better quality. Vendor loyalty may be based on individual and organizational factors that do not conform to the model of a rational buyer.

Bubb and Van Rest cite several subjective reasons why companies continue to buy from the same vendor. Using a study of a new metal product, they found that the most important factors in selecting the same vendor are administrative inertia (reluctance to change to new sources because of an inability to cope with any complications resulting from change), and familiarity (the desire to ensure that unexpected difficulties in purchasing will not occur).[25]

In such cases, the firm is buying because of inertia. Repurchases from the same vendor are not justified by economic criteria. They can only be due to a desire to avoid change, minimize risk, and ensure the organizational buyer's position in the firm.

Summary

In this chapter we considered the nature of purchasing decisions for consumer and organizational buyers. Most of the attention in this book and in the marketing literature has been devoted to the consumer buyer. But the organizational buyer (especially the industrial buyer) deserves attention for two reasons: (1) industrial buying represents more than half of all expenditures in the American economy, and (2) there are enough differences between organizational and consumer buyer behavior to develop separate descriptions of the purchasing process for these two types of buyer.

Consumer and then organizational buyer behavior was described by considering three types of behavior: complex decision making, habit, and low-involvement behavior (inertia). Complex decision making is characterized by high involvement with the product, an active search for information, and careful consideration of alternative brands.

Habit results when the consumer is satisfied with a frequently purchased brand. The consumer buys with little information search or brand evaluation. Continued satisfaction leads .to brand loyalty. Products purchased by habit tend to be high-turnover consumer packaged goods that generate involvement. Marketing strategies for such products generally use advertising and in-store displays for their reminder effect. Distribution is intensive, and price promotions are used to induce consumers to try the company's brand.

In low-involvement buying behavior, a consumer purchases the same brand to avoid the time and effort required in searching for information. Brand preferences are not strong. Since consumers pay less attention to advertising, its role is to create familiarity through repetition and simple themes. Television rather than print should be the primary medium since it is a low-involvement vehicle for communication. Products may be positioned to minimize problems rather than maximize benefits, since a consumer will settle for a brand that is satisfactory rather than optimal.

Industrial buying is much more likely to be conducted on a group basis, to involve negotiations, to require specifications for technically complex products, and to stress service and maintenance. The most important organizational decisions can be characterized by complex decision making. Such decisions are generally made on a group basis and involve selecting a product and a vendor. Price, product quality, delivery, service, and the vendor's reputation are key criteria in these decisions. Industrial buying for more routine purchases can result in vendor loyalty. This is most likely when the buyer is satisfied with the vendor, the value of the order is small, and the vendor's prices are stable. But the same vendor is chosen because of inertia rather than cost efficiencies, so as to work with a familiar source and avoid change.

Having described consumer and organizational buyer behavior, in the next chapter we will consider the development of marketing strategies based on the characteristics and environment of consumer and organizational buyers.

Questions

1. A large manufacturer of kitchen appliances surveys consumers to determine the sequence of decisions along the lines of Figure 5-1. The company identifies three sequences: (1) Certain consumers make a decision for a brand first, then shop for the brand in various stores, and finally decide on product features. (2) Others shop in a certain store and determine the brand and product features in the store. (3) A third group decides on features first, then the brand, and then the store. The first group has more information about alternative brands before going into the store and is composed of better-educated and higher-income consumers. It is also the most price sensitive. The second group tends to have lower income and to be less educated, and relies more on salespeople for information. The third group is more diverse demographically, and emphasizes special product features.

   The company feels that competition for the brand-oriented group is severe. It is considering introducing a line of appliances directed to the second and third groups. What strategies should it use?

2. Use the model of complex decision making in Figure 5-3 to describe the decision-making process you went through in selecting a business school. What are the implications of the decision process you described for a school's

   ☐ positioning strategy,

   ☐ advertising and direct mail campaign,

   ☐ product strategy (development of course offerings), and

   ☐ pricing strategy (tuition level and financial assistance programs)?

3. How might a marketing manager use the model of complex decision making in Figure 5-3 in the following situations?

   ☐ Folgers introduces its coffee line in the East.

   ☐ Mead-Johnson attempts to reposition Metracal, the first diet drink to be introduced, from a medically oriented drink to a line of tasty and nutritious diet products.

   ☐ A company introduces a better fastening disposable diaper.

4. Under what conditions might a consumer change from buying by habit to buying by decision making. If such a change occurs for a substantial portion of the market, what are the implications for

   ☐ product development,

   ☐ advertising strategy, and

   ☐ pricing?

5. If habit is based on repeated satisfaction with a brand, why have certain dominant brands, once purchased by habit, become extinct or experi-

enced a substantial loss in market share (e.g., Chase & Sanborn coffee, Squibb toothpaste, L&M cigarettes)?

6. This chapter suggests that many consumers are not involved with the brand purchased and that decisions are frequently made based on inertia.

   ☐ If this is true, why do most marketing strategies assume an involved consumer?

   ☐ Why is it hard for a marketing manager to believe that most consumers might not be involved in the purchase of the company's brand?

7. (a) Design a general marketing strategy for a new brand of paper towel that is positioned as more economical because it has more sheets at the same price, yet has the same level of quality as other towels. (In most cases, consumers would regard paper towels as a low-involvement product.)
   (b) Now assume the same manufacturer has identified a segment of the paper towel market that is more involved with the product because the segment recognizes situations that require a high-quality towel. The company decides to introduce a heavyweight high-quality towel to this involved segment. How would marketing strategy differ from the strategy for the brand in question 7a?

8. A manufacturer of household cleaners and detergents conducts a study that finds that consumers are not very involved with the company's products. Most consumers view housework as a necessary evil that they frequently do not have time to perform and tend to emphasize convenience rather than pride in the job done. The company is concerned that the low level of involvement in its products means that consumers may be more likely to switch to competitive brands. It decides to try to increase the consumer's level of involvement with its brands. What strategies can the company use to do so?

9. A consumer in the market for a refrigerator has difficulty in deciding among three brands with very similar features and prices. The consumer finally decides on a brand because of the strong recommendation of the store salesperson. Having made a purchase, the consumer then begins to compare the chosen brand to other brands and experiences some dissonance about the choice.

   What strategies might the manufacturer use to reduce postpurchase dissonance?

10. Consider the purchase of a personal computer by an individual consumer versus the purchase of an integrated computer system by an organization.

    ☐ What are the similarities in the decision process?

    ☐ What are the differences?

☐ What are the strategic implications of these similarities and differences for the company marketing the integrated computer system?

11. A pharmaceutical company is considering converting its plant to reduce industrial emissions in order to limit environmental pollution. It is considering proposals from various vendors to adapt its plants. What are likely to be the differences in criteria used to evaluate alternative vendor's proposals by the (a) purchasing agent, (b) engineering department, and (c) production department?

12. A purchasing agent for a large industrial company tends to buy products from the same vendors because of long-established relationships with the salespeople from these companies. The purchasing agent is confident about their products and service reliability.

☐ What are the advantages to the buyer of such vendor loyalty?

☐ What are the potential risks?

Notes

1. Frederick E. Webster, "Management Science in Industrial Marketing," *Journal of Marketing* 42 (January 1978): 21–7.

2. M. Venkatesan, "Cognitive Consistency and Novelty Seeking," in Scott Ward and Thomas S. Robertson, eds., *Consumer Behavior: Theoretical Sources* (Englewood Cliffs, N.J.: Prentice-Hall, 1973), pp. 354–84.

3. Thomas S. Robertson, "Low-Commitment Consumer Behavior," *Journal of Advertising Research* 16 (April 1976): 20.

4. Peter Lawrence Bubb and David John van Rest, "Loyalty as a Component of the Industrial Buying Decision," *Industrial Marketing Management* 3 (1973): 25–32.

5. Leon Festinger, *A Theory of Cognitive Dissonance* (Stanford, Calif.: Stanford University Press, 1957).

6. Judson Mills, "Avoidance of Dissonant Information," *Journal of Personality and Social Psychology* 2 (1965): 589–93.

7. Kenneth E. Runyon, *Consumer Behavior and the Practice of Marketing* (Columbus, Ohio: Charles E. Merrill, 1977), p. 287.

8. There are two excellent reviews on low-involvement consumer behavior. See John C. Maloney and Bernard Silverman, eds., *Attitude Research Plays for High Stakes* (Chicago: American Marketing Association, 1979); and William L. Wilkie, ed., *Advances in Consumer Research*, Vol. 6 (Ann Arbor, Mich.: Association for Consumer Research, 1979), pp. 174–99.

9. Harold H. Kassarjian and Waltraud M. Kassarjian, "Attitudes under Low Commitment Conditions," in John C. Maloney and Bernard Silverman, eds., *Attitude Research Plays for High Stakes* (Chicago: American Marketing Association, 1979), p. 8.

10. Michael L. Rothschild, "Advertising Strategies for High and Low Involvement Situations," in Maloney and Silverman, *Attitude Research Plays for High Stakes*, p. 84.

11. Ibid.

12. Ibid., p.86.

13. Tyzoon T. Tyebjee, "Refinement of the Involvement Concept: An Advertising Planning Point of View," in Maloney and Silverman, *Attitude Research Plays for High Stakes*, p. 97.

14. Herbert E. Krugman, "The Measurement of Advertising Involvement," *Public Opinion Quarterly* 30 (Winter 1966): 584–85.

15. Henry Assael, "The Conceptualization of a Construct of Variety Seeking Behavior," New

York University, Graduate School of Business Administration, Working Paper Series #79–43, May 1979, p. 5.

16. Tyebjee, "Refinement of the Involvement Concept," p. 108.

17. Rothschild, "Advertising Strategies," p. 87.

18. Tyebjee, "Refinement of the Involvement Concept," p. 100.

19. Richard J. Lutz, "A Functional Theory Framework for Designing and Pretesting Advertising Themes," in Maloney and Silverman, *Attitude Research Plays for High Stakes*, p. 47.

20. Harper W. Boyd, Jr., Michael L. Ray, and Edward C. Strong, "An Attitudinal Framework for Advertising Strategy," *Journal of Marketing* 36 (April 1972): 31.

21. Paul D. Converse, *Marketing Methods and Policies* (New York: Prentice-Hall, 1924), p. 147.

22. F. Robert Shoaf, "Here's Proof — The Industrial Buyer Is Human," *Industrial Marketing* 44 (May 1959): 126.

23. John A. Martilla, "Word-of-Mouth Communications in the Industrial Adoption Process," *Journal of Marketing Research* 8 (May 1971): 173–78; and Leon G. Schiffman and Vincent Gaccione, "Opinion Leaders in Institutional Markets," *Journal of Marketing* 38 (April 1974): 49–53.

24. Webster, "Management Science," p. 23.

25. Bubb and Van Rest, "Loyalty as a Component."

CHAPTER **6**

Marketing Strategies Based on Individual and Environmental Buyer Influences

FOCUS OF CHAPTER

This chapter provides a framework for better understanding the development of marketing strategies by describing two major purchase influences: (1) individual buyer influences (factors internal to the consumer such as needs, attitudes, and personality characteristics); and (2) environmental influences (factors external to the consumer such as culture, reference groups, and the family). The focus is on how marketers can use information on the consumer and the consumer's environment to develop marketing strategies.

In the first part of the chapter we will consider individual consumer influences. There are two types: (1) "thought" variables that describe the consumer's state of mind (consumer needs, attitudes, and perceptions), and (2) the consumer's descriptive characteristics (demographics, life-style, and personality). The consumer's thought variables and descriptive characteristics directly influence brand evaluations and purchasing behavior. Therefore they must be measured and used in formulating marketing strategies.

In the second part of the chapter we will consider the consumer's cultural and social environment. Marketers are acutely aware of other people's influences on consumer choice. Advertising frequently portrays the influence of friends, neighbors, and relatives on consumers. Products are also positioned to particular groups on the basis of cultural norms such as youth (cosmetics), power (automobiles), informality (clothing), and slimness (diet foods). Marketers may also design strategies based on purchase influences within the family.

We will consider the strategic implications of environmental influences from the broadest influence (cultural values) to the most specific (family norms and values). In each case the environmental influence and its application in the development of marketing strategies will be described.

Consumer Thought Variables

This section and the next consider the two types of individual influences on buyer behavior, consumer thought variables and consumer characteristics. Consumer thought variables are composed of consumer *needs, attitudes,* and *perceptions.*

CONSUMER NEEDS

Consumer **needs** are forces that direct consumers toward the achievement of desired goals. A theme of this book is that consumer needs identify marketing opportunity and therefore direct marketing strategies. From a marketing standpoint consumer needs can be characterized as benefits that consumers desire from products. Advertising frequently specifies that benefits can be attained from product characteristics (e.g., economy in buying a car can be obtained through low service costs and good gas mileage).

A need has two dimensions — direction and intensity. Consider the cola market. Some consumers may want a highly carbonated cola, others a cola with little carbonation; some consumers may want a sweet cola, others a cola with little or no sweetness. The consumer's desired characteristics (e.g., high to low carbonation or high to low sweetness) is the direction of the need. The other component is the importance or intensity of the need. If a marketer identifies a segment that wants a highly carbonated cola and decides to position a brand to this segment, such a positioning would be relevant only if a significant proportion of the segment says that amount of carbonation is an important consideration in selecting a brand. If it is not, spending advertising dollars to position a cola as highly carbonated would be a misallocation of resources.

Need-Gap Analysis

A gap in a market exists if an important consumer need is not being met. The concept of a gap in the market has led to the development of a means of identifying marketing opportunity known as ***need-gap analysis.*** Assume a manufacturer of hair care products wishes to investigate consumer needs and attitudes toward current brands. The manufacturer conducts a survey and finds that a segment of consumers rates hair care products low on three counts: (1) convenience, (2) keeping hair straight, and (3) avoiding oily hair. The manufacturer decides to test a new product, a two-in-one shampoo and conditioner to meet the needs of women who want a more convenient product that avoids oily and curly hair. The new product is produced in small amounts and is tested on a sample of 500 women who express these three needs.

Figure 6-1 presents sample results of the need-gap analysis. The results are for a single consumer in the sample. The *I* represents her ideal brand. Since she is part of the defined group of target-consumers, she rates her ideal brand as convenient to use, as keeping her hair straight, and as avoiding oily hair. Further, she rates her regular brand of conditioner (represented by *R*) as

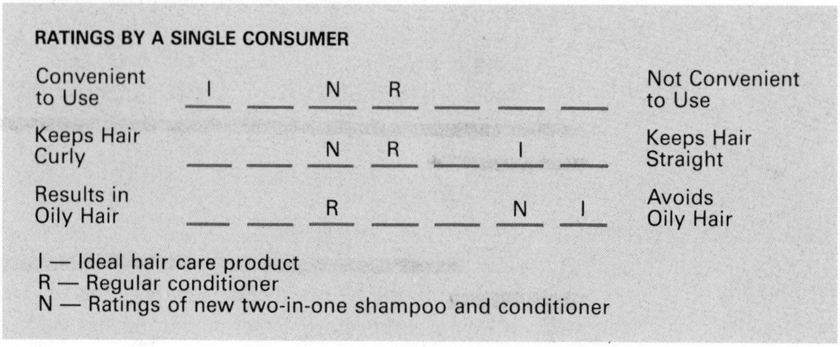

RATINGS BY A SINGLE CONSUMER

Convenient to Use	I _ _ N R _ _ _ _	Not Convenient to Use
Keeps Hair Curly	_ _ N R _ I _	Keeps Hair Straight
Results in Oily Hair	_ _ R _ _ N I _	Avoids Oily Hair

I — Ideal hair care product
R — Regular conditioner
N — Ratings of new two-in-one shampoo and conditioner

FIGURE 6-1
An example of need-gap analysis in the hair care market

acceptable on all three counts. She now tries the new product (*N*) and rates it closer to her ideal on two of the three criteria. This consumer would probably buy the new product since she has rated it closer to her ideal than her regular brand.

Of the sample of 500 women, assume 150 are projected to buy because they rate the test product closer to the ideal than their regular brand. These consumers are identified as the prospect group. Table 6-1 compares the characteristics of the prospect group to those of the rest of the sample. They are somewhat older, are more upscale (higher income and education), are more likely to be working, and are less frequent users of shampoos and conditioners. Further, they have more negative attitudes toward hair care and homemaking chores, are fashion conscious, and are more assertive and independent than

TABLE 6-1
Profile of the Prospect Group Derived from Need-Gap Analysis

	PROSPECT GROUP[a] (30% OF SAMPLE)	ALL OTHERS (70% OF SAMPLE)
Percentage of Working Women	80%	46%
Average Years of Education	12.1 Years	9.3 Years
Average Age	35	28
Average Income	$26,500	$18,000
Frequency of Use	2.1 per Week	3.2 per Week
Attitudes toward Housekeeping	Negative	Neutral
Attitudes toward Grooming	Intermediate/ Negative	Intermediate/ Positive
Fashion Consciousness	Above Average	Below Average

[a] Prospect group is defined as those consumers who rate the test product as closer to their ideal than their regular brand on at least two important criteria.

the rest of the sample. This profile would assist the marketer in targeting the product to the prospect group. The product should be presented for the independent working woman on the go, the woman who does not have time to groom herself, yet who is sufficiently fashion conscious to be concerned about her looks. Media should be selected that are most likely to be read or viewed by the upscale working woman.

Strategic Applications of Consumer Needs

Consumer needs are used to develop an overall strategic approach as well as to guide specific components of strategies. Marketers have used information on consumer needs to develop two broad types of strategy. In one, products are guided by existing needs. This is an ***adaptive strategy*** since the marketer is swimming with the tide. The second is a ***change strategy.*** The marketer attempts to increase sales by changing consumer needs. An adaptive strategy is more likely to succeed than a change strategy because it is easier to reinforce current needs than to change them.

Adaptive strategies

Marketing strategies are most effective when they appeal to existing needs. This is why advertising for diet drinks has been successful, whereas advertising for men's hats and overcoats has not. Diet drinks and diet foods reinforce the need to look slim and young. Men's hats and overcoats are symbols of age and conservatism.

A large telecommunications company followed an adaptive strategy in testing the market for a Picturephone (visual telephone) among business organizations. They first developed a vocabulary of communication needs (precision, speed, directness, service, etc.). They surveyed individuals in organizations responsible for communications and asked them to determine the company's most important communications needs. On basis of these answers they defined four groups of organizations with similar communications needs: efficiency, service/economy, flexibility, and risk-reduction segments (see Table 6-2). They also identified distinctive organizational characteristics of each segment. They then introduced the concept of a Picturephone to the executives in the survey and asked the executives to evaluate it and compare it to other communications alternatives such as the telephone, telex, telegram, mailgram, and mail delivery. Results of these ratings are presented in the next to last row in Table 6-2. The efficiency segment considers the Picturephone and telex as coming closest to meeting company communications needs. The service/economy segment prefers the telephone, the flexibility segment the Picturephone, and the risk-reduction segment the telegram and mailgram.

The company now produces a few prototypes of the Picturephone for product tests. It asks a few companies in each segment to try the product and rate it on telecommunications benefits. The efficiency segment rated the Picturephone concept fairly high, but rated the phone low in actual use (last row

TABLE 6-2
Example of a Need-Adaptive Strategy in the Telecommunications Market

	BENEFIT SEGMENT			
	Efficiency	Service/ Economy	Flexibility	Risk Reduction
Common Communications Needs of Segment	Precision Speed Directness Documentation	Service Maintenance Durability Dependability Economy	Multiple Usage Multiple Channels Nonverbal Messages Complex Messages	Privacy Control No Interference
Common Organizational Characteristics of Segment	New Centralized	Small Retail Older	Large Service Decentralized	Large Manufacturer
Identification of Best Communications Technique in Concept Test	Telex Picturephone	Telephone	Picturephone	Telegram Mailgram
Rating of Picturephone After Trying It	Low	Average	High	Low

in Table 6-2). In other words, the benefits they desired (precision, speed, etc.) were not delivered. But the flexibility segment rated the product high in both the concept and use test. It was identified as the target group because the benefits desired were actually delivered. Future strategies will be directed to this group. This is an example of an adaptive strategy because the product met the existing needs of the flexibility segment.

Change strategies

Although strategies to change needs are harder to implement than adaptive strategies, they are a valid way of influencing purchasing behavior. Marketers can attempt to change the direction of needs and the intensity of needs.

Strategies to change the direction of needs. Directional strategy is the most difficult change strategy to implement since it requires changing the nature rather than the importance of a need. For example, it would be easier to convince consumers who like a strong coffee that strength should be the most important factor in choosing a brand than to get these consumers to like a weaker coffee. Most attempts to change the direction of needs have failed. Several years ago clothing manufacturers banded together to advertise the importance of dressing well. The campaign was an attempt to counteract the trend toward informal clothes after World War II. The campaign failed because it tried to counter a basic change in consumer needs.

Strategies to change the intensity of needs. It is much easier to change the intensity than the direction of needs. This strategy requires changing the importance of a particular attribute rather than changing the desirability of the attribute. The packaging component of many products is rarely one of the most important criteria of selection. Yet Procter and Gamble attempted to increase the importance of the package by introducing Pringle's potato chips in a new cylindrical container as a means of preserving freshness. Such a strategy can be successful only if the company has done prior research to demonstrate that a segment of the market is likely to consider the focus on packaging sufficiently important. The fact that P & G succeeded in increasing the importance of the package but failed to produce a sufficiently good tasting potato chip, demonstrates that a change in one need component cannot be achieved at the expense of another.[1]

BRAND ATTITUDES

Brand **attitudes** are the consumer's tendency to evaluate brands in a consistently favorable or unfavorable way.[2] Whereas needs are used to *identify* marketing opportunity, brand attitudes are used to *evaluate* marketing strategies once the brand has been introduced.

Strategic Application of Brand Attitudes

Brand attitudes are used to evaluate marketing strategies in the following ways:

1. *To evaluate a brand's strengths and weaknesses.* Marketers must determine who buys the brand and if users feel it has delivered on key performance criteria. For example, Kodak would want to know how purchasers rate their disc camera on criteria such as ease of taking pictures, greater opportunity to take pictures, ease of rewinding and reloading, and price of film. Changes in attitudes might indicate future changes in sales. If consumers' attitudes become more negative on a key criterion such as ease of taking pictures, sales are likely to decline. Such a change is more likely as competitors enter the market with improved versions of the product. Management must constantly assess brand attitudes to meet competitive threats.

2. *To evaluate the effectiveness of advertising messages.* Television commercials and print ads are frequently judged by whether they produce a favorable shift in brand attitudes. Brand attitudes are measured before and after exposure to a commercial in a controlled environment, and the degree of attitude shift is used to evaluate the commercial's effectiveness. The marketer of the two-in-one hair care product referred to earlier might wish to test two commercials, one emphasizing manageability in use and the other emphasizing time-saving benefits. Both commercials could be tested by the favorable attitude shift they produce for the product.

3. *To evaluate the total advertising campaign.* Advertising campaigns may have attitude change as a specific objective. Sanka's objective of changing its image of the brand from a medicinal coffee to a more tasty product required careful tracking of the results of the advertising campaign to determine if attitudes toward the brand were changed in the desired direction.

Adaptive strategies

Marketers have developed strategies to adapt to existing consumer attitudes and to change attitudes. As with needs, adaptive attitude strategies are easier to implement and more likely to succeed than strategies that try to change consumer attitudes.

An adaptive advertising strategy attempts to reinforce favorable consumer attitudes. As an example, Nestlé used an adaptive strategy to market a brand of iced tea by appealing to positive attitudes toward the product category. The company conducted a study of iced tea drinkers and found that the heaviest users viewed iced tea as a way of restoring energy and as a good year-round drink.[3] This group represented 17 percent of the market but accounted for 36 percent of iced tea volume. The study identified this heavy-use segment as likely to live in the South, to have two or more children, and to be well educated. Advertising for the iced tea brand reinforced the positive attitudes of the heavy-user group: that iced tea restores energy and is a year-round drink. Each advertising dollar directed to this group was expected to be twice as effective as a dollar spent on the total market, since the group consumed twice as much tea as the average iced tea drinker.

Change strategies

Marketers frequently attempt to change brand attitudes. Attitudes can be altered by changing a brand's characteristics through product development, or by changing a brand's image through advertising. Cadillac changed an important brand attribute by introducing a smaller car. The advertising campaign had to change beliefs that Cadillac was a large car with poor gas mileage to a view of a more compact fuel efficient car. Yet the company had to be careful not to change the car's luxury image.

A change strategy based solely on brand image is illustrated by Sanka's attempt to change beliefs about the brand. The company instituted a "land of origin" campaign emphasizing flavor. For example, it said that Sanka has 100 percent pure coffee flavor.[4] The campaign had little effect over a two-year period. But over a longer period of time, there was movement toward a perception of more flavor. Marketers also try to influence brand attitudes by associating a brand with a positive mood or a pleasant environment. A beer ad might show a group of men drinking the brand after winning some hectic athletic event. If the consumer accepts the association of the product with success, then a favorable attitude has been established. Many cosmetic companies try to induce a mood in advertising — one of mystery, romance, or social success — and to associate the mood with product use. Such associations may be sufficient to change brand attitudes favorably.

CONSUMER PERCEPTIONS

Consumer **perceptions** make up the third thought variable that influences purchasing behavior. Consumer perceptions are the way consumers select, organize, and interpret marketing and environmental stimuli. They are the basis for forming attitudes about a brand. One of the primary concerns in formulating marketing strategy is to determine how consumers perceive advertising, price, and product stimuli. Therefore, an understanding of marketing stimuli is necessary in formulating strategy.

Marketing Stimuli

Marketing stimuli are any communications (advertising, word-of-mouth communications from a friend or a salesperson) or physical stimuli (the product or package) designed to influence the consumer. Advertising is the prime means of conveying information about the product. Continued exposure to advertising is necessary if a brand is to survive in a competitive market. But continued advertising could not be maintained unless enough consumers purchase. Therefore, the ultimate determinant of success is the consumer's experience with the primary stimulus — the product. Once the product has been tested and introduced, most marketing strategy is concerned with communication messages *about* the product to consumers. The key requirement in such communication is a *product concept*.

As noted in Chapter 2, a product concept is a description of a product's characteristics, uses, and intended benefits. These are communicated through words, symbols, and imagery. Communicating a product concept requires the organization of various marketing stimuli into a *product positioning* strategy. As an example of a coordinated set of marketing stimuli, Nestlé positioned its freeze-dried coffee entry, Taster's Choice, as providing the benefits of instant coffee with the taste and aroma of regular coffee. The marketing stimuli were then geared to the intended positioning. The brand name implied taste, the advertising demonstrated the taste benefits of a good instant coffee for the man of the family, and the deep, square jar reinforced an image of hefty taste and masculinity. The essential question is whether consumers perceived the marketing stimuli as intended in the marketing plan. In the case of Taster's Choice, they did, and the brand was highly successful.

Nature of Consumer Perceptions

How consumers perceive marketing stimuli depends on how these stimuli are selected and organized. Consumers perceive information *selectively*; that is, they pick and choose information that best helps them evaluate brands. They are also selective in choosing information that conforms to their beliefs and experiences. Selectivity in choosing and interpreting marketing stimuli means that some advertisements may not be seen or may be misinterpreted. Therefore, marketers must understand the nature of **selective perceptions.**

Marketers must also understand how consumers *organize* information. **Perceptual organization** is the process by which consumers bring together diverse information about a brand, product, store, or company and organize it into an overall image.

Strategic Implications of Consumer Perceptions

The marketer attempts to establish a positive brand, store, or corporate image through advertising to influence sales.

Brand image

The brand image represents the overall perception of the brand and is formed from marketing information and past experiences. Consumers with positive images of a brand are more likely to purchase it. One marketer says, "The more consistent the [brand] image, the more likely it is to have long-term share building strength,"[5]

Small changes in physical characteristics can change the image of an undifferentiated product. An example of how the alteration of a single component can change brand image is provided by Martineau. He states:

> When Procter & Gamble introduced Cheer with adequate advertising proclaiming it as "good for tough-job washing," it was just another detergent going no particular place in sales. . . . Then it was given a blue color, and in the housewife's mind it acquired a completely different character, making it seemingly capable of functional wonders totally uncalled for by anything in the mere color. Thereupon it became a tremendous national success.[6]

Price image

Perceptions of price will affect brand image. Numerous studies have shown that consumers associate higher price with higher quality.[7] This is especially true when the consumer knows little about the product and thus relies on price as a surrogate for other information. Barring knowledge of product specifications, the purchaser of a stereo set or a rug may assume that the higher-priced alternatives are better.

Store image

Consumers also develop images of stores through advertising, store merchandise, shopping experiences, and opinions of others. Store image directly influences brand image. The identical product will be perceived quite differently at Woolco or J. C. Penney than at Neiman-Marcus or Lord and Taylor. Store image and price image are also closely linked. Stores are frequently categorized by price in consumers' minds, and the store's image is formed accordingly.

Consumers will tend to link the brand image more closely to the store under two conditions: (1) if the brand is a private store brand (perceptions of a line of Sears major appliances will be governed by perceptions of the store), and (2) if the brand decision is made in the store (a consumer shopping for carpeting may select the store first and then choose the carpeting within the store, thus linking the carpeting to the store image).

Corporate image

Consumers also organize their information about companies and their experiences with a company's products into corporate images. Companies spend millions of dollars to improve their image with the public primarily for two reasons. First, a positive corporate image will reinforce positive perceptions of the company's products. Such a link is especially important when the brand name is closely associated with the company name. General Electric links its brands to its corporate name; Procter and Gamble does not. Thus, corporate advertising becomes much more important for General Electric. Second, companies attempt to create a favorable corporate image for public relations purposes. Many companies have a vested interest in public issues and seek to maintain favorable relations with their customers to avoid complaints. The oil companies have engaged in heavy advertising to combat any negative image due to high energy costs. For example, Mobil has cited its efforts in solar energy, coal-derived methanol, and petroleum exploration.

Strategic Applications of Consumer Characteristics

Earlier we distinguished between consumer thought variables and consumer characteristics. Marketers use information on consumer characteristics to identify users of their brand and users of competitive brands. Such information permits marketers to reach user and prospect groups more effectively and to develop strategies to appeal to them. Three types of consumer characteristic have been used in developing marketing strategies: demographics, life styles, and personality.

DEMOGRAPHICS

Demographics represent the objective characteristics of the consumer — age, income, education, occupation, location, marital status, and so forth. They are used to segment markets, select media, and identify targets for new products.

Market Segmentation by Demographics

Marketers have used demographics to describe their customers and competitive buyers. Such information will provide guidance in developing advertising appeals and selecting media. Demographics also suggest ways to appeal to users of competitive brands. For example, in 1976 Sylvania completed a study designed to compare the position of their color TV line to those of competitive makes. Purchasers of Sylvania were compared to purchasers of Magnavox, Sony, and Zenith on the basis of demographic characteristics. The objectives of this study were to determine whether demographics might provide insights into the strengths and weaknesses of Sylvania relative to other brands and the appropriate media to use in competing head-to-head against specific competitive makes.

The study showed that if Sylvania is to make inroads against Sony, it must gear its product line to consumers at a higher socioeconomic level. Such a strategy does not necessarily imply moving into higher-quality, higher-priced lines since the study showed that Sylvania is strong in the higher-priced market ($500 or more). Competitive advantage may be gained by developing appeals and product features geared to the needs of the higher-income market without alienating the lower-income group. Therefore, a followup study to ascertain differences in needs and attitudes of higher- versus lower-income groups is warranted. The study also suggested that two separate advertising campaigns may be required, one to the core demographic market and another to an upscale market the company could try to attract. Different ad themes and media would be used in appealing to the two segments.

Identifying Targets for New Products
Demographic characteristics are also used to describe target markets for new products. For example, a large food manufacturer tested a new product concept referred to earlier — a low-calorie breakfast strip designed as a substitute for bacon. The company interviewed 600 respondents in four markets to determine the reaction to a product description. Two demographic segments were most likely to buy: (1) older (fifty-five and up), less-educated respondents, and (2) middle-aged respondents with one or more teenagers in the household. The older segment was more likely to emphasize cholesterol content and health concerns; the middle-aged segment, calories and nutrition. This finding suggested two different advertising campaigns; one positioning the product to the older market on the basis of health benefits (easier to digest, low in cholesterol); another appealing to the middle-aged market with primary dieting and nutritional benefits.

Media Selection
Demographic characteristics also provide guidelines for media selection. The two targets for the breakfast strip would require different media selection. Advertising directed to the health-oriented segment should appear in media with a larger proportion of older downscale readers or viewers (e.g., soap operas, quiz shows). Advertisements to the nutritional segment should appear in media that appeal to more middle-aged families with children (e.g., situation comedies).

LIFE-STYLE CHARACTERISTICS

Life-style characteristics define the consumer's mode of living and are identified by consumer activities, interests, and opinions. Marketers frequently develop an inventory of questions to determine consumers' life-style characteristics. One study developed twenty-two life-style characteristics (see Table 6-3).[8] Consumers were identified as price conscious, child oriented, homebodies, information seekers, dieters, art enthusiasts, and so forth. Consumers can be identified by these characteristics in surveys. Life-style characteristics are then used to (1) identify target segments for new or existing products and (2) develop advertising and product positioning strategies accordingly.

Segmenting by Life-Style Characteristics

The study of the artificial bacon product cited in the previous section demonstrates the use of life styles in identifying consumer segments. Consumers in the diet/nutrition target group tended to (1) be more socially active, (2) eat out frequently, (3) go to more entertainment events, (4) try new products. The life-style profile suggested that the advertising to this group should *not* focus on the fact the product is less messy to prepare or that it is tastier. Rather, it should focus on the social benefits of eating the product — for example, that one will win social approval for being thinner and more attractive.

Product Positioning by Life-Style Characteristics

Life-style profiles have also been the basis for positioning brands and developing advertising campaigns accordingly. They have provided copy writers with a picture of the consumer by suggesting the consumer's needs and social roles. One advertising agency executive described the usefulness of life-style profiles:

> For the creative person, life-style data provide a richer and more lifelike picture of the target consumer than do demographics. This enables the

TABLE 6-3
Sample Life-Style Categories Based on Activities, Interests, and Opinions

1. Price Conscious	12. Self-Confident
2. Fashion Conscious	13. Opinion Leader
3. Child Oriented	14. Information Seeker
4. Compulsive Housekeeper	15. New Brand Tryer
5. Dislikes Housekeeping	16. Satisfied with Finances
6. Sewer	17. Canned Food User
7. Homebody	18. Dieter
8. Community Minded	19. Financial Optimist
9. Credit User	10. Wrapper
10. Sports Spectator	21. Wide Horizons
11. Cook	22. Arts Enthusiast

Source: William D. Wells and Douglas J. Tigert, "Activities, Interests and Opinions," *Journal of Advertising Research* 11 (August 1971): 35.

writer or artist to have in his own mind a better idea of the type of person he is trying to communicate with about the product. This picture also gives the creative person clues about what may or may not be appropriate to the life-style of the target consumer. This has implications for the setting of the advertising, the type and appearance of the characters, the nature of the music and artwork, whether or not fantasy can be used, and so on.[9]

An example of the use of life styles in advertising is a past change in Schlitz's campaign. At one time Schlitz was running an effective campaign based on the theme, "When you're out of Schlitz, you're out of beer." The company felt the campaign was wearing out and searched for a new approach. Results of a life-style survey found that the heavy beer drinker is a "dreamer, a wisher, a guy who is not making it and probably never will."[10] For example, the heavy beer drinker is self-indulgent and takes risks (is likely to take chances, to smoke, to play poker, to go out to parties); is likely to reject responsibility (is not community oriented, is unlikely to save); and has a greater need to demonstrate masculinity (is more likely to agree men are smarter than women, and that men should not do the dishes). Because of this portrait, it was decided that ads should appeal to the heavy beer drinker's sense of masculinity, hedonism, and fantasy. As a result, a "Gusto Life" campaign was developed. Men would be portrayed in roles that would fulfill fantasies (e.g., success in any social role) and demonstrate masculinity (e.g., winning rugged athletic events).

PERSONALITY CHARACTERISTICS

Personality characteristics can also be used by marketers to describe consumers. Personality is more deep seated than life style since **personality characteristics** reflect consistent, enduring patterns of behavior. Because of these patterns, one may assume that personality variables should be related to purchase behavior. But most studies have shown a weak relationship between personality variables like aggression, responsibility, or dependence and purchase behavior. The primary reason is that marketers have used inventories to measure personality characteristics that have been borrowed from psychology rather than developing personality inventories of relevance to the marketing problem. The top of Table 6-4 presents five general personality variables developed in psychology and used in marketing. The bottom of Table 6-4 lists five personality variables developed specifically to identify users of a cosmetic product. We can see that these variables are more relevant to a specific product category than are the variables listed on the top of Table 6-4.

Like life style, personality characteristics are valuable guides in identifying market segments and in developing advertising strategies.

Developing Market Segments by Personality Characteristics

A study by a large insurance company segmented life insurance purchasers by the personality characteristics in Figure 6-2. The data in Figure 6-2 identify a

TABLE 6-4
Sample Personality Variables

General Personality Variables Derived from Psychology	
Achievement:	To rival and surpass others
Compliance:	To accept leadership; to follow willingly
Order:	To have things arranged, to be organized
Affiliation:	To form friendships, to participate in groups
Analysis:	To understand others, to examine motives
Personality Variables Developed for Cosmetics Study	
Appearance Conscious:	Emphasis on social importance of looking properly groomed
Exhibitionism:	Tendency toward self-display and attention seeking
Active:	Need to be on the go
Narcissism:	Preoccupation with details of one's personal appearance
Status:	Personal qualities and attributes that emphasize status

Source: Top of Table from Allen L. Edwards, *Edwards Personal Preference Schedule Manual* (New York: Psychological Corp., 1957). Reproduced by permission. Copyright 1954, © 1959 by The Psychological Corporation. All rights reserved.
Bottom of Table from Shirley Young, "The Dynamics of Measuring Unchange," in Russell I. Haley, ed., *Attitude Research in Transition* (Chicago: American Marketing Association, 1972), p. 62.

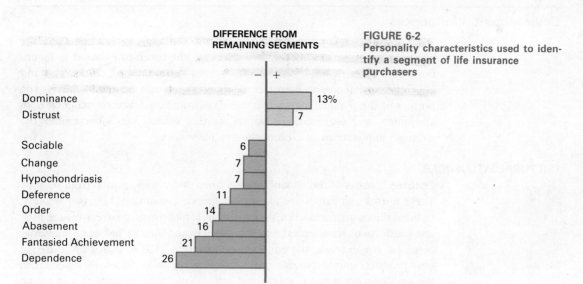

DIFFERENCE FROM REMAINING SEGMENTS

FIGURE 6-2
Personality characteristics used to identify a segment of life insurance purchasers

Dominance — 13%
Distrust — 7

Sociable — 6
Change — 7
Hypochondriasis — 7
Deference — 11
Order — 14
Abasement — 16
Fantasied Achievement — 21
Dependence — 26

Source: Shirley Young, "The Dynamics of Measuring Unchange," in Russell I. Haley, ed., Attitude Research in Transition (Chicago: *American Marketing Association,* 1972), p. 72.

particular segment. For example, this segment scored 13 percent higher on dominance, 7 percent higher on distrust, and 26 percent lower on dependence than the rest of the sample. The segment was described by the researchers as "dominant people who like to have control over situations with which they are involved. They tend to be self reliant (low on dependence and deference) and will follow the counsel of experts only if it meets demands for accuracy and reliability."[11] The personality profile suggests that advertising to this segment should portray a self-confident individual who would like to control the future. One element of control would be to make financial provisions for the family if the individual was no longer there. Therefore, this group should be a good prospect for life insurance.

Developing Advertising Strategies on the Basis of Personality Characteristics

In describing consumer segments, personality characteristics give management guidelines for advertising strategies. The low scores on fantasy and hypochondria for the target segment in Figure 6-2 suggest that insurance advertising should not dwell on the fear of death and its potential for occurring at any time. Rather than relying on such imagery, advertising should be more informational. Further, the greater self-reliance of the target group suggests that spokespersons should not be used to appeal to this segment unless they qualify as experts.

Environmental Influences

The consumer influences marketing strategy not only as an individual but as part of a social and cultural environment. The inverted pyramid in Figure 6-3 shows five environmental influences, from broad cultural, subcultural, and social class influences to narrower reference group and family influences. The bottom of the pyramid shows that these environmental factors influence both consumers and organizational buyers. In this section we will consider the strategic implications of each of the five influences.

CULTURAL INFLUENCES

Culture consists of the widely shared norms and values learned from society. These norms and values are likely to influence consumers' behavior broadly. Cultural values such as individualism, personal achievement, progress, materialism, and youth have characterized American society and directly influence consumer behavior. For example, the emphasis on progress leads to a greater desire for new products and disposable products. Personal achievement is reflected in the emphasis on hobbies, sports, and travel. Youthfulness leads to a stress on the young and new in advertising. Ads for skin creams show young-looking grandmothers; ads for soaps compare the hands of mothers and daughters; ads for hair coloring say, "You're not getting older; you're getting better."

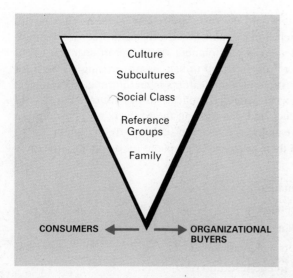

FIGURE 6-3
Environmental influences on consumer behavior

Cultural values influence the consumer's consumption values, which in turn influence the value consumers place on specific product attributes. For example, the desire for informality (cultural value) may lead to emphasis on casualness (consumption value) and on a sporty look (product attribute). The association among culture, consumption, and product-specific values is illustrated by the following example in the automobile market:

Cultural Values	Consumption Value	Product-specific Values
Safety	Dependable	Good brakes Solid
Individualism	High-Performance	Speed Acceleration
Social Recognition	Status-Producing	Luxury Size

APPLYING CULTURE TO MARKETING STRATEGY

Since cultural values sometimes form the basis for product evaluation, they are frequently central to the development of marketing strategies. For example, it would be logical for a furniture manufacturer to segment the market according to the importance consumers place on cultural values such as beauty, social recognition, and comfort.[12] Different product lines and marketing strategies would have to be developed for each segment. The beauty segment would desire highly styled and pleasurable furniture. Advertising symbols for this would be based on product style and integrity with the environment. The social recognition segment would desire furniture that demonstrates status. The furniture would be richer in design, and advertising would use symbols oriented to acceptance in a social environment. The comfort segment might desire furniture that is more practical and utilitarian. Advertising symbols for this segment would demonstrate product features in an informative campaign.

Perhaps the most important strategic applications of cultural values are in tracing recent cultural trends and determining their effects on consumption behavior. In Chapter 3 we noted a number of cultural trends important to marketers in the 1980s and the consequent implications for marketing strategy.[13] These included:

- A trend to a *me* orientation
- A return to a *we* orientation
- Emphasis on self-fulfillment
- Increased acceptance of voluntary simplicity
- Greater skepticism of public institutions.

SUBCULTURAL INFLUENCES

Individuals in a society do not always have homogeneous cultural values. Certain segments of society may be represented as **subcultures** because they have values and customs that distinguish them from others in the community. Because of the diverse nature of American society, it is important that marketers identify subcultures and determine whether specific strategies should be directed to them.

Subcultures in the United States can be identified by demographic characteristics such as age and geography, by national identity, and by race. The definition of subcultures by marketers is determined by common values and purchasing habits that are distinguished from those of the general population.

Age

Marketers have identified a youth market (thirteen to twenty-one) and an elderly market (sixty-five and over). Substantial differences exist in the values and consumption patterns of these age groups, warranting their designation as subcultures. For example, the youth market is more consumption oriented than most groups and is more likely to buy records, cameras, stereo equipment, and personal care products.[14] Elderly consumers are more likely to spend on health care, public transportation, household maintenance, and food consumed at home.[15]

Geography

Sufficient geographic differences in taste and behavior warrant identification of subcultures based on region. For example, Westerners generally like weaker coffee than Easterners, Southerners drink more tea, and consumers in the East and West are more likely to buy rye and whole wheat breads as well as natural foods. Marketers have occasionally adjusted product offerings on the basis of regional tastes. Some soft drink manufacturers use different formulations in different parts of the country to appeal to varying desires for sweetness, thickness, and carbonation.

National Identity: The Hispanic Market

The most distinct subcultures in the United States are identified by national origin and race. The most important group by national origin is the Spanish-speaking market, with close to 10 percent of the United States population and $50 billion in purchasing power.[16] This is not a homogeneous group since it is composed of consumers of different national identities. But traditional values of paternal leadership and strong family ties dominate among Hispanics.

Common characteristics and purchasing behaviors of the Hispanic market can be identified, justifying its description as a subculture. This group tends to live in urban areas, is younger than average, and significantly lower in income and educational level. The Hispanic market spends more on food because of a larger family size and is highly brand loyal. Hispanics are an excellent market because of their emphasis on quality and their brand loyalty.[17] The average Hispanic family spends proportionately more for all types of packaged goods — beverages, canned goods, household cleaners, beauty aids — than other consumers.[18] In shopping Hispanics emphasize the personal interaction with the retailer and prefer shopping in smaller stores.[19]

Several companies have directed products and advertising messages to the Hispanic market. Quaker Oats successfully targeted Masa Harina and Masa Trigo cereals to Hispanic families. Frito-Lay has introduced Sabritas, a wheat snack successfully marketed in Mexico.[20] But the most important effort has been advertising national brands to the Hispanic market through Spanish-oriented media. The Spanish market is easy to target because there is a national Spanish television network (SIN) with 200 affiliates in over 100 markets in 1982. There are an additional 112 local Spanish TV stations and over 80 Spanish-language radio stations.[21] Many leading companies have used these media. Kentucky Fried Chicken and Pizza Hut recognize the greater per capita expenditures by Hispanics on fast-food and advertise extensively on local Spanish TV channels.[22] Anheuser-Busch has extended the sophistication of marketing to Hispanics by producing separate advertising campaigns for Mexican, Puerto-Rican, and Cuban consumers.[23]

Ethnic Subcultures: The Black Consumer Market

Subcultures can also be identified ethnically. The most important and largest ethnic subculture is the black consumer market, representing close to 12 percent of the United States population. It is questionable whether this market is sufficiently homogeneous to be identified as a subculture. There are upper-, middle-, and lower-class blacks, blacks who value self-enhancement over social recognition, blacks who emphasize nutrition over taste, and so forth. In other words, most of the same distinctions that apply to the white market also apply to the black.

Characteristics of the black consumer market

Despite the diversity of black consumers, there is some justification in viewing the black consumer market as a subculture on the basis of the following differences in demographics and purchasing behavior.

Demographics. On average, blacks are younger and have a substantially lower level of income and education. The black consumer market is likely to become more profitable since educational levels are rising and a higher proportion of blacks will be growing into the maximum consumption age range (eighteen to thirty-five). Blacks are also twice as likely as whites to live in central-city areas, making them more accessible to mass media and retail distribution.[24]

Purchase behavior. Blacks spend proportionately more than whites for clothing, personal care, and home furnishings, and proportionately less for medical care, food, and transportation.[25] There are significant differences in products purchased; for example, blacks are much more likely to buy diet soft drinks and regular coffee than whites.[26] Blacks are also more likely to:

- be fashion conscious,[27]
- buy popular brands and be brand loyal,[28]
- shop by mail or phone,[29]
- be unhappy about shopping facilities due to higher prices, overcrowding, and unfriendly employees,[30]
- pay more for the same products, and[31]
- listen to radio, making it the most effective medium to reach blacks.[32]

Strategic Implications of Marketing to Black Consumers

Specific segmentation, product development, advertising, and promotional strategies are required when selling to the black consumer market.

Market segmentation and product positioning

Researchers aware of the diversity of the black consumer market have bemoaned the lack of segmentation and positioning strategies directed to this market. One marketer points out that it is as nonsensical to introduce a product to a single "black market" as it is to introduce a product to a single "white market."[33] One of the few companies that follow a segmentation strategy in marketing to blacks is Johnson Products, one of the largest black-owned companies in the United States. Johnson Products recognizes two broad segments of black consumers, those who strive for white middle-class values (strivers) and those who feel financially blocked from such goals or divorce themselves from the material goods associated with these goals and seek a separate black identity (nonstrivers).[34] Johnson Products has positioned products to both segments. Some of its advertisements are more ethnically oriented, others attempt to portray middle-class values. The two ads for hair coloring in Figure 6-4 provide examples of appeals to each segment. The ad for L'Oreal suggests middle-class values; the ad for Dark & Lovely suggests a denial of such values and a greater focus on black identity.

FIGURE 6-4
Ads directed to strivers versus nonstrivers on the basis of middle-class values

Used by permission.   By permission of Lockhard & Pettus, Inc.

Source: Kelvin A. Wall, "Trying to Reach Blacks? Beware of Marketing Myopia," *Advertising Age,* May 21, 1979, p. 59.

Product development

Some product categories must be geared to the specific needs of black market segments. For example, in 1965 Johnson Products introduced Ultra Sheen, the first product to "remedy the black woman's problem of relaxing curly hair."[35] The fashion editor of *Essence* says that more development work is required to create products that meet the black woman's needs.[36]

Advertising and sales promotion

Companies have used two approaches in advertising to blacks: (1) using blacks to foster black identification and (2) using the same advertising to blacks as to whites, but placing the ads in black media. Undifferentiated ads to blacks are used at times because companies such as Bacardi Rum choose to segment their market by product rather than ethnic criteria (see bottom of Figure 6-5). But in most cases advertisers will try to use symbols and imagery that are relevant to blacks. Ads for Canadian Mist whiskey foster black identity. (See top of Figure 6-5.) The company used research showing that in brand selection for liquor products black consumers reacted more favorably to advertising relevant to their life style. As a result, ads for Candian Mist use black models and high fashion imagery.

SOCIAL CLASS

Social class is another environmental factor that is important to the marketer. It refers to the position of an individual or family on a social scale based on criteria valuable to society. In American society, one's occupation, education, and income generally define one's prestige or power and position as upper, middle, or lower class. Social classes represent broad groups of people with similar occupations, incomes, and educations. Members of a social class do not have to meet, but they are likely to share certain values and attitudes leading to similar patterns of purchasing behavior.

Characteristics of Social Classes

Certain generalizations can be made about the differing norms and values of social class groupings. For example, the upper class represents the social elite, composed of inherited wealth, top managers, or successful professionals. They tend to dress conservatively and avoid ostentatious purchases. The upper middle classes are also professionals and managers, but without the wealth of the upper class. They are career oriented and emphasize educational attainment. They are more likely to appraise product alternatives critically and to be comparison shoppers. The lower middle class is composed of white-collar workers, small businessmen, and well-paid blue-collar workers. They emphasize respectability and conform closely to social norms. They are home and family oriented. The lower classes consist of blue-collar and unskilled workers. They have a routine and dull view of life because of uncreative jobs. The narrow dimensions of their jobs lead to a pattern of impulse purchasing to escape

MISTING.

What is Misting? It's the act of feeling the unique lightness of Canadian Mist,
a smooth and mellow imported Canadian whisky. Get into the feeling. Go Misting.

Used by permission.

Give orange juice
a fresh twist with
Bacardi.

BACARDI. rum. The mixable one.

Used by permission of Bacardi Imports, Inc.

FIGURE 6-5
Advertisements with and without black identity

Source: ''Product Appeal: No Class Barrier,'' *Advertising Age,* May 18, 1981, p. S-4.

from the dull routine. As a result, in-store displays and advertising appeals to fantasy may be particularly effective.

Strategic Implications of Social Class Groupings

The identification of consumers by social class provides implications for the development of market segments, advertising policies, product development, and distribution.

Market segmentation

Marketers seeking to define a target for their brand frequently describe a segment of the market by social class. One study determined that heavy users of bank credit cards were in the upper-middle and upper classes. These individuals were more appearance conscious, achievement-oriented, contemporary in outlook, and willing to take risks.[37] Advertising appeals to heavy bank card users should therefore portray successful, well-dressed individuals in an active setting. Copy might suggest that these individuals became successful entrepreneurs because of a willingness to take risks.

Advertising

Social class characteristics can give direction to advertising. Beer is a good example of a product category whose advertising has been influenced by social class profiles. Heavy beer drinkers are more likely to be in a lower social class and in blue-collar occupations than lighter beer drinkers. One study described the frequent beer drinker as:

> More pleasure-seeking toward life than the nondrinker. He seemed to have less regard toward responsibilities of family and job. More than the non-drinker, he tended to have a preference for a physical/male-oriented existence and an inclination to fantasize.[38]

Michelob and Miller have appealed to the heavy beer drinker by depicting rugged men in strenuous physical activities. The appeal is to masculinity and fantasy. Lowenbrau has appealed to a different social class with the theme "Here's to good friends." The appeal is to a lighter beer drinker and the stress is on sociability. Rather than being oriented to males, the Lowenbrau ads frequently picture couples in a social gathering. The tone and orientation of both advertising strategies depend on the social class definitions of their target markets.

Product development

Social classes react differently to product characteristics and styles providing marketers with implications for product development. A study by AT&T showed that lower-class groups were not interested in different styles and colors for phones.[39] They wanted a utilitarian phone that worked. Interestingly, it was the lower-middle-class that placed the greatest emphasis on phones of different designs and colors. Had AT&T assumed that the higher social groupings were the best market for high-style phones, it would have missed an important target group.

REFERENCE GROUP INFLUENCES

Perhaps the most important environmental influence on consumer behavior is the reference group. **Reference groups** are groups that serve as a reference point for the individual in developing needs, forming brand attitudes, and deciding what to purchase. They are important to the marketer since they are sources of consumer information and influence. Marketers frequently advertise their products in a group setting — the husband and wife having coffee, the neighbor admiring clean laundry, teenagers having soft drinks on the beach, and so forth. Marketers sometimes utilize experts, well-known personalities, and typical consumers in commercials because consumers will more readily believe spokespersons they can relate to than advertisers.

Types of Reference Groups

There are two types of reference groups, **membership groups** and **aspiration groups.** The consumer can be a member of a reference group, like the family, and can aspire to associate with a group of which he or she is not a member (e.g., an organizational trainee emulating higher management, or a tennis buff associating with tennis pros). Membership groups are face-to-face groups. As such, they exert the most important influence because of their frequency of contact with the consumer and the closeness between the individual and group members. The two most important membership groups are the family and various peer groups (close friends, school or business associates, sports groups, etc.). Advertisers frequently portray product consumption in a peer group setting. In the beverage category, diverse products such as Hawaiian Punch, Lowenbrau beer, and Dry Sack sherry all use appeals in a peer group setting. A family context is also used by advertisers. For example, in coffee, Folgers advertised the husband disliking the wife's brew and Mrs. Olsen coming to the rescue with a cup of Folgers; and Sanka advertised an irritable husband or wife in a family setting with Robert Young coming to the rescue with decaffeinated Sanka.

Advertisers have also used aspiration group appeals based on the desire to belong to, or be associated with, other groups. Clothing and cosmetics are frequently advertised within the context of business success and prestige. Well-known personalities that consumers seek to emulate are sometimes used as spokespersons for products not necessarily associated with their field of expertise. For example, Brut cologne has used Vitas Gerulaitis and Joe Namath to endorse its product in an attempt to suggest that use of the product will create the same social success that is associated with these individuals.

Strategic Implications of Reference Groups

Marketers use reference groups in advertising to portray informational, comparative, and normative influence. Groups exert **informational influence** on consumers by supplying them with believable information. Reference groups are a **comparative influence** in permitting consumers to compare their beliefs, attitudes, and behavior to those of the group. Reference groups are a **normative influence** in that they influence members to conform to group norms, and in some cases, use rewards and punishment to gain compliance.

Information influence

Most of the evidence in marketing studies suggests that informational influences come primarily from personal rather than commercial sources because friends and family members are regarded as more credible than advertisers or salespeople.[40] Marketers sometimes use spokespersons to convey information through advertising because they are regarded as credible in their field of expertise. Thus, Rafer Johnson, a former Olympic decathlon champion talks about the benefits of exercise in an advertisement for AMF sports equipment (see top of Figure 6-6). Arthur Ashe as a well-known and credible tennis pro endorses the Head tennis racket.

Advertisers also create their own experts. General Motors has established Mr. Goodwrench as an expert in car maintenance. Betty Crocker was created by General Mills in 1921 and has become a "sort of 'First Lady of Food,' the most highly esteemed home service authority in the nation."[41]

Comparative influence

Consumers constantly compare their attitudes with those of members of their reference group. Advertisers frequently rely on comparative influence by using a "typical consumer" approach. Such an approach requires demonstrating to consumers that other customers have similar needs and then requires offering a solution to these needs. The advertisement for Tylenol in Figure 6-6 is an example.

Another reason for using comparative influence is to encourage a consumer to identify with an individual that he or she would like to be similar to. Brut's use of Vitas Gerulaitis (the third ad in Figure 6-6) is an example of comparative influence based on aspiration group appeals, whereas the Tylenol ad is an example of comparative influence using membership group appeals. In the first case, the consumer would like to be similar to the spokesperson; in the second case, the consumer actually considers himself or herself to be similar to the person in the ad.

Comparative influence has also been used in personal selling. Here the influencers should have characteristics similar to those being influenced. Therefore, there should be some match in characteristics between the buyer and the salesperson. Several studies have found that when a customer sees the salesperson as similar in terms of tastes, attitudes, and even religion, the salesperson is likely to be more effective.[42]

FIGURE 6-6   173
Use of informational, comparative, and normative group influence in advertising

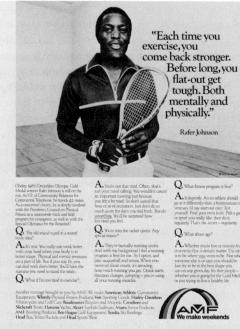

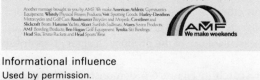

Informational influence
Used by permission.

Comparative influence using "typical consumer"
approach. Used by permission.

Comparative influence using aspirational approach

Normative influence

Courtesy of Vitas Gerulaitis and by permission of Fabergé, Inc. Reprinted with permission of Somerset Importers, Ltd.

Normative influence

Normative influence is based on the ability of the group to reward the individual. The business organization can reward the individual with money and status. The family can reward the child with praise and approval. Social groups can also provide rewards for purchasing behavior. Compliments on one's clothing or looks reinforce the consumer's choice. Normative influence means conformity to group norms. Marketers are interested in such imitative behavior because it implies a **"social multiplier" effect:** once products are accepted by the most influential members of a group, they are likely to be accepted by others. The idea of "keeping up with the Joneses" reflects normative group influence.

Marketers have used normative influence by depicting social approval in advertising. Praise for a good cup of coffee, a shiny floor, glorious hair, good sherry, and a quiet and comfortable automobile ride are all examples of advertising's simulation of social approval. Groups may also exert negative normative influence through coercion rather than reward. The greater the importance of the group, the greater its power to express disapproval and even censure for lack of conformity. Marketers have depicted such coercive power through the use of fear appeals. For example, the fear of social disapproval due to loose dentures is brought out by Poligrip; the fear of group ostracism due to body odor is demonstrated by Dial. In each case use of the product changes disapproval to approval.

The ad for Johnnie Walker scotch in Figure 6-6 demonstrates the use of normative influence. The ad shows the rewards the organization conveys for success by depicting the climb up the corporate ladder in a very original way. The company is trying to link the product with the positive association of group (organizational) rewards.

Opinion Leadership

Reference groups influence consumers through word-of-mouth communication. A central concept in such communication is **opinion leadership.** An opinion leader is one who influences the purchasing behavior of another consumer through word-of-mouth communication. The consumer being influenced is the follower.

Marketers are interested in identifying opinion leaders because of the social multiplier effect. If an opinion leader can be influenced to buy the product, he or she will influence several other consumers, who may in turn influence others in the group to buy. A message reaching the opinion leader from the mass media is therefore likely to have an effect out of proportion to the cost of that message.

It is difficult to identify and reach opinion leaders because they tend to have the same characteristics as the friends and neighbors they are influencing. Marketers have attempted to simulate opinion leadership by showing conversations between typical consumers, one of whom is the opinion leader. Marketers have also tried to stimulate opinion leadership by trying to get consumers to talk about a product. One approach is to encourage consumers to "tell your friends about the product."

FAMILY INFLUENCES

The most important reference group is the family. Not only does the family exert direct influence on consumers; very frequently the family is the decision-making unit. Decisons regarding an automobile, major appliance, or vacation are frequently made jointly by family members rather than by an individual consumer. In this context a family member may play one or more of the following roles in arriving at a decision: (1) gathering information, (2) influencing others, (3) making the final decision, (4) acting as a purchasing agent for others, (5) consuming the product.

From the marketer's standpoint one of the most important distinctions is that between the purchaser and the consumer. Many companies operate on the false premise that the purchaser should provide information on brand satisfaction. Yet frequently the purchaser is not the prime consumer and is buying products for others.

Husband-Wife Influences on Purchase Behavior

Various studies have identified husband dominance, wife dominance, and shared influence in family decisions by product. Husbands dominate decisions for automobiles[43] and insurance.[44] Wives dominate decisions for food, toiletries, and small appliances.[45] Shared decisions are likely for housing,[46] vacations, and furniture.[47] These classifications have important implications for marketers. If a product is in the husband- or wife-dominant category, messages have to be tailored to one spouse or the other. Media have to be selected that are male or female dominant. If the decision is made jointly, the message has to be tailored for the couple and media have to be purchased that are likely to reach both spouses.

The husband's and wife's influence can also vary by the type of decision. One study found that the husband dominates the decision on when to buy a car and how much to spend. The wife is almost as influential as the husband on where to buy the car and the style selected. Similarly, the wife dominates the decision on the style of furniture, but the husband is almost as influential on when to buy furniture and how much to spend.[48]

Parent-Child Influences on Purchasing Behavior

Children play an important part in family decision making for a wide range of products, and in many cases may themselves be the sole decision makers. Younger children may decide on expenditures for candy, snack items, and movies. As the child grows older and his or her purchasing power increases, the child may be the primary decision maker for toys, record albums, and reading material. Teenagers may be decision makers for their clothing and furniture and may begin to exert influence on decisions regarding automobiles, audio equipment, and vacations. Overall, the extent of children's influence is high. What one author referred to as "child power" may be growing with the greater independence of children.[49] Greater affluence and increased divorce rates may be resulting in a greater likelihood that children will get their way.

Strategic Implications of Family Decision Making

Research on family decision making influences every phase of marketing strategy — the advertising message, media, product development, pricing, and distribution.

Advertising messages

The nature of family decision making will influence the content of advertising messages. If the wife, husband, or child is dominant in making the decision, the advertising message must be directed to the needs of the dominant party. One study found that the child directly influences the choice of fast-food restaurants.[50] These establishments must therefore advertise to the child as well as to the parent. Both McDonald's and Burger King consistently portray the whole family. They also directly appeal to children by such characters as Ronald McDonald and the Magic Burger King.

Advertising media

The selection of advertising media will be based on who is involved in the decision. Husband, wife, or child-dominant decisions require the selection of magazines and TV programs that are oriented to a particular member of the family. If the decision is made by the family as a whole, general circulation magazines or prime time TV should be used. Another alternative in joint decisions is to reach each member of the decision unit separately as well as together. This would require using both general and specialized media.

Product development

Products designed for one member of the family provide the marketer with less of a problem than products designed for two or more members. Life insurance was traditionally designed to the specifications of the husband. Currently more life insurance companies are designing insurance to the woman's needs because of the rapid rise in the proportion of working women. Garden tools could be designed to the specifications of either husband or wife since either may make the decision. In designing a trowel or hoe the marketer could introduce a lighter-weight material and an easier grip to facilitate use by the wife. Heavier material and a thicker handle could be introduced to appeal to the husband. The marketer has the option: (1) to segment the market by introducing one product to a certain member of the family, (2) to expand the product line so specific products appeal to individual family members, or (3) to introduce an all-purpose product so the family can buy one item to be used by everyone.

Distribution

If decisions are made jointly, stores may be required to stay open longer to accommodate both the husband and wife. If the product is selected by either husband or wife, separate merchandising displays may be required.

In-store promotional displays must reflect purchase influence as well. One study found that children are more likely to get their preferred brand when they make a request in the store rather than at home.[51] This implies that in-store promotions for cereals, snacks, candy, or toothpaste should be directed toward the child as well as the adult.

Individual and Environmental Influences in Organizational Buying

Consumer thought variables, characteristics, and environmental influences have their parallel in organizational buying. Buyers in organizations develop preferences based on their needs, attitudes, and perceptions. The buyer's organization also has certain characteristics (size, location, centralization, and so forth) that influence vendor and product selection. In addition, organizational buyers are influenced by environmental factors such as organizational and industry norms, the opinions of peers inside and outside the organization, and influences within the buying center. This section describes the (1) needs, attitudes, and perceptions; (2) organizational characteristics; and (3) environmental factors that influence the development of industrial marketing strategies.

INFLUENCE OF THOUGHT VARIABLES IN ORGANIZATIONAL BUYING

The needs, attitudes, and perceptions of organizational buyers are recognized by the industrial firm as important influences in purchasing decisions. These variables are not measured as systematically or used as frequently in industrial marketing as in consumer marketing for several reasons. First, personal selling is the dominant means of communication and influence in industrial marketing. Therefore, it frequently becomes the responsibility of the industrial salesperson rather than the marketing researcher to evaluate a buyer's needs, attitudes toward the vendor, and perceptions of the product line. Such assessments are subjective and are based on the salesman's knowledge of the customer and experience in the industry. Second, products are frequently directed to a handful of potential buyers. In such cases marketing research does not involve surveys or empirical measures of needs and attitudes. Third, industrial marketing research has lagged behind consumer research in developing survey methods and quantitative techniques.

One study illustrates the importance of identifying buyers' needs for a new industrial product, a scientific and technical information (STI) service.[52] The study identified twelve needs based on interviews with 274 scientists and engineers:

speed of information	mode of payment
purchase arrangement	type of supplies
nature of output	language used
output format	topical coverage
mode of search	period coverage
distribution	price

Once information was obtained on the needs of STI buyers, five benefit segments were identified on the basis of similarity in need. The needs and organizational characteristics of each segment are:

- *Segment 1* (48 percent of the respondents in the study) is systems rather than price oriented. It emphasizes the system's language and extent of coverage. Firms in segment 1 are larger and the orientation is more toward information support rather than R&D.

- *Segment 2* (8 percent) is also systems oriented, but this group is more concerned with output format. Firms in segment 2 are smaller. Job responsibility is likely to be with an R&D manager rather than a general manager.

- *Segment 3* (20 percent) is price and systems oriented, emphasizing output format and distribution. Segment 3 is more research oriented and has a greater proportion of employees with advanced degrees.

- *Segment 4* (11 percent) is the most price-sensitive segment. This group assigns responsibility to general managers rather than to R&D.

- *Segment 5* (13 percent) emphasizes speed of information. This group is composed of small firms with emphasis on engineering research.

The study illustrates the importance of identifying needs, since the need segments provide guidelines for product development. The results of the study demonstrate that there is no universally desirable STI system. The researchers suggested using a product-line approach and offering an STI system to appeal to each benefit segment. The alternative would be to offer one flexible basic system with many options that could appeal to all five segments. A third option would be to focus on segment 1 only since it represents almost one-half of all respondents.

USE OF ORGANIZATIONAL CHARACTERISTICS

The organizational characteristics of buyer firms provide the industrial marketer with important information on their size, location, type of business, purchasing responsibilities, and organization. Industrial marketers can use this information to better direct salespeople to prospects, to direct information to appropriate segments, to develop selling and promotional strategies, and to identify those with greatest purchase responsibility within the firm. The study of STI buyers identified the important organizational characteristics of each segment. It demonstrated that the key contact in selling to segment 2 is the R&D manager whereas for segment 4 it is the general manager. The study also suggested that salespeople with advanced degrees might best be directed to segment 3, and those with an engineering background to segment 5.

ENVIRONMENTAL INFLUENCES

Industrial buying behavior has environmental influences similar to those for family buying behavior since in both cases decisions are likely to be made jointly. Since the buying center is the main instrument for joint decision-making, industrial marketers focus on environmental factors that influence the decisions of the buying center. Three types of environmental factor influence the buying center (see Figure 6-7). The broadest is *external influences* such

FIGURE 6-7
Environmental influences on the buying center in the organization

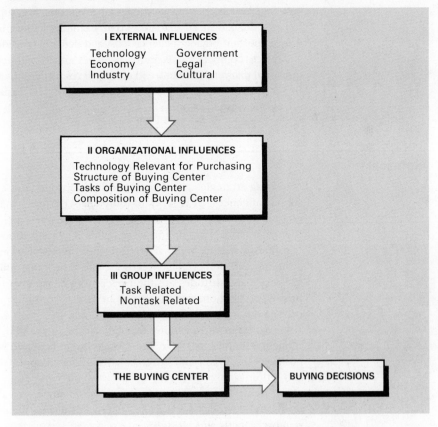

Source: Adapted from Frederick E. Webster and Yoram Wind, "A General Model for Understanding Buying Behavior," *Journal of Marketing* 36 (April 1972): 15.

as the technological state of the arts in the buyer's industry, the state of the economy, competitive intensity, government regulations, and legal and cultural factors that may affect demand. *Organizational influences* that affect the buying center's purchasing decisions (part II in Figure 6-7) are the technology available to the buying center; its structure and organization (centralized versus decentralized, divisional versus corporate responsibilities, limits on decision-making authority, etc.); the goals and responsibilities assigned to each member of the buying center (specific responsibilities for information gathering, decision making, etc.; rewards to members of the buying center); and composition of the buying center (size, organizational position of members).

Group influences (part III in Figure 6-7) are represented by the interaction of members of the buying center. Such influences are divided into task-related interactions (interactions based on the purchasing tasks prescribed by the organization) and nontask interactions (the interplay of personalities, different perceptions of various members' roles, the politics resulting from organizational frictions, etc.).

The external, organizational, and group influences on the buying center influence the marketing strategies of firms that are supplying the industrial buyers (the industrial marketer). For example, if the purchasing agent is the most important buying influence, cost and delivery considerations will dominate and price competition is more likely. If the design engineer is dominant, industrial marketers are more likely to put resources into product development. In such cases markets might be segmented on the basis of the specifications set by the design engineer.

Summary

Marketing strategies are determined by individual and environmental consumer influences. Two types of individual consumer influence are described: consumer thought variables and consumer characteristics. Consumer thought variables are important in guiding strategies because they define the consumer's state of mind. There are three types of thought variable: needs, attitudes, and perceptions. Needs are the forces that guide consumers to specific goals; attitudes are the preferences consumers have for specific brands; perceptions are the means by which consumers organize and interpret marketing information.

Two types of marketing strategy can be developed from consumer thought variables: adaptive and change. In an adaptive strategy, the marketer positions the brand and develops advertising to appeal to existing needs and attitudes. A change strategy seeks to alter needs and attitudes in an attempt to attract new users. In most cases a strategy seeking to change needs and attitudes is much less likely to succeed than a strategy seeking to reinforce needs and attitudes.

Consumer characteristics have been used by marketers to describe users and prospect groups and to develop advertising and media strategies accordingly. Three types of characteristic were described: demographics, representing the objective characteristics of the consumer; life styles, representing the consumer's activities, interests, and opinions; and personality, representing more deep-seated, consistent, and enduring patterns of behavior. Studies using these characteristics for market segmentation, advertising, and product positioning were described.

Marketing strategies are influenced by environmental factors as well as by individual consumer factors. Five types of environmental influence were considered: culture, subcultural influences, social class, reference groups, and the family.

Culture refers to the widely shared norms and values learned from society. These norms and values are likely to influence consumer behavior. For example, the emphasis on youth in American culture has led to purchases of cosmetics, diet drinks, and sports equipment. *Subcultures* are groups with homogeneous norms and values that differ from those of society in general. Subcultures have been identified by age, by geography, by national identity, and by race. The most important subculture in the United States is the black consumer market. *Social class* refers to the position of the consumer on a social scale based on income, occupation, and education. Differences in purchasing behavior of social classes affect marketing strategies. For example, consumers higher on the social scale are more fashion conscious, view furniture and food in a more symbolic context, and are more aware of price and brand alternatives.

Reference groups are the most important environmental influence on the consumer since they serve as a reference point in forming brand beliefs and deciding on purchases. Reference groups serve three important functions: (1) they provide information to consumers, (2) they serve as a basis for consumers to compare beliefs and behavior to those of the group, and (3) they provide support to consumers when they comply with group norms. *The family* is the most important reference group. Studies have classified product decisions according to whether the husband, the wife, or the child is most influential, or whether the decision is made jointly. Such classifications have important implications for the direction of advertising appeals, the media to use, and the development of separate product lines.

Thought variables, characteristics, and environmental influences also provide guidelines for industrial marketers' strategies. The needs of organizational buyers provide industrial marketers with a basis for directing price, product, and service strategies to defined groups of firms. Organizational buyer attitudes help the industrial marketer assess the strengths and weaknesses of the company relative to competition. Identifying the organizational characteristics of defined industrial segments permits the marketer to direct salespeople to prospects and to develop selling and promotional strategies for these firms. Environmental influences affect the joint purchasing decisions of buying centers.

In the last two chapters we considered how consumer behavior determines the marketer's definition of marketing opportunity and how it influences the development of marketing strategies to exploit opportunity. In the next chapter we will describe marketing research as a tool for identifying marketing opportunity and evaluating marketing strategies.

Questions

1. Assume a large paper producer is considering entering the disposable diaper market because the company finds that many consumers are dissatisfied with their regular brand.

   □ How can the manufacturer use need-gap analysis to identify opportunities in the disposable diaper market? (Use Figure 6-1 as a guide in developing a hypothetical example.)

   □ Assume that the need-gap analysis identifies specific demographic characteristics of customers dissatisfied with their regular brand. Use Table 6-1 as a guide in developing hypothetical characteristics of dissatisfied customers (the target segment). What are the strategic implications of these characteristics?

2. The strategic applications of consumer needs cited in the chapter focus on identifying marketing opportunities, whereas the strategic applications of consumer attitudes focus on evaluating marketing strategies.

   □ What is the distinction between identifying marketing opportunity and evaluating marketing strategy?

   □ Relate this difference to the distinction between needs and attitudes.

3. If the telecommunications company producing the Picturephone (see Table 6-2) found that visual communication was relatively unimportant, one option would be to try to change needs by demonstrating the importance of visual communication to businesses through an advertising campaign. What are the pros and cons of such a strategy?

4. The statement is made that a change in a single component of a brand may totally change the image of a commonplace product.

   □ Can you cite an example in which a change in a brand produced a positive or negative influence on the brand's image?

   □ A change in a brand may be made to attract a new or broader segment of the market, but in so doing alienate another more important segment of users. Can you cite an example in which such a change had negative consequences for the brand image?

5. Why are some companies that do not sell directly to the final consumer (e.g., U.S. Steel) concerned with the corporate image they project to the consuming public?

6. The chapter suggests using demographics to define users of a brand or

product category, and to direct marketing strategies accordingly. Should demographics also be used to identify a prospect group (i.e., nonusers who have a greater potential for usage)? Cite an example of the use of demographics for this purpose.

7. What are the marketing implications in using any of the life-style categories cited in Table 6-3 for describing users (or prospective users) of:

☐ a new detergent that advertises that it makes washing easier;

☐ personal care appliances such as curling irons, or facial care appliances;

☐ a new magazine designed to provide up-to-date marketing and financial information to the working woman; and

☐ a new breakfast cereal for the diet conscious and active adult?

8. On what basis could you support identification of the black consumer market as a subculture? On what basis could you argue against such an identification? What are the marketing implications of each position?

9. A leading domestic beer manufacturer is considering buying the rights to produce an imported beer in the United States. The objective is to compete with Lowenbrau, now owned by Miller. How could the manufacturer use social class to (a) define the target market for the new beer, and (b) provide guidelines for advertising?

10. Both the ads for AMF and Brut (see Figure 6-6) use spokespersons. The ad for AMF portraying Rafer Johnson is based on informational influence. The ad for Brut using Vitas Gerulaitis is based on comparative influence.

☐ Why did both advertisers for these two different products use spokespersons?

☐ Why is one based on informational influence and the other on comparative influence?

11. There has been a greater shift toward joint decision making for many product categories that have been within the traditional domain of the husband (autos, financial planning) and wife (appliances, furniture). What are the implications of this shift for (a) new product development, (b) product line strategies, and (c) advertising?

12. Can you draw any parallels between purchasing roles in industrial and family buying decisions?
Cite an example of industrial and family decision making specifying the parallel roles in each case.

Notes

1. "In Spite of Huge Losses, Procter & Gamble Tries Once More to Revive Pringle's Chips," *The Wall Street Journal*, October 9, 1981, p. 29.

2. Gordon W. Allport, "Attitudes," in C. A. Murchinson, ed., *A Handbook of Social Psychology* (Worcester, Mass.: Clark University Press, 1935), pp. 798–844.

3. Henry Assael, "Segmenting Markets by Group Purchasing Behavior: An Application of the AID Technique," *Journal of Marketing Research* 7 (May 1970): 153–8.

4. Joseph W. Newman, *Marketing Management and Information* (Homewood, Ill.: Richard D. Irwin, 1967), Sanka (B) Case, p. 211.

5. "How to Tie Promotions to a Product's Image," *Advertising Age*, June 15, 1981, p. 56.

6. Pierre Martineau, *Motivation in Advertising* (New York: McGraw-Hill, 1957), p. 114.

7. See Douglas J. McConnell, "Effect of Pricing on Perception of Product Quality," *Journal of Applied Psychology* 52 (August 1968): 331–4; and Folke Olander, "The Influence of Price on the Consumer's Evaluation of Products and Purchases," in B. Taylor and B. Wills, eds., *Pricing Strategy* (Staples Press, 1969), pp. 50–69.

8. William D. Wells and Douglas J. Tigert, "Activities, Interests and Opinions," *Journal of Advertising Research* 11 (August 1971): 27–35.

9. Joseph T. Plummer, "The Concept and Application of Life-Style Segmentation," *Journal of Marketing* 38 (January 1974): 33–7.

10. Joseph T. Plummer, "Life Style and Advertising: Case Studies," in Fred C. Allvine, *Combined Proceedings, 1971 Spring and Fall Conference* (Chicago: American Marketing Association, 1972), pp. 290–5.

11. Shirley Young, "The Dynamics of Measuring Unchange," in Russell I. Haley, ed., *Attitude Research in Transition* (Chicago: American Marketing Association, 1972), p. 72.

12. Milton J. Rokeach, "The Role of Values in Public Opinion Research," *Public Opinion Quarterly* 32 (Winter 1968): 547–9.

13. Many of the changes in cultural values cited in the chapter were identified by two research services, Monitor and the Value and Life Style Survey (VALS). See: "Lifestyle's Monitor," *American Demographics*, May 1981, p. 21; and Paul Shay, "The New Consumer Values," *Advertising Quarterly* 56 (Summer 1978): 15–8.

14. Melvin Helitzer and Carl Heye, *The Youth Market* (New York: Media Books, 1970), p. 58.

15. "You Can Sell to the Older Set if You Watch These Trends," *Advertising Age*, August 22, 1977, pp. 33, 42.

16. "A Profile Grows to New Heights," *Advertising Age*, April 6, 1981, p. S-23.

17. Ibid.

18. Ibid.; and "Fast Growing Ethnic Market Nears $5 Billion Annual Sales," *Product Marketing*, June 1982, p. 43.

19. Danny N. Bellenger and Humberto Valencia, "Understanding the Hispanic Market," *Business Horizons* (May–June 1982): 47–50.

20. "Rising to the Hispanic Challenge," *Ad Forum*, April 1982, p. 53.

21. *Advertising Age*, April 6, 1981, p. S-23.

22. *Ad Forum*, April 1982, p. 55.

23. Ibid.

24. Johnson Products Company, *Annual Report*, 1975, p. 4.

25. Raymond A. Bauer and Scott Cunningham, "The Negro Market," *Journal of Advertising Research* 10 (April 1970): 3–13.

26. Carl M. Larson, "Racial Brand Usage and Media Exposure Differentials," in Keith Cox and Ben Enis, eds., *June Conference Proceedings of the American Marketing Association*, Series No. 27 (1968), pp. 208–15.

27. Donald E. Sexton, Jr., "Black Buyer Behavior," *Journal of Marketing* 36 (October 1972): 38.

28. Raymond A. Bauer, "Negro Consumer Behavior," in Joseph W. Newman, ed., *On Knowing the Consumer* (New York: John Wiley & Sons, 1966), pp. 161–5.

29. Laurence P. Feldman and Alvin D. Star, "Racial Factors in Shopping Behavior," in Keith Cox and Ben M. Enis, eds., *June Conference Proceedings of the American Marketing Association*, Series No. 27 (1968), pp. 216–26.

30. John V. Petrof, "Attitudes of the Urban Poor Toward Their Neighborhood Supermarkets," *Journal of Retailing* 47 (Spring 1971): 3–17.

31. Donald E. Sexton, Jr., "Comparing the Cost of Food to Blacks and to Whites — A Survey," *Journal of Marketing* 35 (July 1971): 40–6.

32. Leon Morse, "Black Radio Market Study," *Television/Radio Age*, February 28, 1977, pp. A-1–A-31.

33. "Trying to Reach Blacks? Beware of Marketing Myopia," *Advertising Age*, May 21, 1979, p. 59.

34. Raymond A. Bauer, Scott M. Cunningham, and Lawrence H. Wortzel, "The Marketing Dilemma of Negroes," *Journal of Marketing* 29 (July 1965): 3.

35. Dennis F. Healy, "Johnson Products Company," in M. Wayne DeLozier, *Consumer Behavior Dynamics: A Casebook* (Columbus, Ohio: Charles E. Merrill, 1977), p. 116.

36. *"Essence* Urges Heavier Marketing to Blacks," *Product Marketing,* September 1977, p. 1.

37. Joseph T. Plummer, "Life Style Patterns and Commercial Bank Credit Card Usage," *Journal of Marketing* 35 (April 1971): 35–41.

38. Plummer, "Life Style and Advertising," p. 292.

39. A. Marvin Roscoe, Jr., Arthur LeClaire, Jr., and Leon G. Schiffman, "Theory and Management Applications of Demographics in Buyer Behavior," in Arch G. Woodsdise, Jagdish N. Sheth, and Peter D. Bennett, eds., *Consumer and Industrial Buying Behavior* (New York: North-Holland, 1977), p. 74.

40. See Thomas S. Robertson, *Innovative Behavior and Communications* (New York: Holt, Rinehart and Winston, 1971).

41. Julian L. Watkins, *The 100 Greatest Advertisements* (New York: Dover, 1959), p. 205.

42. F. B. Evans, "Selling as a Dyadic Relationship — A New Approach," *American Behavioral Scientist* 6 (May 1963): 76–9; and Timothy C. Brock, "Communicator-Recipient Similarity and Decision Change," *Journal of Personality and Social Psychology* 1 (June 1965): 650–4.

43. Harry L. Davis, "Dimensions of Marital Roles in Consumer Decision Making," *Journal of Marketing Research* 7 (May 1970): 168–77.

44. Harry L. Davis and Benny P. Rigaux, "Perception of Marital Roles in Decision Processes," *Journal of Consumer Research* 1 (June 1974): 51–62.

45. Haley, Overholser and Associates, Inc., *Purchase Influence: Measures of Husband/Wife Influence on Buying Decisions* (New Canaan, Conn.: Haley, Overholser Inc., 1975).

46. G. M. Munsinger, J. E. Weber, and R. W. Hansen, "Joint Home Purchasing Decisions by Husbands and Wives," *Journal of Consumer Research* 1 (May 1975): 60–6.

47. Davis and Rigaux, "Perceptions of Marital Roles."

48. Davis, "Dimensions of Marital Roles."

49. Daniel B. Wackman, "Family Processes in Children's Consumption," in Neil Beckwith et al., eds., *Proceedings of the American Marketing Association Educator's Conference*, Series No. 44 (1979), p. 651.

50. George J. Szybillo, Arlene K. Sosanie, and Aaron Tenenbein, "Should Children be Seen but not Heard?" *Journal of Advertising Research* 17 (December 1977): 8.

51. Wackman, "Family Processes."

52. Yoram Wind, John F. Grashof, and Joel D. Goldhar, "Market-Based Guidelines for Design of Industrial Products," *Journal of Marketing* 42 (July 1978): 38–42.

CHAPTER 7

Marketing Information Systems and Marketing Research

FOCUS OF CHAPTER

The marketing firm needs a marketing information system to enable it to define and measure opportunity. Information must be obtained from consumers, competitors, and internal company records to obtain a reliable measure of past performance and future opportunities.

A **marketing information system** (MIS) is a set of interacting facilities and procedures designed to provide management with reliable information for defining opportunities and developing marketing plans. The collection and dissemination of information by an MIS facility should be systematic and ongoing, meaning that management should receive information on marketing performance and environmental trends regularly. Information should also be as reliable as possible, meaning that marketing action can be taken on the basis of the information.

As we have seen in the last two chapters, the consumer is the primary source of marketing information. Information on consumer needs, brand awareness, brand attitudes, advertising awareness, demographic and life-style characteristics, and buying intentions is determined by consumer surveys. *Marketing research* is the primary means of collecting consumer information and is the central component of the marketing information system. Marketing research provides the basic input to enable management to develop marketing plans and formulate marketing strategies. Consider the following:

- Procter and Gamble interviews an average of 1.5 million people a year in connection with 1000 marketing research projects to evaluate its current brands and identify new product opportunities.[1] A marketing research study on Downy fabric softener identified a problem: consumers disliked having to run down to their washing machines every rinse cycle to pour in Downy. As a result P&G introduced Bounce, a nonwoven rayon sheet impregnated with softener that is tossed into the dryer with the clothes.[2]

■ Through marketing research Stouffer's identified four objections to diet foods: not tasty, not filling, not enough variety, and not appetizing.[3] As a result Stouffer's developed Lean Cuisine, a successful line of tastier diet foods. The product line was tested on consumer panels and was then introduced into six test markets with positive results before a national launch.[4]

■ Marketing research "played a vital role in the design, development and marketing of Kodak's successful disc camera."[5] The company had the difficult task of identifying opportunity in a market where consumer satisfaction was high. Kodak conducted research to determine when and where consumers were reluctant to take pictures and developed the disc camera to encourage picture taking in these situations. Once having developed the technology, Kodak took prototype cameras to 1000 homes for testing. Responses were positive, but most significantly, after people became familiar with all the features of the camera, intention to buy doubled.[6]

Marketing research is not always successful in helping companies to identify and exploit opportunities. Consider:

■ RCA's overestimation of the demand for videodiscs,

■ P&G's failure to assess the taste disadvantage of Pringle's potato chips, and

■ Polaroid's assumption that there was a need for instant movie cameras.

In each of these cases, the company became enamored of its own technology and ignored danger signals from research.

In this chapter we will first consider the firm's marketing information system as management's basic input in defining opportunity and developing plans. Next we will consider in detail the marketing information needs of managers and the organizations and facilities that satisfy these needs. The rest of the chapter focuses on the most important component of the marketing information system, marketing research, and describes the process of conducting marketing research in both the consumer and the industrial sectors.

The Marketing Information System

Marketing information comes from diverse sources — marketing research studies, internal company data, government agencies, syndicated research services.

Management must combine these sources into an integrated information system capable of providing meaningful and timely data.

Figure 7-1 is a simplified illustration of data sources in a marketing information system. The marketing information system collects data from three sources: the environment, the company, and the consumer. Generally, data collection is the responsibility of marketing research, but at times data from company records and from the environment are fed directly to management.

Figure 7-2 details the components of a marketing information system using the three sources in Figure 7-1. Information is collected from the consumer, the marketing environment, and company sources and is fed into four MIS components: an internal reporting system, a marketing research system, an environmental scanning system, and a government information system. Data are then analyzed to provide information in one or more of the output areas listed. Analysis requires the application of computer facilities and statistical programs as support. Information output deals with marketing opportunity assessment, performance data (profitability, sales, marketing costs), product mix evaluation, and marketing mix evaluation (advertising, sales promotion, price, and personal selling activity). Information is also provided on overall corporate strategies (product mix evaluation, assessment of acquisitions). Information is then presented to management in report form for defining opportunity, evaluating performance, and developing marketing plans.

FIGURE 7-1
Sources of data in a marketing information system

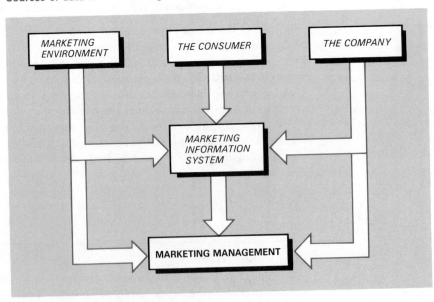

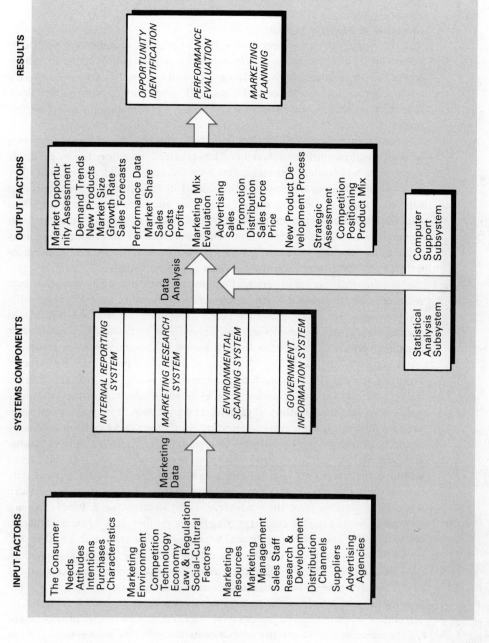

FIGURE 7-2
Components of a marketing information system

COMPONENTS OF THE MARKETING INFORMATION SYSTEM

Each of the four system components of the MIS and its role in opportunity identification and planning will be briefly considered here.

Internal Reporting System

The internal reporting system is designed to provide management with data generated by the company: orders, sales reports, marketing costs, inventory levels, factory shipments. These data are crucial because they provide the basis for information on revenue and costs in the profit and loss statement. Therefore the internal reporting system is the basis for information on actual performance.

Sales information is the most important element of the internal reporting system. The firm must keep track of orders received; inventory levels; products shipped to wholesalers, retailers, and final customers; and prices paid. The physical distribution system to be described in Chapter 16 is the source of this information. Some firms ensure immediate access to orders and shipment data for their managers. For example, "Zone, regional, and sales managers [at General Mills] start their day with a teletype report on orders and shipments in their area the day before. The report also contains percentages to compare with target percentages and the previous year's percentages."[7]

But information on orders and shipments does not easily translate into retail sales. For the industrial firm a shipment to a customer generally represents a direct sale. But most consumer goods companies do not sell directly to consumers. Factory shipments are not synonymous with sales. As a result most consumer goods firms have no internal means of determining sales results.

Because of the need for sales data, an important input into the internal reporting system is information from outside agencies (syndicated services) on retail sales. The two primary sources of sales information for consumer goods firms are **store audits** and **consumer panel data.** Store auditors measure sales by subtracting their end-of-period inventory for a product from inventory at the beginning of the period plus shipments. A. C. Nielsen Company audits a representative sample of food and drug stores nationwide and sells retail store information to many consumer goods companies. Consumer panel data use the periodic reports of a representative sample of consumers to measure sales. Both systems have their advantages and disadvantages. Panel data are sometimes subject to consumer reporting biases, yet they do provide information on where the consumer purchased, what price was paid, and whether the product was bought on deal. Nielsen data are not provided to management until three months after the reporting period. The delay often means management does not have time to react to changes in market conditions. Another service was introduced by Time Inc. to provide quicker sales reports. It is based on warehouse withdrawals (shipments to retailers). Although it does provide more timely information, warehouse withdrawals are still one step removed from actual sales.

The Marketing Research System

Whereas the internal reporting system provides data on actual marketing performance, the marketing research and environmental scanning systems provide information on opportunity and projected performance. The marketing research system collects data on consumers' needs, intended purchases of company and competitive products, and reactions to advertising, price, and promotional strategies.

Figure 7-3 summarizes the role of the marketing research system in marketing planning. It depicts a flow of information from the marketing environment to the marketing organization. Marketing strategies are then introduced by the marketing organization into the marketing environment on the basis of input from the marketing research system.

In the first step a marketing opportunity or problem is identified. An opportunity could be the need for introducing a new product, repositioning an existing product, appealing to new markets, intensifying sales promotions to exploit price elasticity, or increasing the advertising or personal selling budget to increase demand. A problem could be a confused image of the brand, lack of adequate distribution, an advertising campaign that is not reaching the target group, or lack of sufficient advertising or brand awareness. An example

FIGURE 7-3
Role of the marketing research system in marketing planning

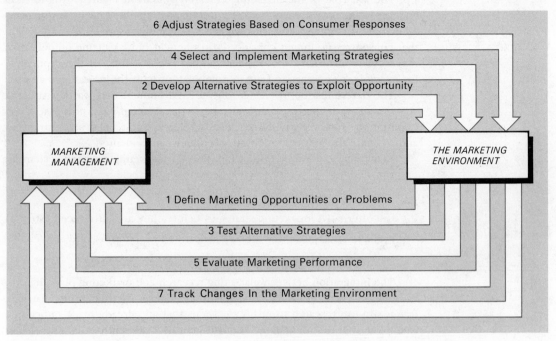

of an opportunity in the soft-drink market is 7-Up's identification of a nutritionally oriented segment that could be appealed to with a no-caffeine claim. An example of a problem is a finding that Parker Pen has a fuzzy image among consumers because of product proliferation.[8]

On this basis management develops several alternative strategies to exploit an opportunity or resolve a problem. For example, management might have considered giving 7-Up a health-oriented appeal, a nutritional appeal, or a taste appeal. Marketing research would be responsible for testing the strategies developed by management to exploit opportunity (step 3 in Figure 7-3). For 7-Up the strategies to be tested would be ads representing different positionings. This **pretesting** phase is designed to determine which strategy is most likely to meet managerial objectives (maximize advertising awareness, improve brand attitudes, gain immediate increases in market share, establish a basis for long-term sales gains, and so on).

Management selects a set of marketing strategies on the basis of the pretest research phase and implements them. It is now marketing research's task to evaluate the results (step 5 in Figure 7-3). This **posttesting** phase is designed to track marketing performance and determine if any adjustments in marketing strategy are required. For example, once the no-caffeine positioning is implemented for 7-Up, research might show that the nutritional segment is buying but that 7-Up is losing the diet segment. Therefore, a logical adjustment in strategy (step 6 in Figure 7-3) would be to extend the line by adding Diet 7-Up. The last role of the marketing research system in Figure 7-3 is to track changes in the environment once the firm has implemented its marketing plans. As competitors introduce their own caffeine-free entries, research might show that consumers no longer consider 7-Up's benefit of no caffeine unique. If so, management may have to consider another repositioning of the product — for example, to emphasize taste in combination with the no-caffeine appeal.

The determination of changes in the environment that warrant strategic adjustment starts the research cycle anew. Management must now assess new opportunities (and competitive threats), develop and test a new set of strategies, and evaluate the strategies that are eventually implemented.

In summary, the four responsibilities of a marketing research system are to:

- define opportunity (step 1 in Figure 7-3),
- test alternative marketing strategies before they are introduced (step 3),
- evaluate strategies once they are implemented (step 5), and
- track the marketing environment (step 7).

The integration between marketing research and marketing planning does not always occur as neatly as depicted in Figure 7-3. Marketing managers frequently use research to justify decisions that are already made rather than to exploit opportunities. Marketing managers also frequently discount research findings because they do not feel they can draw action implications from them or because they mistrust the methods and techniques by which data are collected.

But much of the fault for misusing or neglecting information lies with marketing researchers themselves. Researchers frequently fail to draw out the strategic implications of their findings. As one marketing executive said; "Researchers try to hide behind their numbers. They don't want to interpret data or to be held accountable."[9] Another says, "Research departments' perspective is toward data collection rather than business."[10] And a third says, "Most research people do not know how to suggest ways in which results should be utilized in a relevant way."[11]

Even though the interaction between research and management is far from ideal, the marketing research system is still the primary source of data in defining opportunity and developing marketing strategy. As such, it is in management's interest to ensure that research data are valid, reliable, and most important, actionable.

The Environmental Scanning System

The **environmental scanning system** (sometimes called the marketing intelligence system) tracks changes in the marketing environment that might affect marketing opportunity — competitive activity, changes in technology, economic conditions, the regulatory climate, and changes in social and cultural norms. An environmental scanning system might have:

- encouraged Sears's management to develop videotext technologies because of the promise of in-home shopping,
- identified the risks to RCA of introducing SelectaVision because of competing technologies,
- predicted the effects on automobile safety standards of a decrease in regulation during the Reagan administration, and
- identified the need for soft drink, baby food, and cereal manufacturers to expand their lines into adult-oriented brands because of adverse demographic changes.

In each case, the scanning system is evaluating information on environmental change that will determine future opportunities.

Information is obtained (1) by asking the sales staff and the company's distributors to pass along competitive information, (2) from outside research services that track economic or social trends, (3) by assigning an information manager the responsibility to scan business periodicals, obtain annual reports, acquire competitive products for testing, and read stock reports on competitors. An example of the last is Gillette's hiring of an executive to collect environmental information by reading thirty or forty magazines a month. This executive rarely interviews individuals outside the company, relying on printed material to assess changes in marketing opportunities.[12]

One company that has conducted systematic environmental scanning is Levi Strauss. The company watches closely for relevant environmental change, since its small corporate planning group relies heavily on outside reports for information and forecasts. These reports identify fashion trends, changes in age and geographic distributions of the population, changes in family roles, and prospective government regulations that might affect demand for clothing. The group also tracks economic factors such as clothing imports and technological trends such as improvements in synthetic fibers and in stretch fabrics.[13] These data are used to develop estimates of apparel demand and to assess potential competitive inroads in Levi Strauss's markets.

Government Information System

The government intelligence system is actually part of the environmental scanning system, since government data are used to evaluate legal and regulatory trends, changes in the demographic composition of the United States population, and economic factors. It is treated as a separate system because of the importance of government data, particularly census data.

The government provides a rich storehouse of data that are useful in evaluating marketing opportunity. The Department of Commerce provides information on consumer expenditures for a variety of product categories. Such information is useful in estimating the size of the market for a product category. The Department of Labor provides valuable information on demographic trends such as the proportion of working women. Most important is the demographic information provided by the Bureau of the Census. Information on market opportunities requires a demographic breakdown of consumers by age, income, education, and geographic region. The United States Census provides information on over 200 demographic variables.

DESIGNING A MARKETING INFORMATION SYSTEM

In Figure 7-2 we assumed a marketing information system (MIS) was in place. Such a system must be designed by management. The first step in designing an MIS is to identify the type of information necessary for opportunity identification and marketing planning, and the sources of such data. One author suggests the appointment of a Marketing Information Planning Committee to interview marketing executives and find out their informational needs.[14]

The next step — establishing an organizational responsibility for collecting, analyzing, and reporting marketing data — is more difficult. A marketing executive with the title Manager of Marketing Information Systems should be responsible for this function. The MIS department under this executive's wing should:

- collect data from the various sources listed in Figure 7-2,
- compile the data from these sources into meaningful categories;
- develop statistical and computer capabilities to analyze the data;
- develop models capable of forecasting sales and predicting consumer and environmental changes;

- prepare ongoing reports in areas requiring continuous information (for example, marketing performance; consumer needs, attitudes, and purchasing behavior; and competitors' actions);

- prepare special reports for nonrecurring tasks such as evaluation of markets for entry or assessment of the marketing strengths and weaknesses of acquisition candidates;

- make sure the right information is transmitted to the right decision centers within the organization.

Sources of Marketing Information

In the preceding section we cited the components of a marketing information system. In this section we will examine the sources of information for each of these components in more detail.

Figure 7-4 divides environmental, consumer, and company data sources

FIGURE 7-4
Sources of marketing information

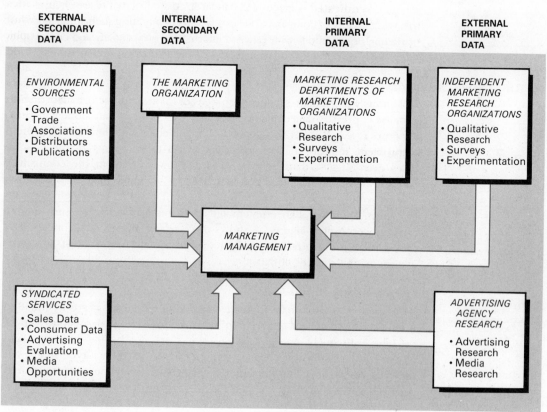

into primary and secondary data. **Primary data** are collected by the marketing organization for its specific purposes: consumer surveys, product and advertising tests, market tests of new products, and so forth. **Secondary data** were collected previously and are not designed to meet the firm's immediate research needs.

Figure 7-4 also distinguishes between internal data (collected by the firm) and external data (collected by sources outside the firm). Internal primary data are obtained through marketing research studies conducted by the firm. Only large firms have marketing research departments that can conduct their own studies. Procter and Gamble has a bank of WATS (Wide Area Telephone Service) lines that it uses to conduct telephone interviews. General Foods conducts many of its product tests. But most marketing organizations commission marketing research firms to conduct research (external primary data). Another important source of external primary data is a firm's advertising agency. Agencies test advertising executions and evaluate the effectiveness of media buys for their clients.

Internal secondary data are systematically collected by the firm for general company use; they include inventory levels, shipments to wholesalers and retailers, sales call reports, and advertising and sales promotion expenditures. External secondary data are obtained by environmental sources and by syndicated services. **Syndicated services** are standardized studies that research firms offer to a wide variety of companies. Research firms conducting such studies provide marketing organizations with valuable information on company and competitors' sales, consumer profiles and trends, advertising evaluation, and media exposure.

NATURE OF SECONDARY DATA

Most firms will evaluate secondary sources of information before incurring the expense of primary data collection. Sometimes secondary data alone will satisfy the firm's research needs. Secondary data might lend insight into the opportunity or problem, indicate the type of primary data to be collected, and in some cases even suggest that the type of survey or experiment the company is considering has already been conducted. Some secondary data such as census data or syndicated services are too expensive or massive for a single company to collect. Therefore a government agency or research firm must provide data to many companies. Figure 7-4 shows three major sources of secondary data: the marketing organization, syndicated services, and government and other environmental sources of data.

The Marketing Organization

As we noted, internal data from the marketing organization are frequently a useful starting point for research. In industrial marketing salespeoples' reports on sales calls might reveal what customers are not buying and why. Sales analysis by territory, by product category, or by customer type might also indicate trouble spots. An internal sales analysis showed one company that 10 percent of its products accounted for 80 percent of its profits. Further, sales of these most profitable products were concentrated among a small, well-defined group of customers. By eliminating many unprofitable products and concentrating sales effort for the remaining product line on a minority of customers, the firm substantially increased profits.

Many organizations do not maintain sales data in enough detail for such an analysis, although the firm's MIS department should be able to do this analysis. Managers should also analyze costs to determine whether the sales effort for a particular product is worth the revenue being produced.

Syndicated Services

Marketing firms have a growing need for data that would be too expensive for one company to collect but that could be collected by a research firm and then sold to many companies. Research firms offer syndicated services that provide information on sales, consumer data, advertising evaluation, and media exposure.

Sales data

As noted, several research firms provide consumer goods companies with information on sales by conducting store audits of product inventory. The largest, A. C. Nielsen, audits about 1600 food and drug stores nationwide every two weeks.

Consumer data

Several firms maintain a panel of households that keep records of their purchases of many food and personal care products. The families that keep these purchase diaries are selected to be representative of all American households. They record brands purchased, store in which purchased, price paid, size purchased, and so forth. Since there is a record of the demographic and, in some cases, life-style characteristics of these households, researchers can determine the characteristics of households buying specific brands. Two of the largest panels are run by National Purchase Diary and the Marketing Research Corporation of America (MRCA).

Rapid changes in cultural values and life styles have also caused some research firms to offer services that track these changes. One, The Monitor Service, interviews 2500 randomly selected respondents every year to determine changes in values. The firm has identified several trends in the 1980s — for example, physical self-enhancement, concern about privacy, a return to nature, a search for community, living for today, and greater personal creativity.[15] Currently 115 companies, including General Foods, General Electric, and CBS, subscribe to the service.

Advertising evaluation

Several research firms also offer services designed to evaluate print and TV advertising. For example, the Starch service measures awareness and readership of advertisements in magazines and newspapers. The service conducts 240,000 interviews each year to evaluate 30,000 ads in magazines and newspapers.[16] It asks respondents whether they have seen the ad, remembered reading about a particular product or company, and read more than half of the copy in the ad.

Companies have also offered services to evaluate TV commercials' effectiveness. In one consumers are brought to a theater to view commercials. Data are gathered on attitudes, preferences, and buying intentions before and after viewing to evaluate the effectiveness of alternative commercials. The second type of service substitutes a test commercial for a regular, on-air commercial. This can be done through split-cable TV in which matched groups of households receive two different versions of a commercial in an attempt to determine the ad's effect on behavior.

Media exposure

Media planners try to select media that are most cost effective in reaching their target group. To do so they need information on the demographic and life-style characteristics of consumers exposed to various media vehicles. The Simmons Market Research Bureau provides the most comprehensive data on media exposure. This company interviews 15,000 respondents yearly and obtains data on readership of 136 magazines and purchases of 500 product categories.[17] It also collects data on newspaper readership and all network TV programming. This information permits marketers to determine the demographic and life-style profiles of magazine and newspaper readers and TV program viewers. They can then select media that most closely match the profile of their target audiences.

Environmental Sources

Government data sources

The largest source of secondary data on the marketing environment is the United States government. Census data provide the most relevant government information. Marketers have used census data to evaluate demographic trends, identify areas of greatest purchasing potential, locate retail and wholesale establishments, develop sales forecasts, and determine sales territories.

Marketers watch census data closely to evaluate demographic trends. In Chapter 3 we noted key demographic changes that have been identified by the census — the increasing proportion of working women, the greater number of singles, the decline in the birth rate, the aging of the baby boom generation. In each case, census-derived information had a profound effect on marketing strategy.

Marketers also use census data for systematic planning purposes. General Motors uses census data to determine which dealerships to close in areas where income and occupational data indicate a reduction in purchasing power. *Time* magazine uses census data to identify zip code areas that have the highest incomes. *Time* then concentrates its subscription solicitation mailings in these areas.[18]

Other environmental sources of data

Researchers have access to other sources of environmental data listed in Figure 7-4. Trade associations frequently publish surveys of industry trends. Marketing researchers can also obtain information on competitors from annual reports and stock analysts' periodic reports on companies. The company's distribution network is a rich source of information on customer reactions and competitive actions. General Motors, Ford, and Chrysler rely on their dealers to provide information on mechanical problems as well as on customer reactions to service.

A particularly important source of information is business publications. *Fortune* publishes a directory of the 500 largest United States corporations, providing information on sales, assets, profits, and employees. *Sales & Marketing Management* provides a yearly survey of buying power that contains data on population, retail sales, and household income by county and city. The magazine develops an index of buying power based on this information for each area.

NATURE OF PRIMARY DATA COLLECTION

In most cases secondary sources of data do not satisfy the firm's research needs. Primary data are required. There are three general approaches to collecting primary data: qualitative research, survey research, and experimentation.

Qualitative Research

Qualitative research does not involve directly questioning consumers or recording information. It is designed to "get a handle" on the problem. Therefore it is most frequently conducted in the early phase of research when the researcher is trying to form some hypotheses about opportunities or problems. Such information is most often obtained in **focus group interviews,** which are open-ended discussions moderated by a trained researcher. The group consists of eight to twelve respondents who are asked to focus on a particular topic. When open-ended interviews are conducted with individual respondents, they are called **depth interviews.**

Another important type of qualitative research is **projective techniques.** These are designed to elicit information when the consumer might be embarrassed to provide it directly or when it is too deep-seated or difficult to be expressed by direct questioning. Rather than asking consumers direct questions they may not be able or willing to answer, researchers give consumers a situation, a cartoon, or a set of words and ask them to respond. Consumers are thus *projecting* from a less involving situation.

Survey Research

Qualitative research frequently leads to more definitive quantitative research. Once a firm has identified opportunities or problems and formed hypotheses, it needs hard data to make a decision. The most important and commonly used type of quantitative research is the consumer survey. Surveys involve selecting a representative sample of respondents from the population of interest; developing a questionnaire; asking the sample questions in person, by phone, or through the mail; and analyzing the results.

Experimentation

In **experimentation** the researcher is trying to establish a cause-and-effect relationship. The most important cause-and-effect relationship is between marketing variables such as advertising, sales effort, or price and sales results. To establish cause and effect, the researcher must attempt to control all extraneous factors so that any variation in the effect (e.g., sales) can be attributed to the marketing factor that is being manipulated (e.g., advertising or price).

Assume a marketer wants to test the effects of in-store displays on sales. Two groups of retail stores are selected and displays are introduced in one group of stores and not in the other. The two sets of stores are matched for size, location, dollar sales, demographic makeup of the neighborhood, and variety of merchandise. Percentage change in sales in the two stores is compared over a two-month period. In the stores without displays sales go up by 5 percent, but in the stores with displays sales go up by 9 percent. Therefore management concludes that in-store displays increased sales by approximately 4 percent. The cost of the displays is compared to the increased revenue, and management decides whether in-store displays are cost effective.

If the stores were not matched, then the increase in sales might have been attributed to another factor. Assume that stores with the displays were in areas where competitive brands had lower market shares. Then the increase in sales might have been caused by competitive weakness, not the effectiveness of in-store displays.

Experimentation is very useful in guiding marketing management decisions. It is used primarily to test specific components of the marketing mix to determine which is most effective (step 3 in Figure 7-3). For example, alternative packages, brand names, advertising executions, or product formulations might be tested on matched groups of consumers to determine which alternative produces the highest score for intention to buy. If the test groups are well matched, management should choose the alternative that results in the highest intention to buy.

Other Methods of Obtaining Primary Data

Two other methods used to collect primary marketing research data are *observation* and *case studies*. Observation can be direct or indirect. Q-tips were created when their inventor observed midwives wrapping cotton around wooden sticks.[19] Curad Battle Ribbon adhesive bandages were developed by watching children decorate bandages with crayons and felt-tip pens.[20] Indirect observation through physical trace measures has also been used. When researchers determined that they could not get reliable estimates of alcohol consumption through direct questioning because of the sensitive nature of the topic, they developed a reliable estimate of consumption by measuring the number of empty bottles in the garbage.[21]

Case studies are comprehensive descriptions and analyses of a situation or series of situations. For example, if RCA had evaluated resistance to the purchase of videodiscs, it might have combined survey research with a series of case studies of consumers who considered videodiscs and decided not to buy. Such case studies might have uncovered some of the basic resistances to purchasing that survey research could have easily overlooked.

The Marketing Research Process: An Example

Since many marketing research studies require the collection of primary data, it is important for the researcher to establish logical steps to ensure the collection of valid and reliable data. Figure 7-5 describes such a process. This section details each of the research steps in Figure 7-5 by citing an actual study of the small-business telephone market conducted by AT&T in 1975.

DEFINITION OF OPPORTUNITY/PROBLEM

In the early and mid-1970s, AT&T was becoming an increasingly market-driven company as a result of increased competition, particularly in the business telecommunications market. The company began to collect data systematically and by 1974 had a comprehensive market information system that included data from customer telephone bills and from research surveys. The company tended to place its customers into three broad categories: large businesses, small businesses, and residential users. It had reasonably good information on its large business and residential customers. It realized, however, that it was fairly ignorant of the attitudes and perceptions of small businesses as to telephone service and equipment, particularly the likelihood that these businesses might begin buying competitive telephone equipment.[22]

The problem that AT&T faced by 1976 was the potential loss of leasing revenue from small businesses unless it learned more about their telecommunications needs and identified those companies most likely to switch to competitive equipment. As a result AT&T identified the following *research objectives*:

1. define the telecommunications needs of small businesses,
2. determine the attitude of these firms toward the local telephone company,

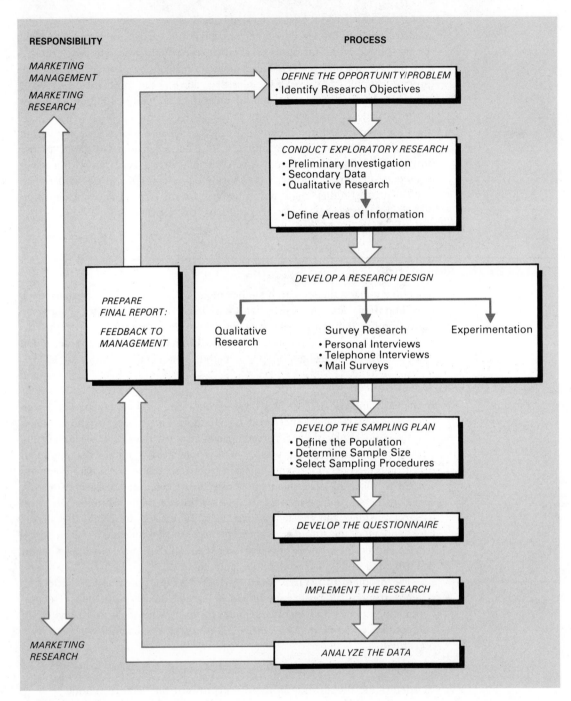

FIGURE 7-5
The marketing research process

3. assess potential inroads from competitors, and

4. predict potential changes in revenue from telephone equipment on the basis of the first three objectives.

EXPLORATORY RESEARCH

The exploratory phase of the research project is designed (1) to clarify the opportunity or problem, (2) to determine whether primary research is required, and if so (3) to identify the areas of information to be collected.

Figure 7-5 identifies three phases in exploratory research. The *preliminary investigation* is designed to determine whether the company has internal data that might be useful and to tap company personnel for their opinions. The first step in the AT&T study was to conduct an internal survey of AT&T personnel who were knowledgeable about the small-business market. These individuals identified 120 informational items (telecommunications needs and use, required services, small-business organizational characteristics, attitudes toward the telephone company, characteristics of the decision maker).

A *search of secondary sources* was conducted next to determine if studies of the telecommunications needs of small businesses had been done previously. A computerized literature search and a review of the Business Periodicals Index identified forty articles, but they were of little help to the researchers.

Qualitative research on small-business people had been conducted in the previous year, and the results were used in defining the problem and areas of information. Eight focus group interviews were conducted with small-business customers in six cities. The findings showed that many small-business people would consider buying their phones from competitors because it cost less than leasing. But a significant number emphasized the security of the local telephone company's repair service. As a result they preferred to keep the existing equipment.

The focus groups suggested that competitive inroads were likely for small businesses that did not depend heavily on the phone or emphasize reliable telephone service. But these interviews did not allow AT&T to make a quantitative assessment of the potential loss of revenue to competition. As a result it was apparent that primary research of the small-business market was necessary.

THE RESEARCH DESIGN

There are two issues in developing a research design: (1) the type of research to conduct and (2) the method of data collection.

Type of Research

In the previous section we described three basic research methods — qualitative, survey, and experimental. The researcher must decide what type of research is best for collecting the information specified by the exploratory phase.

Qualitative research is used most often in the exploratory phase as a means of identifying information to be collected. But it can also be the main data-collection method when the nature of the research problem is too deep-seated, is embarrassing, or is not apparent to the respondent. Studies in which qualitative research was the primary research method found that:[23]

- resistance to purchasing instant coffee when it was first introduced in the late 1940s was a result of the housewife's fear she was shirking her traditional role as a homemaker,

- candy consumption is a source of guilt because of childhood associations with reward and punishment,

- giving blood is sometimes resisted by men because it is associated with a loss of potency, and

- consumers resist using plastic wraps because of a lack of control over the product.

In each of these cases the research objectives were not conducive to a quantitative approach.

Survey Research is used when the objective is to:

1. collect a large amount of well-specified information

2. from a representative sample of consumers

3. for detailed analysis that permits the researcher to identify specific customer groups.

Experimentation is used when the objective is to:

1. evaluate the effects of one or several strategic variables

2. on an important criterion such as sales or intention to buy

3. in a controlled situation so a cause-and-effect relationship can be established

The variables in experimentation are very different from those in survey research. They are marketing strategy variables — package, price, product characteristics, advertising — whereas the variables of primary interest in survey research are consumer thought variables or characteristics. Experimental studies test alternative components of the marketing mix: product tests, tests of advertising executions, evaluation of alternative price levels, tests of sales promotions or in-store displays.

In the AT&T study researchers concluded that a survey was necessary since many variables had to be collected from a representative sample of small businesses to identify customer groups (e.g., small businesses that intend to buy competitive equipment, businesses that are dissatisfied with telephone company service, and so forth).

Method of Data Collection

The method of data collection must be determined for surveys since there are three basic alternatives for conducting interviews — in person, by telephone,

TABLE 7-1
Characteristics of Personal Interviews, Telephone Interviews, and Mail Surveys

	PERSONAL INTERVIEWS	TELEPHONE INTERVIEWS	MAIL SURVEYS
Amount of data	Large	Moderate	Moderate
Complicated questions are feasible	Yes	Limited	No
Visual stimuli can be presented	Yes	No	Limited
Response rate	Moderate	Moderate	Low
Time required to get data	Moderate	Quick	Very slow
Interviewer bias	High	Moderate	None
Response bias	High	Moderate	Low
Cost	Very high	Moderate	Very low

and by mail. Each has its advantages and disadvantages. These are summarized in Table 7-1.

In the AT&T survey all three methods were used. The purpose was to determine which of the three was most efficient for future surveys, since AT&T planned to conduct periodic surveys of small businesses to incorporate into their marketing information system. The results were contrary to the conventional wisdom. Response rates for mail surveys were somewhat higher than for telephone or personal interviews. The reason was that small-business people did not have the time to be bothered at their place of work by a phone call or a personal interview. They frequently refused the interview as a result. But they could take a mail questionnaire home and complete it at their leisure. The low cost of the mail survey, the high response rate, and the fact that a subsequent analysis indicated that response bias (inaccurate responses by the consumer) was not high led AT&T to decide to use mail surveys for future studies of the small-business market.

THE SAMPLING PLAN

Since researchers can rarely interview everyone in the population of interest, they must draw a sample from the population. The primary objective is to ensure that the sample represents the population.

The first question that must be answered to develop a sampling plan is, What is the *definition of the population?* In the AT&T study, the population was defined as all business establishments with three telephone lines or less. Two additional questions form the basis of the sampling plan: (1) What should be the *sample size?* and (2) What procedure should be used to *select the sample?*

Sample Size

Large samples provide the most accurate results for the simple reason that the larger the sample, the closer one gets to the characteristics of the population. But as the sample size increases geometrically, the reliability of the results increase only arithmetically. That is, to double the reliability of sample results would require a fourfold increase in sample size.

Whenever a sample is drawn, some error is expected. **Sampling error** is the difference between the population's value on a certain variable and the sample's value. Since the researcher does not know the population value, the sampling error must be estimated by inference. The larger the sample size, the smaller the sampling error. Therefore the researcher trades off higher reliability for greater cost. In the AT&T study a sample size of 1580 was determined to provide a sufficiently low sampling error. This produced enough reliability to give the researchers confidence in the data.

Sampling Procedure

The sampling procedure determines how respondents are to be chosen. There are two types of procedure, probability (random) sampling and nonprobability sampling. In **probability sampling** scientific rules are used to select the sample to ensure it is representative of the population. As a result each member of the population has a known chance of selection. In **nonprobability sampling** the selection of the sample is based primarily on the researcher's judgment. An important advantage of probability sampling is that scientific inference can be used in evaluating sampling error. This is not possible in nonprobability sampling procedures.

Probability sampling procedures

There are three types of probability sampling procedure, simple random sampling, stratified random sampling, and cluster sampling. In **simple random sampling** the sample is selected from the population as a whole and each member of the population has an equal chance of being selected. The word *random* refers to the fact that respondents are chosen without bias; it is not meant to infer a haphazard method of selection.

The AT&T study used a simple random sampling procedure. The company had a list of all its customers with three lines or less from its billing data. It was a simple matter to select 1580 customers from the list by using a table of random numbers. But what happens when there is no list? Consider a survey of all individuals in the United States sixteen years and over to determine their reactions to existing brands of toothpaste. In this case random-digit telephone surveys are most frequently used. A ten-digit number is selected randomly as a telephone number. The random-number generator is programmed to select only working banks of telephone numbers. In this way all American telephone households can be selected randomly.

Stratified random sampling involves dividing the population into predefined groups (called strata) and then selecting a sample within each stratum.

Suppose Anheuser-Busch wants to conduct a survey of perceptions of premium beers. It estimates that 70 percent of the beer is consumed by males and 30 percent by females. If it used simple random sampling, its sample would be about 49 percent males and 51 percent females. But it wants to select the sample in line with consumption, so it develops two strata, male and female. If its sample size is 2000 then 1400 respondents (70 percent) would be selected from the male stratum and 600 (30 percent) from the female stratum. In each case respondents would be selected randomly. The result would be the same as for drawing two separate simple random samples.

Cluster sampling (frequently called area sampling) is used when there are no lists of respondents but the researcher wants to use personal interviews rather than telephone interviews. The solution is to select large geographic areas randomly, then smaller geographic areas until individual households are identified. For example, in the first stage counties might be selected; in the second stage city-block groupings or rural areas; and in the third stage, individual residences. The Bureau of the Census uses cluster sampling in conducting its periodic surveys.

Nonprobability sampling procedures

In relying on nonprobability sampling procedures, the researcher risks drawing a biased sample. In addition, sampling error cannot be estimated. But nonprobability samples are cheaper and easier to administer. They are most appropriate in exploratory research to develop insights and hypotheses, since in these cases selecting a representative sample is not necessary. There are three nonprobability sampling procedures: quota sampling, judgmental sampling, and convenience sampling.

In **quota sampling** the researcher sets quotas of respondents on the basis of specific criteria. For example, the researcher decides that one-third of a sample will be users of the company's brand, one-third users of the leading competitor, and one-third users of other brands.

Judgmental sampling relies strictly on the judgment of the researcher with no prior constraints. For example, in doing a taste test of a new soft drink, the researcher might decide to interview teenagers in beach areas on summer weekends. **Convenience sampling** is based only on the convenience of the researcher — for example, interviewing the first people to be encountered in a shopping mall.

THE QUESTIONNAIRE

The next step in the research process in Figure 7-5 is developing a questionnaire that incorporates the information areas defined in the exploratory phase. Some basic rules for questionnaire construction can help one avoid biased responses. These include:

- *Avoid leading questions.* Do not ask, "Do you think that Brand X is better than all other brands on the market?"

■ *Do not put the respondent on the defensive.* Do not say, "Why didn't you buy Brand *X* the last time you purchased?"

■ *Do not ask two questions at once.* Do not say, "How much did you buy and why the last time you purchased?"

■ *Avoid assuming the consumer knows what you are talking about.* If you ask, "Have you purchased an expectorant cough suppressant in the last six months?" how many consumers would know what you are referring to?

■ *Do not identify the purpose of the questionnaire.* If you want to determine consumer perceptions of your brand, ask questions on your brand along with questions on other brands in the product category.

■ *If you must identify the purpose of the questionnaire, do so at the end.* This will avoid biasing questions asked earlier.

■ *Ask sensitive questions at the end of the questionnaire.* For example, asking income level at the beginning might be regarded as an intrusion of privacy and cause the respondent to terminate the interview.

■ *Avoid ambiguous questions.* Do not ask, "Why didn't you select your preferred brand instead of the brand you prefer less on your last purchase?"

■ *Select a multiple-choice rather than an open-ended question* when there is an alternative. Rather than asking "What do you like most about Brand *X*?" develop a set of attributes on an attitudinal scale and ask respondents to rate Brand *X*.

The questionnaire developed for the AT&T study was a six-page instrument designed to elicit the following areas of information:

■ nature of business,

■ telephone use and equipment,

■ importance of telephone service,

■ role of telephone in conduct of business,

■ awareness of competitive companies that sell or lease telephone equipment, and

■ intention to buy competitive equipment.

RESEARCH IMPLEMENTATION

Most marketing organizations do not conduct their own research. They commission outside research companies to implement the research. In the case of experimentation this requires conducting product, advertising, pricing, or packaging tests. For survey research, implementation requires controlling the interviewers to ensure that interviews are conducted reliably. Such control involves an attempt to ensure that (1) sample selection procedures are carried out by interviewers and (2) interviewer bias is minimized.

Researchers ensure that sample selection procedures are carried out by monitoring who is being interviewed. In telephone surveys this can be accomplished by controlling the numbers that are called. In personal interviews controls are more difficult. The only control is to make sure the interview was in fact conducted by calling some members of respondents in the sample to see if they were recently questioned (validating).

In the AT&T study a private marketing research company was contracted to conduct the telephone and personal interviews, while AT&T implemented the mail survey. Approximately 10 percent of the personal interviews were validated, and telephone interviews were monitored in a central Wide Area Telephone Service (WATS) facility as they were being conducted.

DATA ANALYSIS

Once the information has been collected, it must be analyzed in order to answer the research questions formulated in the exploratory phase. Analysis requires reducing the data to manageable proportions and then developing relationships between independent variables (e.g., size and type of business, nature of telephone use, satisfaction with service) and one or more dependent variables (e.g., intention to buy competitive equipment).

The simplest analysis is a straight tabulation of the data. In the AT&T study, 13.5 percent of the small businesses said that they had considered buying competitive equipment (see Table 7-2). The next level of analysis is a two-way (cross-) tabulation. A **cross-tabulation** categorizes one variable by another. For example, what variables are likely to increase or decrease the chances of considering competitive equipment. Table 7-2 shows that among those who rate telephone service inadequate, 44 percent consider competitive equipment?

TABLE 7-2
Straight and Cross-Tabulations: AT&T Study of Small Businesses

STRAIGHT TABULATION Percentage of small businesses who considered buying competitive equipment		13.5
CROSS-TABULATIONS Percentage of small businesses who considered buying competitive equipment by:	*Yes*	*No*
1. Whether they felt present telephone service is inadequate	44.2	10.7
2. Whether they considered cost of service very expensive	25.9	11.0
3. Whether they rated quality of service poor	24.9	22.1
4. Whether they rated cost of service most important factor in telecommunications	20.8	10.8

Among those who rate it adequate, about 11 percent consider competitive equipment. Thus dissatisfaction with service increases the chances of considering competitive equipment fourfold. Table 7-2 also shows that the chances of considering competitive equipment are significantly higher among those who consider service very expensive, who rate service poor, and who rate cost of service the most important factor in evaluating the telephone.

To go beyond two-way classifications one must use **multivariate statistical techniques.** These techniques are designed to examine a large number of independent variables and relate them to a dependent variable. In the AT&T study the highest proportion of small businesses that considered competitive equipment were those which rated the cost of service most important *and* the level of service inadequate. Such a finding requires employing multivariate analysis because of the large number of variables in the study and the fact that statistical search procedures are required to select combinations of variables that are most closely related to a dependent variable. Most multivariate techniques used in marketing have one of two purposes: (1) data association or (2) data reduction.

Data Association Techniques

In many cases the researcher is interested in a particular criterion (dependent) variable such as sales and wants to understand what factors are related to it. Certain variables (such as price, advertising awareness, brand attitudes, intention to buy) are hypothesized to be related to the dependent variable (such as sales). Associative techniques determine the degree to which variations in the independent variables explain the variation in the dependent variable. If the association is sufficiently strong, then changes in the independent variables could predict changes in the dependent variable (for example, a downward shift in intention to buy will predict a subsequent decrease in sales.)

Two associative techniques are most widely used, regression analysis and discriminant analysis.[24] In **regression analysis** the dependent variable is continuous (dollar sales). An equation is developed that shows the contribution of each independent variable in explaining variations in the dependent variable. (An example of a regression equation is on page 110.) The strength of the association is measured by the percentage of the variance in the dependent variable that is explained by the independent variables. A typical finding might be that the independent variables explain 80 percent of the variance in sales, and that most of the variance is explained by two or three variables.

Discriminant analysis is similar to regression analysis except that the dependent variable is categorical. For example, rather than determining the factors relating to sales volume (a continuous variable), the problem might be to determine the variables that discriminate between heavy and light users of a product (a two-category variable). Discriminant analysis will produce an equation that assigns a respondent to one of the two groups on the basis of his or her characteristics.

Data Reduction Techniques

Frequently the first step before associating a set of dependent variables to an independent variable is reducing data to manageable proportions. Two techniques for doing so are factor analysis and cluster analysis.[25]

Factor analysis identifies a smaller set of dimensions from the original variables. It does so by identifying variables that are highly intercorrelated and combining them into one variable. For example, income, education, and occupation are highly intercorrelated. Rather than dealing with three separate variables, factor analysis would combine these into one underlying dimension the researcher might label socioeconomic status. The life cycle and personality categories in Tables 6-3 and 6-4 represented dimensions identified by a factor analysis from a larger set of variables.

Cluster analysis groups objects by similarity. It has been used by marketers to identify benefit segments by similarities in the needs of consumers. The cluster program will group consumers to obtain the maximum similarity within a group and the maximum differences between groups to define distinct and mutually exclusive clusters. The four organizational groupings identified by similarity in telecommunications needs in Table 6-2 were determined by cluster analysis.

THE FINAL REPORT AND ACTION RECOMMENDATIONS

The data analysis should be presented to management in a clearly written report devoid of technical details. A two- or three-page executive summary is essential, since this is all that management may get to read. A technical version of the report may be prepared for the Research Department.

It is essential that the management report contain action recommendations. In an earlier section we noted that one of management's criticisms of researchers is their failure to translate findings into action recommendations. Researchers may be hesitant to do so because they view themselves as staff and feel it is management's function to develop action recommendations. They sometimes fail to realize that they are not being asked to make managerial decisions but only to interpret the data in action terms. In the AT&T study action recommendations involved targeting dissatisfied small businesses for service improvements since these businesses were more likely to consider purchasing competitive equipment. Additional recommendations involved suggestions for new products such as pagers and automatic dialers that might fill the specific telecommunications needs of small businesses.

Evaluating the Components of the Marketing Mix

Up to now we have emphasized the type of information collected in marketing research and the research process, particularly survey research. We must realize that a significant part of marketing research's responsibility deals with testing specific components of the marketing mix. In particular, researchers are responsible for the following:

- *Testing new products.*
    - *Concept tests* are first conducted to determine consumer reactions to product descriptions prior to committing funds to production.
    - *Product tests* are then run to evaluate reactions to the actual product.
    - *Test markets* are then conducted in which the product is introduced in several markets to evaluate performance in actual competitive conditions.
- *Testing modifications of existing products* to determine if the product warrants some change.
- *Evaluating alternative packages for new and existing brands.*
- *Testing print and broadcast advertising executions by copy research.*
- *Evaluating media effectiveness by measuring:*
    - advertising exposure to the target group,
    - advertising impact, and
    - cost effectiveness.
- *Testing alternative sales promotional techniques*
- *Estimating consumer responses to alternative price levels*
- *Evaluating sales effectiveness* based on:
    - sales results by customers, products, and territories; and
    - development of new prospects.

Many of these research areas require experimentation because they are testing action-oriented marketing variables on consumers. Thus, copy research is testing the effects of alternative print or broadcast advertisements on consumers by measuring criteria such as consumer recall, changes in brand attitudes, and changes in intention to buy before and after exposure to the advertisement.

These research techniques will be considered in Part III. This is a logical placement since these techniques are closely tied to the development of marketing mix strategies.

Industrial Marketing Research

Marketing research in the industrial sector is conducted in the same way as in the consumer sector. But there are substantial differences in (1) the way marketing research is conducted and (2) sources of research data in industrial firms.

DIFFERENCES IN THE WAY RESEARCH IS CONDUCTED

The nature of industrial goods results in several differences in the way research is conducted and implemented. These are:[26]

- *Importance of personal selling:* Industrial marketing relies heavily on personal selling because of the technical complexity of many products, the large size of many industrial buyers, and the need to communicate to purchasing agents, engineers, and production managers. As a result a significant part of the industrial marketing research effort is devoted to identifying *individual* prospects and analyzing sales effort. Such analysis is frequently based on secondary data and company sales records. In contrast consumer marketers define prospects by identifying large *groups* of consumers as market segments. To do so they require consumer surveys.

- *Technical knowledge:* Industrial marketing research requires more technical knowledge because of the greater complexity of industrial products. Therefore industrial marketing researchers should have an engineering or production background as well as marketing research training to permit them to communicate with technical people in the company.

- *Purchasing influences:* A key task of industrial marketing researchers is identifying industrial buyers with purchasing influence. Several executives in the industrial buying firm may influence the purchase decision. Moreover, the nature of influence may vary.

- *Derived demand:* The industrial marketing researcher is concerned with both the direct demand of the industrial customer and the derived demand of the final consumer. This makes the industrial marketing research task more complicated since data must frequently be collected for two types of customer.

- *The industrial environment:* Industrial markets are composed of fewer and larger buyers than consumer markets. Moreover, buying responsibilities tend to be spread across more individuals and to be better defined. Thus industrial marketing research requires:

  □ smaller sample sizes (at times, a census can be taken rather than a sample); and

  □ more extensive data collection in greater depth (the complexity of the industrial buying process may lead to research that goes deeper into individual buying decisions using a case study approach; whereas in consumer research, data are collected by well-specified questions on a survey basis).

SOURCES OF INDUSTRIAL MARKETING RESEARCH DATA

Primary Data

Table 7–3 shows the type of research conducted by industrial and consumer goods companies on the basis of a study of 110 firms. About the same percentage of industrial marketers conduct surveys as consumer marketers. But such surveys tend to be conducted for different purposes — to identify individuals with purchasing influence, to determine their buying specifications, to assess their evaluation of the services provided by the industrial marketer, to determine their reaction to the company's sales personnel. Industrial market surveys are also less sophisticated than their consumer counterparts because data analysis is not as complex. Segmentation or product positioning analyses involving many variables are less frequent. Where more complex primary research is warranted,

TABLE 7-3
Comparison of Marketing Research Sources and Techniques Used by Industrial and Consumer Goods Companies

	PERCENTAGE USED BY CONSUMER COMPANIES (n = 42)	PERCENTAGE USED BY INDUSTRIAL COMPANIES (n = 68)
Data gathering		
Analysis of trade journal and trade association	91	97
Analysis of internal company records	95	97
Personal interviews	79	75
Telephone interviews	74	74
Mail surveys	79	69
Focus group interviews	81	16
Research Design		
Informal experimental designs	67	13
Formal experimental designs	36	6
Sampling Procedures		
Simple random sampling	76	41
Stratified sampling	69	31
Cluster sampling	43	15
Quota sampling	60	18
Judgmental sampling	52	29

Source: Adapted from Barnett A. Greenberg, Jac L. Goldstucker, and Danny H. Bellenger, "What Techniques are Used by Marketing Researchers in Business?" *Journal of Marketing* 41 (April 1977): 64.

industrial marketing research has lagged behind consumer research in applications of research designs and data analysis.

Table 7-3 shows that industrial marketers rarely engage in qualitative research such as focus group interviews. Yet focus group interviews could be very useful in determining problems industrial buyers might have with the seller's products or service.

Another area of primary research in which industrial marketing research is lagging is experimentation. Industrial marketers do conduct product research by asking buyers to use prototypes or by conducting demonstrations in trade shows or at company facilities. But they rarely do so on the basis of experimental designs. Such an approach might be extremely useful in testing alternative designs of a product on two or three matched groups of buyers to determine which design is best.

Secondary Data

As seen in Table 7-3, almost all industrial companies use internal records to evaluate sales results. Sales are generally divided by salesperson, by territory, by product category, and by customer type to identify trouble spots and opportunities. Industrial marketers also use secondary sources to analyze sales results and identify prospects. Three sources are used most frequently.

1. *Census of Manufacturers and Census of Business.* This data base provides information on the number of establishments in specific industries, quantity of output, value added in manufacturing, number of employees, inventory, and sales by customer class. This information is categorized by a standard industrial classification (SIC) code that breaks businesses into 20 major industry groupings, each having 150 subgroups. The Bureau of the Census also conducts a census of business that provides similar data for retail, wholesale, and service establishments. These data can be used to develop potential sales estimates by SIC code and to evaluate sales results on the basis of potential. SIC categories whose sales are below potential on the basis of their characteristics can be singled out for greater effort. Census data thus become a means for allocating sales efforts to industry groups.

2. *Sales and Marketing Management's Survey of Industrial Purchasing Power.* S&MM conducts a yearly survey of industrial purchasing power by industry group classified by SIC code. It provides information on sales and number of businesses by territory for each SIC group. It also projects sales for the coming year. On this basis an industrial marketer can compute its market share for each SIC group and determine the effectiveness of its sales coverage for each group.

3. *Dun and Bradstreet's Market Identifiers (DMI).* Dun and Bradstreet has an extensive data base of the organizational characteristics of most United States companies. It contains information on sales, number of employees, net

worth, region, type of business, number of years in business and SIC code for each company. Subscribers to DMI can identify the characteristics of their customers. They can then determine companies with similar characteristics that are not buying their products. These would then be prime prospects. For example, if a producer of industrial insulation sells primarily to contractors in the Northwest with 500 or more employees and a net worth of over $50 million, then customers in this category who are not buying from the company would be identified as prospects.

Summary

Identification of marketing opportunity requires establishment of a marketing information system (MIS). The MIS obtains data from the consumer, the marketing environment, and company records. It is composed of:

- an internal reporting system designed to provide management with company data (orders, inventory levels, factory shipments);

- a marketing research system designed to collect consumer information and to test marketing strategies; and

- an environmental scanning system designed to track changes in the environment that might affect the identification of future opportunities.

The marketing information system relies on primary and secondary data. Primary data are collected by the marketing organization or outside marketing research firms to satisfy a specific research objective. Secondary data have been collected previously for purposes other than the specific needs of the marketing organization.

Firms will first evaluate secondary data to determine if they satisfy their research requirements. Secondary sources are (1) internal company data, (2) syndicated services that sell standardized data, (3) government data primarily from the census, and (4) other environmental sources such as trade associations, competition, and publications.

Primary sources are studies conducted by the company's marketing research staff, by outside marketing research firms, or by the company's advertising agency. These studies are (1) qualitative research designed to develop a better understanding of the research area, (2) experiments that test specific marketing variables such as alternative advertising executions, packages, or prices in controlled conditions, or (3) surveys designed to collect consumer data from a representative sample.

In most cases secondary sources are insufficient. Therefore most marketing research studies require the collection of primary data. Primary data collection is the responsibility of the marketing research system. It follows a logical procedure designed to ensure the reliability of the data collected. This procedure involves:

■ defining an opportunity or problem requiring data collection;

■ undertaking exploratory research to clarify the opportunity or problem;

■ developing a research design that specifies:

    □ the type of research to be conducted (qualitative, experimentation, survey, or observational), and

    □ method of data collection (personal or telephone interviews or mail surveys);

■ developing a sampling plan to ensure that a sample will be selected that is representative of the population under study;

■ developing a questionnaire;

■ implementing the research and analyzing the data collected; and

■ developing a final report that includes action recommendations.

Industrial marketing research requires the same procedures, but the nature of industrial products results in several differences in data sources and in the way research is conducted. Industrial marketing research emphasizes sales analysis and identification of individual projects. It also uses surveys with smaller samples requiring less sophisticated data analysis. More technical product knowledge and a more careful identification of purchasing influences are necessary.

In Part III we will consider the development of marketing strategies to exploit opportunities once they have been identified.

Questions

1. How are one or more of the components of a marketing information system (listed in Figure 7-2) used to:

    □ identify marketing opportunities,

    □ track sales,

    □ evaluate marketing strategies, and

    □ monitor changes in the environment?

2. Select a recently introduced product (Kodak disc cameras, Aapri facial scrub, and so forth). Describe the possible interaction between research and marketing planning that might have led to the introduction of the product by citing the seven steps in Figure 7-3.

3. A firm is considering entering the diet foods market with a new line of high-protein, low-calorie breakfast foods. Before conducting primary research it wants to evaluate secondary sources, particularly (a) census data, (b) the Monitor studies, and (c) Simmons data.

☐ What types of information would each of these sources provide the firm to help it evaluate the potential for the new product?

☐ How might these sources help the company define areas of primary data to be collected in a survey?

4. Assume a company is investigating the potential for a snack food line directed to consumers who emphasize nutrition and natural ingredients.

☐ How might the company use (a) focus group interviews and (b) projective techniques to evaluate the potential market?

☐ What is the purpose of each of these techniques?

5. What type of research approach — qualitative, survey, or experimental — would a company be most likely to use in:

☐ identifying the demographic and life-style characteristics of potential buyers of a new fruit-and-nut snack,

☐ determining the sales potential for such a product,

☐ testing two or three formulations of the product on consumers to determine which is most effective, and

☐ determining if consumers might have any deep-seated resistance to accepting fruit as a snack product?

Justify your selection of a research approach in each case.

6. An industrial producer of auto parts finds its sales slipping. Management feels the cause could be an inefficient allocation of sales effort.

☐ How can the company use internal data to investigate the cause of this decline?

☐ What action could the company take based on its sales analysis?

7. How can:

☐ Simmons data be used to select media?

☐ Consumer panel data be used to identify target segments?

☐ Nielsen data be used to evaluate sales results?

8. Assume Coca-Cola conducts a study to investigate the potential for a new diet cola positioned to the male market. It decides to conduct a survey of diet cola drinkers to determine (a) if males are more dissatisfied than females with current diet cola brands and (b) the nature of any such dissatisfaction. Describe the research process the company might have implemented by citing each of the steps in Figure 7-5.

9. The investigation of the small-business market by AT&T warranted the collection of primary data through survey research.

☐ Why was it necessary to collect primary data?

☐ What types of opportunities or problems could be investigated by examining secondary data only? Provide examples.

10. What probability sampling procedure — simple random, stratified, or cluster — would be most appropriate for the following research studies:

☐ an investigation of the attitudes of recent alumni toward the school's fund-raising efforts,

☐ a study of the attitudes of diesel versus regular car owners toward their car's performance,

☐ an investigation of the extent to which consumers sixteen and over have purchased generic and private brands in the last year, and

☐ a study using personal interviews of reactions of smokers to low-tar brands.

11. Why does the evaluation of specific components of the marketing mix (alternative ads, packages, product concepts, prices) require an experimental rather than a survey approach?

12. A large producer of cosmetics and toiletries has recently acquired a manufacturer of industrial generators in an attempt to diversify from its core markets. The firm is research oriented and realizes that conducting research for industrial generators will be very different from conducting research for cosmetics and toiletry products. What changes will be required in:

☐ identifying the research problem,

☐ choosing interviewers to conduct the studies,

☐ developing a questionnaire,

☐ determining the sample size and sampling procedures,

☐ developing an analytical plan, and

☐ reporting results to management?

Notes

1. "At Procter & Gamble, Success Is Largely Due to Heeding Consumer," *The Wall Street Journal,* April 29, 1980, pp. 1, 35.

2. Ibid.

3. "Meticulous Planning Pays Dividends at Stouffer's," *Marketing News,* October 28, 1983, pp. 1, 20.

4. Ibid.

5. "Credit Success of Kodak Disc Camera to Research," *Marketing News,* January 21, 1983, Section 1, pp. 8–9.

6. Ibid.

7. Philip Kotler, *Marketing Management* (Englewood Cliffs, N.J.: Prentice-Hall, 1984), p. 190.

8. "New Chief Pens Bold Plan for a Parker Resurgence," *Advertising Age,* July 25, 1982, pp. 4, 56.

9. "Marketing Researchers and Marketers: Educate Each Other, Show More Respect," *Marketing News,* January 21, 1983, Section 2, pp. 1–2.

10. Ibid., p. 2.

11. "Research Must Meet Greater Demands Than Ever," *Advertising Age,* August 15, 1983, pp. M4–M5, M46–M47.

12. "The Soothsayers: More Companies Use 'Futurists' to Discern What Is Lying Ahead," *The Wall Street Journal,* March 31, 1975, p. 1.

13. David W. Cravens, Gerald W. Hills, and Robert B. Woodruff, *Marketing Decision Making* (Homewood, Ill.: Richard D. Irwin, 1980), pp. 75–77.

14. Kotler, *Marketing Management,* p. 191.

15. Daniel Yankelovich, *The Yankelovich Monitor* (New York: Daniel Yankelovich, 1974); and Lifestyle's Monitor, *American Demographics,* May 1981, pp. 21–22.

16. *Starch: Scope, Method and Use* (Mamaroneck, N.Y.: Starch/INRA/Hooper, 1973), p. 2.

17. *The 1980 Study of Media and Markets* (New York: Simmons Market Research Bureau, 1980).

18. "Businesses Capitalize on Data From Census," *The New York Times,* March 31, 1980, pp. D1–D2.

19. "Using Marketing Research to Explore for Exciting New Product Ideas," *Sales & Marketing Management,* April 4, 1983, pp. 126, 128, 130.

20. Ibid., p. 128.

21. David A. Aaker and George S. Day, *Marketing Research* (New York: John Wiley & Sons, 1980), p. 102.

22. The research project described in this section is presented by permission of AT&T.

23. Henry Assael, *Consumer Behavior and Marketing Action* (Boston: Kent, 1984), p. 272.

24. For an excellent review of applications of multivariate techniques in marketing, see Paul E. Green and Donald S. Tull, *Research for Marketing Decisions* (Englewood Cliffs, N.J.: Prentice-Hall, 1978).

25. Ibid.

26. Robert W. Haas, *Industrial Marketing Management* (Boston: Kent, 1982), pp. 148–50.

Marketing Strategies and the Marketing Mix

Once marketing management has identified opportunities, it must develop strategies to exploit them. The strategic component of marketing management is the central concern of this book. Here we will consider marketing strategy at the product level; in Part IV, at the corporate level.

The development of marketing strategies at the product level is a three-step process as follows:

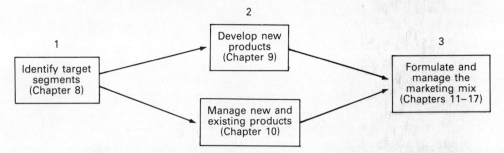

The first step in formulating strategies is identifying market segments to which strategies should be targeted. This is the subject of Chapter 8. The next step is to direct product offerings to defined segments. In Chapter 9 we will consider new product development; Chapter 10 deals with the management and positioning of new and existing products. In the third step, supporting strategies are developed to market the product. Chapters 11 and 12 describe the communications process and the communications mix (advertising, sales promotion, personal selling, publicity). Chapters 13 and 14 then focus on advertising and personal selling respectively. In Chapter 15 we will consider pricing strategies. Chapters 16 and 17 cover the final component of the marketing mix — distribution.

CHAPTER **8**

Identifying The Target Market: Market Segmentation

FOCUS OF CHAPTER

Identifying a target market for a product or service is the first requirement in developing marketing strategies. Most successful products are directed to the needs of a particular segment of consumers. Product, advertising, pricing, and distribution strategies are then based on the needs and characteristics of these consumers.

Vaseline Intensive Care was successful because Chesebrough-Ponds identified a segment of hand lotion users more concerned with therapeutic than cosmetic benefits. Miller Lite beer was successful because Philip Morris not only recognized the importance of a light beer benefit, but also identified a segment of heavy beer drinkers who were ready to try lighter beers.

In each of these cases the market was first segmented by differences in consumer needs and a target segment was then identified. But marketing strategy cannot be based on market segmentation alone. Products must be positioned to these segments. Market segmentation and product positioning must be developed hand-in-hand: products are positioned to meet the needs of a market segment; market segments must be identified by differences in needs to permit effective product positioning.

This chapter deals with market segmentation; in the next chapter we will consider product positioning in the context of new product development. Although we treat them separately, we must remember the link between those two areas. In this chapter we will first consider market segmentation in a strategic context. The requirements for effective segmentation strategies and alternative types of strategies will be described. Methods for identifying segments will then be considered. The chapter concludes by considering market segmentation in the industrial sector.

Market Segmentation Strategy

There are two components to market segmentation, the strategic and the analytical. **Market segmentation strategy** seeks to direct marketing efforts to defined segments on the basis of their needs and characteristics. **Market segmentation analysis** seeks to define target segments to permit such allocations of effort. That is, segments must be defined before marketing strategies can be directed to them. Analysis must precede strategy; but an understanding of the strategic basis for segmentation is necessary before considering the methods of identifying segments.

THE STRATEGIC BASIS FOR MARKET SEGMENTATION

The basis for a strategy of market segmentation is deceivingly simple: customers differ in their needs for a given product and will therefore react differently to different product offerings. The firm can maximize profits by developing products to meet the needs of specific segments rather than by introducing a single product to a mass market.

Market Segmentation versus Market Aggregation

Most firms follow segmentation strategies at least somewhat. But this has not always been the case. Until the mid 1950s firms did not generally direct product offerings to a specific segment. They directed a single product to a more general market. This strategy is known as **market aggregation** since it is designed to aggregate consumer demand on a mass market basis. Market aggregation does not attempt to differentiate between consumer groups; it brings together different consumers under one product umbrella. Before 1950 companies such as Coca-Cola, Hershey, and Chevrolet were essentially one-product companies. Market aggregation is appealing because it achieves economies of scale in production and marketing. An individual product can utilize general media and large-scale distribution, and can therefore enjoy lower per-unit production and marketing costs.

Market segmentation, on the other hand, requires a more fragmented approach: several product offerings directed to specific segments; separate advertising, sales promotion, and pricing strategies for each segment; and higher per-unit production and marketing costs.

Table 8-1 presents market aggregation and market segmentation on a continuum and cites the differences between the two. Market segmentation is most profitable when consumer needs are relatively heterogeneous. The firm maximizes profits by identifying segments with different needs and targeting products to meet these needs. Competitive advantage is based on differentiating market segments and directing unique products to each segment. The economic limits of a strategy of market segmentation are reached when targeting marketing strategies to additional segments is no longer profitable because these segments are too small or too difficult to reach.

TABLE 8-1
Market Segmentation versus Product Differentiation

MARKET AGGREGATION	MARKET SEGMENTATION
Homogeneous needs	Heterogeneous needs
One or a few products directed to a mass market	Specific products directed to defined segments
Competitive advantage based on single offering differentiated by product attributes, advertising or price	Competitive advantage based on market differentiation (unique products to meet needs of a market segment)
Profit maximization by economies of scale in production and marketing	Profit maximization by revenues from new products targeted to additional segments
Limits to profit maximization are additional advertising expenditures	Limits to profit maximization are additional market segments

Market aggregation is most economical when consumer needs are relatively homogeneous. The firm maximizes profits by selling one or a few products to a mass market. The major thrust of marketing strategy is to differentiate the company's single product offering from competitive brands by heavy advertising or a lower price. The economic limits of a strategy of market aggregation are reached when the firm finds that the advertising and other marketing costs required to keep up with competition in a mass market are no longer paying off.

Figure 8-1 further illustrates the basis for market aggregation and market segmentation. The first box shows a market with homogeneous needs. Consider the market for short-haul trucks. Assume that two important criteria used by

FIGURE 8-1
Alternative market conditions affecting strategy

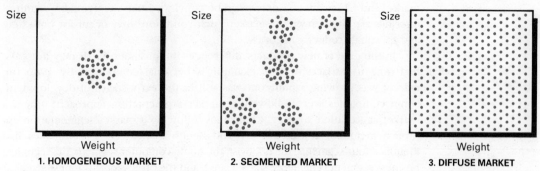

1. HOMOGENEOUS MARKET	2. SEGMENTED MARKET	3. DIFFUSE MARKET

Philip Kotler, *Marketing Management: Analysis, Planning and Control,* 5th edition, © 1984, p. 253. Adapted by permission of Prentice-Hall, Inc., Englewood Cliffs, New Jersey.

shippers in selecting trucks are weight and size. The first box depicts a market in which almost all buyers want medium-sized trucks of average weight. In this circumstance there is no basis for segmenting customers by differences in needs. The truck producer will sell to the total market and try to gain a differential advantage through better warranties, more effective service, price discounts, or possible product improvements such as a more efficient engine and better gas mileage. This represents a strategy of market aggregation.

The second box shows a market that is segmented by differences in needs. Five segments are shown. Three of the segments want a truck that is average in weight, but they differ in the size truck they want. Another segment wants a large, heavy-weight truck, and a fifth segment wants a small, light truck. A manufacturer could appeal to one or two of these segments, or design a full product line to appeal to all of them.

The last box represents a more difficult choice that does not easily lend itself to either market aggregation or market segmentation. Customer needs are so diffuse that they cannot be grouped together into market segments. The marketer would have two choices. The first alternative is to develop a general product to attempt to appeal to as many customers as possible. Such a strategy would not focus on differentiating the product from competition since consumer needs are too diffuse. As a result, product attributes would be deemphasized. Rather, competitive advantage would be gained based on lower price, better distribution, or superior service. The second alternative would be to develop products for individual customers on specification. Such a strategy would be viable in certain industrial markets since individual accounts might be large enough to support producing on specification. It would not be feasible for consumer goods.

Benefits of a strategy of market aggregation

Market segmentation is the dominant strategy today. Few firms follow a policy of absolute aggregation. But a partial aggregation of the market is more profitable if (1) there is little difference in consumer needs across the total market and (2) many consumers can be convinced that the company's limited offerings are the best on the market. Such conditions may occur for both new and existing product categories.

In the case of new products, differences in consumer needs may not have had time to surface. A good example is personal computers. By 1980 the market was growing rapidly but was still in the early stages of development. Some companies were following a market segmentation approach, others a market aggregation strategy. Companies following a market segmentation approach included Hewlett-Packard and Zenith Radio.[1] These companies had identified four segments: the hobbyist, the home computer segment, the technical business segment (engineers, statisticians), and the professional business segment (manager, lawyers, accountants). Hewlett-Packard and Zenith felt they knew enough about the differences between these four segments to direct different products to each. For example, Hewlett-Packard introduced a new personal computer directed to the professional market with capabilities for graphics, forecasting, and information management software programs.[2] Products directed to the technical business segment were more likely to emphasize statistical packages.

Some companies felt that it was too early to distinguish between segments in 1980. The needs of the four major segments were not sufficiently defined for product development. As a result, a single product or a line of products was introduced to appeal to all segments. The appeal was based on price or on product features. Particular products were not directed to specific segments. Two of the largest manufacturers, the Tandy Company and Apple Computer, followed this strategy of market aggregation. *Business Week* reported that Tandy had no segmentation strategy and hoped to ensnare as many users as possible in a "wide net cast out to all potential customers." The president of Tandy said, "We want all of the low end of the computer market that we can possibly achieve." A founder of Apple said, "We subscribe to the model that everyone wants to have his own computer."[3] Both companies were following a *partial* aggregation approach by trying to appeal to disparate consumer groups with a limited set of product offerings.

Companies may also pursue a policy that combines market segmentation and aggregation. For example, Stouffer's Foods' management targeted their Lean Cuisine line to a weight control segment. But they saw this segment as one general group and did not divide it any further. The president of Stouffer's made the case for aggregating weight watchers when he said, "There was no fancy target audience [for the introduction of the company's Lean Cuisine line] because everybody wants to maintain their weight."[4] The advertising theme demonstrated this general approach with the line, "You'll love the way it looks on you."

The rationale for Stouffer's following a policy of market aggregation among weight watchers goes beyond the belief that there are no sharp differences in needs among this group. Management probably felt that any differences in needs could not be translated into different products. Even beyond product differences, the company probably felt that it could not advertise the Lean Cuisine line differently to frustrated dieters or self-confident dieters without an undue increase in advertising costs and potential confusion among dieter segments. Finally, the company might have felt that it would have been unrealistic to develop separate price, sales promotion, and distribution strategies for each dieter segment. Because of the strength of the low-calorie benefits for the Lean Cuisine line, separate marketing mixes for dieter segments were viewed as unnecessary and likely to cause an undue increase in per-unit marketing costs. This reasoning provides the basis for a market aggregation strategy once a broad segment of the market was defined.

Benefits of a market segmentation strategy

The benefits of a market segmentation strategy are illustrated by a study conducted by J. Walter Thompson, a leading advertising agency, for one of its clients, a large food company.[5] Sales for one of the company's products had been stagnant for some time and had to be increased to ensure the product's survival. The product was being advertised on the basis of its strong and distinctive taste. A study was conducted among nonusers who expressed some interest in the product. Five segments were identified based on differences in needs and behavior: (1) impulse buyers, (2) social conformists, (3) bargain hunters, (4) time savers, and (5) health promoters. All except the last segment were eliminated as targets. Purchasing behavior of the impulse buyers was too uncertain to provide a basis for increasing sales. The social conformists were more worried about group norms than taste appeals. Bargain hunters were motivated by price. And time savers were concerned about convenience in food preparation, a benefit that was not the brand's strong point. Health promoters were motivated by health appeals, particularly for the family. Fortunately, the brand's distinctive taste was due to certain natural ingredients. A new advertising campaign was developed based on nutrition, wholesomeness, and natural ingredients and directed to the health promoter segment.

Sales increased as a result of directing advertising to the health-promoter segment because most of the conditions we cited were met: there was a substantial difference in need orientations between current users and health promoters (taste versus nutrition); separate advertising campaigns could be introduced with no confusion or alienation among current users; and different media could be used for each group. A separate product offering to the health segment was not necessary, but a different marketing mix was.

Most important, the increased costs of a separate campaign were more than offset by increased revenue. When a $2 million advertising campaign was directed to current users only, the profit contribution from the brand was $3.84 million. But when the same money was split between current users and health promoters, the contribution was $6.35 million. This represents an estimated increase of $2.5 million in profits based on directing a different product appeal to a new segment.

The J. Walter Thompson study illustrates several benefits of a segmentation strategy:

1. *Segmentation can improve the allocation of marketing resources.* The same amount of advertising expenditures improved sales and profits substantially when allocated to separate segments of the market.

2. *Segmentation permits a better identification of marketing opportunity.* Without a segmentation of prospective users, health promoters would not have been identified.

3. *Segmentation provides guidelines for developing separate marketing campaigns to separate target groups.* The needs of the health pro-

moters guided the advertising campaign, and their demographic characteristics and media habits guided media selection.

4. *Segmentation guides the product's positioning relative to (a) consumer needs and (b) competition.* The segmentation study demonstrated that the product must be positioned as nutritional and whole-
some to appeal to the health segment. Such a positioning would
distinguish the product from competition.

5. *Segmentation provides guidelines for product development.* Appealing
to the health promoter segment did not require the development of a
new product since the existing product had unique nutritional benefits.
If this had not been the case, the company would have had to develop
a new product to appeal to the health-oriented segment.

The Trend to Greater Segmentation

A mass market approach tended to dominate marketing strategy up to the mid-
1950s because there was no pressure on marketers to consider consumer
needs. As we noted in Chapter 1, pressure on the demand side in marketing
was lacking because of the succession of events from a great depression to a
world war, postwar shortages, and the Korean War. The greater availability of
goods after the Korean War coupled with consumer purchasing power permitted
consumers to be more selective and forced marketers to start thinking about
directing products to the needs of specific segments. Market segmentation was
a direct outgrowth of the birth of the marketing concept.

Once marketers recognized the importance of segmentation, the marketing
institutions followed suit. Magazines and radio began to be targeted to particular
groups. Television time began to be purchased with an eye to the specific
characteristics of the viewer. Distribution channels became more specialized.
Moreover, advances in technology lowered production costs in smaller plants
making smaller production runs more cost effective. In short, the marketing
environment permitted a policy of market segmentation.

Figure 8-2 cites the progression of several industries to greater segmentation
over time. During the 1950s leading brands in both the soft drink and beer
industries were following a strategy of market aggregation. Coca-Cola, Pepsi,
Budweiser, Schlitz, and Miller were marketed on an undifferentiated basis. By
the 1960s most of these brands were following a segmentation approach —
Coke and Pepsi being positioned to a youth segment (e.g., the Pepsi generation);
Schlitz and Budweiser being positioned to a large blue-collar segment that
tended to be heavier beer drinkers. Advertising themes reflected a targeted
approach to these segments.

By the 1970s the soft drink and beer industries segmented the market
even further. Companies extended their product lines beyond their original
"cash cows" to target specific segments — low-calorie, fruit flavor, and non-
carbonated segments in the soft drink market, and light, heavy (malt), and

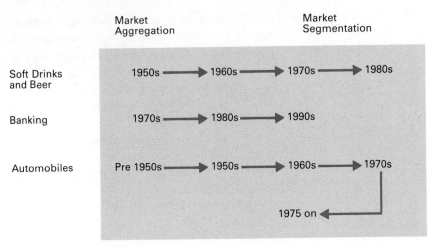

FIGURE 8-2
Increased level of market segmentation in selected industries

super premium (foreign beer) segments in the beer market. Segmentation is being extended even further in the 1980s, particularly in soft drinks. Noncaffeinated brands have been introduced by the major companies. Further, these companies are emphasizing noncola brands as a result of a long-term decline in the cola-drinking teenage population.[6]

The banking industry is also moving toward greater segmentation but is twenty years behind many consumer goods industries. The banks were forced to think in terms of target segments because of potential competition in the money markets. Diverse sources such as brokerage houses, credit card companies, and retail firms were offering customers financial services in competition with the banks. The shift from market aggregation to market segmentation is illustrated by the statement of a president of a large bank-consulting firm:

> In the 1980's banks will no longer be all things to all people. There are simply too many choices in the marketplace and everybody from Merrill Lynch to American Express wants a piece of the action.[7]

One writer adds,

> The Message is clear — any bank or thrift that chooses to stay in the consumer market will have to figure out whom it wants as its customer and how it can best serve that customer profitably.[8]

In other words banks will have to begin defining target segments for services.

Figure 8-2 portrays the shift of banks from an aggregation strategy in the 1970s to a segmentation strategy in the 1980s. The prediction is that as nontraditional sources intensify their competition for financial services into the 1990s banks will have to develop a wider range of services for more specific segments of the market.

Countersegmentation

The industries we have cited have moved from aggregation to segmentation strategies, but a reverse trend has also emerged in recent years — a move from segmentation to aggregation. This trend has been called **counter-segmentation.**[9]

The impetus for countersegmentation has been the greater price sensitivity of consumers in the recessions of the mid-1970s and early 1980s. Consumers are willing to accept lower-priced products that are less tailored to their individual needs. As a result, some marketers have reduced the number of market segments they are willing to target. For example, rather than producing a paper towel for the heavy-duty segment, another for the absorbency segment, and another for the decorator segment, a company will produce a lower-price towel to appeal to all three segments. It may still produce a two-ply towel for a heavy-duty segment, but now the distinction is between an economy and a quality segment. Aggregation is more profitable in a price-elastic market. Prices can be lowered owing to economies of scale, thus appealing to a broad range of price-sensitive consumers.

Figure 8-2 cites the automobile industry as an example of counterseg-mentation. Before 1950 the industry followed a strategy of market aggregation. Most divisions of the large companies produced one dominant model (such as Chevrolet) that was mass marketed. In the 1950s automobile manufacturers began introducing more models and options. Greater competition from foreign makes accelerated the trend to fragmenting the market by the individual needs of consumers. By the early 1970s the industry could boast that it could produce thousands of cars with no two exactly alike. The energy crisis changed the trend to segmentation. Greater emphasis on economy caused manufacturers to reduce prices by offering fewer models and options. They began to group segments together and to define them more broadly.

There are other examples of the trend to countersegmentation as a result of emphasis on economy. The increased number of generic items in supermarkets reflects the trend to offering one item with no distinction between segments. "No frill" furniture and modular housing are other examples of counterseg-mentation. Despite this trend it is likely that a segmentation approach will continue to dominate in marketing strategy. Restricting the number of target markets because of a price appeal is a risky strategy that could cost a company customers. Even companies that are offering a lower-price alternative on a mass market basis are hedging their bets by also offering products to specific segments. Therefore, "the need for countersegmentation coexists with the need to serve smaller market segments."[10]

LEVEL OF MARKET SEGMENTATION

A company pursuing a segmentation strategy must determine the extent to which it wishes to segment the market. Having decided on the level of segmentation, the firm must then determine whether it will target one or several products to specific segments. In this section we will address these strategic issues.

Figure 8-2 suggests that a company has a choice of strategies on a continuum from an absence of segmentation on one extreme (market aggregation) to very specific segmentation on the other (offering a separate product to every segment in the market). Most companies fall in between these two extremes. The key question is how much should the company segment its market.

One approach to determining the appropriate level of segmentation is to use the marginal principles of economics: continue to divide the market as long as the incremental revenue to be gained from the creation of an additional segment is greater than the incremental marketing and production costs required to sell to that segment. Optimal segmentation is defined as the point where the incremental revenue gained from the additional segment equals the incremental cost. The optimal level of segmentation can be stated as:

$$MR_{\Delta s} = MC_{\Delta s},$$

where $MR_{\Delta s}$ is the marginal revenue gained from the last segment (Δs), and $MC_{\Delta s}$ is the marginal cost required to sell to the last segment (Δs).

As an example, assume IBM is considering optimal segmentation for personal computers (PCs). It decides to develop a computer for home use and another for business use. The additional revenue gained in splitting the market in two is greater than the additional cost. It now decides to develop separate personal computers for engineers, managers, and independent businesspeople. The additional revenue of splitting the business market into three segments is still greater than the additional cost. But if IBM develops separate PCs for electrical, civil, design, and production engineers, it finds the additional costs of this higher level of segmentation are greater than the additional revenue. IBM is therefore content with defining three segments in the business market. As competition intensifies and it begins to lose its competitive advantage in the business PC market, IBM may find that it is economical to segment the market further.

TYPES OF SEGMENTATION STRATEGY

In the previous section we considered the level of segmentation. The level of segmentation is the basic consideration in developing segmentation strategies and is translated into three types of strategy: concentrated segmentation, differentiated segmentation, and undifferentiated segmentation.

Concentrated Segmentation

Concentrated segmentation (also known as a market niche strategy) targets a single product to a single market segment. This strategy is illustrated by the first grid in Figure 8-3 using the example of the instant coffee market. Four benefit segments are listed down the side and three product categories across the top. The shaded area defines a particular product offering to a particular segment. In the first grid a company has only one product offering, freeze-dried coffee directed to a taste-oriented segment.

The firm with limited resources is likely to choose a concentrated segmentation strategy to focus its efforts on a portion of the market. It is aiming at a large share of a small market and is avoiding competition with larger competitors. Chapter 1 noted that Block Drug follows this strategy (e.g., targeting effort to a specific niche such as the adult acne remedy segment) to avoid competition with larger pharmaceutical companies.

Differentiated Segmentation

In **differentiated segmentation,** a firm introduces separate products to a variety of market segments (the second grid in Figure 8-3). Nestlé follows a differentiated segmentation strategy for its instant coffee line by offering regular instant, decaffeinated, freeze-dried, and freeze-dried decaffeinated brands. It also offers a chicory-based instant to the consumer that wants a mild coffee. Each product is targeted to a different segment of the instant coffee market. By offering a full line of products to different segments, Nestlé has established a strong identification with the instant coffee category.

Differentiated segmentation requires more resources since separate products and marketing strategies are needed for each segment. The greater marketing, production, and administrative costs required in a differentiated segmentation strategy makes some firms wary of pursuing such a strategy too extensively. The firm must be aware of the economic criteria described in the previous section: continue to segment on a differentiated basis as long as the marginal revenue gained from marketing to each additional segment is greater than the marginal cost of adding that segment. Firms have occasionally oversegmented their markets by fragmenting their resources to the point where marketing to additional segments is no longer profitable.

Undifferentiated Segmentation

Undifferentiated segmentation occurs when a firm targets the same product to several segments simultaneously. In the third grid in Figure 8-3 a company combines two product categories to produce a freeze-dried decaffeinated coffee. It does not position the coffee to any one market segment. Rather, it attempts to appeal to all segments of the instant coffee market by using a general positioning strategy that emphasizes both taste and decaffeinated benefits. In developing a general positioning strategy, the company attempts to widen its market appeal even further by offering frequent coupons and price specials to appeal to the economy segment.

The term *undifferentiated segmentation* may seem contradictory since segmentation requires targeting different products to specific segments. Un-differentiated segmentation is a compromise between market aggregation and

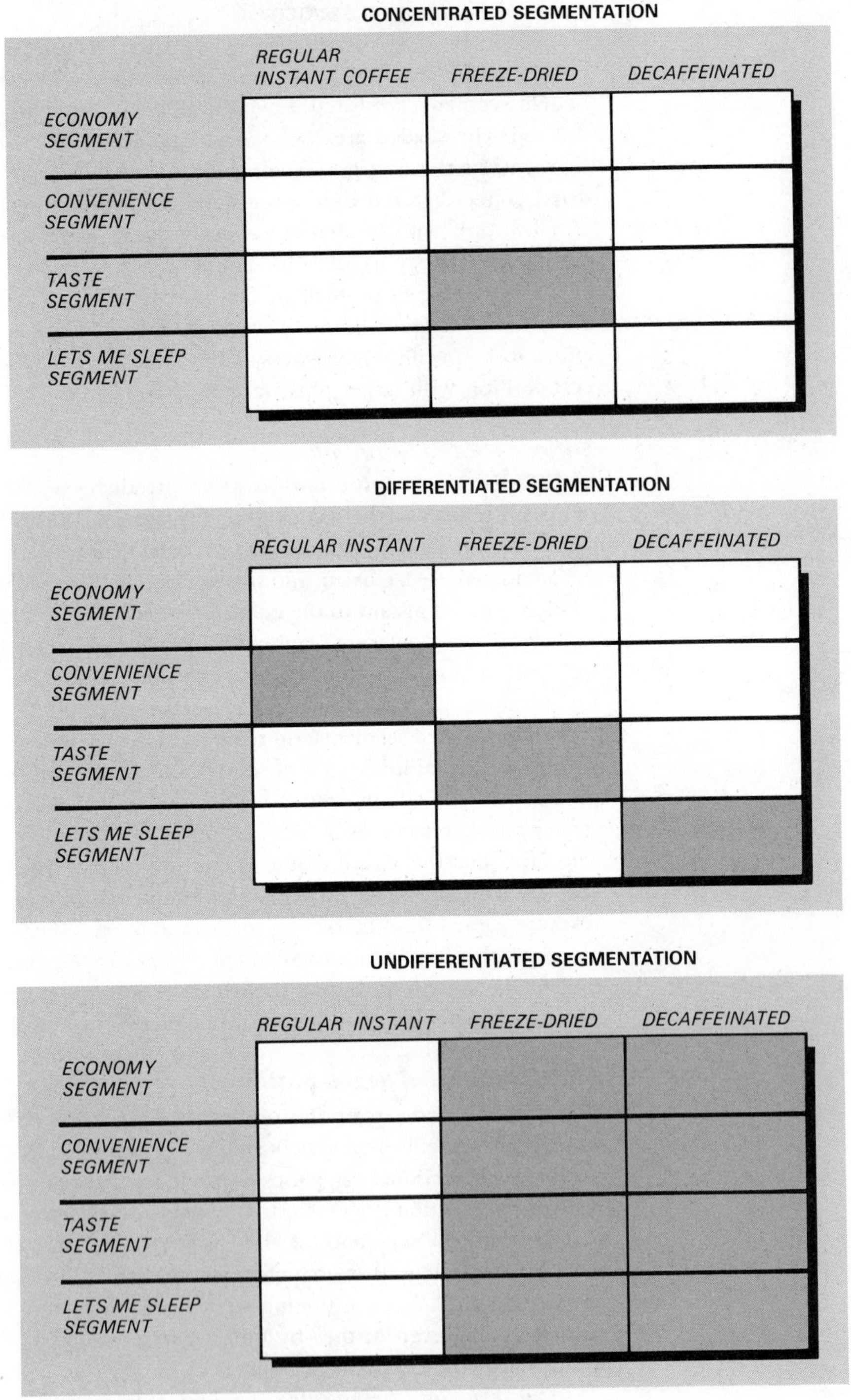

CONCENTRATED SEGMENTATION

	REGULAR INSTANT COFFEE	FREEZE-DRIED	DECAFFEINATED
ECONOMY SEGMENT			
CONVENIENCE SEGMENT			
TASTE SEGMENT		▓▓	
LETS ME SLEEP SEGMENT			

DIFFERENTIATED SEGMENTATION

	REGULAR INSTANT	FREEZE-DRIED	DECAFFEINATED
ECONOMY SEGMENT			
CONVENIENCE SEGMENT	▓▓		
TASTE SEGMENT		▓▓	
LETS ME SLEEP SEGMENT			▓▓

UNDIFFERENTIATED SEGMENTATION

	REGULAR INSTANT	FREEZE-DRIED	DECAFFEINATED
ECONOMY SEGMENT		▓▓	▓▓
CONVENIENCE SEGMENT		▓▓	▓▓
TASTE SEGMENT		▓▓	▓▓
LETS ME SLEEP SEGMENT		▓▓	▓▓

FIGURE 8-3
Three types of segmentation strategies

market segmentation. The firm identifies a broad target (e.g., decaffeinated coffee drinkers) and then aggregates across this broad segment. In so doing, it achieves economies of scale in marketing and production that characterize market aggregation strategies. The risk is that in marketing to a number of segments, the firm may be diluting its effectiveness by attempting to meet various needs with the same product line.

Identifying Target Segments

The identification of market segments must precede the selection of a market segmentation strategy. Segments can be identified on several bases depending on the marketer's strategic objectives. There are three strategic areas in which identifying market segments assists management:

1. determining marketing opportunities for new products,

2. developing marketing strategies for new and existing products, and

3. allocating marketing resources across target segments.

These three areas define the most important strategic tasks of marketing management. A different approach to the identification of market segments will be taken depending on which of these three strategic objectives must be fulfilled in marketing planning.

THREE BASES FOR MARKET SEGMENTATION

Table 8-2 lists three bases for segmenting markets depending on which strategic objective is most important: (1) benefit segmentation, (2) behavioral segmentation, and (3) segmentation by consumer response elasticities.

Benefit Segmentation

If the strategic objective is to identify opportunity for new product development, the first step should be to determine consumer needs. Segments are formed so that (1) consumers with similar needs are placed in the same segments, and (2) each segment has needs that are distinct from other segments. This approach is referred to as **benefit segmentation.** Once benefit segments have been formed, those segments with unmet needs can be identified and new products developed to meet these needs.

Table 8-3 is an example of a benefit segmentation analysis in the snack food market. A large food manufacturer conducted a study of snack food users to identify possible new product opportunities for its nut and chip snack lines. Interviews were conducted with a national representative sample of 1500 snack food users. The company analyzed the data by first grouping consumers by similarity in snack food needs. Six benefit segments were identified: (1) nutritional snackers, (2) weight watchers, (3) guilty snackers, (4) party snackers, (5) indiscriminate snackers, and (6) economy-minded snackers.

TABLE 8-2
Three Bases for Market Segmentation

BASES FOR SEGMENTATION	STRATEGIC APPLICATIONS	CRITERIA	ADDITIONAL SEGMENT DESCRIPTORS
1. Benefits	New Product Development and Product Positioning	Consumer Needs	
2. Behavior	a. Develop marketing strategies for new products	Intention to Buy	Demographics
	b. Develop marketing strategies for existing products	Brand users versus nonusers	Life Styles
	c. Develop marketing strategies for product categories	Product users versus nonusers	Personality
		Heavy versus light users	Product Attitudes and Perceptions
3. Response Elasticities	Level of Marketing Effort to Each Segment	Price Elasticity Deal Elasticity Advertising Elasticity	

The next step was to provide a richer profile of each segment by determining life-style and demographic characteristics. For example, nutritional snackers described themselves as self-assured and controlled, were better educated, and had younger children. The final step was to determine the snacking behavior of each of the six segments. Heaviest users of chip and nut snacks were the party and indiscriminate snackers, whereas nutritional snackers and weight watchers tended to snack on more nutritious, low-calorie foods.

The company wished to extend its franchise beyond the regular chip and nut users to appeal to the nutritional snackers and weight watchers. These segments presented a particularly desirable target since they had similar needs and life-style and demographic characteristics, and could probably be appealed to by the same media and advertising strategies. The company considered two product concepts for testing, a low-calorie, dry roasted nut and a nut and dried fruit product. Both products had nutritional benefits and natural ingredients that would appeal to the two target segments. Further testing confirmed that these concepts could provide an excellent opportunity to extend the company's sales to the target segments. The benefit segmentation analysis in Table 8-3 thus allowed management to identify the segments that represented the greatest marketing opportunity.

TABLE 8-3
An Example of Benefit Segmentation

	NUTRITIONAL SNACKERS	WEIGHT WATCHERS	GUILTY SNACKERS	PARTY SNACKERS	INDISCRIMINATE SNACKERS	ECONOMICAL SNACKERS
Percentage of snackers	22	14	9	15	15	18
Benefits Sought	Nutritious No artificial ingredients Natural snack	Low calorie Quick energy	Low calorie Good tasting	Good to serve guests Proud to serve Goes well with beverage	Good tasting Satisfies hunger	Low price Best value
Life-Style Characteristics	Self-assured Controlled	Outdoor types Influential Venturesome	High anxiety Isolate	Sociable	Hedonistic	Self-assured Price oriented
Consumption Level of Snacks	Light	Light	Heavy	Average	Heavy	Average
Type of Snacks Usually Eaten	Fruits Vegetables Cheese	Yogurt Vegetables	Yogurt Cookies Crackers Candy	Nuts Potato chips Crackers Pretzels	Candy Ice cream Cookies Potato chips Pretzels Popcorn	No specific products
Demographics	Better educated Have younger children	Younger Single	Younger or older Females Lower socioeconomic group	Middle aged Nonurban	Teens	Larger families Better educated

Behavioral Segmentation

Behavioral segmentation uses consumer behavior rather than needs to segment markets. Behavioral segmentation satisfies the second strategic objective listed in Table 8-2 — providing guidelines to develop marketing strategies for: (1) new brands, (2) existing brands, and (3) product categories. Each of these applications will be considered.

Defining market segments for new brands

Once opportunity is identified through benefit segmentation, it is necessary to develop advertising, media, promotional, distribution, and pricing strategies for the product. The most frequent approach in providing initial guidelines for strategy is to segment consumers by their intention to buy the new product and to identify the demographic, life-style, and use characteristics of intenders versus nonintenders. Demographic characteristics of those who intend to buy guide media strategy. Life styles and product attitudes of intenders guide advertising strategy. Shopping behavior of intenders guides distribution strategy. Use characteristics guide in-store promotional strategy. Since intention to purchase is a behavioral criterion, this approach is an example of **behavioral segmentation.**

As an example, a producer of personal care appliances tested a new product concept among women, a facial scrub device. Demographic and life-style characteristics were used to identify those who intended to buy the product. The five segments most likely to buy are presented in Table 8-4. About one-fifth of the consumers said they would definitely buy the product. But among active, career-oriented working women in urban areas, over 50 percent said they would buy. The four demographic and life-style characteristics that define consumers in segment 1 thus double the chances of trying the product.

Segment 2 is made up of younger single women in urban areas who express an interest in buying new products in general. Within this segment 47 percent say they will definitely buy. The third segment is made up of married, nonworking women who describe themselves as sociable and who emphasize grooming. Within this group, 44 percent say they will definitely buy. The two remaining segments are made up of additional working and single women. These groups are also more likely to buy than the average woman.

Important considerations for management are the size and characteristics of these groups. The first three groups make up 18 percent of all consumers, a proportion that is certainly large enough if significant sales can be achieved within each segment. But should each group be targeted? Management decided to direct advertising to segments 1 and 2 only. Both groups are in urban areas and appear to have similar interests and orientations. It would be much harder to select media and develop advertising messages to segment 3 that would also be compatible with segments 1 and 2. Management could expand its promotional net to include all single and working women (all segments except segment 3). This would mean a larger target market, but management would

TABLE 8-4
Market Segmentation by Intention to Buy a New Personal Care Appliance

SEGMENT DESCRIPTION	PERCENTAGE WHO SAY THEY DEFINITELY INTEND TO BUY	PERCENTAGE OF ALL CONSUMERS
All consumers	26	100
Segment 1 Active, career oriented work- ing women in urban areas	53	8
Segment 2 Younger single women in urban areas who are new product oriented (i.e., innovators)	47	4
Segment 3 Married non-working women who are socially oriented and emphasize grooming	44	6
Segment 4 Working women other than those defined in segments 1 and 2	38	12
Segment 5 Single women other than those defined in segments 1, 2 and 4.	31	9
All other women	16	61

lose the capability of appealing to an urban-oriented, active and innovative segment.

Developing marketing strategies for existing products

The same principles apply in using behavioral segmentation to guide strategies for existing as for new products: define the demographic, life-style, and other characteristics of those most likely to buy. The difference is that in this case management can use actual rather than intended behavior as the criterion.

Once a brand is in test market or is being distributed nationally, it can then be segmented by the characteristics of those who purchase. For example, a study by General Motors found that purchasers of the Oldsmobile diesel were likely to be males in a high-income group, mechanically inclined, who keep their car longer, and do more driving.[11] This profile suggests that:

■ media should be selected to reach upper-income males,

■ advertising should concentrate on the utilitarian benefits of the car in technical terms to appeal to the mechanically inclined buyer, and

■ the target market for the Olds diesel should be consumers who empha- size durability and economy.

Developing marketing strategies for product categories

A third application of behavioral segmentation is to direct marketing strategies to users of a product category rather than to users of an individual brand. Table 8-2 lists two criteria used to segment markets by product category — product category use and frequency of use. For example, GM might have segmented the market by ownership of diesels in general rather than by ownership of Olds diesels (product category rather than brand segmentation).

Markets can also be segmented by frequency of use (light versus heavy buyers or users). It is desirable to position a brand to heavy users of the product category since heavy users represent more sales volume. Marketers sometimes refer to the **"heavy half"** in a product category; that is, the 50 percent of the consumers who use a greater than average amount of the product. A frequently stated principle is that the heavy half accounts for at least 80 percent of use in many product categories. One purpose of behavioral segmentation is to identify the heavy half and segment it into smaller target groups.

One study identified the demographic characteristics of heavy versus light users of ten consumer packaged goods. For example, the heaviest buyers of frozen orange juice are college graduates in the higher-income group and between thirty-five and sixty-five. The lightest buyers are the downscale consumers who are under thirty-five or over sixty-five and have two or fewer children.[12] Heavy users of frozen orange juice buy eight times as much as light users.

Products may also be positioned to light rather than heavy buyers. Existing brands may have already preempted the positioning to heavy buyers in a market and the only profitable niche may be a positioning to lighter buyers. Segmenting by frequency of use can provide guidelines for reaching lighter buyers. Demographic characteristics of heavy and light users provide the basis for selecting the media that will reach the targeted use segment.

Segmenting by Response Elasticity

Knowing the needs and behavior of consumers is not sufficient to develop marketing strategies. Management also wants to know consumer reactions to their advertising, prices, sales promotions, and other elements of the marketing mix. Consumers' sensitivity to changes in advertising, price, deals, and so forth, is known as the consumer's response elasticity. (A more formal definition of elasticity will be given in Chapter 15 on pricing.) **Response elasticity** is the third criterion by which markets can be segmented. Marketers may wish to determine which consumers are most likely to switch brands with a change in price (a price-elastic segment) or which consumers tend to buy most frequently by deals (the deal-prone segment). They may also want to know which consumers are most likely to be influenced to buy by an increase in advertising expenditures (the advertising-elastic segment).

Segmenting by response elasticity is designed to group consumers into price-elastic and price-inelastic segments or advertising-elastic and -inelastic segments. This approach provides management with a basis for:

1. directing price or advertising appeals to the most sensitive groups,
2. estimating the groups most likely to reduce purchases with a price increase (an important consideration in an inflationary period),
3. directing deals and coupons to the most responsive consumers, and
4. identifying groups most likely to respond positively to increases in advertising expenditures.

The economic basis for segmenting by response elasticities

Segmenting by response elasticity has its basis in economic theory. The theory of imperfect competition recognized that markets are composed of different demand schedules (different segments) based on the fact that consumers respond differently to price changes. The economist would say that there are several demand schedules (responses to price changes) rather than just one schedule for the total market. The marketer would say there are various market segments that react differently to marketing stimuli (price, advertising, deals). But both are saying essentially the same thing.

Writing in the 1930s the economist Joan Robinson presented the basis for segmenting by response elasticities well before any marketer when she said that markets should be subdivided "until the point is reached at which each submarket consists of . . . a group of buyers whose elasticities of demand are the same."[13] In other words, continue to segment the market until you have groups of consumers who respond to changes in a marketing stimulus (such as price) in the same way. Generally, a manufacturer should direct more resources to a price-inelastic segment since it yields more profits. Consumers in this segment will continue to buy in the face of a price increase, making the inelastic segment more profitable. The manufacturer will continue to allocate marketing dollars to the inelastic segment up to the point where the additional revenue gained from this segment equals the additional revenue gained from an elastic segment. The profit maximization point would be:

$$\frac{MR_i}{MC_i} = \frac{MR_e}{MC_e}$$

where MR_i and MC_i are the marginal revenue and marginal cost, respectively, of the most inelastic segment and MR_e and MC_e are the marginal revenue and marginal cost, respectively, of the most elastic segment. Although the example cites only two segments, the principle applies to any number of segments.

A criterion of response elasticity has been used most frequently to identify price-elastic and inelastic segments. The price-elastic segment would identify consumers more likely to switch out of a brand if there is a price increase; the inelastic segment would identify those consumers more likely to stay loyal. But response elasticity can also be applied to identifying deal- or coupon-oriented consumers. In this way, marketers can direct coupons to segments most likely to redeem them, or run price deals in areas with a larger proportion of deal-oriented consumers. Identifying advertising-elastic consumers would also be useful if they tend to be exposed to certain media or are located in certain TV coverage areas. If so, marketers can then allocate advertising expenditures to those consumers most likely to respond.

An example of segmenting by response elasticity

An example of segmenting by consumer response elasticities is a study design proposed by the New York Stock Exchange when fixed commission rates for the purchase of stocks and bonds were eliminated in May 1975. After that date rates were allowed to fluctuate, making the brokerage market price competitive. The exchange realized that certain stock and bond purchasers would be more sensitive to lower commission rates (price-elastic) whereas others would prefer to pay the same rates if they could be offered more services (price-inelastic). It suggested that brokerage houses conduct surveys of their customers to segment them by price elasticity using a technique known as tradeoff analysis.[14] The survey would ask customers to rate their preference for fewer services at lower commission rates or for more services at higher rates. Four levels of commission rates and four levels of services were offered to consumers (sixteen alternatives) and consumers were asked to rank the six most preferred alternatives. The design is presented in Table 8-5.[15] The four levels of commission rates ranged from 10 percent above the standard commission before the elimination of fixed rates to 20 percent below the standard commission. The service options ranged from full custodial services including investment counseling to no custodial services beyond execution of normal buy and sell orders.

Most customers would of course want the most services at the lowest price (upper left-hand column in Table 8-5). But once having made this selection, the key question is whether a customer would prefer to maintain the lowest price regardless of the service (price-elastic segment) or to keep full custodial services regardless of the price (price-inelastic segment. The extremely price-elastic customer would prefer a commission rate 20 percent below the standard even if it meant receiving no custodial services. Such a customer would rank order his or her preferences from one to four horizontally in Table 8-5. The extremely price inelastic customer would prefer full custodial services regardless of the price, even if it meant paying the highest price for these services. Such a customer would order his or her preferences from one to four vertically in Table 8-5. Most customers would fall in between extreme price elasticity or inelasticity. For example, a customer might be willing to accept full or limited custodial services as long as the commission rate is 10 percent below standard, but once the commission rate increases to the standard level, the customer would prefer no custodial services (a slightly price-elastic customer). Thus, the tradeoff analysis would permit determining a buyer's price sensitivity and segmenting accordingly.

One brokerage house using this design found that the most price sensitive customer was the smaller-volume buyer who was buying for speculation rather

TABLE 8-5
Segmenting the securities market by commission price sensitivity

COMMISSION PRICE ALTERNATIVES	SERVICE ALTERNATIVES			
	Full custodial services such as holding stocks, reinvesting dividends, monthly statements, and including investment counseling	Full custodial services such as in Column 1 but not including investment counseling	Limited custodial services such as safekeeping stocks. Other services at a fee.	No custodial services beyond execution of buy and sell orders
20 percent below Standard Commissions	(1)[a] 1[a]	2	3	4
10 percent below Standard Commissions	(2)			
Standard Commission Rates	(3)			
10 percent above Standard Commission	(4)			

[a] Numbers in parentheses indicate preferences of a price-inelastic consumer.
Numbers without parentheses indicate preferences of a price-elastic consumer.

Source: Adapted from Henry Assael, "Segmenting Markets by Response Elasticity." Reprinted from the *Journal of Advertising Research* © Copyright 1976 by the Advertising Research Foundation.

than long-term growth. Since this was not the type of customer the company wished to retain, it chose to maintain standard commission rates and to offer more services to justify these higher rates. Segmenting by price elasticity thus provided the company with a basis for setting its prices and service packages and identified its target customer.

To summarize, benefit segmentation defines new product opportunities, behavioral segmentation provides guidelines for developing marketing strategies, and segmenting by response elasticity helps direct marketing strategies to those most likely to respond.

DESCRIBING CONSUMER SEGMENTS

Once segments are defined by needs, behavior, or response elasticity, the characteristics of consumers in each segment must be determined. In using behavioral segmentation General Motors defined the demographic characteristics and attitudes of Olds diesel owners versus nonowners. In segmenting by response elasticity the New York Stock Exchange compared the demographic characteristics and buying motives of the price-elastic and price-inelastic segments.

Segments have been defined by the following consumer characteristics (see Table 8-2):

demographics	consumer needs
life styles	product attitudes and perceptions
personality	organizational characteristics (for industrial buyer segments)

These characteristics were described in Chapter 6. In market segmentation strategies they serve as the basis for defining segments — demographics to guide media strategies, life styles and personality variables to guide the tone of advertising, consumer needs to identify benefit segments, and organizational characteristics to identify market segments in the industrial sector.

Industrial Market Segmentation

Market segmentation is as relevant for industrial goods as for consumer goods. There are several differences in strategic emphasis, however. First, industrial segmentation is likely to be more specific than consumer segmentation. Single buyers can be identified, and products are frequently designed to the specifications of these buyers. The third box in Figure 8-1 — diffuse market needs — would be more likely to occur for industrial markets. Second, industrial segmentation is more likely to lead to implications for personal selling. For example, in the segmentation of the market for scientific and technical information systems (STI), cited in Chapter 6, five segments were identified by differences in needs. As a result, companies offering STI systems would have to differentiate their selling strategy by segment.

Third, the criteria for segmentation will remain the same (segmenting by benefits, behavior, or response elasticity), but the descriptors will differ. Organizational characteristics replace demographics, and the organizational environment replaces life-style characteristics as descriptors. Fourth, identification of organizational needs is complicated by the fact that several individuals may have buying influence. The varying needs and perceptions of purchasing agents, production managers, and engineers must be taken into account.

These differences should not prevent the application of market segmentation to industrial marketing strategies. Yet as Wind and Cardozo note, "Industrial marketers by no means use market segmentation strategies as widely or effectively as they might. Segmentation appears to be largely an after-the-fact explanation of why a marketing program did or did not work, rather than a carefully thought-out foundation for marketing programs.[16] One reason why segmentation is less frequent in industrial than consumer markets is that industrial marketing research has lagged behind consumer research. Another is that industrial marketers may feel that segmentation strategies are not necessary when they can operate on a one-on-one basis.

Despite these limitations, segmentation analysis has been applied effectively in the industrial area. The study of STI systems users is a good example of the application of *benefit segmentation* to an industrial product. Most applications are in *behavioral segmentation.* An analysis by AT&T of its business customers is illustrative. The company identified the organizational characteristics of heavier versus lighter users of the telephone.[17] Results of the analysis are in Table 8-6. The average monthly telephone bill for the business customer in the sample is $910, but among companies with more than 500 employees the average bill is $6,033. These companies are only 3 percent of AT&T's business customers, but they represent 20 percent of AT&T's revenues from business accounts. Despite its small size, segment 1 is worth targeting for personal selling and promotional effort.

Another important segment is companies with less than 500 employees that use central switching (PBX) facilities and have at least fifty employees in other locations. These companies represent 8 percent of the business customers

TABLE 8-6
Segmentation of the Industrial Telecommunications Market

ORGANIZATIONAL CHAR-ACTERISTICS OF SEGMENT	AVERAGE MONTHLY TELEPHONE BILL ($)	SEGMENT IS THIS PERCENTAGE OF ALL INDUSTRIAL COMPANIES	SEGMENT ACCOUNTS FOR THIS PERCENTAGE OF TOTAL REVENUE
TOTAL SAMPLE	$ 910	100	100
Segment 1 Companies with 500 or more employees	6,033	3	20
Segment 2 Less than 500 employees, but has PBX facilities *and* 50 or more employees elsewhere	2,412	8	21
Segment 3 Less than 500 employees, but has PBX facilities and less than 50 employees elsewhere	995	46	50
Segment 4 Less than 500 employees and has key facilities	180	43	8

Source: Adapted from Henry Assael and Richard B. Ellis, "A Research Design to Predict Telephone Usage Among Bell System Business Customers," *European Research* 1 (1973): 38–42.

but 21 percent of AT&T's revenue from business accounts. Thus, about 10 percent of AT&T's business customers account for 40 percent of revenue.

Although these results are not surprising, the analysis is valuable in identifying the characteristics of the heaviest telephone users. These characteristics can guide the allocation of the time and effort of AT&T's sales personnel. AT&T has the resources to make personal calls on the large accounts represented by segments 1 and 2. It cannot use personal selling for segments 3 and 4. Segment 3 is particularly important (small businesses with switching facilities). This segment accounts for almost half of all companies and for half of AT&T's revenues from business accounts. The segmentation analysis shows that AT&T will have to rely on advertising to reach this segment. Additional information would be required to better define segment 3 for purposes of selecting appropriate business publications.

Summary

Market segmentation is a key component of marketing strategy since segmentation requires identifying a target group for a product or service. There are two components to market segmentation, the strategic and the analytical. Market segmentation strategy directs marketing effort to defined segments and allocates marketing resources across segments. Market segmentation analysis defines these segments to permit such allocation. In this chapter we first considered segmentation strategies then the means to identify target groups.

Market segmentation became a more important component of marketing strategy with a shift from a sales and production orientation to a marketing orientation in the mid-1950s. The strategic option a firm chooses depends on the breadth of the market and the company's willingness to diversify its marketing strategy and product line across several segments.

Segmentation strategies are more likely to be used when:

- there are substantial differences in needs between segments;
- these differences can be translated into differences in product characteristics and advertising strategies;
- different segments can be reached by different advertising media and distribution channels; and
- different advertising and product strategies to different segments can be justified on a cost basis and are unlikely to cause confusion between segments.

When these conditions are not met, a strategy of market aggregation is more likely (a single product offered on a mass market basis with no distinction in marketing effort between segments).

Market segments have been identified using three general criteria:

1. *Benefit segmentation* defines segments by similarity in needs. It is used to develop and position new products and services.
2. *Behavioral segmentation* defines segments by their intended behavior for new products and by actual behavior for existing products. It is used to provide guidelines for the development of advertising, media, pricing, and distribution strategies.
3. *Segmenting by response elasticity* defines segments by their sensitivity of response to different price, promotional, and advertising levels. It is used to provide guidelines as to the appropriate level of price, deals, or advertising expenditures in marketing strategies.

Benefit, behavioral, and response segments are further described by their demographic, life-style, personality, and attitudinal characteristics. Demographics provide guidelines for media selection; life-style and personality characteristics provide guidelines for developing advertising messages; consumers' brand attitudes provide guidelines for positioning products relative to competition. Industrial segmentation studies rely on organizational characteristics as descriptors of benefit or behavioral segments. We concluded by considering applications of industrial segmentation.

Having defined target segments, we will next consider developing new products to meet the needs of these segments. In the next chapter we will describe the new product development process. In subsequent chapters we will consider specific components of marketing strategy directed to defined segments.

Questions

1. What are the advantages and disadvantages of strategies of market segmentation compared to those of market aggregation?
2. Assume Procter and Gamble is considering offering several new coffee brands in addition to Folgers to appeal to several additional market segments (e.g., decaffeinated coffee users, a convenience segment, an economy segment). What market conditions would be required for such a strategy to succeed?
3. Assume a producer of industrial drills has expanded its product line to meet the needs of specific segments of the market. Much of the pressure for this expansion has come from the sales force because of its desire to attract customers with new products suited to their needs. The vice president of marketing questions the wisdom of developing new products for smaller segments of the market.

□ What criterion can the vice president of marketing use to determine the point at which targeting products to additional segments is no longer profitable?

□ What is the difficulty of applying this criterion?

4. Three industries are cited in Figure 8-2 as shifting from strategies of market aggregation to market segmentation. Can you cite specific companies that have shifted from a one-product aggregation strategy to a multiple-product segmentation strategy?

5. The chapter cites a recent reversal of the trend toward market segmentation, referred to as countersegmentation.

□ What are the reasons for countersegmentation?

□ Does this trend contradict the principle that products should be directed to the needs of defined customer groups?

6. What are the benefits and risks of:

□ concentrated, differentiated, and undifferentiated segmentation strategies?

□ single-product versus product-line segmentation strategies?

7. What benefit segments may be identified for the following markets: (a) soft drinks, (b) household cleaners, (c) personal care appliances, and (d) credit cards?
What are the implications of identifying these segments for:

□ positioning new products, or

□ repositioning existing products?

8. Under what circumstances would a marketer wish to segment by the following behavioral criteria: (a) intention to buy, (b) brand use, (c) frequency of product use?

9. What are the strategic implications of segmenting the detergent market by: (a) deal or coupon sensitivity, (b) sensitivity to changes in package size, and (c) sensitivity to changes in advertising expenditure levels?

10. Table 8-3 cited nutritional, weight-watching, and guilty segments in the snack food market. What would be the strategic applications of identifying each of these segments by (a) demographics, (b) life-style characteristics, (c) benefits sought, and (d) consumption of snack foods?

11. A large food company is developing a strategy to attract additional users to its leading instant coffee brand. Competition has been intense in the last year and the brand has lost market share. One marketing executive argues that the company should direct its resources to those segments in which the brand is weakest since this would represent an opportunity to attract the greatest proportion of users. Another argues that the company should direct its resources to segments where the brand is strongest in an attempt to get consumers in these segments to become users.

☐ What is the rationale for each position?

☐ Under what conditions is one position more likely to be effective than another?

12. What are the differences in strategic emphasis between market segmentation in the industrial versus the consumer sector?

Notes

1. "Discovering a Vast Potential Market," *Business Week,* December 1, 1980, pp. 91, 92, 97.

2. Ibid., p. 91.

3. Ibid.

4. "Bringing Stouffer's to TV," *The New York Times,* May 3, 1982, p. D11.

5. Nariman K. Khalla and Winston H. Mahatoo, "Expanding the Scope of Segmentation Research," *Journal of Marketing* 40 (April 1976): 34–41.

6. "Audience Before Image, Beverage Marketers Urged," *Advertising Age,* August 27, 1979, p. 64.

7. "Now Bankers Turn to a Hard Sales Pitch," *Business Week,* September 21, 1981, p. 62.

8. Ibid.

9. Alan J. Resnik, Peter B.B. Turney, and J. Barry Mason, "Marketers Turn to 'Countersegmentation,'" *Harvard Business Review* 57 (September–October 1979): 100–6.

10. Resnik, Turney, and Mason, "Marketers Turn to 'Countersegmentation,'" p. 101.

11. "Who Buys a G.M. Diesel Car?" *The New York Times,* November 9, 1978, p. D7.

12. Frank M. Bass, Douglas J. Tigert, and Ronald T. Lonsdale, "Market Segmentation: Group versus Individual Behavior," *Journal of Marketing Research* 5 (August 1968): 264–70.

13. Joan Robinson, *The Economics of Imperfect Competition* (London: Macmillan, 1948), p. 186.

14. Henry Assael and Frank J. Conran, *Test Marketing in the Securities Industry,* The New York Stock Exchange, Planning Manual No. 7, 1975.

15. Henry Assael, "Segmenting Markets by Response Elasticity," *Journal of Advertising Research* 16 (April 1976): 27–35.

16. Yoram Wind and Richard Cardozo, "Industrial Market Segmentation," *Industrial Marketing Management* 3 (1974): 153–66.

17. Henry Assael and Richard B. Ellis, "A Research Design to Predict Telephone Usage Among Bell System Business Customers," *European Research* 1 (1973): 38–42.

CHAPTER 9

Developing and Positioning New Products

FOCUS OF CHAPTER

Most companies cannot rely on existing products to ensure long-term profitability. New products must be developed and positioned to meet the needs of defined target segments. Consider the following examples illustrating the importance of new product development:

- Polaroid's earnings went down substantially in the mid-1970s because of a failure to develop new products beyond instant photography.

- Schlitz lost its dominant position in the beer market because of an overly ambitious acquisition program at the expense of a capability to develop new products internally.

- Pennwalt, a chemical and drug conglomerate, underwent a change in management because of a lack of growth. One reason is that the company "has shown little aptitude for internal development."[1] It did not introduce one new product between 1974 and 1982, leading one industry analyst to conclude that the company's internal growth record does not bode well for the future.

- General Foods introduced strategic business units as a basis for marketing planning in the early 1970s because its pace of successful new product introductions slowed considerably. SBUs provided a more effective basis for new product planning.

This chapter describes the process of new product development. The importance of new products and the inherent risks in introducing them are first considered. Each step in the development of a new product is then described, from initial identification of new product ideas to final test marketing and national introduction. Differences in the process for industrial and consumer goods are cited.

What Is a New Product?

Before considering the subject of new product development, it would be wise to clarify what is meant by a new product. A new product does not have to be new to consumers (e.g., personal computers, disc cameras). It can be new to the company. For example, Heinz's introduction of a new line of canned soups did not represent a new product to consumers, but it was new to the company. Additions to existing product lines can also be considered new products to the company. Finally, a revision or improvement of an existing product can be regarded as a new product.

Booz Allen & Hamilton, a leading consulting firm, studied the new product development practices of 700 companies covering 13,000 new product introductions.[2] It classified products by the degree to which they are new to the market and/or new to the company. The classification is in Figure 9-1. The study found that

- 10 percent of the products cited were new to both the company and the market;

- 20 percent of the products cited were new to the company but known to the market;

- 7 percent were repositionings of existing products that were new to the market but not to the company;

- the remaining 63 percent of the new products cited were in an intermediate position. Of these:

  □ 26 percent were additions to an existing product line;

  □ another 26 percent were revisions or improvements of existing products;

  □ the remaining 11 percent were new products that provided similar performance at lower cost.

One factor is common to these four categories of new products — the need for a new development and testing effort. Therefore, a new product can be defined simply as any product that requires a complete development, testing, and planning effort by the firm.

Importance of New Product Development

The Booz Allen & Hamilton study also demonstrated the importance of new product development. The 700 firms studied expected new products to account for 31 percent of profits in the next five years (compared to 22 percent of profits in the five years before the study), and to account for 37 percent of sales growth (compared to 28 percent in the previous period).[3]

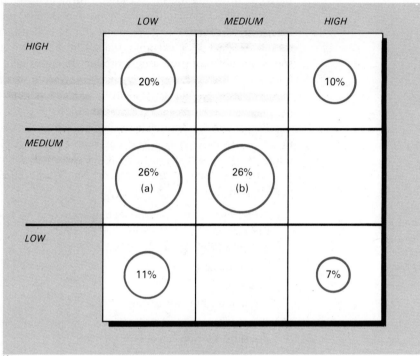

FIGURE 9-1
A classification of new products

Source: Adapted from *New Products Management for the 1980s* (New York: Booz Allen & Hamilton, 1982).

NEW PRODUCT DEVELOPMENT AND PROFITABILITY

New product development is closely linked to profitability for several reasons: the importance of maintaining a flow of new products for sustained growth, the advantage of being first in the market, and the experience gained by continued new product introductions.

Profitability and the Product Life Cycle

The link between new product development and profitability is illustrated in Figure 9-2. The first curve represents the sales volume for a typical product over its life cycle. Products go through periods of introduction, growth, maturity, and decline. The second curve is the profit curve.

During the introductory period, the firm is taking a loss while spending for advertising to create awareness and while recouping research and development costs. If the product is successful, it will enter a growth phase in which sales are accelerating. The product becomes profitable. The maturity phase is marked by a leveling of sales. The effect of a slowdown in sales is magnified by the profit curve. The firm is still making a profit in the maturity phase, but profits are now declining and managers should be forewarned that eventual losses could occur.

The product life cycle will be considered in detail in the next chapter. Its length and shape will vary from brand to brand. But few brands experience such sustained growth that managers do not have to anticipate declining profits. The implication of the profit curve for new product development is clear: sustaining profits for long-term growth requires continual new product intro-

FIGURE 9-2
Profitability and the product life cycle

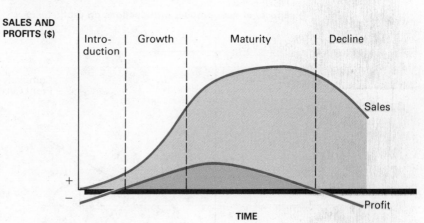

Source: Adapted from *Management of New Products* (New York: Booz Allen & Hamilton, 1968), p. 4.

ductions. The firm must have a planned program that will ensure a constant stream of new products.

The effects of an ongoing process of new product development are illustrated in Figure 9-3. A series of profit curves is depicted over time to illustrate successful new product introductions. A cumulative profit curve shows the firm's total profit position as a result. Profits will rise and eventually level off as the firm reaches the limits of its resources and as some existing products become a drain.

Profitability and the Costs of New Product Introductions

The Booz Allen & Hamilton study found that as a company introduces additional new products the costs of introduction decrease. Specifically, the cost of introducing a second product averages 71 percent of the first, a third 71 percent the cost of the second, and so forth.[4] This means that, on average, if the first product cost $1 million to introduce, the second will cost $710,000, the third $504,000, and so on. Profits from successive new product introductions increase as costs are reduced because of the company's experience.

Profitability and Market Leadership

An additional factor reinforcing the profitability of new product development is the association between profits and market leadership. New products that are innovations tend to be the most profitable. One study of twenty new consumer goods categories over fifteen years found that the first brand to be introduced dominated the market. On average, the second brand into the market did half as well as the innovator, and the third brand one-fourth as well.[5]

FIGURE 9-3
Effects of new product introductions on profitability

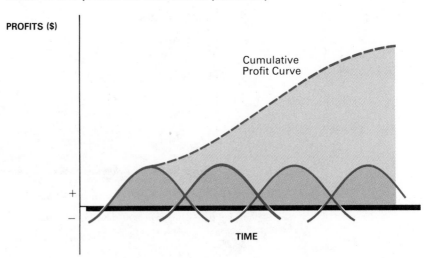

PROFITS ($)

Cumulative
Profit Curve

+

−

TIME

Success Rate Among New Product Introductions

Another factor that links new product development to profitability is the high rate of success among new products *once they are introduced into the market.* Several studies estimate the rate of failure among new products from 60 percent to 98 percent.[6] But these studies are referring to the high proportion of new product *ideas* that fail to reach the market. The Booz Allen and Hamilton study found that once products have been developed, tested, and introduced, two out of three are considered a success.[7]

In summary, new product development is linked to high profitability because:

1. once new products are introduced, they are likely to be successful;

2. such successes generate revenues for the firm and ensure long-term growth;

3. successive new product introductions reduce the cost of development; and

4. leaders in new product introductions in an industry are likely to be in a stronger sales position than followers.

WHY DO NEW PRODUCTS SUCCEED?

There is no blueprint for ensuring the successful introduction of new products. Yet some factors have been identified by managers and researchers as being associated with new product success. These factors are:[8]

- the ability to identify customer needs,

- use of existing company know-how and resources (developing new products in the company's core markets),

- measurement of new product performance during the development process,

- emphasis on screening and testing ideas before spending money on product development,

- coordination between research and development and marketing,

- an organizational environment that encourages entrepreneurship and risk taking, and

- linking new product development to corporate goals (e.g., Eastman-Kodak introducing its disc cameras to ensure its goal of being the leader in amateur photography for the rest of the decade).[9]

The Risks of New Product Development

The emphasis on the benefits of new product development should be balanced by a recognition of the financial risks. The experiences of several companies demonstrate the potential risks. For example:

■ Scott Paper lost substantial sums when it attempted to introduce disposable diapers with different shapes for baby boys and girls. The benefit was not important to mothers.

■ General Foods lost substantially when it introduced Post Cereals with
freeze-dried fruit. Mushy fruit in cereal was not particularly appealing to
children.

■ Rheingold was actually the first company to introduce a light beer, not
Miller. But its Gablinger brand was introduced as a diet beer, not a
light beer, and was meant to appeal to women as well as men. Most
women shunned any beer as being too caloric, and the medicinal con-
notations of a diet beer turned men off as well. Miller positioned Lite
as a male-oriented natural beer that is less filling. The positioning created an immediate success.

Failure of new products once they are introduced is certainly one element
of risk in new product development. The other element is the cost of screening
and testing the variety of product ideas that never reach the market. The Booz
Allen & Hamilton study found that for every seven new product ideas considered,
only one is introduced successfully.[10] If one counts new product ideas that
do not reach the market as failures, this level of performance represents an
86 percent failure rate. In a similar study conducted fourteen years earlier,
the company found that only one product out of fifty-eight new ideas was
marketed successfully, a 98 percent failure rate (see Figure 9-4). New product

FIGURE 9-4
Mortality of new product ideas during the product development process:
1968 versus 1981

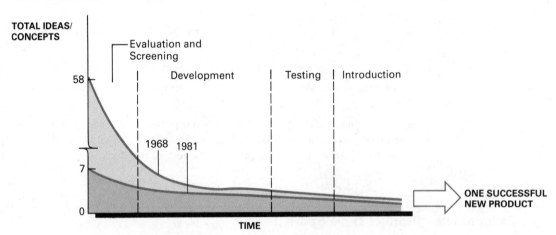

Source: Adapted from "New Product Strategy: How the Pros Do It," *Industrial Marketing,* May
1982, p. 50.

ideas that are eliminated before being tested or marketed cannot really be classified as failures. But even so, screening, concept development, and product development are costly and must be recouped by new product successes.

Although the percentage of new product ideas that are marketed successfully has increased in the last fourteen years, it is likely that the risks of new product introductions will increase into the 1990s because:

- costs will continue to rise,

- competition will intensify, particularly from foreign producers,

- products' life cycles are likely to become shorter as competitors duplicate existing products more quickly,

- the need for a more rapid pace in new product development may not be met by the development of new technologies,

- markets will continue to be fragmented, requiring companies to aim new products at smaller target segments, and

- investment risks are likely to increase because of high interest rates.

The increasing risks of new product development have led many companies to favor a policy of modifying existing products and following innovators into the market rather than incurring the high costs of research, development, and testing. The Booz Allen & Hamilton study showed that only 30 percent of the new products studied were new to the firm. The other 70 percent represented significantly lower risk because they were additions to or improvements in existing product lines. Therefore, companies are gearing new product development more toward low-risk product modifications than high-risk innovations.

The New Product Development Process

The increased risks of new product development have put more pressure on marketing management to develop an effective process for introducing new products. An outline of the new product development process is presented in Figure 9-5.

The logical starting point for the process is the identification of new product opportunities. For example, a large food company identified a need for a low-calorie, nutritious breakfast food among a group of traditional consumers dissatisfied with instant products such as Carnation Slender. Once this opportunity was identified, various new product ideas were developed and screened according to the company's capabilities and the idea's ability to meet consumer needs (idea phase in Figure 9-5). The company considered three ideas: (1) a line of low-calorie omelettes, (2) an artificial bacon product, and (3) a line of low-calorie pancakes and waffles. It selected the artificial bacon product for further exploration because of technological feasibility and the fact that bacon was a

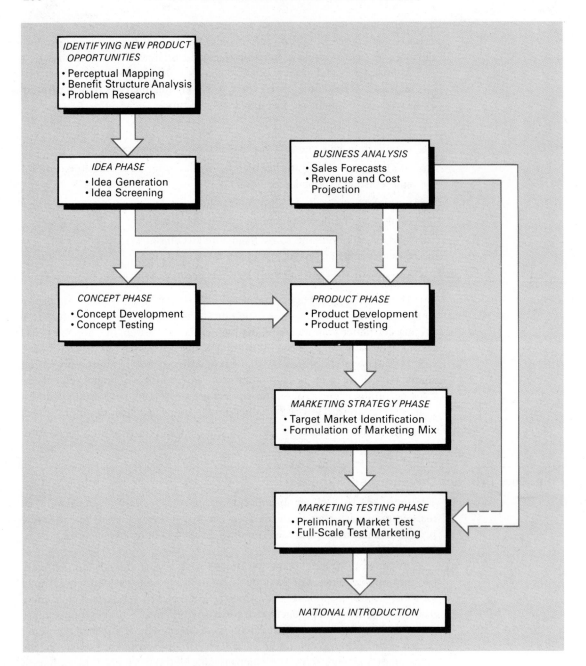

FIGURE 9-5
The new product development process

traditional product that appealed to the target segment. The idea was then translated into several alternative concept statements (concept phase). Each statement positioned the product differently. One emphasized less cholesterol and leanness; a second emphasized fewer calories; and a third the new and unique nature of the product. These concepts were tested on consumers and a positioning emphasizing fewer calories as a primary benefit and leanness as a secondary benefit was selected.

Concurrent with the concept phase, Research and Development investigated the feasibility of producing an artificial bacon product. A prototype of the product was developed and tested on consumers (the product phase in Figure 9-5). Certain problems with the product required reformulation by research and development. The product was then retested. Enough consumers expressed a willingness to buy the reformulated product to warrant a decision to go into test market. A marketing strategy was then developed. A price was established, advertising copy formulated, a media schedule selected, deal and coupon promotions determined, and distribution arranged. The market testing phase first involved a test of the product in a simulated supermarket setting and then introduction into four test cities for a nine-month period. Results of the test market warranted a national introduction.

At each phase of the new product development process, a go—no go decision was made on the basis of consumer responses to the concept and product. A sales forecast was made and a revenue and cost analysis completed (business analysis phase). As the product progressed from the idea phase to market testing, sales forecasts and revenue projections became more reliable. In the remainder of this section we will consider each of the phases in the new product development process.

IDENTIFICATION OF NEW PRODUCT OPPORTUNITIES

The steps cited in Chapter 2 to identify marketing opportunity must be followed in defining new product opportunities. Corporate goals must be considered, the market defined, consumer needs identified, the competitive and technological environment assessed, and company resources evaluated. These preliminary steps feed into the new product development process in Figure 9-5. Of particular importance in identifying new product opportunities is determining "gaps" in the market that might suggest unmet consumer needs. Three methods have been used to determine such gaps:

- perceptual mapping,
- benefit structure analysis, and
- problem research analysis.

Perceptual Mapping

Perceptual mapping is a means of positioning new concepts or existing products on a "map" based on consumer perceptions. A perceptual mapping analysis was conducted by a large food company to determine opportunities for new convenience products in both the snack and main meal markets. Results of the analysis are in Figure 9-6.

The first step in a perceptual mapping analysis is to determine what criteria consumers use in selecting snack foods. Focused group interviews were conducted to determine these criteria. The focused groups suggested eight main criteria for selecting convenience foods. The next step was a survey of 300 consumers. Consumers were asked (1) to rate the importance of each of the eight attributes in their brand selections, (2) to rate six leading brands (brands *A* to *F*) on

FIGURE 9-6
Perceptual mapping to identify new product opportunities

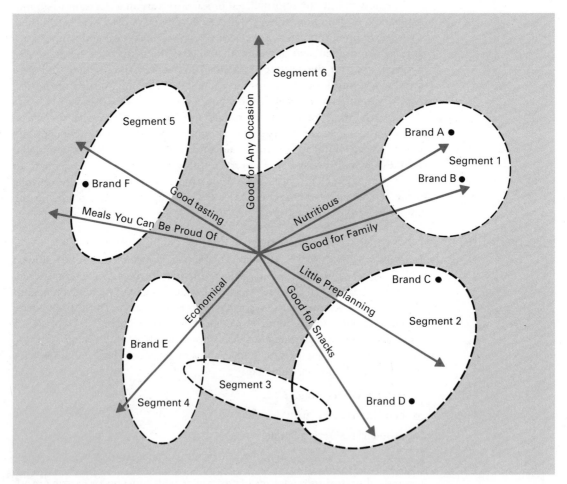

Source: Adapted from Henry Assael, "Evaluating New Product Concepts and Developing Early Predictions of Trial," *Marketing Review* (May 1975): 13.

each of these criteria, and (3) to rank their preferences for each brand. The data from the survey were then entered into a computer program that utilized three analytical techniques to produce the perceptual map in Figure 9-6: multidimensional scaling, property fitting, and cluster analysis. These three programs are described in Exhibit 9-1.

EXHIBIT 9-1
Analytical Techniques Used in Perceptual Mapping

Three programs were used to develop the perceptual map in Figure 9-6: (1) a multidimensional scaling program positioned products in the map, (2) a property fitting program then determined the position of the various attributes such as nutritious and economy, and (3) a clustering program identified the six consumer segments in the map.

Multidimensional Scaling (MDS)

Multidimensional scaling is a group of techniques that attempt to position objects (in this case brands) relative to each other based on some criterion (consumer preferences).[11] The brands in Figure 9-6 were positioned so that if two brands are close to each other it means that consumers who prefer one tend to prefer the other. Thus, consumers who prefer Brand A also tend to prefer Brand B. The analytical problem in MDS is to position brands in a small number of dimensions (two or three) to reflect consumer preferences with a minimum of error. For example, if many consumers prefer both Brands B and E, then the solution in Figure 9-6 would not be adequate. If a third dimension were to be added (that is, representing the brands in a box rather than a flat plane) then the six brands could be positioned to reflect the fact that some consumers prefer Brands A and B and others Brands B and E. The purpose of MDS as represented in Figure 9-6 is to position brands to reflect consumer preferences with a minimum of error.

Property Fitting (PRO-FIT)

Property Fitting is a program designed to position product attributes so they can be related to brands in a perceptual map.[12] For example, Brands A and B in Figure 9-6 are associated with nutrition and good for the family. The PRO-FIT program treats each attribute as a vector in perceptual space and determines where that vector should be positioned. The positioning of the nutritious vector is based on the fact that, on average, consumers rated Brand A highest on nutritious, Brand B next, Brand C third, and Brand D fourth. Similarly, the "good for meals" vector is so positioned because consumers rated Brand D highest in this criterion, Brand C second, Brand B third, and Brand A fourth. Figure 9-6 also suggests that nutritious and good for the family are closely related and are seen as the opposite of economical, and that good tasting is seen as the opposite of little preplanning.

Cluster Analysis

Once brands are positioned on the perceptual map, individual consumers are positioned to reflect their preferences. (Positioning both brands and consumers on the same map requires use of a joint-space multidimensional scaling program.) A consumer is positioned to be closest to the most preferred brand and furthest from the least preferred brand. If a consumer is positioned next to Brand A, it means that he or she prefers Brand A most, Brand B second, Brand C third, and Brand F least. Since 300 consumers were surveyed in the study, there would be 300 points on the map, each point representing a particular consumer. A cluster program is then used to group consumers by similarity in their preferences. As noted in Chapter 7, cluster analysis groups consumers into segments so that those who are most similar on a set of variables (e.g., preferences) will be in the same group. As seen in Figure 9-6, the cluster program produced six segments; segment 1 preferring Brands A and B, segment 2 Brands C and D, and so forth.

Figure 9-6 shows that brands *A* and *B* are associated with nutritious and good for the family, Brand *C* is positioned midway between nutritious and good for snacks, Brand *D* is seen as particularly good for snacks and involves little preplanning, Brand *E* is viewed as economical, and Brand *F* is rated a good-tasting product that one could be proud to serve. The circles in Figure 9-6 represent segments of consumers based on their ranking of preferences and rating by importance. The circle around *A* and *B* represents consumers who preferred these brands and identified them with nutrition and good for the family (segment 1). Segment 2 is a larger segment that preferred brands *C* and *D* and rated them "good for meals" and requiring little preplanning, and so forth.

The company was most interested in those circles not associated with existing brands. These represented segments of consumers with unmet needs. Two such gaps existed. One was the failure of any product to be perceived as good for any occasion (main meals, in-between meals, after dinner). A new convenience food positioned so that it could be eaten both as a snack and at mealtimes might best appeal to this segment. The second gap suggested the need for an economical snack, since consumers in segment 3 want both snacking and economy benefits and must buy separate brands to achieve each. Thus the perceptual mapping analysis identified two new product opportunities based on unmet consumer needs.

Benefit Structure Analysis

Benefit structure analysis focuses on the degree to which key benefits are being met.[13] The principle is relatively simple: determine the proportion of consumers who consider a key benefit to be important and the proportion who are receiving the benefit. The wider the gap between what people want and what they are getting, the greater the opportunity to position a product to meet this need. Using four of the criteria in Figure 9-6, a survey of consumers might produce the following results:

	Percentage of Consumers Who Consider the Benefit Very Important	Percentage of Consumers Who Consider Benefit Important and Feel Current Brand Is Fulfilling Benefit	Percentage of Consumers Who Consider Benefit Important and Feel Current Brand Is Not Fulfilling Benefits
Good for any occasion	52	18	34
Economical	76	46	30
Good tasting	81	66	15
Nutritious	83	69	14

These results suggest that even though "good for any occasion" is not the most important benefit, it is a benefit that is not being delivered by existing brands (that is, it has the greatest benefit deficiency). A new brand could therefore be positioned to meet this benefit.

Problem Research Analysis

Products can be positioned to solve problems as well as to deliver benefits. As noted in Chapter 6, a consumer who is not involved with a product frequently selects the brand that is least likely to cause problems — the plastic wrap that will not shred or stick together, the shaving cream that will not irritate skin, the moisturizer that will not make oily skin break out. Problem research analysis identifies problems such as these through focused group interviews.[14] Consumers are then surveyed to determine the magnitude of the problem and whether existing brands are viewed as solving it. If enough consumers see a problem and feel existing brands do not provide a solution, an opportunity exists for a new product.

THE IDEA PHASE

The idea phase is designed to generate many new ideas and then screen them down to a few alternatives for further consideration. One question that arises frequently is whether an opportunity should be defined first through research and the idea and concept developed after, or whether the idea and concept should be developed first and the need for the product determined after.

The marketing concept suggests that consumer needs should be determined first and new products positioned to meet these needs. In the majority of cases it is the reverse. A company will develop an idea or technology and will then determine if there is a need. For example, Monsanto developed a synthetic ribbon for industrial use. As an afterthought, it felt it might make a good substitute for grass. It designed a mounting, a padded base, and a drainage system and thus developed Astroturf.[15] Testing occurred after the idea was born and after the product was developed. Developing the idea and the product first does not violate the marketing concept. The company may have discovered the idea by accident (as with Astroturf) or developed a technology with several applications. As long as the company realizes the product must be tested to meet consumer needs and must be positioned to a defined target segment, it does not really matter whether the opportunity or idea phase comes first.

Idea Generation

New product ideas can come from many sources: research and development labs, management, marketing research, consumers, competitors, and miscellaneous other sources such as the sales force, consultants, and industrial publications.

Research and development

Many companies invest heavily to develop technologies that will provide them with a competitive edge. Investment in R&D is not restricted to high-technology companies. Philip Morris relies on its research and development group to offer ideas for brands.[16] Merit, a leading low-tar brand, originated with the R&D group. The marketing department then researched consumer acceptance.

Marketing research

Surveys of consumer needs and attitudes frequently provide new product ideas. One company has used focused group interviews with consumers to develop new product ideas. Focused group interviews uncovered the need for a cold remedy that was efficient, yet free of the antihistamine ingredients in many cold tablets. The result was Sine-Aid.[17] In another application focused groups identified the problem coffee drinkers had with a bitter aftertaste in many coffees. As a result, General Foods emphasized the development of a chicory based coffee.[18]

Consumers

Generally, consumers are not sources of new product ideas. Some companies do encourage ideas from consumers. For example, IBM seeks out software packages developed by their users through an Installed User Program (IUP).[19] IUP hears of promising programs developed outside the company, either from customers or from the IBM sales force, and sometimes acquires the right to these consumer-developed programs.

Competitors

Companies try to monitor the new product development of competitors. Products introduced into test markets by competitors quickly become known to companies. Competitors' products can then be purchased and tested in company labs before the competitive product is introduced nationally. Distributors, wholesalers, and sales representatives are also sources of information since they come into contact with many companies. Companies must make sure their executives are acting legally in acquiring information on competitive products.

Idea Generating Techniques

Some companies have decided they cannot rely solely on the sources cited above for new product ideas. These companies have introduced techniques to ensure that new product ideas will be generated internally. These techniques generally involve company personnel rather than consumers, competitors, or trade associations. A group of managers, scientists, production personnel, and any others involved in new product development come together and are given ground rules for idea generation. The most frequently used techniques have been:[20]

- **Brainstorming:** A specific problem area is defined. Ideas related to the problem are elicited in a freewheeling atmosphere. Wild ideas are encouraged. The more ideas the better. Criticism of ideas is discouraged.

- **Synectics:** This technique was developed because some researchers felt that ideas generated through brainstorming were not thorough enough. A very general problem area is defined, and through associations with familiar objects, ideas become more specific until new product ideas associated with the problem area are identified.

- **Morphological Analysis:** A problem is explicitly formulated and the parameters of the problem identified. All possible combinations of dimensions of the problem are examined and solutions generated. The feasibility of each solution is considered. This method was used to generate ideas for new types of jet engine. Six dimensions were identified in developing jet engines, producing 576 possible new product ideas. These were reduced to several viable new product alternatives.

Other techniques have been used as well, but they all:[21]

- establish openness and participation,
- encourage many and diverse ideas,
- allow participants to build on each other's ideas, and
- have discussion oriented to a problem.

Idea Screening

The 576 ideas for new types of jet engines cannot all be seriously considered by management. A screening procedure is required to identify a few viable alternatives that warrant concept development and testing. New product ideas can be screened by (1) managerial judgment and (2) consumer evaluations. Sometimes both methods are used in sequence.

Managerial judgment

Management frequently screens new product ideas by rating each idea on its potential for using existing financial resources, distribution capabilities, marketing know-how, and so on. The company is more likely to pursue an idea if it converges with company resources. Although useful, convergence with existing company resources is not a sufficient basis for evaluating new product ideas. Other factors such as market size, projected growth, potential for competitive entry, and cost effect must be evaluated. A more complete set of criteria used by the Owens-Corning Fiberglass Research Labs is presented in Table 9-1.[22] The variables used to judge new product ideas are listed down the side. Three criteria are used to judge each variable: (1) the importance of the factor, (2) how well the new product idea meets the requirements specified by the factor, and (3) the reliability of the information used in making the judgment. Using a ten-point scale, a 6-10-2 rating on market size means that a large market size is moderately important, that managers feel the new product idea has excellent market potential, but that there is little information to support this conclusion.

Owens-Corning does not rate every new product idea using Table 9-1. Usually, the process starts out with about 500 ideas, which are reduced through managerial discussion to perhaps ten viable ideas. These are then rated using Table 9-1 and perhaps one or two then become eligible for concept evaluation.

Consumer evaluations

Although managers may have good insight into the industry, they cannot always gauge what may appeal to consumers. Therefore, it would be logical for management to do an initial screening to weed out products the company cannot produce and then ask consumers to evaluate the ideas that are feasible. Mobil Chemical used this approach. It developed a large list of ideas and identified twenty viable new product prospects in six product categories: (1) storage bags, (2) trash bags, (3) pet products, (4) disposable white goods, (5) bug killers, and (6) convenience baking products. Consumers heard taped descriptions of each product idea and were asked to evaluate it against competition and to state their intention to buy the product. Ideas rated highest against competition and highest on intention to buy are selected for concept evaluation.

THE CONCEPT PHASE

The next series of steps in new product development require translating product ideas that survived screening into product concepts and then testing these concepts. Before considering concept development and testing, we should distinguish between a new product idea and a concept. A new product idea is a general description of a product. For example, one of the product ideas selected by Mobil for further testing was called Super Temp, a storage bag that can also be put into the oven in temperatures of up to 450°F. The product

TABLE 9-1

Management Rating System Used by Owens-Corning to Evaluate New Products

CRITERIA	IMPORTANCE OF CRITERION (TEN-POINT SCALE)	RATING OF PRODUCT IDEA (TEN-POINT SCALE)	RELIABILITY RATING (TEN-POINT SCALE)
General			
1. Value Added Potential			
2. Entry Options			
3. Regulatory			
4. Social Contribution			
5. Wall Street/Shareholders			
Product Section			
1. Key Attributes of Product			
2. Potential Product Differentiation			
3. Description of Competitive Products			
4. Product Variation Impact on Manufacturing Cost, Inventory, Etc.			
Marketing			
1. Market size			
2. Projected Growth			
3. Potential Owens-Corning Fiberglas Market Share			
4. Key Factors in Market Success			
5. Owens-Corning Fiberglas Customers			
6. Market Development Exposure			
Competitive Section			
1. Describe Competition			
2. Competition's Channels of Distribution			
3. Ability of Competition to React			
Technology Section			
1. Key Technologies			
2. Technology Development Exposure			
Organization			
1. Owens-Corning Divisional Fit			
2. Owens-Corning Resources Available			
3. Contact Program			
Manufacturing Fit			
1. Key Element in Manufacturing Success			
2. Competitive Manufacturing Processes, Advantages & Disadvantages			
3. Manufacturing Cost Breakdown Trends & Problems			
4. Manufacturing Exposure			
Financial Section			
1. Outline of Profit and Loss Statement			
2. Investment Required			

Source: John W. Muncaster, "Picking New Product Opportunities," *Research Management* (July 1981): 82.

concept represents the positioning of the product. The concept must state the key benefits of the product on the basis of the needs of the target segment. Alternative concepts could be developed for Super Temp depending on the benefit emphasized. One might focus on the economy of having a storage and cooking bag in one product, another might emphasize the convenience, a third the cooking advantages. The concept phase is meant to develop and test these alternative concepts so that the product can then be positioned appropriately for the target segment.

Concept Development

Translating a product idea into a concept requires developing several alternative positionings. For example, a large food company was considering introducing a line of casserole dishes that required only the addition of boiling water. The casserole would be ready in three minutes. Management developed four alternative positionings for the product (see Figure 9-7). Two of the concepts described the product as a casserole-for-one, emphasizing the convenience of a single serving. The other two described the product as a three-minute meal, emphasizing the quick preparation. Within this basic positioning there were variations in the secondary appeal. One concept positioned the product for active people; another positioned it for lunch; a third positioned it as good for noontime and nighttime; and a fourth focused on the advantage of not having to put it in the oven. The key requirement in the concept development phase is formulating alternative positionings such as those in Figure 9-7. Management must determine the combination of factors to introduce into a concept. The four concepts in Figure 9-7 could have been positioned in many more ways than those depicted; for example, a three-minute hot meal that is perfect for people on the go at any time of the day. Two techniques have been used to help marketers select the combination of product features to introduce into a concept: conjoint analysis and trade-off analysis. These are described in Exhibit 9-2.

Concept Testing

The concept development phase is designed to formulate concepts and to narrow down the number of concepts to be tested. Once the concepts are screened to a manageable few, they will then be tested on consumers to.

1. select the best positioning for the product among the alternative concepts,
2. identify the target group (consumers who say they are most likely to buy),
3. determine the concept's position relative to competitive brands, and
4. on this basis develop sales and revenue estimates and determine whether prototype production is warranted so that an actual product can be tested.

1 INTRODUCING CASSEROLE-FOR-ONE
THE 3-MINUTE HOT MEAL
FOR PEOPLE ON-THE-GO

New Casserole-for-One is a delicious 3-minute meal that you make and eat right in its own bowl. Each is made with the finest noodle, meat, and vegetable ingredients, then blended with home-style sauces. The result is an instant meal that tastes so good everyone will think you made it from scratch.

Casserole-for-One offers you the perfect hot meal that tastes homemade yet is ready in minutes when you're too busy to cook and clean up. Away from home, it's the perfect carry-along—to work, play, or on family outings.

New Casserole-for-One comes in a variety of flavors everyone will love:

Noodles with beef and onions in a rich tomato sauce
Noodles with chicken and mushrooms in a light cream sauce
Noodles with ham and peas in a mild cheese sauce
Noodles with tuna and celery in a special seafood sauce

2 INTRODUCING CASSEROLE-FOR-ONE
THE 3-MINUTE MEAL
THAT'S THE PERFECT HOT LUNCH

New Casserole-for-One is a delicious 3-minute meal that you make and eat right in its own bowl. Each is made with the finest noodle, meat and vegetable ingredients, then blended with home-style sauces. The result is an instant meal that tastes so good everyone will think you made it from scratch.

Casserole-for-One offers you the perfect lunch for several reasons. It's a complete hot meal. It's quick and easy, yet actually tastes homemade. It's just the right amount for one person. And it's far more satisfying and more substantial than a bowl of soup or a salad.

New Casserole-for-One comes in a variety of flavors everyone will love:

Noodles with beef and onions in a rich tomato sauce
Noodles with chicken and mushrooms in a light cream sauce
Noodles with ham and peas in a mild cheese sauce
Noodles with tuna and celery in a special seafood sauce

3 INTRODUCING 3-MINUTE MEAL
THE HOT MEAL FOR ONE
THAT'S PERFECT—NOONTIME & NIGHTTIME

New 3-Minute Meal is a delicious single-serving meal that you make and eat right in its own bowl. Each is made with the finest noodle, meat and vegetable ingredients, then blended with home-style sauces. The result is an instant meal that tastes so good, everyone will think you made it from scratch.

3-Minute Meal offers you a quick and easy meal that's perfect almost anytime. It's great for lunch because it's hot, filling, and just the right amount for one person. It's also great for those light or late evening meals when you want something satisfying but not too heavy. No matter when you eat it, 3-Minute Meal offers you a great homemade taste in an instant.

New 3-Minute Meal comes in a variety of flavors everyone will love:

Noodles with beef and onions in a rich tomato sauce
Noodles with chicken and mushrooms in a light cream sauce
Noodles with ham and peas in a mild cheese sauce
Noodles with tuna and celery in a special seafood sauce

4 INTRODUCING 3-MINUTE MEAL
THE HOT MEAL FOR ONE
THAT COOKS ITSELF IN ITS OWN BOWL

New 3-Minute Meal is a delicious single-serving meal that you make and eat right in its own bowl. Each is made with the finest noodle, meat and vegetable ingredients, then blended with home-style sauces. The result is an instant meal that tastes so good everyone will think you made it from scratch.

New 3-Minute Meal comes in a variety of tempting flavors:

Noodles with beef and onions in a rich tomato sauce
Noodles with chicken and mushrooms in a light cream sauce
Noodles with ham and peas in a mild cheese sauce
Noodles with tuna and celery in a special seafood sauce

FIGURE 9-7
Four alternative concept positionings for a new casserole

EXHIBIT 9-2
Methods for Developing Product Concepts Based on Consumer Preferences

A requirement in developing a product concept and eventually a product is determining the combination of product features to include. Two techniques have been used to provide consumer input in determining the best features to include in a product: conjoint measurement[23] and trade-off analysis.[24] Both techniques determine the optimal set of product features based on consumer preferences.

Conjoint Measurement

Consider the casserole dishes in Figure 9-7. The problem is what factors to include in the concept and the final product positioning. The company has the following options:

- call the brand "Three-Minute Meal" or "Casserole for One"; (two alternative attributes),
- position it for working women, for children, or for people on the go (three alternative attributes),
- position it as perfect for lunch, for dinner, or for both occasions (three alternative attributes),
- emphasize the convenience of either quick serving or not having to put it in the oven (two alternatives),
- emphasize a variety of flavors or focus on one flavor (two alternatives).

These five factors produce seventy-two possible concepts ($2 \times 3 \times 3 \times 2 \times 2$ attributes). Obviously, the marketer cannot ask a consumer to rate seventy-two different concepts. A smaller set of concepts will be rated, say twelve, as follows:

	COMBINATIONS OF PRODUCT FEATURES IN CONCEPTS				
Concept	Brand Name	Occasion	Person Positioning	Convenience Positioning	Flavor
1	Casserole for One	Lunch	Working Wife	Quick Serving	Variety
2	Casserole for One	Dinner	Child	No Oven	Variety
3	Casserole for One	Both	On the Go	Quick Serving	Variety
4	Casserole for One	Lunch	Child	No Oven	Single
5	Casserole for One	Dinner	On the Go	Quick Serving	Single
6	Casserole for One	Both	Working Wife	No Oven	Single
7	Three Minute Meal	Lunch	Working Wife	Quick Serving	Variety
8	Three Minute Meal	Dinner	Child	No Oven	Variety
9	Three Minute Meal	Both	On the Go	Quick Serving	Variety
10	Three Minute Meal	Lunch	On the Go	No Oven	Single
11	Three Minute Meal	Dinner	On the Go	Quick Serving	Single
12	Three Minute Meal	Both	Working Wife	No Oven	Single

Each of the twelve concepts is placed on a card and consumers are asked to order the cards by their preferences from most to least preferred. The preference ratings for consumers in the sample are entered into the **conjoint measurement program.** Even though only twelve of the possible seventy-two concepts were rated, the program extrapolates the results to all seventy-two concepts by producing a utility score for each attribute. The utility scores might be as follows (on a scale from zero to one):

Brand Name		*Person Positioning*		*Flavorings*	
Casserole for One	.3	Working Woman	.2	Variety	.7
Three Minute Meal	.4	Child	.8	Single	.2
		On the Go	.1		

Occasion		*Convenience Positioning*	
Lunch	.9		
Dinner	.2	Quick Serving	.5
Both	.3	No Oven Required	.5

Based on these utility scores, the preferences for any combination of attributes can be extrapolated.

These results demonstrate that the consumer did not have a strong preference for either brand name or for either convenience positioning. But consumers did prefer the product as a lunchtime meal for children that emphasizes a variety of flavors. Notice that these combinations of attributes were not actually tested, but that the conjoint measurement program identified them as being the optimal positioning based on the utility consumers placed on each feature.

Trade-Off Analysis

Trade-off analysis is a useful alternative to conjoint measurement when the consumer is asked to choose between mutually exclusive product features. Table 8-5 in the previous chapter is an example of trade-off analysis. Investors are asked to choose either lower commission rates and fewer services or higher commission rates and more services. Table 8-5 presents four price and four service alternatives. Investors are asked to rate their preference for each of the combinations from one to sixteen. Based on these ratings, a utility score is determined for each feature — in this case, price and service. On this basis, the researcher can determine whether the investor places more emphasis on price, on service, or falls somewhere in between. This analysis would help a brokerage firm decide whether to maintain or increase the commission rates and offer more services, or to reduce commission rates and offer fewer services. It also indicates the optimal rate and service level (e.g., would consumers prefer moderately lower rates, say a 10 percent reduction, if the firm were to eliminate investment counselling services).

A good example of a concept test is a large auto manufacturer's study of 1000 car owners in one of their foreign markets. The purpose was to determine the best positioning for new car models relative to competitive makes and to define the characteristics of the target segment for each prospective entry.

Concept testing in the automobile market is particularly important because the investment required to produce a test model is substantial. Three new economy-car concepts were presented to consumers (concepts *S*, *T* and *U*) as well as four existing makes. Concept *S* was designed to compete with the Renault R-12 and the VW Brazilia, Concept *U* with the R-12, and Concept *T* with the Datsun 1600. The VW Beetle was included in the analysis as a leading economy car at the time. Respondents were given specifications and positioning statements for each concept and existing make and were asked to rank their preference for each of the seven cars. The data were analyzed in a multidimensional scaling program. Results are presented in Figure 9-8.

FIGURE 9-8
Testing alternative economy car concepts

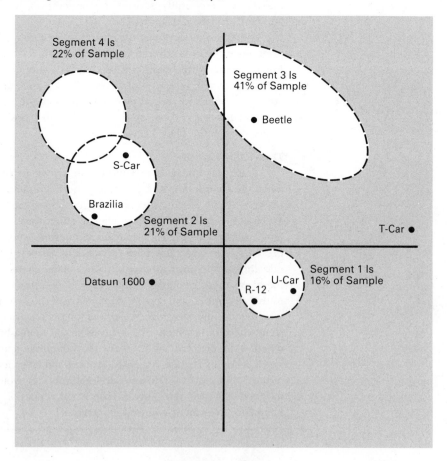

Based on the analysis the *T* car was eliminated because few consumers preferred it. The *U* car was also eliminated because of the small size of segment 1, even though the concept was positioned as intended against the R-12. The *S* car was a viable prospect because (1) it was positioned well against one of the market leaders (the Brazilia) and (2) it straddled two segments representing 43 percent of all economy-car prospects. The differences between segments 2 and 4 suggested two separate positionings to each segment; one describing the technical specifications of the *S* car, the other emphasizing styling and comfort. From the concept test, the company:

- identified the best potential entry into the market,
- evaluated positioning strategies relative to existing makes,
- estimated the size and characteristics of target segments for prospective entries, and
- assessed whether preliminary sales and revenue estimates for the prospective entry warranted prototype production.

THE PRODUCT PHASE

The product phase requires translating the concept into a physical product (product development) and testing the product to determine consumer acceptance.

Product Development

Product specifications based on the concept test are generally submitted to Research and Development so that prototypes of the product will be developed. One of the most difficult tasks in new product development is translating consumer preferences into physical product attributes. Several years ago, Liggett and Myers attempted to translate consumer preferences into cigarette blends. After hundreds of tests they found few physical properties that could be related to typical consumer benefits such as smoothness, lightness, and absence of harsh aftertaste. General Foods successfully translated consumer preferences for a "bold, vigorous, deep tasting coffee" into several test blends, but only after its R&D labs spent many months and dollars working to develop a corresponding taste.[25] Even then the product was too expensive, and attempts to make it cost/effective compromised its flavor, leading the company to withdraw the brand.

These experiences suggest the difficulty of a one-to-one translation from concept to physical product. One of the problems in this respect is lack of integration between R&D and marketing. R&D personnel tend to prefer standard components with longer lead time for development. Marketing would prefer to see greater variety in response to consumer needs with a shorter lead time to get the product on the market.[26] These differing perspectives make it all the more difficult to translate consumer preferences in concept tests into products.

Product Testing

Once a prototype is ready, it will be tested to determine consumer acceptance. Product tests can be conducted (1) in a controlled laboratory situation, (2) in shopping centers and malls, or (3) in the home.

Type of product tests

Lab tests are sometimes necessary to control the situation in which the product is being used. For example, in conducting a taste test, it may be desirable to have a respondent pause between tasting several formulations of a product to ensure no decrease in taste discrimination. Consumers can also be recruited in shopping centers and malls. Many research companies invite consumers into trailer facilities stationed in malls and shopping centers for product testing. This procedure permits careful screening of respondents and also allows for control of test conditions. Products can also be given to consumers to be used in the home. In-home tests are the most realistic since consumption takes place in a natural setting. They also allow for consumers to use the product over time and evaluate it against their regular brand. But the researcher has little control over the way the product is used.

The procedures required of consumers in product-use tests are similar to those in concept tests: ranking of preferences for the test product and competitive brands; rating of the test product on key evaluative criteria such as economy, convenience, taste; and stating intention to buy. The basic difference is that the consumer is being exposed to the actual product rather than an idea. Because of the greater realism in product use tests, sales and revenue forecasts based on intentions to buy are likely to be more reliable than estimates from the concept test.

The product-concept fit

A key issue in product testing is the degree to which the benefits described in the concept are actually delivered once the consumer uses the product. The **product-concept fit** can be determined by comparing results of the concept and product tests. For example, in testing an artificial bacon product, the company developed a perceptual map positioning the bacon concept against three leading brands. The dots in Figure 9-9 show the position of the concept and three existing brands on four key attributes. The concept was seen as having fewer calories and as being more convenient. It did not have any particular advantage over existing brands on nutrition and appetizing.

After the concept test, the artificial bacon product was given to those consumers who said they would definitely buy the concept. The arrows in Figure 9-9 show the position of the artificial bacon product after consumers used it. The perception of the concept deteriorates after it is used. It is rated more negatively on both low calories and nutrition. Consumers expected more of these key benefits because of the concept description than they received. The right side of Figure 9-9 shows that there was no change in perceptions

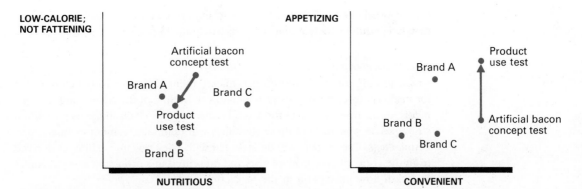

FIGURE 9-9
Determining the concept-product fit for an artificial bacon product

of the convenience of the new product, and consumers saw the products as more appetizing in use than they were led to believe by the concept description.

Apparently, the concept description conveyed the impression of a nutritious but not particularly appetizing product. When consumers used the product, they found it fattier but more tasty than expected. Since the product was meant to be positioned as nonfattening, the in-home test strongly suggested further product modification. The product was sent back to R&D, and was modified and retested. Further tests of the reformulated product showed it was rated acceptable on "low calorie." Sales and revenue projections based on the last in-home product use tests suggested that introduction into test markets was warranted.

MARKETING STRATEGY PHASE

Once the product is developed and tested, management must formulate an integrated marketing strategy to introduce it.

Target Market Identification

Strategy formulation requires identifying the target market for the product. In the opportunity identification phase, the target is identified by benefit segmentation; for example, identifying a nutrition-oriented segment as a target for the low-fat artificial bacon product. In the marketing strategy phase, targets are identified by behavioral segmentation. The most important behavioral criterion is intention to buy. The target is defined as those consumers who say they will definitely buy the new product. The demographic, life-style, and product use characteristics of those who intend to buy will be determined. For example, consumers who say they will definitely buy the artificial bacon product might be upwardly mobile, active, young adults who are concerned with fitness. This profile would guide management in the type of advertising strategy (show active, successful, young people), the main appeals in the advertisement (a low-fat breakfast food that is tasty), and media selection (magazines directed to young adults and working women; late-hour TV shows).

The Marketing Mix

Given the identification of a target, management will have to develop a plan for market introduction. This plan includes an outline of the advertising strategy, media, distribution and sales force requirements, price level, and sales promotion strategies. Formulation of these strategies will help management estimate marketing costs. These costs will be included with sales revenue estimates derived from the concept and product tests and presented in a profit and loss statement and cash flow projection in the marketing plan.

The components of the marketing mix will be considered in Chapters 10–17. Particularly important in the formulation of strategy for the new product is the selection of the brand name and the package.

Brand name selection

The brand name should convey product benefits (Pampers disposable diapers, Right Guard deodorant, Easy-Off oven cleaner). This is not always feasible. For example, the decay-prevention properties of Crest or the packaging advantages or Pringle's potato chips could not be conveyed descriptively in a brand name. In such cases the company will formulate many names and determine which has the most positive connotation. At least three methods have been used to select brand names: managerial judgment, consumer name tests, and focused group interviews.

The idea for the name Walkman was developed by a *management team* at Sony.[27] At first several names such as "Hot-Line" and "Sound-About" were discussed and rejected because the team felt they would not appeal to consumers. Another idea, "Stereo Walkie," had to be rejected because a competitor, Toshiba, had already registered the name "Walky." But the team liked the name "Walk," particularly a logotype with two legs sticking out from the bottom of the A in "walk" that was developed by the ad agency. Someone suggested that the "Walk" be combined with "Man" and in the final stages of discussion, the team selected this name.

The danger in using a management team to select a brand name is that the name may be rejected by consumers well into the strategy development phase. It would be safer to select several alternatives and *test them on consumers*. Before selecting the name Gainesburgers, General Foods tested several alternatives such as Dog Burgers, Dog Patties, Prime Burgers, and Prime Patties. Consumers thought the burger conveyed a hearty image, but there were problems in using Dog and Prime as a prefix. The brand name of the existing dog line — Gaines — was then suggested as a prefix, was tested on consumers, and received positive ratings.[28]

A third approach to name selection is to use *focused group interviews* to identify key benefits and to develop names accordingly. One research company selects many names based on factors such as memorability, innovativeness, and interest. The list is reduced by judgment, and then consumers are paid to give their reaction to each name.[29] Nestlé selected Taster's Choice as the name of its first freeze-dried coffee because focused groups showed that consumers felt regular instant coffee did not provide the taste benefits of ground roast coffees.

Package development

Another key consideration early in the marketing strategy phase is package development. In addition to providing convenience, protection, and ease of use packaging should serve these strategic objectives:

- *Provide a competitive edge for an otherwise standardized product category.* Bleach is a standardized product, but Clorox could establish product differentiation by a distinctive package and by packaging improvements over time, particularly the introduction of a safer plastic bottle.

- *Reinforce a positive brand image.* Miller-Morton, producers of Chapstick, successfully extended Chapstick's positive image into lipstick and then into facial makeup and powder by introducing the Lip Quencher, Face Quencher, and Skin Quencher lines. Packaging was crucial. A single look for the Quencher line was developed with a silver and black carded package.[30] The packaging was meant to establish a link to Chapstick and to convey the key moisturizing benefit of the line. The president of the company cited the importance of packaging in introducing the Quencher line: "With all due respect to advertising, packaging is probably more important. Packaging is probably remembered more. . . . It gives the product personality."[31]

- *Establish an association with product benefits.* Hershey did not advertise for many years because of a distinctive package that had instant recognition. Widespread distribution and the reminder effect of the package was the substitute for advertising.

- *Provide consumers with information on ingredients and size.* Many companies provide such information voluntarily. But inadequate labeling of some food products led the Food and Drug Administration to require more information on packages in rules formulated in 1975.

MARKET TESTING PHASE

Before a new product can be introduced, management needs information on consumer reactions to the product in a realistic market setting. Concept and product tests ask consumers "What if" questions — namely, whether they will buy if the product is introduced. In market testing, the product is actually introduced in selected areas, and the consumer has an opportunity to buy. Information on consumer purchases is a much more reliable basis for predicting sales and revenues than information on consumer intentions.

There are several purposes in market testing:

■ *To determine consumer reactions in a realistic market environment.* Advertising and sales promotions for the product are run in the market(s) used for testing. The product is distributed and available in stores. Consumers are exposed to the product in a realistic in-store environment in which they can compare it to competitive brands.

■ *To evaluate marketing strategy before national introduction.* The market test is likely to run for a period of time, permitting evaluation of the effectiveness of advertising, media, sales promotion, distribution, and pricing strategies.

■ *To project sales and revenues to the national market from test market areas.* Some market tests are designed to select areas representative of the national market. Sales results are then projected to the national level to estimate revenues and permit cash flow projections.

■ *To introduce the product in test areas as a stepping stone to national introduction.* Products are sometimes introduced into test areas with the intention of expanding distribution on a step-by-step basis if results in test markets are positive. Such rollouts reduce the risk of a quick national introduction, but increase the risk of competitive duplication.

Preliminary Market Tests

There are two types of market test; preliminary and full-scale. Until about 1970 companies generally went from product testing to either full-scale test markets or national introduction without any market tests. Full-scale test markets required introducing the product into two to four cities or areas for an extended period of time (six months to a year). Cities or areas were selected to produce reliable projections of national sales. An extended period of time was required to estimate the rate of repeat purchases as well as the initial trial rate.

Many companies felt that test marketing was a costly and risky step in new product development. Costs in excess of $1 million for full-scale test markets, errors in projecting sales at the national level, and the opportunity for competition to duplicate the product because of the extended time required for testing caused some companies to seek alternative procedures. Some companies decided to forego test marketing. For example, Philip Morris avoids introducing cigarette brands into test markets and prefers to go from taste tests to national distribution to discourage competitive duplication.[32] Other companies began using newly developed market testing techniques that were less costly and quicker than full-scale test markets. These techniques, called preliminary market tests, are sometimes used instead of or as a lead-in to full-scale test marketing. When they have been used as a lead-in to full-scale testing, these techniques have reduced the cost and time required for test marketing, thus decreasing the risk of competitive entry. Three types of preliminary market test are used frequently: (1) **controlled market tests**, (2) **simulated market tests**, and (3) **sales wave experiments.**

Controlled market tests

In controlled market tests, one or two test cities are selected and the product is distributed to stores on a controlled basis. A research organization ensures proper distribution, and in-store promotions are implemented. The research organization then tracks sales in the stores and reports results back to the client. In full-scale test markets, the company ships the product directly to stores in the area with little control over in-store handling.

Controlled market tests (sometimes called minimarket tests) are quicker and less expensive than full-scale test markets. They also provide the facility for testing specific components of the marketing mix. For example, two or three matched sets of stores might be selected in a market and variations in price or in-store promotions introduced in each set of stores. In one experiment a heavier advertising campaign was tested in one city and a lighter campaign in another. Two sets of stores were selected in each city and the product sold with and without in-store pricing promotions in each set of stores. Since distribution was controlled, the company could regulate the in-store promotions. The results showed that lower advertising expenditures in combination with in-store price promotions produced the greatest profits.

Simulated market tests

Several research firms have established experimental supermarket facilities in which new products are introduced. Consumers are given a small amount of money and invited to shop in the store. They are told they may buy any brand in the product category being tested, or they may keep the money. Before entering the store they are asked several questions about brand preferences and attitudes and are then shown a series of commercials for the test brand and competitive brands. After shopping, the consumers are asked their reasons for buying a brand or for not buying at all. After enough time has passed to use the product, consumers are interviewed by phone to determine what brand they intend to buy next and are given an opportunity to buy the new product.

The method has the advantage of measuring initial trial in the supermarket and subsequent repeat purchase rates. Data on trial and repeat purchases have been used in models designed to predict market share with some accuracy.[33] The method is also speedy and does not expose the product to competition as would occur if the product were introduced in actual stores.

Sales wave experiments

Sales wave experiments require the new product to be placed in the home. Consumers are asked to use the product and evaluate it as in the typical in-home product use test. They are then given a chance to buy the new product or competitive products at reduced prices. Consumers may be allowed to repurchase up to six times (six sales waves). As with simulated test markets, sales waves can be conducted inexpensively and quickly. They can also be implemented before final product and packaging decisions have been made. Therefore they can be run early in the market testing phase. There are several disadvantages: (1) consumers may be biased by repeated contacts; (2) sales waves do not test advertising and promotional strategies; and (3) they are conducted in artificial conditions. As with simulated supermarket tests, they tend to be used to support rather than replace full-scale test markets.

Full-Scale Test Marketing

Procedures for test marketing

A full-scale **test market** is a dress rehearsal for a national introduction. Two or more cities are selected, and a full advertising campaign and promotional program are introduced. The company's sales force will distribute the product and make sure stores are adequately stocked. Sales will then be measured by auditing store inventory at the retail level or warehouse withdrawals at the wholesale level. Test markets must be long enough to determine the repurchase rate for the product. For example, a test for aftershave lotion would have to be longer than a test for toothpaste because the former is purchased less frequently. Yet the length of test markets must be shortened if competitors threaten to enter the market quickly.

Test markets must also be projectable to the national market if results are to be used to estimate sales. Selection of test cities is therefore crucial. Table 9-2 presents a worksheet used to select test cities. St. Louis is used as an example. The first criterion is projectability. St. Louis represents 1.29 percent of United States households. Its demographic characteristics are average (an index of 100 is average in Table 9-2), with the exception that Spanish-American households are grossly underrepresented. In addition, media provide good coverage in the area. The second factor in test market selection in Table 9-2 is control. The test city should be sufficiently isolated so there is no "spill-in" of advertising from other major markets or "spill-out" of advertising for the new product into markets where the product is not being tested. Market share for competitive brands should also be close to the national average. The third factor in Table 9-2 is measurement. The test area should have facilities to measure sales results through warehouse withdrawals, store audits, scanner data, or consumer surveys. The final consideration in test market selection is cost. In summary, test markets should be:

- long enough to account for the repurchase rate,
- short enough to avoid the risk of competitive duplication,
- projectable to the national market,

TABLE 9-2
Criteria for Selecting Test Markets

	1 ST. LOUIS	2	3
I. Projectability			
1. Market Size _____ % of U.S. households in market	1.29		
2. Demographic representations: Index U.S. = 100			
Age — head of household: Under 35	94		
35–54	100		
55 and over	105		
Disposable income: 0–$14,999	93		
$15,000 and over	107		
Ethnic composition: Spanish-American	17		
Non-white	100		
Effective buying/income/household in dollars	$17,623		
3. Media availability			
Number of TV stations	6		
% Cable penetration	12		
Number of metro radio stations required for 50%			
share of adult listeners	5		
Number of daily newspapers in market	8		
II. Control			
1. Media isolation			
% spill-in	2%		
% spill-out	5%		
1. Competitive balance:			
(market share of major competitors indexed to			
national/regional)			
1.			
2.			
3.			
4.			
III. Measurement	Research Firms		
Availability of research services:			
Warehouse withdrawals	SAMI		
Audits	Nielsen		
Scanner item movement	TRIM		
Mail diary panel	Custom		
Scanner consumer panels	TRIM/MSA		
IV. Cost			
Estimated cost for the period of the test	$_____		

Source: Adapted from "Improve Test Market Selection With These Rules of Thumb," *Marketing News*, January 22, 1982, Section 1, p. 8.

■ sufficiently isolated to avoid contamination from other markets, and

■ equipped with research facilities to measure sales results.

Risks of full-scale test marketing

In addition to being costly, full-scale test marketing is risky because competitors might purposely affect results. Competitors might slash prices, increase their advertising or couponing, and give out free samples to steal potential customers from the new product. Ralston Purina has the reputation of finding out where a new competitive product is being test marketed and then handing out thousands of coupons for free bags of Purina Dog Chow.[34] Competitors may also send individuals to buy large quantities of the test product to give the impression the market is greater than it actually is. When American Can test marketed a premoistened toilet paper, consumers ignored it but competitors bought it up in such quantity that the company considered introducing it nationally.[35]

The greatest risk in test marketing is that of competitive entry. Competitors can quickly obtain a product in test market and send it to their labs for analysis. Helene Curtis successfully test marketed a baking soda–based deodorant called Arm-in-Arm only to find that Arm and Hammer had beat it to national introduction with a similar product with no test marketing.[36] These risks have spurred the use of preliminary test market methods, particularly controlled market tests, as substitutes for full-scale test markets.

NATIONAL INTRODUCTION

If sales forecasts derived from the market tests are high enough, the company will introduce the brand nationally. The following schedule would be typical for the national introduction of a consumer packaged good:

Management approval	November 1984
Begin production for test market	February 1985
Test market	April 1985–December 1985
Approval for national introduction	January 1986
Production for national introduction	February 1986
National distribution begins	March 1986
Trade release and publicity	April 1986
Start of national advertising	May 1986

The national introduction is the most crucial decision for the company since it involves a substantial investment in marketing effort and possibly new plant facilities. A "go" decision requires the company to choose between a region-by-region rollout or an immediate national introduction. Most companies choose a rollout to minimize risk. The regions first selected are those in which competition is weakest. Procter and Gamble rolled out Folgers coffee from its strong regional base in the West across the center of the country. The East coast was the last region in which the brand was introduced because General Foods' Maxwell House brands were strongest in the East.

Another important consideration in the national introduction is integration of the marketing strategy components. In 1981 Gillette introduced Aapri, a facial scrub meant to compete with Noxzema, Ponds, and Oil of Olay. A well-integrated marketing plan was implemented. In June 1981 network TV advertising was begun.[37] In August, full-color two-page ads appeared in national magazines. In September 15 million samples were distributed by mail. Retail trade support in the form of early-buy allowances and cooperative advertising was provided during this period to ensure adequate stocks.

BUSINESS ANALYSIS

Sales forecasts and revenue and cost estimates must be developed at frequent intervals in new product development. This requirement is illustrated in Figure 9-5 by the dotted line, indicating revenue and cost estimates in the product and market testing phases. As the product is developed and tested, sales forecasts and cost estimates become more reliable. The final estimates will be developed after market testing and incorporated into the marketing plan for national introduction.

Sales Forecasts

Sales are first projected on the basis of intentions to buy in the concept and product tests. They are then based on actual behavior in the market testing phase. When forecasts are based on actual behavior, they become more reliable and serve three important purposes:

1. They provide a more definite basis for determining whether the product should be introduced nationally.

2. They permit more specific projections of revenues and costs.

3. They provide a basis for refining marketing strategy.

Sales forecasts based on full-scale test markets

Test markets are used both to project and to forecast sales. A sales projection is a sales estimate to a broader population (the national market) from a sample (the test market). In Table 9-2 national sales would be projected from results in St. Louis and two other test cities. Test markets are also used to forecast what future sales will be. Most forecasting methods attempt to predict market share and then estimate future sales from share forecasts. Market share predictions are based on estimates of the new product's (1) initial trial rate and (2) repeat purchase rate. A brand will eventually attain a market share based on:[38]

$$MS_{it} = p_{it}\, r_{it}\, b_i,$$

where

$\quad MS_{it}$ = market share for brand i in time t,
$\quad\quad p_{it}$ = the ultimate trial rate of the brand in time t,
$\quad\quad r_{it}$ = the ultimate repeat purchase rate of the brand in time t, and
$\quad\quad b_i$ = a buying rate index for the brand, where an index of one
$\quad\quad\quad$ is an average for the product category.

For example, assume that from test market results management estimates that 40 percent of potential buyers will try brand i and that 20 percent of these triers will be repeat purchasers. Further, buyers tend to be heavy users, so that the buying rate index is estimated at 1.2 (that is, buyers of the brand purchase 20 percent more units in a shopping trip than the average consumer). The predicted market share is 8.6 percent (trial rate of 40 percent times repeat rate of 20 percent times buying index of 1.2).

If the test market is run long enough, management can obtain a good estimate of the ultimate trial and repeat rate. But the costs of long test markets have led researchers to use results from preliminary market tests to forecast market share.

Sales forecasts based on preliminary market tests

Various forecasting methods have been developed to estimate market share and then sales based on preliminary market tests, particularly simulated market tests. The problem in using simulated market tests is in estimating repeat purchases since consumers do not have an opportunity to repurchase over time. One technique called ASSESSOR estimates a consumer's probability of repurchasing the test brand based on the strength of preference for the new brand after having tried it.[39] The stronger the preference for the new brand relative to other brands in the market, the greater the probability of repurchasing. Once repeat purchases have been estimated, market share can be predicted since the trial rate of consumers going through the simulated store is known. Models such as ASSESSOR have sometimes proven to be as accurate as test market results in forecasting market share and sales, yet at significantly less cost.[40]

Changes in Sales and Cost Estimates

Sales and cost estimates will change during new product development as forecasts become more reliable. Such changes are particularly likely during the market testing phase since the company is first testing its marketing strategy. Changes in marketing strategy are likely to affect sales and cost estimates.

For example, results from concept tests for the artificial bacon product suggested two separate advertising campaigns: one directed to young adults who emphasized fitness and nutrition, and a second directed to an older segment who emphasized low cholesterol content and health benefits. Separate campaigns were introduced in one test city and a combined campaign was introduced in another. The market test showed that the separate campaigns produced only marginally greater sales and were not worth the additional costs.

The new strategy prompted a reformulation of the sales forecast and a reestimation of costs. Costs for advertising would be lower, but in-store promotional costs might be higher because of the costs of coupons to obtain initial trial.

Industrial New Product Development

New product development is no different for industrial products than for consumer goods. Figure 9-5 applies to both. In fact, many of the findings on the factors related to product success and failure were derived from industrial product experiences. In the Booz Allen & Hamilton study of seventy firms, 60 percent were industrial manufacturers and 40 percent were consumer goods manufacturers split between durables and nondurables.[41]

What does differ in industrial new product development is the nature of R&D and the relative emphasis on product and market tests. Industrial goods firms rely more heavily on research and development to develop new product ideas and technologies. A good example is Elscint, an Israeli firm that is a leader in medical technology. Elscint developed the CAT-scan, a device that is likely to replace X-ray machines. It has taken the lead in developing nuclear medicine. Its objectives are to "develop a new generation of nuclear medical instruments that will enable Elscint to assume technical leadership in the field."[42]

Devices such as the CAT-scan and radiation monitors are unlikely to be market tested. It would be very expensive to introduce such products to limited markets for trial. Such tests would also invite competition because of the high technology involved. Industrial companies, particularly high technology companies, emphasize use tests more than market tests. They will first develop a concept of the product and test it on customers with purchase influence. They will then develop prototypes if the concept tests warrant the expenditure. Prototypes will be given to a small group of customers to be used for a limited time either at their location or at the company's plant site. Trade shows are frequently used to test new products. Thus, Elscint probably developed a few prototypes of the CAT-scanner and gave it to several local hospitals to try it out.

Some industrial companies use test markets on a limited basis, especially if the risks are high. They may produce a limited supply of the product and give it to the sales force to sell in specific markets. But the investment required in limited production and the risk of competitive entry generally discourages industrial firms from using test markets.

Summary

New product development is essential to the marketing firm because it is closely linked to profitability. Companies cannot always rely on existing products for sustained growth. Further, the ratio of new product success has been fairly high once a product is introduced, particularly if it is the first brand on the market. Companies have also experienced cost efficiencies by gaining experience in developing and marketing new products.

Emphasis on new product development must be balanced by a recognition of the risks. New product failures frequently cost millions of dollars. Further, over 80 percent of new product ideas that are developed and tested do not reach the market. Such development and testing is costly to the firm. Overall, the risks of new product development are likely to increase in the coming years, causing some companies to seek alternatives such as line extensions or a follow-the-leader policy.

The importance of new product development and the risks have prompted companies to develop effective processes for introducing new products. There is no specific blueprint for new product success, but an effective new product development process requires the following steps:

1. *Identification of new product opportunities.* Several approaches were described in identifying new product opportunities. These approaches used either unmet needs or unsolved problems as the basis for opportunity identification.

2. *Generating and screening new product ideas.* New product ideas are generated from sources such as management, R&D, consumers, and marketing research. Once generated, these ideas are then screened with internal company criteria (company resources, market size, growth) and external consumer assessment.

3. *Developing and testing alternative new product concepts.* New product ideas that survive the screening process are translated into concepts. Once developed, alternative concepts are then tested on consumers to determine the best positioning for the product and to identify the target group most likely to buy.

4. *Developing and testing the new product.* If results of the concept test are positive, the concept is then translated into a physical product and tested. The actual product is tested in controlled facilities or by placing it in the consumer's home. Consumer evaluations of the product will

determine whether the company will make the major investment in production required for market testing and introduction.

5. *Development of a marketing strategy.* Management must develop an integrated marketing strategy for the product before introducing it. It is especially important to choose an effective brand name and package since these components are so closely tied to the consumer's image of the product.

6. *Market testing.* The product is introduced on a limited market basis to obtain the consumer's reaction in a realistic market setting. Market testing is the basis for projecting sales and revenues to the national market and often serves as the first step in a national rollout of the product.

7. *National introduction.* Once the decision to introduce the product has been made, the company must decide between a region-by-region rollout and an immediate national introduction. Various components of marketing strategy must also be coordinated with market introduction.

8. *Business analysis.* Management will attempt to forecast sales at each step in the new product development process. Revenue and cost estimates are developed to determine whether national introduction is warranted.

In the next chapter we will consider the management of new and existing products and the development of product strategies within the framework of the product's life cycle and the company's product lines.

Questions

1. Why are new products so important to the profitability of many firms?

2. The president of a firm that manufacturers small appliances says:

   New products are one road to profitability, but not the only road. The problems with investing heavily in new product development are that (a) it is expensive, (b) it is risky because competition can follow you in very easily, and (c) it opens you up to losses due to changes in technology. I would prefer to let the other fellow take the lead and then follow when I think the market is ripe.

   □ What are the pros and cons of this position?

3. Cite some examples of brands that were successful as the first brand into the market, and brands that were not. Why do some brands succeed as market leaders and others do not?

4. What are the common denominators in the three new product failures cited on page 256?

5. Some companies have reacted to the increasing risks of new product

introductions by increasing the efficiency of the new product development process; others by relying less on new products. In what ways
have companies:

- ☐ improved the efficiency of new product development, and

- ☐ developed strategies to reduce the reliance on new product introductions?

6. Identify the marketing opportunities in Figure 9-6. Develop one product
   concept to meet each of the opportunities you have identified.

7. Consider the four alternative concepts for the new casserole product depicted in Figure 9-7. Develop a proposal to determine which of
   the four concepts should be selected as a basis for positioning the new
   product.

8. This chapter cited the importance of a product-concept fit.

   - ☐ What is meant by this term?

   - ☐ Why is a product-concept fit important?

   - ☐ What are the alternatives if a product-concept fit is weak?

9. Which of the three types of preliminary market test — controlled test
   markets, simulated test markets, and sales waves — would you use to
   determine:

   - ☐ the effects on sales of two alternative price levels with and without
     price off coupons?

   - ☐ consumer evaluation of a new hair conditioner and the repurchase rate
     over five or six trials?

   - ☐ changes in consumer preferences and intentions after being exposed
     to a new therapeutic hand lotion in an in-store environment?

10. A company is trying to decide whether to introduce a new type of jog-
    ging shoe nationally. Consumers have reacted very favorably to the new
    shoe in preliminary product tests. Management is debating whether to
    test market the product first or to introduce it immediately on a na-
    tional basis.

    - ☐ What are the pros and cons of test marketing versus a national introduction?

11. Assume the company in the previous question decided to test market
    the new jogging shoe. How would you use Table 9-2 in selecting three
    or four key test markets?

12. Why have many companies come to rely more on preliminary market
    tests and less on full-scale test marketing in evaluating new products?

Notes

1. Pennwalt, "Shedding Losers and Betting Big
   on Pharmaceuticals," *Business Week*, February
   22, 1982, pp. 76–78.

2. "New Product Strategy: How the Pros Do It,"
   Industrial Marketing, May 1982, pp. 49–60.

3. "Despite Mixed Record, Firms Still Pushing for New Product," *The Wall Street Journal*, November 12, 1981, p. 31.

4. *Industrial Marketing*, May 1982, p. 58.

5. Bernard D. Kahn, "Five Reasons Why Originals Win — Imitators Lose!" *Marketing Times*, July/August, 1981, pp. 13–15.

6. See for example, *Management of New Products* (New York: Booz Allen & Hamilton, 1968), p. 9.

7. *Industrial Marketing*, May 1982, p. 59.

8. For factors related to new product success, see R. G. Cooper, "Identifying Industrial New Product Success: Project NewProd," *Industrial Marketing Management* 8 (1979): 124–35; R. G. Cooper, "The Dimensions of Industrial New Product Success and Failure," *Journal of Marketing* 43 (Summer 1979): 93–103; and *Industrial Marketing*, May 1982, p. 50.

9. "Kodak Shows New Disk Cameras," *The New York Times*, February 4, 1982, p. D4.

10. *Industrial Marketing*, May 1982, p. 50.

11. For a description of multidimensional scaling applications in marketing, see Paul E. Green and Frank J. Carmone, *Multidimensional Scaling and Related Techniques in Marketing Analysis* (Boston: Allyn and Bacon, 1970).

12. For a description of property fitting techniques, see Ibid., pp. 58–59.

13. James H. Myers, "Benefit Structure Analysis: A New Tool for Product Planning," *Journal of Marketing* 40 (October 1976): 23–32.

14. Edward M. Tauber, "Discovering New Product Opportunities with Problem Inventory Analysis," *Journal of Marketing* 39 (January 1975): 67–70.

15. "New Products: The Push is on Marketing," *Business Week*, March 4, 1972, p. 76.

16. "Philip Morris: The Hot Hands in Cigarettes," *Business Week*, December 6, 1976, p. 62.

17. "Creating Products For the Marketplace," *The New York Times*, December 10, 1981, p. D22.

18. Ibid.

19. Eric Von Hippel, "Get New Products from Customers," *Harvard Business Review* 60 (March/April 1982): 117–22.

20. Glen L. Urban and John R. Hauser, *Design and Marketing of New Products* (Englewood Cliffs, New Jersey: Prentice-Hall, 1980), pp. 140–45.

21. Ibid., p. 140.

22. John W. Muncaster, "Picking New Product Opportunities," *Research Management* (July 1981): 26–29.

23. For a description of the conjoint measurement procedure described in Exhibit 9-2 see Paul E. Green and Yoram Wind, "New Ways to Measure Consumers' Judgments," *Harvard Business Review* 53 (July–August 1975): 107–17.

24. For a description of trade-off analysis, see Richard M. Johnson, "Trade-off Analysis of Consumer Values," *Journal of Marketing Research* 11 (May 1974): 121–27.

25. *Maxwell House Division (A) Case* (Boston: Intercollegiate Case Clearing House, 1970), Case #13M83.

26. Paul A. Carroad and Connie A. Carroad, "Strategic Interfacing of R&D and Marketing," *Research Management* (January 1982): 28.

27. "The Selling of the 'Walkman,'" *Advertising Age*, March 12, 1982, p. M-37.

28. *General Foods Post Division (B) Case* (Boston: Intercollegiate Clearing House, 1964), Case #10M9.

29. "Concocting Zingy New Names Starts Turning Into a Business," *The Wall Street Journal*, August 5, 1982, p. 19.

30. "Chapstick 'Quenches' More Consumer Thirst," *Product Management*, July/August 1977, pp. 8–10, 12.

31. Ibid.

32. *Business Week*, December 6, 1976, p. 62.

33. Alvin J. Silk and Glen L. Urban, "Pre-Test Market Evaluation of New Packaged Goods: A Model and Measurement Methodology," *Journal of Marketing Research* 15 (May 1978): 171–91.

34. "Fighting It Out in the Test Market, *Dun's Review*, June 1979, p. 70.

35. Ibid., p. 70.

36. Ibid., p. 69.

37. "Gillette Spends $17.4 Million to Introduce Aapri, Gain Foothold in Skin Care Market," *Marketing News*, May 29, 1981, p. 6.

38. J. H. Parfitt and B. J. K. Collins, "Use of Consumer Panels for Brand Share Prediction,"

Journal of Marketing Research 5 (May 1968): 131–46.

39. Silk and Urban, "Pre-Test Market Evaluation of New Packaged Goods," pp. 171–91.

40. Urban and Hauser, *Design and Marketing of New Products,* p. 403.

41. *Industrial Marketing,* May 1982, p. 49.

42. "Elscint Combines High Technology R&D, International Marketing Network to Yield 35% Annual Growth Rate," *Marketing News,* October 17, 1980, Section 2, p. 2.

CHAPTER 10

Product Management and Strategy

FOCUS OF CHAPTER

New product development naturally leads into the management of existing brands as new products become established. Firms must develop marketing strategies for their brands on an ongoing basis. In this chapter we will consider the product as a central component of marketing strategy. In succeeding chapters we will consider other components of the marketing mix: advertising, personal selling, pricing, and distribution.

There are actually three levels at which product decisions are made: the individual brand, the product line, and the product mix. Product management at the individual *brand level* requires formulating and implementing marketing strategies for new brands and considering possible changes in strategies of existing brands. For example, Bon Ami, once a leader in the cleanser market but now with a share less than 5 percent, is being repositioned as an odor-free, nonpolluting product designed to appeal to a young, environmentally conscious segment of the market.[1] Companies spend millions of dollars to maintain brand identity and to ensure continued brand awareness. Maintaining a brand in a top competitive position is a key requirement of marketing management.

Decisions affecting corporate profitability are also made at the *product line level.* Here the firm decides on the brands it will add or delete in a given product category. For example, as part of its program of expansion, General Mills extended its line of cereals by introducing Crispy Wheat 'n Raisins.

The firm's *product mix* is represented by all its offerings. Decisions regarding changes in the product mix affect future growth, the cash-generating ability of the firm, and profitability. For example, Airwick was a one-product company in 1975, relying on its room air freshener for sales. It then embarked on a program of product expansion. Today it has new lines such as rug cleaners, bathroom cleansers, and breath fresheners. As a result of the change in its product mix, sales increased over sixfold in four years.[2]

In this chapter we will first consider the three levels of product strategy and management: brand, product line, and product mix. We will then focus on marketing strategies at the first two levels. In a later chapter we will take a more detailed look at the firm's total product mix within the framework of strategic marketing planning.

The Product Management Hierarchy

Decisions about the brand, product line, and product mix can be viewed as a product management hierarchy. Table 10-1 presents management's responsibilities for each of the three decision areas, from the narrowest level (the brand) to the broadest (the product mix).

Figure 10-1 suggests that the flow of product planning goes from the product mix to the product line to the brand, and then back in the other

FIGURE 10-1
Product planning by management level

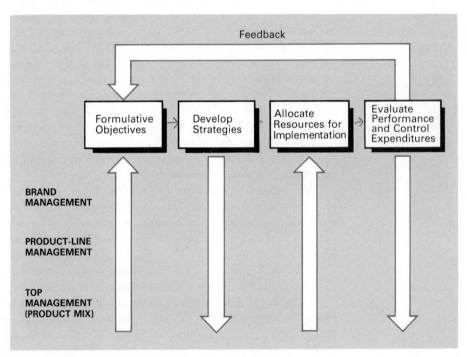

TABLE 10-1
The Product Management Hierachy

PRODUCT LEVEL	MANAGEMENT LEVEL	RESPONSIBILITIES
Brand	Brand manager (product manager)	Develop marketing strategies for a new brand Recommend changes in strategy for an existing brand Develop a positioning for the brand Identify target segments for the brand Evaluate the effect of alternative marketing strategies on brand performance
Product line	Product line manager (product group manager)	Evaluate products in a given line Consider extensions of the line to different types within the product category Assess an expansion of the line to other product categories Consider candidates for deletion from the line Consider the effects of additions to and deletions from the line on the profitability of other products in the line
Product mix	Top management or SBU management	Evaluate existing product lines in the firm's product mix Evaluate the mix of new and existing products Consider the relative emphasis on new versus existing products Consider the effects of line additions and deletions on the profitability of other lines in the mix Consider the introduction of new product lines

direction. Top management formulates corporate objectives that become the basis for planning the product line. Product line managers formulate objectives for their line to guide brand managers in developing the marketing mix for individual brands. Brand strategies are then formulated and incorporated into the product line plan, which is in turn incorporated into the corporate plan. The corporate plan details changes in the firm's product lines and specifies strategies for growth. Once plans have been formulated, financial allocations flow from top management to product line and to brand management for implementation. Implementation of the plan requires tracking performance and providing data from brand to product line to top management for evaluation and control. Evaluation of the current plan then becomes the first step in the next planning cycle (feedback in Figure 10-1) since it provides a basis for examining the firm's current offerings and recommending changes as a result of past performance.

THE BRAND

Decisions at the first level of product management involve the marketing mix for an individual brand. These decisions are the responsibility of a brand manager (sometimes called a product manager). Table 10-1 shows that the brand manager reports to the product line manager.

The Brand's Marketing Mix

Decisions regarding the marketing mix for a brand are represented in the brand's marketing plan. The plan for a new brand would specify price level, advertising expenditures for the coming year, coupons, trade discounts, distribution facilities, and a five-year statement of projected sales and earnings. The plan for an existing product would focus on any changes in marketing strategy, namely:

- a change in the brand's positioning (repositioning 7-Up from "the Uncola" to a caffeine-free soft drink);

- a change in the brand's target market (Miller's shift from targeting the higher-income, infrequent beer drinker to the blue-collar, heavier beer drinker);

- changes in advertising and promotional expenditures (increasing the advertising budget for 7-Up to emphasize the new positioning);

- changes in brand characteristics (strengthening decay prevention in Crest by increasing the fluoride content);

- a change in price level (reducing the price of Gillette's Cricket lighter to meet the challenge from Bic's lighter); and

- recommended changes in distribution strategy (additions of new wholesalers or retailers or changes in trade discounts).

In developing brand strategies the brand manager must justify these recommendations by projecting their effect on sales and earnings (how will a
change in the Crest formula affect market share?). The brand manager should
consider alternative approaches (e.g., no change in Crest, a moderate change
in the formulation, or a major change) and their projected effect. Further,
once the plan is implemented, the brand manager will be responsible for
tracking performance and further refining brand strategy in the next planning
cycle.

The Brand Management System

Management of the firm's product offerings is anchored in the brand managers
who are responsible for individual brands. The **brand management system**
was first developed by Procter and Gamble over fifty years ago and has since
been adopted by many of the leading consumer goods firms. The system assigns
responsibility for brand performance to one person. At General Mills the brand
manager "acts as a business manager, collecting all the internal and external
information that might affect the brand, setting goals for it and plotting strategies
and tactics to achieve them."[3] Not only consumer goods have adopted the
brand management system; many industrial and service firms have found it an
efficient means of assigning profit responsibility at the brand level. The United
States Post Office embarked on a program to become more consumer oriented
in the 1970s. Part of the program was developing new products and services
(express mail, electronic mail, self-service equipment, stamp-collecting services).
Each new product or service was assigned to a product manager with responsibility to:

- establish plans to stimulate sales for the particular plan or service,
- determine customer needs for the new service,
- modify related services to better meet customer needs,
- develop marketing plans and programs for the assigned products or
  services,
- recommend marketing budgets,
- be responsible for marketing research,
- be accountable for volume and revenue results of these activities, and
- assess the net contribution to earnings of the product or service and
  project future contributions to earnings.[4]

Although developed for the United States Postal Service, this statement of brand
management responsibilities is equally relevant at Procter and Gamble, General
Mills, or General Electric.

The brand management system is fairly pervasive, but its usefulness in
generating creative marketing strategies at the brand level, and more importantly
as a means of generating a pool of talent for future top management positions,

has been questioned. Brand managers frequently come out of MBA programs, join the firm as assistant brand managers, and achieve brand manager positions within two years. Top management is reluctant to assign profit responsibility to these individuals because of lack of experience. Although the brand management system requires profit responsibility, at General Mills brand managers have "very little real authority and virtually no financial risk."[5]

In addition, the system has been faulted for discouraging risk taking. Brand managers are judged by product performance, and it is sometimes safer to overresearch the product. A third criticism is that brand managers "cannot look beyond the confines of their own product; they do not see the total marketing plan."[6] Furthermore, they are not always given sufficient responsibility to recognize the interaction between marketing and other business functions such as finance, accounting, and production.

In spite of these criticisms the brand management system has worked effectively in generating brand strategies and developing top management material in many firms. Although real responsibility lies at a higher level at General Mills, some executives have risen rapidly because of the initiative they demonstrated as brand managers. For example, one brand manager was promoted quickly to marketing director because he convinced General Mills to buy a small Michigan company with a license from a French dairy company to manufacture a tasty yogurt called Yoplait.[7] Backed by General Mills's promotional clout, the line was phenomenally successful. Another brand manager moved up quickly after she revitalized a forty-year-old cereal called Kix by recognizing its potential because of its low-sugar content and lack of artificial flavoring. Repositioned to the natural foods segment, the brand achieved a twenty-year high in sales.[8]

THE PRODUCT LINE

Product-line decisions are concerned with the combination of individual products offered in a given line. Table 10-1 shows that the responsibility for a given product line resides with a product line manager (sometimes called a product group manager) who reports to marketing management at the SBU level. The product-line manager supervises several product managers who are responsible for individual products in the line. Decisions about a product line are usually incorporated into a marketing plan at the divisional or SBU level. Such a plan specifies changes in the product lines and allocations to products in each line. Product-line managers have the following responsibilities:

- *Consider expansion of a given product line.* (Dristan, one of the first cold remedies to have an antihistamine, expanded its line to include twenty-one cold remedies under the Dristan name.)[9]
- *Consider candidates for deletion from the product line.* (Welch Foods, producers of Welch's grape juice, found its product line overextended. Consumers were switching to lower-priced products, yet supplies of

grapes from cooperative growers were at record levels. As a result, Welch eliminated 50 percent of its line including Sunshake drinks and all Welchade fruit drinks except grape.)[10]

■ *Evaluate the effects of product additions and deletions on profitability of other items in the line.* (When Hanes Corp. introduced L'Eggs, a less expensive pantyhose in a unique, egg-shaped package, it experienced a 20 percent drop in the volume of its more expensive hosiery. Consumers were switching from one product in the line to another.[11] That is, L'Eggs was **cannibalizing** sales from other company products. But the phenomenal success of L'Eggs more than counterbalanced any loss in revenue.)

■ *Allocate resources to individual products in the line on the basis of marketing strategies recommended by product managers.* (When General Mills introduced Crispy Wheat 'n Raisins, it allocated $10 million to the introductory promotional campaign. Recommendation for the expenditure would be the responsibility of the product line manager, who would base the decision on a marketing plan developed by the product manager.)

THE PRODUCT MIX

Product-mix decisions are concerned with the combination of product lines offered by the firm. Management of the firm's mix of offerings is the responsibility of top management or SBU management, depending on whether the planning focus is at the corporate or SBU level. Basic product-mix decisions involve:

■ *The mix of existing product lines.* In addition to its existing product lines, General Mills has fast-growing positions in restaurants with its Red Lobster Inns and York Steak Houses, in toys with Parker Brothers and Lionel Trains, in apparel with Izod/Lacoste and Foot Joy, and in yogurt with its new Yoplait line.)[12]

■ *The addition of new lines and deletion of existing lines in the product mix.* (General Mills has tried to diversify away from foods, by acquiring over forty nonfood lines since 1969, so that today more than half its profits come from nonfood items. But it must be aware of nonperformers. For example, its Ship 'n Shore line of blouses and shirts has been losing money, making the line a candidate for deletion. Top management is hoping to retain it by broadening the line, closing inefficient plants, and instituting better financial controls.)[13]

■ *The relative emphasis on new versus existing product lines in the mix.* (General Mills's top management has emphasized the addition of new lines to counterbalance projected decreases in cereal consumption due to a decreasing birth rate.)

■ *The relative emphasis on internal development versus external acqui-*

sition in the product mix. (General Mills has generally emphasized external acquisition. But once it has acquired a new product, the company has encouraged internal development by product-line managers. For example, Yoplait yogurt was acquired but the products in the line have been developed internally.)

■ *The effects of adding or deleting a line on the profitability of other lines in the product mix.* (Would keeping the Ship 'n Shore line of blouses and shirts represent a cash drain on other lines? Direct competition between Ship 'n Shore and Izod might be a reason for deleting Ship 'n Shore.)

■ *The effects of future environmental change on the firm's product mix.* (General Mills foresaw that when the baby boom generation became young adults in the early 1970s, cereal consumption would decrease. This was an important rationale for beginning its diversification into nonfood lines in 1969.)

In the rest of this chapter we will consider planning and strategy at the brand and product-line levels. Product mix strategies will be described in Chapter 19.

Brand Identification

The basic purpose in developing brand strategies is to identify the brand with positive consumer benefits. Advertising can create awareness of the brand when it is introduced. But repeat purchasing and loyalty to the brand can be gained only by convincing the consumer that the product is worth its price. The primary function of the brand manager is to ensure positive brand identification by the target segment.

ADVANTAGES OF STRONG BRAND IDENTIFICATION

In addition to the obvious advantage of ensuring a core of loyal users, a strong brand identity has several other important benefits.

■ *Brand identification can create a strong brand image.* Brands have come to be associated with specific benefits (Crest with cavity prevention, Charmin paper products with softness, Head and Shoulders with dandruff removal). Identification of a brand with such positive benefits creates a brand image that is likely to encourage trial and repeat purchasing.

■ *Brand identification ensures in-store recognition.* When a purchase is not planned, seeing a familiar brand in the store might remind the consumer to buy. Brands with strong identities have an edge on the store shelf because of this reminder effect.

- *Brand identification helps position the product relative to competition.* A strong identification of the brand with a consumer benefit can provide a unique positioning. If 7-Up establishes a new brand identity based on a caffeine-free benefit, it might effectively position itself against Coke and Pepsi.

- *Brand identification can result in a price advantage.* If consumers are sufficiently loyal to a brand, they are less likely to be sensitive to price increases. Therefore, the company may be able to maintain a price differential with competition.

- *Brand identification ensures distribution and shelf position.* Strong brand identity will prompt wholesalers and retailers to stock the brand because of consumer demand. P&G's success in introducing Pampers, the first disposable diaper, ensured shelf space for the brand in supermarkets. Competitive brands have had a hard time breaking into the market, because disposable diapers are bulky and most supermarket managers will allocate space to only one or two brands.

BRAND IDENTIFICATION STRATEGIES

The role of the corporate name in product strategy raises the issue of the approach a company should take in establishing brand name identification. Companies have several options in trying to establish a strong brand identity depending on whether (1) the brand is part of a product line and (2) the brand is linked to the corporate name. These alternatives give rise to the four brand identification strategies in Figure 10-2.

Individual Brands

Companies can try to establish brand identification without reference to an integrated product line or to the corporate name. Each brand is sold individually

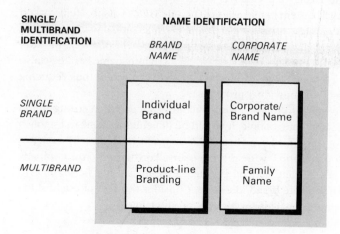

SINGLE/
MULTIBRAND
IDENTIFICATION

NAME IDENTIFICATION

FIGURE 10-2
Brand identification strategies

	BRAND NAME	*CORPORATE NAME*
SINGLE BRAND	Individual Brand	Corporate/ Brand Name
MULTIBRAND	Product-line Branding	Family Name

and stands or falls on its own. Procter and Gamble follows this strategy. It will identify a new brand with the P&G name only for the first few months of advertising. After that it discontinues all reference to P&G. Further, there is no strong product-line connotation in brand names. P&G's detergents — Tide, Bold, Dash, Cheer, Duz — are all sold as separate brands. P&G's brand-identification strategy is dictated by the policy that each brand is regarded as a profit center. A former P&G chief executive officer describes the approach as follows:

> We are dedicated to the concept that our business is run by brands. By that I mean we regard each brand as a separate business. Each brand is expected to stand on its own feet in the competitive struggle. And each brand is expected to earn money.[14]

One important result of this approach is that P&G is less likely to use product portfolio analysis in evaluating individual brands, because it is unwilling to transfer funds from a cash cow to a star or a problem child. Each brand is accountable for costs and revenue, and if a brand is not performing according to ROI and payback standards, the company is quick to eliminate it. In the words of the same executive;

> One thing we do not do is borrow from one brand to support another. The principle of running each brand as a separate business provides a discipline which prevents such actions in the employment of our funds. This discipline is extremely important to us.[15]

Family Name

The opposite of an individual-brand-name strategy is a strategy that includes the firm's total product mix under one **family name.** Brand names are not emphasized. Products are identified by the corporate name and the product category. Thus, one refers to a General Electric toaster or a GE refrigerator or dishwasher. Similarly, Heinz's 57 varieties include Heinz catsup, Heinz baked beans, etc. A family name strategy is feasible if the company has a strong corporate identity and views its products within the context of a total product mix rather than as independent profit centers. A family-name strategy also permits advertising a wide range of products in one campaign, thus reducing the advertising costs for individual products.

Companies are likely to follow a family-name strategy when strong brand identification is difficult. For example, it would be difficult for Heinz to establish a strong brand association for baked beans. An umbrella of Heinz's 57 varieties permits an overall association with the company. Further, when a company has many brands in the same general product area, it may not be feasible to attempt to establish separate brand identities. Consider the cost of establishing fifty-seven advertising campaigns for Heinz's product line.

Product-Line Branding

A strategy of product-line branding is midway between an individual-brand and a family-name strategy. All brands within the product line have a common name. For example, Nestlé introduced a new line of low-calorie foods under the product-line name, New Cookery. There were thirty products in the line when it was introduced, among them New Cookery chili and New Cookery pasta.[16] Product-line branding is used when a company produces diverse product lines that require separate identification. Nestlé's product mix cannot be identified by the Nestlé name alone, because it includes coffees, foods, and soups. But an individual line can have a name identification, providing some benefits in multiproduct advertising campaigns.

Corporate/Brand Name

Some companies link their name with the brand name. Such a strategy associates a strong corporate entity with a brand while maintaining the brand's individuality. If successful, it provides the advantages of both a family-name and an individual-brand strategy. For example, Kellogg's Rice Krispies and Kellogg's Raisin Bran link the corporate logo to the brand.

SOURCE OF BRAND IDENTIFICATION

Most of the examples of brand identification have referred to brands marketed by manufacturers. These brands are called national brands to distinguish them from store brands owned and marketed by distributors (retailers and wholesalers). Further complicating the picture is the possibility of a manufacturer's producing an unbranded product and distributing it with no promotional expenditures (a generic brand). These alternatives are classified in Figure 10-3 by the brand's source (manufacturer versus distributor) and the presence or absence of a concerted marketing strategy.

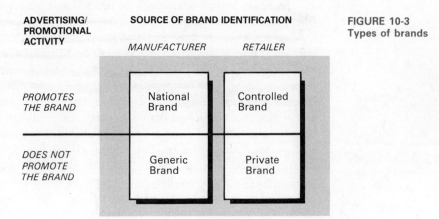

ADVERTISING/ PROMOTIONAL ACTIVITY

SOURCE OF BRAND IDENTIFICATION

MANUFACTURER   *RETAILER*

	MANUFACTURER	RETAILER
PROMOTES THE BRAND	National Brand	Controlled Brand
DOES NOT PROMOTE THE BRAND	Generic Brand	Private Brand

FIGURE 10-3
Types of brands

National Brands

National brands are marketed by manufacturers with an integrated marketing mix, frequently involving advertising expenditures in the millions of dollars per year. Although called national brands, they are sometimes only regional (e.g., Coors beer in the Midwest, Folger's coffee in the West until the 1970s). Most of the references in this chapter are to national brands.

Controlled Brands and Private Brands

Controlled and private brands are sold under the label of a wholesaler or retailer. These distributors generally do not manufacture these items. They purchase them, frequently from leading manufacturers of brand names such as Heinz or Scott paper, and put their own store name on the product. Therefore they are sometimes called store brands. **Controlled brands** are advertised and promoted, but private brands are not. Sometimes advertising expenditures for controlled brands approach those of national brands; for example, A&P's Ann Page coffee or Sears' DieHard battery are advertised heavily. Controlled brands are also more heavily promoted within the retail stores through coupons, price promotions, and displays. Most of these brands are sold only in the retail store represented on the label, but some are distributed more widely. Because of this important distinction between controlled and private brands, it is surprising that most marketers continue to refer to controlled brands as private brands. They do so because the marketing mix is within the control of the retailer or wholesaler sponsoring the brand.

Private brands are generally distributed by wholesalers and retailers who cannot afford the costs of advertising. They tend to be sold in local areas. Thus, a small clothing, liquor, or appliance store will frequently sell under its own store label with minimal advertising in the local area, whereas a controlled brand will be sold by a large retailer, sometimes using television commercials on a regional or national basis.

There are several advantages for retailers and wholesalers in selling their own brands. Controlled and private brands have a distinct price advantage over national brands since marketing costs are lower. Prices for private and controlled brands have been estimated to be 15 percent to 30 percent below those of national brands.[17] Generally the product quality and price of controlled brands are higher than those of private brands, but the price is still significantly below that of national brands. Consumers have become more value conscious and realize that controlled brands in particular are often as good as national brands. Large retailers purchase products from leading manufacturers and try to duplicate national brands. Thus, Safeway claims that its White Magic laundry detergent is the same as Tide, its Truly Fine deodorant soap is a copy of Dial, and its Nu-Made mayonnaise is the same as Hellmann's.[18] Retailers selling controlled or private brands will generally give them more and better shelf space, and can display them more prominently than national brands.

The battle of the brands

Because consumers in an inflationary economy are more conscious of price and value, controlled brands have grown more than national brands in recent years. In one study, over one-third of all respondents interviewed reported a shift from buying national brands to the store's own brand.[19] Because of consumer acceptance private and controlled brands now account for 20 percent of sales in food stores.[20]

The increased competition between controlled and national brands has come to be called "the **battle of the brands**." The "battle" is over shelf space and the consumer's dollar. Retailers have the advantage in this battle by controlling shelf space and offering price advantages. They sometimes package their own brands to make them look very similar to the leading national brands, thus encouraging comparisons. For example, Woolco's baby shampoo and baby powder look like those of Johnson & Johnson, the market leader in both categories. Manufacturers claim that national brands have higher quality. However, controlled brands are gaining in this battle because consumer loyalties to national brands are decreasing as their price sensitivity increases.

Manufacturers' reactions

Manufacturers have reacted by fighting the trend or by joining it. Some manufacturers have fought the controlled brands head-on by offering higher discounts to the trade in an effort to gain more shelf space. CPC International follows this policy. Procter and Gamble has fought the controlled brands by offering discounts to consumers rather than to the trade through coupons and promotions. P&G has the leverage with retailers to demand good shelf position; therefore, they do not feel the need to offer trade discounts.

Manufacturers have also reacted by joining the trend to store brands. Many such as Ralston-Purina manufacture heavily for store brands. In so doing, they ensure utilization of their production facilities and hold down per-unit production costs. They also reduce marketing costs, since advertising and distribution are the responsibilities of the retailer or wholesaler. Manufacturers of store brands also protect themselves from price competition at the retail level.

Other manufacturers, such as Kellogg, refuse to produce for controlled or private brands. They cite their product superiority and sales leadership as evidence that their effort should be directed to their own brands. They view manufacturing for store brands as self-defeating since these brands will compete with their own national brands for shelf space. Overall, the trend is toward manufacturing for store brands. In some cases as much as 40 percent of the output of manufacturers of national brands goes to producing store brands.[21]

Generic Brands

The fourth category in Figure 10-3 is generic brands. Actually the term generic "brands" is a misnomer since these products are unbranded. They are frequently in stark white packages with large black letters. The packages are labeled "detergent," "paper towels," or "cooking oil," with no brand name designation, only the generic name of the product category.

Generics are produced and distributed by manufacturers, but receive no advertising, promotion, or sales support because they are unbranded products. The name of the manufacturer will be listed in small print on the box. Generics were introduced in Europe in the mid 1970s and in the United States in 1978. In three short years generics grew to account for 12 percent of sales in food stores.[22] Acceptance by consumers is also reflected in a 1980 survey; it found that 60 percent of all consumers who tried generics planned to purchase them again.[23] Consumers have accepted generics for the same reasons they previously accepted store brands: greater price sensitivity and value consciousness. On average, generics are priced 40 percent below national brands and 15 percent to 20 percent below store brands.[24] The deep recession in the early 1980s further increased the acceptance of generics.

Generics have been most successful in product categories where brands receive little loyalty from consumers (e.g., paper towels, toilet tissue, paper napkins, canned fruit, fabric softeners, and detergents). They have not been able to make inroads in areas where consumers see significant differences between brands (e.g., drug, cosmetic, and toiletry items).[25]

Manufacturers have split sharply in their willingness to produce generics. Some have decided to produce them for the same reasons they produce controlled brands — to utilize production capacity and avoid the high costs of advertising and marketing. Cost and price pressures in times of recession are added reasons. Generally these manufacturers are not the leaders in the industry and might have experienced declining sales. For example, Liggett and Myers (L&M) has come out with a generic simply called "filter cigarettes," sold for ten to twelve cents less per package than national brands. The company had experienced several new product failures and declining sales. Because of L&M's smaller share in the cigarette market, generics are less likely to compete with L&M products than with competitors. "Inflation, the shaky economy, and a growing acceptance of other generic products have helped Liggett's [generic] cigarette," said one executive.[26]

Manufacturers in a stronger sales position have chosen not to produce generics but have found it necessary to react to the increased price competition by offering lower-priced branded products. For example, Procter and Gamble's new line of low-priced paper towels, Summit, was introduced primarily because of the inroads generics have made in paper products. The company is introducing the line without advertising to permit a lower price that is competitive with controlled brands and generic products. Some marketers feel that national brands that are not market leaders will experience greater difficulties in the future as a result of price pressure from both controlled brands and generics. One executive predicted that manufacturers will be forced to withdraw advertising support from these brands and allocate it to the marketing leaders, leading to fewer national brands.[27]

Brand Strategy and the Product Life Cycle

The previous section provided a classification of brands, but did not deal with marketing strategies for individual brands. In this section we will focus on marketing strategies that are primarily for national brands.

An important concept in determining the marketing strategy for a brand is the **product life cycle.** A brand's position on the life cycle directly influences positioning, advertising, pricing, and distribution strategies. As a product (or brand) goes through introduction, growth, maturity, and decline, it requires changes in marketing strategies to meet changing consumer demand and competitive conditions.[28] Brand strategies tend to progress over the life cycle from (1) brand development in the introductory stage to (2) brand reinforcement in the growth stage to (3) brand repositioning in the maturity stage to (4) brand modification in the decline stage. These strategies will be described in the order of their occurrence in the product life cycle.

BRAND STRATEGIES

Brand strategies can be categorized on two dimensions: (1) whether strategy requires a new/modified brand or an existing brand, and (2) whether strategy is directed to new or existing markets.

Brand Development

A brand-development strategy requires developing a new brand for new market segments or making major changes in an existing brand to appeal to a broader market. Generally this strategy is associated with the introductory phase of a product's life cycle since a product development process is required as a lead-in to product introduction. Procter and Gamble's Wondra hand lotion was a totally new product for the company and was aimed at a segment it did not currently appeal to — therapeutic hand lotion users. When an existing brand is changed substantially, it can be thought of as a new product requiring an initial brand development phase. P&G's introduction of Crest in gel form can be seen as a new product for the company designed to appeal to a new segment — gel users.

Brand Reinforcement

A brand follows a strategy of reinforcement to support a new brand in the growth phase of its life cycle. Its positioning strategy has been set, and it is maintaining or increasing its advertising and distribution support. The basic rationale is to maintain a "winning combination" in the marketing mix. If the brand's growth is curtailed by poor positioning, intense competition, or other environmental factors, management might consider an immediate repositioning or modification strategy to prevent an early decline.

Brand Repositioning

Brand repositioning is implemented when the company sees opportunities for revitalizing an existing brand by marketing it to new segments. For example, Philip Morris repositioned 7-Up as a caffeine-free soft drink when its initial attempt at competing directly with Pepsi and Coke failed. The company did not have the advertising impact or the strength with bottlers that was required. As a result, it sought a new market segment, soft drink users concerned with natural ingredients and nutrition.

Brand Modification

A brand modification strategy involves some substantial change in the brand requiring a new marketing strategy but to essentially the same market. At one time, Nestlé reformulated Nescafé to provide a richer, more granular coffee. It changed its advertising theme to emphasize dark, rich granules. This change enhanced the perception of taste benefits and strengthened the brand's position among current users.

THE PRODUCT LIFE CYCLE

Figure 10-4 shows the traditional life cycle curve for a product or brand. The sales curve will vary by product, but the bell-shaped curve is typical. The marketing strategies just described are listed in Figure 10-4 for each of the four basic periods in a product's or brand's life cycle. There will be exceptions to these strategies. For example, a brand may continue to be reinforced into the maturity phase. Some brands are never repositioned or modified, and others may be repositioned long before they go into decline. But the strategies listed in Figure 10-4 tend to be typical for each stage of the life cycle.

Introduction

In the introductory stage the main purpose of marketing strategy is to establish the brand. Product strategy is still developmental to ensure a high enough standard of quality for consumer acceptance. The main purpose of advertising is to create consumer awareness of the brand. The marketer must ensure sufficient distribution so that the product will be available on the shelf after it is advertised. When distribution is not ensured, trade discounts and cooperative advertising allowances are offered to convince distributors to stock the brand.

Pricing will follow a **penetration strategy** (below competition) if the objective is to make competitive inroads quickly, or a **skimming strategy** (above competition) if the objective is to maintain a quality image and appeal to a select market. Penetration is more likely if demand is elastic and competition is intense. Under such conditions the firm must price at or below competition

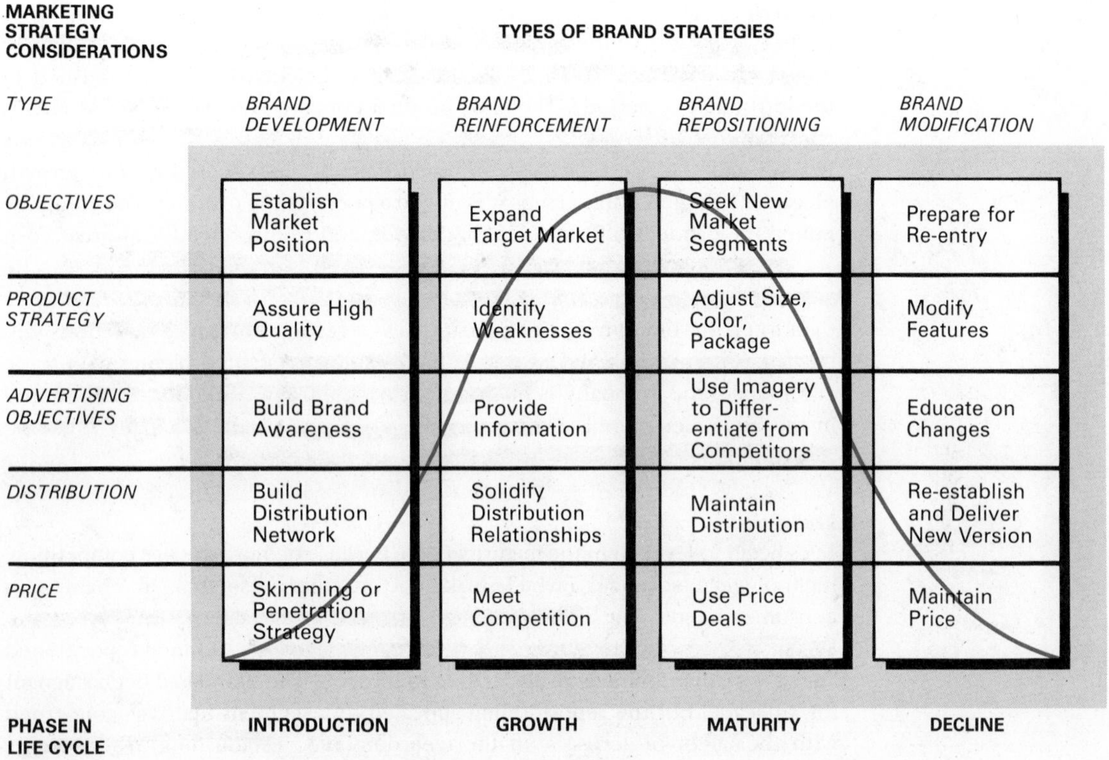

MARKETING STRATEGY CONSIDERATIONS

TYPES OF BRAND STRATEGIES

TYPE	BRAND DEVELOPMENT	BRAND REINFORCEMENT	BRAND REPOSITIONING	BRAND MODIFICATION
OBJECTIVES	Establish Market Position	Expand Target Market	Seek New Market Segments	Prepare for Re-entry
PRODUCT STRATEGY	Assure High Quality	Identify Weaknesses	Adjust Size, Color, Package	Modify Features
ADVERTISING OBJECTIVES	Build Brand Awareness	Provide Information	Use Imagery to Differentiate from Competitors	Educate on Changes
DISTRIBUTION	Build Distribution Network	Solidify Distribution Relationships	Maintain Distribution	Re-establish and Deliver New Version
PRICE	Skimming or Penetration Strategy	Meet Competition	Use Price Deals	Maintain Price
PHASE IN LIFE CYCLE	INTRODUCTION	GROWTH	MATURITY	DECLINE

FIGURE 10-4
Changes in brand strategy over its life cycle

Source: Adapted from Ben M. Enis, Raymond La Grace, and Arthur E. Prell, "Extending the Product Life Cycle," *Business Horizons* 20 (June 1977): 53. Copyright 1977 by the Foundation for the School of Business at Indiana University. Reprinted by permission.

unless it has a unique product advantage. A penetration strategy would require widespread distribution facilities to ensure reaching a broad market. Skimming is more profitable if the company is directing its appeal to a smaller, select group of customers willing to pay a higher price. A skimming strategy assumes the product has some competitive advantage, resulting in price inelasticity and brand loyalty. Distribution is more selective.

A product in its introductory stage is Gillette's Aapri facial scrub. When Aapri was introduced in 1981 Gillette provided heavy initial advertising support to ensure brand awareness and followed a penetration pricing strategy by setting the price well below that of competitive brands. The initial concern was to provide product quality in the developmental process to ensure that the brand could deliver on its promise of effective cleansing action without irritation. The strategy was to convey this appeal to as broad a market as possible.

Growth

In the growth phase the basic purpose of brand strategy is to establish loyalty among those who have tried the brand (if sufficient trial was established in the introductory period). The main product concern is to identify deficiencies once consumers have had a chance to use the product for a period of time. Procter and Gamble quickly determined that the unexpectedly short growth phase for Pringle's potato chips was due to a poor-tasting product. The company pulled the product off the shelf, modified it, and reintroduced it at great cost.

Several changes in marketing strategy occur in the growth phase. The advertising objective is now to educate the consumer on specific benefits rather than to create brand-name identification. As a result advertising insertions will not be as frequent and will be more informational. Further, having won trade acceptance, the company is likely to cut back on any trade discounts offered in the introductory phase. Price may be decreased, if the company followed a skimming strategy, to try to head off competitive entry.

Maturity

Sales begin to level off in the maturity phase because of more intense competition, technological advances (which make the product obsolete), or changes in consumer needs. The most frequent strategy for revitalizing the product in this stage is repositioning to secure new market segments. Mennen repositioned Speed Stick deodorant as an alternative to aerosols. The brand had been stagnant for a decade, but the repositioning appealed to a segment that was concerned with the effect of aerosols on the environment.[29] Establishing a new target segment revitalized the brand.

Greater competition frequently results in more difficulty in establishing a unique position in the marketplace. As a result, marketers often have to rely on advertising to ensure market position. Advertising campaigns tend to shift from an informational base to imagery in an attempt to differentiate the brand from a greater number of competitors. Minor changes might be made in packaging or product design — for example, putting blue flakes in detergents or changing the shape of the package.

Decline

When sales begin to decline, the company must choose between totally redesigning the product or withdrawing it. Withdrawal might be preceded by a **harvesting strategy** to milk the brand for additional profits by withdrawing all marketing expenditures.

If the brand is to be modified, the main purpose of marketing strategy is to reintroduce the brand. This strategy requires formulation of a new marketing mix. For all intents and purposes, the brand is treated as a new product. The main purpose of advertising is to educate consumers on the brand's improvements. Distributors may have to be convinced to stock the new brand, especially since sales have been declining. Trade discounts and advertising allowances may again be in order. Consumers might be offered coupons and price promotions to induce trial, since many former consumers might have been lost during decline.

Product-Line Evaluation and Strategy

Marketing planning at the product-line level requires coordinating the marketing strategies of the various brands that make up the product line. Before we consider the evaluation of the product line, we need to understand the importance of grouping brands into product lines.

IMPORTANCE OF A PRODUCT LINE

Grouping brands into a product line gives the firm several important advantages in formulating marketing strategy:

1. *Product lines provide economies of scale in advertising.* Several products can be advertised under the umbrella of one line. Rising media costs increase the advantages of product-line advertising.[30]

2. *Advertising a product line enhances the corporate name.* When a product line uses the corporate name (e.g., Heinz's 57 varieties) product-line advertising is corporate advertising.

3. *A product line allows for package uniformity.* All packages in the line should have a common look without causing them to lose their individual identities. Thus one item in the line can advertise another.[31]

4. *Product lines provide an opportunity for standardizing components,* thus reducing manufacturing costs. For example, many of the components Samsonite uses in manufacturing its folding tables and chairs are used in its patio furniture.[32]

5. *Product lines facilitate sales and distribution.* Sales personnel can provide a full range of product alternatives to customers. Distributors and retailers are more willing to stock the company's products if a full line is offered. Transportation and warehousing costs are likely to be less for a product line than for individual brands.

PRODUCT-LINE EVALUATION

To evaluate the product line the product-line manager must consider its *depth, length,* and *consistency.*

Depth

A line's **depth** defines the extent of coverage of the product category. Some companies seek to provide full coverage of a product line, whereas others might specialize in one or two items. Bristol Myers has capitalized on the strength of Ban deodorant by introducing seventeen Ban products in its deodorant line, including four pump sprays, two "dry" roll-ons, three solid sticks, and six Ultra Ban products. In addition, Bristol Myers has other deodorant brands in the line (e.g., an oversized ball roll-on).[33] Procter and Gamble has much less depth of coverage in its deodorant line. Line managers seek a full line to satisfy consumers' desire for a range of alternatives, to satisfy dealers who want to avoid lost sales because of missing items in the line, and to preempt competitors from finding gaps in the company's line. A full line is particularly important for industrial marketers. For example, there may be hundreds of variations of industrial valves or fasteners. Lack of a full line may cause a purchaser to switch to an alternative vendor.

There are problems with adding items to the line to ensure depth. First, additional items increase the chances of cannibalization. A new product may steal sales from others in the line, resulting in no net increase in revenue. This is most likely to happen if the new product is not sufficiently different from existing products in the line. Second, as additional items are added, costs of inventory, processing, and transportation increase. Maintaining profitability of the line becomes more difficult. Third, too many items may confuse customers. It is up to the product-line manager to justify additional items on the bases of customer needs and cost.

Product-line managers frequently carry unprofitable products in the line to ensure depth. They fail to justify new and existing items on the bases of cost and customer demand. An analysis of profits by item might identify candidates for deletion.

Length

The **length** of the product line refers to its diversity. Lengthening a line means "stretching" it beyond its current range, whereas deepening the line means adding items within the current range. An important means of lengthening a line is through **brand leveraging.** Leveraging is taking advantage of a strong brand name by introducing related items under the brand name. Arm & Hammer leveraged its strong position in baking soda by introducing a deodorant, oven cleaner, laundry detergent, and washing soda under the Arm & Hammer name. By lengthening its line the company pushed earnings up threefold in the mid-1970s.[34]

Brand leveraging does not always work. Certs tried to leverage its strong position as a breath freshener by introducing Certs chewing gum. The line extension was a failure because competition in the market was too strong, the cost of entry high, and manufacturing capacity limited.[35]

Certs's experience demonstrates the product-line manager's responsibility to evaluate additions to the line on the basis of planning procedures that ensure adequate consideration of market conditions and reliable projections of sales and profits.

Consistency

Consistency of the product line refers to how closely related the individual items are in terms of end use. The Ban line is fairly consistent, because all the products are deodorants. The Arm & Hammer line is much less consistent, because many of the items are in unrelated categories (a deodorant, baking soda, and laundry detergent). Generally, the greater the length of the line, the lower its consistency. A consistent line is desirable because it can be advertised under one umbrella. Ban could advertise several deodorant types in one ad. Arm & Hammer must advertise its items separately, increasing the costs of advertising.

PRODUCT-LINE STRATEGIES

Product-line strategies may seek to maintain the existing line or to modify it through additions and deletions. Figure 10-5 shows that because each of these three options can be directed to existing markets or to new markets, there are six product-line strategies.

Line-Maintenance Strategies

Firms may seek to maintain the current offerings in a line by appealing to existing markets through a holding strategy or to new markets by revitalizing current offerings.

A *holding* strategy means simply maintaining the status quo. The line remains the same, and there are no major changes in marketing strategy. A *revitalization* strategy requires changing the marketing strategy to appeal to

FIGURE 10-5
Product-line strategies

MARKET CATEGORIES	PRODUCT LINE CHANGE		
	MAINTENANCE	*ADDITIONS*	*DELETIONS*
EXISTING MARKET CATEGORIES	Line Holding	Line Extensions	Line Pruning
NEW MARKET CATEGORIES	Line Revitalization (Repositioning)	Line Expansion	Line Retrenchment

new markets with the existing line. Seiko is following a holding strategy for its line of quartz watches in the Japanese market, but it is following a revitalization strategy in the American market. The company sees little prospect for growth in Japan. It is following a defensive strategy by holding on to its current markets against smaller rivals. But the company sees significant room for growth in the American market and is "stepping up its international marketing drive."[36] It has expanded the American market by revitalizing every element of the marketing mix. It has offered an up-to-date product line, outspent every watch company except Timex in advertising, held price increases to a minimum, and built a strong distribution network by signing up fifteen watch distributors to sell Seiko watches exclusively.[37]

Line revitalization frequently requires *repositioning* to appeal to new market segments. For example, Scott Paper found its sales of toilet tissues and paper towels decreasing in the late 1970s. It was relying on a high-priced, high-quality line while consumers were becoming more price sensitive and switching to lower-priced products. It was also saddled by a follow-the-leader mentality in duplicating P&G's introduction of new paper products. Scott reacted by moving away from its reliance on high-priced items to lower-cost goods.[38] The company reduced the price of its existing line by changing the paper composition. It then promoted the lower-cost line heavily. By the early 1980s Scott had regained its market share in toilet tissue and paper towels.

Product-Line Additions

Figure 10-5 shows two strategies to add products to the line, line *extension* and line *expansion.* Firms extend their product line by adding new versions of existing products or by modifying these products to provide a fuller line to an existing market. Expanding the product line involves adding new products to appeal to different market segments. Line extension adds depth to the line, whereas expansion adds length. The introduction by Gillette of Silkience deep conditioner for the hair was an extension of the Silkience conditioner line. It represented a variation of the basic product to provide conditioner users with a fuller range of products. Gillette's introduction of Silkience shampoo was an expansion of the line because the company used the success of Silkience conditioners to appeal to a new market category, shampoo users.[39]

Product-Line Deletions

Products can be deleted from a line because of overextension into existing markets or overexpansion into new markets. A cutback in offerings as a result of overextension requires *pruning* the line, whereas cutting back because of overexpansion requires *retrenchment.*

At times, companies have been overzealous in establishing a full product line. Pressure from salesmen to provide customers with a full range of product alternatives and fear of competitive encroachment have led companies to add too many items to the line. Three conditions signal a need for line pruning:

1. Items in the line are not making an adequate contribution to earnings because,

   □ sales are not high enough to warrant retaining the item, or

   □ sales are adequate, but the item is cannibalizing other items, resulting in little net addition in revenue.

2. Financial and manufacturing resources can be used on more attractive alternatives.

3. Items become outdated because of technological improvements.

At one time, executives of Sun Oil's Lubrication Division conceded, "Product proliferation got totally out of hand."[40] Line pruning resulted in a reduction of metal working oils from 1150 grades to 92, lubes from 1000 grades to 200, and greases from 225 grades to 29.

Retrenchment of a product line may also be required as a result of attempts to expand the line into new markets. In the late 1970s Univac sought to expand its customer base by introducing several new computer series. The problem was that these offerings required incompatible operating systems and software packages. As a result, Univac had to retrench by merging nine hardware systems into two and paring down fourteen operating systems to three.[41]

Summary

Product strategies are developed on three levels: the brand, the product line, and the product mix. This chapter focused on the first two. The product mix represents the firm's total offerings and will be considered in Chapter 19 in the context of strategic marketing planning.

Product strategies at the brand level require decisions about the brand's marketing mix. These are the responsibility of the brand manager. The brand manager must implement marketing strategy and is accountable for the brand's performance.

Most of the examples in the chapter deal with national brands marketed by manufacturers, but distributors can also market brands. Controlled brands are store brands that are advertised and promoted under a retailer's or wholesaler's label. Private brands are distributors' brands that are not promoted. The competition between controlled brands and national brands for shelf space and for the consumer's dollar has been called the "battle of the brands." Another category of products recently introduced in the American market are "generics." These are unbranded items distributed by manufacturers with no marketing support and sold at very low prices. Generics are making inroads into both national and distributors' brands.

Brand strategies rely on the establishment of a strong brand identity through advertising and product performance. Brand strategies can be directed to (1) developing and introducing the brand into the marketplace, (2) reinforcing the brand once it has been introduced, (3) revitalizing the brand through repositioning strategies, or (4) modifying the brand to create additional benefits and to appeal to an expanded market. These strategies can be associated with the brand's position in the life cycle, development occurring in the introductory stage, reinforcement during growth, repositioning during maturity, and modification when the brand is in decline and an attempt is made to revitalize it.

Development of product-line strategies requires evaluating the depth, length, and consistency of the line. The depth of the line refers to the extent of coverage within the product category. The length represents the diversity of the line — that is, its extension into other product categories. Consistency refers to the interrelationship of the items in terms of end use. Consistency is desirable because it permits multiproduct advertising and economies of scale in marketing effort. Product-line strategies can be classified depending on whether the current line is being maintained, expanded, or retracted, and whether strategies are directed to the same market segments or to new segments. Six strategies were discussed based on these alternatives.

In the next three chapters we will shift our focus from product strategy to another essential element in the marketing mix — promotional strategy.

Questions

1. What are the advantages and disadvantages of a brand-management system?

2. The chief executive officer of a firm producing industrial goods does not believe in a brand (product) management system. The executive explains his position as follows: "Brand managers are fine for a multiproduct consumer goods firm that spends millions of dollars on brand identification. But we emphasize the corporate, not the brand name. So why do we need brand managers?"

   □ Do you agree with the executive's position?

   □ How can the company maintain profit accountability without a brand management system?

3. Consider the following statement: "Advertising plays an important role in establishing brand identification, but not the only role, and frequently, not even the most important role."

   □ Explain.

   □ Under what conditions is advertising likely to have a less important role in brand identification than other components of the marketing mix?

4. Procter and Gamble follows an individual brand strategy, whereas Heinz and General Electric follow a family brand strategy. What are the advantages and disadvantages of each approach?

5. Most consumer goods manufacturers produce national brands and frequently spend millions of dollars to establish positive brand identification.

   □ If this is so, why would a manufacturer produce products to be sold by distributors as private or controlled brands or produce generic products?

   □ Why have more manufacturers produced private or controlled brands and generics since 1980?

6. Some manufacturers have refused to manufacture private brands or generics. How have these manufacturers reacted to the inroads being made by lower-priced alternatives?

7. How can the concept of a product life cycle be used in establishing a brand's marketing strategy?

8. In this chapter we associated brand development strategies with the introductory phase of the product life cycle, brand reinforcement with growth, brand repositioning with maturity, and brand modification with decline. When might each of these generalizations *not* be true? Cite specific examples.

9. What is the changing role of advertising over the product life cycle? What is the changing role of price?

10. What are the advantages and disadvantages of a full product line?

11. What is brand leveraging? What are the risks of such a strategy?

12. Distinguish between a strategy of product-line extension and product-line expansion.

   □ Are the strategies mutually exclusive? Why or why not?

   □ Under what conditions is a company likely to follow one or the other strategy?

Notes

1. "Bon Ami Now Scratches for Soap Market Share," *The New York Times,* March 21, 1983, pp. D1, D7.

2. "Airwick's Discovery of New Markets Pays Off," *Business Week,* June 16, 1980, pp. 139–140.

3. "The General Mills Brand of Managers," *Fortune,* January 12, 1981, p. 99.

4. Intercollegiate Clearing House, *United States Postal Service (A1),* Harvard Business School, 1975, pp. 9–10.

5. *Fortune,* January 12, 1981, p. 99.

6. "Product Manager: Adman's Friend or Foe?" *Advertising Age,* August 17, 1981, p. 43.

7. *Fortune,* January 12, 1981, p. 106.

8. Ibid.

9. "Line Extensions Mean Big Profits for Name Brand Product Makers," *Product Marketing,* December 1979, p. 1.

10. "Welch Drops 50% of its Items," *Advertising Age,* November 16, 1981, p. 103.

11. Michael G. Harvey and Roger A. Kerin, "Diagnosis and Management of the Product Cannibalism Syndrome," *University of Michigan Business Review* 31 (November 1979): p. 18.

12. "General Mills: All-American Marketer," *Dun's Business Month,* December 1981, p. 72.

13. Ibid., p. 73.

14. "P&G: Past Is Prolog," *Advertising Age,* January 11, 1982, p. 47.

15. Ibid.

16. "Nestlé: Centralizing to Win a Bigger Payoff From The U.S.," *Business Week,* February 2, 1981, pp. 57–58.

17. "What's in a Name Brand?" *Money,* February 1974, p. 41; and "Fragmented Markets Complicate Setting New HBA Product Positions," *Product Marketing,* March 1981, p. 8.

18. *Money,* February 1974, p. 42.

19. "Shopping Smart," *Progressive Grocer,* April 1975, p. 50.

20. "Plain Labels Challenge the Supermarket Establishment," *Fortune,* March 26, 1979, p. 71.

21. *Advertising Age,* September 30, 1974, p. 66.

22. "Paper Towel Battle: Generic Savings vs. Brand Quality," *The New York Times,* September 1, 1981, p. D4.

23. "Mum's the Word for the New Generics," *The New York Times,* July 5, 1981, p. F17.

24. *The New York Times,* September 1, 1981, p. D4.

25. "Lack of Brand Identification Stymies 'No Name' HBA Goods," *Product Marketing,* October 1981, p. 23.

26. "New Cigaret Gets No Name, No Promotion," *The Wall Street Journal,* December 11, 1980, p. 29.

27. *Fortune,* March 26, 1979, p. 76.

28. Ben M. Enis, Raymond La Garce, and Arthur E. Prell, "Extending the Product Life Cycle," *Business Horizons* 20 (June 1977): 53.

29. "The Outsiders' Touch That's Shaking Up Mennen," *Business Week,* February 1, 1982, p. 59.

30. Joseph A. Morein, "Shift from Brand to Product Line Marketing," *Harvard Business Review* 53 (September–October 1975): 60.

31. Ibid., p. 61.

32. "Expanding Product Lines: A Winning Strategy," *Industry Week,* February 4, 1974, p. 42.

33. *Product Marketing,* December 1979, p. 6.

34. "The New Face of Arm & Hammer," *Business Week,* April 12, 1976, p. 60.

35. "Brand Leveraging: One Way to Deal With Diminishing Markets in 1980's," *Marketing News,* January 9, 1981, p. 4.

36. "Seiko's Smash," *Business Week,* June 5, 1978, p. 87.

37. Ibid., p. 92.

38. "Scott Paper Fights Back, At Last," *Business Week,* February 16, 1981, pp. 104, 108.

39. "No Sweat, Gillette," *Sales & Marketing Management,* August 17, 1981, p. 31.

40. "The Squeeze on the Product Mix," *Business Week,* January 5, 1974, p. 54.

41. "Univac Takes It Slow — But Very, Very Steady," *Computer World,* June 4, 1979, pp. 1, 6.

CHAPTER 11

Marketing Communications

In Chapter 1 we defined marketing as including all activities directed to identifying and satisfying consumer needs. To satisfy consumer needs one must develop and communicate product benefits. The major part of the marketing budget is devoted to communications.

Marketers communicate through four basic elements: advertising, personal selling, sales promotion, and publicity. These are combined into a promotional mix designed to inform and influence the customer. The promotional mix is frequently the most important component of the brand's marketing mix because marketing communications are required for the consumer to act. Marketing communications are designed (1) to create and maintain brand awareness, (2) to induce trial of new products, and (3) to influence the consumer to repurchase the product.

In this chapter we will first describe a marketing communications model to provide an understanding of how the various components of the promotional mix work. In the rest of the chapter we will consider each component of the marketing communications model: the source of the message, the message itself, transmitting the message through media, and evaluating the effects of the message on the consumer. The focus throughout is on the strategic issues in developing communications.

The Marketing Communications Process

Any type of communication requires a source, a message, a means of transmitting the message, a receiver, and an evaluation of the message's effects. These requirements are presented as a communication model in the top of Figure 11-1. Translated as strategic requirements, the communication model suggests that marketing communicators must:

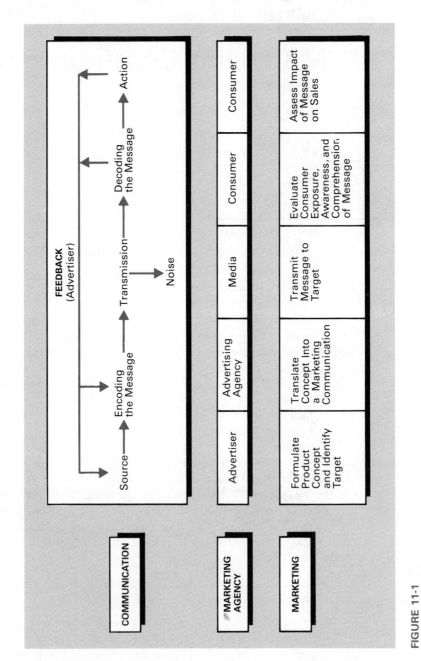

FIGURE 11-1
A marketing communication model

1. Formulate a product concept to meet consumer needs and identify the appropriate target audience,

2. Develop messages to communicate the benefits to the target audience,

3. Transmit messages through print and broadcast media and salespeople,

4. Determine consumers' comprehension of and reaction to these messages, and

5. Try to estimate the effect of marketing messages on sales.

THE SOURCE

Figure 11-1 indicates the marketing agency with primary responsibility for each of these communication functions. In the first step, the source (the manufacturer of the brand) has responsibility for developing the product concept, the product itself, and the product's positioning. As an example, in 1980 Chesebrough-Pond's introduced a new perfume called Chimère as part of its Prince Matchabelli line. The company had perfumes positioned to the romantic middle-American woman (Wind Song), to the individual self-confident woman (Cachet), and to the sensual woman (Aviance). Because over 50 percent of women were in the work force, management felt that a new perfume positioned to the achieving working woman might be successful. The product manager described the target as a woman who is a "cool decision-maker, efficient action-taker coping with the demands and pressures of daily life."[1]

ENCODING

The second step in Figure 11-1 requires an advertising agency to translate the product's positioning into a strategy that will communicate product benefits to consumers. In communications terms this is known as **encoding** the message. Messages are developed in the context of an overall promotional mix designed to communicate benefits and encourage product trial. Chesebrough-Pond's advertising agency developed an advertising campaign that showed a working woman in her professional role — self-confident and assertive — and then in a more private and sensual role (see Figure 11-2 for an example of the advertising). The benefits of the product were communicated to the sales force before the launch. An integrated sales promotion campaign was also developed involving a scented direct-mail piece sent to 5 million women as well as counter displays and price promotions. The Public Relations Department announced the brand to the trade press and to distributors through mailouts.[2] Therefore, each of the four components of the promotional mix was represented.

TRANSMISSION

The third step in Figure 11-1 requires transmitting the message to the target consumer through media vehicles. The advertising agency will develop a media plan that is meant to reach the target segment most effectively. The media plan will require selecting a mix of vehicles — broadcast and print. The most

Chimère Perfume. To the world, it's discreet, elegant. But up close, it's something else.

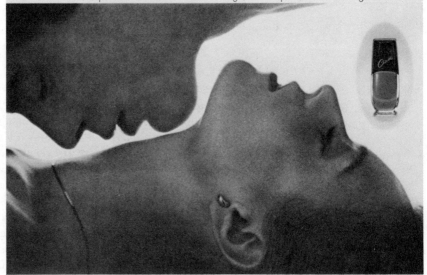

FIGURE 11-2
Advertising message for Chimère

Used by permission of Chesebrough-Pond's, Inc.

important media are the TV stations (local, network, and possibly cable), radio, magazines (both specialty and general readership), and newspapers. A natural outgrowth of the communications process is noise — that is, interference with message transmission. Noise can be due to competitive clutter resulting from the many messages directed to the consumer. Interference with the communications process can also occur in the encoding or decoding phases of communications. Perhaps the agency did not adequately convey product benefits, perhaps the message was not directed to the right target audience, or perhaps the consumer misunderstood the message.

In the case of Chimère, the media objective was to reach 95 percent of all women over eighteen in the United States at least eight times in the introductory period. To do so the company would spend $4.5 million on advertising, almost 90 percent of it ($4 million) on TV and the rest on print. Most of the TV advertising was to be spent on thirty-second spot commercials on the national networks. Print advertising appeared in women's magazines such as *Vogue, Mademoiselle,* and *Glamour.* All advertising carried the same basic theme: "Chimère Perfume. To the World It's Discreet, Elegant. But up Close It's Something Else".[3] Carrying the same theme ensured coordination of all elements of the communications mix.

DECODING AND ACTION

In the last two steps in Figure 11-1 the consumer (receiver) decodes the message and may or may not take action as a result. In **decoding** consumers acquire information and process it. In so doing, they are *exposed* to a message, are *aware* of it, *comprehend* it and *retain* its meaning so that they can use the information at some future time. Marketing communicators must evaluate the consumers' perception of and reaction to the message. Key questions are:

- Did the message reach the intended target group?
- Was the message found to be credible, believable, acceptable?
- Was the message interpreted in the manner intended by the advertiser?
- What portions of the message were retained?
- Did the message lead to action?

FEEDBACK

The message's effect on sales is represented by a feedback loop in Figure 11-1 from consumer action to the source and sender. The marketer will evaluate sales results and adjust the promotional campaign accordingly. This is easier said than done. The link between advertising and sales is the most important one in Figure 11-1, yet it is the most difficult to evaluate. It is the most important because the purpose of a marketing communication is to influence the consumer to act. Although exposure, awareness, comprehension, and retention are used to measure a message's effectiveness, they are the means to the end — sales.

In the case of Chimère, advertising appeared to be highly successful, since the brand delivered over $100 million in gross revenue in 1981 and is still growing. But the difficulty in linking advertising to sales results is that management can never be sure to what degree sales are due to advertising, to price, to competition, or to a host of other environmental factors beyond its control. It is almost certain that advertising will have an effect on sales, but the key questions are How much of an effect? and What components of the promotional mix are most successful? A statement made by John Wanamaker over a hundred years ago is still true today: "I know that half my advertising is working, but I don't know which half."

In the next few sections we will consider in more detail each of the components of the marketing communications model described above:

- the source,
- the message (encoding),
- the media (transmission),
- the consumer's processing of information (decoding) and subsequent action, and
- feedback (evaluating the communications).

Source Effects in Marketing Communication

Figure 11-1 is focused primarily on the advertiser as the source of marketing communications. But the communication model is equally relevant for other sources and other forms of communication. For example, in a buyer-seller interaction the salesperson would be the source of the message, the encoder, and the transmitter. The effective salesperson would first gauge the needs of the buyer, determine products in the line that might meet these needs, formulate a message to convey product benefits, transmit the message, evaluate the customer's reaction to the message, and then adjust the message on the basis of customer feedback.

TYPES OF SOURCES

Consumers are exposed to many sources of information — for example, messages from different companies and from friends and neighbors.

Marketing information comes from three types of source:

1. *Commercial* (advertising, personal selling, sales promotions, publicity — in short, the promotional mix);
2. *Personal* (friends, relatives, acquaintances who transmit product information through word-of-mouth); and
3. *Neutral* (impartial testing agencies, government sources, news and editorial sources).

Most research studies agree that the commercial sources of information are most important in providing product information, but that personal and neutral sources have a more powerful influence on consumer actions.[4] Advertising is a weaker influence than word-of-mouth and neutral sources for two reasons: (1) less source credibility and (2) less source attractiveness.

SOURCE CREDIBILITY

Credibility is associated with believability, trustworthiness, and expertise. Advertising is not viewed as very credible because of the advertiser's obvious desire to sell the brand. Neutral sources are regarded as credible because they have no vested interest in the brand. They make no attempt to change attitudes or influence behavior. Newscasters and editorial sources have a high degree of credibility. Walter Cronkite, the former newscaster, has been cited in polls as the most credible individual in the eyes of the American public. Personal and neutral sources are viewed as more credible, because they are regarded as trustworthy sources of information.[5] Consumers are more likely to accept the brand judgments of family and friends, particularly those viewed as opinion leaders for the product category.

Studies have found that the greater the credibility of the source in consumers' eyes, the greater the likelihood the message will be accepted.[6] It would benefit advertisers to increase their credibility by using the following strategies:

1. *Use spokespersons and sales personnel that convey expertise.* Research has shown that salespeople who are viewed as experts have credibility in sales situations. Marketers should therefore ensure that their sales staff is totally familiar with the product. Expertise is particularly important in industrial sales because of the technical complexity and service and maintenance requirements of many industrial products. The same principle can also be applied to spokespersons in consumer advertising: use an expert to provide a testimonial for your product. Arthur Ashe appearing for tennis rackets, Ella Fitzgerald for Memorex tapes, and Rafer Johnson, the former Olympic decathlon champion for AMF sports equipment (see Figure 6-7) are examples of experts lending credibility to the product.

2. *Do not say the product is good for everything.* Emphasize its advantages but also state some of the disadvantages. Research has shown that such a two-sided approach increases the credibility of the source.[7]

3. *Emphasize information in the message.* Advertising and sales presentations using facts are more credible than those relying on imagery. The use of doctors in ads to provide factual material on over-the-counter drugs is an example. Mercedes-Benz takes an informational approach in their print advertising by detailing the specifications and performance results of the car.

4. *Use publicity to get the message across.* The use of publicity increases the advertiser's credibility because the product's message appears in neutral

media such as newspaper stories, magazine articles, or TV talk shows. A good public relations department will get as much play for the product from such impartial sources as possible. One public relations executive effectively states this advantage: "Advertising has never had credibility and never will have. With advertising, people are always on their guard. They're always wary because they know the purpose of advertising is to sell. But public relations — that's something different.[8] Such publicity is most likely to occur if there is some public-service value to the consumer. Perhaps the most famous case is the public-relations benefit obtained by Procter & Gamble when the American Dental Association endorsed Crest toothpaste as a more effective agent for reducing tooth decay because of the introduction of fluoride. The ADA's endorsement received wide publicity at no cost to P&G and enhanced the credibility of P&G's advertised claim.

SOURCE ATTRACTIVENESS

Another reason why advertising is a weak form of communication is that it has little attractiveness for the consumer. Attractiveness increases with the similarity of the source to the receiver, the believability of the source, and its prestige. On this basis marketers can use the following strategies to increase source attractiveness:

1. *Emphasize the similarity between the source and the receiver.* Research has shown that when consumers see salespersons as similar to themselves, they are more likely to accept and be influenced by the salesperson's message.[9] The salesperson is seen as a friend or peer and becomes more attractive. Advertisers have used this principle by portraying "typical consumers" using and endorsing the product. Diverse brands such as Tylenol analgesics, Nikon cameras, and Dove soap have used this approach (for example, see Figure 6-6).

2. *Enhance prestige through the use of spokespersons.* Consumers are sometimes attracted to and influenced by dissimilar communicators, particularly prestigious people. These may not need to have expertise in the product category as long as they have prestige in the eyes of the target group. One of the first persons American Express used when it kicked off its "Do you know me?" campaign was William Miller, Barry Goldwater's running mate in the 1964 presidential election. Even though not widely known, Miller added prestige to the campaign.[10]

When the communication is direct (e.g., a salesperson) similarity seems to be best, but when the communication is indirect (e.g., advertising) dissimilarity is sometimes effective in increasing source attractiveness. One study found that combining similarity and expertise produces the greatest message acceptance.[11]

3. *Enhance likeability by the use of empathetic personalities.* Bill Cosby has been rated high on persuasiveness for Jell-O pudding and other children-

oriented commercials because he is a likeable character. But respondents found him less effective as a spokesman for Ford Motor Company.[12] Nancy Walker portrays a likeable lunch-counter waitress in ads for Bounty and also scores high on persuasiveness. Both individuals tend to increase the attractiveness of the source.

Message Effects in Marketing Communications

Marketing communications are meant to inform and persuade. *Informational objectives* are:

- announcing a new product,
- communicating changes in existing products,
- informing consumers of the product's characteristics,
- comparing the brand to competitors, or
- providing information on price, promotions, and store availability.

Some *persuasive objectives* are:

- convincing the consumer of the product's superiority,
- inducing trial,
- associating the product with positive thoughts and feelings, or
- reducing uncertainty after the purchase is made.

Certain aspects of message content bear directly on the likelihood that these objectives will be fulfilled. The following questions are particularly important in developing advertising messages and other forms of marketing communications:

1. Should the message take an emotional or rational approach?
2. What are the advantages of using fear appeals?
3. What is the appropriate role of humor in advertising?
4. Should messages be clear-cut or ambiguous?
5. Should the message be one-sided or two-sided?
6. Is comparative advertising (naming a competitor in the ad) more persuasive than noncomparative advertising?

Each of these message effects will be briefly considered.

EMOTIONAL VERSUS RATIONAL APPEALS

In a recent seminar of advertising executives, the strategic issue cited as most deserving immediate attention was when to use emotional and rational appeals.[13] The reason for this concern was the frequency of emotionally based advertising in the 1980s coupled with the lack of guidelines for strategically positioning promotional strategy on an emotional-rational continuum. Minute Maid Orange Juice pictures a young mother assuring her five-year-old son that she loves him as much as his newborn brother. Cannon Mills shows a montage of happy people with the slogan "Cannon Touches Your Life." General Foods decided to sack Cora, its more rational spokeswoman who explained the benefits of Maxwell House coffee, for a campaign based on such emotional vignettes as a harried commuter pausing for coffee after missing his train. In none of these cases was there any attempt to directly inform consumers of the specific benefits of the product (a rational approach). Rather, product benefits were communicated indirectly through good feelings, sympathetic scenes, and attempts to portray typical consumers in everyday situations (emotional appeals).

Why is there a trend away from the traditional gospel of directly communicating product benefits? There are at least four reasons:

1. "Many advertisers have turned to sentiment because they've run out of compelling appeals to logic. Their own sales pitches have lost their punch and, for the increasing number of products that don't differ markedly from their competitors, new arguments are hard to find."[14] When most competitors are using the same appeals, the only distinctive positioning may be emotionally based.

2. More rigorous regulation of advertising has narrowed the scope of benefits that advertisers can claim. One creative director says, "In hair care and cosmetics products, the ability of the advertisers to make stronger specific claims is dramatically reduced . . . due to increased scrutiny of their advertising by the networks and the government."[15]

3. Rational appeals have sometimes been equated with a hard sell. Repetitive appeals of product benefits can be irritating and lose their attention-getting value. The "ring around the collar" campaign for Wisk detergent clearly communicates the cleansing benefits of the product. But it is regarded as one of the most irritating and abrasive commercials on the air.[16]

4. The trend to emotional appeals reflects advertisers' recognition that many of their products are low involvement categories unrelated to consumers' ego needs. Emotional appeals attempt to increase the individual's association with the product category. As the creative director of the Cannon Mills' campaign said, "A towel is an insignificant thing until you relate it to a person's involvement with it [create an emotional situation]."[17]

If emotional appeals are used to increase involvement for unimportant products, can they work for products more closely related to the consumer's self-image? Frequently, yes. For example, ads for perfumes, automobiles, and clothing use emotional appeals to build a positive image. But such products cannot be sold on sentiment alone. The financial risk in buying an automobile, the social risk in buying a perfume or deodorant, or the product risk in buying a drug item dictates the need for a more rational, benefit-communications approach. For example, the ad agency for Bayer aspirin found that when it used an emotional approach, the ad bombed. Bayer switched to a stone-faced announcer with this unemotional pitch: "Nothing works better than Bayer. Nothing."[18]

FEAR APPEALS

Another issue in marketing communications is the use of fear appeals to persuade consumers to buy. Most marketing communications attempt to inform consumers of the benefits of using a product. Fear appeals do the opposite: they inform consumers of the risks of using a product (e.g., cigarettes) or of not using one (e.g., deodorants).

Fear appeals are least likely to be effective when consumers' anxieties associated with the product are either too high or too low. If the anxiety about the use or lack of use of a product is too high, the consumer will simply avoid the anxiety-producing information. Public-service advertising to discourage cigarette smoking with appeals from terminal cancer patients or to discourage drunken driving with detailed scenes of car crashes were ineffective because of the high anxiety they produced. Cigarette smoking did not decrease after health warnings became public because many smokers simply chose to ignore them.[19]

When there is little or no anxiety associated with the message, fear appeals are again likely to fail. A fear appeal for floor cleaners picturing neighbors commenting on a dirty floor is not likely to work these days because homemakers are just not very concerned. However an appeal based on social ostracism for having bad breath or loose dentures might work because many consumers are concerned about these issues, but not concerned enough to avoid the message.

Fear appeals are therefore most likely to influence the consumer when anxiety is moderate.[20] They are also most likely to succeed when the consumer has a choice. They may influence nonsmokers to stay away from cigarettes or light smokers to quit. But they will not influence the behavior of addictive smokers. Nor are they likely to influence teenagers who are under heavy peer pressure to smoke. These teenagers may feel they have no choice but to conform to group norms.

HUMOR IN MARKETING COMMUNICATIONS

There are pros and cons to using humor to inform and persuade consumers. One research company found humorous ads to be more memorable and persuasive.[21] This is because humor is a good attention-getting device and may create a positive mood toward the advertiser.[22] But unless the humorous appeal is clearly linked to the product and is communicating product benefits, it may distract the consumer and do more harm than good. One of the better-known commercials based on humor was the use of "Bert and Harry Piels" played by the comedians Bob and Ray to advertise Piels beer. Although recall of the ads was high, consumers focused more on the characters than on the product. In this case humor could not be said to be effective. The advertising got their attention but did not persuade consumers to buy.

AMBIGUOUS APPEALS

Sometimes advertisers introduce ambiguity into their appeals so that the message can mean different things to different people. Consumers who do not hold strong beliefs about the brand are more likely to accept an ambiguous message. Ambiguity also allows consumers to project their own needs to the brand. If the message is too explicit, the consumer has little room for projecting and the marketer may be unnecessarily restricting the potential market. The Lenox China and Crystal ad at the left in Figure 11-3 is an example of an ambiguous appeal. The purpose of the advertisement is to enhance the female ego and allow almost any motive to be projected to the ad. The theme "Live the legend" and the imagery can mean many things to women. Some informational content

FIGURE 11-3
Examples of ambiguous and unambiguous advertising

By permission of Lenox China & Crystal, Inc.   By permission of Mobil Oil Corp.

is required; otherwise the message may be misunderstood. The Lenox ad is clearly conveying an image of quality and luxury. But excessive ambiguity will cause the consumer to have difficulty understanding the ad or relating to it. The symbolism might be so remote as to have no meaning. An example is the case of a lower-priced beer that attempted to establish a quality image by using a fox hunt as a setting.

On the other side of the coin, marketers should be explicit in their advertising if the product's benefits are clear-cut and the product is targeted to a well-defined segment. An example of an unambiguous ad is at the right in Figure 11-3. The ad refers to one basic benefit directed to drivers concerned with gas economy. The information is clear and readily understood by consumers interested in this benefit. Information dominates and ambiguity is held to a minimum. Industrial advertising tends to be less ambiguous than consumer advertising because it is more heavily balanced toward informational content than toward symbolism.

TWO-SIDED MESSAGES

Two-sided messages provide both positive and negative information about a product. There are two approaches to two-sided communications. First, the negative information is not important and is discounted. Second, the negative information presents and then refutes competitive claims.

Presenting and then discounting negative information about the company's product is an infrequent strategy in advertising. It does increase credibility, but it could also point to product deficiencies and discourage consumers from buying. Such a strategy can be quite effective if discounting a negative factor actually reinforces the benefits of the product. Avis uses a two-sided discounting strategy by first stating that it is not the largest company and then discounting it by saying, "We try harder." (See Figure 11-4.) The Avis campaign actually turned an unimportant negative into a positive benefit by convincing many consumers that being number two prompted the company to pay more attention to its customers.

Refutational ads state competing appeals and then refute them by communicating the product's benefits. The classic refutational campaign was Volkswagen's advertising for the Bug. Competing cars emphasized roominess and luxury. Volkswagen met this claim head-on by recognizing a lack of luxury and claiming high quality. Similarly, Mutual of New York (MONY) refuted the idea that people would be better off putting their money in stocks and bonds rather than life insurance with the following copy: "I'm in stocks and bonds. I'll take them over life insurance [the competitive claim]. But a MONY man gave me a new look at life insurance. As an investment cornerstone it would protect my family ... and build cash, too!" [the refutation].[23]

Two-sided messages tend to be effective as a means of defusing the competitive appeal.[24] Thus, if a salesperson mentions some of the minor disadvantages of the company's product, it takes the edge off any such mention by a competitive

Avis is only No.2.
But we don't
want your sympathy.

It hasn't come to this.

Have we been crying too much? Have we overplayed the underdog?

We didn't think so till David Biener, 11 years old, sent us 35¢, saying, "It may help you buy another Plymouth."

That was an eye-opener.

So now we'd like to correct the false impression we've made.

We don't want you to rent Avis cars because you feel sorry for us. All we want is a chance to prove that a No. 2 can be just as good as a No. 1. Or even better. Because we have to try harder.

Maybe we ought to eliminate the negative and accentuate the positive.

Instead of saying "We're only No. 2 in rent a cars," we could say "We're the second largest in the world."

©AVIS RENT A CAR SYSTEM, INC.

FIGURE 11-4
Example of a two-sided message
Increasing source credibility
Used by permission.

salesperson. Two-sided ads also tend to be most effective with well-educated consumers.[25] Such consumers are likely to be skeptical when only one side of the story is presented. But two-sided communications are not always more effective. Evidence suggests that a one-sided message is most persuasive when the consumer (1) agrees with the advertiser's position or (2) is loyal to the advertised brand.[26] In such cases the one-sided message reinforces the consumer's current beliefs. But consumers are becoming more skeptical and less brand loyal, suggesting that the use of two-sided advertising is likely to increase.

COMPARATIVE ADVERTISING

Comparative advertising has been used more often since the networks removed a ban on its use in the mid 1970s and the Federal Trade Commission formally endorsed its use in 1979. In 1981 23 percent of the radio and TV commercials on ABC were comparative ads.[27] Most comparative advertising is one-sided; that is, presenting only the strengths of the advertised product and weaknesses of the competitive product. For example, 7-Up blasts other sodas for having caffeine, Minute Maid berates Country Time as the "no-lemon lemonade," and Pillsbury's Totina pizza contends the crust on other frozen pizzas tastes like cardboard.[28]

There are pros and cons to the use of comparative advertising. Benefits have been cited for both consumers and advertisers. The FTC cites the main consumer benefit: more rational purchase decisions.[29] For example, in 1975 Bristol-Myers launched a comparative campaign for Datril, its nonaspirin analgesic in competition with Tylenol, by advertising that the two products were identical except that Datril was cheaper. The advertising informed the consumers of price differences, but more important, caused Tylenol to reduce its price to consumers by about 30 percent.[30]

For the advertiser the main benefit of comparative advertising is the potential of increased sales as a result of greater attention to comparative claims and the possibility of drawing users of competitive products.[31] For example, the "Pepsi challenge" campaign in which Pepsi taste tests showed consumers preferred it to Coke boosted Pepsi sales in some markets by 35 percent. And Burger King's sales increased by 16 percent in January 1983 after a four-month comparative campaign attacking McDonald's for having 20 percent less meat and frying rather than broiling their hamburgers.[32] In each case the company in the second or third position in the market attacked the market leader successfully.

Most marketing analysts have concluded that comparative advertising is most likely to be successful when a challenger attacks a leader. But there may be serious drawbacks to its use. Comparative advertising sometimes confuses rather than clarifies. A study by Ogilvy and Mather, a large advertising agency, found that consumers were more likely to misidentify the sponsor of the ad as the market leader. The study also found that comparative advertising is no more persuasive than noncomparative advertising.[33]

A key strategic question faced by market leaders is how they should react to comparative attacks. The conventional wisdom is to do nothing and weather the storm since attacking weaker competitors draws attention to their claims and does more harm than good. This principle was violated by Coca-Cola and McDonald's probably to their detriment. Coca-Cola embarked on some comparative advertising of its own, citing caloric advantages for Coke over Pepsi.[34] McDonald's chose to take Burger King to court, but the mass media began reporting the battle between the two, giving Burger King free publicity. Burger King estimates that the company got $20 to $30 million worth of free publicity from newspaper, radio, and television coverage of the "battle of the burgers."[35]

Media Effects in Marketing Communications

The third component in the communications model in Figure 11-1 is message transmission through media. Most marketers use paid media, but the Burger King example points out the benefits of no-cost publicity. A key requirement in the communication model is that the message reach the intended target. The target segment's demographic and life-style characteristics must be identified and media must be selected to best reach these segments. Media selection and strategy will be considered in the next chapter.

This section describes types of media used in marketing communications — television, radio, newspapers, magazines — and their advantages and disadvantages. Another factor in media effects is the media vehicle. For example, there are substantial differences between the image, editorial content, and prestige of various magazines. An ad suitable for the *New Yorker* is not likely to be suitable for *Reader's Digest.*

MEDIA EFFECTS BY TYPE

The broadest divisions by type of media are between (1) broadcast versus print media and (2) in-store versus mass media. In this section we will consider each of these and will then look at specific types of mass media.

Broadcast versus Print

Broadcast media (TV and radio) are better at communicating imagery and symbolism but not as effective as print (newspapers and magazines) in communicating detailed information. As a result, TV is more suitable for developing a mood or establishing a good feeling about the product. Print is more effective in directly conveying information. Print is particularly appropriate in industrial advertising because of the need to communicate product specifications.

Broadcast media (particularly TV) have been described as low-involvement media because the rate of viewing and understanding is out of the viewer's control. There is little opportunity to dwell on a point in television advertising. The consumer can sit back and absorb the message without being actively involved. As one marketer said, "The public lets down its guard to the repetitive commercial use of television. . . . [The public] easily changes its ways of perceiving products and brands and its purchasing behavior without thinking very much about it at the time of TV exposure."[36] In other words, consumers receive marketing communications from TV commercials in a more passive state than from print media but do absorb the information and may act on it once they are in a purchasing situation.

Print media (particularly magazines) have been described as more involving because they allow the reader to set the pace.[37] The reader can choose whether to be exposed to the advertisement and has more opportunity to think about the points made in the advertising. The main benefits of the product can be read, considered, and related to the consumer's needs. Print is more appropriate when specific information must be communicated in combination with symbols and imagery (automobiles, clothing, cameras, sound equipment). Most national advertisers use a combination of print and broadcast media, because they have several objectives and want to reach several audiences.

In-Store versus Mass Media

Media can be classified as marketing communications that occur in the store in the form of point-of-purchase advertising (displays and in-store TV) or as communications through the mass media (print and broadcast). The product package can also be regarded as a form of point-of-purchase advertising, since consumers frequently obtain information from the package in the store.

Point-of-purchase (POP) advertising gives marketers difficulty because it is within the control of retailers, and retailers do not always use the displays, shelf racks, signs, and banners provided by the manufacturer. Yet it is a crucial part of the promotional mix because it represents the last point of influence before the purchase. Its importance is reflected in the fact that advertisers spent about $5.5 billion on point-of-purchase material in 1982.[38]

The diversity of point-of-purchase media may be illustrated by a hypothetical shopper faced with Coca-Cola's well-integrated POP campaign: As our customer crosses the parking lot, there is a special price offer for Coke announced on the store window. The cart he or she pulls is decorated with a "have a Coke ..." sign on its side. The consumer flips open the baby seat to put in some groceries and up pops a convenient shopper's desk for lists and coupons. Under its laminated top is "Enjoy a Coke now." Proceeding down the aisle the consumer passes another shopper on whose cart the front ad reads (you guessed it) "Buy a Coke." In the soda aisle, displays beckon. From the ceiling hangs a mobile. All their messages are telling our consumer about Coke.[39]

Types of Mass Media

There are five major types of mass media: television, radio, newspapers, magazines, and direct mail. Advertising expenditures in 1983 in dollars and as a percentage of all expenditures for these types are listed below:[40]

	1983 Expenditures *(in millions)*	*% of* *Total*
Newspapers	17,694	26.6
Television	14,329	21.5
Direct Mail	10,319	15.5
Radio	4,670	7.0
Magazines	3,858	5.8

Other forms of advertising (outdoor, transit) account for about one-fourth of expenditures. The reason that newspapers top the list is the large amounts spent by retailers on day-to-day announcements of sales and merchandise. On a national basis television is clearly most important. Each medium has its strengths and weaknesses as we shall see.

Television

Television's greatest strength is that it is a visual medium in sound, color, and motion that can demonstrate product usage and consumer reactions. Another strength is its reach. Over 97 percent of United States households have TV sets. In an average day 88 percent of these households watch TV.[41] TV is regarded as the most effective selling medium for mass-market products.[42] The national scope of network TV makes it particularly effective in creating quick awareness of new brands. The massive network TV campaign for Diet Coke made it a household name almost overnight.

The national scope of TV is also a potential weakness. The medium is not selective in pinpointing target segments. If a food manufacturer identifies the target segment for its new brand of yogurt as well-educated, high-income, weight-conscious young adults, then a saturation blitz on TV might be wasteful. Perhaps 70 percent of advertising expenditures would be directed to consumers who are not in the target group.

TV is an expensive medium; a thirty-second spot in prime time costs over $100,000. TV costs have also increased faster than those of other media, rising almost 2 1/2 times between 1970 and 1982.[43] As a result, many advertisers are switching from TV to magazines, radio, and cheaper local and nonprime-time TV.

Cable TV

One development that many marketers are closely watching is cable TV. It offers the selectivity that network TV lacks. Cable channels are often oriented to specialized interests such as news, sports, cultural programming, and movies. Commercials can therefore be directed to more specific and well-defined audiences. As a result, cable TV has come to be referred to as **narrowcasting** as opposed to the mass media's *broadcasting.* Another advantage of cable TV is that commercials can be much longer and more detailed because of lower costs and the more specialized interests of the audience. Three- or four- minute commercials are the norm — for example, advertising a food product by showing its use in a recipe. As a result, such advertising has come to be called **infomercials** in contrast to network TV's *commercials*.

Advertising expenditures on cable TV are limited at this point, representing only a small fraction of total expenditures on network TV. But the growth of cable TV homes (over 30 percent of American households now have it) and the advantages of the medium as a selective means of communication have prompted most large advertising agencies to establish cable TV divisions, signaling increased use of the medium.

Radio

A panel of advertising experts found that radio's key advantages are immediacy, economy, and flexibility.[44] Radio provides immediacy because it offers room-to-room coverage. There are an average of five radios per household. It is frequently turned on for news, music, or sports, with the average consumer listening to over three hours of radio per day. It also offers flexibility in reaching audiences when other media cannot — namely at wakeup time and while driving. The medium also offers the flexibility of reaching specialized audiences. The diversity of radio stations and their local reach prompted one advertising executive to describe radio as "the original narrowcaster, enabling advertisers to reach teenagers, senior citizens, housewives, blacks, Hispanics, and other target audiences."[45]

These advantages prompted advertisers to spend $4.2 billion on radio commercials in 1982, one-third the total expenditures for TV. Campaigns for True Value hardware stores and Shasta soft drinks have relied primarily on radio. True Value uses radio because it can more easily tie in with local hardware retailers and sponsor local special events. Shasta effectively used radio locally and nationally while spending only a fraction of what the most popular brands spent on their campaigns.[46] Yet it became one of the top ten soft drinks.

Radio does have its disadvantages. It is not visual or involving. Most people listen to radio as background while reading, working, or driving. But the medium is cost effective in reaching specialized audiences.

Magazines

Magazines are as selective as radio in reaching a target group. The trend since the early 1970s has been to specialty rather than general-audience magazines. Magazines are best at reaching audiences with special interests (fashion, sports, autos, electronics, and so forth). They have also been introduced to meet the needs of specific demographic groups; for example, working women (*Working Mother, Enterprising Woman*), blacks (*Black Family, Black Enterprise*), and Hispanics (*Vanidades*).

Magazines have one major advantage over other media — permanence.

Most magazines are saved, picked up more than once, and passed along to others. As a result, a consumer may be exposed to a magazine ad more than once, and a single ad is likely to be seen by more than one reader. Magazines also offer the power of the printed word, the ability to attract a reader by a headline or illustration and to keep the reader's attention by copy that is directly related to his or her needs. Honda uses magazines to target car enthusiasts as an effective means of conveying its benefits of quality and economy.[47]

An important category of magazines for industrial marketers is specialized business publications such as *Iron Age, Aviation Week,* and *Engineering and Mining.* These publications are the primary medium for industrial advertisers since they direct ads to industrial buyers with purchasing influence.

Newspapers

Retail advertising accounts for most of the advertising in newspapers. Retailers advertise day-to-day changes in prices, special offers, sales, coupons, and merchandise. Despite the dominance of retail advertising, however, national advertisers are beginning to spend more on newspaper advertising. National advertisers see newspapers as an excellent medium for providing detailed information to consumers. Product advertising by manufacturers in newspapers is growing, and is close to total expenditures for magazines. Added to this is the credibility of newspaper advertising. Television and radio are regarded as entertainment media. Newspapers are news media. Advertising in newspapers is therefore more likely to be believed.

These advantages led Peugeot's advertising agency, Ogilvy and Mather, to develop an advertising campaign for the car in which 80 percent of advertising expenditures were allocated to newspapers.[48] The reason is that the target audience was defined as intelligent, well-educated information seekers. The agency concluded, "Newspapers work well because we want to provide our target audience with a lot of information, and we have a lot of excellent information to give."[49] Another plus was flexibility. The campaign could tailor the amount of advertising to the level of Peugeot's penetration in each market.

Direct mail

The mails are another important communication medium. Direct-mail advertising is a $6-billion-per-year business. The main advantages of direct mail are that it can target communications to a specific group and that it is less expensive than the mass media. Mailing lists have been developed that can pinpoint specific markets. For example, The Life-Style Selector, a Denver-based company, has a data base of 10 million names and addresses that includes consumption and demographic data for each name.[50] The company can develop a list for a particular target. If an advertiser wants to promote darkroom equipment through direct mail, the Life-Style Selector can identify photographers in the higher-income group who own their own homes. Use of direct mail ensures that the message will get through to the group with the highest purchase potential. Its effectiveness is illustrated by the fact that 30 to 35 percent of Americans have responded to direct-mail ads, and that such responses doubled between 1977 and 1983.[51]

MEDIA EFFECTS BY VEHICLE

Media effects vary not only by type, but by vehicle within type. Marshall McLuhan's statement, "The medium is the message," implies that media vehicles communicate an image independent of any one message they contain.[52] Magazines like *New Yorker*, *Reader's Digest*, and *Playboy* have different images based on different editorial content, reputation, and subscribers. The interpretation of an advertising message is therefore a function of the vehicle by which it is transmitted as well as the content of the message.

The role of the media vehicle in marketing communications is illustrated by the fact that the same advertisement will result in different communications effects when run in two different vehicles. A study by Aaker and Brown placed identical ads in two magazines, *New Yorker* and *Tennis World*.[53] The two magazines were chosen as contrasts, *New Yorker* representing a prestige magazine and *Tennis World* a specialty magazine. The study found that *New Yorker* was more effective in persuading nonusers to consider a product when the ad stressed product quality. *Tennis World* was more effective when the ad stressed reasons for use. These findings suggest that the vehicle's environment conveys a message: specialty media were more effective in conveying information; prestige media were more effective in conveying image.

The Aaker and Brown study suggests that the vehicle's environment conveys a mood that might affect reaction to particular product categories. Another study found that some product categories were definitely more appropriate for some media vehicles because of the vehicle's mood and image. For example, food products do well in situation comedies but poorly in mysteries and adventure programs. Analgesics do well in adult Westerns and situation comedies.[54]

Consumer Effects in Marketing Communications

The fourth link in the marketing communications chain in Figure 11-1 is the consumer (receiver). The consumer is the crucial element in the chain. For marketing communications to be effective, enough consumers must process the information and act on it. How they process and act on marketing communications is the basis for the last step — feedback and evaluation.

CONSUMER PROCESSING OF MARKETING COMMUNICATIONS

Figure 11-5 presents a model of the processing of marketing communications. The consumer is first exposed to a marketing communication. Exposure can result from the passive receipt of information (sitting in front of the television

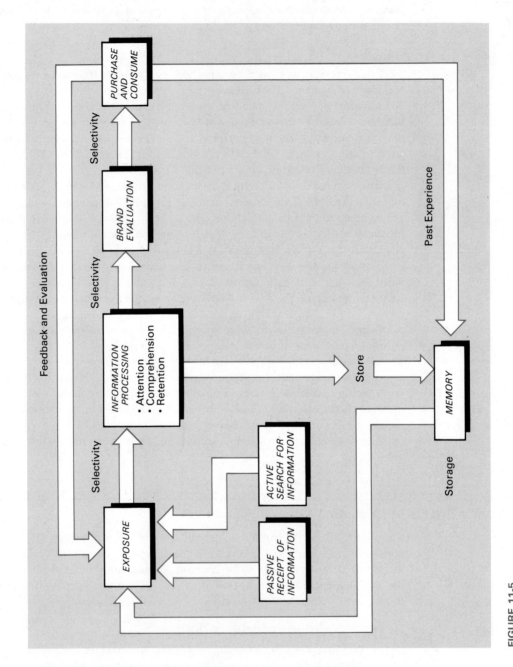

FIGURE 11-5
Consumer processing of marketing communication

set and seeing a commercial) or active information search (visiting a car dealer's showroom). In most cases, marketing information will be processed through attention, comprehension, and retention. As a result of retention the information is stored in memory.

Information processing leads to some effect on the perception of the brand — either reinforcing existing beliefs and attitudes or changing them. The 7-Up campaign centering on the caffeine-free benefits of the soft drink might reinforce some consumers' beliefs that caffeine in soft drinks should be avoided. Awareness of the caffeine-free benefit of 7-Up might lead these consumers to buy. Others might first become aware that soft drinks have caffeine and become more sensitive to the need to avoid it. Such attitude change might also lead to trial. Yet others might consider caffeine in soft drinks a nonissue and maintain existing attitudes with little prospect of trial. In all cases the campaign was evaluated through attention, comprehension, and retention.

On the basis of brand evaluation the consumer decides whether to purchase or not. A purchase will result in a consumption experience that is also stored in memory. Memory feeds back into exposure in that consumers can call up the information in memory for future use.

Each step in Figure 11-5 is selective because each person chooses information and interprets it differently as a result of his or her unique combination of needs, attitudes, experiences, and personal characteristics. Selective processing of information means that the identical advertisement, package, or product may be perceived very differently by two consumers. One consumer may believe the claim that Bayer is a safer and faster-acting aspirin; another may regard such a claim as untrue and believe that all aspirin products are the same.

Selectivity also extends to physical stimuli such as taste. Studies have shown that most consumers cannot discriminate between the taste or smell of various brands of beer, cigarettes, soft drinks, or coffee when these brands are unlabeled. But once the brand is labeled, the same consumers express strong taste and quality preferences.[55] Consumer reactions are not based on the physical properties of the brand in these cases; they are based on consumer associations derived from advertising and word-of-mouth communications from friends. The consumer who cannot tell the difference between Coke and Pepsi but expresses a strong preference for Coke when it is labeled, is doing so on the basis of advertising and social stimuli.

COMPONENTS OF INFORMATION PROCESSING

In this section we will consider the steps in information processing, namely:

- exposure,
- attention,
- comprehension, and
- retention.

These steps will be considered from the strategic perspective of the marketing communicator, since they have direct implications for product positioning, message development, media selection, and promotional evaluation.

Exposure

Exposure requires only that the consumer be present when a marketing stimulus occurs. Consumers occasionally sit in front of a TV set without really seeing a commercial or flip through a magazine without noticing an ad. One study found that three-fourths of consumers who were not alone when watching TV were talking to someone.[56] In such cases exposure occurs without much attention. Generally, some level of attention does follow exposure.

Information search

In most cases consumers are exposed to marketing communications passively while doing something else — seeing a billboard while driving, seeing a commercial while watching TV, noticing an ad while reading a magazine, hearing about a product while talking to a friend, noticing a new product on the shelf while shopping. But in some cases, the consumer is motivated to search for information. Such search may involve seeking out ads in specialty magazines, visiting stores to comparison shop, or asking friends about products, prices, and stores. Studies have found that information search is most likely when:

- *The price of a product is high.*[57] (A higher price means more economic benefits from information search.)
- *There are substantial differences between brands.*[58] (More benefits are gained from comparison shopping when significant differences exist between brands.)
- *The product is important to the consumer.*[59]
- *The perceived risk in purchasing is higher.*[60]
- *The consumer has less past experience,* requiring information search for an informed choice.[61]

High-priced items such as cameras, stereo equipment, and automobiles, and high-involvement items such as perfumes, toiletries and clothing are most likely to lead to information search and exposure to marketing messages. Yet active search is limited even for these products. One study found that appliance buyers use only 24 percent of the information available.[62] Another found that 50 percent of the purchasers of cars and appliances visit only one showroom[63] and that over 40 percent of these buyers consider only one brand.[64]

Strategic implications of information search

Advertisers can assist in consumers' information search by providing catalogs, brochures, and informational advertising. For example, a furniture manufacturer might provide retailers with brochures describing the line and its features, and individual flyers to be distributed to customers. Advertising might also stress the functional benefits of the line. One study found that purchasers of rugs and carpets felt uneasy about buying these items because they did not know what criteria to use to evaluate alternative makes. They were willing to search for information because of the high risk and cost, but they did not know what questions to ask salespeople.[65] A manufacturer could gain a competitive advantage by using an informational campaign that instructed the consumer on product attributes and cited the advantages of the company's line.

Marketers must realize that in most cases information search is limited. Limited search means that marketers must establish awareness of existing products and recognition of new products through passive means. Repeated advertising on TV is the most effective way to establish enough awareness to encourage consumers to try the product. This is particularly true of packaged goods, since these are inexpensive items that do not warrant active information search.

Limited search also points to the importance of trial as a means of obtaining information.[66] If the product is inexpensive and uninvolving, it may be cheaper and easier to try it than to search for information. A cost-effective communication strategy in such cases is to put additional dollars into free samples and price promotions instead of advertising. Because sales promotion has been emphasized more than advertising in recent years, many marketers are following this strategy.

Attention

Attention is the process of noticing a marketing communication or certain portions of the communication. It is a screening mechanism that controls the quantity and nature of the information perceived. Only a small portion of a communication the consumer is exposed to gets through the attention filter. In one study consumers utilized only 2 percent of their information presented to make their brand decision.[67]

Attention is selective since consumers are most likely to look at information relevant to their needs and to communications that agree with their beliefs and attitudes. For example, one study asked consumers to rate several products and then choose one as a gift.[68] After making their choice, consumers were given a research report citing the good and bad characteristics of each of the products in the study. They noticed the positive characteristics of the chosen product and the negative characteristics of the rejected products. Attention was selective in reinforcing their choice.

Attention should not be a communication objective in itself. It is easy to draw attention to an ad without drawing attention to the product or its benefits. A good-looking model, a striking scene, or eye-catching graphics will draw the consumer's eye to the ad. But unless attention encourages comprehension of the message, it is meaningless. The Bert and Harry Piels ads cited earlier got attention because of their humor but did not lead to comprehension of product benefits.

Comprehension

Comprehension is the organization and evaluation of information so that it can be used to evaluate brands or it can be stored in memory for future use.

Organization and Evaluation of Information

To comprehend information, one must first organize it. Consumers simplify this process by putting information into categories. Brand logos such as Coca-Cola or Ivory Soap are associated with the product and provide a shorthand for categorizing information. Johnson & Johnson has established the basis for categorizing baby powders with its square, white plastic container and blue lettering. When information is new, the easiest method of categorizing it is by generalizing to something familiar. When the automobile was first introduced, consumers categorized it with their former means of transportation and called it the "horseless carriage."

Once information is organized, it is then evaluated. A governing principle in evaluating information is **perceptual equilibrium** — that is, the interpretation of information to conform to current beliefs and attitudes. The consumer who rejects Coke in an unlabeled test but prefers it when the label is shown is selectively evaluating information (the label) to conform to his or her past experiences (brand preference for Coke).

Strategic Implications of Comprehension

The manner in which consumers organize and evaluate information provides several important implications for promotional strategy. Marketing communicators should seek to facilitate the organization of information by ensuring that:

■ *the product is easily categorized* (prominently display the product and symbols associated with it for easy identification in the advertising);

■ *information is consistent with the brand image* (do not confuse the consumer by frequently shifting symbols and imagery); and

■ *various components of the promotional mix are telling the same story* (do not advertise the item as a luxury product and then use sales promotions to run sales and price specials).

The marketing communicator should also facilitate evaluation of the message by ensuring that it is communicating consumer benefits. Even emotionally oriented appeals or ambiguous messages that do not directly communicate benefits should be tested to determine whether they do so indirectly. Does the harried consumer stopping for a cup of Maxwell House convey a benefit of refreshment and relaxation? Does the Lenox China ad convey the benefits of prestige and luxury from product ownership? In short, is the consumer decoding the message as the advertiser intended?

Retention

A message may be noticed, evaluated, and quickly forgotten. Messages relevant to consumer needs are more likely to be **retained;** but most information is not retained. Advertising has a quick wear-out effect even after comprehension. One study reported that many respondents could not identify a commercial they saw less than two minutes before. Among those who remembered seeing the advertisement, recall of commercial content averaged 12 percent or less.[69]

Studies have found that repetitive advertising reminds the consumer of the brand and is more likely to be retained. An important function of advertising is such a reminder effect.[70] But advertising frequency promotes retention in decreasing increments. Therefore, advertisers must balance increasing frequency with increased costs. Studies have also suggested that retention is improved if advertising is spaced over time rather than concentrated in several periods.[71] This means that advertisers should be wary of concentrating too much of their budgets in the initial introduction if this means depleting advertising expenditures later.

Feedback and Evaluation

The final steps in the communications process in Figure 11-1 are action and feedback to the advertiser to evaluate the effectiveness of marketing communications. The advertiser can try to establish a direct link between message effectiveness and purchase behavior. As noted, this is extremely difficult because management cannot isolate the effects of marketing communications from other factors that may influence sales. In addition, marketing communications have a cumulative effect on the consumer. It is difficult to determine to what extent sales may be caused by current advertising or by the cumulative effects of past advertising.

These difficulties have led marketers to try to evaluate marketing communications by their effects on the consumer's information processing rather than on sales. Exposure, attention, comprehension, and retention thus become the criteria by which advertising and sales messages are evaluated. These are called indirect measures because they are assumed to be steps leading to sales. Thus, it is assumed that a consumer exposed to an advertising campaign is more likely to buy than one not so exposed. A consumer who has paid attention to the campaign is even more likely to buy; one who has comprehended the message is yet more likely to buy; and so forth. The path from exposure to action is illustrated in Figure 11-6 and has been called a **hierarchy of effects** because of the assumption that each step is more likely to lead to action.[72]

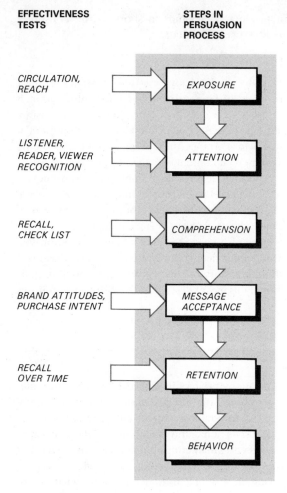

EFFECTIVENESS TESTS

CIRCULATION, REACH

LISTENER, READER, VIEWER RECOGNITION

RECALL, CHECK LIST

BRAND ATTITUDES, PURCHASE INTENT

RECALL OVER TIME

STEPS IN PERSUASION PROCESS

EXPOSURE

ATTENTION

COMPREHENSION

MESSAGE ACCEPTANCE

RETENTION

BEHAVIOR

FIGURE 11-6
Measures of feedback in consumer information processing

Source: Adapted from William J. McGuire, "An Information-Processing Model of Advertising Effectiveness," in H. L. David and A. J. Silk, eds., *Behavioral and Management Sciences in Marketing* (New York: Ronald/Wiley 1978), p. 161. Copyright © 1978 John Wiley & Sons, Inc. Reprinted by permission of John Wiley & Sons, Inc.

This hierarchy is the basis for evaluating marketing communications using the information-processing criteria in Figure 11-6.

Figure 11-6 also summarizes the type of feedback provided to the advertiser at each step of information processing. *Message acceptance* is added to the steps described earlier to illustrate that the message is not only comprehended but is accepted.[73] Message acceptance is likely to increase the chances of message retention.

Figure 11-6 shows that *exposure* can be measured by a magazine's circulation or a television program's reach. *Attention* can best be measured by recognition of an advertisement. For example, the Starch service asks consumers whether they noticed an advertisement. There is also a seen-associated measure in which consumers are asked to associate the ad with a brand or manufacturer. The noted and seen-associated measures provide some assurance that the consumer was attentive to the ad at the time of exposure.

Comprehension is measured primarily by tests of recall of copy points. The Gallup and Robinson readership service asks respondents to recall and describe sales messages of specific ads. In this manner comprehension of the ad's theme can be evaluated. Checklists can also be used to determine whether respondents remember seeing particular components of an ad. Such checklists represent aided recall since they cue consumers to what was in the ad. Message acceptance is best measured by its effect on brand attitudes and purchase intentions. It should be reflected in more positive brand attitudes or an increase in purchase intent.

Retention is measured by recall of the advertising message, but after a period of time. Since marketing communications are likely to "wear out" over time, retention is an important determinant of communications effectiveness.

These measures evaluate specific messages indirectly on the basis of information processing. But the marketer is most interested in the overall effects of a promotional campaign, its effect on sales, and its profitability. These questions will be considered in the next chapter as part of advertising management.

Summary

Marketing communication is central to informing and influencing consumers and must be understood in the development of marketing strategies. Marketing communications require (1) a source (the advertiser), (2) message development (the responsibility of the advertising agency), (3) transmission of the message through the mass media, (4) receipt and evaluation of the message by the consumer through information-processing steps, and (5) feedback to the advertiser of the consumer's reaction to the message.

The strategic implications of each of these five steps was described. Key issues regarding the source of the message are its credibility and attractiveness. Advertisers are less credible than other sources because of their obvious desire to sell their products. They are also less attractive because they do not have the prestige and likeability of other sources such as friends and relatives, news media, and government sources. Various means of increasing advertising credibility and attractiveness were described.

The content of marketing *messages* also affects how these communications are received and whether they lead to sales. Various issues regarding message content were considered, namely:

■ whether messages should take an emotional or rational approach,

■ whether fear appeals are useful,

■ what role humor plays in advertising,

■ whether messages should be clear-cut or somewhat ambiguous,

■ whether messages should be one- or two-sided, and

■ what advantages and disadvantages comparative advertising has.

The third requirement in marketing communications is transmission of the message through *media* to the right target audience. The advantages and disadvantages of the five most important types of mass media — television, radio, magazines, newspapers, and direct mail — were considered. In addition, differences between vehicles within a particular type of medium (e.g., the difference between the editorial content and image of the *New Yorker* and those of *Reader's Digest*) were described.

The consumer's role in evaluating marketing communication was described in the context of *information processing*. For marketing communications to be effective, enough consumers must process information and act on it. Consumers process information through steps leading to action, namely exposure to the information, and attention, comprehension, and retention of the message.

The final step in the communication process — feedback — links marketing communications and sales results. Because it is difficult to establish such a link, feedback to the advertiser generally takes the form of determining to what extent each of the steps in information processing has been achieved. Has the message gained exposure, received the consumer's attention, been comprehended in the manner intended by the advertiser, and been retained so the information can be used in the future?

In this chapter we emphasized advertising's role in marketing communication. In the next chapter we will consider the total mix of elements that marketers can use in their promotional plan — advertising, personal selling, sales promotion, and publicity.

Questions

1. Figure 11-1 cites three basic tasks in the marketing communication process:

   ☐ translating product concepts into effective marketing communications,

   ☐ transmitting marketing communications to target groups, and

   ☐ evaluating the effects of marketing communications on consumers.

   What problems might marketers face in accomplishing each of these communication tasks?

2. Assume that state and local agencies in California wish to undertake an educational campaign to alert the public to the dangers of earthquakes. They use several ads to show the devastation that earthquakes can produce to try to convince the public of the importance of an educational

campaign. What factors are likely to encourage and discourage the acceptance of the message?

3. Assume that Exxon introduces a new high-performance gasoline. Most consumers think that brands of gasoline are pretty much alike. What strategies could Exxon use to convince consumers of the credibility of its claim of better performance?

4. Cite some fear appeals that have and have not worked.

   □ Why have they worked or not worked?

   □ What are the circumstances that make some fear appeals succeed and others fail?

5. One advertising executive says, "Ads should be clear-cut and directly convey consumer benefits. The problem with mood [emotional] advertising is that it is too vague. I'd prefer to have something to hang my hat on. Mood advertising is just too risky." What are the pros and cons of this statement?

6. Another advertising executive says, "I follow two basic principles in communicating a marketing message: (1) Only say good things about the client's product; (2) don't advertise the competition, even if you have bad things to say about them. As a result, I totally reject both two-sided and comparative advertising." What are the pros and cons of this statement?

7. Under what circumstances would an advertiser use primarily broadcast media? Print media? What are the relative advantages and disadvantages of each?

8. One media expert says, "Advertising expenditures on cable TV will increase for the rest of the 1980s. Why? Because cable TV is closer to a print than to a broadcast medium." Explain.

9. One of the concerns of advertisers is that the message may not be processed and interpreted by consumers in the manner intended by the marketer. What are some reasons why consumers misinterpret marketing communications?

10. What are the marketing strategy implications if consumers are more likely to be passive information receivers than active information seekers?

11. Categorization is an important requirement in processing marketing communications.

    □ Can you cite any examples when consumers did not categorize a product as it was intended by the manufacturer?

    □ What strategies can marketers use to help consumers categorize new products?

12. Because of the difficulties in evaluating an advertising message's effects

on a consumer's purchase decision, advertisers have used the measures in Figure 11-6 (exposure, attention, and so forth) as criteria of effectiveness. What are some of the limitations of using the measures in Figure 11-6 in this way?

Notes

1. "Prince Matchabelli: The Scent of Success," *Marketing Communications,* April 1982, p. 25.

2. Ibid.

3. Ibid.

4. See Thomas S. Robertson, *Innovative Behavior and Communications* (New York: Holt, Rinehart and Winston, 1971); Joseph W. Newman and Richard Staelin, "Information Sources of Durable Goods," *Journal of Advertising Research* 13 (April 1983): 19–29; and Henry Assael, Michael Etgar, and Michael Henry, "The Dimensions of Evaluating and Utilizing Alternative Information Sources," Working Paper, New York University, March 1983.

5. See Assael, Etgar, and Henry, "The Dimensions of Evaluating"; and C. Samuel Craig and John M. McCann, "Assessing Communication Effects on Energy Conservation," *Journal of Consumer Research* 5 (September 1978): 82–88.

6. See W. Watts and William McGuire, "Persistence of Induced Opinion Change and Retention of the Inducing Message Contents," *Journal of Abnormal and Social Psychology* 68 (1964): 233–241; G. Miller and J. Basehart, "Source Trustworthiness, Opinionated Statements and Response to Persuasive Communication," *Speech Monographs* 36 (1969): 1–7; and C. Samuel Craig and John M. McCann, "Assessing Communication Effects on Energy Conservation," *Journal of Consumer Research* 5 (September 1978): 82–88.

7. Robert B. Settle and Linda L. Golden, "Attribution Theory and Advertiser Credibility," *Journal of Marketing Research* 11 (May 1974): 181–85.

8. *Advertising Age,* January 5, 1981, p. S-10.

9. Timothy C. Brock, "Communicator-Recipient Similarity and Decision Change," *Journal of Personality and Social Psychology* 1 (June 1965): 650–54; and Arch G. Woodside and J. William Davenport, Jr., "The Effect of Salesman Similarity and Expertise on Consumer Purchasing Behavior," *Journal of Marketing Research* 11 (May 1974): 198–202.

10. "Campaign — American Express: They Got What They Deserve," *Madison Avenue,* April 1982, pp. 44–58.

11. Woodside and Davenport, "The Effect of Salesman Similarity"; and Paul Busch and David T. Wilson, "An Experimental Analysis of a Salesman's Expert and Referent Bases of Power in the Buyer-Seller Dyad," *Journal of Marketing Research* 13 (February 1976): 3–11.

12. "People Appreciate Good Ads, an Agency Survey Concludes," *The Wall Street Journal,* April 28, 1983, p. 33.

13. First Advertising Research Colloquium, New York University, March 1983.

14. "If Logic in Ads Doesn't Sell, Try a Tug on the Heartstrings," *The Wall Street Journal,* April 8, 1982, p. 27.

15. "There's a Song in Their Art," *The New York Times,* May 2, 1982, p. 4F.

16. " 'Ring Around the Collar' Ads Irritate Many Yet Get Results," *The Wall Street Journal,* November 4, 1982, p. 33.

17. *The Wall Street Journal,* April 8, 1982, p. 27

18. Ibid.

19. "Study Finds Nonsmokers Living 2 Years More by Heeding Alerts," *The New York Times,* September 22, 1979, p. 6.

20. See W. J. McGuire, *Effectiveness of Appeals in Advertising* (New York: Advertising Research Foundation, 1963); and John R. Stuteville, "Psychic Defense Against High Fear Appeals: A Key Marketing Variable," *Journal of Marketing* 34 (April 1970): 39–45.

21. "Funny Commercials," *The Wall Street Journal,* October 2, 1982, p. 31.

22. Brian Sternthal and C. Samuel Craig, "Humor

in Advertising," *Journal of Marketing* 37 (October 1973): 12–18.

23. David A. Aaker and John G. Myers, *Advertising Management* (Englewood Cliffs, N.J.: Prentice-Hall, 1982), p. 282.

24. George J. Szybillo and Richard Heslin, "Resistance to Persuasion: Inoculation Theory in a Marketing Context," *Journal of Marketing Research* 10 (November 1973): 396–403.

25. Mark I. Alpert and Linda L. Golden, "The Impact of Education on the Relative Effectiveness of One-Sided and Two-Sided Communications," in Bruce J. Walker et al., eds., *Proceedings of the American Marketing Association Educators' Conference,* Series #48 (1982), pp. 30–33.

26. Carl I. Hovland, Arthur A. Lumsdaine, and Fred D. Sheffield, *Experiments on Mass Communication,* (New York: John Wiley, 1949), pp. 182–200; and W. E. J. Faison, "Effectiveness of One-Sided and Two-Sided Mass Communications in Advertising," *Public Opinion Quarterly* 25 (1961): 468–69.

27. "Comparative Ads Are Getting More Popular, Harder Hitting," *The Wall Street Journal,* March 11, 1982, p. 29.

28. Ibid.

29. "Comparative Ads: Better Than ... ," *Advertising Age,* September 22, 1980, p. 59.

30. "Comparative Ads: The Headaches of the Analgesics," *Advertising Age,* October 6, 1980, p. 64.

31. William L. Wilkie and Paul W. Farris, "Comparison Advertising: Problems and Potential," *Journal of Marketing* 39 (October 1975): 7–15.

32. "Some New Ads May Rekindle Burger Battle," *The Wall Street Journal,* March 4, 1983, p. 4.

33. Philip Levine, "Commercials That Name Competing Brands," *Journal of Advertising Research,* 16 (December 1976): 7–16.

34. "Comparative Ads: Battles That Wrote Dos and Don'ts," *Advertising Age,* September 29, 1980, p. 64.

35. "Campaign: The Battle For Hamburger Hill," *Madison Avenue,* January 1983, p. 61.

36. Herbert E. Krugman, "The Measurement of Advertising Involvement," *Public Opinion Quarterly* 30 (Winter 1966): 584–85.

37. Herbert E. Krugman, "The Impact of Television Advertising: Learning Without Involvement," *Public Opinion Quarterly* 29 (Fall 1965): 354.

38. "Cosmetics Display Walls Spearhead Boom in Point-of-Purchase Media Use," *Marketing News,* February 18, 1983, p. 18.

39. "Inside the Store, the Selling Never Stops," *Advertising Age,* March 15, 1982, p. M-30.

40. "100 Leaders' Media Expenditures," *Advertising Age,* September 9, 1982, p.

41. Figures from the Television Bureau of Advertising, Inc.

42. "Advertisers Growing Restless Over Rising Cost of TV Time," *The Wall Street Journal,* January 27, 1983, p. 29.

43. "Agency, Advertiser Reps Tell What Advantages They Find in Using Radio," *Marketing News,* December 10, 1982, p. 14.

44. *Marketing News,* December 10, 1982, p. 14.

45. Ibid.

46. Ibid.

47. "Honda — Where Success Lies in Simplicity," *Marketing & Media Decisions,* Spring 1982 special issue, pp. 51–66.

48. "Peugeot's Newspaper Relaunch," *Marketing & Media Decisions,* July 1982, pp. 48, 49, 222.

49. Ibid., p. 49.

50. "New Mail-Order Techniques," *The New York Times,* July 30, 1983, pp. 33, 43.

51. "Potential of Lists is Growing," *The New York Times,* April 28, 1982, p.

52. Marshall McLuhan, *The Medium is the Message* (New York: Random House, 1967).

53. David A. Aaker and Phillip K. Brown, "Evaluating Vehicle Source Effects," *Journal of Advertising Research* 12 (August 1972): 11–16.

54. Lauren E. Crane, "How Product, Appeal and Program Affect Attitudes Toward Commercials," *Journal of Advertising Research* 4 (March 1964): 15.

55. R. I. Allison and K. P. Uhl, "Influence of Beer Brand Identification on Taste Perception," *Journal of Marketing Research* 1 (August 1964): 36–39.

56. "Who Watches Commercials," *The Wall Street Journal,* May 20, 1982, p. 29.

57. W. P. Dommermuth and E. W. Cundiff, "Shopping Goods, Shopping Centers and Selling Strategies," *Journal of Marketing* 31 (October 1967): 32–36; and Joseph W. Newman and Richard Staelin, "Pre-Purchase Information Seeking for New Cars and Major Household Appliances," *Journal of Marketing Research* 9 (August 1972): 249–57.

58. John D. Claxton, Joseph N. Fry, and Bernard Portis, "A Taxonomy of Prepurchase Information Gathering Patterns," *Journal of Consumer Research* 1 (December 1974): 35–42.

59. Jacob Jacoby, Robert W. Chestnut, and William A. Fisher, "A Behavioral Process Approach to Information Acquisition in Nondurable Purchasing," *Journal of Marketing Research* 15 (November 1978): 532–44; and William L. Moore and Donald R. Lehmann, "Individual Differences in Search Behavior for a Nondurable," *Journal of Consumer Research* 7 (December 1980): 296–307.

60. William B. Locander and Peter W. Hermann, "The Effect of Self-Confidence and Anxiety on Information Seeking in Consumer Risk Reduction," *Journal of Marketing Research* 16 (May 1979): 268–74.

61. Moore and Lehmann, "Individual Differences."

62. Noel Capon and Marian Burke, "Individual, Product Class, and Task-Related Factors in Consumer Information Processing," *Journal of Consumer Research* 7 (December 1980): 314–26.

63. Compiled from five studies in David L. Loudon and Albert J. Della Bitta, *Consumer Behavior* (New York, McGraw-Hill, 1979), p. 463.

64. Newman and Staelin, "Pre-Purchase Information Seeking for New Cars."

65. Neil H. Borden and Martin V. Marshall, *Advertising Management: Text and Cases* (Homewood, Ill.: Richard D. Irwin, 1959), p. 126.

66. C. Whan Park and Henry Assael, "Has the Low Involvement View of Consumer Behavior Been Overstated?" Working Paper, University of Pittsburgh, April 1983.

67. Jacob Jacoby, Robert W. Chestnut, Karl C. Weigl, and William Fisher, "Pre-Purchase Information Acquisition," in Beverlee B. Anderson, ed., *Advances In Consumer Research*, vol. 3 (Atlanta: Association for Consumer Research, 1975), pp. 306–14.

68. J. E. Brehm, "Post-Decision Changes in the Desirability of Alternatives," *Journal of Abnormal and Social Psychology* 52 (July 1956): 384–89.

69. Leo Bogart, *Strategy and Advertising* (New York: Harcourt Brace Jovanovich, 1967), Chapter 5.

70. Alan G. Sawyer, "The Effects of Repetition: Conclusions and Suggestions about Experimental Laboratory Research," in G. David Hughes and Michael L. Ray, eds., *Buyer/Consumer Information Processing* (Chapel Hill: University of North Carolina Press, 1974), pp. 190–219.

71. Leo Postman, "Verbal Learning and Memory," *Annual Review of Psychology* 26 (1975): 291–335.

72. R. Lavidge and Gary A. Steiner, "A Model for Predictive Measurements of Advertising Effectiveness," *Journal of Marketing* 25 (October 1961): 59–62; and Michael L. Ray, "Marketing Communication and the Hierarchy of Effects," in P. Clarke, ed., *New Models for Mass Communication Research* (Beverly Hills, Calif.: Sage Publications, 1973), pp. 147–75.

73. William J. McGuire, "An Information-Processing Model of Advertising Effectiveness," in H. L. Davis and A. J. Silk, eds., *Behavioral and Management Sciences in Marketing* (New York: Ronald/Wiley, 1978), pp. 156–80.

CHAPTER 12

The Promotional Mix

FOCUS OF CHAPTER

The description of marketing communications in the last chapter tended to emphasize advertising. But marketers do not rely on advertising alone in communicating product benefits to consumers. In most cases, personal selling, sales promotion, and publicity are combined with advertising as part of a total promotional mix. These elements are further divided. For example, we could refer to an advertising mix composed of brand, product, corporate, and cooperative advertising; or a sales promotion mix composed of coupons, premiums, price promotions, and free samples.

The importance and diversity of these promotional elements are illustrated by the following examples:

- *Brand advertising.* Xerox was searching for a way to communicate the complex benefits of its 9200 color copier to a mass market without being overly technical. The ad agency came up with the idea of a monk making 500 copies of an illuminated manuscript for his abbot with the tagline "It's a Miracle." The campaign was an immediate success; it communicated the benefits of fast reproduction, automatic feed, sorting, collating, and binding features in a simple and effective storyline.[1] Sales of the 9200 zoomed.

- *Corporate advertising.* GTE found that its corporate name did little to enhance its reputation among customers. Therefore it embarked on a corporate advertising campaign to demonstrate its broad product line and emphasize its technological achievements in telecommunications.[2] The ads portrayed a consumer surprised at the company's innovations, leading to the tagline, "Gee! No, GTE." The campaign links the corporate name with innovations, not only in the consumer's mind but in the minds of the company's stockholders and employees as well.

- *Retail cooperative advertising.* Champion increased its advertising allowances to retailers to encourage them to advertise the company's sparkplugs. Champion felt there was little difference between the sparkplugs advertised nationally. One way to communicate the quality of its product was through the "little guys — service stations and small auto stores."[3] As a result, the company spent more to support retailer cooperative advertising than to advertise its own national brand.

- *Personal selling.* The Fort Howard Paper Company recognized the need to strengthen its promotional mix by acquiring additional sales representation. As a result, it bought the Maryland Cup Corporation because of the "marketing punch and sales servicing skills for which Maryland Cup is known."[4]

- *Sales promotion.* Revlon used a sales promotion device — a sweepstakes — to increase awareness of its Chaz cologne for men. First prize was a custom Ferrari advertised by Tom Selleck, star of the TV show Magnum P.I. Participants had to visit the Revlon store display to determine if they won any of the prizes.[5] The campaign increased consumer awareness, reinforced the image of the brand through the use of Selleck as a spokesman, and stimulated interest by the trade, thus facilitating distribution.

- *Publicity.* Bacardi boosted public awareness of its Puerto Rico rum through a well-orchestrated publicity campaign centering on food and dessert recipes requiring rum. The recipes appeared widely in newspapers and magazines, reached about 5 million consumers, and increased sales.[6]

In this chapter we will first consider the factors that determine a company's promotional mix. Promotional campaigns differ in emphasizing advertising, personal selling, sales promotion, or publicity. These allocations frequently depend on the nature of the product and the competitive environment it faces. The marketing manager must determine not only the content of the promotional mix but also the amount of money to be devoted to the promotional effort. Therefore, in the next section we will consider various ways of (1) establishing the promotional budget, and (2) allocating the budget to the components of the promotional mix. In the rest of the chapter we will review the elements of the promotional mix. The strategic purpose of each element will be emphasized. Because advertising and personal selling are so important, in the following two chapters we will consider these in more detail.

Determinants of the Promotional Mix

A key responsibility of the marketing manager is allocating resources to the four key components of the promotional mix. Companies vary widely in their emphasis on advertising, personal selling, sales promotion, and publicity. For example, in cosmetics, Avon relies almost totally on its door-to-door sales effort, allocating only about 1.5 percent of sales revenue to advertising, whereas Noxell spends almost 20 percent of sales revenue on advertising.[7] There are also wide differences in allocations within each component. In automobiles, General Motors spends most of its money on television, whereas Peugeot allocates 80 percent of its advertising budget to newspapers. The effectiveness of each of the components of the promotional mix will vary by:

- type of product,
- consumer characteristics, and
- stage in the product life cycle.

TYPE OF PRODUCT

The nature of the product largely determines the emphasis placed on personal selling, advertising, or sales promotions. For example, *personal selling* tends to be the dominant element in the mix if the product:

- is technically complex (direct selling is required to communicate product specifications);
- involves negotiations over price, warranty, or maintenance;
- is purchased on specification (requiring direct contact between buyer and seller);
- requires postpurchase contact such as installation, maintenance, and monitoring performance;
- requires demonstration;
- is expensive (high risks require direct contact);
- is so important that some direct contact is required through a salesperson; or
- is directed to only a few customers, making advertising an inefficient means of promotion.

These characteristics identify industrial goods. It is not surprising that personal selling is by far the most important component of the promotional mix for most marketers of industrial goods.

Advertising tends to be the most important element in the marketing mix when:

- a relatively simple set of benefits must be communicated;
- such communication is required on a mass-market basis;

- product specifications and terms of sale are fairly standardized;
- products are purchased frequently, meaning the consumer has had recent experience with a standardized product and therefore expects the same performance on the next purchase;
- the marketer relies on a brand name to sell; or
- there are few significant differences in product characteristics between competitors, resulting in more emphasis on advertising as a means of gaining a competitive advantage.

These characteristics are associated primarily with consumer goods, and more with consumer packaged goods than with durables.

Yet advertising is not always the most prominent element in the promotional mix for consumer packaged goods. Expenditures for sales promotions are frequently greater than those for advertising. For consumer goods, *sales promotions* tend to be most important when:

- price elasticity is high (consumers are more likely to be attracted by coupons and price specials);
- brand loyalty is low (resulting in greater willingness to try alternative brands because of price); or
- product decisions are made in the store (consumers are thus influenced by in-store sales promotions such as coupons or price specials).

CONSUMER CHARACTERISTICS

The size, geographic dispersion, and stage in the customer's decision process influence the relative effectiveness of components in the promotional mix. If the target market is large and widely dispersed, advertising is the most economical way to reach it. This is characteristic of consumer goods. If the target market is small and geographically concentrated, mass media would be wasteful. Personal selling would be cost effective if the average order per sales call is sufficiently high. Many industrial firms sell to large, geographically concentrated buyers. But personal selling is likely to be combined with advertising in business publications.

The stage in the decision process will also affect the promotional mix. In Chapter 11 we noted that advertising is most successful in creating brand awareness and in conveying information, whereas word-of-mouth communications are more influential in making the final decision. In situations where personal selling is used (e.g., for industrial goods), advertising should pave the way by creating awareness of the company's line, whereas personal selling should be used to close the sale.

STAGE IN PRODUCT LIFE CYCLE

In Chapter 10 we noted that marketing strategies change over the life cycle of a product. Therefore, the promotional mix will also change. In the introductory stage advertising expenditures are likely to be heavier, because the objective is to create awareness of the brand. If the brand is a consumer packaged good in a price-sensitive market, sales promotion expenditures are likely to be heavy to stimulate trial. In the growth phase, the purpose is to consolidate gains and encourage brand loyalty. Advertising expenditures will probably be maintained, but sales promotions will be reduced because trial has been established. Continued use of price promotions might cause the consumer to view the brand as a low-priced and possibly low-quality entry.

In the maturity phase advertising continues to be maintained, but its role changes from reinforcing brand loyalty to persuading competitive users to switch to the company's brand. The basis for competitive advantage shifts from the product to advertising since most products are similar. Sales promotion again becomes important, but this time as a means of getting consumers to switch rather than as a means of inducing trial. Further, more of the budget is devoted to trade than to consumer promotions in an attempt to hold dealer support.

Decline is marked by a cutback in all promotional expenditures. The exception occurs when the company modifies the brand to attempt revitalization. Then the company might risk maintaining promotional support in the face of declining sales.

These relationships are illustrated in Figure 12-1. Sales promotion and advertising tend to be on a par in both the introductory and the maturity

FIGURE 12-1
Typical advertising and sales promotion expenditures over the product life cycle

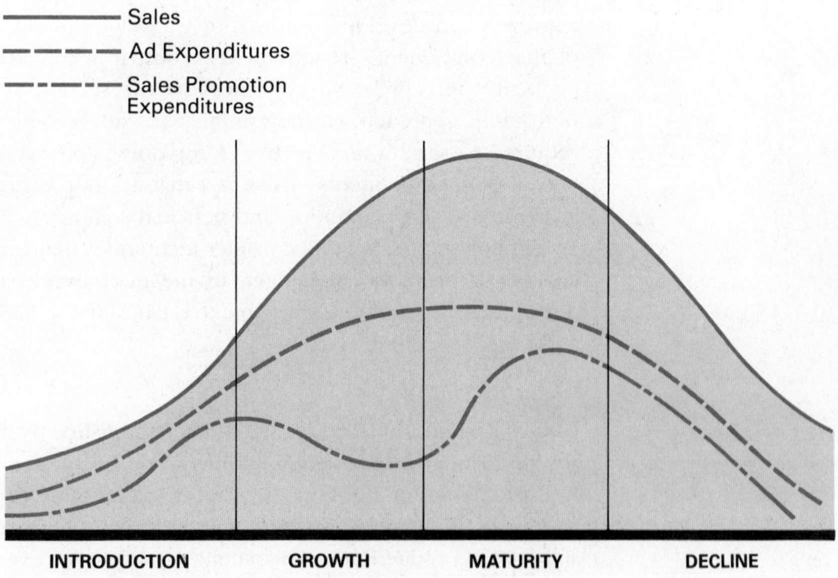

INTRODUCTION   GROWTH   MATURITY   DECLINE

phases, but for different reasons. Advertising is the predominant element in the growth phase. We must remember that these are generalizations and that, on occasion, advertising or sales promotion might be the dominant factor in the promotional mix during any phase of the product life cycle.

Setting and Allocating the Promotional Budget

In considering the components of the promotional mix we assume that marketing management has established a promotional budget and allocated this budget to the specific components of the mix. Determining the size of the promotional budget must therefore precede considerations of the makeup of the promotional mix. A company that cannot afford to advertise a brand on prime-time TV should determine this fact before developing an optimal mix that might include such an unaffordable component. In this section we will consider establishing the amount in the promotional budget, and then allocating this amount across the promotional mix.

SETTING THE PROMOTIONAL BUDGET

In Chapter 3, we cited two general approaches in setting a marketing budget, a top-down approach and a bottom-up approach. The same approaches are used in setting the promotional budget. The assumption in this chapter is that a top-down approach is used. The very term *promotional mix* assumes that a total budget is determined and is allocated to the components of the mix. The advantage of this approach is that the firm can view advertising, sales promotion, personal selling, and publicity as parts of an integrated marketing plan on the basis of common objectives. On the other hand, a bottom-up approach can develop a budget for each component of the mix on the basis of that component's requirements. Thus, if a key advertising objective is to attain 80 percent brand awareness by the second year after introduction, a bottom-up approach can determine what advertising frequency and reach is required to reach this objective. A top-down approach muddies the waters by considering components of the mix that are not as crucial in achieving brand awareness (sales promotion and personal selling).

In this section we will consider techniques that can be used in establishing an overall promotional budget. In the next two chapters we will consider techniques that are more amenable to establishing specific budgets for advertising and personal selling.

Optimal Method

Ideally, a promotional budget would be established by determining the marginal revenue obtained from each additional dollar spent on the promotional mix. It is profitable for the firm to continue to increase promotional expenditures as long as the marginal revenue is greater than the marginal cost of promotions and related production and marketing activities. For example, assume a company determines that the marginal revenue from each additional dollar spent on promotions is $1.40, and that the production and marketing costs associated with generating the additional $1.40 in revenue are 30 cents. This means that the marginal contribution to profits is 10 cents from the additional dollar spent on promotions ($1.40 − [$1.00 + .30]). As long as additional promotional dollars are increasing the contribution to profit, promotional expenditures should increase. The optimal promotional expenditure level occurs when marginal revenue equals marginal cost.

The problem with this approach is in determining marginal revenue. The firm cannot know how much revenue is being obtained from each additional dollar spent on promotions, since this requires establishing a relationship between promotional expenditures and sales. The point that is frequently made is that the marketing environment is too complex for the firm to isolate the effects of promotional expenditures on sales. Too many other factors affect sales results.

Because the promotional budget must be established on a less-than-optimal basis, four frequently used methods to determine the amount to be budgeted for the promotional mix will be considered:

1. Develop the budget on the basis of promotional objectives and the proposed strategies to meet these objectives (an **objective-task approach**);

2. Set the budget as a percentage of last year's sales or of next year's sales forecast;

3. Determine expenditures on the basis of what the most important competitors in the industry are doing (a **competitive parity approach**); or

4. Spend as much as you can reasonably afford, or use some arbitrary method to set the budget.

Objective-Task Method

The objective-task method requires defining promotional objectives, determining the strategies (tasks) required to meet these objectives, and deciding on the promotional expenditures required to implement the strategy. To justify the proposed budget, the marketing manager must state the assumptions behind the objectives and demonstrate how proposed strategies are likely to meet them. Only then is top management likely to approve the budget.

Pillsbury used an objective-task method in setting the ad budget for its Totino's frozen pizza line. The overall objectives were to increase sales by 30 percent and profits by 100 percent by increasing product quality, distribution, and consumer preferences. The promotional objectives included a 70 percent increase in brand awareness, a 20 percent increase in trial, and a 40 percent increase in the repurchase rate.[8] The strategy involved a change in the promotional mix from an emphasis on trade allowances (a **push strategy**) to greater TV advertising (a **pull strategy**). This made more money available to increase consumer preferences.

Percentage of Sales

One way to estimate the advertising budget is as a percentage of last year's sales or next year's forecasts. It is the most frequently used method for several reasons. First, it is simple. Second, promotional expenditures vary with brand performance. Third, the general use of this method means that competitive promotional expenditures are predictable. Competitors are less likely to increase or decrease promotional costs suddenly.

However, there are several distinct disadvantages in using percentage of sales as a basis for setting promotional budgets:

- It is an illogical method for estimating expenditures. Using percentage of sales means that sales determine the promotional mix. The opposite should be true — the promotional mix determines sales.

- Sales may not reflect profitability. Products with the lowest margins sometimes have the highest sales. But these products receive the greatest promotional support at the expense of more profitable products.

- When the budget is based on a percentage of future sales, it encourages managers to inflate sales forecasts to guarantee promotional funds for the brand.

- Using a percentage-of-sales approach sometimes inhibits management from trying to transform a promising brand into a star. Such a strategy would require spending more on promotion than is warranted by the sales performance of the brand.

These problems have not inhibited some of the largest companies from using percentage of sales. Automobile and oil companies tend to use this method.[9] Sears set its advertising budgets for 1983 so that advertising expenditures would be 3 percent of forecast retail sales. Advertising expenditures for its catalog were set at 5.75 percent of forecast catalog sales.[10]

Competitive Parity

Another approach to setting the promotional budget is to keep pace with competitors. This is generally done by determining promotional expenditures as a percentage of sales for two or three key competitors or for the industry as a whole and using this figure as a basis for setting the company's advertising budget. Although such a figure may represent the best thinking of competition, there is no guarantee that it is a reasonable figure for the company. As one marketer said, using the industry's average percentage of sales "incorporates the errors of competitors into the advertiser's own budgeting process. Opportunities for gaining competitive advantage may be lost."[11]

Arbitrary Methods

Many companies do not have a formal planning process requiring the establishment of promotional objectives. These companies often feel that the relation of promotional expenditures to sales cannot be determined, so arbitrary methods are used to fix the budget. One basis for budgeting is to determine what the company can afford to spend. Another is to increase promotional expenditures by a fixed percentage each year. These are weak methods since they are not tied to promotional effectiveness or product performance. But in the absence of formalized planning procedures, sound managerial judgment may be the best recourse. One study found that among industrial advertisers, arbitrary methods were most frequently used for setting promotional budgets.[12]

ALLOCATING THE PROMOTIONAL BUDGET

Once the promotional budget is set, the marketing manager must allocate it to advertising, personal selling, sales promotion, and publicity. Further allocations are also required by type of effort (e.g., the amount of the sales promotional budget to be spent on coupons, sweepstakes, and so forth).

In determining the optimal allocation of the promotional budget, management can again use the principle of operating at the margin. **Optimal allocation** requires that management direct resources to the component of the promotional mix that produces the greatest marginal revenue in relation to marginal cost. For example, assume a firm obtains $1.20 for each additional dollar spent on advertising a particular brand, and $1.30 for each additional dollar spent on sales promotions for that brand. The firm will allocate more money to sales promotions than to advertising. As it does so, the effectiveness of sales promotions will begin to diminish (the marginal revenue will begin to decrease), because there is a limit to the number of coupons or deals the consumer will accept. The firm will continue to increase sales promotion expenditures until the marginal revenue gained from each additional dollar in expenditures equals that for advertising. Similarly, within the sales promotion budget, if coupons are more cost effective than deals (they produce more marginal revenue relative to marginal cost), the firm will allocate more sales promotion dollars to coupons than to deals. The optimal-allocation principle can be stated as:

$$\frac{MR_{pm1}}{MC_{pm1}} = \frac{MR_{pm2}}{MC_{pm2}} = \frac{MR_{pm_n}}{MC_{pm_n}}$$

where

MR_{pm1} ; MR_{pm2} ; MR_{pm_n} are the marginal revenues for the 1st, 2nd, and nth promotional mix components, respectively, and

MC_{pm1} ; MC_{pm2} ; MC_{pm_n} are the marginal costs for the 1st, 2nd, and nth promotional mix components.

In other words, the promotional budget is allocated so the marginal revenue is in the same proportion to the marginal cost for each component of the promotional mix.

Another way of stating the **optimal-allocation principle** is that expenditures should be allocated on the basis of the relative effect of the promotional mix component on sales. If incremental advertising expenditures are producing twice as much additional revenue as incremental sales promotional expenditures, then the appropriate allocation criterion would be two-to-one in favor of advertising.

Marketing managers strive for the optimal promotional allocation and intuitively recognize the marginal principles involved. They will try to allocate funds to those promotional components they *think* produces the highest marginal revenue relative to marginal cost. The problem is that they rarely *know* the marginal revenue produced by each promotional component, because they cannot establish its effect on sales. As a result, they must rely on product and environmental factors cited in the previous section to guide their promotional allocations.

Promotional Planning

Developing an effective promotional campaign requires systematic planning and management. The promotional plan is a component of the overall marketing plan and requires the same basic steps in the planning process, specifically:

- *Setting promotional objectives.* These might include:
  - ☐ creating brand awareness,
  - ☐ communicating product information,
  - ☐ maintaining brand recognition, and
  - ☐ providing postsales reinforcement.
- *Defining a target audience.*
- *Developing the means to reach the target audience,* namely:
  - ☐ mass media for advertising,
  - ☐ a directed personal-selling effort, and
  - ☐ coupons and deals targeted to the right audience through direct mail and in-store distribution.
- *Formulating a promotional strategy to meet the objectives.* For example, if the objective is quick awareness of a new product, most of the initial effort will be to immediately penetrate the market through an intensive advertising campaign. If an additional objective is immediate trial in a highly competitive market, more of the budget will be allocated to deals and coupons.

- *Establishing and allocating the promotional budget.*
- *Evaluating the effectiveness of the promotional effort* and adjusting future objectives and strategies accordingly.

In developing a promotional plan management must ensure that the components of the plan are integrated. The salesperson must reinforce the advertising message. Attempting to establish a different positioning for a product will just confuse the consumer. The sales promotion effort must be consistent with the image that advertising and the personal selling effort are trying to convey. For example, countering competition with coupons and price deals will not work if management has attempted to establish a luxury image for a brand.

Components of the Promotional Mix

In the rest of this chapter we will consider the four basic elements in the promotional mix: advertising, personal selling, sales promotion, and publicity. We will also look at the activities associated with each of these components.

ADVERTISING

Most advertising effort is directed to stimulating demand for a particular brand. The successful campaigns most frequently cited — such as the Marlboro Cowboy, Miller Time, Coke Is It — are examples of brand advertising. However, three other types of advertising can be as important in attaining the communication objectives of the firm: product, corporate, and cooperative advertising.

Brand Advertising

Brand advertising attempts to increase sales of the company's brand by:

- attracting users of competitive brands (influencing Hertz users to rent from Avis);
- influencing nonusers of the product to try the brand (getting consumers who ordinarily do not rent to try Avis by convincing them renting is cheaper than alternative modes of transport);
- increasing use among current users (Why rent just for business reasons? Consider renting from Avis for weekends and vacations at a special introductory rate); and
- maintaining satisfaction among current users (Avis doesn't take its customers for granted; we still try harder).

These objectives are geared to increasing the market share for the brand (i.e., stimulating **selective demand** by holding present customers and attracting competitive customers). But, in the process, brand advertising may also enlarge the market for the product category (i.e., stimulating **primary demand**). If Avis attracts customers who do not ordinarily rent or convinces existing customers to rent more frequently, it is not gaining sales at the expense of competition; it is increasing the size of the car rental market.

The first objective of brand advertising is to stimulate selective demand. But at times an equally important purpose is to increase the demand for the product. A company that is introducing a new product category (such as the Sony Betamax) will place just as much emphasis on advertising the product category as on advertising the brand name. Companies that are market leaders stimulate both primary and selective demand. Because of their large share of market they would benefit most from an increase in demand for the product category. For example, with over 80 percent of the canned soup market, Campbell Soup Company would profit from any increase in the demand for canned soups. At one time, Campbell attempted to increase the consumption of canned soups with primary demand themes such as "Soup for Lunch." The advertising featured the Campbell's Soup logo, illustrating a dual purpose — stimulating primary and selective demand. The company has continuously advertised the nutritional value of soup in general to broaden the market for canned soups.[13] Another example of such a dual purpose is in Figure 12-2. Pampers, the leading disposable diaper brand, is using a comparative advertising approach to influence users of cloth to switch to disposable diapers and specifically to Pampers. It is attacking a competitive product category, not a competitive brand, in an attempt to enlarge the disposable diaper market.

Brand advertising has a third objective — to create brand loyalty. Loyal customers buy the brand repeatedly, ensuring sales among a core group of users. Few brands can survive without the assurance of repeat purchases from loyal consumers. Many marketers view brand advertising as a long-term capital expenditure designed to establish a brand franchise — that is, a loyal group of sufficient size and stability to ensure long-term profitability. An advantage of brand loyalty is that it sometimes leads to price inelasticity. The loyal user of a brand may be willing to pay more for it than for a competitive brand, even if the brands are nearly identical. The loyal user is also less likely to be attracted to competitive deals and promotions. Effective brand advertising protects the brand's franchise against such attempts to induce trial of competitive products.

Product Advertising

The sole purpose of product advertising is to increase primary demand for the category. There are two types of product advertising: (1) educational campaigns designed to inform consumers about new or existing products, and (2) cooperative campaigns sponsored by trade associations to increase industrywide demand.

Educational campaigns

Education campaigns are frequently necessary to inform consumers of the nature of new product categories. Kodak's introductory advertising of the disc

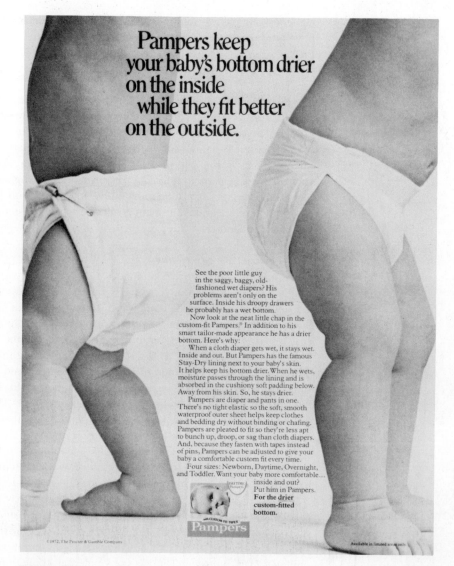

FIGURE 12-2
An attempt to stimulate both brand and product demand
Courtesy of the Procter & Gamble Company.

camera was meant to inform consumers of the features and advantages of the new product. Kodak has the advantage of being the first to introduce the product. But its success is also encouraging competitive entry. As competitive makes are introduced, Kodak will switch its emphasis from product to brand advertising.

Educational campaigns are not limited to new products. At times, companies may educate consumers about the benefits of existing products. Celanese Corporation began advertising polyester fibers in 1982 using the theme "Look what polyester is doing now."[14] The purpose was to increase primary demand for polyesters in the face of decreasing sales and rising foreign imports. The campaign was a marked shift from past promotional emphasis on brand names. One company spokesman said, "We are not backing off [brand advertising]. It's just that now our commitment is to educate the consumer about polyester's fashionability and easy care."[15]

Industrywide advertising

Companies sometimes band together in an industrywide effort to stimulate product demand. Such advertising is frequently motivated by a decreasing demand trend. Under such circumstances, attempts to gain market share through brand advertising might be counterproductive. The solution is not to gain a larger share of a shrinking pie but to try to prevent the pie from shrinking further. Shortly after World War II a group of clothing manufacturers agreed on an industrywide campaign to counteract the decreasing demand for men's suits, overcoats, and hats as a result of the postwar fashion trend toward informality. One of their ads is shown in Figure 12-3. The campaign was a failure for several reasons. First, it used a fear appeal that was too stark — a daughter ashamed of her father because of the way he dresses. But more important, the campaign was attempting to counteract a basic cultural trend toward informality. Advertising is most effective when it conforms to consumer needs and values. It is ineffective in changing deep-seated cultural trends.

A recent industrywide attempt to advertise coal may be more successful. In 1982 the coal industry, suffering from a slump in demand, decided to embark on a campaign to sell coal as a consumer product. Two trade groups and the United Mineworkers solicited donations from coal companies to pay for the million-dollar campaign. The ads are "aimed at community leaders who presumably would rally their neighbors to support new, coal-fired power plants and legislation that promotes coal."[16] The campaign represents a marked shift for the industry. As one executive said, "Coal companies can no longer view themselves as miners. Gradually, the smarter ones are viewing themselves as sources of energy."[17] This campaign is more likely to be successful than that of the clothing industry because it is not in conflict with consumer needs and values. The campaign could lead to an increase in the demand for coal because of the greater energy consciousness of the American public.

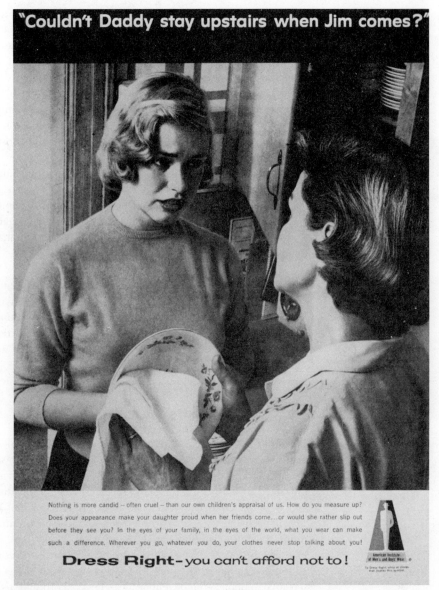

FIGURE 12-3
Example of an industrywide campaign to stimulate product demand

Cooperative Advertising

Cooperative advertising is a third type of product-related advertising. Manufacturers offer retailers allowances to advertise the manufacturers' products, permitting retailers to insert the name of the store and, in some cases, short messages about the retail establishment. Cooperative advertising differs from brand and product advertising in representing a "push" rather than a "pull" strategy. Manufacturers are encouraging retailers to stock and to more aggressively sell their products by offering advertising allowances. In brand and product advertising, manufacturers are directly influencing consumers to go to the store without seeking the intervention of the retailer.

Cooperative advertising is advantageous to both manufacturers and retailers. It provides manufacturers with a local outlet for advertising their products. It also offers retailers a basis for advertising their store name in the mass media. Without manufacturers' advertising allowances, many retailers could not afford to advertise on a regular basis in newspapers and regional magazines, and on local TV.

The importance of cooperative advertising is reflected in the over $7 billion offered to retailers for such advertising in 1983 (only half of which was used by retailers). Diverse companies such as Fram automotive filters, Levi Strauss, Apple Computers, and Bristol-Myers run extensive cooperative campaigns, sometimes exceeding their expenditures for national advertising. Apple Computer is "making an all-out effort in co-op, providing co-op advertising materials, sending bimonthly statements to retailers about co-op activity, establishing new regional advertising programs, ... and setting up media schedules."[18]

Corporate Advertising

Corporate advertising — that is, advertising the corporate name, image, or position on certain issues — has become important for several reasons. First, the creation of large conglomerates such as Norton Simon and TRW has resulted in a need to inform the public about who these companies are, what they do, and what products they offer. Second, top management has begun to realize that advertising should be directed not only to potential customers but to other "corporate publics" such as investors, legislators, opinion leaders, and its own employees. These publics directly influence the corporate environment and indirectly influence sales. Third, top management has become increasingly sensitive to public opinion. Public awareness of corporations as potential polluters and energy wasters has resulted in a more negative view of American business. Many companies have begun to present their position on these public issues.

These factors reflect three types of corporate advertising with very different purposes: (1) corporate patronage advertising, (2) corporate image advertising, and (3) corporate issue advertising. These three types are illustrated in Figure 12-4.

Corporate patronage advertising
Used by permission.

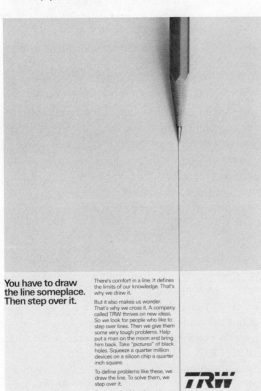

Corporate image advertising
Used by permission.

FIGURE 12-4
Three types of corporate advertising

Ten timely truisms

Our dictionary defines a truism as "... a statement that almost everybody knows is true."

Want to find out if you go along with "almost everybody"? Try these 10 truisms on for size.

Truism 1 holds that the more money invested in our business, the more oil and gas we can find, produce, process, and sell.

Truism 2 says the opposite is true, too; i.e., less money invested means less oil and gas.

Truism 3 makes the obvious point (because it's a truism, naturally) that money is thus a raw material we need a lot of to keep functioning. It has been estimated that the domestic energy industry will need $850 billion in new capital over the next decade.

Truism 4 says that may be so, but the petroleum industry isn't laying its hands on anywhere near that amount of money. This threatens energy malnutrition a few years from now that could show up in the form of gasoline lines, cold homes, and unemployment resulting from factory shutdowns.

Truism 5 notes that to stave off energy malnutrition, we must get more capital from (1) profits plowed back into our business, (2) borrowing, and (3) selling stock to the public.

Truism 6 is that everything, then, depends on profits. If your company doesn't earn a profit, you have nothing to plow back into the business. Lenders won't lend to you. Investors won't buy your stock.

Truism 7 concludes that profit formation is the key to capital formation—a favorite topic these days of editorial writers, economists, and other pundits.

Truism 8 reminds us that public opinion polls, giving the lie to all the preceding truisms, show that most Americans are suspicious of profits and believe they are too high. Too high? Worldwide, Mobil makes only a penny and a half on every gallon of petroleum products we sell.

Truism 9 warns that people who snipe at profits are unwittingly taking potshots at their own jobs, their own savings, their government's tax revenues, and their standard of living.

Truism 10 is that what's true about the petroleum industry applies equally to other industries.

What's the upshot of our 10 truisms? Since a truism is something almost everybody knows, maybe it's that we ought to spread the word to folks who haven't got the message yet. Like some members of Congress.

And let's all try to keep an open mind about profits. As Judge Learned Hand once said, "The mutual confidence on which all else depends can be maintained only by an open mind and a brave reliance upon free discussion."

Mobil

Corporate issue advertising

© 1975 Mobil Oil Corporation. Reprinted with permission of Mobil Corporation.

Corporate patronage advertising

Many companies advertise the corporate name to encourage customers to patronize the firm. For example, General Electric advertises, "We bring good things to life." The purpose of the campaign is to develop positive associations for all of GE's products. One GE executive describes the campaign as "umbrella advertising," because the purpose is to convey a perception of quality for all GE products.[19] Similarly, General Motors has run a patronage campaign based on the theme "People building transportation to serve people." The ads deal with GM cars in general and attempt to influence consumers to consider GM models.

Corporate image advertising

Corporate image advertising is designed to establish a corporate identity in the eyes of the company's various publics. Corporate identity is particularly important for large, diversified companies whose operations may be diffuse and ill defined. For example, TRW, the seventy-first corporation in size in the United States, did a study in 1973 that showed hardly anyone knew what it was. As a result, TRW began corporate image advertising to inform the public it was a leading producer of automotive parts, electronic components, satellites, spacecraft, and many other related products and services.[20] The campaign doubled the number of people who identified TRW with its principal product areas. Other companies such as GTE, Singer, and Grumman have used corporate advertising to educate the financial community and other relevant targets about the company.

Corporate image advertising can also be used to change an image. Both Philip Morris and the Liggett Group decided that their images were tarnished by the sale of cigarettes. Therefore they began to advertise to show their other products and interests to broaden their image beyond cigarettes.[21]

Corporate issue advertising

Corporate issue advertising states a company's position on a social issue of public importance. It frequently does so in a way that "supports the position and interests of the sponsor while ... downgrading the sponsor's opponents and denying the accuracy of their facts."[22] Generally, the purpose is to counteract negative stories and bad press about the company.

Most companies do not engage in corporate issue advertising, preferring to avoid public controversy, and feel it is a misuse of corporate resources. The chairman of ITT says, "Our money shouldn't be spent on political issues; it's not fair to those stockholders whose views are different. ... We do our advocacy selling in speeches and if they get publicity, fine!"[23]

One company that strongly disagrees with this view is Mobil Oil. According to Mobil's chairman, "An idea not opposed sooner or later will be accepted. Participation in vigorous dialogue is appropriate for a corporation."[24] As a result Mobil has engaged in issue-oriented advertising since 1970 and covers subjects as diverse as a wasteful Congress, government expenses, taxes, and political action committees.

Type of Advertising by Source

Our four-part classification of advertising is somewhat of an oversimplification because it does not deal with the sources of advertising. For example, each of the four types could be divided into consumer and industrial advertising. There is also the distinction in each between product and service advertising. For example, service companies such as Citibank, Merrill Lynch, and Prudential can advertise the benefits of their services (brand advertising), the company name (corporate advertising), or the benefits of life insurance or stock ownership in general (product advertising). The distinctions between consumer versus industrial and product versus service are important since advertising objectives, executions, and media will differ. But the basic types of advertising remain the same.

One distinction not covered in the preceding section is between commercial and noncommercial advertising. The examples cited were all commercial. But nonprofit agencies such as the American Cancer Society or the United Negro College Fund will advertise to encourage contributions, political candidates will advertise for votes, and public agencies may advertise to influence a change in behavior (such as decreasing energy consumption). Not-for-profit advertising is reviewed in the last chapter.

PERSONAL SELLING

Personal selling is complementary to advertising since it is directed to individuals rather than large groups and is conducted by company sales representatives on a personal basis rather than by the mass media. Personal selling is the one component in the promotional mix that permits the marketer to have face-to-face contact with the consumer. A preestablished message does not have to be developed as in advertising. The salesperson can assess the consumer's needs, develop a sales message accordingly, evaluate the consumer's reaction to the message, and adjust his or her approach. Because of the face-to-face nature of personal selling, it is more likely to elicit the attention of the buyer and to result in some sort of response, even if it is not a final sale.

The personal sales effort will vary depending on whether the items being sold are consumer products, industrial products, or services. As noted, selling industrial goods tends to be much more complex than selling consumer goods. More complex selling tasks require:

- greater customer interaction,
- a higher level of technical knowledge,
- contact with more diverse customers,
- more prospecting for customers, and
- greater involvement in postpurchase followup and service.

Industrial purchases may also involve a buying group whose members frequently have conflicting goals. This further complicates the industrial salesperson's task.

Sales of consumer goods are generally simpler. The consumer is frequently presold through advertising. The salesperson then simply acts as order taker. Even if the consumer is not presold, the fact that most consumer goods are standardized makes it easier for a salesperson to tell the consumer about a product and to demonstrate it.

The complexity of the sales task for consumer goods varies widely. The sale of an automobile might approach that of an industrial product in complexity because of the importance of performance specifications and service. Automobile manufacturers therefore spend much more money on maintaining sales effort through their dealer network than they do on advertising. In general, however, personal selling takes a back seat to advertising for consumer goods.

Personal selling is also essential in the sale of services. Financial and banking services, professional services, and services related to travel and entertainment all require personal selling. Service institutions view personal selling much more broadly than consumer goods companies and even industrial firms since the delivery of the service will determine the level of satisfaction. As a result, personal selling also tends to be the most important element of the service institution's promotional mix. Personal selling is fully considered in Chapter 14.

SALES PROMOTION

Sales promotions represent the largest expenditures in the promotional mix for consumer packaged goods, exceeding expenditures for advertising and personal selling. Overall, sales promotional expenditures are about one-third higher than those for advertising. (Sales promotional expenditures in 1981 were $46.6 billion compared to $31.3 billion for advertising).[25]

Purposes of Sales Promotions

These expenditures in sales promotional activities are represented by large investments in cents-off coupons, sweepstakes offers, premiums, refunds, and free samples. For example, 120 billion coupons were distributed to the American public in 1982.[26]

Sales promotion and advertising are complementary promotional tools. The purpose of advertising is to create brand awareness and to develop a positive brand image over time. Advertising is a cumulative technique. Little can be accomplished by one exposure, but over time a strong brand franchise can develop. Consider the strength of Coca-Cola, Crest, or Campbell's soups for this reason. In contrast, sales promotions are "short-term incentives designed to immediately encourage consumers to purchase a product."[27] Advertising takes time but promotions do not. Further, advertising attempts to influence cognitive activities — communicate information about a brand, convey a mood, develop good feelings about the brand through imagery and symbolism. Sales promotions are not intended to influence attitudes or to communicate product information (other than price). Once the consumer is convinced to try the product, beliefs and attitudes may change as a result of consumption.

Importance of Sales Promotions

Sales promotions not only represent a greater part of the promotional budget than advertising for many firms, they are also rising more rapidly than advertising expenditures for several reasons:[28]

1. Product parity has become more common for many categories. Unique product "niches" are harder to achieve. Sales promotions are a means of attracting buyers in a parity situation.

2. It is difficult for brands to gain and maintain an advertising advantage over competitors. Media costs are so high that the cost effectiveness of advertising and particularly television is open to question. Marketers are beginning to view sales promotions as a more cost effective way to obtain trial.

3. There have been increasing price pressures on national brands, particularly from generics and private labels. As a result, marketers of national brands have recognized the importance of the price incentives that sales promotions offer in combatting the inroads of lower priced products.

4. Consumers have become more price sensitive and less brand loyal, partly as a result of the cycle of inflation and recession in recent times. Coupled with this price sensitivity is a search for quality. Sales promotions are an excellent tool in a price-sensitive economy.

The importance of sales promotional tools is illustrated by two very different campaigns; one for the introduction of the TRAC II razor by Gillette, the other for the reintroduction of Tylenol after the cyanide poisonings in September 1982. In the early 1970s Gillette introduced its new twin-blade shaving system. It realized that trial was essential to win over a potentially skeptical male audience from established shaving habits. It started off with a $4 million advertising and sales promotion budget for four months. The product was launched with a heavy advertising campaign on TV and radio during the World Series and in national magazines. The company used three sales promotion tools: (1) distribution of over 12 million free samples, (2) a one-dollar consumer refund, and (3) retail promotional aids such as streamers and flags for high point-of-purchase effect during the World Series. The result? "Almost overnight, TRAC II became the bestselling razor in the nation."[29]

Johnson & Johnson, producers of Tylenol, faced a unique problem. Should they bury their leading analgesic after a series of cyanide deaths in September 1982 that the company was not at fault for; or should they try to recapture their leading position in the analgesic market? Many marketing experts felt the brand was dead. But the company decided to reintroduce it aggressively, not with an advertising campaign, but with sales promotions. The company gave away millions of coupons worth $2.50, the price of a small bottle of Tylenol. These coupons were distributed to 40 million American households.[30] The company correctly realized that once repeat purchases of competitive brands began to occur, it would be difficult to recapture lost customers. Therefore, it lost no time in distributing the coupons. The emphasis on coupons seems to have worked. By early 1983 Tylenol had regained its former market share.

Types of Sales Promotions

Consumer promotions represent one of three general types of sales promotions. The other types are: (1) promotions to the sales force such as bonuses, sales contests, and sales rallies, and (2) promotions to the trade such as buying allowances, dealer sales contests, and allowances for advertising and promotional displays. These two types will be described in Chapter 14 on sales and Chapter 16 on distribution. The major types of consumer promotions will be described here.

Coupons

Coupons are by far the most important sales promotion device. Figure 12-5 shows that almost two-thirds of all sales promotion activity is represented by coupon offers. Coupons are meant to encourage consumers to try the product because they offer a discount on the regular price. But studies suggest that coupons do not provide enough incentive to make consumers permanently switch brands. They are good for immediate sales but not as a means of inducing brand loyalty.[31] Therefore, coupons are frequently used to support short-term sales for weak brands.[32]

Although coupons are an established means of gaining immediate sales, they have several disadvantages. First, they are expensive. The average coupon requires a twenty-cent discount on a brand.[33] Further, most coupons appear in expensive newspaper and magazine space. One single-page four-color coupon insert in 236 Sunday newspapers cost $550,000.[34] Second, most coupons are not redeemed. In fact, average redemption is only about 4.5 percent of the coupons distributed.[35] Third, the market is becoming saturated with coupons, diminishing their effectiveness. Some critics describe the trend as "coupon madness" and see it as a largely unprofitable defensive measure against competitors.[36] Yet coupons are a powerful tool and are likely to increase in the face of consumers' price sensitivity.

Premiums

Premiums are products offered free or at a reduced price as an incentive to buy other products. They should be related to the product itself to be effective. For example, Citicorp increased sales for its travelers checks by giving consumers who bought at least $600 worth of checks a Travel Savings Coupon

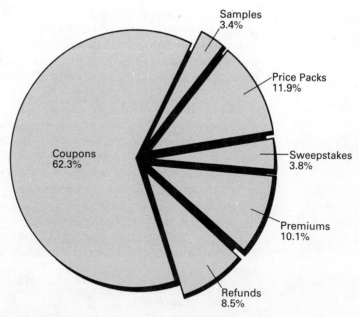

Samples
3.4%

Price Packs
11.9%

Sweepstakes
3.8%

Premiums
10.1%

Refunds
8.5%

Coupons
62.3%

FIGURE 12-5
Distribution of types of sales promotions in 1981 (based on 6147 promotions reported)

Source: Adapted from Dancer Fitzgerald Sample's monthly consumer promotion reports, 1981; and "It's on the Package," *Advertising Age,* May 17, 1982, p. M-27. Copyright 1982 by Crain Communications, Inc.

Book valued at more than $2500. The coupons could be used to buy brand-name travel products and services. This premium was supported by a nationwide magazine ad campaign.[37]

Premiums have their limitations. Like coupons, they are more likely to result in immediate sales than in repeat purchases since many buyers are more attracted to the premium than the product. They are also expensive. Yet their use, like that of coupons, is increasing.

Refunds

Refunds are another means of obtaining quick sales. They began to be used more widely when auto companies began giving rebates. Chrysler made a startling comeback in the early 1980s through promotional tools such as rebates and obtained 12 percent of the auto market largely as a result. Some analysts feel, "Chrysler has been buying its market share with rebates and other incentives," and that it might not obtain a 12 percent share of market in normal times.[38]

The use of rebates in the auto and appliance industries spurred other industries to use them. American Can began offering refunds to purchasers of its Gala paper towels, giving certificates worth up to seven dollars in free groceries. The promotion increased sales and won trade support.[39] Generally, consumers view refunds as disguised price cuts and incorporate the refund into their evaluation of the product's price. But the technique proved popular during the recession in the early 1980s as a means of offering price incentives.

Sweepstakes

Sweepstakes lend excitement to sales promotions and appeal to the American consumer's gamesmanship. Their use was limited because a company cannot legally require a purchase to participate. They were a good means of increasing brand awareness but not necessarily trial. Marketers got around this restriction by introducing the in-pack instant-winner card games in which the prizes are printed on the package itself. Pepsi and Coke have the prizes printed under the bottle caps. Hunt's tomato sauce has the prize printed on the inside bottom of the can. C&H sugar has game cards inside five-pound bags. These in-pack promotions increased the use of sweepstakes as a means of spurring immediate sales.[40]

Cents-off packages

Sometimes a price discount is printed on the package. Like refunds, these promotions are viewed as price cuts and are effective in producing short-term sales effects. Some marketers use cents-off promotions so frequently that they become part of the established price and lose their effect. A consumer who becomes used to seeing twenty cents off on the label might be discouraged from buying when the promotion is temporarily halted. Overuse may therefore have a negative effect on brand loyalty and long-term sales.

Free samples

Free samples are an important means of inducing trial of new products (as illustrated in the introduction of the TRAC II razor) or in revitalizing existing brands (as illustrated by the reintroduction of Tylenol capsules). They are one of the few sales promotion tools that may be effective in gaining brand loyalty. A new product that is given to the consumer is frequently used and may lead to repeat purchases. But many free samples are wasted, either because of a lack of interest or because they are given to people who already use the product. As a result sampling is frequently a shotgun approach and is extremely expensive.

Sales Promotion Management

Each of the components of the promotional mix requires planning and management. Management of the advertising and personal selling efforts will be considered in the next two chapters. In this section we describe the planning and management process for sales promotions. Because expenditures on sales promotions are so large, it is surprising that so few firms have a rational process for sales promotion management. It is frequently left to advertising agencies ill equipped to handle coupon redemptions, refund offers, or the contacts with retailers required to implement these tools. Only a few of the larger firms such as Procter and Gamble, General Mills, and General Foods have internal sales promotion staffs.

Sales promotion management should require:

1. *Establishing sales promotional objectives.* These might include some combination of:

   ☐ obtaining trial among nonusers of the product,

   ☐ encouraging continuity of use among current or occasional users,

   ☐ encouraging increased product use among current users, and

   ☐ reinforcing the advertising and personal selling effort.[41]

2. *Selecting the combination of sales promotion tools.* If the objective is to gain trial for a new product, free samples should be emphasized. If it is to counter competitive price activity, cents-off package should be emphasized. If it is to try to generate product interest and awareness, sweepstakes should be considered.

3. *Coordinate the promotional plan with advertising.* Sales promotions are generally used in conjunction with advertising. The two should reinforce each other — advertising by increasing brand awareness, and sales promotions by encouraging trial to convince consumers of product benefits. Generally a good sales promotion plan will increase awareness of the advertising campaign, and an effective advertising campaign will encourage coupon redemptions.

4. *Evaluate the sales promotional program.* Management must try to estimate the incremental sales produced by the sales promotion campaign. One research service, known as Sales Promotion Analysis Reporting (SPAR) attempts to do just that.[42] SPAR estimates what sales would have been without the promotional campaign and then compares this figure to actual sales results during the campaign. Hypothetical results of a SPAR report are presented in Table 12-1. The analysis estimates that sales during the sales promotion period are $500,000 higher than they would have been without a promotion. But sales decreased before the promotion because retailers reduced orders in expectation of better prices during the promotional period. Sales also decreased after the promotion because retailers built up inventories during the promotional period. These costs plus the actual costs of the promotional incentives result in a total promotional cost of $600,000. On this basis the promotion actually produced a $100,000 loss, despite the net gain in sales during the period.

TABLE 12-1
Evaluation of a Sales Promotion Program

	(IN MILLIONS)
Sales results during promotion	$3.0
Sales results had no promotion occurred (as estimated by SPAR)	2.5
Net Sales from promotion	0.5
Costs of promotion decrease in sales before promotion due to retailer expectations of promotion	0.2
decrease in sales after promotion since consumer is stocked up	0.1
cost of promotional program	0.3
Total costs of promotion	0.6
Net Gain (or Loss) from promotion	(0.1)

Source: Based on description of SPAR in "SPAR Service Evaluates Promotion Effectiveness, Profitability," *Marketing News,* December 12, 1980, p. 6.

PUBLICITY

Publicity is the fourth major component of the promotional mix. It involves releasing to the mass media news stories about a product or service. These may be in the form of news releases for magazines or newspapers, films for TV news shows, or appearances by corporate executives. Publicity has only recently been recognized as an important component of promotional strategy. Today many firms launch publicity campaigns in conjunction with advertising campaigns. "It complements the other marketing efforts, but serves a distinct and unique purpose, often giving a product, service or marketer added credibility, exposure and newsworthiness." [43]

Even with this new recognition publicity is largely underutilized. The responsibility for publicity lies with the Public Relations Department, located in corporate headquarters. As a result, it tends to be divorced from marketing functions, making coordination with other components of the promotional mix difficult.

Publicity is most effective when it is newsworthy. The Potato Board, a cooperative association of potato growers, launched an effective publicity campaign to convince opinion leaders that potatoes are a good source of vitamins and minerals and are not fattening. Many stories were generated about the potato for television and women's magazines, recipes were distributed, and *The Potato Lover's Diet Cookbook* was offered to audiences. [44]

Publicity offers several other advantages to marketers:

1. *Publicity is credible.* The American press has a reputation for skepticism, so if a publication writes about a product's advantages, the implication is that the product is worth looking into. [45]

2. *Little cost is involved.* There are few media costs in publicity. It provides free exposure. The only costs are those of public relations staffers and some minimal out-of-pocket expenses.

3. *Publicity supports the sales force* by paving the way for a sales call. Good product or service publicity facilitates the sales task.

4. *Publicity supports the advertising campaign.* It increases advertising awareness and, most important, advertising believability.[46]

There are also several drawbacks to the use of publicity. First, it is not within the company's control. As one PR executive says, "When we're dealing with the media, we don't have the final say about the product. If, for example, a newspaper uses a press release, the editors make the final decision about what appears."[47] Second, coordination between publicity and other elements in the promotional mix tends to be poor because of the distance between the PR department and marketing.

Summary

Marketing management must determine the mix of promotional elements required to market a brand or product line. Such a mix is composed of advertising, personal selling, sales promotion, and publicity. The appropriate mix of these elements is determined by the type of product being promoted, the characteristics of the target group, and the stage of the product in its life cycle. For example, personal selling tends to be the dominant element for industrial goods, whereas advertising is dominant for consumer goods. More money is spent on advertising and sales promotion in the early phase of a product's life cycle to gain brand awareness and encourage trial.

Management must determine the size of the promotional budget and then allocate it to the various components of the promotional mix in order to implement promotional strategies. Various methods of determining the budget were reviewed — objective-task, percentage of sales, and competitive parity. Once the budget is set, it must be allocated to the promotional mix components in accordance with the nature of the product and the environment in which it is marketed.

Having considered the importance of establishing a promotional mix, we then reviewed each of the four major components of the mix. Various types of *advertising* were considered:

- Brand advertising is designed to stimulate sales of the company's brand.
- Product advertising is designed to stimulate demand for a product category.
- Corporate advertising is meant to:
  - advertise the corporate name,

□ enhance the corporate image, and

□ state a company's position on a social or public issue.

■ Cooperative advertising involves manufacturers offering retailers allowances to advertise the manufacturer's products.

Whereas advertising is a means of promoting to the mass market, *personal selling* is designed to influence customers on a one-to-one basis. The salesperson assesses the needs of the individual customer and develops a sales approach accordingly. The personal sales effort will vary depending on whether it is for a consumer good, an industrial product, or a service.

Sales promotions are short-term incentives designed to encourage consumers to try the brand. Most sales promotions involve price incentives. The hope is that once a consumer tries the brand, he or she will become a loyal customer. Sales promotions represent the greatest part of the budget for many consumer packaged-goods firms. Expenditures on sales promotions are increasing more than those for advertising. Such promotions may involve coupons, premiums, refunds, sweepstakes, or free samples.

Publicity, the last component of the promotional mix to be considered, involves news releases, articles, and appearances that benefit the company. It is highly credible and involves little cost.

In the next chapter we will consider the most important component of the promotional mix — advertising. The process of planning for and managing advertising strategies will be described.

Questions

1. Which of the main components of the promotional mix — advertising, personal selling, or sales promotion — is likely to be most important for:

   □ a company trying to revitalize a cereal brand whose share has been declining?

   □ a coffee brand trying to combat competition from lower-priced brands?

   □ a producer of automobile parts trying to create awareness for a new line of electrical accessories?

   □ a manufacturer of household products trying to get consumers to buy a new detergent?

2. What is the ideal method to determine the:

   □ optimal level of the promotional budget?

   □ allocation of the budget to promotional mix components?

   What is the problem with implementing this ideal?

3. What are the problems with a (1) percentage-of-sales approach and (2) competitive parity approach as a basis for establishing the advertising budget? Since these problems exist, why are these approaches so widely used in setting promotional budgets?

4. Under what circumstances would a manufacturer wish to stimulate demand for a product category (such as disposable diapers) rather than (or in addition to) demand for the company's brand (such as Pampers)?

5. Why have many industrywide advertising campaigns failed to arrest a downward slide in industry demand? Under what circumstances have some of these campaigns been successful?

6. One manufacturing executive who considered offering retailers advertising allowances stated why he chose not to do so as follows:

   Why should I offer retailers advertising allowances? When I do, half of them don't use it and the other half use it in the wrong way (wrong ads, wrong media placements). We spend millions of dollars trying to establish a national image. I want to control my advertising to maintain this image. Retailer cooperative advertising does not permit me that control.

   What are the pros and cons of this statement?

7. The chairman of ITT does not think a corporation should advertise its positions on public issues, whereas the chairman of Mobil Oil strongly supports such advertising. What are the pros and cons of corporate issue advertising?

8. How are advertising, personal selling, and sales promotion complementary tools (tools designed to fulfill different objectives of the promotional plan). Under what circumstances can one of these components be considered as a substitute for the other?

9. Why are expenditures for sales promotions increasing more rapidly than those for advertising? What are the strategic implications of this increase?

10. Which sales promotion methods (coupons, premiums, free samples) should be used in the following circumstances, and why?

    ☐ Supporting short-term sales for a weak brand.

    ☐ Influencing customers to try a new brand.

    ☐ Tying two related product categories together.

11. Consider Table 12-1. On what basis are sales promotions evaluated? What assumptions are made in evaluating sales promotions?

12. What are the advantages and disadvantages of emphasizing publicity in the promotional mix?

Notes

1. "Campaign: Needham Creates the Brother Dom Phenom," *Madison Avenue,* August 1982, pp. 44–55.

2. Thomas F. Garbett, "When to Advertise Your Company," *Harvard Business Review* 60 (March–April, 1982): 103.

3. "Heavy Spending Propels Champion Campaign," *Advertising Age,* March 7, 1983, pp. M-18–M-20.

4. "Fort Howard: New Marketing Muscle from Maryland Cup," *Business Week,* July 18, 1983, p. 132.

5. "Best Promotions of the Year," *Advertising Age,* May 9, 1983, p. M-54.

6. "PR Ripens Role in Marketing," *Advertising Age,* January 5, 1981, p. S-10.

7. "100 Leading National Advertisers," *Advertising Age,* September 8, 1983, p. 166.

8. Malcolm A. McNiven, "Plan for More Productive Advertising," *Harvard Business Review* 58 (March–April 1980): 131.

9. Philip Kotler, *Marketing Management* (Englewood Cliffs, N.J.: Prentice-Hall, 1980), p. 499.

10. "Sears Eyes Lower Ad-to-Sales Ratio," *Advertising Age,* December 4, 1978, pp. 3, 8.

11. "Common Sense Rules in Setting Ad Budgets," *Industrial Marketing,* December 1979, p. 54.

12. Andre J. San Augustine and William F. Foley, "How Large Advertisers Set Budgets," *Journal of Advertising Research* 15 (1975): 11–16.

13. "How Campbell Keeps Media on Schedule," *Marketing & Media Decisions,* January 1983, p. 57.

14. "Polyester Tries on a New Image," *Advertising Age,* March 14, 1983, p. 43.

15. Ibid.

16. "Coal Industry Tries Consumer Marketing to Improve Its Product's Image and Sales," *The Wall Street Journal,* August 9, 1982, p. 17.

17. Ibid.

18. *Advertising Age,* March 7, 1983, p. M-11.

19. "How GE Puts It All Together," *Marketing & Media Decisions,* January 1980, p. 132.

20. "Building Image for a Company Called TRW," *Madison Avenue,* February 1983, pp. 60–63.

21. Garbett, "When to Advertise Your Company."

22. S. Prakash Sethi, "Institutional/Image Advertising and Idea/Issue Advertising as Marketing Tools: Some Public Policy Issues," *Journal of Marketing* 43 (January 1979): 70.

23. "Corporate Advertising: Speaking Out Can Be Good for Your Corporate Health," *Madison Avenue,* February 1983, pp. 72–80.

24. Ibid., p. 76.

25. "Seeds of Promos' Future Planted in Year's Events," *Advertising Age,* March 2, 1981, p. 50.

26. "Coupons in Danger, P&G Exec Warns," *Advertising Age,* March 23, 1983, p. 3.

27. "Exploring Some Myths, Realities About Strategy of Sales Promos," *Advertising Age,* July 2, 1979, p. 37.

28. "Strategic Promotion Planning Yields More Bang for the Marketing Buck," *Marketing News,* October 30, 1981, pp. 1, 13.

29. "Trac II: Marketing Key to Success of an Innovative Idea," *Marketing Times,* January/February, 1983, pp. 38–40.

30. "Special Recovery: Tylenol Regains Most of No. 1 Market Share," *The Wall Street Journal,* December 24, 1982, p. 1.

31. *Sales and Marketing Executive Report,* March 1982, pp. 7–8.

32. "Retailing May Have Overdosed on Coupons," *Business Week,* June 13, 1983, pp. 147, 149.

33. "The Supermarket Coupon War," *The New York Times,* September 30, 1981, pp. D1, D15.

34. *Business Week,* June 13, 1983, p. 147.

35. *The New York Times,* September 30, 1981, p. D15.

36. Ibid.

37. "Best Promotions of the Year," *Advertising Age,* May 9, 1983, p. M-58.

38. "Chrysler Is Upbeat as Market Share Rises, but Some Doubt It Can Maintain Success," *The Wall Street Journal,* April 22, 1982, p. 31.

39. "The Year's Best Promos," *Advertising Age,* August 10, 1981, p. 40.

40. "Effective Promotions Not Always 'A First,'" *Advertising Age,* December 14, 1981, p. 50.

41. *Marketing News,* October 30, 1981, p. 13.

42. "SPAR Service Evaluates Promotion Effectiveness, Profitability," *Marketing News,* December 12, 1980, p. 6.

43. *Advertising Age,* December 12, 1980, p. S-10.

44. Joseph M. Coogle, Jr., "Media, Advertising, and Public Relations," in Gerald Zaltman and Thomas V. Bonoma, eds., *Review of Marketing 1978* (Chicago: American Marketing Association, 1978), pp. 481–84.

45. "Planning Product Publicity Pays Off," *Nation's Business,* September 1978, p. 35.

46. "Public Relations Gets Short Shrift from New Managers," *Marketing News,* October 15, 1982, p. 8.

47. *Advertising Age,* January 5, 1981, p. S-10.

CHAPTER 13

Advertising Management and Strategy

FOCUS OF CHAPTER

Advertising is often regarded as the most important component of the promotional mix, particularly for consumer goods, because it can reach large groups of consumers with the same message. Advertising is mass communications, yet it is selective enough to target messages to market segments. For example, General Motors views Chevrolet as a car for the mass market and advertises it heavily on a nationwide basis. In the words of Chevrolet's general marketing manager, "Chevrolet's contribution to General Motors should be as a strong anchor in the mass market. It's a role no other division is suited to play."[1] But advertising's mass-marketing capability still allows the Chevrolet division to choose media according to the market segment the division wants to reach: business publications for the executive and professional market, specialty car magazines for the teenage car enthusiasts, TV news programs for the upscale market, and local TV spot commercials for specific geographic markets.

In this chapter we will first cite the importance of advertising based on level of expenditures. Then we will consider the advertising management process — that is, the decisions that advertisers must make to inform and influence their target markets. Advertising management involves decisions regarding:

1. advertising objectives,
2. the advertising budget,
3. advertising strategies,
4. media selection, and
5. the effectiveness of the advertising campaign.

Each of these five areas will be considered. Special attention will be devoted to advertising strategy because of the importance of fulfilling communications objectives by implementing advertising campaigns.

Importance of Advertising

The importance of advertising can be illustrated by level of expenditures and scope of activities. Total expenditures for advertising were $67 billion in 1982, $73 billion in 1983, and an estimated $83 billion in 1984.[2] They are expected to rise fourfold to $320 billion by the turn of the century.[3] Advertising expenditures have consistently been about 2 percent of the gross national product in recent years.

Advertising and sales promotion represent most of the promotional expenditures for consumer goods. The top twenty advertisers sell primarily consumer goods, each having spent $250 million or more on advertising in 1982 (see Table 13-1). Many of these companies spend a substantial share of their sales revenues on advertising. Drug, toiletry, food, and other consumer packaged-goods firms typically spend over 5 percent of sales revenues whereas the leading auto companies and retail chains spend 2 percent or less on advertising (see Table 13-1).

McDonald's is a good example of the importance of advertising. The company spent over $260 million on advertising in 1983. Advertising expenditures have risen more than tenfold since 1970 and represent 3.4 percent of gross sales.[4]

TABLE 13-1
Advertising Expenditures by the Top Twenty Advertisers for 1982

RANK	COMPANY	ADVERTISING EXPENDITURES (IN MILLIONS)	ADVERTISING AS A PERCENTAGE OF SALES
1	Procter and Gamble	726.1	5.8
2	Sears, Roebuck and Co.	631.2	2.1
3	General Motors Corp.	549.0	.9
4	R. J. Reynolds Industries	530.3	4.1
5	Philip Morris Inc.	501.7	4.3
6	General Foods Corp.	429.1	5.2
7	AT&T Co.	373.6	.6
8	K Mart Corp.	365.3	2.2
9	Nabisco Brands	335.2	5.7
10	American Home Products Corp.	325.4	7.1
11	Mobil Corp.	320.0	.5
12	Ford Motor Co.	313.5	.9
13	PepsiCo Inc.	305.0	4.1
14	Unilever U.S.	304.6	10.3
15	Warner-Lambert Co.	294.7	9.1
16	Beatrice Foods Co.	271.0	2.9
17	Johnson & Johnson	270.0	8.2
18	Colgate-Palmolive	268.0	5.5
19	McDonald's Corp.	265.5	3.4
20	Coca-Cola Co.	255.3	4.1

Source: "100 Leading National Advertisers," *Advertising Age*, September 8, 1983, pp. 1, 166. Reprinted with permission. Copyright 1983 by Crain Communications, Inc.

Advertising is subsidized by contributions from McDonald's franchisees, with local advertising handled by about one hundred ad agencies supervised by McDonald's regional advertising managers. National advertising is run by Leo Burnett Company, a large agency located in Chicago.

The importance of advertising is also shown by the energy and attention devoted to it by marketing management. Brand and product managers devote practically all their time to three areas: advertising, sales promotions, and distribution. Marketing managers spend a good deal of their time coordinating with advertising agencies to translate a product's positioning objectives into a viable communication strategy. And top management's increasing concern with company image is reflected in its greater attention to corporate advertising.

Advertising Management

In the rest of this chapter we will describe the advertising management process — that is, the decisions that must be made to develop and implement an advertising campaign. This process is summarized in Figure 13-1. The first step is to establish the objectives for the advertising campaign. For example, in Stouffer's successful introduction of Lean Cuisine, a low-calorie line of frozen entrees, the initial objective was to change consumer perceptions of low-calorie foods as tasteless, not filling, and lacking in variety.[5] Moreover, the advertising described the line as a calorie-controlled food rather than as low calorie to get away from the stigma of poor-tasting diet foods.

The second step, establishing the advertising budget for Lean Cuisine to meet objectives, required heavier initial expenditures and then a constant stream of advertising once the brand was established. The budget for the introductory period was $1.5 million.[6] Budgetary allocations called for advertising

FIGURE 13-1
The advertising management process

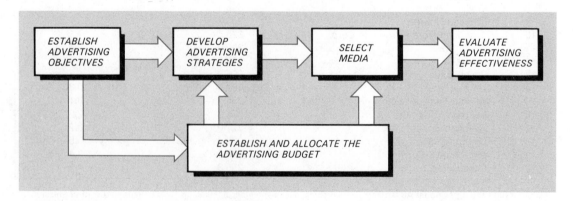

to appear fairly evenly over the year after the introductory period. The lack of seasonal demand for the line meant that the company did not have to advertise more heavily in certain times of year.

The third requirement in Figure 13-1 is developing an advertising strategy to fulfill the objectives. The initial advertising was informationally oriented. It explained that the line had less than 300 calories, the meats had less than 10 percent fat content, and the result was a tastier low-calorie product that looked good (see left of Figure 13-2). Once the concept of a good-tasting diet food was accepted, the campaign took on more of a "cosmetic or high-fashion look."[7] The advertising still emphasized the benefits of less than 300 calories, but there was much less copy and the emphasis shifted to a new appeal: "You'll love the way it looks on you." (See right of Figure 13-2.)

The fourth requirement in the advertising management process is to develop a media plan to reach the target audience. The best target for low-calorie

FIGURE 13-2
Introductory and later advertising for Lean Cuisine

Introductory information-oriented advertising for Lean Cuisine

Used by permission.

Subsequent fashion-oriented advertising for Lean Cuisine

Used by permission.

frozen foods is primarily women between twenty-five and forty-five and with $25,000 or more in income.[8] But the media plan should not exclude the male market. The media plan called for a combination of magazines, newspapers, and spot TV. A scattered schedule of magazines over the year included *Better Home and Gardens, Good Housekeeping, Cosmopolitan, Glamour,* and *Working Women.* More general publications like *People* and *Reader's Digest* were also used. Daytime TV spots tended to focus on news and educational programming to reach the upscale woman.[9] The frequency objective of this media schedule was to reach 90 percent of the target audience four times a year.

The last step in the advertising management process is evaluating the effectiveness of the campaign. Management must determine awareness of the advertising, beliefs about the brand, whether the message is reaching the target group, and ultimately, the effects of the campaign on sales. Stouffer's seems to have been successful in overcoming consumer skepticism about a good-tasting low-calorie entree. The low-calorie segment of the frozen food market went from 7 percent at the time of Lean Cuisine's introduction to 17 percent; and sales were $125 million in the first year.[10]

The five areas in Figure 13-1 will be described in the next section. Although described in sequence, some of these steps occur simultaneously. Setting the advertising budget is a function of advertising strategies, so both steps occur simultaneously. Similarly, the media plan must be set in conjunction with advertising strategies.

Establishing Advertising Objectives

Establishing advertising objectives is a crucial first step in the advertising management process for several reasons:

1. The objectives should determine the advertising expenditures required to meet them.

2. Advertising objectives provide guidelines for advertising strategy and media schedules. Strategy represents the messages developed to meet the objectives; media represent the vehicles used to target the strategy.

3. A good set of advertising objectives should provide the basis for establishing measurement criteria to evaluate the campaign. If an objective is to change consumer beliefs about a product on certain criteria (e.g., that low-calorie foods can be good tasting), then one measure in evaluating the campaign is the amount to which it has in fact changed consumer beliefs on this criterion.

CHARACTERISTICS OF ADVERTISING OBJECTIVES

Because advertising objectives are the basis for evaluating the campaign, they should have several characteristics. They should be:

1. *Measurable.* An objective such as reaching 90 percent of households with four impressions is measurable. An objective such as attracting users of competitive brands is not, unless the company can in some way determine advertising's role in inducing a switch in brands.

2. *Targetable.* Objectives should be stated in terms of a target audience. Lean Cuisine could target its objectives to an upscale, young to middle-aged group that is weight conscious. Changes in beliefs about low-calorie foods should be measured for this target. Changing beliefs of consumers with a low probability of purchase cannot be counted toward achieving the company's objectives.

3. A *benchmark.* In many cases, advertising objectives are framed in terms of change: change beliefs, improve attitudes, increase the level of use, encourage brand switching, and so on. These objectives require a benchmark measure at the start of the campaign and in subsequent periods to determine if they are being met.

TYPES OF OBJECTIVES

There are three types of advertising objectives; they deal with (1) message effects, (2) media effects, and (3) behavior. These objectives are illustrated in Figure 13-3 with specific operational criteria. The behavioral objectives are most important since they reflect sales results. But as noted, they are hardest to measure because: (1) advertising is only one of many influences on the consumer, and the effects of advertising cannot be isolated; and (2) advertising has a long-term effect on sales, and it is difficult to sort out the effects of past advertising from that of the current campaign.

These difficulties have led two marketing authorities to conclude, "Advertising objectives that emphasize sales are usually not very operational because they provide little practical guidance for decision makers."[11] As a result, marketers have used intervening objectives as measures of advertising effectiveness, primarily the message and media criteria in Figure 13-3.

Despite the difficulties in establishing an advertising-to-sales relationship, advertisers have not given up on behavioral measures. Rather than talk in terms of sales increases, advertisers can shorten their sights and talk of attracting new users, increasing the level of use, or increasing brand loyalty. These behavioral measures are still more difficult to operationalize than intervening measures such as brand awareness, but they are not so difficult as sales. For example, it is possible to determine if advertising a new use for a product (e.g., cold soup as a refresher) has led to adopting this idea, or to determine whether naming a competitor in an ad has led some of the competitor's customers to switch to the company's brand. These are behavioral goals that can be measured. But trying to measure the effect of the overall campaign on sales is difficult at best.

Because message effects are more operational than behavioral objectives, advertisers also recognize that these objectives are more limited. Message

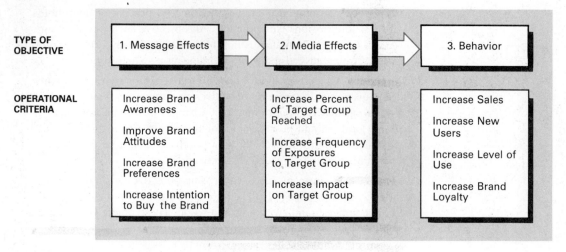

FIGURE 13-3
Types of advertising objectives

effects are designed to measure parts of the overall campaign; behavioral objectives are designed to measure the effects of the campaign as a whole. It is more desirable to measure the effect of the total campaign, but barring that, advertisers frame objectives in more limited terms to assess particular components of the campaign.

Setting and Allocating Advertising Budgets

To determine an advertising budget managers can use the same approaches they used to determine a total promotional budget: an objective-task method, a percentage-of-sales approach, a competitive parity approach, or some arbitrary method. The difference is that in determining an advertising budget, management has chosen a bottom-up approach — that is, determining a budget for each component of the promotional mix. Management has rejected a top-down approach that would establish a total promotional budget and then allocate part of it to advertising.

As in setting a promotional budget, the objective-task method seems effective, because it relies on criteria of advertising effectiveness. The other three methods are based on fixed or arbitrary criteria that may have little to do with how effective advertising is.

One other approach that has been used in setting the advertising budget involves quantitative modeling of an advertising-to-sales relationship. As we saw in Chapter 12, if management can estimate a relationship between a promotional component (such as advertising) and sales, it can then set the budget so the marginal revenue from advertising equals the marginal costs associated with generating that revenue (advertising, marketing, and production costs).

Several quantitative models have been developed to estimate the most efficient level of advertising expenditures. Determining this level requires establishing a relationship between advertising and sales. An example of a model relating sales response to advertising is one developed by Vidale and Wolf, and illustrated in Exhibit 13-1.[12] From this model a company can estimate the effects of advertising expenditures on sales results. The company can determine the effects of incremental advertising expenditures on sales and estimate the advertising expenditures that will maximize profits. Using the model in Exhibit 13-1 it is estimated that an increase of $2.0 million in advertising expenditures will generate an additional $2.6 million in sales. But consider that alternative expenditure levels produce the following figures (in millions of dollars):

1.	2.	3.	4.	5.
Advertising Expenditure Level	Proposed Change in Ad Expenditure Level	Increase in Other Costs	Increase in Revenue (based on model in Exhibit 13-1)	Marginal Contribution to Profits [column 4 − (columns 2 + 3)]
$6.0	(Current Level)	0.00	0.00	0.00
$6.5	+0.50	+0.05	+0.58	+0.03
$7.0	+1.00	+0.20	+1.25	+0.05
$7.5	+1.50	+0.40	+1.90	0.00
$8.0	+2.00	+0.70	+2.60	−0.10

These figures show that increasing the firm's advertising budget by $2 million actually results in a negative contribution to profits of $100,000 (an increase of $2.6 million in revenue minus the $2 million increase in advertising expenditures *and* the $700,000 increase in associated marketing and production expenses). The company's decision rule would be to continue to increase advertising expenditures up to an additional $1.5 million but not beyond, because up to this point additional advertising expenditures are still contributing to profit. Therefore, the firm sets its advertising budget at $7.5 million. This is where marginal revenue equals marginal costs and the marginal contribution to profits from advertising is zero.

The problem with such models is that they must assume an advertising-to-sales relationship (the *r* parameter in Exhibit 13-1). Attempts have been made to estimate the advertising-to-sales relationship by trying to control advertising expenditures in the field, by simulations, and by statistical analysis. In each case, there is no certainty that advertising has in fact been controlled and the cumulative effects of advertising have been accounted for. In short, the use of quantitative models to determine the advertising budget runs up against the same basic problem of isolating the effects of advertising on sales.

EXHIBIT 13-1 A Quantitative Model to Estimate the Advertising-to-Sales Relationship[a]

In this model, a change in sales is a function of advertising expenditures and market potential. The relationships are:

$$\Delta S_t = rA\,\frac{M - S}{M} - \lambda S$$

where

S = sales volume at time t,

A = advertising expenditures,

r = a sales response constant (the sales generated per advertising dollar when the rate of sales volume is zero),

M = the level of sales when the market is saturated, and

λ = a sales decay function (the percentage loss in sales in time period t).

The model says that sales will increase at a more rapid rate if (1) advertising expenditures are increasing, (2) sales response to advertising is high, (3) there is untapped sales potential in the market (as represented by saturation level M minus the sales volume, S), and (4) the sales decay function is low. With this model, one can estimate sales from proposed advertising expenditures and the other variables listed above. For example, assume a company introduces a new product. It estimates the total market for the product category is no greater than $10 million (the saturation level). Initial sales for the brand are $1 million ($S$). From test market results, the company estimates sales response to advertising (r) to be 1.5 ($1.50 in sales can be generated from an additional $1.00 in advertising). The company estimates it will lose sales at the rate of 10 percent per year if it does no advertising ($\lambda = 0.1$). It is considering increasing the advertising budget from its current level of $6 million to $8 million (a $2 million increase) and wants to estimate the effect on sales. This is estimated as

$$\Delta S = 1.5(2)\frac{10 - 1}{10} - 0.1(1) = 3.0(0.9) - 0.1 = \$2.6 \text{ million}$$

Therefore, on the basis of an increase in advertising expenditures of $2 million the company estimates it can gain an additional $2.6 million in sales. If the additional expenses involved in generating the additional sales are less than $600,000, the increase in the ad budget by $2 million will produce a contribution to profit.

[a]See H. L. Vidale and H. B. Wolfe, "An Operations Research Study of Sales Response to Advertising," *Operational Research Quarterly* 5(1957):370–381.

ALLOCATING THE ADVERTISING BUDGET

Once the advertising budget has been set, it must be allocated. Allocating the budget requires specifying (1) the timing of advertising expenditures, (2) the advertising strategies required to fulfill objectives, and (3) the media to be used in delivering the message. Advertising strategies and media will be considered next. In this section we will consider the timing problem.

Seasonality

An important issue in timing advertising expenditures is seasonality in product category sales. Most products have some seasonality based either on variations in consumption (iced tea in the summer) or special events (watches or cameras for graduation and Christmas). The advertiser must decide whether advertising should precede or coincide with seasonal sales. For example, many clothing manufacturers begin advertising their lines before the buying season. On the other hand, gift advertising tends to occur during the buying season.

Another decision is the level of advertising during the heaviest buying period. If 30 percent of camera sales occur during Christmas, should camera advertisers devote 30 percent of their budget to this time period? Gearing seasonal advertising expenditures to the level of purchasing activity is reasonable. But the danger is that heavy expenditures at one time of year may mean low advertising activity the rest of the year and decreased levels of brand awareness.

Continuity versus Pulsing

Another aspect of timing is whether advertisers should spend most of the budget in a few large bursts at various times of the year (**pulsing**) or choose a steady level of expenditures over the year (continuity). For example, if a strategy calls for running 104 thirty-second spot commercials on network television over one year, should about nine be run during a one-week period every month (pulsing), or should the ads be run twice a week over the whole year (continuity)? Many advertisers feel that pulsing has a greater effect on the consumer, since increased learning occurs when information is presented in concentrated segments. Others feel that the brand should be consistently advertised to ensure brand awareness and maintain a reminder effect through continuous exposure.

One authority believes that continuity should win out over pulsing under the following conditions:

1. When the objective is to maintain brand awareness;

2. When the product is purchased frequently (a continuous reminder effect is necessary); and

3. When the consumer is likely to forget the brand in the absence of some stimulus (the higher the forgetting rate, the more important it is to keep the brand in front of the consumer).[13]

Advertising Strategies

Advertising strategy is the key element in advertising management since it is the means of implementing objectives. Advertising strategies differ on many dimensions: the information communicated in the ad, the way the message is presented, the imagery and symbolism used, the use of spokespersons, and so forth. The diversity of strategies makes it difficult to classify them. But two major questions can help:

1. Is the campaign meant to maintain or to change market conditions?
2. Is the campaign meant to communicate information or imagery and symbolism?

Advertising strategies may be designed to maintain and reinforce current brand images and attitudes in order to keep present users and ensure the continued strength of the brand. For example, cash cows such as Pampers, Jell-O, and Taster's Choice seek to maintain their market positions and use advertising for a reminder effect to reinforce current users. But most advertising strategies are meant to produce some change: to inform consumers of new products or changes in existing products, to improve brand images and attitudes, or to increase involvement with the brand.

The second criterion in classifying advertising strategies is the nature of the message. The basic distinction is between messages that are meant to inform and messages that are meant to convey imagery and symbolism. Informational advertising is meant to sway beliefs about a brand. Advertising that uses imagery and symbolism is meant to influence feelings.

These two dimensions produce the classification in Figure 13-4. The strategies listed under each of the four headings will now be described using specific advertising campaigns as examples.

MAINTENANCE STRATEGIES

Brand maintenance strategies are divided into those which communicate information about the characteristics of the brand and those which create brand images.

Informational Strategies

Companies can maintain their current strength by continuing to advertise the characteristics that convey product benefits. Mercedes has been saying the same things about its cars in the same way for twenty years and doing so almost entirely on an informational basis. Bruce McCall, the original copywriter on the account remembers, "There was an early realization that we couldn't tell the Mercedes story without using long copy."[14] The result was a campaign "packed with lots of technical facts." The media plan reflected the informational orientation of the campaign — primarily print, newspapers first and then an

PURPOSE

MESSAGE EXECUTION

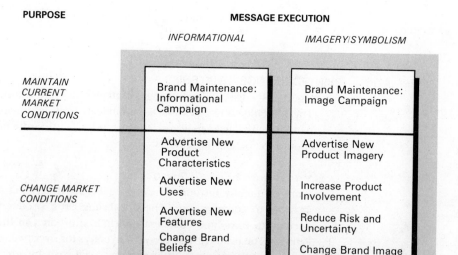

INFORMATIONAL   *IMAGERY/SYMBOLISM*

FIGURE 13-4
Types of advertising strategy

emphasis on magazines. The consistency of the campaign over the years reflects the maintenance strategy. In McCall's words:

> We've written to the consumer for years as if he's a smart guy. And he's responded to us. People are capable of understanding a technical message if it's couched in benefit terms. The look of the ads won't be different, but the content will. A change without changing."[15]

Brand Image Strategies

Brands can maintain their current position by continuing to reinforce the same brand image. One of the best examples of this strategy is the Marlboro cowboy campaign, a campaign that has used the same imagery — masculinity, the outdoors, independence — for over twenty years to sell Marlboro cigarettes. Many cigarette campaigns have followed Marlboro's lead in using a maintenance strategy based on imagery. The strategy is described by *Ad Forum,* an advertising trade publication:

> In contrast to the product attribute advertising of the 1970's, much of to-day's [cigarette] advertising emphasizes an image ... Most companies have chosen to buoy existing brands in this fashion rather than gamble ... to launch new brand names.[16]

This switch from informational to image campaigns is illustrated by the fact that the number of cigarette claims decreased by 25 percent while the number of ads emphasizing smoking pleasure went up by 50 percent in a two-year period.[17]

INFORMATION-ORIENTED CHANGE STRATEGIES

Figure 13-4 lists several change strategies that are informationally oriented. These include strategies that communicate new information (new products, new uses, new features for existing brands) and that attempt to change beliefs about new or existing brands.

New Product Characteristics

Firms frequently introduce new products by describing their characteristics in order to communicate benefits. Sterling Drug, producers of Bayer aspirin, decided to introduce their first aspirin-free product in the American market, Panadol. The product has been sold overseas for over twenty-five years. Sterling introduced the product on an informational basis by advertising that:

- the product is a thousand milligrams strong,
- it will not upset the stomach, and
- it was sold in seventy countries and is now made in America.[18]

New Uses

Companies have attempted to increase demand by advertising new uses for their brands. The classic example is Arm & Hammer baking soda. After a series of depth interviews with consumers in the early 1970s about uses of baking soda, the theme of sweetening and freshening kept coming up. The idea of using baking soda to eliminate odors was not new. But odor control implied the consumer was a poor homemaker. Once the company emphasized the benefits of freshness and sweetness rather than odor control, reported use of baking soda in refrigerators went from 1 percent of American households to 57 percent. Advertising additional uses for baking soda such as keeping the freezer fresh and as a way to drain sinks was similarly successful. By 1981 the product was used for its original purpose — baking — only 6 percent of the time.[19]

New Features

Another strategy to stimulate demand is to emphasize new features for existing products. When Philip Morris launched its "No caffeine: never had it, never will" campaign in 1982 for 7-Up, the brand began to gain market share for the first time in six years.[20] But Pepsi and Coke quickly followed with caffeine-free brands, nullifying 7-Up's advantage. The company responded by emphasizing yet another new feature — no artificial flavors and colorings — and launched a new campaign on this basis in 1983.[21]

Belief Change

Another strategy is to try to change beliefs about a brand or product category through an informational campaign. Maytag used an educational campaign to convince consumers that appliances can be energy efficient. Volkswagen tried to change beliefs that small cars are uncomfortable.

IMAGE-ORIENTED CHANGE STRATEGIES

Change strategies can attempt to influence consumers' feelings about brands through symbolism and imagery. Figure 13-4 lists four such strategies:

1. introducing new products by emphasizing brand image,
2. communicating product involvement through the advertising,
3. reducing any risk and uncertainty consumers might have about purchasing, and
4. changing the consumer's image of the brand.

Use New Product Imagery

New products can be introduced on the basis of imagery rather than product information. Such a strategy is relevant if the product category is not new and the brand has no unique claims. Anheuser-Busch introduced Budweiser Light in 1982 on an imagery basis. Anheuser-Busch held only 17 percent of the light beer category compared to Miller's 60 percent before introducing Budweiser Light. The brand brought no new benefits to the light-beer category. It was meant to put Anheuser in a more competitive position in light beers.

Anheuser used the symbolism of an athlete winning after initial setbacks with the theme "Bring out your best." This theme was meant to challenge light beer drinkers to bring out the best in themselves.[22]

Increase Product Involvement

Change strategies are also designed to increase consumer involvement with the product category. A brand that can generate excitement in a stable category would have a decided competitive advantage. American Express attempted to generate involvement with its credit card (a product that has the negative association of paying bills) by using exciting people whom consumers could relate to. The purpose was to develop a campaign that "would engender personal involvement."[23]

Reduce Risk and Uncertainty

Another change strategy is to reduce the consumer's risk and uncertainty in purchasing. IBM introduced its personal computer line using Charlie Chaplin as its advertising symbol because the character conveyed friendliness and security:

In developing an advertising strategy, IBM knew it wanted to break down widespread public fear of the computer, demonstrate the essential simplicity of its operation and popularize its many applications.[24]

And that is where Charlie Chaplin fit in. By using Charlie Chaplin, IBM reduced the fear of a personal computer. IBM was estimated to have spent $13 million in 1983 on the campaign.[25]

Change the Brand Image

Advertisers frequently seek to improve their brand image to increase sales. At times this objective is prompted by a change in social or cultural norms that has resulted in an outdated image. For example, the ads for Charlie perfume first pictured an independent, liberated woman. Recently the Charlie woman has been portrayed as having a serious romance and considering marriage. Why the change in image? Because there has been a shift in values reflected in "more interest in traditional relationships, marriage and families."[26]

Media Selection

Having developed an advertising strategy, management must select the media to transmit the message. The advertising strategy is not developed separately from the media plan. The creative group that developed the Charlie Chaplin campaign for IBM first formulated sixty-second spot TV commercials designed for prime time. They then began developing print ads retaining the Chaplin theme but providing more detailed information about the computer and its applications.[27] Thus the strategy was developed with the media plan in mind.

In Chapter 11 we saw the strengths and weaknesses of various media. Here we will consider the media plan and the criteria managers use to select media.

COMPONENTS OF THE MEDIA PLAN

The media plan requires specifying:

1. allocations to various types of media (TV, magazines, radio, etc.),
2. selection of specific media components; for example, for TV and radio:
   - □ program versus spot commercials,
   - □ if spot, thirty- or sixty-second commercials,
   - □ network versus local, and
   - □ advertising in prime time, weekends, day, or late night;

   for newspapers:
   - □ type,

    □ size,

    □ use of Sunday supplements, and

    □ national versus local newspapers;

  3. frequency of insertions in each media vehicle; and

  4. the cost of reaching a particular target group for each of the media vehicles specified in the plan.

MEDIA SELECTION CRITERIA

Five criteria have generally been used in selecting media vehicles:

1. advertising exposure,
2. advertising impact,
3. wearout,
4. nature of the target audience, and
5. cost.

Advertising Exposure

The number of exposures created by a media plan are determined by **reach** and **frequency.** Reach is the number of people exposed to one or more of the vehicles in the media plan. Frequency is the average number of times an individual is exposed to the message as a result of the media plan. The reach times the frequency yields the number of exposures produced by the media plan. This figure is generally stated in terms of **Gross Rating Points (GRPs).** In the Lean Cuisine campaign described earlier, the media objective was to reach 90 percent of the target audience four times a year, representing a GRP of 360 (90% $\times$ 4). Advertising exposures must be measured in terms of effectiveness in reaching the target audience; otherwise the figure has little value.

  An important issue is the trade-off between reach and frequency. Within an advertising budget greater emphasis on reach means less emphasis on frequency and vice versa. The balance between the two depends on the advertising objectives. One authority states that frequency is a more important objective under the following circumstances:[28]

■ When introducing a new brand, frequency is required to build brand awareness.

■ If the brand is not in a dominant position, frequency creates more awareness relative to the market leaders.

■ If brand loyalty is low, frequency can improve brand attitudes.

■ If competitive advertising is intense, frequency is required to maintain brand visibility.

■ When a new campaign is introduced, frequency is required to establish advertising awareness.

■ If a message is unique or complex, frequency is required to gain comprehension.

These are not hard and fast rules. For example, if a new brand is introduced by a penetration strategy (low price, mass market), then reach becomes more important than frequency. But it is important for media planners to specify the relative weight given to each.

Advertising Impact

The problem with using advertising exposure as a criterion of media effectiveness is that it may not be related to the impact of the message — awareness, comprehension, and retention. Advertising impact is more closely related to the message than to the media. But if the medium is sometimes the message, then advertising impact should be a criterion for media selection. In Chapter 12 we saw that different media vehicles may produce different levels of awareness and comprehension for the same message. An ad for a tennis racket in *Sports Illustrated* is likely to produce greater awareness than one for the same product in *Time*, even though the latter may produce greater exposure. Therefore, media planners should take account of the medium's impact as well as exposure, using awareness, comprehension, and retention as criteria.

Wearout

Another problem with using advertising exposure as a criterion for selection is that it assumes all advertising insertions have equal value. But as the number of insertions (frequency) in a particular medium increases, the effect of each additional insertion decreases. There are various opinions as to the speed and importance of such **advertising wearout.** One writer feels that for most campaigns three exposures is enough. The first creates awareness, the second comprehension, and the third reinforces exposure by serving as a reminder.[29] Others argue for more frequency.[30]

Whatever the position taken, it is important to assess the potential wearout of both the message and the medium. Generally wearout is more a function of the message. Some messages easily lose their effect or are sufficiently irritating to be avoided. But media can also affect wearout. For example, the advertiser who sponsors an involving TV program is more likely to keep the attention and interest of an audience over time than is the advertiser who relies on TV spots. Similarly, a campaign using magazines that have lively editorial content relevant to the advertised product is more likely to avoid wearout than a campaign using general audience magazines. If wearout for the same message can vary by media, then planners should consider the effect of wearout in their media choices.

The Target Audience

Media must be selected with a specific target audience in mind. The target market for the brand is usually defined by demography and life style. Media are then selected that can best reach these groups.

How do companies make these media selections? They must first define the demographic and life-style profile of the potential or actual consumers of their brand by conducting consumer surveys. They must then ascertain the demographic and life-style profiles of TV audiences and magazine readers by purchasing data from syndicated services such as the Simmons Market Research Bureau. These services conduct large-scale studies to determine what TV programs consumers watch and what magazines and newspapers they read. They also obtain demographic and life-style information permitting them to identify profiles of TV program viewers and magazine and newspaper readers. This allows advertisers to match the characteristics of the target segment with the characteristics of media audiences.

Cost

Media must be evaluated on the basis of cost. Media planners use two cost-related criteria in evaluating media vehicles: (1) the cost per gross rating point and (2) the cost per thousand.

Cost per gross rating point

The cost per gross rating point is the cost of a set of commercials divided by the GRPs (reach times frequency) the commericals are likely to achieve. For example, McDonald's 1979 media plan called for achieving 140 GRPs aimed at children on weekend TV, split between sixty- and thirty-second commercials.[31] Suppose the company estimated the following:

Time	Spots per Month	Type of Spot	Estimated GRPs	Total Cost	Cost per GRP
Sat. morning	5	60 sec.	45	$225,000	$5,000
Sat. morning	3	30 sec.	30	$ 90,000	$3,000
Sun. morning	5	60 sec.	40	$180,000	$4,500
Sun. morning	3	30 sec.	25	$ 70,000	$2,800
Totals	16		140	$565,000	

On this basis it would pay the company to put more money into thirty-second spots since they give more GRPs per dollar. It would also pay to switch a few spots from Saturday to Sunday morning since the cost of achieving GRPs is lower on Sundays.

This type of analysis requires estimating the GRPs a media vehicle will achieve for the target audience. The assumption is that the media planner can adjust the schedule to obtain GRPs in the most cost-effective manner. This is not always possible. For example, if McDonald's campaign required a sixty-second spot to explain a special offer or to announce new food offerings, then the media planner would be constrained to select a certain number of longer spots regardless of cost per GRP.

Cost per thousand

Cost per thousand (CPM) is the cost of reaching 1000 members of the target audience. For example, if it costs $25,000 to put a full-page, black-and-white ad in the *New Yorker* magazine and the ad reaches 5 million members of the target group, then the cost per thousand is:

$$\frac{\text{Cost} \times 1{,}000}{\text{Circulation to target group}} = \frac{\$25{,}000 \times 1{,}000}{5{,}000{,}000} = \$5.00$$

Cost per thousand is generally used to evaluate print media, whereas cost per GRP is used to evaluate broadcast media. The reason is that frequency is a much more important criterion in selecting broadcast than print media. Cost per GRP takes account of frequency, whereas cost per thousand only takes account of the number of people reached.

A weakness of a CPM basis for evaluating print media is that it does not take account of the medium's circulation. For example, an advertiser of a prestige line of clothing might find that the *New Yorker* is the least expensive magazine in reaching the target group, because the profile of the *New Yorker* reader is almost the same as that of the purchaser of the company's line. Yet the circulation of the *New Yorker* is low. Therefore, the company will have to supplement its media schedule with higher-priced general circulation magazines to reach a broader audience. Management realizes that using general circulation magazines will mean reaching a large number of nonpurchasers. But it is willing to accept the cost inefficiencies to obtain a broader cut at the market.

QUANTITATIVE MODELS FOR MEDIA SELECTION

Developing a media schedule is a complex task. Because of the combination of media types, specific vehicles, timing, and number of insertions, the number of media alternatives is almost infinite. Some advertisers have attempted to develop quantitative models to select optimal combinations of media. These models have several things in common. First, they define an objective function that specifies a value for a set of media based on the advertiser's objectives. Second, they set constraints to limit the alternatives that can be considered. The budget is the most important constraint, but there are others dictated by the plan's objectives. For example, the McDonald's plan required more sixty-second spots to get the message across. Other constraints may specify that a certain proportion of the budget should go into one type of medium (e.g., 80 percent of Peugeot's advertising going into newspapers). Third, these models have decision rules that systematically search the combinations of media schedules to find the one that will optimize the objective function.

One such model, presented in Exhibit 13-2, is based on linear programming.[32] The purpose of the model is to maximize exposures (E) in four magazines (X_1, X_2, X_3, X_4) subject to various constraints. One constraint is the advertising budget of $500,000. Another is the requirement that at least $200,000 must be spent on magazine X_1 and $100,000 on magazine X_2. A third is the number of times each magazine comes out. Within these constraints, a mathematical solution will determine the optimal allocation of the $500,000 budget across the four magazines.

EXHIBIT 13-2 A Linear Programming Model for Media Selection

Linear programming has been used to select a media mix based on a specified objective and constraints. In this example the purpose is to maximize the exposures across four magazines.[a] This objective is subject to several constraints. For example, assume the objective is to maximize the following function:

$$\text{Exposure} = 4.2X_1 + 3.3X_2 + 2.5X_3 + 1.1X_4$$

These numbers represent the effective exposures (in millions) per vehicle. Thus, magazine 1 gives 4.2 million effective exposures per issue. Attempts at maximizing this function are subject to the following constraints:

1. $20,000X_1 + 8,000X_2 + 5,000X_3 + 1,600X_4 \leq 500,000$
2. $20,000X_1 \geq 200,000$
3. $8,000X_2 \geq 100,000$
4. $X_1 \geq 4$
5. $X_1 \leq 12$
6. $X_2 \leq 52$
7. $X_3 \leq 52$
8. $X_4 \leq 24$

These constraints mean: (1) The advertising budget of $500,000 must be spread across the four magazines whose average cost of an insertion per issue are $20,000; $8,000; $5,000; and $1,600 respectively. (2–3) At least $200,000 must be spent on magazine 1 and at least $100,000 on magazine 2. (4–5) Magazine 1 comes out monthly. The media planner wants to put in at least four insertions in magazine 1 but not more than 12. (6–8) Magazines 2 and 3 come out weekly and magazine 4 bimonthly. As a result, insertions must be limited to no more than 52 for magazines 2 and 3, and 24 for magazine 4.

[a]See James F. Engel and Martin R. Warshaw, "Allocating Advertising Dollars by Linear Programming," *Journal of Advertising Research* 4 (September 1964): 41–48.

Another media model, known as MEDIAC, relies on more advertising and marketing variables to estimate the expected number of exposures (GRPs) produced by one insertion in a particular media vehicle.[33] Exposures are estimated for particular market segments. For example, MEDIAC might attempt to estimate the exposures from a full-page four-color ad in *Cosmopolitan* among the target group for Lean Cuisine (upscale women between twenty-five and forty-five). The estimated number of exposures in the target group is a function of:

- the likelihood a member of the target group will be exposed to an advertisement in *Cosmopolitan,*
- the percentage of people in the target group who read *Cosmopolitan,* and
- the size of the target group.

These models have been of some assistance to media planners. But by far the most prevalent method of developing the plan is managerial judgment based on cost, target audience, and exposure criteria.

Evaluating Advertising Effectiveness

The last step in the advertising management process in Figure 13-1 evaluates advertising effectiveness by measuring (1) communications effects and (2) sales results. As noted, sales results are the ultimate criterion of advertising effectiveness, but because of the difficulty in relating advertising to sales most of the emphasis has been on assessing communications effectiveness.

EVALUATING COMMUNICATIONS EFFECTS

Communications effects research involves evaluating a single commercial or ad. As noted in Chapter 11, communications criteria such as attention, message comprehension, message retention, and purchase intent are used to evaluate messages. This research area is known as *copy research* because of the emphasis on the spoken or printed word. Different copy research techniques have been developed for print and broadcast advertising. In each case a distinction is made between research designed to test the message before the campaign (pretesting) and to evaluate its effectiveness during the campaign (posttesting). Pretesting is designed to evaluate alternative advertising executions so the best can be selected for the campaign. Posttesting is meant to evaluate the message's actual effect on the consumer.

Techniques for Evaluating Print Ads

Several techniques are designed to pretest print advertisements. The most commonly used are **portfolio tests** in which respondents are given a dummy magazine or portfolio of ads and asked to look through them. They are then asked to recall the ads and play back copy points. Print ads could also be tested through physiological techniques. *Pupil dilation* measures are the most common. Dilation of the pupil is supposed to reflect consumer interest and arousal. Some researchers feel this is an unbiased measure of communication effects since it is involuntary and does not require a consumer response.

The most common posttest of print ads is the *in-magazine recognition test.* Several syndicated services ask consumers whether they remember seeing ads in magazines. As noted in Chapter 7, the most commonly used and the oldest is the Starch service.

Techniques for Evaluating Broadcast Ads

Two techniques have been frequently used to pretest TV ads. One is a *theater test* in which an audience is recruited to view TV shows including test ads. Respondents are asked about brand preferences and intention to buy before and after seeing the ads. Improvements in brand preferences and buying intent measure the effectiveness of the ad. Another technique is the *trailer test.* Trailers are parked in shopping malls and consumers invited in to see TV programming and test ads. Both techniques measure the relative effectiveness of alternative ads. An ad that increases purchase intent by 10 percent is not expected to increase the brand's market share by 10 percent if it is introduced. This figure merely indicates that the ad is a better performer than one that produces, say, a 5 percent increase in purchase intent.

The most common method of posttesting TV ads is the *day-after recall* method. Consumers are interviewed the day after a TV ad appeared and are asked if they can remember any ads they saw the day before. They are asked to recall and report everything they can remember about these ads.

EVALUATING SALES EFFECTS

Advertising's effect on sales can be measured in certain situations. If the advertisement requires an immediate response, it can be related to sales. For example, catalog and direct-mail advertising can be related to sales through consumer responses. The effectiveness of advertising with coupons can be determined on the basis of redemptions. Retail newspaper advertising announcing sales can be evaluated by consumer turnout during the sales period. In each of these cases response can be due only to advertising. The difficulties of determining the sales effects of brand and corporate advertising have been cited previously. Despite these difficulties, advertisers have made some strides in measuring sales effects. They have taken three approaches:

1. field experiments,
2. analysis of historical data, and
3. quantitative models.

Field Experiments

One of the most promising approaches in determining sales effects is to control advertising expenditures so that some areas receive no advertising, others the usual amount, and others more than usual. Anheuser-Busch used this approach starting in the late 1960s. They found that sales for Budweiser were significantly higher in areas with advertising, but not high enough to warrant the current levels of expenditure. As a result, they reduced advertising expenditures with very little effect on their market share.[34] The problem with this approach is that very few firms are willing to eliminate advertising expenditures, even if only in certain areas of the country, and that such experiments must run for several years to determine the sales effects of advertising.

One promising development is the use of split cable TV to deliver two different campaigns to families in the same city. The sales results of each campaign can be tracked because these experiments are run in cities with scanner facilities. The combination of cable TV and scanner data permits researchers to compare sales results from two different ad campaigns.

Historical Data

Researchers have attempted to link advertising expenditures to sales with historical data using econometric techniques. One such analysis traced the relation of advertising expenditures to sales for Lydia Pinkham's Vegetable Compound from 1908 to 1960.[35] But this study was rare because few marketing or competitive factors other than advertising were operating to affect sales. As a result, advertising's effect could be more easily determined. In most cases historical analysis is not feasible because of confounding market factors.

Quantitative Models

Quantitative models designed to estimate the advertising-to-sales relationship were described as a means of determining the optimal level of advertising expenditures (see Exhibit 13-1). These models are also used to evaluate sales response to advertising. The major difficulty is again in isolating the effects of advertising from other factors that affect sales results.

Agency-Client Relationships

Advertising management involves the advertising department of the company (the client) and its advertising agency. The client determines the objectives, plans overall advertising strategy, and determines the budget. The agency prepares and evaluates the advertisements and develops the media plan.

The relationship between the client and the agency has been likened to a marriage. Some clients and agencies have established long-term relationships; for example, Pepsi-Cola has used the same agency for over twenty years. Perhaps the stormiest part of the relationship is when the client seeks a divorce.

The main reason advertising executives cite for moving their business to another agency is a failure to produce "motivating, persuasive advertising."[36] An agency handling a client for too long could become stale in its creative approach leading to "creative ideas that are off target, based on faulty market strategy, poor strategic thinking."[37] The agency could be very effective for other clients, but might go sour on one account.

As an example, McDonald's, one of the top twenty advertisers, switched its account from Needham, Harper & Steers, even though the agency got the company off the ground in the 1960s. The company felt that it was losing its competitive edge and that its basic theme — "You deserve a break today" — no longer made it distinctive.[38]

Some advertisers view the agency's responsibilities seriously enough to go through a formal evaluation procedure periodically. Companies such as Lever Brothers, Ford, DuPont and General Mills undertake such reviews to ensure that their communications strategies are being adequately implemented.[39]

Industrial Advertising

The role of advertising in the industrial promotional mix is very different from its role in the consumer promotional mix. Industrial advertising "does not sell the product per se, but paves the way for the salesman."[40] Advertising is designed to ensure that the industrial buyer is aware of the company and its products so that a subsequent visit by a salesperson is more likely to lead to a sale. In contrast, consumer advertising plays a dominant rather than a supportive role in the promotional mix. It is designed to influence the consumer to try the product.

Given this basic distinction, we will now explore the differences between industrial and consumer advertising and consider media used by industrial advertisers.

DIFFERENCES BETWEEN INDUSTRIAL AND CONSUMER ADVERTISING

Industrial advertising differs from consumer advertising in at least five important respects:

1. Industrial advertising tends to support personal selling.
2. It is a less important part of the promotional mix.
3. Industrial advertising is more likely to be corporate advertising.
4. It is more likely to be used to stimulate derived demand.
5. It is more likely to be directed to several buyers or to a buying group.

Facilitates Personal Selling

The importance of advertising in laying a foundation for a salesperson's call is illustrated by the McGraw-Hill advertisement in Figure 13-5. The ad depicts

"I don't know who you are.

I don't know your company.

I don't know your company's product.

I don't know what your company stands for.

I don't know your company's customers.

I don't know your company's record.

I don't know your company's reputation.

Now—what was it you wanted to sell me?"

MORAL: Sales start **before** your salesman calls—with business publication advertising.

McGRAW-HILL MAGAZINES
BUSINESS • PROFESSIONAL • TECHNICAL

FIGURE 13-5
An illustration of the difficulty of selling to industrial buyers without advertising

Used by permission.

the difficult task the industrial salesperson faces without an advertising campaign behind the first sales call. McGraw-Hill has effectively supported the use of business publications with this campaign.

Several studies have suggested that industrial advertising is cost effective in increasing the likelihood of a sale. One large-scale study found that when an industrial buyer is exposed to the advertising campaign before a sales call, dollar sales increase by almost 30 percent.[41]

Advertising is also a means of reducing the cost of a sales call. McGraw-Hill estimates that the average cost of a business sales call is $205, whereas an ad in a business publication may cost only 17 cents per customer.[42] Advertising can reduce this cost by increasing the chances that a prospect will receive the salesperson and by decreasing the time required to make the sales presentation.

Plays a Subsidiary Role in Influencing Demand

The fact that personal selling is dominant in industrial communications means that advertising is less influential. One study found that the most important influence on industrial buyers came from other executives in the firm. The second most important influence was direct contact by the industrial salesperson. Next came colleagues in other firms, trade shows, and promotional materials mailed by industrial sellers. Advertising was the least important item mentioned as influencing industrial buyers.[43] This study supports the fact that industrial advertising is not designed so much to influence purchases as to create product and company awareness.

The lesser role of advertising in industrial as compared to consumer firms is demonstrated by the fact that only 10 percent of industrial marketers have a systematic plan to evaluate their advertising.[44] One industrial advertiser says that despite the money spent on industrial advertising, "few companies really consider it an integral part of their marketing and selling effort."[45]

Emphasizes Corporate Image

Industrial marketers are more likely to advertise the company than are consumer goods marketers. They realize that industrial buyers prefer long-standing relationships in which product reliability and delivery are ensured. Creating corporate awareness and goodwill is as important as advertising product benefits. One study found that 88 percent of industrial marketers planned corporate advertising campaigns, compared with 29 percent of consumer durable goods firms and only 18 percent of consumer packaged goods firms.[46]

Stimulates Derived Demand

Industrial marketers sometimes attempt to stimulate the demand for their customers' products. Stimulating derived demand will stimulate direct demand.

Glass, steel, and aluminum manufacturers advertise to persuade consumers to buy drinks in glass bottles or steel or aluminum cans.[47] In so doing, industrial advertisers are playing the same role as consumer advertisers in influencing the demand of the final consumer.

Reaches Multiple Purchasing Influencers

Most consumer advertising is directed to an individual consumer rather than to a buying group. But as we saw in Chapter 5, a good deal of industrial buying is done through a buying group. Therefore, industrial advertising must be directed to several purchasers — purchasing agents, engineers, production supervisors. In some cases, different media will be used to reach different groups in the same firm. For example, production supervisors may read *Plant Engineering,* and purchasing agents may read *Purchasing Week.*[48] In such a case, the same ad will appear in both magazines.

BUSINESS PUBLICATIONS

The primary medium for industrial advertisers is business publications. One source estimates that from 60 to 70 percent of industrial advertising budgets is spent on print advertising in business publications.[49] Most of the rest of the budget is spent on direct mail, general-circulation magazines, and industrial directories. Only one percent of the budget is spent on television, in marked contrast to consumer advertising.

Business publications are divided between general business magazines such as *Fortune, Business Week, The Wall Street Journal,* and *Forbes* on the one hand, and trade journals on the other. Trade journals can be divided into vertical and horizontal publications. Vertical trade publications such as *Iron Age,* or *Engineering and Mining Journal* serve a particular industry. Horizontal publications cut across industry lines at one functional level of business.[50] Examples are *Advertising Age* and *Purchasing Magazine.*

Business publications can be extremely selective in reaching executives with purchase influence. There are several thousand such magazines with a combined circulation of over 60 million. One study found that over 80 percent of executives with buying influence cited business publications as a source of information about a product or company.[51] Such advertising can reach buying influencers who might not be willing to see salespeople.

The selectivity of business publications permits industrial advertisers to select them with a great deal of precision. Data exist to match a business publication's readership to specific industries based on their Standard Industrial Classification code. Magazines can thus be chosen that are most likely to reach prospective purchasers in a cost-effective manner.

Summary

Advertising is the primary means of informing and influencing large groups of people. Its importance is illustrated by the money spent ($73 billion in 1983), and by its role in the marketing mix.

To implement advertising campaigns, firms must decide on advertising objectives, the advertising budget, advertising strategies, media plans, and the effectiveness of the projected advertising campaign. These five decision areas represent the advertising management process. There are three types of *advertising objectives* — message, media, and behavioral. Behavioral objectives are the most important since they reflect sales, but they are the hardest to measure.

To fulfill objectives, management must *set and allocate advertising budgets.* Budgets must be allocated to implement strategies, to transmit these strategies through media vehicles, and to time the campaign on the bases of seasonality and effect.

The central requirement of the advertising management process is setting *advertising strategies*. Two types of strategies were considered: those designed to maintain and reinforce positive brand images and attitudes, and those designed to change images and attitudes. Various strategies for maintenance and change were considered. Advertisers can maintain their current images through informational campaigns or through imagery and symbolism. Strategies for change include advertising new products, promoting new uses for existing products, changing brand beliefs and images, and increasing product involvement.

Once strategy has been determined, media must be selected to transmit the message. Most advertisers *select media* by determining the demographic or life-style characteristics of their current or prospective users, and then trying to find broadcast or print media most likely to reach this target audience. Media are selected according to the number of people they reach, their influence, and their effectiveness in reaching the target audience. The final step in the advertising management process is *evaluating advertising's effectiveness*. The effectiveness of advertising hinges on sales results. But because it is difficult to establish an advertising-to-sales relationship, most attention has been focused on specific communications objectives such as awareness, comprehension, preference for the company's brand, and intention to buy the brand.

Industrial advertising differs sufficiently from consumer advertising to deserve separate attention. It is designed to support the personal sales effort, unlike consumer advertising, which is designed to induce a direct sale. As a result, industrial advertising receives less attention in the promotional mix. It is also more likely to be corporate advertising, whereas consumer advertising is primarily product advertising. Industrial advertising must also deal with several purchasing influences, whereas consumer advertising is generally directed to individual purchasers.

In the next chapter, we will consider another essential component of the promotional mix, the personal selling effort.

Questions

1. Consider the companies in Table 13-1 with the highest advertising-to-sales ratio (companies with advertising representing over 5 percent of sales). What do they have in common? Now consider companies with the lowest advertising-to-sales ratio (less than one percent). What do they have in common? What are the risks of a high advertising-to-sales ratio?

2. Develop a set of advertising objectives for an actual or hypothetical brand that reflects (1) message, (2) media, and (3) behavioral objectives.

3. Demonstrate that some or all of the objectives you developed in question 2 (1) are measurable, (2) are targetable, and (3) provide a benchmark for evaluation.

4. Consider the following statement by a marketing authority quoted in the chapter:

   Advertising objectives that emphasize sales are usually not very operational because they provide little practical guidance for decision makers.[52]

   ☐ Explain.

   ☐ How have advertisers reacted to the difficulty of establishing advertising objectives that emphasize sales?

   ☐ Does the use of advertising objectives other than sales entail any risks?

5. How can a firm estimate its advertising budget from the model in Exhibit 13-1? What is the problem in applying models such as those in Exhibit 13-1 to determine the advertising budget?

6. Under what circumstances should an advertising campaign schedule be developed based on pulsing? based on continuity?

   ☐ Can an advertiser use both pulsing and continuity in a single campaign?

   ☐ Give an example.

7. Under what circumstances might a company use an informational (rather than image-oriented) advertising strategy in introducing a new product?

8. Under what circumstances would an advertiser stress reach over frequency in allocating the advertising budget? Frequency over reach?

9. What are the problems in using gross rating points (reach times frequency) as a measure of the effectiveness of a media plan?

10. How do companies select media that are most likely to reach the target groups for their brands?

11. How do the objectives of industrial advertising differ from those of consumer goods advertising?

12. Given the differences in objectives described in question 11, how does industrial advertising differ from consumer goods advertising in terms of:

☐ the media mix?

☐ the content and makeup of the advertisements?

☐ the process of evaluating advertising effectiveness?

Notes

1. "Chevy Drive Shoulders GM Load," *Advertising Age,* November 1, 1982, p. 67.

2. "Coen Details Surge in Ad Spending," *Advertising Age,* July 18, 1983, pp. 3, 73.

3. Robert J. Coen, "Vast U.S. and Worldwide Ad Expenditures Expected," in *The Shape of Things to Come: The Next 20 Years in Advertising and Marketing"* (Chicago: Crain, 1980), pp. 10–16.

4. "The Mammoth, Marvelous, Money Machine," *Marketing & Media Decisions,* Spring 1982, Special Edition, pp. 114–15; and "100 Leading National Advertisers," *Advertising Age,* September 8, 1983, p. 166.

5. "Stouffer's Lean Cuisine Fattens Up Frozen Food Market," *Madison Avenue,* March 1983, p. 94.

6. Private communication from Stouffer Inc.

7. *Madison Avenue,* March 1983, p. 96.

8. "Frozen Foods Get Hot Again," *Newsweek,* May 23, 1983, p. 96.

9. "Stouffer's 300-Calorie Coup," *Marketing & Media Decisions,* Spring 1982 Special Issue, pp. 157–64.

10. *Madison Avenue,* March 1983, p. 94.

11. David A. Aaker and John G. Myers, *Advertising Management* (Englewood Cliffs, N.J.: Prentice-Hall, 1982), p. 94

12. H. L. Vidale and H. B. Wolfe, "An Operations Research Study of Sales Response to Advertising," *Operational Research Quarterly* 5 (1957): 370–81.

13. Philip Kotler, *Marketing Management* (Englewood Cliffs, N.J.: Prentice-Hall, 1984), p. 519.

14. "Campaign: Mercedes — Classic Copy for a Class Act," *Madison Avenue,* February 1983, p. 66.

15. Ibid., p. 70.

16. "Cigarette Makers Puff Up Images," *Ad Forum,* October 1982, p. 5.

17. Ibid., p. 61.

18. "Sterling Drug Plans to Challenge Tylenol After Years of Overcaution, Misjudgment," *The Wall Street Journal,* April 29, 1983, p. 35.

19. "The Ongoing Saga of Mother Baking Soda," *Advertising Age,* September 20, 1982, p. M-2.

20. "Another Hardball Campaign From Seven-Up," *Business Week,* June 6, 1983, p. 30.

21. Ibid.

22. "Budweiser's 'Must Win' Attitude," *Marketing & Media Decisions,* Spring 1982 special issue, p. 26.

23. "Campaign: American Express — They Got What They Deserve," *Madison Avenue,* April 1982, p. 48.

24. "Using Yesterday to Sell Tomorrow," *Advertising Age,* April 11, 1983, p. M-4.

25. Ibid.

26. "Why Revlon's Charlie Seems to be Ready to Settle Down," *The Wall Street Journal,* December 23, 1982, p. 11.

27. *Advertising Age,* April 11, 1983, pp. M-4, M-5.

28. "What Level Frequency," *Advertising Age,* November 9, 1981, pp. S-4, S-6, S-8.

29. Herbert E. Krugman, "What Makes Advertising Effective?" *Harvard Business Review* 53 (March–April 1975): 96–103.

30. Darrell B. Lucas and Steuart Henderson Britt, *Measuring Advertising Effectiveness* (New York: McGraw-Hill, 1963), p. 218.

31. "McDonald's 1979 Plan: Beat Back the Competition," *Advertising Age,* February 19, 1979, p. 89.

32. See James F. Engel and Martin R. Warshaw, "Allocating Advertising Dollars by Linear Programming," *Journal of Advertising Research* 4 (September 1964): 41–48.

33. John D. C. Little and Leonard M. Lodish, "A Media Planning Calculus," *Operations Research* 17 (January–February 1969): 1–34.

34. Russell L. Ackoff and James R. Emshoff, "Advertising Research at Anheuser-Busch, Inc. (1963–1968)," *Sloan Management Review* (Winter 1975): 1–15.

35. Kristian S. Palda, *The Measurement of Cumulative Advertising Effects* (Englewood Cliffs, N.J.: Prentice-Hall, 1964).

36. "A Profile of the Bad Agency," *Advertising Age,* November 23, 1981, pp. 53–54.

37. Ibid., p. 53.

38. "Why McDonald's Switched," *Advertising Age,"* October 19, 1981, p. 1.

39. "Grading Madison Ave.," *Dun's Review,* May 1979, pp. 88–93.

40. "Industrial Advertising — It Ain't What It Used to Be," *Industrial Marketing,* May 1981, p. 78.

41. John E. Morrill, "Industrial Advertising Pays Off," *Harvard Business Review* 48 (March–April 1970): 4–15.

42. "Cost of Industrial Sales Calls Reaches $205.40," *Labreport* (New York: McGraw-Hill Research, 1983), 4 pp.

43. A. Parasuraman, "The Relative Importance of Industrial Promotion Tools," *Industrial Marketing Management* 10 (1981): 277–81.

44. "Research a Basic Issue," *Advertising Age,* June 8, 1981, pp. S10–S12.

45. "How To Measure Your Advertising's Sales Productivity," *Industrial Marketing,* February 1983, pp. 54–60.

46. "Telling the Corporate Story," *Industrial Marketing,* March 1981, pp. 43, 44, 46, 48.

47. Robert W. Haas, *Industrial Marketing Management* (Boston, Mass.: Kent, 1982), p. 271.

48. Ibid., p. 275.

49. Ibid., p. 274.

50. Maurice I. Mandell, *Advertising* (Englewood Cliffs, N.J.: Prentice-Hall, 1980), p. 400.

51. Haas, *Industrial Marketing Management,* p. 278.

52. Aaker and Myers, *Advertising Management,* p. 94.

CHAPTER 14

Sales Management and Strategy

FOCUS OF CHAPTER

Personal selling provides the direct approach to customers that advertising lacks. Direct sales are particularly important in industrial marketing since terms of sales (price, specifications, delivery) must frequently be negotiated and followup services offered. But direct contact with customers is also essential in consumer marketing. Most consumer firms sell directly to distributors and retailers, requiring a company sales staff or a sales agent to represent the company. Some consumer goods companies are emulating their industrial counterparts by going directly to consumers through catalogs, telephone orders, and door-to-door sales. And in many cases consumer goods companies use salespeople either directly or through retailers to sell to the final consumer — for example, in the sale of appliances, electronics, and clothing.

The importance of personal selling is reflected in the increased emphasis many companies give it. Consider the following:

■ Xerox's introduction of its personal computer prompted the company to sign up fifty-five independent dealers and distributors to increase its sales capabilities to retailers and provide support for the company's 500-person sales force.[1]

■ Swift, the food company, consolidated fifteen sales forces into one national sales force to deal more effectively with its customers. The move from a divisional to a corporatewide organization permitted a sales account to deal with one salesperson for all of Swift's products.[2]

■ FWD, a manufacturer of heavy construction vehicles, saw sales decrease substantially as a result of the recession in the early 1980s. Rather than cut back on selling costs, management enlarged the sales force and increased bonuses. One result was a 30 percent sales increase in 1982 and a company in the black after having gone through bankruptcy proceedings.[3]

This chapter focuses on the two key individuals in the sales process, the salesperson and the sales manager. Description of the salesperson centers on the selling process; description of the sales manager centers on the sales management process. Key to the selling process is the role of the salesperson and his or her interaction with the customer. The sales manager has two primary responsibilities: (1) managing the sales process and (2) managing the sales force. The central components in managing the sales process are determining sales objectives, identifying prospects, establishing sales strategies, and evaluating sales performance. Managing the sales force requires recruiting, training, motivating, and supervising salespeople.

Importance of Personal Selling

Personal selling activities represent a large part of the American economy. Estimates of expenditures on personal selling effort range from $150 to $200 billion, meaning that companies spend more than twice as much on personal selling as on advertising. Moreover, approximately 8 million individuals are employed as salespeople.

Most of this effort is accounted for by industrial sales. Selling expenses as a percentage of sales volume are much higher in industrial than in consumer goods companies. For example, they are 12 percent in the office supplies industry, 8 percent in printing, 7 percent in computers, and 4 percent in light machinery. They are less than 2 percent in foods and major household items.[4] The opposite is true for advertising. Advertising expenditures as a percentage of sales are higher for consumer than industrial goods.

Another factor illustrating the importance of personal selling of industrial goods is the cost of the selling effort. As noted in Chapter 13, an average sales call was estimated to cost $205 in 1983.[5] Further, on average, a sale is made in only one out of ten cases.[6] This means that it costs a company an average of $2,050 to make a sale through face-to-face contacts. Clearly, industrial companies selling high-priced items are willing to spend substantial sums on personal contacts. But direct selling is also very important in consumer goods firms. A survey of executives in consumer durable and packaged goods firms found that selling was 1.8 times more important than advertising in their companies' marketing efforts for consumer durable goods and about equal to advertising in importance for packaged goods.[7]

Several market and organizational developments have also increased the importance of personal selling. First, both consumer and industrial products are becoming more complex, requiring more sophisticated and better trained salespeople. The transformation of the home into an electronic center in the 1980s and 1990s will require direct selling. It will also enhance the capabilities for personal selling by phone and by interactive TV. In industrial selling many salespeople must have an engineering background; they are becoming sales consultants to their customers in an attempt to meet their complex needs. The standardized (canned) presentation and the hard sell are becoming less frequent.

Industrial buying has also become more complex. Important purchases are now made by buying teams rather than by a single purchasing agent. Individual buyers are more carefully evaluating the quality, service, and cost effectiveness of sellers. As a result, sales personnel are undergoing careful scrutiny. Top management is devoting more attention to evaluating the personal selling effort and to the management process required to select, train, and motivate the sales force.

The Salesperson and the Selling Process

Personal selling varies according to the selling task and the characteristics and abilities of the salesperson. Despite this diversity, some common sales roles can be described as well as a general model of the selling process.

SALESPERSON ROLES

The major role of the salesperson is, of course, to sell the company's product line. But other responsibilities may be even more important than selling. These are:

- *Determining customer needs.* When approaching a new buyer, the salesperson has, as a first task, to listen. The salesperson should then help the customer find his or her own combination of products and specifications to satisfy needs, even if it means recommending competitive products. In the words of one sales authority:

  By listening, observing, understanding nonverbal communication, and asking the right questions, salespeople can let customers find their own reasons for buying. Salespeople who do this will increasingly view themselves as "consultants" to buyers. They won't try to overpower customers with talk, talk, and more talk.[8]

  The role of the salesperson as a consultant — that is, an expert interested in solving the customer's problems — is winning greater acceptance, particularly in industrial sales.

- *Prospecting.* Salespeople must try to identify potential buyers as well as to service existing buyers. The natural inclination for a salesperson is to rely on existing accounts to increase sales. This is a less risky means of gaining commissions than prospecting for new accounts. Yet prospecting is the only way to ensure future sales and profitability.

- *Providing marketing intelligence.* Salespeople must report changes in needs, buying behavior, and competitive actions to their sales managers. They should also be encouraged to make recommendations regarding product design and additions to or deletions from the product line based on buyer feedback. McCormick & Company's Grocery Products Division has formalized such feedback by forming a Sales Board composed of twenty salespeople who serve for one year. The Sales Board makes recommendations on ways to increase sales or reduce costs. Salad bars in food stores was a profitable idea that came from the Sales Board.[9]

- *Communicating information to buyers.* Salespeople must communicate information to buyers on company capabilities including product lines, product specifications, price, delivery, and service.

- *Providing service.* "Each customer buys three things ... the product and what it will do, the reputation of the manufacturer, and the treatment and service provided by the salesperson."[10] Often service outweighs other factors in gaining sales. In many product categories, specifications and price are fairly standard. The good salesperson must then concentrate on factors that could differentiate his or her company from others — technical assistance, financing, delivery, postpurchase maintenance.

- *Implementing trade or consumer promotions.* In many consumer goods companies, the salesperson's primary task is to get wholesalers and retailers to use company promotions. This activity — called **merchandising** — "is the first line salesperson's primary responsibility ... at companies such as CPC's Best Foods Division, Procter & Gamble, and R. J. Reynolds Tobacco."[11] When a P&G sales representative goes into a supermarket chain, he or she does not have to sell Pampers or Crest or Folgers. These are leading brands that are stocked by most food stores. The salesperson is serving only as an order taker for these items. The creative task is to get the retailer to use the company's displays, to run a price promotion, or to stock the brand prominently in the store.

- *Supporting advertising.* Salespeople should also support the other component of the promotional mix — advertising. The sales approach should be consistent with the advertising appeals. Salespeople who refer to the advertising reinforce its message, having more of an effect on the buyer. One marketer believes, "An 'educated' sales force can give your advertising program an extra 18 percent to 20 percent in effectiveness".[12] Industrial salespeople are particularly reliant on advertising. They view industrial ads as the calling card for new accounts.

SHORTCOMINGS OF THE SALESPERSON'S ROLE

The description of the salesperson's role is one of a professional who knows his or her field, can plan and coordinate selling and prospecting tasks, and can develop sales strategies based on customer needs. Frequently this level of professionalism is lacking.

These shortcomings are reflected in negative perceptions of sales personnel. A McGraw-Hill study of 881 sales managers found that one-fourth believed their salespeople were communicating poorly.[13] A survey of more than 10,000 buyers found that two-thirds felt salespeople were indifferent and 90 percent said they did not know their products.[14] Confirming these perceptions of salespeople was a study of the sale of refrigerators and TV sets that found that in over 50 percent of the cases salespeople did not ask customers any questions.[15]

The lack of the desired professionalism in selling generally betrays the lack of a consumer orientation. Companies that develop marketing strategies based on consumer needs must convey a consumer-oriented approach to their sales staff. Such an approach was only recently adopted by Alcoa. In the past, Alcoa sales personnel had demonstrated little concern for customer needs on the assumption that the customer needed Alcoa more than Alcoa needed the customer. They viewed aluminum as a seller's market. As one customer said, "If we had any problem with their product, their attitude was that there was something wrong with our equipment."[16] A decrease in demand for aluminum and an increase in foreign competition in the early 1980s led Alcoa to review its sales approach. It incorporated the concept of adjusting sales strategies to customer needs. Now Alcoa sales personnel "regularly ask for a list of things they can do better for their customers."[17]

Despite its shortcomings, the personal sales process is being improved, particularly in industrial sales. Top management is devoting more attention to personal selling. Recruitment, training, and evaluation are becoming more rigorous. As a result, it is important to describe a customer-oriented sales process.

A MODEL OF THE SALES PROCESS

Figure 14-1 describes a customer-oriented sales process.[18] In the first step (impression formation) the salesperson combines past knowledge of the customer with specific information gained from the current contact to form an impression of customer needs. Using this impression, the salesperson formulates a strategy. The strategy can be based on meeting or changing customer needs and attitudes. As in advertising, a change strategy is more difficult to implement. Such a strategy might require that the salesperson attempt to change customer beliefs about a product or the priority of customer needs.

As an example of the sales process, a salesperson for a producer of fork-lift trucks visits a regular customer and determines that the customer's priorities have changed. The customer is not as concerned with price. More emphasis

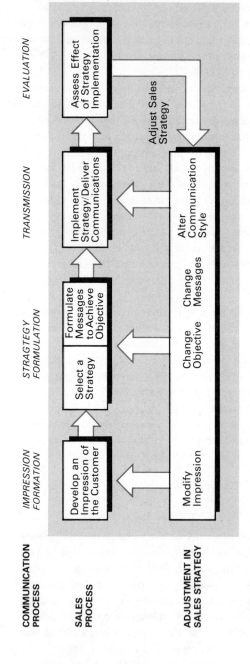

FIGURE 14-1
A model of the sales process

Source: Adapted from Barton A. Weitz, "The Relationship Between Salesperson Performance and Understanding of Customer Decision Making," *Journal of Marketing Research* 15 (November 1978): 502. Reprinted with permission from the *Journal of Marketing Research.*

is being placed on heavier loads and greater mobility. Both the salesperson and the customer know that the two needs are not entirely compatible. Greater load weight means more limited mobility. Therefore the salesperson's strategy is to educate the customer on the various trade-offs that can be achieved between load weight and mobility. He formulates a message to educate the customer but without alienating him. In so doing he tries to communicate the company's options in terms of these two criteria.

In the third step the salesperson transmits the message and waits for a reaction from the customer. The customer expresses interest in several heavy-duty models that do not really satisfy mobility requirements. On further questioning, the customer admits that mobility is not as important a criterion as load weight. There is no need for the salesperson to adjust his sales strategy since the buyer is a long-standing customer and took no offense at his educational approach. Further feedback establishes price level, delivery requirements, and service needs.

The result of this interaction was not a sale; the buyer decided to look into several competitive lines. But the salesperson's objectives were met, since he established the options that his company could offer and the terms of sale. Further, because the buyer perceives the salesperson as customer oriented and views the company as a reliable and quality-oriented manufacturer, the salesperson knows the chances of closing the sale are high.

Figure 14-1 shows that the salesperson must evaluate the customer's response to the sales process at each step and make the proper adjustments. Because of what the customer says, the salesperson might modify his or her impressions of the customer, change the objectives of the sales presentation, change the message being transmitted, or alter the way the sales message is being presented.

As a model of the sales process, Figure 14-1 is also a communications process, since personal selling is (or should be) communication. This is illustrated by the parallel between the basic communications model in Figure 11-1 and the sale process model. The steps are essentially the same: the source (e.g., the salesperson who develops an impression of the customer), message development (formulation of a strategy and message by the salesperson), transmission of the message, evaluation by the receiver (that is, the buyer), and feedback.

The Sales Management Process

The sales manager has two interrelated responsibilities: (1) managing the selling effort and (2) managing the sales force. Managing the selling effort involves a planning process to implement sales strategies. Managing the sales force requires recruiting, training, motivating, controlling, and evaluating salespeople so that sales strategies can effectively be implemented. In the rest of this chapter we will consider these two responsibilities as represented in Figure 14-2.

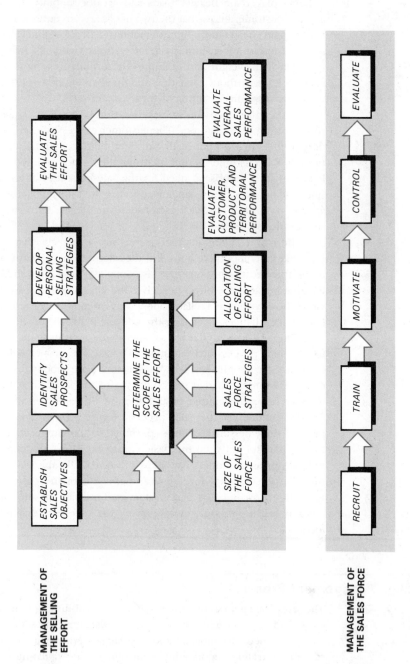

MANAGEMENT OF THE SELLING EFFORT

MANAGEMENT OF THE SALES FORCE

FIGURE 14-2
The sales management process

Management of the Selling Effort

The first step in planning the selling effort is establishing sales objectives. These are generally stated in terms of dollar sales goals and contribution to profits. The next step in Figure 14-2 is to determine the size and nature of the sales force, and the allocation of selling effort by customer types and geographic areas. Once the level of sales effort is established, prospect groups will be identified on the basis of potential sales. Salespeople will be guided in their search for new accounts by data specifying the characteristics, industry categories, and locations of the best prospects. Sales strategies will then be formulated to guide salespeople in effectively approaching prospects and existing customers. The final step in evaluating the sales effort is to determine if objectives were met.

A comparison of Figure 14-2 with Figure 13-1 shows that the steps required to manage the selling effort are almost identical to those required to manage the advertising campaign.

Sales Management	*Advertising Management*
Establish sales objectives	Establish advertising objectives
Determine size and allocation of sales effort	Establish and allocate the advertising budget
Define sales prospects and direct effort accordingly	Define target consumers and direct messages accordingly
Develop sales strategies	Develop advertising strategies
Evaluate sales effectiveness	Evaluate advertising effectiveness

We can see that the components of the promotional mix have similar planning requirements — defining target groups, developing communications strategies to these groups, and evaluating the effectiveness of the communications strategy. Let us consider each of the steps in managing the selling effort.

ESTABLISHING SALES OBJECTIVES

The most frequently stated sales objective is a volume target. The volume target is generally derived from a sales forecast that is allocated by sales territory or by customer type. Frequently, salespeople receive a quota that is based on volume goals. Because volume objectives are derived from the sales forecast, methods of forecasting directly affect sales objectives. (Sales forecasting methods will be considered in Chapter 20.)

Although volume targets are the most frequently stated objectives, they are not always the most relevant. Sales managers have a vested interest in attaining volume goals to demonstrate the effectiveness of the selling effort. But sales volume is not always related to profitability. Higher sales can be achieved by increasing marketing costs to unprofitable levels. Therefore, sales efforts should be evaluated according to their contribution to profit.

Sales objectives are tied to marketing strategies. For example, a large chemical company expanded its line of fiber products. The sales objectives reflected the line expansion strategy as follows:

- Immediately increase sales volume for the product by 50 percent and expand this goal to 100 percent as quickly as possible.

- Shift salespeople from geographic to end-use specialization.

- Establish joint marketing-technical teams for each major end-use business area.[19]

SCOPE OF THE SALES EFFORT

The next step in the sales management process is determining the scope of the sales effort. Three important decisions must be made: (1) the size of the sales force, (2) sales force strategies, and (3) allocation of the sales effort on the basis of these strategies.

Size of the Sales Force

Alternative methods of determining the optimal size of a sales force are similar to those used to determine the advertising budget.

Objective-task method

The size of the sales force is based on the required effort to reach existing and prospective customers (the objective). For example, assume the company estimates the number of sales calls per month (the task) for large, medium, and small customers as follows:

	Large	Medium	Small
Number of customers	100	200	400
Required sales calls per customer	× 10	× 5	× 1
Total number of calls per month	1,000	1,000	400

The total calls average 2400 per month. If a salesperson averages 100 calls per month, the size of the sales force should be 24. This method can be refined by weighting accounts by potential rather than current sales. The weakness of the approach is that number of sales calls is not always related to profitability and may in some cases be inversely related.

Percentage of sales

The size of the sales force is based on a percentage of sales. This method has the same weakness as in advertising: sales determine the selling effort, whereas the selling effort should determine sales.

Competitive parity

The size of the company's sales force is based on the size of competitive sales forces. This is the simplest and least defensible basis for determining sales force size. It assumes that the company's market potential and sales effectiveness are the same as its competitors', a dangerous assumption.

The marginal approach

Two additional methods have been used to estimate sales force size — one using a marginal approach and a second determining size from a quantitative model of the effects of sales effort on profits. These methods have the advantage of not relying on fixed criteria, which are sometimes hard to support.

The marginal approach parallels that used to estimate size of the advertising budget. It requires establishing a relationship between selling expenses and sales results in order to maximize the net profit contribution from sales. The principle is to continue to expand the sales force as long as the marginal revenue gained from adding a salesperson is greater than the associated marginal cost. The optimal size is achieved when the marginal revenue equals the marginal cost. This should also be the point at which the net profit contribution (gross contribution minus selling costs) is maximized. This would be at about ninety-five salespeople in Figure 14-3.

FIGURE 14-3
Relationship between sales force size and profitability

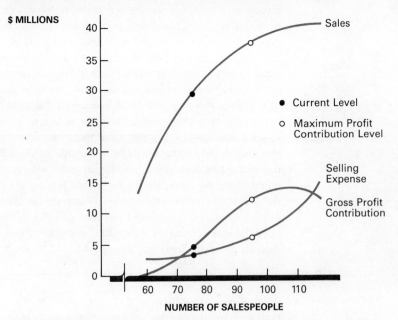

Source: David W. Cravens, Gerald E. Hills, and Robert B. Woodruff, *Marketing Decision Making* (Homewood, Ill.: Richard D. Irwin, 1980), p. 387. Used by permission.

Determining optimal sales force size from Figure 14-3 requires estimating a relationship between number of salespeople and dollar sales. Such an estimate is necessary since the company does not know what sales will be past its current level of seventy-five salespeople. Selling expenses and profit contribution are also estimated by size of the sales force. Past the optimal sales force level of ninety-five, each additional salesperson will cost more than his or her profit contribution (the sales expense curve is rising faster than the gross profit curve).

Quantitative models

A quantitative model developed by Montgomery and Urban determines the optimal size of the sales force as follows:[20]

$$Z = PQ(X) - C_1(Q) - C_2(X)$$

where

Z = profits
X = sales force size
P = selling price
Q = number of units sold as a function of selling effort
$C_1(Q)$ = total cost of producing and marketing Q units
$C_2(X)$ = total cost of selling effort by size of the sales force

The model determines size of the sales force (X) that maximizes profits (Z), and estimates revenue (PQ) and costs $(C_1$ and $C_2)$ as a function of the sales force size. Profits are maximized at the point where the difference is greatest between revenue (as a function of size of the sales force) and sales and production costs associated with this selling effort.

The difficulty in both the marginal and quantitative modeling approaches is the same as that in estimating advertising expenditures — establishing a link between sales results and selling effort. Without such a link the optimal size of the sales force cannot be determined. The problem of establishing a link between selling effort and sales is not as severe as establishing an advertising-to-sales relationship. But the same questions arise: Was the sale a function of the price level or the result of a creative selling effort? To what extent was the sale a function of the missionary sales efforts of others? To what extent might there be cumulative effects that influence current sales (for example, the efforts of former salespeople to cultivate the customer)? Can the influence of advertising be separated from that of sales in estimating the effect of the personal sales effort? In short, the methods of estimation just described are difficult to implement, but attempts should be made to estimate the effect of sales effort on profits.

Sales Force Strategies

One way to look at the selling effort is to consider the combination of the size and the nature of the company's sales force. The size of the company's sales force can be decreasing, staying the same, or increasing. The sales effort can be based on the company's own sales force or on outside sales facilities such as manufacturers' agents (independent salespeople who work for a commission) and distributors (wholesalers). These two considerations produce the five sales force strategies illustrated in Figure 14-4.

Companies relying on their own sales force may be following strategies of retrenching, consolidating, or expanding the sales effort. Companies using outside sales facilities could be replacing their own sales staff with manufacturers' agents or distributors. Companies could also be supplementing their own sales force by using outside facilities.

Relying on the existing sales force

Various companies have followed the sales force strategies illustrated in Figure 14-4. For example, Garland Corporation, a marketer of women's sweaters, was "snatched from the jaws of bankruptcy in 1980" by a cost-cutting and *retrenchment* program that included reducing its sales staff from thirty-two people to eight. Salespeople who were kept on sold a leaner but more profitable product line.[21]

A second strategy for companies relying on their own sales force is *consolidation.* The size of the sales force does not change. Rather, the sales force is reorganized for greater efficiency. Swift's reorganization of fifteen divisional sales forces into one national sales force is an example.[22] As noted earlier, the move permitted Swift's customers to deal with one salesperson for all of its product lines.

FIGURE 14-4
Sales force strategies

CHANGE IN SIZE OF COMPANY'S SALES FORCE	NATURE OF SALES EFFORT	
	USE COMPANY SALES FORCE	USE OUTSIDE SALES FACILITIES (MANUFACTURER'S AGENTS OR DISTRIBUTORS)
SMALLER	Retrench	Replace
SAME	Consolidate	Supplement
GREATER	Expand	Supplement

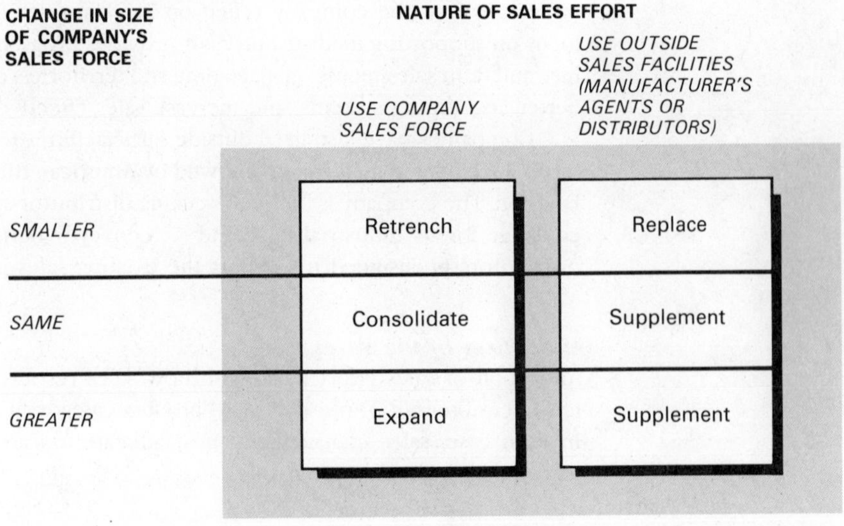

Avon, the largest door-to-door marketer in the United States, is following a strategy of *expansion.* It is looking for worldwide growth in its sales force of 10 percent a year to keep earnings growing. "The company's main method of building its force is to shrink the size of sales territories once an area is covered, which serves to intensify sales efforts."[23]

Increasing the use of outside sales facilities

Many companies have relied more on sales facilities outside the company, namely manufacturers' agents and distributors. Use of manufacturers' agents and distributors to support a company's sales force has several advantages. They can reduce selling costs by contacting less profitable and more geographically dispersed accounts that may be sapping the effort of the existing sales force. Further, agents and distributors can contact prospects that might not ordinarily be contacted by the company's sales force.

There are disadvantages, however, particularly if the company relies solely on outside facilities. First, agents and distributors may not be as highly motivated to sell the company's line. Most work for more than one manufacturer. Second, they may not be as knowledgeable about the company's line. Their technical expertise is likely to be less. Third, they are less knowledgeable about customers and prospects than the company's sales force. Fourth, a switch to outsiders may cause a negative reaction among the company's customers.[24] They may feel they will be getting less information and service.

Companies can follow two strategies in using outside facilities, replacing or supplementing the company sales staff. Airwick decided to *replace* its network of sales offices for its institutional line of products with distributors. Its ten sales offices were divided into twenty-eight new distributorships.[25] The company now relies on ninety-three independent distributors for sales. The reason for the replacement strategy was the lack of evidence of greater sales penetration in areas where the company relied on its own sales force. Now Airwick can focus on supporting its distributors. It provides programs that help distributors hire and train salespeople, manage time and territories, control inventory, install better accounting systems, and increase sales effectiveness.[26]

Companies have also used outside sales facilities to *supplement* their sales force. Such a strategy is being followed by American Biltrite's Industrial Rubber Division. The company is "actively seeking distributor-specialists to supplement coverage for its industrial hose and ... conveyor belting."[27] Increased use of distributors is designed to support the existing sales organization.

Allocation of the Sales Effort

Allocation of sales effort deals with how sales resources should be deployed to (1) customers, (2) prospects, (3) product categories, and (4) sales territories. In each case, sales management must allocate a scarce resource — its sales force — to maximize profits.

Customer allocations

Sales management generally allocates sales resources to customers on the basis of the customer's sales potential. Sales potential can be estimated from the customer's market share, demand for the customer's product, and territorial factors if the customer is regional. Many companies have computerized models to estimate customer potential and allocate their sales efforts accordingly. One model — called CALLPLAN — deals with the customer allocation problem by attempting to determine the optimum number of sales calls per customer. The model estimates the expected sales volume from various customers as a function of the number of calls made on the customer.[28] Salespeople are asked to estimate sales potential if they were to call on the customer say one, three, six, ten, and fifteen times during the year. The model then calculates the optimum number of sales calls to make to each account to maximize profits.

Prospect allocations

The question of allocating time between new and existing accounts is also crucial. Most salespeople would prefer to minimize prospecting because of uncertainty. They feel that commissions are more likely when visiting current customers. Any method that can demonstrate the profitability of contacting prospective accounts is valuable.

Most sales managers will estimate a prospect's potential on the basis of the prospect's past purchases, estimated growth rate, credit rating, and reputation among salespeople. A more empirical basis for estimating the potential of a prospect is derived from investment theory.[29] This method attempts to:

1. Determine the present value of a prospect's future income (Z). (Estimating Z would require determining the average expected revenue from the prospect in future years and then discounting this revenue to present value.)

2. Estimate the number of calls (n) and the cost per call (c) of converting the prospect to a customer.

3. Estimate the probability (p) that the prospect will be converted to a customer. (This will be influenced primarily by the number of calls.)

Once the prospect's present value (Z) is estimated, the investment that is justified to convert the prospect into a customer (nc) can be determined. This figure can then be used to estimate the potential value of the prospect's business (V) as follows:

$$V = pZ - nc$$

In other words, the prospect's value is the estimated present value of the revenue that can be obtained from the prospect (Z), weighted by the probability of the prospect becoming a customer (p), less the total cost of converting the prospect (nc). The salesperson's time will then be allocated on the basis of the estimated value of the prospect.

Product allocations

Sales management is also concerned about the appropriate allocation of effort across products. Many companies find that salespeople tend to focus on the line they know best or the one with which they are most comfortable rather than on the most profitable lines. As a result, salespeople often find it easier to generate commissions in less profitable products.

Sales management must provide guidelines as to which products salespeople should be concentrating on. These guidelines should be based on (1) profitability of the product line, (2) the needs of the particular customer, and (3) the salesperson's ability to sell the particular product.

Territorial allocations

Sales management also seeks to allocate sales effort by geographic region. Such allocations are particularly important if the sales force is organized territorially. A logical basis for territorial allocations is the sales potential of each territory. Census data can help one estimate territorial potential for various product categories by region. *Sales & Marketing Management,* a business publication, also publishes a *Survey of Industrial Purchasing Power* for industrial goods and a *Survey of Buying Power* for consumer goods that provides indexes of sales potential by region on the basis of past purchases.[30]

IDENTIFY PROSPECTS

In order to allocate sales effort between new and existing accounts, a firm must identify new customers. Therefore, the next step in the sales management process in Figure 14-2 is identifying prospects.

Sales management realizes that long-run profitability requires allocating effort to prospecting. Yet in most cases they feel their salespeople are not spending enough time to attract new accounts. A study of over 3500 salespeople and sales managers found that managers felt their sales staff should spend about 40 percent more time on prospecting.[31]

Several factors have increased the importance of prospecting. Many industries have experienced increased competition, particularly from foreign producers. To maintain their market shares, these companies must find new accounts. Second, because of slow growth in the late 1970s combined with inflation, profitability rather than sales volume has been emphasized as a criterion of sales effectiveness. Ensuring profitability requires more emphasis on prospecting. As a result, the natural predisposition of salespeople to spend more time with their current accounts has met with increasing resistance from sales managers. Third, the rapid pace of technological change has meant that a company's customer base is constantly changing. AT&T is entering into data processing, Xerox is going into personal computers, Polaroid is entering into many industrial product areas. If salespeople relied on their old customers, sales of new product lines would be severely curtailed.

Companies use two methods for prospecting: (1) relying on the salesperson to identify prospects from his or her contacts, and (2) developing a data base.

Sales force as a source of prospect identification

A survey of sales representatives of major domestic computer companies found that the most frequently used sources for prospecting are (1) other salespeople in the firm, (2) referrals from satisfied customers, and (3) the engineering departments of potential customers.[32] When sales reps were asked which was the most effective source in identifying prospects, two stood out: referrals from satisfied customers and referrals from other salespeople in the firm who were *not* selling the same line as the sales rep. The sales rep might have found information from colleagues not selling the same line more useful because salespeople selling the same line might be competing for commissions from new accounts.

Data based methods for identifying prospects

Industrial and consumer goods companies are turning increasingly to outside data bases such as Census data or broad-based customer files sold by service companies to identify prospects. One such data base is *Sales & Marketing Management's Survey of Industrial Purchasing Power.* This is used to identify industrial sales prospects. Some of the information provided in the Survey is shown in Table 14-1. The ten largest industrial classifications are listed with 1980 sales and the percentage increase forecast for 1981 (last column). For example, electronic computing equipment, the eighth ranked industry, had $24 billion in sales in 1980 with a projected increase of 26 percent in 1981.[33] The industry has 531 plants with an average of $45 million in sales per plant.

An industrial marketer selling parts and materials to manufacturers of electronic computing equipment might use S&MM's figures to give the following hypothetical results:

Sales Region	Number of Computer Equipment Firms	Number that are Company's Customers	% Coverage	Market Share
Western region	150	120	80	8.0%
Northcentral region	100	80	80	7.5%
Southern region	80	70	87	8.0%
Eastern region	201	130	65	5.5%
Total	531	400	75	7.0%

These data show that the company's coverage is relatively good except in the Eastern region. The company's market share reflects the weaker sales effort in the East. The seventy-one Eastern companies not being contacted are identified from the S&MM survey and the Eastern sales manager is asked to direct prospecting efforts to these companies.

TABLE 14-1
Sample Output of the Survey of Industrial Purchasing Power

1980 RANK	SIC	INDUSTRY	1980 SHIPMENTS (MILLIONS OF DOLLARS)	TOTAL PLANTS	SHIPMENTS PER PLANT (THOUSANDS OF DOLLARS)	1981 FORECAST SHIPMENTS
1.	2911	Petroleum refining	156,406	334	468,283	NA
2.	3711	Motor vehicles & car bodies	67,229	162	414,994	+30%
3.	3312	Blast furnaces & steel mills	50,564	341	148,280	+22
4.	2011	Meat packing plants	38,797	1,112	34,890	+13
5.	3714	Motor vehicle parts & accessories	31,531	1,244	25,347	NA
6.	2869	Industrial organic chemicals, NEC	30,158	449	67,168	+15
7.	3079	Miscellaneous plastics products	25,632	4,547	5,637	NA
8.	3573	Electronic computing equipment	24,176	531	45,530	+26
9.	3662	Radio & tv communication				
10.	3721	Aircraft	22,832	99	230,621	−2

NA = Not Available

Source: "How Prospecting for Profitable Sales Pays," *Sales & Marketing Management*, April 27, 1981, *Survey of Buying Power*, p. 12. © 1981. Further reproduction prohibited.

In most cases the number of potential customers in an industry is much greater than 531 and the number of sales regions greater than 4, complicating the prospecting task. In such cases, *S&MM's Survey of Industrial Purchasing Power* is even more useful.

DEVELOP PERSONAL SELLING STRATEGIES

Once prospects have been identified, sales management can develop strategies to guide the efforts of the sales force.

Types of Strategies

Sales strategies can vary by the salesperson's approach to the customer. Salespeople can approach customers by trying to emphasize their product expertise, or by trying to establish empathy and to emphasize their similarity to the customer. If the salesperson is trying to establish expertise, he or she should take a more informational approach by communicating product specifications and capabilities. A salesperson taking an empathetic approach should establish rapport and friendship while delivering the sales message. After examining the literature and conducting several studies, Weitz concluded that expertise should be established if:

- the salesperson has the product knowledge and credentials legitimately to be seen as an expert,
- the customer is engaged in a high risk, complex buying task that requires expertise, and
- the salesperson does not regularly sell to the buyer, creating more of a need to establish his or her credentials.[34]

Strategies emphasizing expertise
Sales strategies can also vary depending on whether the salesperson is trying to reinforce existing customer needs and beliefs, or trying to change them. These alternatives — expertise versus empathy and reinforcement versus change — combine to produce the selling strategies in Figure 14-5. If the salesperson decides to emphasize expertise to meet existing needs (first column in Figure 14-5), he or she must identify and meet those needs. If the salesperon decides that a change strategy would best fill customer needs, he or she can attempt to change beliefs about existing products, change needs, or provide information on new brands or new features of existing brands.

FIGURE 14-5
Personal selling strategies

APPROACH TO CUSTOMER'S NEEDS AND BELIEFS	APPROACH TO CUSTOMER	
	EMPHASIZE KNOWLEDGE AND EXPERTISE	*EMPHASIZE EMPATHY*
REINFORCE NEEDS AND/OR BELIEFS	Identify and Meet Existing Needs	Demonstrate Similarity to Customer
CHANGE NEEDS AND/OR BELIEFS	Change • Beliefs About Products • Consumer Needs Provide Information on • New Products • New Features	Change Customer Perceptions of Buyer-Seller Interaction

Strategies emphasizing empathy

If the salesperson decides to emphasize empathy in an interpersonal context, the best approach to meeting existing needs is to establish his or her similarity to the customer. Personal relations are then established on the customer's perception of empathy, and the salesperson can then proceed to determine how to best meet customer needs from the company's product line. A change strategy would be required if the salesperson feels that the proper interpersonal relationship has not been established to make a sale. The salesperson would then attempt to change the customer's perceptions to establish similarity and empathy.

Sensitizing the Salesperson to Alternative Strategies

The sales manager's task is to sensitize the salesperson to the dyadic relationship with the customer. First, the salesperson should be aware of the continuum between expertise and empathy. Most effective sales approaches combine elements of both, but when in the sales presentation to emphasize each element is a matter of training and experience. For example, studies have found that in the sale of life insurance, expertise is more effective, whereas in the sale of paint, interpersonal relations are more likely to produce sales results.[35] This is logical since the sale of life insurance requires communicating information on many dimensions of this service. Interpersonal relations might make the difference in the sale of paint since it is a more standardized product.

The sales manager's second task is to make the salesperson sensitive to the customer's frame of mind and set of needs. The purpose is to enable the salesperson to select a maintenance or a change strategy, and if a change strategy, to select the optimal strategy.

The Customer-Salesperson Interaction

The strategies cited in Figure 14-5 assume an interactive relationship between the customer and salesperson. The salesperson listens, evaluates needs, forms a strategy, and adjusts the strategy on the basis of customer feedback. But other strategies are sometimes followed. One writer characterized these strategies by the degree to which the salesperson or the buyer is controlling the selling situation as follows:[36]

Salesperson
Controls
Situation   *Buyer Controls Situation*

	No	Yes
No	Inactive	Reactive
Yes	Proactive	Interactive

An inactive situation involves no creative sales process. The seller makes a canned approach and may take an order. In a reactive situation, the buyer is in control. The salesperson presents the buyer with the product he or she wants and makes every effort to fulfill service, price, and delivery needs. In a proactive situation, the salesperson is in control. He or she informs the buyer of market conditions, and recommends the products, models, and even specifications best suited to the buyer's needs. In an interactive situation, the seller and buyer work together to solve the buyer's problems by determining how the buyer's company can best respond to and develop favorable long-term market conditions.[37]

A good example of an inactive approach is Alcoa's former sales strategy of filling orders with little concern for customer needs. Alcoa then moved to a reactive strategy by getting salespeople to "ask for a list of things they can do better for their customers."[38] AT&T has moved from a relatively inactive sales approach to a proactive approach. In the past, salespeople tended to emphasize technical efficiency and relied on AT&T's monopoly position for sales results. By the early 1970s AT&T forecast increased competition in telecommunications equipment and service and began encouraging salespeople to communicate new products and service capabilities.[39] The recent divestiture of AT&T and its move into data processing and transmission makes communication from salespeople to buyers even more important.

A shift from an inactive to an interactive approach is demonstrated by Dana Corporation, producers of parts for the transmission and control of power machinery. The company shifted "from merely selling products to promoting the services of an expanded Dana Industrial Sales Force."[40] Dana's sales approach requires interactive problem solving with its buyers. Their salespeople, described as sales engineers, are trained to handle 90 percent of the design requirements of buyers. The salesperson is required to be involved with the buyer right in the buyer's plant. To support its sales engineers, Dana mounted a $1 million advertising campaign to create a stronger corporate identity. The campaign increased the number of buyer inquiries thirtyfold.[41]

EVALUATE THE SALES EFFORT

The last step in the sales management process is evaluation of the sales effort. The sales effort can be evaluated by customer, product, or territory. It can also be evaluated using sales volume and profits.

Evaluating Customers, Products, and Territories

The planned distribution of sales efforts by customers, products, or territories should be compared to actual results. If sales are below the estimated potential, the sales manager must make adjustments. For example, GTE developed a prospect identification system that was meant to estimate potential sales for existing customers from their organizational characteristics. (Organizational characteristics of customers were obtained from Dun & Bradstreet's large data base of companies known as *Dun's Market Identifiers.*) Potential sales for each account were then adjusted by the account's market share and by inputs from sales reps and management about the customer's situation. Actual sales were then compared with the customer's potential as the basis for evaluating sales performance. Assume the following data for five existing purchasers of high-intensity lamps:

	Potential Sales (based on D&B data and other factors)	Actual Sales	Index of Sales Performance (actual sales divided by potential)
Customer 1	$240,000	$320,000	133
Customer 2	$130,000	$150,000	115
Customer 3	$180,000	$182,000	100
Customer 4	$110,000	$ 80,000	73
Customer 5	$ 90,000	$ 50,000	55

Using this data, the sales manager asks why sales for customers 4 and 5 are well below potential. The reason could be one or two inefficient salespeople. Or there could be a more widespread pattern of ignoring smaller accounts. Or factors internal to these two customers could make the difference. Adjustments within the control of the sales manager would be made; for example, increasing sales calls to these customers or providing more information before sales calls.

Sales results by product line and by territory would also be compared to projected sales. If sales of a certain product category are only 70 percent of potential, was it the fault of the sales force, of inadequate direct mail, of an ineffective advertising campaign, of a poorly designed product, or of market factors beyond the control of the company (e.g., competitive efforts or an advance in technology)? Once again, the sales manager would be concerned with adjusting sales allocations and strategies to meet potentials.

Evaluating Overall Sales Results

The ultimate criterion of the sales effort's effectiveness is profitable sales. As in advertising, management would like to relate dollars expended to dollars returned. But establishing a sales-effort-to-sales relationship runs into the same problems as those encountered in establishing an advertising-to-sales relationship — trying to isolate the effects of the personal selling effort on sales, and accounting for the cumulative effect of past selling efforts.

There have been few attempts to relate personal selling effort to sales on an empirical basis. The quantitative approaches used to determine the optimal size of the sales force assume the relationship between selling effort and sales is known (the X term in the equation on page 424). Several approaches to estimating the relationship between sales response and selling effort have been used, including (1) estimating a historical relationship between the two,[42] (2) using field experiments to control for the effects of alternative selling efforts on sales,[43] and (3) using simulation.[44] But quantitative models to estimate a sales-effort-to-sales relationship are not as advanced as those designed to estimate an advertising-to-sales relationship.

Sales Force Management

While establishing and evaluating the selling effort, the sales manager must also direct the efforts of the sales force. Figure 14-2 showed four components of sales force management: recruiting, training, motivating, and evaluating the salesperson.

RECRUITMENT

The quality of the sales force depends on the effectiveness of recruiting procedures. Effective recruitment can reduce the turnover of the sales force and increase sales volume. One study analyzed recruiting costs in a pharmaceutical firm and concluded that the firm should increase its recruiting budget to thirteen times its present size to increase sales productivity and profits.[45]

Sales managers must determine what criteria to use to select salespeople. If personal characteristics could be related to effective sales performance, these criteria could be used in hiring salespeople. But few such characteristics have been identified. Factors such as age, education, intelligence, sociability, and experience have yielded mixed results. For example, one study of life insurance salespeople found that experience is positively related to performance, whereas another study found that it was not.[46] Similarly, one study of oil company salespeople found that their intelligence was related to performance, but another found it was not.[47] As a result of such conflicting results, most firms rely on managerial judgment, which is based on personal interviews with candidates, their past references, and previous job experience.

Some firms have sought more empirical bases for recruiting. One door-to-door sales organization considered developing a model to predict the sales performance of its applicants. It would analyze current salespeople's demographic characteristics to determine if they were related to performance. If so, these characteristics would be used to predict the potential performance of applicants. Assume the model produced the following results:

Average sales performance of existing sales personnel: $28,000/year
Effects of demographic characteristics on performance:

Age 30–40	+ $6,000
Married	+ $2,000
Income under $25,000	+ $3,000
Urban	− $4,000
Completed college	− $6,000

This analysis shows that the best salespeople are married, middle-aged, somewhat downscale individuals who do not live in cities and did not complete college. According to this model, if an applicant was a twenty-six-year-old, single city dweller who completed college with an income of $22,000, her projected yearly sales would be:

$$\$28,000 \text{ (average sales)} - \$4,000 \text{ (for urban)} - \$6,000 \text{ (for college grad)} + \$3,000 \text{ (for income)} = \$21,000 \text{ (predicted sales)}$$

Predicted sales are well below average, and the applicant would not be hired.

Such methods are valid as long as personal characteristics can be shown to be related to sales. Since this is the exception rather than the rule, recruitment procedures are likely to continue to be based on managerial judgment and referrals.

TRAINING

Because of the substantial costs of training salespeople — $15,000–$20,000 per person is typical — sales managers must scrutinize the objectives and methods of training programs. Such scrutiny was spurred by greater cost consciousness of sales managers in the face of inflation and a weaker economy in the late 1970s.

The primary objective of most training programs is *not* to teach recruits how to sell. Some sales executives feel these skills can be discussed but not really taught. A survey of industrial companies found that the most frequently mentioned reason for training was to convey knowledge of the company's product line.[48] Such information is essential to enable salespeople to meet customer needs.

The question sales management must answer in evaluating training programs is "To what degree do they pay?" A firm always has the option of hiring experienced salespeople rather than training new ones. The comparative costs of these alternatives should be analyzed. Most firms favor training new staff rather than hiring experienced personnel. Experienced salespeople cost much more, and there is always some loss in transferring their skills to another company. But in some cases, such costly hires are necessary to fill gaps in the sales force and to establish new capabilities.

Attempts should also be made to determine the effect of training on sales volume, sales force turnover, development of new accounts, and contribution to profits.

MOTIVATING

Recruitment and training procedures are meaningless if the salesperson is not motivated to perform. The key questions are whether (1) performance goals are viewed as attainable, and (2) the rewards for performance are considered satisfactory. These motivational issues can be represented as follows:

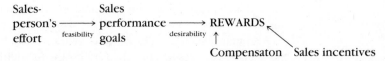

The salesperson will be motivated if sales goals (generally in the form of quotas) are viewed as feasible and if the rewards for performance are viewed as desirable. Rewards are of two types, compensation plans and special incentives to stimulate sales on a shorter-term basis.

Compensation

Three methods of compensation have been used to reward salespeople: straight salary, straight commission, and a combination of salary and commissions. One study found that about one-fourth of the companies paid straight salary, another fourth straight commission, and about one-half a combination.

There are advantages and disadvantages to each. *Straight salary* plans are simple and less costly to administer, and they facilitate revenue projections since sales expenses for the coming year are known. But straight salary may not stimulate performance. The best salespeople may be discouraged since their compensation may not be commensurate with their sales volume.

Straight commission plans provide financial incentives tied to sales volume. These methods encourage salespeople to increase sales and to more effectively use their selling time. The basic difficulty is that selling is not the only thing salespeople do. A straight commission plan gives the salesperson very little incentive to fill out call reports, supply intelligence, do missionary work, or prospect. Salespeople are not rewarded for such activities. Further, a decrease in sales could demoralize the sales force under straight commission plans: salespeople would see their compensation decreasing because of factors beyond their control.

Deficiencies in a straight salary or commission approach have led most companies to adopt a *combination plan*. Such a plan attempts to balance the security of salary and the maximum incentive of commissions and bonuses. It also reflects a balance between the sales manager's desires to stimulate sales through commissions and to control sales expenses through a salary plan.

Sales Incentive Programs

Sales incentive programs are shorter-term motivators such as sales contests and recognition programs designed to stimulate sales. They are effective in maintaining sales effort in a recession or to counteract increased competitive activity. In the words of one sales executive who increased his sales incentive activities, "We're putting increased emphasis on short-term sales because of the more competitive environment."[49] One survey found that three times as many firms increased sales incentive expenditures as decreased them during the deep recession in the early 1980s. The reason was that sales executives viewed such programs as "sure-fire stimulants to greater sales effort" in depressed markets.[50]

Programs such as sales contests or travel may be valuable in stimulating immediate sales results, but they are costly. In addition, some sales managers feel that they simply shift sales volume that would have occurred anyway into the contest period.

EVALUATION AND CONTROL

The last steps in the management of the sales force require evaluating the performance of individual salespeople and controlling sales operations.

Salesperson Evaluation

The sales manager has the dual responsibility of evaluating the overall sales effort and the efforts of individual salespeople. The criteria used to evaluate a salesperson's performance vary widely from firm to firm. A survey of industrial companies found sales volume to be the most widely used criterion. A more effective measure is the relation of sales volume to sales quotas to determine if the salesperson has fulfilled the potential in his or her territory.

The weakness of volume and quota criteria is that they may not be related to profitablility. Sales quotas might have been achieved at excessive costs. A more effective measure of performance would be to determine the salesperson's contribution to profits. A survey of industrial companies found that whereas two-thirds of the firms interviewed used sales volume criteria, only about one-fourth used profit criteria. Perhaps some firms have inadequate records to determine the contribution a particular salesperson makes to profits by product and territory.

Profitability measures should be used with other criteria in evaluating sales performance. The following criteria could be used in evaluating the salesperson's allocation of time and fulfillment of administrative assignments:

- number of calls per customer,
- expenses per sales call,
- number of new customers,
- number of lost customers,
- completion of call reports, and
- fulfillment of postpurchase service and maintenance requirements.

Control

The sales manager's primary concern in the area of control is expenses, particularly for travel and entertainment. These expenses must be controlled to maximize profitability. A second area of control is the salesperson's time. One sales executive estimates that the average salesperson spends one-fourth of the time selling, another fourth doing administrative tasks assigned by the sales manager, and half of the time traveling, waiting, or servicing accounts.[51] Because so much time is spent on tasks that do not generate revenue, the sales manager must try to develop more effective allocations of salespeople's time.

A third area of control is ensuring that salespeople fulfill necessary administrative tasks like making out call reports or developing prospect lists.

Summary

Personal selling gives marketers the means of obtaining face-to-face contact with the customer. Such contact is particularly important in industrial selling because of the need for negotiations, postpurchase service, and product specifications for complex and expensive products.

The selling task can vary from creative problem solving, requiring close interaction with the customer, to simple order taking. Common roles in the sales process are determining customer needs, prospecting, providing the firm with marketing intelligence, and providing service. A communications model described the sales process as requiring the salesperson to form an impression of customer needs, formulate a strategy to meet those needs, transmit a message, evaluate the customer's response, and adjust subsequent communications to the customer accordingly.

In the rest of the chapter we considered the sales management process. The sales manager has two responsibilities, managing the selling effort and managing the sales force. Managing the selling effort requires:

1. *Establishing sales objectives.* These are based on sales volume, profitability, cost, and product mix criteria.

2. *Determining the scope of the sales effort.* This requires (1) estimating the optimal size of the sales force and (2) allocating sales effort by customer, product, and territory.

3. *Identifying prospects* through salespeople, customer referrals, and direct inquiries. Some firms are beginning to use data bases such as the *Survey of Industrial Purchasing Power* to identify prospects for subsequent contact by sales representatives.

4. *Developing personal selling strategies.* Such strategies can be classified according to whether the salesperson is trying to meet the existing needs of the customer or to change these needs by offering new information or changing beliefs about existing brands.

5. *Evaluating the sales effort.* Sales efforts are analyzed by evaluating sales results by customer, product, or territory to determine whether sales potentials have been achieved. The sales manager must also attempt to evaluate overall sales results by establishing a relationship between sales effort and sales. Such a relationship is difficult to establish

because the effect of the sales effort cannot be isolated from other factors such as advertising and price.

The sales manager must also direct the efforts of the sales force. This requires recruiting, training, motivating, controlling and evaluating salespeople.

In the next chapter we will consider another strategic element of the marketing mix — price.

Questions

1. Industrial selling accounts for more dollars than any other component of the promotional mix. Why then has more attention been devoted to advertising both in business schools and by the business community?

2. A salesperson for a pharmaceutical company says:

   The most difficult part of the selling process isn't developing a sales message; it is overcoming customer resistance to what is new and unfamiliar. For example, it is difficult to try to sell a new high-potency nonprescription pain reliever when the druggist is used to Bayer, Bufferin, and Tylenol. The creative part of selling is adjusting to the customer's frame of reference or trying to change it.

   □ Do you agree with this statement? Why or why not?

   □ Using Figure 14-1, estimate the adjustments the salesperson would have to make in a sales presentation in an attempt to influence druggists to carry a new nonprescription pain reliever.

3. What are the shortcomings of developing sales objectives based on dollar sales volume?

4. What are the limitations of determining the size of the sales force from:

   □ required sales calls to customers?

   □ a percentage of last year's sales?

   □ competitive parity?

   Given these limitations, why is each approach frequently used as a basis for estimating sales force size?

5. In the chapter two approaches were described as superior for determining optimal sales force size — a marginal method and a quantitative modeling approach.

   □ Why are these approaches superior to those mentioned in question 4?

   □ If these approaches are superior, why are they used so rarely?

6. What are the pros and cons of using outside sales facilities to support or replace a company's sales staff?

What types of companies are most likely to develop outside sales facilities rather than their own sales staff?

7. A sales manager for a producer of hydraulic lifts believes that prospecting is going to become more important in the coming decade. The company is a leader in the field, but the sales manager is concerned that new entrants will have more innovative and technically oriented salespeople who are better able to identify prospects.

 □ Is the sales manager's concern well founded?

 □ Why is prospecting likely to become more important in the next decade?

8. A manufacturer of auto parts and accessories asks *Sales & Marketing Management* to break down purchases of parts and accessories by region using S&MM's *Survey of Industrial Purchasing Power*. Data are to be categorized by number of customers and dollar sales per region. (See page 430 for similar data for computing equipment). How can the manufacturer use this data to:

 □ identify sales prospects?

 □ allocate sales calls to prospects by region?

9. Which of the sales strategies listed in Figure 14-5 would be most appropriate when:

 □ selling perfume on a door-to-door basis?

 □ demonstrating personal computers to small businesses that are used to maintaining files and accounts manually?

 □ selling a new type of high-speed film to professional photographers?

 □ trying to convince retailers to provide more shelf space for an up-and-coming food company that is getting an increasing share of the diet foods market?

10. Sales strategies were classified on page 432 as inactive, reactive, proactive and interactive. Which of these would best describe each of the following, and why?

 □ A seller of custom-made hydraulic lifts uses the specifications formulated by the customer's engineering department as a basis for submitting terms of sales for the proposed product.

 □ The sales force for a large telecommunications firm is instructed to communicate the firm's new capabilities in information processing and office systems.

 □ The sales staff for a leading drug wholesaler generally takes orders from drug chains. It provides little service or information, since buyers for the drug chains know the products they want.

 □ A seller of pollution control systems works jointly with the buyer in developing specifications to the buyer's needs. Both the salesperson and buyer are trained engineers who work together with their design staffs in developing, installing, and servicing the system.

11. What are some of the problems sales managers face in hiring salespeople? Can any empirical bases be developed to predict a salesperson's performance?

12. What are the advantages and disadvantages of a straight salary versus a straight commission plan?

Notes

1. "Xerox's Bid to be No. 1 in Offices," *Business Week,* June 22, 1981, p. 77.

2. "A Swift Kick in the Sales Force," *Sales & Marketing Management,* May 14, 1979, p. 33.

3. "Sales and Marketing to the Rescue," *Sales & Marketing Management,* April 4, 1983, p. 39.

4. "Selected Tables from S&MM's Survey of Selling Costs," in *Managing Costs for More Productive Selling* (New York: Sales & Marketing Management, February 1981).

5. "Cost of Industrial Sales Calls Reaches $205.40," *Labreport* (New York: McGraw-Hill Research, 1983), 4 pp.

6. "Training, Employee Orientation Hike Sales Rep Performance," *Marketing News,* November 13, 1981, p. 1.

7. Jon G. Udell, *Successful Marketing Strategies in American Industry* (Madison, Wis.: Mimir, 1972).

8. "Taking Orders Isn't Enough: Direct Salespeople Must Become Marketers," *Marketing News,* January 8, 1982, p. 6.

9. "To Find Out What Will Sell, Try Going to the Source — the Sales Force," *Sales & Marketing Management,* July 7, 1980, p. 75.

10. *Marketing News,* January 8, 1982, p. 6.

11. "Manage the Sales Force to Make the Most of Your Promotion Investment," *Sales & Marketing Management,* August 1978, p. 58.

12. "The Medium is the Salesman," *Advertising Age,* June 9, 1980, p. S-23.

13. "Salespeople are Communicating Poorly," *Marketing News,* April 1, 1983, p. 2.

14. "Training, Employee Orientation Hike Sales Rep Performance," *Marketing News,* November 13, 1981, p. 1.

15. Richard W. Olshavsky, "Customer-Salesman Interaction in Appliance Retailing," *Journal of Marketing Research* 10 (May 1983): 208–9.

16. "Alcoa's Dominance in Aluminum Industry Wanes as Rivals Grow, Markets Get Tight," *The Wall Street Journal,* March 25, 1982, p. 31.

17. Ibid.

18. Barton A. Weitz, "The Relationship Between Salesperson Performance and Understanding of Customer Decision Making," *Journal of Marketing Research* 15 (November 1978): 501–16.

19. Harry J. Demas, Richard A. Bobbe, and Phyllis E. Connolly, "Developing End-Use Marketing Teams," *Industrial Marketing Management* 8 (1979): 313.

20. David B. Montgomery and Glen L. Urban, *Management Science in Marketing* (Englewood Cliffs, N.J.: Prentice-Hall, 1969).

21. *Sales & Marketing Management,* April 4, 1983, p. 36.

22. *Sales & Marketing Management,* May 14, 1979, p. 33.

23. "Avon Crosses Its Fingers," *Financial World,* November 15, 1979, p. 26.

24. "Converting to Reps Without Trauma," *Sales & Marketing Management,* April 4, 1983, p. 56.

25. "Airwick Drops Sales Offices to Increase Sales," *Marketing News,* February 8, 1980, p. 6.

26. Ibid.

27. "Rebuilding American Biltrite," *Sales & Marketing Management,* November 12, 1979, p. 35.

28. Leonard M. Lodish "Callplan: An Interactive Salesman's Call Planning System," *Management Science,* 8 (December 1971): 25–40.

29. Philip Kotler, *Marketing Management* (Englewood Cliffs, N.J.: Prentice-Hall, 1980): 568–69.

30. "How Prospecting for Profitable Sales Pays," *Sales & Marketing Management,* April 27, 1981, pp. 6–18.

31. Terry Deutscher, Judith Marshall, and David Burgoyne, "The Process of Obtaining New Accounts," *Industrial Marketing Management,* 11 (1982): 173–81.

32. "High-Tech Can't Forget Sales Prospecting," *Industrial Marketing,* November 1981, p 78.

33. *Sales & Marketing Management,* April 27, 1981, p. 12.

34. Barton A. Weitz, "Effectiveness in Sales Interactions: A Contingency Framework," *Journal of Marketing,* 45 (Winter 1981): 85–103.

35. Paul Busch and David T. Wilson, "An Experimental Analysis of a Salesman's Expert and Referent Bases of Social Power in the Buyer-Seller Dyad," *Journal of Marketing Research* 13 (February 1976): 3–11; and Timothy C. Brock, "Communicator-Recipient Similarity and Decision Change," *Journal of Personality and Social Psychology* 1 (June 1965): 650–54.

36. Peter W. Pasold, "The Effectiveness of Various Modes of Sales Behavior in Different Markets," *Journal of Marketing Research* 12 (May 1975): 171–76.

37. Ibid.

38. *The Wall Street Journal,* March 25, 1982, p. 31.

39. "Selling is No Longer Mickey Mouse at AT&T," *Fortune,* July 17, 1978, p. 102.

40. "Dana Industrial Marketing," *Sales & Marketing Management,* January 12, 1981, p. 18.

41. Ibid.

42. Henry C. Lucas, C. B. Weinberg, and K. Clowes, "Sales Response as a Function of Territorial Potential and Sales Representative Workload," *Journal of Marketing Research* 12 (August 1975): 298–305.

43. Arthur Meidan, "Optimizing the Number of Industrial Salespersons," *Industrial Marketing Management* 11 (1982): 63–74.

44. Montgomery and Urban, *Management Science in Marketing,* p. 253.

45. Rene Y. Darmon, "Sales Force Management: Optimizing the Recruiting Process," *Sloan Management Review* 20 (Fall 1978): 47–59.

46. Donald Baier and Robert D. Dugan, "Factors in Sales Success," *Journal of Applied Psychology* 41 (February 1957): 37–40; and Robert Tanofsky, R. Ronald Shepps, and Paul J. O'Neill, "Pattern Analysis of Biographical Predictors of Success as an Insurance Salesman," *Journal of Applied Psychology* 53 (April 1969): 136–39.

47. John B. Miner, "Personality and Ability Factors in Sales Performance" *Journal of Applied Psychology* 46 (February 1962): 6–13; and Thomas W. Harrell, "The Relation of Test Scores to Sales Criteria," *Personnel Psychology* 13 (Spring 1960): 65–69.

48. Alan J. Dubinsky and Thomas E. Barry, "A Survey of Sales Management Practices," *Industrial Marketing Management* 11 (1982): 136–37.

49. "Inspiration at the Right Price," *Sales & Marketing Management,* April 6, 1981, p. 61.

50. Ibid., p. 59.

51. "Controlling Territory Time Costs," in *Managing Costs for More Productive Selling* (New York: Sales & Marketing Management, February 1981).

CHAPTER 15

Price Determination and Pricing Strategies

FOCUS OF CHAPTER

One of marketing management's main responsibilities is establishing a price level for a brand or product line within the context of a dynamic pricing strategy. Dynamic pricing strategies can anticipate market forces such as consumer demand, competitive actions, economic conditions, and the legal and regulatory climate, and then determine prices accordingly. Such a dynamic approach recognizes price as a key determinant of long-term profits. As such, price should be one of marketing management's most important concerns.

Yet it was only in the 1970s that price became a dominant concern in formulating a marketing mix. Before that, nonprice factors such as advertising and sales promotion were more important. A survey of managers in the 1960s found that they did not select price as one of the five most important factors in determining a company's marketing success.[1] Price determination at the time was fairly routine and was often based on what competitors did. But now many firms are following new pricing strategies, ones characterized by "flexibility and a willingness to cut prices aggressively to hold market share. On the way out of the window are many of the pricing traditions of the U.S. industrial giants."[2] Consider the following examples that demonstrate this new pricing flexibility:

- Airlines, long sheltered by government regulations, have been engaged in price wars to try to protect shrinking profits.
- The steel industry had long been characterized by a follow-the-leader approach to pricing, usually led by United States Steel. But the stable pattern of prices has given way to more flexibility in the face of stiff foreign competition. An example is Armco's reduction of 20 percent off list price, with other steel companies reluctantly following Armco's lead.[3]

■ The auto industry's historic reliance on setting prices based on a pre-specified target return on profits helped create an average $1,500 price differential between American and Japanese compacts in 1982.[4] The industry is now beginning to moderate its rigid targets and to show signs of greater price flexibility in an attempt to more effectively compete with imports.

In this chapter we will look at the process of determining prices and establishing pricing strategies for brands and product lines. Such a process requires:

■ setting price objectives,

■ evaluating the market and corporate influences on price,

■ selecting a method for determining the price level,

■ evaluating consumer responses to price, and

■ adjusting and controlling pricing strategies on the basis of consumer responses.

A key element in this process is developing a pricing strategy that will guide managerial actions. Alternative pricing strategies and competitive responses to these strategies will be described.

The Increasing Importance of Price

Before we consider the process of determining price, we should explore why price has become a more important element in marketing strategy. Management has always regarded price as important. An elementary fact is that the total revenue equals price times quantity; and revenues and costs determine profit. Therefore price is a key ingredient in the profit equation. But until the 1970s management was more concerned with the quantity side of the equation than the price side. In the 1950s and 1960s, the primary emphasis was on stimulating demand through advertising and product development. Pricing was more a function of costs than of demand. Companies determined their costs, set price on the basis of a target return on investment, and only then determined if consumers were willing to buy at that price.

The energy crisis in 1973 and the subsequent periods of alternating inflation and recession created something of a revolution in the role of price. Shortages of raw materials substantially increased costs. Foreign competition decreased the demand for many domestically produced products. The recession of the mid-1970s and early 1980s depressed purchasing power. Competition increased in the face of shrinking demand. The result was a profit squeeze in many major industries — automobiles, airlines, steel, aluminum — that also began to extend to consumer packaged goods. What was the marketers' initial response to changed environmental conditions?

> [It was] a confused attempt to pass on cost increases in an unthinking way — an effort to retain target rates of return [on investment] but in an atmosphere requiring higher and higher prices. But with unused capacity around the world, there was just too little demand and too much competition to allow target return pricing to work. Indeed, 1975 and 1976 were marked by repeated retreats from announced industrywide price boosts in steel, paper, aluminum, and chemicals.[5]

These repeated retreats from fixed pricing policies caused management to view pricing in a new light. Companies began to show a willingness "to adjust prices, or profit margins, on specific products as market conditions varied. ... They are juggling prices among products — raising some, lowering others — to get the maximum mix of sales and profits."[6]

This newfound flexibility required demand-oriented pricing rather than a strictly cost-oriented approach. Demand-oriented pricing meant more frequent price adjustments and pricing independent of competitors' actions. As one marketing planner said, "The worst thing a company can do now is price identically to its competitors."[7] Because of increasing risk and uncertainty, companies can no longer assume that what is good for their competitors is good for them.

Other factors also increased the importance of price:

- *Greater consumer price sensitivity* in inflationary and recessionary periods has made price a much more important consideration in the final purchase decision.

- *An increase in the purchase of private brands and generics* has created downward price pressures on national brands.

- *An increase in the pace of new product introductions* requires constant reevaluation of the prices of existing products.

These factors have all increased the importance of pricing strategies. But they have not had a uniform effect on price levels. Foreign competition and recessions have had a dampening effect, but inflation has resulted in upward price pressures. Consumer price sensitivity has resulted in some drive to reduce prices, but many of these consumers are emphasizing more value for their money. Thus some segments are willing to pay more if they think a product is worth it.

The Process of Price Determination

A flexible process of price determination is illustrated in Figure 15-1. The first step is to establish pricing objectives. For example, Eli Lilly's pricing objective

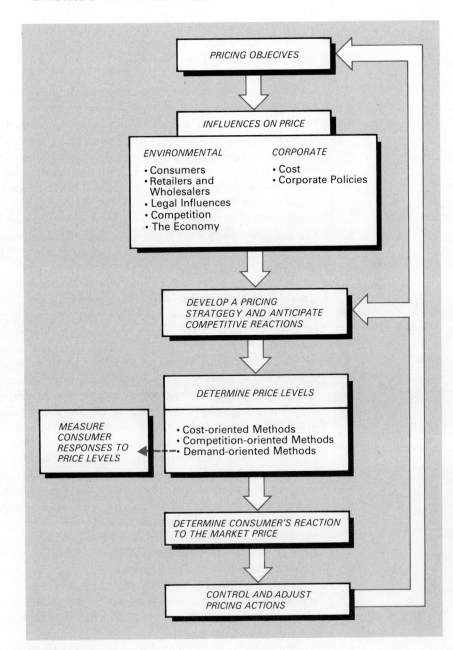

FIGURE 15-1
The price determination process

for Treflan, an agricultural herbicide, was to increase its market share for the product before its patent expired in the mid 1980s. As a result, the company reduced the price of the product in 1982 for the first time since the mid-1970s.[8]

The next step in Figure 15-1 is to evaluate the environmental forces that affect price. Most important is the consumer. Lilly would want to determine farmers' sensitivity to a price change and the possibility that sales would increase enough to warrant a price decrease. Determining its distributors' reactions to a price decrease would also be warranted, especially since the price decrease meant a reduction in dealer margins. Competitive reactions must also be considered. Will Monsanto and American Cyanamid decrease prices on their agricultural herbicides? One concern is that Lilly's price decrease might spark a price war.[9] Legal and regulatory factors must be considered. For example, companies must make sure they offer the same trade discounts to all buyers; otherwise they might be in violation of the Robinson-Patman Act, which forbids price discrimination.

Internal corporate factors must also be considered. Most important are costs. Given Treflan's costs of production, will the price decrease required to increase market share prove profitable? What effect will a price decrease have on other products in Lilly's line? Would a price decrease conflict with any corporate objectives such as maintaining a high-price, high-quality image?

The third step in setting prices is developing a pricing strategy for the brand. Clearly, Eli Lilly's strategy calls for a price reduction and anticipated response to competitive price moves. Such responses might involve maintaining the lower price, increasing advertising, offering greater discounts to retailers, or trying to outflank competition by offering additional herbicide brands at varying price and quality levels.

Once actions and anticipated reactions are established, a price level should be determined. The price might be based on a cost- or demand-oriented approach. If a demand-oriented method is used, consumer responses to price changes must be evaluated as input to price determination. Consumers can be asked to respond to proposed price changes — for example, determining farmers' responses to reductions of 5, 10, 15, and 20 percent in Treflan. Prices can also be tested in simulated store conditions or test markets. (Lilly decided on a 12 percent cut in Treflan prices.)[10]

Once the price has been set, the company must try to assess the effect of price on sales. Consumer responses to price should be evaluated by tracking sales and determining if consumers are changing purchasing patterns on the basis of price changes.

The last step in Figure 15-1 is controlling and adjusting pricing strategies. If sales goals are not being met, management might consider adjusting prices by rescinding price increases or decreases, or by changing prices further. Control over pricing actions also requires ensuring that pricing policies are implemented by the sales force and evaluating price-related strategies dealing with discounts and price promotions. Consumer reactions to price and the company's adjustments in pricing strategies will then affect pricing objectives and strategies in the next planning cycle (the feedback loop in Figure 15-1).

In the rest of this chapter we will consider each of the steps in the price determination process in Figure 15-1.

Establishing Pricing Objectives

Like other elements of the marketing mix, the first step in setting prices should be to establish objectives. Pricing objectives are particularly important since they are closely related to corporate goals. A company that sets a corporatewide goal of a 20 percent return on stockholders' equity is also transmitting a signal to its marketing managers that product pricing should contribute to this goal. A company that establishes a corporate strategy of market dominance is telling its marketing managers to price low enough to maintain high market shares.

COST- AND COMPETITION-ORIENTED OBJECTIVES

Cost-oriented pricing objectives rely on internal company criteria rather than external, market-driven criteria for pricing. The company establishes an objective of recouping costs and obtaining a predetermined target return on investment. Another cost-oriented objective is to maintain sufficient price margins to finance advertising and sales promotions. For example, Alberto-Culver used to subscribe to a strict one-price policy that allowed for high enough margins to finance heavy advertising expenditures. Both these objectives require cost as the basis for establishing price.

Price can also be established on the basis of competitive objectives. One objective might be to maintain the competitive status quo. Such an objective would be particularly suitable for a market leader. For example, at one time American Can's objective in pricing was to maintain its 55 percent share of the can market.[11] Another objective likely to be followed by a market leader is to price low enough to discourage competition. A third competition-oriented objective is to maintain price parity with leading competitors to avoid "rocking the boat." In each case, competitive objectives dictated pricing policy.

DEMAND-ORIENTED PRICING OBJECTIVES

In the early 1970s companies began to realize the limitations of cost- and competition-oriented objectives. Long-term profit maximization might not be achieved by rigid target returns, by duplicating competitors' actions, or by maintaining the status quo through price stabilization. Flexible pricing approaches required more demand-oriented objectives.

Demand-oriented objectives aim at setting prices on the basis of consumer responses. The firm's objective is to establish a demand curve for the brand (a price-quantity relationship) by investigating consumer responses to prices through market tests. In most cases the firm that establishes demand-oriented objectives recognizes differences in price sensitivities among various market segments. Profits can be maximized if companies introduce different brands to different segments with prices geared to the price sensitivities of each segment. Separate product lines can be established and prices set to meet the needs of each segment. A one-price, mass-market strategy would mean losing out on the profits to be made in appealing to higher and lower price segments.

Factors Influencing Pricing Decisions

Once the firm has established pricing objectives, it must evaluate the factors that affect its pricing decisions. There are two sets of pricing influences, environmental and corporate. The main environmental influence is the consumer. The consumer's awareness of alternative prices and sensitivity to price changes must be determined before prices can be established. Only then can the firm forecast the market's response to its pricing strategies.

CONSUMER INFLUENCES

The marketer should be aware of two components of consumer reactions to prices: consumer price perceptions and consumer responses to alternative price levels. Price perceptions relate to the way consumers see and interpret price; pricing responses relate to the consumer's actual behavior.

Price Perceptions
The marketer must determine the consumer's price awareness, price expectations, and any price-quality relationship the consumer may see for the product.

Price awareness
Generally the consumer's price awareness is low. But price awareness of inexpensive brands and of generics has been increasing as a result of greater price sensitivity. Price awareness among industrial buyers is greater because of the need to negotiate price and terms of sale.

Price expectations
Consumers develop expectations about a normal price level and a price range for a brand. They develop a **standard price** for many items — what they regard as fair. They also develop an **acceptable price range.** They will be reluctant to buy above this range because the product is not worth it, and they will be reluctant to buy below the lower limit because they fear something may be wrong with the product if it is priced too low.

The average standard price for the segment the marketer is aiming at becomes the baseline for setting a price level. If the marketer is introducing a prestige item, the upper limit of the acceptable price range is the highest possible price. If an economy brand is being introduced, or if the regular brand is going on sale, the lower end of the acceptable price range should be the lowest possible price.

The price-quality relationship

Another important strategic pricing question is whether consumers regard the price level as an indication of the product's quality. If so, reducing price may attract buyers in the short term, but may also lose customers who feel that product quality has been compromised.

The evidence suggests that consumers tend to use price as an indicator of quality when they lack product experience,[12] there is little basis for making direct product comparisons,[13] and they see the purchase as risky.[14] A consumer with adequate information for brand comparisons is unlikely to assume the highest-priced products provide the best quality.

Industrial buyers are unlikely to make price-quality assumptions. They are more likely than consumers to have adequate information to make direct product comparisons.[15]

The evidence suggests that marketers should be wary of assuming that a high price will necessarily convey product quality. Pricing above the competitive norm should be based on some product advantage.

Consumer Price Responses

If marketers are to set prices in a customer-oriented manner, they should be aware of the consumers' level of demand at various prices (the price-quality relationship) and their sensitivity to price changes (the consumer's price elasticity of demand).

Consumer demand

Consumer demand for a hypothetical brand is illustrated in Figure 15-2. Assume the brand is selling for two dollars. The company is considering two alternative strategies to counteract increased competition: reducing price or increasing advertising and sales promotion while maintaining the $2.00 price. In pursuing the first strategy, the company tests two price levels on consumers — $1.70 and $1.90. From these tests it estimates that a 5 percent reduction in price to $1.90 will result in a 3 percent increase in volume. But a 15 percent reduction in price to $1.70 will attract many more consumers, resulting in a 30 percent increase in volume to 13 million units. (See demand curve D_1D_2 in Figure 15-2.) At $2.00 the company's total revenue is $20 million. At $1.70 it is $22 million ($1.70 × 13 million units). The extra $2 million in revenue is partially offset by labor and material costs in producing additional output, but still yields a net profit.

The other strategy, increased advertising and sales promotion, results in an expansion in demand at the $2 price. Advertising and sales promotion budgets were increased in several markets. From these test areas, the company

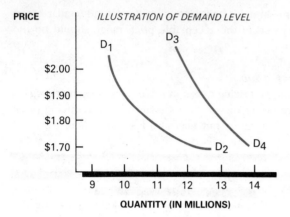

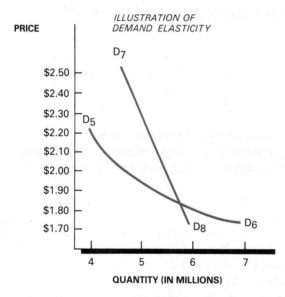

FIGURE 15-2
Illustration of demand level and demand elasticity

projects a 20 percent increase in demand to 12 million units. This means that the demand curve has shifted to the right to position D_3D_4 in Figure 15-2 because of the advertising effort, which yielded an additional $4 million in revenues ($2 price × 12 million in sales = $24 million total revenue, an increase of $4 million over the baseline revenue of $20 million). But the estimated additional cost of the new advertising and promotional campaign is 3.5 million and the additional costs of producing 1.2 million units are estimated at $600,000, meaning that the company stands to lose money if it attempts to increase demand by a nonprice strategy (advertising and sales promotion). Therefore, it opts to meet competition by reducing price to $1.70.

Price elasticity of demand

Price elasticity is measured by the percentage change in quantity resulting from a percentage change in price. It is represented as an index:

$$\text{Price elasticity} = \frac{\text{Percentage change in quantity}}{\text{Percentage change in price}}$$

When the percentage change in quantity is less than the percentage change in price, consumers are relatively price insensitive and demand is inelastic (e.g., if price increases by 10 percent and the resultant quantity decrease is only 3 percent, consumers are inelastic and the price elasticity index is less than one). When the percentage change in quantity is more than the percentage change in price, consumers are price elastic (price elasticity greater than one).

Marketers reduce their prices when they believe demand to be elastic because quantity will increase proportionately more than the decrease in price. As a result, total revenue rises. A price increase would be optimal when demand is inelastic, since the decrease in quanitity purchased is proportionately less than the increase in price. Such a situation would also result in an increase in total revenue.

Upside and downside elasticity

Consumers may have different elasticities for a price increase than for a decrease. A consumer may decrease consumption if price increases, but may not necessarily increase consumption when price decreases. When coffee prices increased sharply in the mid-1970s, many consumers switched to instant coffee or to tea. When prices began to decrease, some of these consumers continued to drink other products. These consumers demonstrated upside price elasticity (sensitivity to increases in price) and downside inelasticity (insensitivity to decreases in price). Conversely, when gasoline prices increased in the early 1970s, most consumers demonstrated upside price inelasticity by maintaining their rate of driving. The marketer's ideal situation would be upside inelasticity (no substantial change in consumption as prices go up) and downside elasticity (increased purchases as prices go down). Many consumers demonstrated these "ideal" characteristics when buying gas in the 1970s.

Marketers encourage upside price inelasticity through advertising by trying to convince consumers their product is the best on the market and is worth any price differential being charged. Brand loyalty is a reflection of upside inelasticity. Loyal consumers are willing to pay more for their favorite brand. But marketers must be wary of assuming demand inelasticity. Misreading the market by increasing prices could prove disastrous.

The automobile industry assumed that demand for compact cars was inelastic in the face of rising gasoline prices. In 1981 pricing strategy was based on a belief that "demand is relatively insensitive to price changes and that even a sharp increase in prices such as occurred over the past year (1980) will not depress sales much, if at all, and will result in a substantial increase in revenue."[16] But Detroit misread the public's price sensitivity as reflected by the popularity of cheaper Japanese imports. One analyst questioned Detroit's belief that demand is inelastic and concluded that it was wishful thinking based on "desperation since profits are down and cash flow is abominable."[17]

Figure 15-2 shows that demand is inelastic at $1.90, since volume increases by 3 percent when price decreases by 5 percent. Total revenue at this price decreases. But at $1.70 demand is elastic, since volume increases by 30 percent when price decreases by 15 percent. Total revenue therefore increases.

Elasticity by market segment

The demand curve D_1D_2 in Figure 15-2 assumes that the firm is marketing a brand to a segment with relatively homogeneous demand. But suppose the market segment identified by demand curve D_1D_2 can be split into two segments, one that is price sensitive and another that is more price insensitive. This is illustrated in the bottom of Figure 15-2. The market segment represented by demand curve D_5D_6 is much more price sensitive than that represented by D_7D_8. At $1.70 the price-elastic segment would buy 7 million units and the price-inelastic segment would buy 6 million units. But if the price were to go up to $2.50, the quantity purchased by the elastic segment would go from 7 million units to less than 4 million, whereas purchases for the inelastic segment would go from 6 million to 5 million units. Price went up almost 50 percent, but volume went down only about 15 percent for the inelastic segment. Thus, the firm can maximize profits by setting one price for the elastic segment and another for the inelastic segment.

OTHER ENVIRONMENTAL FACTORS INFLUENCING PRICE

Several other environmental factors affect pricing decisions: reactions of retailers and wholesalers, legal constraints, competition, and economic conditions.

Retailers and Wholesalers

Although the marketer is most concerned with consumer reaction to prices, few marketers sell directly to consumers. The immediate buyers are wholesalers (distributors) and in some cases retailers. Manufacturers must price with an eye to retailers' and wholesalers' reactions to the margins offered in the list price. Sometimes manufacturers do not have the leverage to convince wholesalers and retailers to stock a new product. Their only recourse might be to offer these intermediaries attractive margins. But in satisfying the retailer's desire for a high margin, the manufacturer may be cutting prices to the bone and reducing profits below corporate targets.

Another factor that is frequently overlooked by students of marketing is the manufacturer's inability to enforce a retail price. Some retailers might charge prices higher than that suggested by the manufacturer if they are located in out-of-the-way areas, if they have established a prestige image, or if they offer special services. Retailers may also price substantially below the manufacturer's suggested list. Some retailers use popular brands as loss leaders by pricing below cost to encourage consumers to enter the store and buy other items. Manufacturers dislike **loss-leader pricing** because it detracts from a brand's image and may create doubts about product quality.

Manufacturers have several options in attempting to control prices at the retail level. One is to avoid discounters and sell to retailers and wholesalers willing to conform to suggested list prices. Another is to franchise retailers to ensure uniformity in pricing policies and service. A third is indirectly to reward retailers and wholesalers who conform to suggested prices by giving them better service or quicker delivery. But if such rewards take the form of discounts or allowances, they may be violating the Robinson-Patman Act's prohibition against offering price discounts to some intermediaries and not to others.

Legal Influences

Two laws bear directly on marketers' pricing practices; the Sherman Antitrust Act and the Robinson-Patman Act.

Sherman Antitrust Act

The Sherman Act prohibits price fixing and the use of price to establish a monopoly position. In **horizontal price fixing** competitors agree on a price and maintain it. **Vertical price fixing** involves an agreement between manufacturers and retailers that the manufacturer's suggested price will be charged at the retail level. Vertical price fixing was considered to be in restraint of trade. But during the Great Depression, pressure came from manufacturers and retailers to permit vertical price fixing as a means of ensuring manufacturers' profits and retail margins. As a result, the *Miller Tydings Act* was passed in 1937 allowing vertical pricing fixing. States were permitted to pass fair trade acts (also known as resale price maintenance) that allowed manufacturers to enforce suggested list prices at the retail level. But many economists felt fair trade laws to be anticompetitive, and in 1976 Congress passed the *Consumer Goods Pricing Act,* which again made vertical price fixing illegal on a nationwide basis. The Carter administration vigorously prosecuted manufacturers who attempted to engage in vertical price fixing, whereas the Reagan administration has been less forceful in prosecuting cases of vertical price fixing.

The Sherman Act also prohibits predatory pricing to drive competition out of markets. A company that attempts to establish market dominance by pricing below cost may cause the failure of many of its competitors, and then raise prices once competition has decreased. The Federal Trade Commission brought action against General Foods for **predatory pricing** in 1976. It contended that GF priced its Maxwell House coffee too low in areas where it enjoyed a high market share, driving out existing competitors and deterring new competitors from entering the market.[18] General Foods countered with the claim that it was competing in good faith against Procter and Gamble's introduction of

Folgers coffee into the Eastern market. Whether the FTC's attempt to induce GF to increase coffee prices was in the consumer's best interest is open to question, especially since Maxwell House is not in a monopoly position.

Robinson-Patman Act

The Robinson-Patman Act of 1936 prohibits price discrimination. Specifically it says that a seller cannot charge different prices for the same products to competing buyers (e.g., retailers in the same trading area). The main exceptions are if (1) price differences have some cost justification such as differences in transportation costs or savings for quantity purchases, (2) the seller is meeting the low price of a competitor, or (3) the product has undergone some change such as perishability or obsolescence.

The Robinson-Patman Act is the law that is most likely to be violated by companies, in most cases unwittingly. Overzealous salespeople might offer discounts to one buyer but not to another, or executives may be pressured by large buyers to provide discounts beyond those justified, on the basis of economies of scale.

Competition

Marketers must consider competitive reactions when setting prices. In the next section we will consider various competitive strategies in response to a company's pricing actions. Competitors might meet or exceed a price decrease, might not follow a price increase, or might react through nonprice strategies such as increasing advertising or introducing new product lines. Competitive action and reaction is illustrated by Hattori and Timex in the watch market. Hattori has been very aggressive in introducing new, lower-priced lines. The watches are priced from $12.95 to $49.95. Partly in response to this price competition, Timex nearly doubled its advertising budget to $22 million in 1982.[19] As noted in Chapter 3, Gillette and Bic have been engaged in a competitive duel in the shaver and pen market for several years. Gillette countered Bic's entry into the razor market by introducing a line of low-priced pens to compete with the Bic pen. Gillette's pen was introduced at a price lower than Bic's. Bic "is fighting back. Rather than following Gillette's prices down in pens, it has quietly been marketing a new line of stick pen, called the Biro — a pen which looks very much like Gillette's pen."[20] In each of these cases, competitive reaction should have been anticipated in setting prices and developing product lines.

Economic Conditions

Economic conditions will directly affect pricing decisions. Inflation, recession, and shortages have a direct and sometimes contradictory effect on prices. In an inflationary period upward pricing pressures lead marketers to emphasize quality rather than price. In a recession price tends to be emphasized. The combination of inflation and recession in the late 1970s and early 1980s (known as stagflation) resulted in a profit squeeze and a pricing quandary for many manufacturers. One result was a shift from a cost to a profit orientation in establishing objectives and setting prices.

CORPORATE FACTORS INFLUENCING PRICE

Two corporate factors will influence pricing decisions — costs and policy constraints on pricing actions.

Costs

Marketers must determine costs to establish price levels. Costs are not always obvious. The firm may easily determine the costs of material and labor in producing a particular item. But how should overhead be allocated when a plant produces more than one product? Allocation of joint costs also affects price levels. Joint costs are a particular problem for firms that advertise and distribute many products under a corporate umbrella. A slight change in the method of allocating such costs could make a substantial difference in the price level if a cost-oriented pricing approach is used. (Cost factors will be considered further when we discuss methods of price determination.)

Policy Constraints

Corporate policy sometimes places constraints on the marketing manager's pricing actions. For example, top management might specify that a product should be introduced at a low price to penetrate the market. Such a strategy may be in the interest of long-term profit maximization but might violate the price a marketing manager would set on the basis of shorter-term profit criteria. Corporate management might also decide that a particular product should be "harvested" by continuing to charge a higher price rather than by following competition down in price. The purpose would be to reap short-term profits and then delete the product. A third example of corporate policy constraints deals with the brand's position in the product line. Management may decide to price a brand relative to other products in the line (known as price lining) rather than to establish an independent price. A price based on a product-line strategy may not be optimal for the brand, but it may benefit other brands in the line.

Pricing Strategies and Competitive Response

The third step in price determination (Figure 15-1) is developing an overall pricing strategy for the brand and anticipating competitive responses to the strategy. In many cases management's future reactions to the anticipated moves of competitors are more important than the initial pricing strategies. For example, Xerox provoked a price war in the copier market in the mid 1970s by slashing prices.[21] Xerox must have anticipated that its chief rivals would follow suit. But the question was whether Xerox would keep up the price pressure. It chose to do just that, thus ensuring the intensity of price competition in the industry through the early 1980s. Further, it extended competition to nonprice methods by trying to sign up as many office equipment dealers as possible to lock out competition.[22]

Pricing strategies can be simply classified into those which maintain the prevailing price, those which seek to undercut competition through price reductions or the introduction of economy-oriented brands, and those which seek to increase price for existing products or introduce higher-priced, quality products. These three strategies are illustrated in Figure 15-3.

Of more interest is the range of competitive pricing reactions to the marketer's initial price actions. Figure 15-3 shows four types of competitive reactions to pricing actions and the strategies that result.

In this section we will consider examples of these price strategies and the competitive reactions they have provoked. They are considered here because it is important for the price setter to anticipate possible competitive moves *before* arriving at a final price.

FIGURE 15-3
Pricing strategies and competitive responses

COMPETITIVE REACTIONS	PRICING ACTIONS		
	STABLE PRICES	PRICE REDUCTIONS	PRICE INCREASES
1. MAINTAIN CURRENT PRICES	No Change	Hold the Line	Hold the Line
2. FOLLOW COMPETITOR'S ACTIONS	• No Change • Follow the Leader	• Meet Price Decreases • Follow the Leader	• Meet Price Increases • Follow the Leader
3. CHALLENGE COMPETITOR'S ACTIONS • By Pricing Actions • By Nonprice Actions	• Increase or Decrease Prices • Increase Advertising and Sales Promotions • Introduce New Brands	• Exceed Price Cuts • Initiate Price War • Increase Advertising and Sales Promotions • Introduce New Brands	• Exceed Price Increases • Increase Advertising and Sales Promotions • Introduce New Brands
4. OUTFLANK COMPETITOR'S	Establish a Pricing Niche	Establish a Pricing Niche	Establish a Pricing Niche

STABLE PRICE STRATEGIES

Some large companies have tried to maintain stable prices in their industries to avoid price competition. These companies have assumed the role of price leaders and have encouraged competitors to follow their price changes. United States Steel, Alcoa, Owens-Illinois, and Dow Chemical have assumed price leadership in the steel, aluminum, glass container, and chemical industries as a means of achieving price stability. Although price leadership tends to produce price stability, there are significant variations from industry to industry. Historically, U.S. Steel has tried to hold prices steady in good times and bad and has changed prices reluctantly. Dow prices more aggressively. "Dow will not hesitate to slash prices when and where demand is slack and raise them as high as possible when and where demand is strong."[23] Therefore, a follow-the-leader strategy in chemicals means more frequent price changes.

Material shortages and foreign competition have inhibited stable pricing strategies. For example, steel prices are becoming much more flexible. Smaller steel companies are beginning to show price boldness by discounting prices of steel products without fear of retaliation from giants such as U.S. Steel. Traditional patterns of price leadership are also breaking down in the glass container industry. Owens-Illinois increased its list prices on containers by 4.5 percent in the late 1970s, expecting most companies to follow. But smaller companies did not follow. In fact they did the reverse by offering discounts. The president of one of Owens' competitors said, "The smaller companies became the price leaders."[24] In short, price stability is harder to maintain.

A strategy of price stability is not limited to oligopolies. In other industries companies sometimes maintain prices over time in the face of competitive price increases to gain a market advantage. Some candy bar manufacturers have maintained prices by reducing the size of their candy bars in small increments that are hard to notice. Hershey placed enough importance on a strategy of price stability in 1981 to advertise that it "was holding the line on candy bar prices." Similarly, McDonald's announced it would freeze prices for the first six months of 1982 in an attempt to emphasize the broadening price gap between its products and those of its leading competitors, Burger King and Wendy's.[25]

PRICE-REDUCTION STRATEGIES

Many industries have experienced downward price pressures as a result of (1) more intense foreign competition (e.g., steel, automobiles, aluminum), (2) inroads made by lower-priced private brands and generics (paper goods, pet foods, canned foods), and (3) greater price sensitivity on the part of the consumer (gasoline, appliances). As a result, many companies have checked the inflationary price increases of the 1970s and have begun to emphasize strategies of price decreases. For example, Arco lowered prices by abolishing credit cards for gasoline. As a result, most of the major refiners established a two-tier pricing system, offering discounts for cash purchases.

Some companies are following reduced-price strategies by producing for private brands and generics. Sherwin-Williams is selling its paints to K-mart, creating price pressures on other paint manufacturers.[26] Liggett and Myer's generic cigarettes now have 2.1 percent of the market.[27] When companies have sought a competitive advantage through price reductions or introduction of lower-priced brands, these actions provoked immediate competitive reactions. Competitors followed the four strategic reactions described in Figure 15-3.

Maintain Prices

When lower-priced Japanese watches began to be widely accepted, competitors were slow to respond. Bulova has maintained its prices, whereas Timex has responded by increasing advertising expenditures. Similarly, increased acceptance of Japanese compacts produced a sluggish response on the part of American auto manufacturers. In each case consumers demonstrated a level of price sensitivity that was exploited by foreign competitors.

Follow Price Decreases

Competitors will often meet price decreases but not challenge them by further reductions, because they want to avoid price wars. Initial price decreases by TWA in 1976 were met by American and United. Eventually price reductions became widespread. Yet the airlines' experiences have shown that it is increasingly difficult to avoid price wars in the face of competitive price decreases.

Challenge Price Decreases

In the 1980s the norm seems to be to challenge price decreases by either initiating price wars or by intensifying nonprice competition. When Arco reduced prices by eliminating credit cards, competitors quickly responded by discounting even further. One trade magazine believes that as a result, "the stage is set for a modern-day gas war, unlike any before."[28]

Other companies have responded to price decreases by intensifying nonprice competition. Seagram reduced the price of its Paul Masson wines to challenge Gallo's market leadership.[29] Gallo is reacting by expanding its product line and attempting to position some of its wines as premiums. Reducing its prices to challenge Seagram could harm its current attempts to build a quality image.

Outflank Competition

Another competitive response to downward price pressures is to try to outflank competition by finding a pricing niche in the marketplace that is not being exploited. *Business Week* cites Hewlett-Packard as "the best example of a successful 'market niche' strategy. . . . In the highly competitive pocket calculator market where price cutting is rampant, H-P has been able to thrive by offering high-priced products for a select segment of the market."[30] Whenever competition comes in and undercuts H-P's price, the company varies its product line and offers new models.

PRICE INCREASE STRATEGIES

Companies have also followed higher-price strategies by either increasing prices of existing brands or introducing quality brands aimed at a more value-oriented, price-inelastic segment. Many companies have increased price as a result of higher material and labor costs. Such across-the-board price increases cannot be regarded as strategic pricing actions, since they are industrywide responses to maintain target returns in the face of increasing costs. In some cases, companies have attempted to increase price as a strategic move in the expectation that competition will follow. If it does not, the company generally scales backs its prices. Thus, Miller attempted to increase its beer prices in 1980, but Anheuser-Busch's refusal to follow suit resulted in scaling prices back.[31]

Companies have also followed high-price strategies by introducing quality-oriented products. Although price consciousness is increasing, marketers have identified segments that are willing to pay more for products that are perceived as providing value. Stouffer's introduced Lean Cuisine to appeal to a value-conscious segment that is willing to pay for the convenience of low-calorie, single-serving foods. Price is not as important to working couples and singles because they emphasize time-saving convenience. Competitors have reacted by following Stouffer's lead. Swift is introducing International Entrees and Kraft is marketing À La Carte entrees.[32] Such strategies are successful only if the company has identified a relatively price-inelastic group that sees the value of the product.

ADDITIONAL STRATEGIC PRICING CONCERNS

Two strategic pricing areas are not adequately covered by the strategies described in Figure 15-3 — strategies for pricing new products and for pricing product lines.

New Product Pricing Strategies

Two types of pricing strategy for new products have been referred to previously — a skimming strategy and a penetration strategy.[33]

Skimming strategies

A skimming strategy works best if demand for the new product is inelastic. Polaroid could introduce its instant cameras and film at a high price because of the uniqueness of the product. Interested consumers were insensitive to the high price. Several other factors also encouraged Polaroid to follow a skimming strategy. First, it had a patent that protected it from competitive entry until 1975. Second, the product was a true innovation, warranting a higher price. Third, product acceptance was likely to be slow, precluding a mass-market approach. Fourth, the company could identify a price-inelastic segment that was likely to adopt the innovation. Over time the company had the option of reducing price to expand the market. It could develop a product line by maintaining expensive cameras positioned to the quality-oriented camera buff and less-expensive cameras for the less-serious picture taker.

In the absence of patent protection, price decreases can be rapid after an initial skimming strategy. When Texas Instruments introduced its 99/4A home computer in mid-1981, the suggested retail selling price was $525. By the summer of 1983 it was $100.[34] The home computer industry is moving from a skimming to a penetration strategy as a result of a rapid diffusion process for home and personal computers and intense competition.

Penetration strategies

A penetration strategy is most effective when demand is elastic, when there is no patent protection and competitive entry is easy, and when the market cannot be segmented by price. Coca-Cola could follow a penetration strategy in introducing Diet Coke because it met the above criteria. The product was priced competitively and was introduced nationwide with an intensive advertising campaign.

DuPont follows a penetration pricing policy for new products to build up a customer base over the long term. The objective is to obtain profits through volume rather than through higher margins. Even if a company has patent protection, it may prefer to forego initial profits to secure volume.[35] The reasoning is that a lower initial price will attract customers, increase the potential for brand loyalty, and enhance long-term profits. Prices can be increased later, once sufficient brand loyalty has been established.

Product-Line Pricing Strategies

Some firms develop pricing strategies within the context of a product line. R. J. Reynolds introduced a lower priced cigarette to compete with generics. In establishing a low-priced entry, it was following a policy of **price lining.** Price lining is introducing various brands in a product line at different price points. In following such a strategy the company is "covering the demand curve" by marketing products to appeal to the quality-conscious consumer, the average consumer, and the economy-minded consumer. Consumers with different elasticities can thus find the right product at the right price.

Price lining is an important decision for companies using product-line strategies. Heublein used price lining when its competitor, Wolfschmidt, lowered its price. Rather than follow suit, Heublein increased the price of Smirnoff and introduced a lower-priced brand, Relska, to compete with Wolfschmidt.[36]

Marketers following a price-lining strategy must carefully assess the effect of a new addition to the line on the other brands. The primary concern is the possible cannibalization of sales from other products in the line.

Methods of Price Determination

Figure 15-1 shows that once the general direction of price strategy has been established and competitive reactions assessed, the marketing manager is ready to establish a specific price level for the brand. Three approaches to price determination will be described: cost-oriented, competition-oriented, and demand-oriented methods. Methods based on cost and competitive pricing actions have a major drawback: they do not account for the consumer's reaction to the price level. However, they are the most widely used methods because they are simplest to apply and encourage price stability.

COST-ORIENTED PRICING METHODS

Two widely used cost-oriented methods of pricing will be considered — cost-plus and target-return pricing.

Cost-Plus Pricing

Cost-plus pricing simply requires determining costs and adding a fixed margin. For example, assume a firm estimates a markup of 30 percent will cover its profits and unallocated expenses in pricing a new detergent. Further, assume it allocates fixed costs at 10 percent of variable costs. Then the price for an item could be determined as in the following example:

Variable costs per unit	$2.00
Allocated fixed costs per unit (10% of variable costs)	.20
Average cost per unit	$2.20
Allowable margin (30% of average costs)	.66
Selling price	$2.86

Markup pricing is a variation of cost-plus pricing as applied to wholesale and retail prices. The only difference is that the margin is based on the final selling price rather than the total cost. Using the same figures as above for an item being priced in a retail store, the price would be:

$$\frac{\text{Average cost of the unit}}{1 - \text{the margin}} = \frac{\$2.20}{1 - .3} = \$3.14$$

At a price of $3.14, there would be a 94-cent margin over cost, which is 30 percent of the selling price.

Cost-plus pricing has several advantages. It is a simple method of determining prices. Further, it tends to encourage price stability since most competitors will arrive at similar prices. Yet price stability is by no means assured, especially if certain competitors are willing to price below cost to gain immediate market share. Also if prices are not fixed in advance, cost overruns may alienate the buyer and lose the company future sales.

Target-Return Pricing

In **target-return pricing,** the firm specifies a target return on total costs at a specific volume level and then determines the price that would produce the target return. A breakeven chart is required to determine the target return price as in Figure 15-4. Total revenue is a straight line from the zero point since it is price times quantity. Total cost is fixed plus variable costs and is a curve that rises sharply as production approaches capacity.

In this example assume the firm has a capacity of 1.5 million units. Further assume the firm's best estimate of sales for the coming year is one million units (meaning the firm would be operating at 67 percent of capacity), and that at this level the cost of production is $22 per unit. Total cost at one million units is $22.0 million. The firm's target return on costs is 20 percent, a rate above the estimated return the firm could make on alternative investments. Therefore, the target return is $4.4 million (20 percent of $22 million) and the total revenue required to achieve the target return at one million units is $26.4 million ($22.0 + $4.4 million). The price is simply the required revenue divided by the estimated quantity or $2.64.

Target-return pricing has the same advantages as cost-plus pricing; it is simple and encourages price stability. It also assures the firm of a fair return on investment. These advantages have led target-return pricing to be the most popular method in use. One analyst estimates that roughly half of the producers

FIGURE 15-4
Target-return pricing

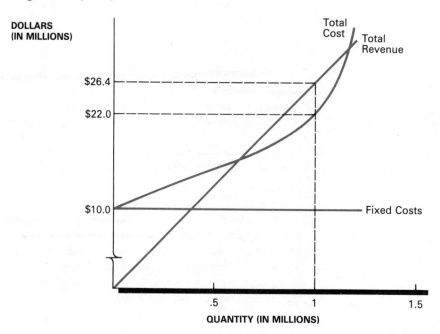

of industrial goods use target-return pricing. But the method has the same basic flaw that has limited the use of percentage-of-sales approaches in estimating advertising and selling expenditures — it is circular. Sales must first be estimated to determine price. Yet price plays a large part in determining the sales level. The total revenue curve in Figure 15-4 simply does not take account of consumers' price elasticities, since there is no assurance consumers will buy one million units at a price of $2.64.

Despite this limitation, target-return pricing is the method that price leaders generally use in establishing the market price. It is also the predominant method of pricing in the automobile industry, as illustrated by the typical costs used in pricing a 1982 compact in Figure 15-5. But currently the use of target return pricing seems to be decreasing. As noted, price leaders are becoming more reluctant to maintain stable prices in the face of new competitive pressures. The result seems to be a shift to more efficient demand-oriented pricing methods. In fact, one study concluded that companies are using target-return pricing more as a reference point for price levels than as a fixed means of setting prices.[37]

The shift from target-return pricing may cause problems for smaller competitors. Target-return methods generally produce higher prices and act as a price umbrella for small, sometimes inefficient companies. Now with the large

FIGURE 15-5
Target-return pricing for a 1982 compact

HOW A SMALL CAR'S PRICE GROWS FROM THE ASSEMBLY LINE TO THE SHOWROOM

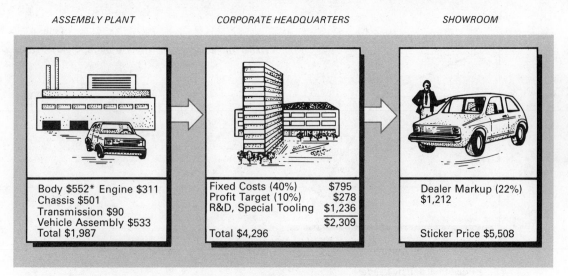

Source: "Why Detroit Can't Cut Prices," *Business Week,* March 1, 1982, p. 111. Reprinted from the March 1, 1982 issue of *Business Week* by special permission, © 1982 by McGraw-Hill, Inc.

companies unwilling to provide such an umbrella, some of the smaller companies may go under, increasing concentration in certain industries.

COMPETITION-ORIENTED PRICING METHODS

Companies frequently base their prices on what competitors do. Many of the strategies in Figure 15-3 are reactions to competitors' actions. Such reactive strategies are typical of companies that follow a price leader or those which simply go along with a general industry trend. Three types of competitor-oriented pricing methods will be described: a follow-the-leader approach, prices pegged to prevailing industry levels, and prices based on estimates of competitive actions.

Follow-the-Leader Pricing

Companies follow a price leader when they seek protection from price competition. Such protection is generally sought in oligopolistic industries producing relatively standardized products. Upside demand is elastic because an increase in price will result in lost business (no one will follow the price increase unless the increase is proposed by a price leader). Downside demand is inelastic because a decrease in price will be matched by most competitors, producing no net gain in volume. In the absence of a price leader, an oligopoly will therefore create downward price pressures and the possibility of destructive price wars. The solution is to maintain price stability through a follow-the-leader approach.

Upside elasticity and downside inelasticity produce a "kink" in the demand curve as demonstrated in Figure 15-6. The point at which the kink occurs is

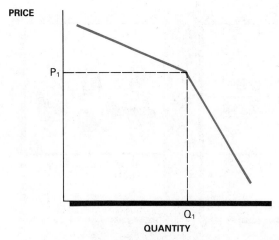

FIGURE 15-6
Typical kinked demand curve in oligopoly industries

P_1 = Price Charged by Leader
　　(i.e., Market Price)
Q_1 = Industry Demand at P_1

the market price established by the leader. If the price leader changes price, the point of the kink will move resulting in a change in the quantity demanded. Following the leader in pricing avoids the problem of having to assess how competitors might react if the company were to establish its own price. But it is essentially a reactive method of pricing that assumes that what is good for the price leader is good for other members of the industry. There is little opportunity to use pricing strategies to establish a competitive advantage. And there is no opportunity to adjust to changes in the environment such as greater foreign competition or a change in consumer demand, independent of the price leader.

Pegged Pricing

In some industries prices are based on competitive actions but without a price leader. Frequently companies will *peg* their prices to the prevailing industry price. Sometimes they will price a certain percentage above or below the industry price if they wish to establish a pricing niche or if they are differentiating themselves on the basis of quality on the high side or economy on the low side.

Prices Based on Estimated Competitive Actions

Firms can also set price levels based on their evaluation of competitive responses. Assume that a company such as Kodak is setting a price for a new product such as the disc camera. One of the key considerations is the likelihood of entry of other camera manufacturers such as Minolta or Canon. The lower the price set by Kodak, the less likely that other manufacturers will enter quickly to try to undercut Kodak's initial price. Now assume Kodak considers seven alternative prices from $40 to $100 as in Table 15-1. It determines its return

TABLE 15-1
Price Setting Based on Estimated Competitive Actions

PRICE	ESTIMATED RETURN ON INVESTMENT	PROBABILITY OF COMPETITORS NOT ENTERING MARKET			PROBABILITY OF NO COMPETITOR ENTERING (PROB. OF A × B × C)	EXPECTED ROI (PROBABILITY OF NO COMPETITIVE ENTRY × ACTUAL ROI)
		FIRM A	FIRM B	FIRM C		
$40	9%	100%	98%	100%	98%	9%
$50	17%	98%	95%	90%	84%	14%
$60	23%	95%	90%	85%	73%	17%
$70	29%	80%	50%	55%	22%	6%
$80	33%	40%	30%	25%	3%	1%
$90	38%	20%	10%	5%	0	0
$100	41%	5%	0%	0%	0	0

on investment (ROI) at each price and asks its managers to estimate the probability that any of the top three competitors will enter the market at that price. For example, at a price of $40 there would be a 98 percent chance that none of the three would enter the market in the first year, and at $50 there would be an 84 percent chance that no one will enter. Once the price reaches $70, there is a sharp drop in the likelihood of no competitive entry.

The probability that Kodak will have the market to itself times the ROI produces an expected ROI (last row in Table 15-1). The price with the highest expected ROI is $60. If the company had priced lower, there would have been an even lower chance of competitive entry in the first year, but at too high a cost in lost profits. The price of $60 thus maximizes the expected return on the basis of anticipated competitive reactions.

DEMAND-ORIENTED PRICING METHODS

The major flaw in cost- and competition-oriented pricing methods is that they do not assess consumer responses to the proposed price. There is no indication that consumers will buy enough at the suggested price to meet profit targets. Greater consumer price consciousness and the profit squeeze created by intense competition and frequent recessions have caused companies to pay more attention to demand-oriented pricing methods.

As Figure 15-1 shows, these methods require some measure of consumer response to varying price levels. Therefore, techniques of determining consumer price sensitivities will be considered before describing price-setting methods.

Estimating Consumer Responses to Price Levels

Marketers use two approaches in estimating consumer price sensitivities *before* the price is set: one based on consumer intentions, the other on actual behavior.

Measures of consumer intent rely on what the consumer says he or she will do at various price levels. For example, consumers might be asked their favorite brand of soft drink. If a consumer says Coke, he or she would be asked how much of a price decrease for Pepsi would induce a switch to that brand, how much of a price decrease for Royal Crown Cola would induce a switch, and so forth. If the perceived price differential for Coke is much higher among Coke users (price inelasticity is high) the company might have room to raise its price.

The problem with asking consumers to react to various price levels is that they do not always do what they say. One study found that gasoline purchasers said they would drive less frequently when gas prices first started going up in the early 1970s. But followup interviews found these consumers did not decrease consumption.[38] As a result, marketers have measured consumer pricing responses by offering actual products at alternative prices in test markets, simulated stores, or in sales wave experiments after product tests. These techniques were described in Chapter 9. They can be used to project sales at various price levels, permitting the firm to select an optimal price based on consumer responses.

Pricing Methods

Three methods of demand-oriented pricing will be considered: modified break-even analysis, marginal-revenue pricing, and segmented pricing. In each case, consumer responses must be determined at various price levels to establish the optimal price.

Modified break-even analysis

Price setting by modified break-even analysis is illustrated in Figure 15-7. The method is an extension of the break-even analysis required for target-return pricing in Figure 15-4. The difference is that the firm starts out by considering four alternative prices. (In target-return pricing, one price level is considered on the basis of the required ROI.) A total-revenue curve is drawn for each of the four prices in Figure 15-4. This is easily done since total revenue is simply price times quantity. The firm has conducted market tests to determine consumer demand for the product at each of the four prices. These demand levels are indicated by X's. Demand at \$2.00 is at Q_4, demand at \$2.50 is at

FIGURE 15-7
Pricing by modified break-even analysis

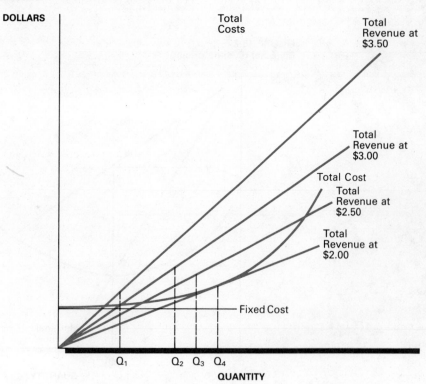

Q_3, etc. The difference between total revenue and total cost is greatest at the
$3.00 price level. At this price, the firm projects it will sell Q_2 based on its
market tests. The best price ($3.00) was therefore determined on the basis
of consumer responses to price levels obtained in prior market tests.

Marginal-revenue pricing

Marginal-revenue pricing sets prices based on the basic economic principle
that prices should be increased as long as marginal revenue from each additional
unit sold is greater than the marginal cost of producing and marketing that
unit. This is logical, because as long as there is a positive marginal contribution
to profit (marginal revenue is greater than marginal cost) from each additional
unit sold, the firm should increase prices. Conversely, prices should be decreased
as long as marginal cost is greater than marginal revenue. The profit-maximizing
price would therefore be at the point where marginal revenue equals marginal
cost and the marginal contribution of the last unit sold is zero.

Figure 15-8 illustrates the application of this marginal principle to price
setting. The marginal-revenue curve is derived from the average revenue curve
because it is the revenue gained from each additional unit sold (marginal
revenue is the slope of the average revenue curve). Average revenue is the
same as the demand curve. Why? Because the average revenue is the price

FIGURE 15-8
Marginal-revenue pricing

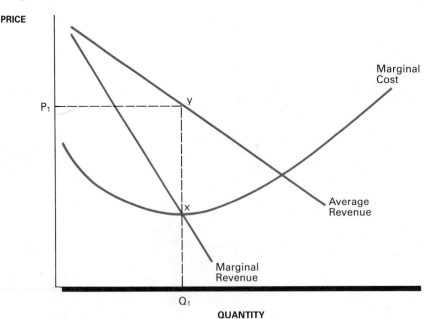

P_1 = Profit Maximizing Price

the firm obtains at each quantity level. The demand curve is exactly the same thing — the price the consumer is willing to pay at various quantity levels.

This means that in order to determine the marginal-revenue curve, the firm must first establish the demand curve (average-revenue curve) for the brand. To establish the demand curve, consumer responses must be determined at various price levels through market tests. This is why marginal-revenue pricing is a demand-oriented method.

The marginal-cost curve is relatively easy to establish. If the firm can determine the marginal-revenue curve, then the optimal price level can be identified. The optimal price level in Figure 15-8 is at p_1. This was established by first determining the intersection of the marginal cost and revenue curve (at point x) and then projecting that position up to the demand (average revenue) curve (at point y). The profit-maximizing price is at P_1 at which point the firm estimates that consumers will buy Q_1 units of the brand.

Marginal-revenue pricing is efficient because it establishes the profit-maximizing price. The problem is the difficulty in determining a demand curve for a brand. This would require estimating consumer responses at enough price points.

Segmented pricing

Marginal principles can also be applied to pricing across segments. Profit maximization would be achieved by increasing prices for inelastic segments and decreasing prices for elastic segments until marginal revenue equals marginal cost in each segment. This principle was illustrated in Figure 15-2 when the market for a brand was split into inelastic and elastic segments, and separate prices were determined for each segment. An alternative approach to segmented pricing would be to introduce separate brands to elastic (economy) and inelastic (quality) segments. Such a product-line strategy would require price lining; that is, setting prices differentially on the basis of the price elasticities of each segment. This would require setting prices in each segment by the demand-oriented approaches illustrated in Figure 15-7 or 15-8.

TACTICAL CONSIDERATIONS IN SETTING PRICES

The previous sections were concerned with pricing strategies and price levels. The marketer may also have to decide on more specific and shorter-term (tactical) issues dealing with price. The following can be considered tactical pricing issues:

- using odd/even and multiple prices,
- offering discounts, and
- using price as a promotional tool.

Odd/Even and Multiple Pricing

Odd/even pricing is used by manufacturers and retailers in the belief that consumers are more likely to buy if the price ends with an odd number just under a round number (e.g., a price of $2.99 instead of $3.00). **Multiple pricing** offers several items at one price (e.g., four for 79 cents instead of 20 cents each). These pricing policies are sometimes called *psychological pricing* because they rely on consumers' sensitivity to certain price points.

There is some evidence that both odd/even and multiple pricing affect consumer responses. One study found that the odd price level was seen as being lower by consumers than the even price only for certain product categories.[39] A study of multiple pricing found that the consumers are likely to buy in multiples as long as they recognize a clear saving. If the multiple price becomes too complicated, consumers will not buy.[40]

Discounts

Manufacturers frequently offer discounts to retailers and wholesalers as incentives to purchase. Three types of discount are frequently offered. One is a trade or functional discount given to intermediaries for services they perform, such as handling, storage, or transporting. A second type is a quantity discount. Such discounts encourage the buyer to purchase in bulk and allow marketers to better predict production and distribution costs. A third type of discount is offered when payments are made in a specified time, a typical offer being 2 percent off if payment is made within ten days. These discounts are sometimes used as adjuncts to aggressive pricing strategies. For example, Coke sharply increased volume discounts to retailers as a partial response to the Pepsi Challenge campaign.[41] Marketers must ensure that these discounts are offered to the trade on a uniform basis; otherwise they might violate the Robinson-Patman Act.

Manufacturers can also offer discounts directly to consumers. As noted, gas companies are offering discounts for using cash rather than credit cards.

Promotional Pricing

Marketers use sales promotion strategies as forms of price cutting. Coupons, premiums, sweepstakes, and cents-off deals are extensions of a firm's pricing strategies. (See Chapter 12.) Gasoline marketers have begun to use these techniques in the face of declining demand. For example, Sunoco gave out 4.5 million iced tea glasses and 11 million Gillette razors to its customers.[42] These promotional giveaways reflect the increased importance of pricing strategies as the result of a transformation from a seller's to a buyer's market in gasoline.

Determining Consumer Responses to Price

In a previous section we discussed the necessity of estimating consumer responses to price *before* the product is introduced. But consumer responses to price must also be determined *after* the product is on the market.

The firm will track sales after setting the price level for a new product or changing the price of an existing product, and try to determine the effect of price on sales. But the same difficulty arises as in attempts to evaluate advertising and selling effects — the marketer is never sure how much of a change in sales is due to a change in price. Environmental and marketing mix factors are likely to affect sales, thus obscuring the direct effect of price. One solution is to try to track consumer responses on the individual consumer level rather than the aggregate sales level. Consumer responses to price can be evaluated by analyzing panel data. Such data provide a record of day-to-day consumer purchases of specific items, prices paid, and the store from which the item was purchased. Changes in the quantity consumers purchase or switches to other brands can then be related to changes in price. Similarly, the effects on purchases of price promotions such as coupon offers, premiums and cents-off deals can be evaluated.

Another source of information on consumer responses to price is scanner data. By using the universal product code on packages, scanner data record the price paid. In many areas consumers shop in the same store and can be identified by store credit cards, thus permitting a link between the quantity they purchase and changes in price.

Controlling Prices

The final step in price determination in Figure 15-1 is controlling prices and changing price levels and strategies if necessary. The first step in control is to determine whether sales goals are being met, and if not, whether price is at fault. Consumer responses to price based on panel or scanner data will help determine whether price levels should be changed. Such data will help indicate whether the company misread the consumer demand curve and assumed more inelasticity than warranted in the case of a price rise, or more elasticity than warranted in the case of a price decrease. In each case, a misestimation of elasticity would adversely affect profits. Consumer panel data can also tell management whether it is losing customers to other brands because of too high a price, or possibly because of too low a price if a low price is associated with low quality.

Other market responses in addition to consumer reactions might serve as danger signals requiring adjustments in price levels and strategies. For example:

- the firm may not be offering retailers and wholesalers enough discounts or promotional allowances when compared with competitors;
- the price differential between products in a line (price lining) may not be related to the relative value of the items;
- price changes may be too frequent, or too many price options may be offered, causing confusion among buyers;

- lower price policies may be alienating loyal buyers by creating a low-quality image; or

- pricing information may not be conveyed accurately by salespeople.

Each of these circumstances requires corrective action by management.

Another requirement in the process of control is to ensure that pricing strategies are coordinated with other elements in the marketing mix. Price should be coordinated with:

1. advertising strategy to ensure that it is in line with the product value being communicated;

2. product development to ensure that it reflects product value; and

3. distribution policies since the manufacturer's price determines the retailer's margin (higher margins can be used to ensure that the product will be stocked and gain a favorable shelf position).

Industrial Pricing

The preceding discussion of pricing strategies and price determination focused primarily on consumer goods. Price is also a key component of the marketing mix for industrial goods.

IMPORTANCE OF PRICE IN INDUSTRIAL MARKETS

In many cases price is a more important determinant of sales for industrial than for consumer goods. Price assumes this importance for at least four reasons. First, industrial buyers are more likely to use cost criteria in evaluating alternative products and will assess price relative to product specifications to obtain the best value for the company's money. Second, prices set by different suppliers are likely to show much more variation because of differences in specifications and terms of sale. Therefore, price setting becomes a crucial determinant of sales. Third, negotiated prices are more likely in industrial sales. Negotiation frequently centers on price levels and discounts. A fourth factor that makes price important in industrial marketing is the frequent request for bids put out by buyers.

DIFFICULTY OF DETERMINING PRICE

Not only is price frequently more important in industrial than in consumer marketing, price determination is often a more difficult process. Industrial demand is derived demand; that is, it depends on the demand for products in other industries. When a manufacturer of food-processing machinery tries to estimate demand, such estimates are contingent on the sale of consumer processed foods. The sale of steel, aluminum, automobile accessories, and industrial generators is contingent on the level of demand at the next stage in the industrial process. Therefore, industrial marketers have more than one industry and one demand curve to worry about when they try to assess demand levels in fixing prices. The fact that derived demand tends to be more subject to cyclical swings than final demand does not make the pricing task any easier.

Another complicating factor is that the production process may be much longer for industrial than consumer goods. The development, sale, and installation of an air pollution control system for a large manufacturer may take several years. Costs, regulatory rulings, and specifications may change markedly during this time. An industrial company cannot lock itself into a fixed price for such complicated products. As a result, price level becomes a major concern over a prolonged period of time.

METHODS OF DETERMINING PRICE

The same price determination methods are used by both consumer and industrial companies — cost-plus, target-return, follow-the-leader, breakeven, and marginal-revenue pricing. But the emphasis placed on these methods differs. The volatility of industrial demand has made implementing demand-oriented pricing methods difficult. One study of industrial marketers in Canada found that few firms attempted to assess customer demand, and those which did were hampered by volatile demand and unpredictable competitive reactions.[43] It is not surprising that the study found most firms using cost- and competition-oriented methods of pricing. A factor that encourages the use of follow-the-leader pricing is the greater predominance of oligopolistic industries producing standardized products — for example aluminum, steel, copper, chemicals.

Although many methods of price determination are similar for industrial and consumer goods, three are particular to industrial marketers: (1) bid pricing, (2) unbundled pricing, and (3) delayed-quotation pricing.

Bid Pricing

Industrial buyers frequently send out requests for proposals (RFPs) that invite prospective sellers to bid on a set of specifications developed by the buyer. Buyers use a bidding system because they feel it will provide the most reasonable price and that the sellers invited to bid are reliable. The lowest bid usually gets the sale, but not always. One study found that the lowest bidder won out about 60 percent of the time. Two reasons were given for not buying from the lowest bidder: (1) the low bidder's product did not meet specifications, and (2) the low bidder's product was not interchangeable with company equipment.[44] Pricing practices also vary between companies. A study of several industrial companies found that in one the lowest bidder was awarded the sale 40 percent of the time, whereas in another the lowest bidder won out 90 percent of the time.[45]

The seller must balance the desire to win the contract with the desire to maintain profit targets in setting the price level. In so doing it must try to estimate the level of competitive bids. The same probability method described in Table 15-1 can be used here. The seller can estimate competitive bids and develop a probability estimate that the company will get the sale as follows:

Company's Bid	ROI	Probability of getting sale with this price	Expected ROI (actual ROI × probability)
$20,000	6%	.9	5.4%
$22,000	7%	.8	5.6%
$25,000	12%	.6	7.2%
$30,000	20%	.2	4.0%

Based on the estimated probability of getting the sale and the profit return at that price, the optimal price is $25,000, even though there is only a 60 percent chance of getting the contract at this price level. The company would prefer to accept a lower probability of getting the contract than increase that probability by lowering profit levels.

Unbundled Pricing

In **unbundled pricing,** some or all elements of the product-service mix are priced separately. Transportation costs, installation, maintenance, and the cost of training operating personnel are charged separately. Separate charges are required because these costs are high and vary significantly between buyers. For example, the cost of transportation can be significant for heavy industrial goods, and the seller cannot absorb the differences between shipping to a buyer close to the plant and one located thousands of miles away. As a result, transportation costs might be quoted FOB (freight on board) mill, meaning that the buyer is responsible for transportation costs from the mill. Or transportation might be charged from some intermediate point; for example, FOB Chicago means the buyer pays for transportation from Chicago, even though the plant is located elsewhere. There are many other bases for establishing transportation costs, reflecting the fact that transportation and other services are open to negotiation in unbundled pricing.

Delayed-Quotation Pricing

As noted, the long production lead times required for many industrial goods make it too risky for sellers to commit to a price at the start of the production process. As a result, they will delay quoting a price until delivery. In effect, this process passes the risk of cost overruns and faulty production schedules to the buyer. Some sellers are willing to negotiate their commitment to a fixed price in advance. One solution is to quote a wide price range and assure the buyer that the final price will be within this range. But frequently this is akin to having the seller quote the higher level in the price range in advance of production. Both delayed-quotation pricing and unbundled pricing are means used by industrial sellers to reduce the risk of price setting.

Summary

Price is an essential component of the marketing mix and has received increased attention because of the energy crisis and alternating periods of recession and inflation. The result has been more flexible pricing policies in the 1980s.

Given the importance of price, marketing management must engage in a rational process of price determination. Such a process requires:

- establishing pricing objectives,
- evaluating the environmental and corporate influence on price,
- establishing pricing strategies and forecasting competitive responses,
- determining a price level,
- evaluating consumer responses to price, and
- controlling pricing strategy.

In this chapter we considered each of these six steps.

Pricing objectives must be established on the basis of ROI, market share, and profit goals. Once such objectives are established, the marketing manager must evaluate the *factors influencing price.* These can be divided into environmental influences (the consumer, retailers and wholesalers, competition, legal requirements, the economic climate) and corporate influences (costs and corporate policy). The marketing manager must also develop an overall *pricing* strategy for the brand and anticipate competitive responses to this strategy. Various competitive responses to stable prices, price increases, and price decreases were considered. Specific pricing strategies for new products and for product lines were described.

The fourth step is determining a *price level* for a brand or product line. Three approaches to price determination were described: cost-oriented, competition-oriented, and demand-oriented methods. The two most widely used cost-oriented methods of pricing are cost-plus and target-return pricing. The most common methods of pricing based on competitive actions are following an industry price leader or pegging price at a certain percentage above or below prevailing industry prices. Pricing methods based on cost and competition have one major drawback; they do not account for consumer demand. Therefore, managers are paying more attention to demand-oriented pricing methods. Methods such as marginal revenue pricing and segmented pricing are potentially more profitable but are difficult to implement because they require determining consumer responses to price levels as a basis for price setting.

The final steps in the pricing process require *determining consumer responses* to price levels and *controlling pricing actions.* Consumer responses can be determined from panel and scanner data. Control over price is necessary because prices may have to be changed to adjust to consumer demand or to react to unforeseen contingencies such as customer confusion over price levels.

We concluded the chapter by considering pricing of industrial products. Pricing is generally a more important component of the marketing mix for industrial products. Pricing industrial goods may also be more difficult because of the greater cyclical swings in industrial demand and the fact that long production times create cost and other environmental uncertainties.

In the next two chapters, we will consider the last key component of the marketing mix — distribution.

Questions

1. Since the mid-1970s many industries have shifted from rigid to flexible pricing policies.

   □ Why?

   □ What price determination methods are most likely to be used under rigid and under flexible pricing policies?

2. Assume IBM is trying to determine a price for its Peanut portable computer, a smaller and less-expensive version of its regular PC. Using Figure 15-1, describe the steps that IBM might go through in developing a price for the Peanut.

3. A manufacturer of rugs and carpets prefers to price on the high side because, in the words of one executive, "Consumers maintain a strong price-quality association for consumer goods. Our price reflects a quality image. If we come out with a lower-priced line, this may alienate our best customers."

   □ Do you agree with this executive that consumers are likely to establish a price-quality association for rugs and carpets? Why or why not?

   □ What are the pros and cons of the high-price strategy described by the executive?

4. A company is considering two alternative strategies to combat competition. The first is to lower price; the second is to try to increase market share for the brand by increasing advertising expenditures. The first strategy depends on whether the company has correctly evaluated the consumer's price elasticity for its brand. The second depends on whether the company has correctly evaluated the demand for its brand.

   □ Explain this statement by referring to the demand curves in Figure 15-2.

   □ What are the pros and cons of each strategy?

5. Apply the concepts of upside and downside price elasticity to setting prices in an inflationary and a recessionary market. Can a marketer assume that if a consumer is elastic on the upside, the same consumer will be elastic on the downside? What are the dangers of such an assumption?

6. A basic principle in pricing is that if the price elasticities of two or more target segments differ, the marketer can better maximize profits by pricing separately to each segment rather than by charging one price across all segments.

   ☐ Explain.

   ☐ What principle is the marketer using in following a segmented pricing policy?

7. Under what circumstances is a company likely to follow a skimming strategy when introducing a new product? A penetration strategy? What are the risks of each strategy?

8. Why have competitors in oligopolistic industries gravitated to a follow-the-leader pricing approach? (Explain by using the concept of the kinked demand curve in Figure 15-6.)

9. Both target-return pricing (Figure 15-4) and modified break even analysis (Figure 15-7) use the total revenue and total cost curve as a basis for price determination.

   ☐ How do these methods differ?

   ☐ Why is one called cost-oriented and the other a demand-oriented approach?

10. Marginal revenue pricing requires the firm to estimate a demand curve.

    ☐ Explain why.

    ☐ What is the difficulty in estimating a demand curve?

11. A typical condition in bid pricing by industrial sellers is that the higher the price, the lower the probability of getting the contract. How can the industrial seller balance the desire to maximize profits with the desire to get the sales contract? Specifically, what method would you propose for achieving this balance?

12. Although pricing methods in industrial and consumer markets are similar, price determination is a riskier process for industrial than for consumer goods.

    ☐ Why?

    ☐ What methods do industrial sellers use to shift some of the price risks to the buyer?

Notes

1. Jon G. Udell, "How Important is Pricing in Competitive Strategy," *Journal of Marketing* 28 (January 1964): 44–48.

2. "Flexible Pricing," *Business Week,* December 12, 1977, p. 78.

3. Ibid., p. 81.

4. "Why Detroit Can't Cut Prices," *Business Week,* March 1, 1982, p. 111.

5. *Business Week,* December 12, 1977, p. 79.

6. Ibid.

7. Ibid., p. 80.

8. "Lilly Cuts Prices 12% on Major Herbicide to Lift Market Share," *The Wall Street Journal,* December 15, 1982, p. 10.

9. Ibid.

10. Ibid.

11. Robert F. Lanzillotti, "Pricing Objectives in Large Companies," *American Economic Review* 48 (December 1958): 921–40.

12. Kent B. Monroe, "The Influence of Price Differences and Brand Familiarity on Brand Preferences," *Journal of Consumer Research* 3 (June 1976): 42–49.

13. Douglas J. McConnell, "Effect of Pricing on Perception of Product Quality," *Journal of Applied Psychology* 52 (August 1968): 331–34.

14. V. K. Venkataraman, "The Price-Quality Relationship in an Experimental Setting," *Journal of Advertising Research* 21 (August 1981): 49–52.

15. Phillip D. White, "PM's and the Price-Perceived Quality Relationship," *Journal of Purchasing and Materials Management* 14 (Winter 1978): 9–12.

16. "Detroit's High-Price Strategy Could Backfire," *Business Week,* November 14, 1980, p. 109.

17. Ibid.

18. Victor E. Grimm, "Some Legal Pitfalls," In Earl L. Bailey, ed., *Pricing Practices and Strategies* (New York: The Conference Board, 1978), pp. 19–23.

19. "New 'Watchword' is Marketing," *Ad Forum,* August, 1982, pp. 12–14, 28.

20. "How Bic Lost the Edge to Gillette," *The New York Times,* April 11, 1982, p. F7.

21. "Xerox Touches Off a Price War," *Business Week,* November 3, 1975, p. 29.

22. "The Squeeze on Copier Dealers," *Business Week,* July 6, 1981, pp. 78–79.

23. *Business Week,* December 12, 1977, p. 84.

24. Ibid., p. 81.

25. "McDonald's to Freeze Prices," *Advertising Age,* November 9, 1981, pp. 1, 93.

26. "Caution Wet Paint," *Forbes,* December 8, 1980, pp. 89–90.

27. Shaun Assael, "No Frills Savings," *Daily News,* August 3, 1983, p. 3.

28. "Gas Marketers are Over a Barrel," *Ad Forum,* November 1982, pp. 12–18.

29. "Masson Moves to Boost its Share," *Advertising Age,* December 13, 1982, pp. 4, 56.

30. *Business Week,* December 12, 1977, p. 84.

31. "Beverages," *Forbes,* January 5, 1981, pp. 216–17.

32. "New Tastes Spark Food for Thought," *Advertising Age,* pp. M-16, M-18.

33. Joel Dean, *Managerial Economics* (Englewood Cliffs, N.J.: Prentice-Hall, 1951).

34. "Computer Firms Push Prices Down, Try to Improve Marketing Tactics," *The Wall Street Journal,* April 29, 1983, p. 35.

35. Robert J. Dolan and Abel P. Jeuland, "Experience Curves and Dynamic Demand Models: Implications for Optimal Pricing Strategies," *Journal of Marketing* 45 (Winter 1981): 60.

36. Philip Kotler, *Marketing Management* (Englewood Cliffs, N.J.: Prentice-Hall, 1980), p. 405.

37. "The Myths and Realities of Corporate Pricing," *Fortune,* April 1972, p. 88.

38. Robert E. Pitts, John F. Willenborg, and Daniel L. Sherrell, "Consumer Adaptation to Gasoline Price Increases," *Journal of Consumer Research* 8 (December 1981): 322–30.

39. M. Alpert, J. McGrath, and J. Alpert, "Magic Prices: An Extension," *Proceedings of the Western AIDS Conference,* March 1984.

40. "How Muliple-Unit Pricing Helps and Hurts," *Progressive Grocer,* June 1971, pp. 52–58.

41. "Coke's Big Marketing Blitz," *Business Week,* May 30, 1983, pp. 58–64.

42. "Oil Companies Hustling Again as Price of

Gasoline Declines," *The Wall Street Journal,* January 6, 1983, p. 19.

43. Isaiah A. Litvak, James A. Johnson, and Peter M. Banting, "Industrial Pricing — Art or Science," *The Business Quarterly* (Autumn 1967): 43.

44. J. Patrick Kelly and James W. Coaker, "The Importance of Price as a Choice Criterion for Industrial Purchasing Decisions," *Industrial Marketing Management* 5 (1976): 285.

45. J. Patrick Kelly and James W. Coaker, "Can We Generalize About Choice Criteria for Industrial Purchasing Decisions," in Kenneth L. Bernhardt, ed., *Proceedings of the American Marketing Association Educators' Conference,* Series 39 (1976), p. 332.

16

Distribution Management and Strategy

Distribution is an essential marketing function because it attempts to get the right set of products to the right market segments at the right place and at the right time. Its importance is reflected in the fact that distribution costs average from 10 percent to 25 percent of sales revenue.[1] Few manufacturers can carry out all the activities involved in distribution, although some do sell directly to the final customer. Most must use the services of intermediaries — retailers, wholesalers, agents, and brokers. These intermediaries are organized into a channel system that ensures a process of consumption. As a result marketing management must make key decisions regarding what types of intermediaries to use, how to motivate them to sell the company's products, how much money to spend on channel (trade) support, and what intensity of distribution to use to ensure product availability.

The importance of distribution decisions is reflected in the following examples:

- The successful introduction of personal and home computers was largely based on a change in the method of distribution. Computer manufacturers such as IBM, Xerox, Control Data, and Digital Equipment had to discard the direct sales approach used in selling high-cost computers to larger companies. They developed their own computer retail stores to facilitate selling to smaller customers.[2]

- The rapid growth of Perrier in the United States "from an obscure product sold only in gourmet shops into a major beverage that competes with U.S. soft drink giants ... was based heavily on a strategic channel management plan that enabled Perrier to get its products into thousands of U.S. supermarkets."[3]

■ 7-Up's success in introducing Like, its caffeine-free cola, also depended on distribution. The company had to line up bottlers that distribute to retail stores. The problem: existing bottlers are constrained by franchise contracts with Coke, Pepsi, and RC Cola to handle only one cola brand.[4]

In this chapter we will view distribution from the standpoint of the manufacturer; in the next we will consider distribution from the perspectives of the retailer and wholesaler. First we will describe the channel of distribution as a system, consider types of channel systems, and show how they operate. Then we will describe the management of the distribution system as a process of (1) selecting channels of distribution, (2) managing the intermediaries that make up the system, and (3) implementing the physical distribution process required to move the goods through the channel system. A central element in this process is the development of channel strategies that define the scope of the distribution effort and use distribution to maintain a competitive advantage.

The Distribution Channel System

Channels of distribution are interdependent businesses that perform the functions necessary to move products from producer to consumer. The manufacturers, wholesalers, retailers, and sales agents that might comprise such a channel represent a system because they work together to buy, sell, deliver, store, and assemble the products customers desire. Producers usually manage distribution channels since they have the responsibility of ensuring that the product is distributed to the consumer. But sometimes large retailers such as Sears or wholesalers such as Foremost-McKesson operate as the channel leaders because they can exert control over producers.

In this section we will consider the types of distribution channel typically used, the functions they perform, and the consequent cooperation and conflict between channel members.

TYPES OF CHANNEL SYSTEM

As we have noted, channel systems are made up of the manufacturer, intermediaries, and customers. These can be linked in different forms of channel arrangements as shown in Figure 16-1.

Types of Intermediaries

The four boxes in Figure 16-1 represent the four types of institutions in the distribution system: manufacturers, retailers, wholesalers, and agents and brokers.

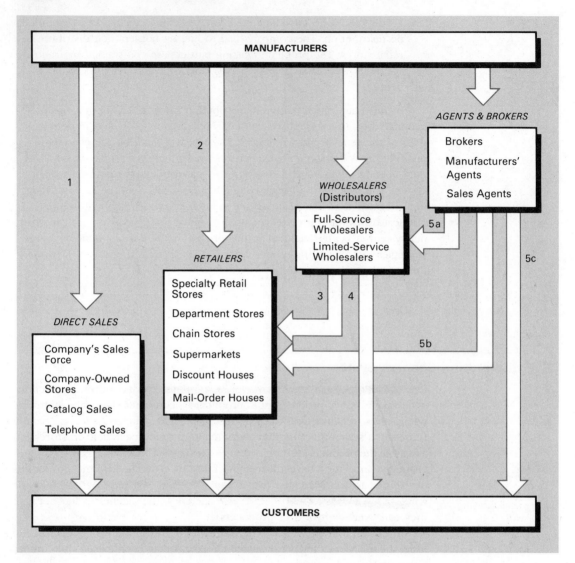

FIGURE 16-1
The marketing distribution system

The first box is not actually an intermediary, since it represents means of distribution directly owned by the *manufacturer.* These include personal selling efforts by the company's own sales force, company-owned retail outlets such as the computer retail stores owned by Xerox and Control Data, catalog sales through the mails, and telephone orders made directly to the manufacturer.

The second box represents *retail institutions.* Specialty retail stores are those which deal in a particular product line. They include diverse outlets such as automobile dealers, clothing stores, and computer stores. Retail institutions also carry diverse items; examples are department stores, discount houses, and chain stores, as well as supermarkets and smaller food stores. **Retailers** are distinct from other intermediaries in that they sell directly to the final consumer. As such they are used by consumer goods, not industrial companies. Retail sales totaled $957 billion in 1980 and are over one trillion dollars today.

Wholesalers (the third box in Figure 16-1) represent institutions that buy and resell merchandise to other businesses. Wholesalers can sell to other wholesalers, to retailers, or to industrial buyers. In other words, they sell to anyone except the final consumer. Wholesalers are often called distributors or jobbers, but these terms are used more frequently for wholesale outlets in industrial channels. Wholesalers are of two general types: full service and limited service. **Full-service wholesalers** perform all the distribution functions required of an intermediary: selling, extending credit, storage, delivery, and even advice to buyers on shelf displays, inventory control, and accounting procedures. **Limited-service wholesalers** offer buyers savings by cutting out some of these services. For example, cash-and-carry wholesalers require customers to come to them and pay cash for goods.

The fourth category of intermediary in Figure 16-1 is *agents and brokers.* They do not take title to the goods but facilitate distribution by bringing buyer and seller together. Agents differ from brokers by serving as an extension of the manufacturer's sales effort. They specialize in certain lines of trade and offer this expertise to manufacturers on a commission basis. Figure 16-1 lists two types, **manufacturers' agents** and **sales agents.** Manufacturers' agents sell a company's product offering in a specific geographic area, often on an exclusive basis. They carry product lines of several noncompeting manufacturers and restrict their activities to selling to wholesalers, retailers, and industrial buyers. Manufacturers' agents are used most frequently by producers of industrial machinery and equipment, automotive accessories, clothing, and food products as extensions of the company's sales organization.

Sales agents have fuller authority to set prices and terms of sale. Sometimes they even assume the manufacturers' total marketing effort by specifying promotion and distribution activities for the product line. Sales agents are used by producers of industrial goods and are rarely found in consumer goods industries. **Brokers** differ from agents in having no continuous relationship with one seller. They inform sellers of possible buyers and negotiate deals directly with buyers on a commission basis. They are used most frequently where producers are not continuously trying to sell their product or services and a permanent sales staff is unnecessary; for example, financial securities, real estate, insurance, and seasonal food items.

Alternative Channels of Distribution
Manufacturers can form various channel systems to distribute their goods. Five of the most common are represented in Figure 16-1.

Manufacturer direct to customer (1)

As we saw in Chapter 14, the cost and complexity of many industrial goods requires direct contact between buyer and seller. Frequently, intermediaries are not necessary because there are too few buyers in the industry. Also, many industrial marketers have mixed distribution systems, selling to large customers through their own sales force and to smaller customers through distributors.

Direct distribution is less frequent for consumer goods. Some companies have sought to control distribution at the retail level by financing their own stores. Sherwin Williams has relied on company-owned stores for retail distribution of its paints. The automobile companies own many of the dealerships in large metropolitan areas because it is costly for independent retailers to finance operations there. Direct ownership is also a way for automobile companies to control prices and inventories in these large selling areas.

Other forms of direct selling are also used by consumer goods companies. Avon built its reputation through door-to-door selling. Some products such as stereo components, seeds, and artist's materials can be purchased directly from manufacturers' catalogs. Direct distribution of consumer goods may become more prevalent because of the potential for in-home telephone ordering through interactive cable TV systems.

Manufacturer-retailer-customer (2)

Many large manufacturers of consumer goods sell directly to large retailers. Such a channel system is efficient because economies of scale can be achieved between buyer and seller. Companies like Procter and Gamble and General Foods have large sales staffs that can sell directly to food chains and supermarkets. Their sales personnel not only sell directly, they also ensure that the company's brands are in a favorable shelf position and that in-store displays for the brand are visible.

Large appliance, clothing, and furniture manufacturers sell directly to department store chains such as Bloomingdale's and Lord & Taylor, and to high volume discount houses. Manufacturers also sell directly to mail order operations such as Sears-Roebuck or Montgomery Ward.

Manufacturer-wholesaler-retailer-customer (3)

The third channel system in Figure 16-1 uses wholesalers to reach retailers. Manufacturers sell to wholesalers either because they are too small to sell directly to retailers, or because the retailers are too small to make direct sales economical. Rather than selling to thousands of small retailers, it is much more economical to sell to a handful of wholesalers who stock a broad number of items from various companies. These wholesalers can sell to retailers more efficiently because they offer a single retailer the variety that cannot be provided by a single manufacturer. Most of the large consumer goods manufacturers that sell directly to retailers also use wholesalers to achieve more complete distribution.

But wholesalers are not always economical. Manufacturers have stopped using wholesalers at one time or another in the drug, food, petroleum, electrical products, and farm equipment industries. In each case, manufacturers or retailers assumed the wholesale function because it was either more economical or because wholesalers were not providing adequate service. In foods, large retailers and buying cooperatives could achieve economies by buying direct from manufacturers. In the television and electrical products industries, manufacturers assumed the wholesale function because the technical services offered by independent distributors were insufficient.[5]

Manufacturer-wholesaler-customer (4)

Manufacturers of industrial products frequently rely on wholesalers (**distributors**) to sell directly to customers. For companies with small sales staffs, distributors can act as extensions of their own sales organizations. Airwick's institutional division, American Biltrite's industrial rubber division, and Amweld Building Products have expanded the use of distributors. In each case, these companies have attempted to strengthen their network of independent distributors through managerial assistance, training, and promotional sales aids. Similarly, companies such as 3M, Pfizer, Norton Simon, IBM, and Xerox use distributors to sell directly to industrial customers because of the high cost of personal sales calls.[6]

Using distributors to sell to industrial buyers is risky because the manufacturer does not have direct control over sales. Product specifications, warranties, and installation and maintenance may be better negotiated between a company sales representative and the buyer. Use of independent distributors is most likely to be effective when:[7]

- there are many buyers having standardized requirements,
- the item is easily stocked,
- quantity of sales is small (in such cases, distributors can assemble small orders from many different buyers into larger ones), and
- products can be bought on a routinized basis.

Use of agents and brokers (5)

The fifth channel system in Figure 16-1 involves the use of agents or brokers. These intermediaries can sell to wholesalers (system 5a), to retailers (5b), or direct to customers (5c). Agents are most frequently used by industrial-goods producers that are too small to support a full sales staff, or by larger firms that cannot effectively reach smaller and more geographically dispersed industrial buyers.

Agents are occasionally used by consumer goods firms as well. The Cumberland Packing Company, producers of Sweet 'n Low, uses a network of sales agents nationwide. In 1965 the brand was a lackluster sugar substitute with sales of under $3 million. The company hired a sales consultant who devised a distribution system made up of sales agents. Largely as a result, sales increased to $36 million by 1978.[8]

Multiple Channel Systems

Figure 16-1 may give the impression that a company selects one channel system to distribute its goods. Actually, most companies use more than one system. A multiple system frequently used by larger manufacturers is to sell direct to large retailers or industrial buyers and to use wholesalers to sell to smaller accounts. IBM sells its lower-priced office and computer products through independent distributors, mail orders, and company-owned retail stores, and relies on its own sales staff to sell higher-priced products.[9]

Vertically Integrated Channel Systems

The channel systems in Figure 16-1 are **vertical systems** because institutions at different levels combine to distribute goods. A horizontal system is one in which companies at the same level cooperate in the distribution process — for example, a retail buying cooperative.

Although channel systems are vertical, they are not always integrated. Integration requires the management of the distribution system so that common objectives (e.g., adequate inventory, quick delivery) are attained and conflicting objectives (e.g., level of discounts, use of company's promotional aids) are resolved. There are three ways to achieve integrated operations: by direct corporate ownership of different levels in the channel, by administration of independent intermediaries, and by contracts with independent intermediaries.

Corporate-owned systems

The most direct way to control the channel system is to own it outright. As noted in Figure 16-1, some companies own their own retail stores. Manufacturers might also acquire distributors. These are examples of forward vertical integration. Forward vertical integration occurs because manufacturers (1) want to assure themselves of outlets, (2) can better control the way their products are handled at the wholesale or retail level, or (3) determine that they can perform wholesale and retail functions more cheaply. Backward integration occurs when retailers such as Sears, J. C. Penney, and A&P acquire wholesale or manufacturing facilities. Large wholesalers can also acquire manufacturing facilities. Both retailers and wholesalers acquire these facilities to reduce the costs of goods purchased, thus increasing traditionally tight operating margins.

Administered systems

In an administered channel system, one or more members of the system attempt to coordinate distribution functions. The role of coordinator or channel leader is generally assumed by the most powerful member of the channel. Integration occurs when channel members cooperate in achieving goals that sometimes conflict. Without cooperation, inefficiencies occur — delayed deliveries, inefficient administration of warranty claims, ineffective use of a manufacturer's promotional aids, use of ineffective selling techniques, and so forth.

Alfred Sloan, Jr., president of General Motors in the 1920s, developed a distributive strategy making GM the channel leader. He attempted to lay the groundwork for a cooperative administered system with GM's network of dealers. He felt GM should assist dealers in every way possible — financial, managerial, and promotional. Yet the level of cooperation proposed by Sloan was not always implemented. In the past automobile manufacturers have sometimes been heavy-handed in their contacts with dealers, forcing excess inventory on them in economic downturns.[10] Other dealer grievances such as inadequate availability of parts, lack of acceptance by manufacturers of dealer warranty claims, and control by manufacturers of promotional allowances demonstrate that the automobile channel system was not always truly integrated and that manufacturers did not always fulfill their role as channel leaders.[11]

Contractual systems

Another method of integrating distributive functions is through contractual arrangements. There are three types of contractual systems: retailer-sponsored cooperatives, wholesaler-sponsored voluntary chains, and franchise systems. **Retailer-sponsored cooperatives** came into being because smaller retailers wanted to protect themselves against larger chains. They did so by acquiring and operating wholesale facilities. This permitted them to obtain quantity discounts available to the chains. **Wholesaler-sponsored voluntary chains** are groups of retailers organized by a wholesaler into a chain operation. The wholesaler can provide goods and services more economically to this voluntary chain than if it had to deal with each retailer separately.

Franchise systems are one of the fastest growing forms of distribution. A parent company (usually a manufacturer) grants a wholesaler or retailer the right to sell the company's products and to be the exclusive representative in a certain area. Manufacturers grant franchises to retailers in the automobile, petroleum, appliance, and fast-food industries. Such franchised establishments account for about one-third of all retail sales. Many industrial manufacturers also provide exclusive franchises to distributors to strengthen direct sales to industrial buyers. In consumer goods, soft-drink manufacturers offer exclusive franchises to wholesalers that bottle and distribute their products.

INTERMEDIARIES' FUNCTIONS

With the exception of direct sales, the channel systems in Figure 16-1 employ intermediaries between producer and consumer. These intermediaries are used because they perform distributive functions more efficiently than manufacturers. Their efficiency lies in their ability to make goods widely available to target markets. This ability is illustrated in Figure 16-2. Assume four different manufacturers sell directly to four consumers. Sixteen transactions are required.

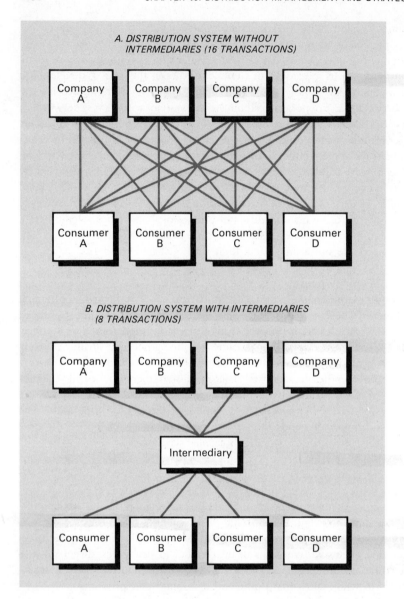

FIGURE 16-2
Reduction of transactions with an intermediary

The introduction of one intermediary reduces the number of transactions to eight. The intermediary thus assembles large quantities of goods from many sources, builds up an assortment of brands, and then offers this assortment to buyers in smaller quantities. In so doing the intermediary creates time, place, and possession utility, since the products are available when consumers want them, where they want them, and with the facility for taking possession of them in the right quantities.

TABLE 16-1
Marketing Functions Performed by Intermediaries

I *Transactional*

    Selling: Promoting a product to potential customers

    Buying: Purchasing products from various sellers usually for resale

    Risk Taking: Absorbing business risks, especially risks of maintaining inventories, product obsolescence, etc.

II *Logistical*

    Assorting: Providing an assortment of items for potential customers
    Storing: Protecting a product and maintaining inventories to offer better customer service

    Sorting: Buying a quantity of items and breaking bulk items into desired amounts

    Transporting: Physically carrying products from manufacturer to end user

III *Facilitating*

    Financing: Offering credit to customers to facilitate a transaction; providing funds to sellers to help finance their activities

    Grading: Judging and labeling products as to quality

    Obtaining market information: Obtaining information needed by manufacturers about market conditions (e.g., demand, fashions, prices)

Source: Adapted from Frederick E. Webster, Jr., *Marketing for Managers* (New York: Harper & Row, 1974), p. 192; and Thomas G. Kinnear and Kenneth L. Bernhardt, *Principles of Marketing*. Copyright © 1983 by Scott, Foresman and Company. Reprinted by permission.

In creating time, place, and possession utilities, intermediaries must perform various functions: buying, selling, transporting, storing. These functions are divided in Table 16-1 into transactional, logistical, and facilitating functions. They are carried out by intermediaries as long as they can be performed at a cost savings to the manufacturer. When they cannot, the manufacturer will consider bypassing the intermediary and assuming these functions. A manufacturer can eliminate an intermediary from a channel system, but not the distribution functions it performs.

COOPERATION AND CONFLICT

Manufacturers and their intermediaries depend on each other to distribute products. Procter and Gamble needs wholesalers to reach small retailers, and it needs thousands of retail outlets to reach the final consumer. Conversely, most store managers would regard their assortment of food and household products incomplete without P&G brands. Similarly, General Motors, the largest manufacturing entity in the United States, needs its network of close to 20,000 dealers to distribute its cars. It would be economically infeasible to distribute cars directly through company-owned stores on a nationwide basis. And GM dealers cannot do business without the company's cooperation in providing a sufficient inventory of cars and the necessary financing to buy them.

This interdependence links manufacturers and intermediaries into a channel system that requires cooperation. But as in any social system — families, peer groups, political parties, nations — cooperation goes hand-in-hand with conflict. Cooperation is necessary to perform the basic distributive functions in Table 16-1. Conflict results because of differing economic objectives and methods of operation between manufacturers and intermediaries.

Cooperation

Any channel system requires cooperation between its members in establishing terms of sale, maintaining storage facilities, ensuring adequate inventory, ensuring delivery, and informing other channel members about market trends.

Cooperation frequently goes beyond the necessary functions in Table 16-1. The concept of a channel leader or captain implies that the most powerful member of the channel system will view distribution strategy as an attempt to optimize profits of the total channel rather than to optimize profits of one member. Industrial manufacturers that rely on distributors (e.g., Amweld, American Biltrite) recognize the commonality of interest with their distributors by providing them with:

- training in sales techniques,
- cooperative advertising,
- promotional sales aids,
- programs to manage time and territories,
- programs for inventory control,
- accounting systems, and
- technical information.

Cooperation also occurs in consumer goods channels. Automobile manufacturers are no longer as heavy-handed with their dealers as they were in the 1950s and 1960s. Today they provide managerial training in store operations and more liberal financing of inventory.

Conflict

Conflict occurs between members of a distribution system because of (1) the national product-oriented perspective of manufacturers versus the local store-oriented perspective of their intermediaries, (2) differing economic objectives, and (3) differing views of who should perform distributive functions.

National product versus local store perspective

Manufacturers are interested in selling their products on a nationwide basis. They spend millions in advertising and have a vested interest in ensuring that the brand is visible in the store and that promotional displays and advertising allowances are used by retailers. Manufacturers also want to ensure that store personnel correctly represent the quality, features, and price of the product and that store operations reinforce the product's image.

Retailers and wholesalers frequently sell many items besides the manufacturer's line. They are interested in presenting their total assortment of goods. Further, they are concerned with local competitive conditions that affect store sales, not with national market conditions that affect product sales.

As a result of these differences, manufacturers frequently try to exert some control over store operations. They may pressure retailers to stock their items, to put their products in a prominent place in the store, and to use promotional displays and allowances. Just as frequently retailers resist such moves as intrusions on their independence. The more powerful the manufacturer, the more likely it is to pressure intermediaries. For example, consider the following description of Procter and Gamble's relationships with its intermediaries:

> Aware of its strength, the company can force retailers to stock its Tide, Crest, Pampers, Crisco and other brands. "When they [P&G] enter a market with an item, you've got to carry it," declares an executive at a leading wholesaler. As a result, the trade charges that P&G is rigid and arrogant in its policies and ignores legitimate grievances.[12]

The grievances most often raised by retailers are P&G's intense scrutiny of store performance, and inadequate trade allowances.

Similarly, Coca-Cola has the power over bottlers and retailers in its distributive network and has used it to force bottlers to use national promotions on the local level. As one bottler in Rochester, New York, said, "In wintertime we were forced to buy water skiing TV commercials even if we were sitting in the middle of a blizzard."[13]

Recently both Coca-Cola and P&G have attempted to resolve these conflicts by loosening the strings on their intermediaries. They have given retailers more flexibility in determining local promotions. P&G is also providing more liberal trade allowances and discounts.[14]

Differing economic objectives

Another reason for conflict in the channel system is differences in the economic objectives of manufacturers and their intermediaries. Manufacturers desire stabilized production rates at levels that are high enough to cover fixed costs. Yet many of these manfacturers operate in industries with unstable demand. The desire for stabilized production in the face of unstable demand means periods of overproduction and inventory buildups. The question is: At what point in the channel will excess inventory be absorbed?

Retailers and wholesalers would argue that the manufacturer should take the risk of cyclical demand since the manufacturer gets the most profits in the distribution system. Why should intermediaries bear the brunt of poor demand estimates and overproduction? Manufacturers would argue that intermediaries are part of the channel system and should bear part of the risk of inventory buildups. In past years these differences in economic objectives have led manufacturers to force excess inventory on automobile dealers, service station operators, and TV distributors. If dealers refused inventory, manufacturers could threaten to stop all deliveries. Electrical distributors and food retailers had also been subject to pressures to take inventory.[15] But such pressures were ineffective because electrical and food intermediaries have such broad lines that they could refuse to take the inventory of a single manufacturer.

Many of these practices have ceased in recent years. But not entirely. Japanese manufacturers of motorcycles misjudged demand in the United States in 1982. The result was 1.5 million leftover motorcycles. The companies began putting pressure on their 6000 dealers to absorb the excess inventory. One dealer described "horrendous pressure" from the manufacturers. Another dealer said "I was told to order 700 bikes or they would find a dealer who could."[16] As a result dealers had to cut prices substantially in 1983. In effect manufacturers shifted a substantial amount of the risks of production onto their dealer network.

Performance of distributive functions

A third major reason for conflict in channel systems is different views over who should perform distributive functions. One member of the channel may take on the functions of another when it becomes economical to do so. The intermediary being bypassed will of course try to protect its position in the channel. Manufacturers have bypassed wholesalers in the television and electrical products industries by establishing company-owned wholesale outlets. In the food industry the large retail chains and buying cooperatives have assumed the wholesale function.[17]

Manufacturers have also bypassed wholesalers and retailers in specific areas. As noted, automobile manufacturers own dealerships in large metropolitan areas. Further, they bypass their independent dealers by selling directly to major leasing and rental companies such as Hertz.[18]

Conflict resolution

An effective channel leader will take the initiative in resolving conflicts. In most cases this responsibility will fall on the manufacturer, but sometimes large retailers will seek to resolve conflicts with their suppliers. The following methods of conflict resolution have been used in several industries:

- *Redefine channel responsibilities.* After a period of conflict with its dealers in the mid-1950s General Motors redefined their responsibilities. Dealers were allowed to administer cooperative advertising programs, were given greater independence in administering warranty claims, and were given greater latitude in ordering new cars, parts, and accessories.[19]
- *Reallocate channel resources.* One way to resolve conflict is to give intermediaries more of the economic resources in the channel. This is

what P&G did when it gave its retailers more liberal trade allowances and discounts.

- *Improve communications with intermediaries.* In the food industry some manufacturers have appointed "liaison personnel" whose sole function is to interpret company policy to wholesalers and retailers and to report grievances to the manufacturer.[20] General Motors and Ford have dealer councils to provide a forum for expressing grievances. After the period of conflict with its dealers in the 1950s GM strengthened these councils to provide more direct communication with the company.[21]

- *Voluntary arbitration.* Although not typical, manufacturers and intermediaries can seek outside arbitration of disputes. In one case TV manufacturers, distributors, and dealers agreed to abide by rules established by the Federal Trade Commission to reduce channel conflicts. Five conflict areas were arbitrated: tie-in sales, price fixing, forcing inventory, discriminatory billing, and favoritism in rebates and discounts.[22]

Selecting Channel Systems and Strategies

In the rest of this chapter we will consider the management of the channel system. Figure 16-3 shows that there are three basic decision areas in distribution management: (1) selecting the channel system, (2) managing channel intermediaries, and (3) implementing physical distribution activities.

The process of selecting a channel system requires (1) establishing distribution objectives, (2) determining environmental and corporate influences on the channel system, (3) selecting the intermediaries in a channel system, (4) formulating distribution strategies, and (5) evaluating and, if necessary, modifying the channel system. In this section we will briefly consider each of these five steps in channel selection.

ESTABLISHING DISTRIBUTIVE OBJECTIVES

Distribution objectives should specify the target markets to be reached, the penetration of these markets, and the support to be given to intermediaries. For example, both Xerox and IBM might have established the following hypothetical objectives in distributing small computers:

- Maintain control over all facets of distribution to ensure proper servicing;

- Develop a common distribution facility for the small-business and home-computer markets;

- Develop separate training and servicing support for each segment; and

- Attain market coverage of 35 percent of American households through retail outlets in large metropolitan areas.

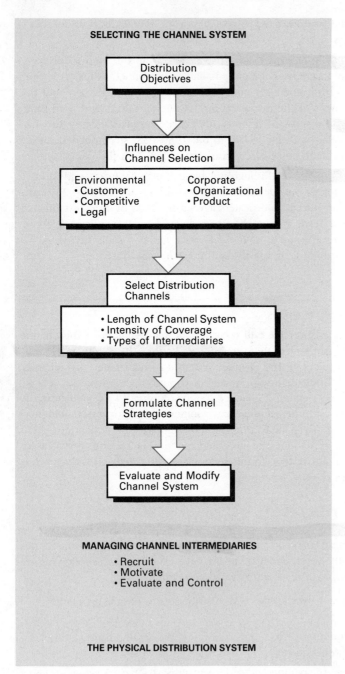

SELECTING THE CHANNEL SYSTEM

Distribution
Objectives

Influences on
Channel Selection

Environmental
• Customer
• Competitive
• Legal

Corporate
• Organizational
• Product

Select Distribution
Channels

• Length of Channel System
• Intensity of Coverage
• Types of Intermediaries

Formulate Channel
Strategies

Evaluate and Modify
Channel System

MANAGING CHANNEL INTERMEDIARIES
• Recruit
• Motivate
• Evaluate and Control

THE PHYSICAL DISTRIBUTION SYSTEM

FIGURE 16-3
Management of the channel system

These objectives would have led both companies to establish a nationwide network of company-owned stores to sell personal and home computers, and to establish separate training and service staffs for each market.

EVALUATING FACTORS THAT INFLUENCE CHANNEL SELECTION

Several environmental and corporate factors influence the length of the channel and intensity of coverage.

Environmental Factors

The customer's characteristics, competition, legal regulations, and the state of the economy are environmental factors that influence channel decisions.

Customer characteristics

Direct channels are most effective when customers are few, large, and geographically concentrated. In these cases direct contact by the company's sales staff is economically feasible. If the company has many small, geographically dispersed customers, it needs intermediaries to assemble diverse products and sell them to buyers in various areas.

Competition

Marketing channels used by competitors will influence channel selection. Most manufacturers want their products to compete in the same outlets. Some companies base distribution strategies on the opposite idea — avoid competitive products to establish a unique distributive niche. Consolidated Foods' Hanes Hosiery division was highly successful in using such a strategy when it distributed L'Eggs through supermarkets and food stores.

Legal regulations

There are several important legal restrictions in the development of channel systems. Five areas stand out:[23]

1. **Exclusive dealing** is the seller's requirement that its customer will handle only the company's line of products. Such arrangements violate the Clayton Antitrust Act when courts interpret these arrangements as lessening trade. For example, if exclusive dealing contracts exclude competitive products from a market, they will be regarded as illegal.

2. **Tying contracts** require a buyer to take other products in a manufacturer's line in order to obtain the products desired. An automobile manufacturer may insist that a dealer take a certain quota of less popular models to get the most popular ones. These arrangements are also illegal under the Clayton Act if they lessen competition. Most courts have considered them anticompetitive and illegal per se.

3. **Full-line forcing** is a requirement that an intermediary carry a full line of the manufacturer's products in order to buy from the manufacturer.

Such a contract is not illegal unless it is combined with an exclusive territory contract.

4. **Exclusive territories** are sometimes offered by manufacturers to ensure that a wholesaler or retailer is the only one in an area selling a manufacturer's products. It is a means of protecting intermediaries from competition. A recent Supreme Court ruling held that such arrangements should be judged on a case-by-case basis depending on whether they restrict competition. In 1980 the soft-drink industry won a long fight for legislation to give manufacturers the right to grant exclusive territories to bottlers. The beer industry is seeking a similar ruling.[24]

5. *Vertical integration,* that is, the acquisition of intermediaries by manufacturers or the reverse, may violate the Sherman Antitrust Act if it tends to promote monopoly.

Economic conditions

The state of the economy will affect channel selection. In a recession manufacturers may try to decrease costs by bypassing wholesalers and retailers and selling directly. But the high cost of personal selling should make manufacturers wary of shortening the channel to save costs in an economic downturn.

Company Factors

Two company factors will affect channel selection: the nature of the product and the company's characteristics.

Product characteristics

The following product characteristics encourage direct marketing rather than use of intermediaries:

- *Perishability:* perishable products require quick delivery, necessitating direct marketing by suppliers.
- *Bulk:* bulky products require channel systems that minimize transportation and handling. Selling through a company sales force will minimize the number of transactions and will reduce transportation costs if the company has a nationwide network of branch offices.
- *Complexity:* complex products such as automated production systems require technical expertise that can best be supplied by the company's sales staff.
- *High price:* high-priced industrial products such as an industrial generator involve more organizational risk. Industrial buyers often insist on dealing directly with the company rather than through an intermediary when buying such products.

The opposite characteristics — namely, smaller, standardized, lower-priced products with a high shelf life — would increase the likelihood of using intermediaries.

Certain characteristics will also encourage more intensive distribution. If a product is purchased frequently, it should be generally available. Milk, paper towels, toothpaste, and many other packaged goods are purchased frequently and quickly. These products are distributed through channel systems that provide widespread coverage. On the other hand, cars, appliances, and furniture are purchased infrequently and require more deliberation. As a result these products are distributed more selectively through fewer intermediaries.

Company characteristics

Company characteristics will influence the length of a channel. Large, powerful companies can deal directly with customers and can determine which functions they want to delegate to intermediaries. Financially weak companies are frequently forced to use distributors or manufacturers' agents because they do not have the resources for their own sales staffs. Companies with a full product mix are also better able to deal directly with customers since they do not need wholesalers to offer a complete assortment of goods. Buyers are less likely to deal directly with companies offering limited product lines.

A company's characteristics also affect the control it has over its channels. A large, financially sound company is more likely to be a channel leader. Such a company will attempt to administer the channel system to ensure systemwide profit maximization. But a financially powerful company can also create conflict by attempting to maximize profits at the expense of its intermediaries.

SELECTING DISTRIBUTION CHANNELS

Once the manager has considered the influences affecting the distribution system, he or she is in a better position to determine the makeup of the channel. Three decisions must be made: (1) the length of the channel system, (2) the intensity of the coverage provided by the channel system, and (3) the types of intermediaries to use.

Length of the Channel System

The length of the channel refers to the different levels of intermediaries to be used (retailers only; retailers and wholesalers; retailers, wholesalers, and agents). Industrial channel systems are likely to be shorter than consumer goods systems. Fewer intermediaries are required for industrial goods because fewer buyers buy in large quantities. Selling directly or through an extension of the company's sales force such as agents is more likely. The bulk, complexity, and higher prices of industrial goods also encourage shorter channels because of high transportation and handling costs.

Shorter channels also give manufacturers greater control over intermediaries. In consumer goods, automobile companies and large appliance manufacturers use only one level in the channel — dealers — to sell to consumers because they want some control over the way their goods are sold. Consumer packaged goods companies do not have the luxury of shortening their channels for the sake of control. Most of them have to sell through wholesalers or brokers to reach smaller stores. But even here some have tried to deal directly with retailers to retain control. For example, Goya Foods, a manufacturer of Hispanic specialty food items, uses its 120 salespeople to deal directly with their 9300 grocery store clients. It pays special attention to the mom-and-pop stores that dot Hispanic neighborhoods.[25] It does so to keep the personal touch with its clients. Most other food companies use intermediaries, particularly food brokers, to sell to the smaller stores.

If a company shortens its channel to maintain control over distribution, it must then assume the distribution functions that would ordinarily be performed by intermediaries. One supermarket executive describes Goya Foods as an "old-time wholesale grocer" because it has assumed the functions of a wholesaler.[26] It writes orders, extends credit, restocks the store's shelves, and offers suggestions to managers. Larger companies such as P&G, Campbell, and Pillsbury also sell directly through their salespeople, but only to large retailers. They use wholesalers to sell to smaller stores. Goya is unusual in maintaining a short channel system to small retailers.

Intensity of Distribution

The intensity of distribution can vary from a high level in which most outlets in an area carry a product to low intensity in which one dealer is given exclusive territorial rights. Between the two extremes of intensive and exclusive distribution is selective distribution in which a select number of dealers will carry the company's line.

Intensive distribution

Intensive distribution is most likely for inexpensive, frequently purchased, widely used items. Manufacturers of food and drug products use intensive distribution because, in most cases, if a store does not have a particular brand, a consumer will buy an alternative. Therefore, intensive distribution is necessary to avoid losing customers. The fight for shelf space in supermarkets is another indication of the importance of intensive distribution. If a substantial number of retailers do not stock an item or if they give it poor shelf position, the brand might fail.

Selective distribution

In **selective distribution** the marketer selects a limited number of intermediaries who can provide the desired sales support and service. Selective distribution is most often used for durable goods like small appliances, stereo equipment, musical instruments, and furniture. Consumers are likely to shop around for these goods because they are higher priced and the risks are greater. Brand loyalty is also high, permitting manufacturers to limit distribution. Selective distribution is beneficial to these manufacturers, since it allows them to control how their products are sold and to extend service to customers through a limited number of retailers. It also decreases the likelihood of price competition between intermediaries which can tarnish the companies' quality image.

Many furniture companies are following the lead established by Ethan Allen Furniture in the 1960s by moving to selective distribution. The purpose is to establish a prestige image for their line and better control the way retailers present the product. For example, Pennsylvania House went from 3000 to 350 outlets in the past decade.[27] In electronics Sony moved to selective distribution when it found many of its retailers selling to discounters to get rid of inventory. Lower prices tarnished Sony's quality image. Sony finally decided to cancel all of its dealers. It reinstituted some under a franchise agreement which allowed it to prevent dealers from reselling to other retailers.[28]

Exclusive distribution

Some manufacturers grant dealers exclusive territorial rights. The advantage to the retailer is the exclusion of other retailers selling the same brand. The advantage to the manufacturer is more direct control over retail operations and a greater sales commitment from the retailer. But there are disadvantages. The retailer may lose some independence in store operations. The manufacturer may lose some sales because of limited distribution. **Exclusive distribution** is most likely for high-priced products with a quality image — cars, jewelry, appliances.

Both selective and exclusive distribution are widely used by industrial marketers. A smaller number of customers buying high priced and technically complex items permits more limited distribution.

Selection of Intermediaries

Marketing management must decide whether to use intermediaries, and if so, what types.

Determine whether to use intermediaries

The distribution of consumer goods almost always requires intermediaries. Direct marketing to many final consumers is too costly. But in industrial marketing the manager must frequently decide whether to distribute through intermediaries (manufacturers' agents and/or distributors). If intermediaries can provide the same support and coverage as the company sales force, then the decision can be based on cost criteria. For example, suppose manufacturers' agents receive a 5 percent commission on sales. Company sales representatives receive a 3 percent commission. But sales support and administration of the company's sales force adds $500,000 a year to the cost of direct sales. Management asks at what sales level either manufacturers' agents or company sales representatives are more economical. It can determine this by setting the costs for agents versus company sales representatives equal to each other as follows:[29]

$$0.03x + \$500,000 \text{ (the cost of the company's sales force)}$$
$$= 0.05x \text{ (the cost of manufacturers' agents)}$$

where x = sales volume.

Solving for x, sales volume equals $25 million, meaning that below $25 million the use of manufacturers' sales agents is cheaper, but above $25 million in sales, use of the company's sales representatives is cheaper. This is because as sales increase the fixed costs of a company-owned sales force are defrayed. The key question is whether the company forecasts sales to exceed $25 million.

Evaluate alternative intermediaries

If a company decides to use intermediaries, it must then find the potential revenue and the relative costs of using one type of intermediary versus another. The marketing manager must (1) project sales for each type of intermediary, (2) determine the distribution costs incurred by alternative intermediaries, and (3) compute the resulting contribution to profit.

An example of cost and revenue projections for two intermediaries being considered by a cosmetics company is in Table 16-2. It is apparent that drugstores are substantially less costly because they do not need to employ salesclerks. But department stores are projected to generate more sales revenues and to make a greater contribution to profit. Developing sales projections for alternative intermediaries is difficult, but it should be attempted if alternative intermediaries are to be selected on the basis of rational economic criteria.

The difficulty of estimating sales and costs for alternative intermediaries has led management to use other methods to select channel members. One simple approach is to have management rate alternative intermediaries. If management is considering using manufacturers' agents or distributors, it will rate them on factors such as effectiveness in reaching the target market, co-operation likely to be extended, investment required, and projected profits in using each. Management will select the intermediary that scores highest on the most important of these criteria. Another approach used to select inter-

TABLE 16-2
Comparing Two Intermediaries on the Basis of Cost and Revenue Projections

	DRUGSTORES (IN MILLIONS)	DEPARTMENT STORES (IN MILLIONS)
Sales Forecast	$4.5	$6.0
Cost of Goods Sold	2.2	2.1
Cooperative Advertising	0.3	0.8
Salesclerks' Salaries	0	1.0
Commissions	1.5	1.4
Contribution to Profits	0.5	0.7

mediaries is quantitative models. One model based on mathematical programming determines the type of intermediary, the margin to seek from each type, and the number of outlets to employ.[30]

FORMULATING COMPETITIVE CHANNEL STRATEGIES

Once a channel system has been selected and is in place, management should consider its strategic role in the marketing mix. The main question is whether management wants to influence consumers through the channel system (as in personal selling and trade promotions) or outside the system (as in advertising). Using intermediaries to stimulate customer demand is known as a **push strategy** because the product is being pushed through the channel of distribution, first by the manufacturer and then by intermediaries. Influencing consumers outside of the channels of distribution is known as a **pull strategy** because the consumer is influenced to go into the store by advertising and is "pulling" the product out of the channel system.

Most companies will rely on both strategies to sell their products. The important question is where the emphasis will be. Vassarette, a manufacturer of intimate apparel, is an example of a company that changed its emphasis. The company "traditionally allocated its communications budget to its sales force, conforming to the push-through approach rather than the pull-through tactics of package goods marketers."[31] But a shrinking market share and a decrease in consumer awareness of its line led Vassarette to put more emphasis on advertising. The company has now opted for a consistent advertising campaign with the objective of creating "a brand awareness for the line, to make clear that it carries all the categories ... that are important to the trade."[32]

Push Strategies

Manufacturers can use various strategies to influence their intermediaries to push the product. They can:

- provide higher margins as an incentive to sell the product;
- offer cooperative advertising allowances;
- grant higher quantity and trade discounts than competitors;
- provide contests and bonuses to stimulate sales;
- offer training programs to improve operations in areas such as inventory control, shelf stocking, and accounting;
- offer exclusive dealerships; and
- provide promotional displays and point-of-sale aids.

Industrial marketers are most likely to use push strategies because of the importance of personal selling. Small and financially weak companies are also more likely to use a push strategy to influence distributors to stock their items. Stormaster, a new producer of steel boxes for industrial use, is offering distributors a margin that is 15 percent higher than that of competitors to induce them to carry the line. It is also offering distributors advertising support and assistance from its sales representatives in the form of joint sales calls.[33]

Pull Strategies

Manufacturers use the following types of pull strategies to attract customers:

- national advertising;
- coupons, premiums, cents-off and other promotions to attract consumers to the store;
- product quality to create brand loyalty;
- service;
- warranties; or
- a full product line.

In each of these cases the manufacturer is trying to establish brand loyalty through product and promotion rather than distribution strategies.

Pull strategies tend to be used by large and powerful companies that do not have to cater to their intermediaries. For example, as a result of a $726 million television advertising budget, Procter & Gamble is able to pull consumers into stores.[34] It does not have to worry about influencing retailers to stock the company's products. Similarly, when Philip Morris bought 7-Up, it cut back on promotional support to bottlers and retail stores. It also reduced discounts to the trade. As a result one bottler said, "Philip Morris hasn't recognized that this industry requires as much 'push' at the local level as 'pull' through national ads."[35] More recently 7-Up has begun to have a more balanced push and pull approach. It has increased incentives to bottlers and has implemented a system designed to tailor merchandising needs to specific retailers.[36]

A pull approach is not restricted to large, financially powerful companies. Some furniture companies feel they can no longer rely on retailers to promote their products. White Furniture has launched a print advertising campaign to strengthen its brand name, demonstrating a shift from a push to a pull approach.[37]

EVALUATING AND MODIFYING THE CHANNEL SYSTEM

The last step in channel selection is to evaluate the performance of the channel and determine whether modifications in the channel system are necessary.

Evaluation

In evaluating the channel system the marketer must determine whether intermediaries are performing key functions effectively. The basis for such an evaluation should be a comparison of the actual performance of a set of intermediaries to projected performance. The revenue and cost estimates for drugstores and department stores in Table 16-2 could be used to evaluate the performance of these two types of intermediaries. If revenues fall below projections or costs above projections, then some change in distribution policy may be required.

The purpose of such evaluation is not to change any single wholesaler or retailer that may not be performing effectively; it is to determine if a change should be made in the channel system. The basis for any such change should be a *channel audit*. Such audits should be comprehensive evaluations of each class of intermediaries used by the company. The result of such an audit could be a decision to change the distribution process — for example, Xerox's decision to change its method of distributing small computers from direct sales to company-owned stores. Decisions of such magnitude must be approved by management in the top echelons of a company. But the channel audit might also come up with smaller recommendations, such as changing the margins or discounts being offered to intermediaries, or giving intermediaries more latitude in administering cooperative advertising and in-store promotional programs.

Modification

Frequently a channel audit will result in a recommendation for a change in the channel system. If the company opts to modify the channel, then a rational stategy for modification should be adopted that is in line with the company's overall marketing plan. Figure 16-4 presents various strategies for changing the intensity of distribution coverage and for changing the types of intermediaries used. Strategies for changing intensity are categorized into increasing, sustaining, and decreasing distribution coverage. Strategies for changing intemediaries are classified by companies that do or do not introduce new intermediaries into the system. These options produce the six strategies in Figure 16-4.

Extension

A company may decide to increase the intensity of distributive coverage using its existing intermediaries. Warner-Lambert decided to pursue such a course when it bought Entenmann's Inc., a bakery distributing products in the Northeast and Florida. The company had sold its products directly to retailers, using its own trucks and drivers. It would be costly to extend such a system beyond a regional base. But within months of acquiring the company, Warner-Lambert decided to add trucks, warehouses, and production facilities to make nationwide distribution a possibility. The result was the profitable introduction of Entenmann's products into the Midwest.[38]

Acquisition/development

A company could also increase the intensity of coverage by adopting new intermediaries, either through the acquisition of another company or through the developement of a revamped channel system. One of the reasons that Nabisco and Standard Brands merged was that "Nabisco's distribution system,

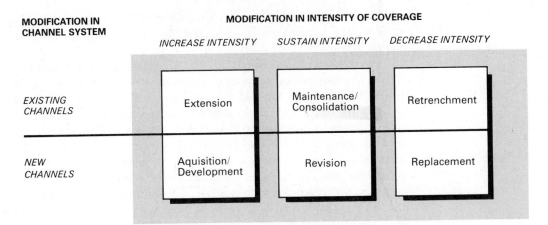

FIGURE 16-4
Channel modification strategies

coupled with Standard Brands' research capabilities, makes the merged company stronger than they were separately."[39] Standard Brands now has a more extensive base for distribution coverage.

A company can also gain more extensive coverage by changing its channel system. Mitsubishi Motors agreed to let Chrysler distribute its cars in 1971. But years of poor sales performace by Chrysler caused Mitsubishi to develop its own dealer network.[40]

Maintenance/consolidation

Companies may not seek a change in either the intensity of distribution coverage or the types of intermediaries used. Such companies can actively maintain their existing distribution network, and in some cases consolidate it to improve performance. Frito-Lay is following a maintenance strategy by distributing its products through the company's existing channel system — a 9500-member force that sells directly to retailers and stocks and services them an average of fifty-five times a year. The company recently bought Grand Ma's Foods, a producer of sweet snacks, and plans to distribute the products of the new acquisition through its current channel system.[41]

Sun-Diamond Company, a cooperative of fruit growers, has consolidated its existing channel sytem by combining four smaller companies into one larger one.[42] As a result Sun-Diamond can buy in larger quantities, achieving cost savings through quantity discounts.

Revision

Another strategy in Figure 16-4 is to sustain intensity of coverage while changing the channel system. North American Systems introduced Mr. Coffee, an electric drip coffee maker, through appliance stores, department stores, and mail orders. Management soon realized that replacement filters were a major source of profits. But customers did not go to appliance and department stores often enough to buy filters. Therefore its channel system had to be revised to allow for the sale of filters. The company hired food brokers to distribute the filters. Now 65 percent of sales are through food and grocery outlets.[43]

Retrenchment/replacement

The last two channel modification strategies in Figure 16-4 represent a reduction in the intensity of distribution coverage. These strategies by no means imply a reduction in sales effort. They could in fact result in more effective selling by moving from intensive to selective distribution. When Sony eliminated most of its dealers to control price cutting, it followed a policy of retrenchment. But the result was a leaner, more efficient dealer network that was easier to control.

A reduction in the intensity of distribution coverage can also be accompanied by a change in the channel system. For example, an industrial marketer might decide to reduce the number of distributors it uses and change to an exclusive distributor system. The purpose would be to ensure that distributors will fully stock the company's line and more effectively push it to customers.

Managing Channel Intermediaries

The second basic area of responsibility in distribution management is managing the intermediaries in the channel system. The responsibilities here are essentially the same as managing the company's sales force — recruiting, motivating, and evaluating — but some of the issues and techniques differ.

RECRUITING CHANNEL MEMBERS

The manufacturer must identify specific intermediaries that can perform the required distribution functions. The following criteria could be used to select intermediaries:

- contacts and relationships with the company's target segments,
- past sales performance and current sales capabilities,
- reputation and capability for service and delivery,
- caliber of management,
- financial status,
- equipment and facilities for handling the company's products,
- willingness to carry a full line of products,
- number of years in business,
- growth record and growth potential, and
- reputation for cooperating with suppliers.

Manufacturers may wish to weight these criteria by importance and then rate intermediaries on the criteria to obtain an overall score as a basis for selecting channel members.

MOTIVATING CHANNEL MEMBERS

Most intermediaries carry more than one line of products. Therefore, a manufacturer must motivate an intermediary to sell its products over competing lines. Stormaster, the producer of industrial steel boxes, motivated its distributors by offering them higher margins. 7-Up tried to repair its relations with its distributors by increasing discounts. Beech-Nut motivated its food brokers by offering training programs that helped them increase their business skills. Toyota introduced an elaborate dealer incentive program to motivate its dealers to buy genuine Toyota parts.[44] Other important motivators are cooperative advertising and trade allowances, financial assistance, and sale contests.

EVALUATING PERFORMANCE

The manufacturer must evaluate the performance of channel members. Evaluation of individual members could be part of the periodic channel audit. The basic criterion of evaluation is sales results. Channel members can be evaluated on three sales criteria:

1. current compared to past sales,
2. actual sales compared to quotas, and
3. sales compared to other intermediaries.

Other criteria are also important in evaluating performance; for example:

- customer delivery time,
- adequacy of inventory levels,
- cooperation in company advertising and promotional programs, and
- service fulfillment.

Where performance is below par the manufacturer should investigate the causes and provide assistance to improve the intermediary's performance. In the extreme the manufacturer must consider replacing the intermediary.

Physical Distribution

The third decision area in the distribution management process in Figure 16-3 is physical distribution. **Physical distribution** encompasses those activities required to move products from producers to consumers. Physical distribution activities are a major part of our economy. One study estimates that physical distribution functions represent 20 percent of the gross national product.[45] Physical distribution costs average 13.6 percent of sales for manufacturers and

25.6 percent for intermediaries.[46] The biggest chunk of these expenditures is for transportation. A trade report estimates that physical distribution costs are categorized as follows:[47]

transportation	45 percent
inventory	25 percent
storage (warehousing)	20 percent
order processing and management	10 percent

Because of the high costs of transportation for industrial products, it is not surprising that industrial marketers view physical distribution as one of the most important functions. One study showed that industrial buyers rate physical distribution second only to product quality in evaluating alternative suppliers.[48] Physical distribution is increasing in importance because of a steady rise in transportation and storage costs. Inventory costs are also increasing because the trend to segmentation means smaller and more frequent orders. Moreover, customers are placing more emphasis on service. Industrial buyers in particular emphasize quick delivery. For many industrial buyers the starting point in selecting a vendor is not identifying the company offering the best price but the company with the best delivery and service reputation.[49]

Physical distribution is becoming more important for consumer goods as well. Decreasing brand loyalty and greater price sensitivity among final consumers means that out-of-stock situations are more costly. Consumers are no longer reluctant to switch to another brand when their preferred brand is not available. Poor delivery and inadequate inventory levels can be very costly to manufacturers.

THE PHYSICAL DISTRIBUTION SYSTEM

Physical distribution activities are a subsystem of the total channel system because they facilitate the movement of goods through intermediaries to the customer. Operation of the physical distribution system is illustrated in Figure 16-5. A customer places an order which is processed by the manufacturer. If the quantity requested is large enough, the order can be filled directly from inventory — that is, from the plant or a supplier's distribution center. If quantities will not fully load a vehicle, it may be more cost efficient to distribute the merchandise through a warehouse. The manufacturer attempts to locate warehouses strategically to minimize transportation and handling costs. Once the items have been assembled from inventory or from warehouses, they are shipped to the customer by a particular mode of transportation. The customer evaluates the service provided by the seller. Satisfaction with order processing, handling, and delivery serves as feedback to the decision whether to use the same supplier in the future.

Distribution Efficiency
Figure 16-5 represents a system because there is a common goal driving it — distribution efficiency. Distribution efficiency is measured by (1) the inputs

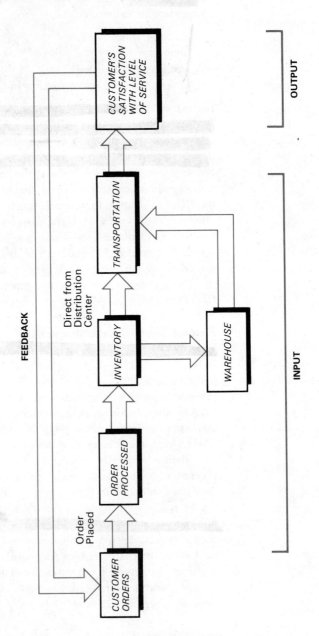

FIGURE 16-5
The physical distribution process

into the system — that is, the cost required to perform the four functions in Figure 16-5 — and (2) the output — that is, the customer's satisfaction with the distribution services. The problem is that no physical distribution system can simultaneously maximize customer service while minimizing distribution costs. Maximizing customer service means larger inventories, speedier transportation methods, and many warehouses, all of which escalate physical distribution costs.

Distribution Trade-Offs

A second reason Figure 16-5 is a system is that the activities are interrelated and involve trade-offs. For example:

■ inventory costs can be decreased by speeding up delivery, but speeding delivery means using air freight services, thus increasing transportation costs;

■ storage costs can be reduced by decreasing the number of warehouses, but such a decrease would mean increased inventory levels in more centralized warehouses and increased costs of transporting goods greater distances; and

■ transportation costs can be decreased by using rail over air transport, but since rail is slower it ties up working capital, delays customer payments, and may aggravate customers.

Minimizing Distribution Costs

Despite the complexity of these trade-offs, management must attempt to develop a physical distribution system that provides adequate customer service at reliable cost. As with other components of the marketing mix, management must determine the effort required to deliver adequate customer service and then allocate the required effort to components of the physical distribution system. One author states the problem as minimizing distribution costs in terms of:[50]

$$D = T + FW + VW + S$$

where:

D = total distribution costs of the proposed system,
T = total freight costs of the proposed system,
FW = total fixed warehouse costs,
VW = total variable warehouse costs, and
S = total costs of lost sales due to average delivery delay under the proposed system.

Distribution costs associated with alternative systems are determined, and the system that minimizes distribution costs at a target level of customer service is selected.

Although the preceding formula states the problem, it does not provide a solution for arriving at an optimal system. Few programs have been developed to simultaneously determine least cost alternatives for physical distribution activities for a specified service target. The reason is that these interrelationships are extremely complicated. As a result applications have tended to focus on one element of the physical distribution system. For example, mathematical programs have been developed to determine the optimal number and location of warehouses and optimal inventory levels and reorder points.[51]

PHYSICAL DISTRIBUTION MANAGEMENT

The manager of the channel system must also manage the physical distribution system. This requires (1) setting objectives, (2) establishing each of the four major physical distribution functions in Figure 16-5 and (3) evaluating the system.

Physical Distribution Objectives

Management should establish customer service (output) and cost (input) objectives for physical distribution. For example, service objectives might be to:

■ transmit orders within twenty-four hours of receipt,

■ deliver requested goods to customers within one week of the order,

■ ensure that out-of-stock conditions occur in less than 3 percent of all orders,

■ deliver special orders within forty-eight hours by air freight at customer's request, and

■ ensure that 99 percent of all goods are delivered in perfect condition.

Cost objectives might be stated as a percentage of sales (for example costs of physical distribution should not exceed 15 percent of sales). The cost of various functions might also be controlled (for example, transportation costs should be no greater than 50 percent of costs of physical distribution). Such a criterion would attempt to ensure that the company is not incurring excessive transportation costs to satisfy requests for quick delivery.

Physical Distribution Functions

Channel management must decide on the nature of the four main physical distribution activities and the cost allocations to these functions. Decisions must be made on:

■ developing a system to process orders,

■ deciding on stock reorder points and maintaining adequate inventory levels,

■ determining the need for storage through warehouses and their locations, and

■ determining the mode of transportation.

Order processing

Order processing requires (1) filling out an order and transmitting it to a stockroom or warehouse, (2) preparing a bill and checking the customer's credit, and (3) filling the order from inventory and ensuring delivery.[52] An important development in physical distribution management is the widespread adoption of computerized order-processing systems. In one system salespeople transmit the order, which is entered on a computer. A printout is on its way to the warehouse to select and ship the item, and the order is ready to be billed. All this occurs the same day. Through computer terminals managers have instant access to information on the status of each order, items in inventory, and each customer's sales and purchasing history.[53]

Inventory

Inventory management has received more attention from managers in the 1980s because of greater emphasis on profit rather than sales criteria. Sales-oriented management can increase sales volume by maintaining high inventory levels to ensure that all orders, even marginally profitable ones, can be covered. But sales volume is obtained at the expense of distribution efficiency, resulting in lower returns on investment.[54]

Efficient inventory management requires decisions on the following:

1. *How much to reorder.* Firms try to balance the carrying costs of maintaining high inventories with the danger of being out of stock. The optimal reorder quantity varies directly with (1) the amount of market demand (the greater the demand, the greater the required inventory) and (2) order-processing costs (high processing costs create pressures to maintain higher inventory levels to reduce the number of times the product must be reordered). Optimal reorder quantities vary inversely with the inventory carrying costs (higher carrying costs create pressure to reduce inventory). These relationships give an optimal order quantity (Q) estimate of:

$$\frac{D \text{ (annual demand)} \times S \text{ (order processing costs)}}{IC \text{ (inventory carrying costs)}}$$

The relationship is stated as:

$$Q = \frac{2DS}{IC}$$

because demand and order-processing costs count twice as much as carrying costs in arriving at the optimal order quantity.

2. *When to reorder.* The decision when to reorder depends on (1) the optimal reorder quantity and (2) the annual sales forecast. If a company determines that the optimal reorder quantity is 4,000 units and the yearly sales forecast is 40,000 units, the product should be reordered ten times a year or about every fifth week.

3. *Minimizing stockouts.* The cost to a firm of being out of stock can be high. One study found that the margin lost on a unit when it is out of stock ranged from 1.9 percent for canned peaches to 17 percent for deodorants.[55] A safety stock level should be detemined — that is, a certain percentage above the normal stock level. The safety margin takes account of the possibility that demand was underestimated and reduces the probability of stockouts.

Warehousing

Companies maintain warehouses close to centers of demand to minimize transportation and handling costs and to increase the speed of delivery and service calls. Warehouses are either privately owned or are public facilities. *Private warehouses* are used when a firm has special storage needs, wishes to maintain control over its storage operations, and has a constant and high volume of goods moving through.[56] *Public warehouses* are used to reduce storage costs. They give firms more flexibility in shipping to different areas since they are more numerous.

Some firms use **distribution centers** in addition to, or in place of, warehouses. These facilities are centralized and serve broader markets than warehouses. They maintain full product lines, consolidate large shipments from different production points, and usually have computerized order-handling systems.[57] They also differ from warehouses in turning inventory over more rapidly.

The costs of storage are substantial. When Coors beer moved into the South, distributors had to make substantial investments to build refrigerated warehouses. Some spent as much as $500,000. As a result, "they had all their assets wrapped up in fixed costs and couldn't afford to back the brand."[58]

Transportation

Transportation costs are influenced by locational decisions about plants and warehouses. If a company adds weight and bulk in production, then locating plants and warehouses closer to the point of demand would reduce transportation costs. If the final product weighs less and is less bulky than the raw materials going in, transportation costs would be reduced by locating closer to the sources of supply.

The importance of reducing transportation costs by locating close to sources of demand is also illustrated by Coors. The company's expansion into the Sunbelt is proving expensive because it is shipping beer from its single refinery in Colorado. Transportation costs are $7 to $8 a barrel compared to an average of $3 a barrel for the industry. As a result Coors is considering constructing or buying a brewery in the area.[59]

In addition to location the key decision to be made by management is on the mode of transportation. Management should evaluate modes of transportation on criteria such as speed of delivery, availability in different locations, dependability, ability to handle different products, frequency of service, and cost.

Evaluation of the Physical Distribution System

Once decisions have been made on order handling, inventory, warehousing, and transportation, channel management must evaluate the operation of the physical distribution system. Such an evaluation should be conducted as part of a channel audit that would monitor distribution costs and determine performance on key customer service factors such as delivery, product availability, and product condition. Management should be aware of certain danger signals in evaluating the performance of the physical distribution system, for instance,

- *Slow inventory turnover.* Distribution inventories should turn over between six and twelve times a year in most companies. Inventories that turn less than six times a year frequently signal control problems.

- *Intrawarehouse shipments.* Such transfers require double handling, increasing distribution costs. A significant number of such transfers could indicate a lack of control in the physical distribution system.

- *Premium freight charges.* A system that relies on premium freight may be incurring unnecessary distribution costs.

Distribution of Industrial versus Consumer Goods

So far we have described the distribution of both industrial and consumer goods and have attempted to indicate the differences between the two. These differences are important enough to summarize here.

1. *Types of channel system.* Figure 16-6 divides the channel systems in Figure 16-1 into those used by industrial and consumer goods manufacturers. As we can see, certain types of intermediaries are used for either industrial or consumer goods. Retailers are particular to the distribution of consumer goods since they sell directly to final consumers. Manufacturers' agents and sales agents are used primarily in the distribution of industrial products since they serve as extensions of the manufacturer's sales force and specialize in particular lines.

2. *Length of channels and intensity of coverage.* Industrial channel systems are shorter than consumer goods systems because direct selling is more likely. Industrial channels are also more likely to be selective in their coverage. Industrial marketers do not need the intensity of coverage of most consumer goods channels because there are fewer buyers and sales are less frequent. The need to offer industrial buyers technical information and special services such as installation, maintenance, and product repairs requires either direct sales or a few well-placed intermediaries. Industrial marketers are also more likely to offer exclusive territories to their distributors as a means of ensuring effective sales. In consumer goods markets such exclusive arrangements are limited because manufacturers need more widespread coverage for their products.

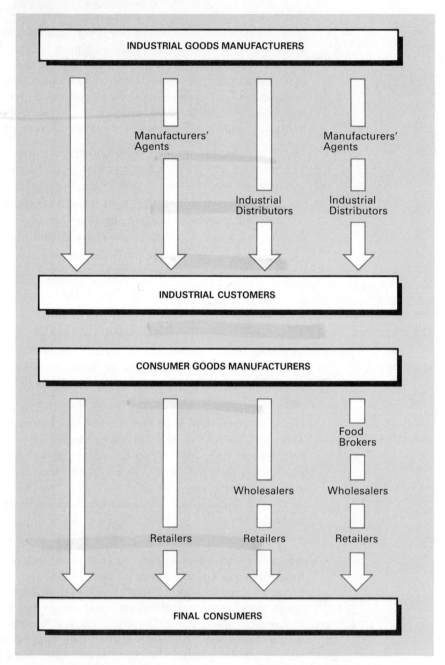

FIGURE 16-6
Channel systems characteristic of industrial and consumer goods

3. *Distribution conflict.* Conflict between a manufacturer and its intermediaries is less intense in industrial distribution than in consumer goods. A study of the historic pattern of distributive conflicts in several industries found that the most intense conflicts have occurred in the drug, automobile, petroleum, and food industries, all consumer goods industries.[60] One simple reason for this is that these industries use retailers. Conflicts are created by the localized perspective of the retailer and occur over store management, cooperative advertising allowances, and in-store promotions. Such conflicts are less likely to exist in industrial distribution.

4. *Distribution strategies.* Industrial marketers are more likely to use push than pull strategies because personal selling and distribution are more important components of the marketing mix than advertising. The industrial marketer must directly influence the buyer through its own sales force or its intermediaries. Rarely will an industrial marketing plan rely on advertising to pull the product through the channels by influencing buyers to contact salespeople and distributors. Industrial advertising is used more to support personal selling and distribution efforts as a means of paving the way for a personal selling effort. The purpose is to create awareness to facilitate the push, not to create buying influence to facilitate the pull.

5. *Physical distribution.* Control of physical distribution activities is much more important for industrial goods compared to consumer goods because of their higher transportation and handling costs.

Summary

Marketing management must develop a channel system to make sure its goods are received by target segments at the right place and time. In most cases intermediaries must be used to distribute goods. There are three basic types of intermediaries: (1) retailers, (2) wholesalers, and (3) agents and brokers. These intermediaries are formed into channel systems that vary in length (the number of types of intermediaries used) and intensity (the coverage the company seeks). Channel systems perform certain key functions in providing time, place, and possession utilities to the consumer. Channel members buy and sell products, transport goods, store them, and maintain inventory.

By their nature as social systems, channels of distribution promote both cooperation and conflict. The channel leader (usually the manufacturer) assists its intermediaries by offering training, financing and promotional programs. Conflict occurs because of differing economic objectives of manufacturers and intermediaries, the national perspective of the manufacturer compared to the more local orientation of retailers and wholesalers, and different views as to who should perform distributive functions.

Marketers must manage the distribution system to ensure that channel functions are performed and conflicts are minimized. Distribution management involves (1) selecting the channel system, (2) managing channel intermediaries, and (3) managing physical distribution activities. *Selecting the channel system* requires:

- establishing distribution objectives,
- determining the environmental and corporate influences on channel selection,
- selecting the types of intermediaries and determining channel length and intensity of coverage,
- determining the relative emphasis on push and pull strategies, and
- evaluating and modifying the channel system.

Managing channel intermediaries requires recruiting, motivating, and evaluating them. *Managing the physical distribution process* requires:

- establishing distribution-cost and customer-service objectives,
- developing a physical distribution system that must:
  - □ establish an order-handling system,
  - □ develop an inventory control system to maintain inventory levels and determine reorder points,
  - □ determine types and locations of warehouses, and
  - □ determine modes of transportation; and
- evaluating the physical distribution system.

In the next chapter we will examine distribution management and strategies from the perspective of the wholesaler and retailer.

Questions

1. What are the advantages and disadvantages to an industrial marketer of selling through a company-owned sales force rather than manufacturers' sales agents? How can the manufacturer determine whether a company-owned sales force or manufacturers' agents are more economical?

2. A manufacturer of industrial pipe insulation sells to many small buyers. Sales are frequently tied to reorder points determined by automated inventory control systems. Order sizes tend to be small, and sales are routinized.

   □ What type of distribution system is this manufacturer likely to develop?

□ What factors might cause this manufacturer to change the distribution system it is currently employing?

3. Administered channel systems and franchised operators were developed as means for manufacturers to control their intermediaries.

□ In what ways do manufacturers exert this control?

□ Why is control over intermediaries so important to many manufacturers?

4. What are the basic causes of conflict in a channel system? Cite specific causes.

5. An automobile executive cites the changing nature of company-dealer relations as follows:

Twenty years ago we would go in and tell the dealer "Take so many cars or parts and accessories; handle warranty claims in this or that way"; and so forth. The company's attitude was that if the dealers didn't like it, let them find someone else to supply them with cars. Today it is totally different. We recognize the dealer as an independent businessperson who might have legitimate grievances, and we try to accommodate our policies to the legitimate economic interests of our dealers.

□ Why do you suppose this automobile manufacturer shifted to a more dealer-oriented view?

□ What are some recent policies that reflect a greater dealer orientation?

□ Do some manufacturers of consumer products still force dealers to follow their policies?

6. A manufacturer of personal care appliances (hair dryers, electric mirrors, curlers) has been using company salespeople to demonstrate its line for years. What environmental factors might cause the company to consider selling through manufacturers' agents or distributors?

7. Is intensive, selective, or exclusive distribution most likely to be used for the following products? Why?

□ paper towels

□ antacid tablets

□ an electric foot massager

□ personal computers

Can a company gain an advantage by using either more intensive or more selective means of distribution than its competition? Cite an example.

8. A manufacturer of over-the-counter pharmaceutical items is considering introducing a new line of medicated hair shampoos. It is evaluating two alternative forms of distribution to drug chains: through distributors or direct selling. The company has traditionally used distributors because

it never developed a strong sales staff. It now feels that the economics of selling direct warrants considering developing its own sales capability.

☐ Do the pros and cons of selling direct differ for industrial and consumer goods?

☐ What specific criteria could management use in evaluating the benefits of direct selling?

9. When Philip Morris first began to distribute 7-Up, one bottler commented, "Philip Morris hasn't recognized that this industry requires as much 'push' at the local level as 'pull' through national ads."[61]

☐ What are the dangers of too much push and not enough pull? Of too much pull and not enough push?

☐ When is a company less likely to be concerned with pushing the product through the channels of distribution?

10. What are the pros and cons of modifying a channel system by acquiring a new company instead of changing existing channel facilities?

11. Why are physical distribution activities described as a system? What are some of the trade-offs in the physical distribution system?

12. What are some differences between distribution of industrial and consumer goods described in this chapter? Specifically, what are the differences in terms of:

☐ length of distribution channels,

☐ intensity of distribution,

☐ types of channel systems used, and

☐ nature of distribution strategies?

Notes

1. "Distribution: Industrial Marketing's Neglected Opportunity," *Marketing News,* June 25, 1982, Section 2, p. 10.

2. "A Funny Thing Happened on the Way to the Computer Store," *Sales & Marketing Management, Special Report, Managing Costs for More Productive Selling,* December 8, 1980.

3. "Educators Stressing Importance of Channels," *Marketing News,* July 23, 1982, Section 1, p. 8.

4. "Seven-Up's No-Caffeine Cola ... Gambling on Erasable Ink," *The Wall Street Journal,* March 25, 1982, p. 31.

5. Henry Assael, "The Political Role of Trade As-

sociations in Distributive Conflict Resolution," *Journal of Marketing* 32 (April 1968): 22–23.

6. James D. Hlavacek and Tommy J. McCuistion, "Industrial Distributors — When, Who, and How?" *Harvard Business Review* 61 (March–April 1983): 96.

7. Ibid., p. 97.

8. "Regional Sales Agents Help Cut Rising Staff Costs for Big Firms," *Product Marketing,* May 1979, p. 6.

9. "No. 1's Awesome Strategy," *Business Week,* June 8, 1981, p. 85.

10. Henry Assael, "Constructive Role of Interor-

ganizational Conflict," *Administrative Science Quarterly* 13 (December 1969): 573–82.

11. Ibid.

12. "Why P&G Wants a Mellower Image," *Business Week,* June 7, 1982, p. 60.

13. "Coke's New Program to Placate Bottlers," *Business Week,* October 12, 1981, p. 48.

14. Ibid.; and *Business Week,* June 7, 1982, pp. 60, 64.

15. Assael, "The Political Role of Trade Associations," pp. 22–23.

16. "Wheeling & Reeling," *Sales & Marketing Management,* May 16, 1983, p. 50.

17. Assael, "The Political Role of Trade Associations," pp. 22–23.

18. Louis W. Stern and Adel I. El-Ansary, *Marketing Channels* (Englewood Cliffs, N.J.: Prentice-Hall, 1982), p. 226.

19. Assael, "Constructive Role of Interorganizational Conflict," p. 579.

20. Albert Adler, Herbert Johnson, Jr., and William Meschio, "The Food Industry," in Henry Assael (ed.), *The Politics of Distributive Trade Associations: A Study in Conflict Resolution* (Hempstead, N.Y.: Hofstra University Press, 1967), p. 195.

21. Assael, "Constructive Role of Interorganizational Conflict," p. 578.

22. Robert G. Biedermann and Richard L. Tabak, "The Television Receiver Industry," in Henry Assael (ed.), *The Politics of Distributive Trade Associations* (Hempstead, N.Y.: Hofstra University Press, 1967), pp. 280–82.

23. This section is largely based on Stern and El-Ansary, *Marketing Channels,* pp. 365–82.

24. "Antitrust Exemption for Beer Draws Fire," *The New York Times,* August 30, 1983, p. D1.

25. "Goya Foods Inc., No. 1 in Hispanic Market Aims to Broaden Base," *The Wall Street Journal,* March 23, 1983, p. 1.

26. Ibid., p. 24.

27. "Home Furnishers Polish Strategies," *Ad Forum,* October, 1982, p. 41.

28. Stern and El-Ansary, *Marketing Channels,* p. 228.

29. This example is based on a communication from Prof. Roger A. Kerin, professor of marketing, Southern Methodist University, March 15, 1984.

30. Marcel Corstjens and Peter Doyle, "Channel Optimization in Complex Marketing Systems," *Management Science* 25 (October 1979): 1014–25.

31. "Vassarette Tries New Hands-On Approach," *Advertising Age,* February 15, 1982, p. 30.

32. Ibid.

33. "Stormaster Comes on Like 'Gang Boxes,'" *Sales & Marketing Management,* March 16, 1981, pp. 41, 42, 45.

34. *Business Week,* June 7, 1982, p. 60.

35. "A Slow Rebound for Seven-Up," *Business Week,* October 12, 1981, p. 107.

36. "Like to Shift as Seven-Up Plots Growth," *Advertising Age,* April 4, 1983, pp. 3, 75.

37. *Ad Forum,* October 1982, p. 41.

38. "How Warner-Lambert's Recipe Helps Entenmann's Go National," *The Wall Street Journal,* October 23, 1980, p. 37.

39. *Business Week,* July 19, 1982, p. 186.

40. "Mitsubishi Revs Up to Go Solo," *Business Week,* May 3, 1982, pp. 131–32.

41. *Business Week,* July 19, 1982, p. 186.

42. "What Makes Sun-Diamond Grow," *Business Week,* August 9, 1982, p. 83.

43. "Grocers' 'Middlemen' Step to the Forefront," *Advertising Age,* October 11, 1982, p. M-17.

44. "Toyota Sells Parts With Perks," *Sales & Marketing Management,* September 13, 1982, pp. 106, 108.

45. *Measuring Productivity in Physical Distribution* (Chicago: National Council of Physical Distribution Management, 1978).

46. B. J. LaLonde and P. H. Zinszer, *Customer Service: Meaning and Measurement* (Chicago: National Council of Physical Distribution Management, 1976).

47. "Distribution Can Greatly Boost Productivity," *Distribution Worldwide,* January 1979, pp. 39–40.

48. "Changes in Segmentation, Distribution, Logistics, Demand Analysis Challenge Industrial Marketers," *Marketing News,* June 26, 1981, Section 2, p. 9.

49. Ibid.

50. Philip Kotler, *Marketing Management* (Englewood Cliffs, N.J.: Prentice Hall, 1984), p. 594.

51. A. Keuhn and Michael J. Hamburger, "A Heu-

ristic Program for Locating Warehouses," *Management Science*, 9 (July 1963): 657–58; and Martin K. Starr and David W. Miller, *Inventory Control: Theory and Practice* (Englewood Cliffs, N.J.: Prentice-Hall, 1962).

52. Ronald H. Ballou, *Basic Business Logistics* (Englewood Cliffs, N.J.: Prentice-Hall, 1978), p. 310.

53. "The Best Defense is Offense," *Industrial Distribution*, November 1982, pp. 63–65.

54. Stern and El-Ansary, *Marketing Channels*, pp. 173–74.

55. David P. Herron, "Managing Physical Distribu-

tion for Profit," *Harvard Business Review* 57 (May–June 1979): 123.

56. James L. Heskett, Nicholas A. Glaskowsky, Jr., and Robert M. Ivie, *Business Logistics* (New York: The Ronald Press, 1973), pp. 607–8.

57. Stern and El-Ansary, *Marketing Channels*, pp. 169–70.

58. "Coors Charts Path Over a Rocky Road to Growth," *Advertising Age*, July 11, 1983, p. 4.

59. Ibid., p. 59.

60. Assael, "The Political Role of Trade Associations," pp. 21–28.

61. *Business Week*, October 12, 1981, p. 107.

CHAPTER **17**

Retail and Wholesale Management and Strategy

FOCUS OF CHAPTER

In the last chapter we dealt with manufacturers' distribution strategies. In this chapter we will view distribution strategy and management from the perspective of the intermediaries in the channel system — retailers and wholesalers. In the past retailing and wholesaling have been viewed as bastions of conservative marketing governed by "old fashioned" management that has failed to react to environmental opportunity or to adopt modern research and planning techniques. This view is rapidly changing. Since the early 1970s there has been an evolution (some might call it a revolution) in strategy and planning, particularly in the retail sector. Retail management has begun to utilize techniques of strategic marketing planning. It has adopted the same types of corporate growth strategies as manufacturers: diversification, market expansion, and in some cases selective retrenchment. As a result many of the old retail classifications — discount houses, department stores, general merchandisers — are becoming blurred as retail management changes its scope and methods of operation. Consider the following:

■ Retail management has begun to shift its focus from sales to return on investment. At key retailers such as J. C. Penney, Sears, and Montgomery Ward, management has begun to evaluate investments in terms of marketing opportunities.

■ As a result retailers are beginning to adapt to a changing environment. Dayton-Hudson, a well-established department store chain, recognized consumers' greater price sensitivity in the inflationary 1970s. It moved heavily into discounting. Today revenue from its discount stores dwarfs that from its traditional department stores. In 1977 discount operations accounted for less than 50 percent of sales; in 1983 they were 69 percent.[1]

523

■ Sears, the number one retailer in the country, has also become the number one purveyor of financial services by diversifying from its base as a general merchandiser. In 1981 it acquired the largest real estate organization in the country and the fifth largest stock brokerage house to add to its ownership of Allstate Insurance.[2] The reason? A recognition of the limits of rapid growth in the retail sector.

■ The strategic revolution in retailing is also spawning a technological revolution. Large retailers are beginning to offer electronic funds transfers and automatic checkout services. In the near future consumers will also be able to retrieve store catalog information on interactive TV terminals and place their orders directly from their homes.

In each of these cases management has (1) established corporate objectives, (2) evaluated marketing opportunity, (3) formulated corporate strategies for profit and growth, (4) developed store marketing strategies accordingly, and (5) instituted the means to evaluate and control their strategies. In this chapter we will be concerned with these five phases of strategy development for retailers and, to a lesser extent, wholesalers. Before considering the process of retail strategy and management, we will consider the importance of retailing and types of retailers. The last part of the chapter describes types of wholesalers, and strategy and management at the wholesale level.

Importance of Retailing

Retailing is the sale of goods to a final consumer. As such it assumes a central role in a free-market economy. In the previous chapter we noted that retailers perform the crucial functions of assembling diverse goods from various sources and making them available at locations and in quantities permitting consumers to buy.

The importance of retailing is reflected in its economic magnitude. Total retail sales in the United States in the mid-1980s were over one trillion dollars, with sales made by close to 2 million retail establishments. Table 17-1 lists sales for the top twenty-five retailers in the United States in 1981. The largest retailers are dominated by general merchandisers (Sears, Penney, Woolworth), supermarket chains (Safeway, Kroger, A&P), and discount stores (K-Mart). Sears' traditional lead as the largest retailer is being challenged by Safeway and K-Mart.

The importance of retailing goes beyond the dollar sales. Retail strategies directly affect the types of goods available to consumers, the variety, and the price. The decision by K-Mart (formerly S. S. Kresge) in the early 1960s to move from a variety store to a broadly based discount operation meant that

TABLE 17-1
Twenty-five Largest Retailers in the United States, 1981

Rank	1981 RETAIL SALES (000)
1. Sears	$16,865,000
2. Safeway	15,102,700
3. K-Mart	14,204,400
4. J. C. Penney	11,353,000
5. Kroger	10,316,741
6. F. W. Woolworth	7,218,000
7. A&P	6,989,529
8. Lucky Stores	6,468,682
9. American Stores	6,419,884
10. Federated Department Stores	6,300,686
11. Montgomery Ward	5,500,000
12. Winn-Dixie	5,388,979
13. City Products	4,462,000
14. Southland	4,294,100
15. Jewel Companies	4,267,922
16. Dayton-Hudson	4,033,536
17. Wickes	3,919,436
18. Grand Union	3,626,000
19. May Department Stores	3,149,800
20. Albertson's	3,039,129
21. Carter Hawley Hale	2,632,921
22. Supermarkets General	2,628,851
23. R. H. Macy	2,373,531
25. Melville	2,332,244
25. Allied Stores	2,267,711

Source: "Trends in Retailing, 1982," *Marketing Communications,* February 1982, p. 54.

many customers could now buy quality merchandise at discount prices. The decision by Sears to offer insurance policies, real estate brokerage services, and stock purchasing services in 250 of its retail outlets means that these services will be available to many consumers who might not ordinarily consider them.[3] The rash of failures of discount houses in the early 1980s (e.g., Woolco, Korvette, Goldblatt) means that fewer consumers will have the no-frills, low-price option. In each of these cases retail decisions have directly affected product alternatives and consumer behavior.

The importance of retailing is also reflected in the fact that, for the manufacturer, the retailer is the essential link to the final consumer. Without retailers, manufacturers would have to invest millions of dollars to reach consumers directly.

Types of Retailers

Retailers have been classified as department stores, discount houses, general merchandise stores, supermarkets, specialty stores, and convenience stores. One of the problems with this classification is that it is too static. The distinctions among discount stores, department stores, and general merchandisers have become blurred as discounters such as Caldor and Target Stores have begun to offer more services and better-quality merchandise, and department stores such as Macy's and Saks are offering lower prices to become more competitive. General merchandisers such as Montgomery-Ward and J. C. Penney found themselves in a profit squeeze between discounters and department stores. Both have reacted by upgrading their product mix and moving closer to department stores. As a result it would be difficult to label Penney and Ward clearly as either general-line merchandisers or department stores.

Another problem with these classifications is that they refer to the retail store but not to retail corporations. Many retail corporations are spread across department, discount, and specialty stores. For example, Woolworth started out as a variety store, moved into discount operations in the early 1960s with its Woolco chain, eliminated Woolco in 1983, and is now concentrating on acquiring specialty stores such as Kinney Shoes and The Shirt Closet.[4] Today it has more specialty stores than variety or discount stores.

A third problem with these classifications is that they do not reflect the importance of nonstore retailing. Consumers frequently buy products from door-to-door salespeople, through catalogs, and by phone.

Bearing these limitations in mind, in this section we classify retailers into three broad categories: merchandisers, food stores, and nonstore retailers. Figure 17-1 lists merchandisers and food stores by (1) level of service, (2) price, (3) breadth of assortment (number of product lines carried by the store), (4) variety of products in a given line, and (5) size of establishment.

MERCHANDISERS

Merchandisers are on a continuum from small, specialized, high-priced, service-oriented stores (specialty stores in Figure 17-1) to large, mass-merchandise, low-price, self-service stores (discount houses).

Specialty and Department Stores

Specialty stores (clothing stores, furniture outlets, florists, computer stores, etc.) carry few product lines but a broad range of goods within a given line. Specialty stores have been a fast-growing segment of the retail sector. Their emphasis on specific lines appeals to the quality-conscious consumer who prefers a broader variety of models or styles than department stores or discount houses might provide.

Department stores are full-service establishments that carry several product lines (generally clothing, furniture, household goods) in some depth. Department

MERCHANDISERS

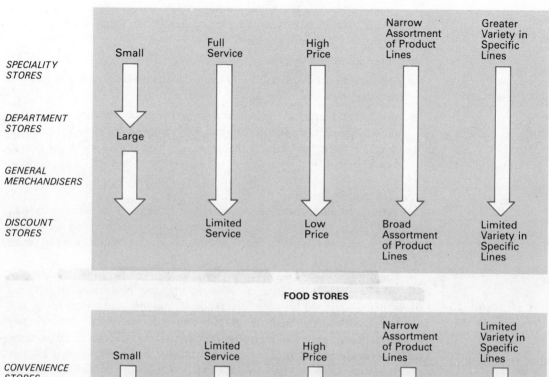

FOOD STORES

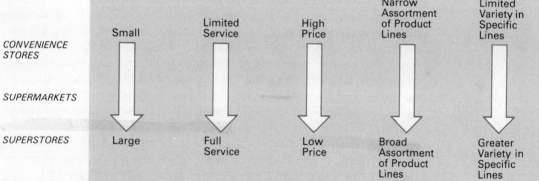

FIGURE 17-1
Characteristics of retailers by type of store

stores have not fared as well as specialty stores in recent years because of (1) price pressures from discount houses, (2) loss of customers to specialty stores, and (3) the deterioration of central cities, which has made downtown shopping less appealing. Some retail experts have concluded that as a result of being attacked at the high end by specialty stores and at the low end by discount houses, department stores may cease to exist.

Department store chains have reacted to these threats by:

- opening bargain basements to deflect price pressures from discount houses (Filene's, a traditional Boston retailer, has exported its bargain basement to other Eastern cities by opening nine "bargain basement" department stores);[5]

- acquiring discount stores;

- emphasizing catalog sales to counteract declining sales in downtown shopping areas; and

- introducing boutiques and specialty departments as a means of meeting the challenge from specialty stores. (Bloomingdale's, a New York department store, has perfume boutiques, clothing boutiques, and a gourmet food shop.)

General Merchandisers

General merchandisers provide a broader assortment of goods than department stores (e.g., Sears sells items as diverse as tires, clothing, and washing machines). They are positioned between department stores and discount houses in terms of price and service.

The largest retailers — Sears, Montgomery Ward, J. C. Penney — are general merchandisers. They have encountered the same problem as department stores, being squeezed between "professionally run discount chains at one end and high-fashion department or specialty stores at the other."[6] J. C. Penney was the first among the big three general merchandisers to react to this squeeze with a strategic plan. Starting in the mid 1970s it attempted to shed its "low priced Middle America image" with a shift to higher-priced, fashion-oriented items.[7] The chain is eliminating its household appliances, auto equipment and accessories, hardware items, and garden equipment lines. It has signed an exclusive contract with Halston, the high fashion designer, to carry that clothing line. The shift in the product mix is designed, according to Penney's former chairman, to make the company "the only truly national department store chain in the country."[8] In other words Penney is narrowing its assortment of product lines and providing more variety per line at a greater range of prices, putting it closer to the definition of a department store in Figure 17-1.

Discount Stores

Discount stores offer goods at the lowest prices on a self-service basis. But low price should not imply shoddy merchandise. Most discounters offer well-known national brands. The reason merchandise is offered at a lower price is that stores operate in low-rent areas, provide minimum facilities, and are not concerned with decor and fixtures.

The largest discounter in the country, K-Mart, has been successful by keeping costs down while scaling up its merchandise. As a result it has built a strong reputation among its customers for "value, price, and merchandising quality."[9] Department store chains have watched K-Mart's success and realized the potential for profits in "upscale discounting," that is, offering some of the same high quality items they sell in their department stores in separate, no-frill discount stores at lower prices. These companies "are increasingly oriented toward spending their capital where they get the best return on investment, and that means upscale discounters rather than department stores."[10]

Discounters who have not followed this trend have suffered. Woolco went out of business because of a combination of inadequate cost controls and an inability to maintain a quality image in competition with more successful discounters.

FOOD STORES

Figure 17-1 lists the three most important types of food stores — convenience stores, supermarkets, and superstores — and their characteristics.

Convenience Stores

Convenience stores are so named because they are conveniently located near residential areas and stay open longer than other food stores. They carry a limited line of high-turnover convenience items and charge higher prices because of higher costs of operation.

Convenience stores have enjoyed tremendous growth in recent years because of (1) the greater number of working women, resulting in more off-hours shopping, (2) the growing number of single shoppers who demand fast service for smaller purchases, and (3) the growth of fast-food establishments which has meant that consumers are less likely to eat at home and tend to purchase smaller amounts of food, primarily for convenience. As a result, convenience stores grew from 2,000 in 1957 to 36,000 in 1981.[11]

Supermarkets

Supermarkets are by far the most important food store establishments, representing nearly 80 percent of grocery store sales.[12] The average supermarket is over six times the size of a convenience store and carries over eight times as many items. Supermarkets are low-cost, high-volume operations with an average stock turnover of 25 times a year. Yet they operate on a very small margin, averaging only 1 percent profit on sales.

Higher costs, more intense competition, and shrinking margins have caused supermarket management to:

- expand their product mix into higher-margin nonfood items, a trend that has come to be known as **scrambled merchandising** (for example, Safeway has introduced gift centers, liquor barns, home improvement centers, photography sections, and flower markets);[13]

- diversify into more profitable areas (e.g., Stop & Shop of New England owns a general merchandise chain, drugstores, tobacco shops, apparel stores, and a food manufacturing company);[14]

- upgrade their facilities (the Byerly supermarket chain in the Midwest is targeting its stores to young, affluent shoppers by carrying a much greater variety of high quality food items); and

- reduce reliance on lower-margin national brands by emphasizing private-brand merchandise (at Safeway, the store's own brands account for 30 percent of sales).[15]

Superstores

Superstores are very large supermarkets that engage in extensive scrambled merchandising. They are at least twice as large as supermarkets (30,000 square feet and up compared to 17,000).[16] The largest superstores, those over 100,000 square feet, are called *hypermarkets*.

The main advantage of superstores is one-stop shopping. These stores carry a wide variety of drug items, hardware, beauty aids, and soft goods, as well as food. Kroger and Safeway are building superstores in the expectation that the consumer's emphasis on convenience will make these outlets profitable. The stores provide supermarket chains with higher profit margins, but there are risks, namely the high cost of construction and higher operating costs. The failure of a superstore means the loss of millions of dollars.

NONSTORE RETAILING

The retail categories we have listed all describe stores. Yet nonstore retailing has grown faster than store retailing in recent years and accounts for about 12 percent of consumer purchases. The following nonstore retailing methods have been used widely:

- mail-order,

- telephone,

- door-to-door selling,

- buying services that enable consumers who become members to buy a wide variety of products at a discount, and

- vending machines.

The nonstore retailing facility with the greatest potential is *in-home electronic marketing*. As we noted in Chapter 3, videotext systems permit consumers with interactive cable TV to purchase merchandise displayed on their television screen by simply ordering through a small terminal. Some retail experts believe that by the end of this century, "almost all food and other basic household needs will be acquired through the use of in-house television computer systems, and shopping choices will be made after viewing ... brands on the television screen."[17] Sears is the retailer doing most to develop this facility. It tested in-home electronic shopping jointly with AT&T and Knight-Ridder newspapers in the early 1980s and is currently testing a videotext system with IBM and CBS designed for home computers. One analyst predicts that by 1990 Sears' nonstore sales (both catalog and electronic shopping) will be greater than its store sales.[18]

Although electronic shopping and nonstore retailing in general are likely to grow further, many marketers express doubt that they will ever approach store sales. They cite the following limitations to nonstore retailing:

- consumers like to see, touch, feel and examine products first-hand, as well as to make comparisons to other products;

- consumers prefer to have someone to turn to for information;

- shopping is a pleasant experience for many consumers;

- delivery of products is required, increasing uncertainty; and

- stores offer services that cannot be offered by most nonstore marketers (e.g., demonstrations, consultation, sampling).

Limits to Retail Growth

The difficulties faced by many of the largest retailers in recent years suggest that growth in the retail sector may be limited. Until the early 1970s "retailers in the United States [were] confronted with an ever-expanding market. The population was growing, real per capita incomes were constantly climbing, and the suburbs awaited new retail stores. However, by the mid-1970s, the magic of growth vanished."[19] Retailers were caught in a profit squeeze between downward price pressures from discounters and rising costs. In addition:

1. consumers became more price conscious;

2. population growth was decreasing in most urban areas ouside the Sunbelt;

3. the high cost of capital made it difficult for retailers to expand, since high interest rates eat into traditionally low margins; and

4. competition intensified.[20]

As a result, "it was the consensus of retail analysts that the 1980s would be characterized by flat or, at best, moderate growth curves."[21]

Many retailers have reacted to shrinking margins by emphasizing high-quality, high-margin items. Thus, food stores carry nonfood items and discount houses have engaged in **"upscale discounting"** by carrying higher-quality merchandise. But in so doing these retailers run the danger of losing their identity and, as a result, their core markets. Other retailers (such as Stop & Shop) have begun to diversify into unrelated areas. But there is danger here too, as retail management enters unfamiliar fields. After a rash of diversifications many of these retailers have decided to go back to their core business.

The economic pressures on retailers have moderated with the economic recovery after 1982. But the experiences of two major recessions within seven years left retailers with a fear of low growth potential and increased competition. As a result, many retailers have recognized a need to be more efficient in developing marketing plans by carefully evaluating marketing opportunities and designing strategies to exploit them. In the next section we will look at a process of retail planning and strategy development designed to promote growth in a more competitive environment.

Retail Planning and Strategy

Figure 17-2 depicts a process of planning to develop and implement retail strategies. The retail planning process is similar to the marketing planning process described in Chapter 3. The first step is to define retail objectives. For example, Limited Inc., a specialty women's apparel retailer, wanted to ensure its steady growth by expanding its market beyond its traditional base of young, price-conscious, working women. Its evaluation of market opportunity (the second step in Figure 17-2) suggested the existence of a profitable market niche in (1) special sizes, particularly among middle-aged women, and (2) mail-order catalog sales. As a result, Limited developed a corporate strategy of store expansion (step 3 in the planning process). It decided to acquire a retail chain that targeted the special-size market and had mail-order capabilities. The result was the acquisition of 207 Lane Bryant stores, a privately owned chain merchandising large-size women's apparel.[22]

The next step in the retail planning process is to define target segments and position retail stores accordingly. The typical customer in the Lane Bryant store was a lower-income, overweight woman who bought clothes infrequently. Limited wanted to reposition the store to appeal to an upscale, fashion-conscious woman in line with the parent company's positioning of its own stores. This positioning strategy directly affects the fifth step in Figure 17-2, development of strategies at the store level. The company plans to reduce the number of lines carried, but increase the depth per line.[23] It also plans to reduce advertising in order to cut costs and to expand the mail-order capability of Lane Bryant.

The final step in the retail planning process is evaluation of retail performance and control over implementation of strategies. Limited will have to track retail and mail-order sales at Lane Bryant and keep a careful watch over costs, particularly since it incurred a high level of debt to acquire the company.

RETAIL OBJECTIVES

Retail objectives should be broad enough to guide overall corporate strategy (e.g., a statement of corporate mission), yet specific enough to measure retail performance at the store level.

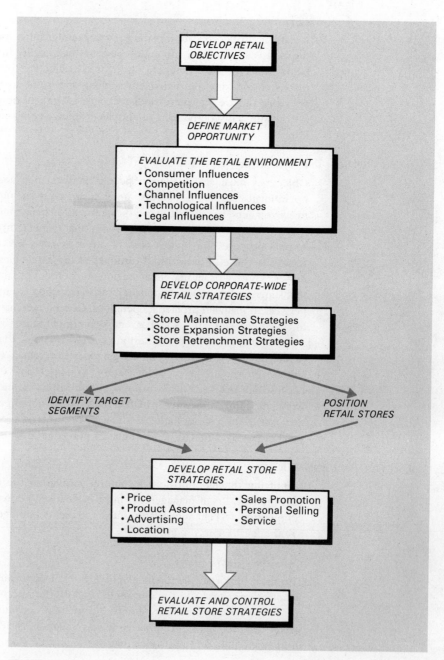

FIGURE 17-2
The retail planning process

Corporate Mission

A statement of corporate mission for a discounter might be to give consumers the best value for their money by offering high-quality merchandise at prices below those of local competition. A broad objective for a department store that is considering alternative investment opportunities might be to restrict operations to areas of merchandise expertise. Such an objective would permit it to acquire a discount chain, but not an insurance company or a manufacturing firm.

Performance Goals

Objectives must also be fairly specific. Performance goals can be stated in operational and financial terms. *Stock turnover* is an important criterion for many retailers, because it is the only means for maintaining reasonable profit levels with low margins. One study found that manufacturing firms obtain high returns because of a higher ratio of profit to sales, but retailers obtain high returns because of more rapid turnover of the assets employed in their businesses.[24] With a profit margin averaging one percent of sales, it is not surprising that supermarkets must obtain stock turns averaging twenty-five to thirty times per year to maintain profitable operations. General merchandisers require fifteen to seventeen stock turns a year, and department stores require even fewer.[25]

Another performance criterion is *profit margin,* that is, net profits as a percentage of sale. But profit margin does not reflect turnover of assets. A supermarket might have a profit margin of one percent yet be highly profitable because of a very high stock turnover. A more effective measure of performance would be *return on assets,* which is the product of the profit margin and asset turnover. Thus a supermarket with an asset turnover of twenty-five and a one percent profit margin is achieving a 25 percent return on assets.

THE RETAIL ENVIRONMENT

Identifying retail opportunities requires evaluating the company's operating environment. Retail management must evaluate (1) consumer influences, (2) competition, (3) channel relationships, (4) the technological environment, and (5) the legal environment.

Consumer Influences

The most important factor in identifying retail opportunity is the consumer. Retailers must evaluate the consumer on both the micro and macro level. On the micro level retailers are interested in how consumers select a store in which to purchase. On the macro level retailers must identify broad changes in demographics and life styles that may influence store choice.

Store choice

Consumers select stores by identifying certain shopping needs (e.g., availability of their favorite brands, convenient locations, good value). They then form images of stores because of the store's advertising, their experience with the store, and opinions of friends and relatives. Consumers will select the store that is perceived as most closely filling their shopping needs. To develop appropriate marketing strategies, the retailer must:

1. determine the store's image,
2. assess the effect of in-store stimuli and advertising on store selection, and
3. identify store-loyal consumers.

Store image can be determined by asking customers to rate the store on its reputation, decor, product variety, value, store service, and so on. Figure 17-3 shows the results of a 1975 study that positioned several department stores and general merchandisers by consumers' store image. Penney was positioned as a medium-priced store carrying a broad assortment of products.

FIGURE 17-3
Relative position of six retailers on the basis of store image

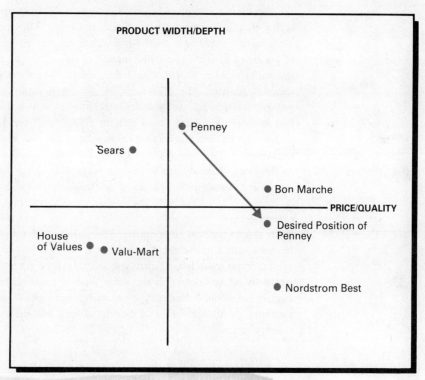

Source: Adapted from Ricardo L. Singson, "Multidimensional Scaling Analysis of Store Image and Shopping Behavior," *Journal of Retailing* 51 (Summer 1975): 38–52.

Penney's current strategy to reposition itself as a store carrying more limited but higher-quality lines is represented by the arrow in Figure 17-3. If consumers shift their image of Penney in accordance with the arrow, Penney's strategy has been successful.

In-store stimuli and advertising influence store image and selection. The spartan decor of K-Mart stores encourages an image of a low-priced, no-frills discounter. But K-Mart also spent close to $18 million on network TV in 1980 to convince customers that it provides high quality as well as low price.[26]

Store loyalty is important to retailers. Stores with more loyal customers tend to be more profitable since they attract more consumer expenditures.[27] But inflationary pressures and frequent economic downturns have reduced store loyalty. In a study by a large research firm, almost half of all shoppers interviewed said that between 1980 and 1982 they switched from their favorite supermarket to one that offered lower prices.[28] A decrease in store loyalty is likely to increase the profit squeeze on retailers through the 1980s, further decreasing the potential for growth.

Demographic and life-style trends

Retailers must identify broad changes in demographics and consumer life styles that may affect store choice behavior. The increasing proportion of working women has caused Kroger and Safeway to increase their assortment of goods to provide the convenience of one-stop shopping. The rapid shift to the suburbs after World War II resulted in the development of the suburban shopping center. The growth of the "me generation" with its orientation to self-gratification has caused department stores to emphasize product quality and in-store decor. Macy's Cellar in New York "has been reprogrammed to provide an exciting, sensuous environment to ... younger Manhattan life-style segments."[29] The search for more leisure time has caused some merchandisers to develop technologies to reduce shopping effort. One result has been an increase in catalog shopping and toll-free telephone ordering of merchandise.

Competition

With the exception of specialty stores that have found a niche, competition has intensified in the retail sector since the mid-1970s. Competitive pressures are reflected in increased intratype and intertype competition. **Intratype competition** occurs between the same type of retailer. **Intertype competition** occurs between different types of stores selling the same merchandise — for example, drugstores, general merchandisers, and discounters selling drug and toiletry items.

Intratype competition

Competition between larger retailers has been primarily price competition. Stores that are directly competitive generally use price cuts leading to even tighter profits. For example, A&P's WEO (Where Economy Originates) campaign in the early 1970s involved heavy price cuts which were duplicated by many chains. The figures below indicate the disastrous results of the price-cutting strategy for both A&P and its closest competitors:[30]

Profits as a % of Net Sales

	1970	*1971*	*1972*	*1973*
Chains with little A&P competition	1.4	1.5	1.5	1.4
Chains competing with A&P	0.9	0.8	0.2	0.4
A&P	0.9	0.3	−0.8	0.2

A&P's actions in the early 1970s reflected a policy of price leadership. But the result was losses for the chain and its competitors in the face of shrinking margins. Other retailers have tried to be merchandise rather than price leaders by improving the quality of their goods. Dayton-Hudson's Mervyn discount chain has followed an upscale discounting strategy by increasing the quality of its product line.

Some competitors have followed a reactive strategy. One of the problems at Montgomery Ward was that over a twenty-year period, newly hired executives from Sears kept following Sears's strategies, with the result that Ward has a very fuzzy image in consumers' minds.[31]

Intertype competition

Intertype competition has intensified with the increase in scrambled merchandising. Margins on products sold on an intertype basis have begun to shrink, however, as a result of greater competition. One study found that margins on items such as baby products, hair care products, men's toiletries, and cosmetics have decreased by at least 15 percent as these products began to be sold in different types of stores.[32] The irony is that as margins shrink the rationale for engaging in such intertype competition disappears.

Reactions to increased competition

One way for large retailers to increase profits in the face of increased competition is to improve productivity. Safeway's reaction to more stagnant growth in the late 1970s was to try to "whittle costs and boost productivity with new labor-saving systems." These range from computerized distribution centers to electronic checkouts.[33] Increases in productivity will require improved inventory control, distribution cost analysis, and information on market trends.

Another reaction to increased competition has been increased emphasis on market share. If retailers cannot look to an expanding market, they must then look to expanding their share of the existing market. The rationale for more emphasis on market share was provided by one study that linked high retail market share to higher ROI. Consider the following data:[34]

Retail Market Share	*ROI (percent)*
Greater than 14 percent	29.0
8–14 percent	20.0
Less than 8 percent	8.4

One retail expert believes that retailers will be more successful in obtaining market share if they follow a **strategic leveraging** approach; that is, determining what one does better than competition and then committing whatever resources are necessary to this area.[35] Following a strategic leveraging approach has led many retailers to deemphasize diversification into unrelated businesses as a strategy for coping with low growth and greater competition. They have decided instead to emphasize gaining market share in their core businesses.

Channel Influences

Retailers must evaluate channel relationships in identifying marketing opportunities. Relationships with manufacturers and wholesalers in the channel system and decisions about the makeup of the channel system will directly affect a retailer's profits.

In the last chapter we discussed manufacturer-retailer relationships and the conflicts that arise. In most cases the manufacturer is the larger and more economically powerful unit. Manufacturers, as channel leaders, try to ensure that retailers will stock and effectively sell their goods by offering a wide range of concessions to gain retailer support. Manufacturers provide assistance such as price discounts, cooperative advertising allowances, training programs, and financing. They also help retailers reduce risk through consignment selling, return allowances on unsold goods, and territorial protection through selective or exclusive distributorships. Retailers decide which manufacturers to buy from by the type of assistance provided as well as the price and quality of the manufacturers' merchandise.

In some cases the retailer will be the larger and more dominant member of the channel system. Retailers such as Sears, Penney, and K-Mart can exert control over wholesalers and sources of supply. Some of these retailers have integrated backward by acquiring manufacturers in order to control their sources. For example, Sears obtains over 50 percent of its merchandise from manufacturers in which it has an equity interest. It has substantial ownership in Whirlpool, Kellwood apparel, Armstrong Rubber, and EASCO hand tools.[36] Revco, the largest discount drugstore in the United States, has acquired manufacturers of vitamins, food supplements, cough syrup, shampoos, and liquid antibiotics. Profits from their manufacturing operations are higher than those from their retail operations.[37]

Large retailers do not have to own their sources of supply to serve as channel leaders. Department stores, general merchandisers, and supermarkets frequently offer many of the same types of aids we have described (for example, financing, managerial assistance, and risk reduction programs) to smaller manufacturers.

Technological Influences

Several technological innovations have given retailers opportunities to expand in-home sales and to reduce their costs of operation. In describing nonstore retailing we cited two such technological advances — in-home shopping via cable TV, and computerized buying services.

Additional technologies that offer retailer opportunities are:

- *Merchandise handling systems.* Some large retailers that own their own warehouses have installed computerized, automated warehouse conveyor systems. K-Mart and Safeway improved their turnaround time from order receipt to delivery after installing such systems.[38]

- *Checkout scanning.* The introduction of scanner facilities in many supermarkets (see Chapter 7) has increased productivity because stockers do not have to price each item and because cashiers can work faster. Another benefit is that scanners provide retailers with a rich source of purchase data.

- *Electronic funds transfer.* Electronic retail payment systems are likely to become widespread. Dahl's Foods, a Des Moines supermarket, is testing such a system with National Cash Register. The system enables customers to pay for groceries electronically by using a bank card to transfer funds from their account to the supermarket's.[39] The ability to complete the transfer of funds at the moment of purchase accelerates the retailer's cash flow and reduces fraudulent charges and bad checks.

- *In-store television.* Some supermarkets are installing closed-circuit TV monitors over checkout counters to transmit commercials for national advertisers. This new method of advertising may be more effective since it reaches the consumers while they are shopping. Such monitors can also be used to supply shoppers with price and product information.

Legal Influences

Retailers must consider legal constraints on their actions, particularly in two areas — pricing and distribution.

Pricing

The same pricing constraints that apply to manufacturers also apply to retailers, specifically:

1. *Price fixing.* Retailers are prohibited from engaging in **horizontal price fixing,** that is, competitive retailers cannot agree on a common price in a given area. For example, three of the largest supermarket chains in Cleveland

were indicted for conspiring to fix food prices from 1976 to 1978.[40] Retailers are also prohibited from conspiring with manufacturers to fix retail prices (**vertical price fixing**). Although fair trade laws permitted manufacturers to stipulate the price retailers should charge, such actions are now illegal.

2. *Price discrimination.* Retailers must be careful not to violate the Robinson Patman Act's prohibition of **price discrimination.** If a manufacturer offers a particular retailer a lower price or a discount not offered to similar retailers, the manufacturer is guilty of offering the discriminatory price and the retailer is guilty of accepting it. At times larger retailers might put pressure on smaller manufacturers to obtain preferential prices. A&P was involved in a five-year battle with the FTC over charges that it tried to force its suppliers to grant it lower prices than those charged to other buyers.[41]

3. **Deceptive pricing.** Retailers are prohibited from using deceptive prices. Some retailers advertise products at unusually low prices (loss leaders) to get consumers into the store and then claim they are out of the item. They then encourage consumers to look around for other merchandise. If such practices are systematic, they are illegal. Advertising low prices and then adding hidden charges also constitutes deceptive pricing.

Distributive relationships

Retailers are affected by various laws regarding distributive relationships. If retailers agree to carry a manufacturer's line to the exclusion of others, and if such action lessens trade, it is illegal. Further, granting an exclusive territory to a retailer may be judged illegal by the courts. Because of the increase in franchising, retailers entering such an arrangement should be aware that the franchisor has no right to set the retail price at which goods are sold or to require the franchisee to purchase materials and supplies from the franchisor.

CORPORATE RETAIL STRATEGIES

Once retailers have evaluated their environment, they are in a better position to consider strategy development. Figure 17-2 distinguished between retail strategies at the corporate and store level. Corporate strategies deal with overall operations and may involve more than one type of retailer. For example, Woolworth's corporate strategies involve variety, discount, and specialty-store operations. Retail-store strategies are used to get consumers to shop at the store. Corporate strategies are used to outline a systematic course of action to ensure future growth and profits across all stores.

Figure 17-4 outlines various corporatewide retail strategies using two dimensions: (1) the level of store operations (whether the company is maintaining, expanding, or reducing the number of stores in operation); and (2) the level of new market activities (whether the company is continuing to focus on existing markets, entering new markets, or entering new lines of business). As with other types of strategies, retailers may follow more than one strategy simultaneously in developing a rational strategic plan for growth.

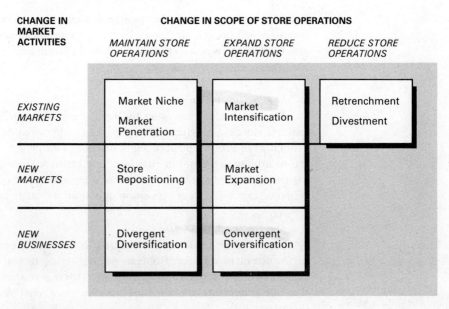

CHANGE IN MARKET ACTIVITIES

CHANGE IN SCOPE OF STORE OPERATIONS

	MAINTAIN STORE OPERATIONS	EXPAND STORE OPERATIONS	REDUCE STORE OPERATIONS
EXISTING MARKETS	Market Niche Market Penetration	Market Intensification	Retrenchment Divestment
NEW MARKETS	Store Repositioning	Market Expansion	
NEW BUSINESSES	Divergent Diversification	Convergent Diversification	

FIGURE 17-4
Corporatewide retail strategies

Maintenance Strategies

Because of the sluggish growth in retailing in the 1970s and early 1980s, most retailers have opted to maintain rather than expand store operations. Yet such a strategy need not constrain profits. Retailers can intensify their activities in existing markets (market penetration), attempt to appeal to new markets with existing stores (repositioning), or enter new nonretail businesses as a hedge against a slow growing retail sector (divergent diversification).

Market penetration

Market penetration is a market share strategy. The firm is seeking to gain a larger share of an existing market through existing stores. A successful penetration strategy requires strategic leveraging — that is, finding a basis for operating retail stores that will outperform competitors. A good example is Southland, owner of 7-Eleven stores. The company has won a competitive advantage by offering late hour and weekend shopping in convenient locations in over 7,000 stores. The company plans to penetrate existing markets further as a base for future expansion. The vice-president of marketing described Southland's strategy:

> If we do the right kind of marketing job, then we can take the existing base of stores and substantially increase our sales and dollars per square foot. And by doing that, we can make each business unit more productive, allowing us to open more locations successfully.[42]

Southland's strategy for further penetrating existing markets involves increasing its advertising budget, directing advertising to well-defined demographic groups, and expanding its product mix to combine the advantages of greater product assortment with convenience.

Store repositioning

Retailers can increase sales by appealing to new market segments through existing stores. An extension of the store's appeal to new market segments generally requires a repositioning of the store's image. J. C. Penney's repositioning to a higher-quality but narrower line of merchandise was an attempt to expand its base to attract more upscale consumers. The company has no plans for store expansion. It is repositioning within its existing base of stores.

Divergent diversification

Several large retailers have reacted to slow retail growth by maintaining their current base of retail operations, but trying to find profit opportunities outside of retailing. Such a strategy is called divergent diversification to contrast it to one in which retailers acquire other types of retail businesses (convergent diversification).

The leader in divergent diversification has been Sears. The company's profit margin in its retail stores decreased from 4.9 percent in 1977 to 2.9 percent in 1982.[43] The company faced the same competitive squeeze as J. C. Penney, but failed to position itself to well-defined demographic targets. Whereas Penney repositioned its existing stores, Sears sought to expand its higher-profit financial service operations.

Since 1981 Sears has expanded its financial services beyond its property and life insurance subsidiary, Allstate Insurance. Financial services now include:[44]

- mortgage life insurance;
- savings and loan operations in California;
- Dean Witter Reynolds, the country's fifth largest stock brokerage firm;
- Coldwell Banker, the largest real estate broker;
- personal lending facilities to rival finance companies and banks;
- United States government money market funds;
- a debit card to offer banklike savings and checking services; and
- automated teller machines in Sears retail stores.

The company has no plans to expand its network of 831 retail stores and 2388 catalog outlets. But it is expanding financial services by offering them in many of its retail stores. Shoppers can purchase securities, insurance, and real estate in 250 Sears stores, representing the ultimate in scrambled merchandising (see Figure 17-5).[45] Sales in the in-store financial centers have exceeded management's expectations.

FIGURE 17-5
An Example of Divergent Diversification

Source: The New York Times Special Features, Tom Meyer cartoon. Reprinted by permission.

Expansion Strategies

Some retailers have identified opportunities for expansion by increasing the number of stores in existing areas (market intensification), expanding into new geographic areas (market expansion), or acquiring other retail companies (convergent acquisition).

Market intensification

By having more stores in a given area, a retail chain gains economies of scale in distribution and the potential to be the strongest retailer in the area. Walgreen, the first drugstore chain in the United States, is using a strategy of market intensification after having tried divergent diversification in the mid-1970s. Diversification "saddled the company with an array of unprofitable peripheral businesses."[46] As a result, in 1978 top management asked itself, "What is our strength?" The answer was drugstores. The resulting divestiture of many of its acquisitions gave Walgreen the base for expanding its stores. The company saw an opportunity to capitalize on its name and strong customer loyalty. Since the change in direction Walgreen added 35 percent more stores so that by 1983 it had close to a thousand stores nationwide. But store expansion occurred in existing markets. For example, the company went from 100 to 180 stores in Chicago.[47] Market intensification has three advantages for Walgreen: (1) economies of scale in advertising, (2) economies of scale in distribution, resulting in cheaper warehouse and transportation costs per store,[48] and (3) more efficient regional supervision of store managers.

As part of its strategy the company has doubled its advertising budget in areas of market intensification and is continuing to resist the trend toward scrambled merchandising. Since Walgreen's move to return to its base business, earnings have tripled.

Market expansion

Market expansion increases the retailer's store base in additional geographic areas. Retailers following strategies of market intensification and expansion tend to see opportunities for growth in their core businesses and shun diversification as a growth strategy. K-Mart is an example. The number two retailer in the country has been successful in offering national brands at the lowest prices. It rode the tide of the inflationary 1970s with increased sales because of a more price conscious public. As a result it has been generating excess cash. The cash has been plowed back into K-Mart's core business, discounting. In the late 1970s the company was opening an average of 170 new stores each year[49] and is now challenging Sears's position as the largest American retailer. By 1981 the company's expansion into new markets slowed, and it began concentrating its new stores in existing markets — moving from a strategy of market expansion to market intensificaton.[50] But it still avoids using its excess cash to acquire peripheral businesses.

Convergent diversification

Some retailers have reacted to slow growth in their areas by identifying opportunity in other retail areas. Department store chains in particular have sought to expand their retail base by going into discounting. Federated opened a chain of Gold Circle discount stores, May's opened its Venture discount chain, Dayton Hudson acquired Mervyn discount chain, Associated Dry Goods acquired Caldor, and Rich's opened a chain of Richway discount houses.[51] In each case department stores saw an opportunity to fill a gap between traditional discounters such as K-Mart and their own higher-priced lines. As a result they went into upscale discounting by offering higher quality merchandise than the discounters and filling a void in the mid-price range. These retailers also chose convergent over divergent diversification, because they could transfer their department store expertise to upscale discounting.

Retrenchment and Divestment Strategies

Some retailers have recognized the need to scale back operations for greater efficiency in a limited-growth situation. Such a strategy may require scaling back the number of stores to eliminate smaller and less efficient operations (retrenchment). A&P is using retrenchment, eliminating its smaller stores in favor of larger, more efficient stores that can maintain enough stock turns to ensure profitability. It has eliminated 2300 stores since 1974 and moved out of key markets such as Chicago and Philadelphia in an attempt to cut back to a profitable core of stores.[52]

A more common strategy for many retailers who followed a strategy of divergent diversification is the divestment of these acquisitions. Zale, a large jewelry chain with 840 stores, is divesting itself of shoe, drug, and sporting goods businesses to finance more stores.[53] As did Walgreen, Zale's management realized that the best path to growth lay in going back to their core businesses.

MARKET SEGMENTATION AND STORE POSITIONING

Establishing corporate growth strategies permits a retailer to focus on strategies at the store level. Retailers must first ensure that they have identified the appropriate target segments for their merchandise and that their stores are positioned to meet the needs of these segments. As Figure 17-1 illustrated, market segmentation and store positioning strategies will influence marketing strategies at the store level. Merchandise, price, service, location, and advertising must be consistent with the image the store is trying to convey to its target segment.

For example, Jordan Marsh, a regional chain based in Boston, had an image of a conservative store with a solid 130-year-old reputation that appealed to a vast middle market that "drove midsize cars and lived in houses behind little picket fences."[54] The company realized that if it was to compete effectively with its close rival, Filene's, it would have to appeal to a younger, more affluent, and fashion-conscious target. As a result, in 1979 it began to reposition its stores. The company launched a $30 million campaign to:[55]

- upgrade the physical decor of its stores to "get away from the barnlike look";
- select high-visibility brands known for quality and fashion;
- streamline an expanded TV campaign to emphasize a modern, youthful, and active look;
- develop catalog and print material that is coordinated with its ad campaign; and
- introduce a new magazine, *JM*, to show Jordan Marsh products in fashion-oriented settings.

MARKETING STRATEGIES AT THE STORE LEVEL

A store's positioning strategy provides guidance for setting marketing strategies. Stores must establish strategies in each basic marketing area:

- price,

- product assortment,

- advertising,

- sales promotion,

- personal selling and service, and

- location.

Price

Stores follow a general pricing policy to reflect their image — for example, maintaining a high-price policy to convey a high-fashion, status-oriented image. But retailers must also price specific items. Because of the large number of items in a retail store, it would be difficult to price each item on a demand-oriented basis by studying consumer responses to different price levels. Most retailers price using a markup approach. They add a certain margin to the cost of the item to cover their expenses and to try to meet profit goals. (See Chapter 15).

Markups will be higher when (1) demand is seasonal, requiring a higher price to overcome the risk of not selling, (2) the item is specialized and sold through fewer outlets, (3) demand for the product in inelastic, and (4) storage and handling costs are high.[56] A typical markup is 50 percent of the selling price, but the percentage markup does not have to be consistent. Lower-priced items can carry lower markups because they are likely to turn over faster. Some stores also use price lining — carrying different price ranges in a given line. For example, a store might carry higher-priced suits with three price lines (say $400, $325, and $280) and mid-priced suits with two price lines ($250 and $180). Price lining facilitates the price-setting process, since the store buyer knows that purchases have to conform to these five lines. It also allows the consumer to compare alternatives.

Pricing decisions must also be made about the level and timing of *mark-downs*. Retailers that emphasize low margins and high turnovers are likely to mark down merchandise early. Such markdowns speed the movement of goods and finance the purchase of more saleable merchandise. Stores that do not mark down on a daily basis run holiday sales or semiannual clearances to sell slow-moving merchandise. The magnitude of the markdown is based on the retailer's judgment on what price decrease is required to move the item. Retailers sometimes mark down their merchandise in stages, offering a greater markdown as the item remains in stock longer.

Product Assortment

Retailers must make decisions about the variety of products they offer (width of product assortment) and the depth of offerings in individual product lines. The importance of product assortment is illustrated by the different positioning strategies followed by Penney and Sears. Penney believes, in the words of one retail expert, "The mass merchants' formula for presenting a store with a full assortment of goods is really obsolete."[57] As a result the company has reduced its product assortment by announcing that it will no longer offer major appliances, paint, hardware, fabric, lawn and garden supplies, and automotive products in its stores. Instead, it is increasing the depth of offerings in a limited assortment of soft goods.

Sears, on the other hand, shows no sign of giving up its franchise as the country's most comprehensive retailer. The company is continuing to sell appliances, hardware, automotive supplies, and apparel. It has added a higher-fashioned line of sportswear with the names of famous athletes such as Evonne Goolagong Cawley and Arnold Palmer, and has asked designer Diane Von Furstenberg to lend her name to bedroom furnishings, dinnerware, textiles, and wall coverings. Sears is not targeting its line to specific demographic groups. Rather, it is relying on the fact that two out of three American adults will visit a Sears store at least once a year.[58]

Advertising

Retail advertising is of two general types. Institutional ads attempt to sell the store by building a store image. Promotional ads sell the merchandise in the store by advertising price and special sales on a short-term basis. Promotional advertising generally appears in newspapers, because newspapers are well suited for advertising price specials and sales.

Institutional advertising is more likely to be used by national chains. Large retailers such as Sears, Montgomery Ward, K-Mart, Penney, and Federated spend millions on network TV. These ads are as sophisticated as those for national brands.

Sales Promotion and In-Store Decor

In-store stimuli such as displays, promotions, and decor influence consumers to patronize a store. Merchandise displays are particularly important since many purchase decisions are made in the store. One study found that over 50 percent of food items purchased in supermarkets were unplanned and over 60 percent of the decisions for health care and beauty items were unplanned.[59] Another study found that retailers can increase unplanned purchases by using:

- displays (27 percent of the respondents in the study bought more unplanned items because of displays);
- product demonstrations (35 percent of the respondents bought more unplanned items because of demonstrations); and
- price promotions (56 percent bought more on an unplanned basis because of price promotions).[60]

In-store decor (sometimes called atmospherics) is also an important influence on store image and consumer behavior. Penney's attempt to upgrade its image to compete with higher-quality department stores relied heavily on improving the decor of its stores.

Personal Selling and Service

The level of service offered by a retail store can be the most important factor in attracting consumers. As one retail executive said, "If people can buy the same merchandise in a number of stores ... it stands to reason that service must be the single ingredient that will create [store-] loyal customers."[61]

The most important service factor is the quality of sales help. In some cases the salesperson is essentially an order taker. But salespeople can influence the consumer for specialty goods, appliances, furniture, and hard goods. Because of this important role, it is not surprising that many retail experts identify the quality of sales help as the biggest problem in retailing today. The problem stems from reduced sales staffs, inadequate employee training, widespread expansion, and indifference on the part of sales personnel. Concern with this problem caused some retailers to fear that the erosion in selling quality could hurt the business turnaround taking place in 1983.[62]

Some retailers have increased training of sales employees. Department stores such as Filene's, Bloomingdale's, Saks Fifth Avenue, and Dayton-Hudson have instituted sales-training programs to sensitize salespeople to high service standards. The importance of factors such as sales help, wrapping, credit, and delivery are illustrated in a study of the reasons for consumers switching stores. Seven of the eleven most important reasons were service related.[63]

Locational Decisions

An element of a store's marketing strategy that is sometimes taken for granted is the location of new stores. The starting point for this decision must be the store's definition of its target segment. For example, The Broadway, a department store chain based in Los Angeles, appeals primarily to upscale working women. New store locations would be optimal in upscale areas with a high proportion of working women. On the other hand, the location of convenience stores such as 7-Eleven cannot be targeted so precisely. These stores must be in enough locations to provide the convenience of easy accessibility.

Area selection

A retailer engaged in a locational analysis should first identify the most attractive communities in which to locate by the degree to which they represent the retailer's target segment. For example, Yamaha determines the demographic characteristics of various areas being considered for dealerships and then matches them to the demographic profile of a Yamaha owner.[64] It develops a sales forecast for each area on this basis. For example, if the typical Yamaha owner is a male high school graduate, eighteen to twenty-one years old, living in a rural area, then regions with a high proportion of individuals fitting this description would be prime candidates for dealerships.

Site selection

After determining the area the retailer must choose a specific site. Sites should be evaluated on factors such as size of the site, traffic flow, distance to the site, and number of competitive retailers in the area.

Huff developed a model of site location that focused on two of these factors — size and distance. The model predicted that the proportion of consumers who would shop in a prospective store is directly proportionate to the size of the store and inversely proportionate to the distance of the store's site from the average consumer.[65] Assume a retailer is considering two sites of 100,000 and 40,000 square feet. The larger site is in an outlying area that is twice as far from the average consumer as the smaller site. The proportion of consumers that would shop at each store can be computed as follows:

$$P_{ij} = \frac{S_j/D_{ij}^2}{\Sigma S_n/D_{in}^2}$$

where:

P_{ij} is the proportion of consumers in area i that shop in site j,

S_j is the size of site j,

D_{ij} is the average distance of consumers in areas i from site j, and

$\Sigma S_n/D_{in}^2$ is the sum of the size of each site being considered divided by the distance squared.

In our example the proportion of consumers that would shop in the larger, more distant site is:

$$\frac{100,000/2^2}{100,000/2^2 + 40,000/1^2} = 38\%$$

The proportion of consumers that would shop in the smaller site is:

$$\frac{40,000/1^2}{100,000/2^2 + 40,000/1^2} = 62\%$$

Therefore, even though the more distant site is more than twice as large, it would attract substantially fewer customers. A refinement of the model takes account of factors other than distance and store size, such as population of transients who might be attracted to the site, traffic flow, and consumer perceptions of the area.[66]

EVALUATION AND CONTROL

The last step in the retail planning process in Figure 17-1 is evaluation of performance and control over retail operations and strategies. Retail performance must be compared to performance objectives such as stock turnover, profits as a percentage of sales, and return on assets or inventment. Such evaluation requires a retail information system that permits management to track revenue and expenses and to estimate future sales.

Retail Information System

A retail information system should record sales data by store, type of merchandise, and price paid. Scanner data will facilitate tracking sales in supermarkets. Most large retailers have also computerized their sales records, permitting store and department managers to access sales data on terminals. Such data are effective only if they are updated. Tandy requires its 5600 Radio Shack stores to supply sales data weekly and profit and loss statements monthly.[67] Costs must also be recorded and joint costs such as advertising and overhead allocated to stores and to lines within stores. (See Chapter 20 for allocation of joint costs.)

A retail information system must also monitor a retailer's assets (inventory, accounts receivable, cash, and fixed assets). Sales performance can be evaluated on the basis of utilization of assets, for example:

- sales per dollar invested in inventory (a measure of stock turnover),

- sales per square feet of selling space (a measure of space productivity, and

- sales per dollar invested (a measure of asset productivity).[68]

A retail information system should also enable management to compare its performance to that of its competitors. Competitors' sales, promotional expenditures, prices, and merchandise mix should be determined on a systematic basis.

Evaluation of Corporate and Store Strategy

On a more general level retailers should assess the effectiveness of strategy both on the corporate and store levels. To evaluate corporate strategy a company must have a strategic marketing plan that states the company's corporate mission and sales, market share, and ROI objectives. Many of the larger retailers are in a weak position today because they failed to develop such a strategic plan. For example, the former president of Woolworth "kept his plans for the company's future to himself. [He] shared, with only two or three colleagues, nothing more than the broad outline of a plan for expansion of specialty retailing, including acquisitions and startup ventures."[69] When he died, the company was left without a strategic plan.

A new management team tried to get Woolworth on track by establishing a strategic plan that involved divesting the company of its unprofitable Woolco discounting division and following through with the acquisition of specialty stores. Strict financial criteria for new operations have been established: a 14 percent return on investment and a maximum five-year payback.[70]

At the store level retailers must monitor advertising expenditures and attempt to evaluate the effectiveness of advertising and sales promotion campaigns. The retailer must also evaluate the product mix and prune it when necessary. One of the problems at Sears in the 1970s was the lack of control over unprofitable lines. The company is now requiring that product lines be justified on a profit basis. Prices must also be monitored, particularly the timing of markdowns. Failure to mark down merchandise adequately could spell disaster for a retailer that relies on fast turnover.

Finally, inventory and distribution costs must be carefully evaluated. At Radio Shack stores inventories are audited every three months and an automatic reorder system assures stores of a four-month supply of goods.

Controls and Corrective Action

The retail information system should indicate when corrective action is required. Such action is required when performance is significantly below objectives. For example, if a supermarket's stock turns are at twenty when twenty-five is the norm, management must determine if there is a problem in pricing certain lines, in maintaining adequate inventories, in the shelf positions of high-turnover items, or in checkout services. Similarly, if a division such as Woolco is consistently falling below ROI objectives, the company must undertake an intensive audit to determine the reason for poor performance and determine whether corrective action or divestment is warranted.

The general orientation among retailers today is toward evaluation and control in strategic planning. As one retail expert said, "There's increased focus on return on investment, on improving the productivity of assets in place today. There's better scheduling of personnel, better inventory control."[71]

Wholesaling

Wholesaling is the sale of goods to other businesses for resale. Wholesalers of consumer goods generally sell to retailers; industrial wholesalers (distributors) generally sell to manufacturing companies or to commercial users such as building contractors.

As we noted in the previous chapter, wholesaling is essential because (1) many manufacturers are too small to sell directly to retailers or industrial users, and (2) wholesalers can perform the distribution function more efficiently because of their wider range of retail contacts and larger assortment of goods.

Wholesaling was not always considered as important as it is today. As producers and retailers grew in the early part of this century, they began to question wholesalers' efficiency. The term "bypassing the wholesaler" began to be heard more frequently. Wholesale sales began to decrease in the 1930s. But after World War II, many of these manufacturers found direct distribution too expensive and reverted to reliance on wholesalers. Today wholesale sales are outpacing retail sales. In 1981 total sales in the wholesale sector were $1.2 trillion. Almost 60 percent of all manufacturers' products shipped in that year went through wholesalers.[72] Sales growth in wholesaling is expected to rise at an annual rate of 13 percent in the 1980s, outpacing a projected 11.5 percent annual increase in manufacturing.[73]

Wholesalers today are split into two broad groups: those who see their function primarily as order takers and those who are more marketing oriented and sensitive to customer needs. Since the early 1970s this latter group has grown and began to adopt more efficient management techniques, marketing plans, and cost-reducing physical distribution processes such as automated warehousing. Although wholesalers lag behind retailers and manufacturers in their marketing planning abilities, a management and marketing revolution is occurring that parallels that in retailing. Many wholesalers are seeking to provide more efficient customer services at lower costs.

In this section we will first consider types of wholesalers and then consider the split between the more traditional order taker and the newer marketing-oriented wholesaler.

TYPES OF WHOLESALERS

Figure 17-6 lists the types of wholesalers in both the consumer and industrial sector. The first distinction is between companies that establish their own wholesale outlets (manufacturers' sales branches or retail warehouse centers), and independent wholesalers. Among independent wholesalers a second distinction is between those who take title to goods (merchants) and those who do not (agents and brokers). Among merchants a third distinction occurs between those who provide a fuller line of services (full-function wholesalers) and specialized (limited-function) wholesalers.

Company-Owned Wholesale Outlets

Some manufacturers have taken on the wholesale function by establishing sales branches that carry inventory for resale. Sales branches represent 11 percent of all wholesale outlets but almost 40 percent of sales, because manufacturers generally locate these branches in high-volume market areas.[74] These manufacturers use independent wholesalers to distribute their products to smaller customers in dispersed areas.

IBM uses eighty sales branches to sell smaller computers and office products to retailers. These branches have also begun to function as retail stores by selling to final customers.[75] IBM also sells to independent distributors to cover areas not represented by its company-owned outlets. One potential problem in such an arrangement is competition between the distributors and the company's own sales branches.

Large retailers can also assume the wholesale function by integrating backward. Some supermarkets have established company-owned warehouses and distribution centers that permit them to buy directly from manufacturers. These facilities provide retailers with lower costs, more variety, better quality and inventory control, and quicker delivery.[76]

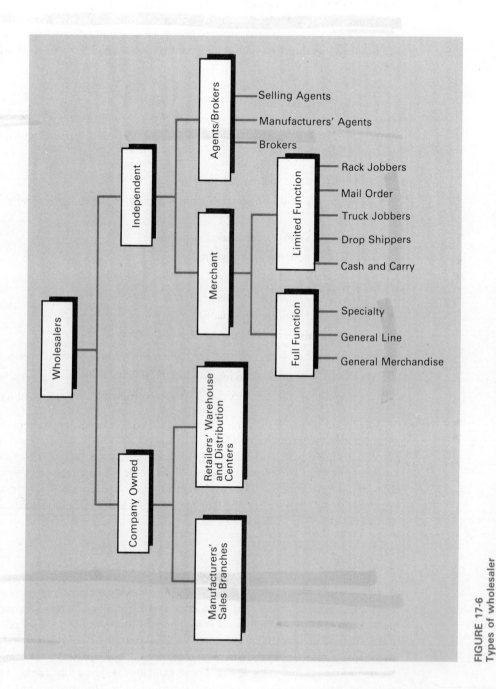

FIGURE 17-6
Types of wholesaler

Source: Adapted from Thomas C. Kinnear and Kenneth L. Bernhardt, *Principles of Marketing* (Glenview, Ill.: Scott, Foresman and Company, 1983), p. 372.

Independent Wholesalers

Independent wholesalers are divided into merchant wholesalers, and agents and brokers. Agents and brokers were described in the previous chapter. Here we will focus on the two types of merchant wholesaler: full service and limited service.

Full-service wholesalers

Full-service wholesalers perform all wholesaling functions. Foremost-McKesson, the largest wholesaler in the nation, helps the manufacturers it purchases from by:

- providing a sales staff to sell their goods,
- taking on the risk of maintaining an inventory of the manufacturer's products,
- collecting and analyzing market data, and
- researching new uses for products.

It assists retailers by:

- offering shelf management plans,
- leasing them electronic ordering equipment,
- providing a full sales staff that sets up racks of goods in their stores,
- providing help in bookkeeping and marketing analysis, and
- cooperating in the use of cable TV to advertise the retailer's products.[77]

Figure 17-6 showed several types of full-service wholesaler. General-merchandise wholesalers carry goods across many product lines. Grocery and drug wholesalers are typical. For example, in servicing drugstores Foremost-McKesson carries both drug and nondrug items. General-line wholesalers carry several lines, but offer greater depth of assortment in each line. Specialty wholesalers specialize in carrying part of one line, for example, heavy-duty industrial cable, auto accessories, or health foods.

Limited-service wholesalers

Limited-service wholesalers specialize by service whereas general-line and specialty wholesalers specialize by product. *Cash-and-carry* wholesalers require their customers to come to them to buy and pick up goods on a cash-only basis. **Drop shippers** obtain orders for goods without storing or transporting them. They deal with bulky products such as lumber or coal. *Truck jobbers* distribute perishable items from their own trucks. **Rack jobbers** sell nonfood items in grocery and drug stores. They maintain inventory on display racks, relieving the retailer of the necessity to stock the items. *Mail-order wholesalers* sell out of catalogs they distribute to their customers. They sell to buyers in outlying regions where personal selling would be costly.

WHOLESALE MANAGEMENT

The major issue facing wholesalers is whether they can provide services to their suppliers and customers in a cost-effective manner. The issue is reflected in the split between a traditional order-taker mentality and a newer focus on wholesale productivity.

The Traditional Wholesaler

As recently as the mid-1970s most wholesalers were essentially order takers who were not concerned with marketing planning. For example, Foremost-McKesson, the drug wholesaler, "merely took manufacturers' goods and resold them to small retailers, a humdrum process of warehousing, transportation, and simple marketing that offered thin profits."[78] Traditional wholesalers priced on the basis of a static 20 percent markup that allowed for net profits averaging 3 percent of sales. Few attempted to develop marketing strategy to sell manufacturers' goods. Materials handling and order processing tended to lag behind available technology. These conditions led one industrial marketer to predict that unless wholesalers began improving productivity through more effective marketing and cost cutting, one in seven would go out of business.[79]

The Progressive Wholesaler

Wholesalers began to improve operations as a result of increasing costs and more intense competition, particularly from company-owned outlets. Operations improved in two ways: (1) the development of more effective marketing practices, and (2) the application of new technologies to increase productivity.

Improved marketing practices

Wholesalers began to improve their marketing practices by researching their markets to identify target segments. They also began pruning their product lines by eliminating unprofitable items. Market analysis was extended to an evaluation of sales territories and systematic sales forecasts. One study of 250 wholesalers found that the most profitable were providing a "superior product service package — marketing analyses, promotion, technical support, and delivery." This was true of both large and small wholesalers. The author of the study concluded, "Distributors had better get with modern marketing and financial management techniques or they might as well fold up their tents."[80]

Improved technologies

The greatest strides in wholesale management have been made in applications of new technologies. In 1976 Foremost-McKesson decided to invest heavily in sophisticated technology "in order to make the company so efficient at distribution that manufacturers could not possibly do as well on their own."[81]

It was attempting to ensure its survival by being more cost effective than manufacturers' sales branches. As a result the company:[82]

- automated seventy-two of its warehouses to streamline ordering, delivery, and invoice procedures;
- centralized inventory analysis of its 1200 chemical products;
- established direct computer links with thirty-two drug manufacturers;
- set up a computerized accounts-receivable program for pharmacists to enable them to offer customers charge accounts; and
- provided drug stores computer terminals for ordering inventory.

Other wholesalers have followed Foremost-McKesson's technological lead. Wetterau, the nation's fourth-largest food wholesaler, provides its customers with electronic checkout scanners that are hooked into its computers. This permits Wetterau to provide sales information, updated prices, and reorder requirements to its retail customers.[83]

Summary

Retailers can be broadly categorized as merchandisers, food stores, and non-store retailers. Retailer types within each of these categories have been undergoing marked changes in marketing plans and growth strategies. Some recent developments have been:

- diversification by department store chains and general merchandisers into upscale discounting because of pressures from specialty stores on the high end and discount houses on the low end;
- the increased profitability of specialty stores;
- the vulnerability of discount houses that have not scaled up their merchandise while holding down cost;
- the growth in scrambled merchandising as supermarkets try to increase their small profit base by carrying nonfood items;
- the introduction of superstores as the ultimate in one-stop shopping; and
- the growth of nonstore retailing and the potential for in-home shopping through interactive cable systems.

Overall, however, growth in the retail sector has been limited because of increased competition, losses from diversification into unrelated areas, and higher costs.

Most of the chapter was concerned with retail planning and management. The retail planning process was described in six steps:

1. *Develop retail objectives.* Retailers must define the corporate mission and establish performance criteria such as stock turnover, profit margins, and return on assets.

2. *Evaluate the retail environment.* Retail management must evaluate consumer influences, competition, channel relationships, the technological environment, and the legal environment.

3. *Develop corporate retail strategies.* Retailers have followed corporate-wide strategies that maintain the current scope of store operations (e.g., market penetration, store positioning), expand operations (market intensification, market expansion, diversification), or cut back operations (retrenchment or divestment).

4. *Define segments and store positioning.* Having developed a corporate-wide strategy, retailers must be sure that they have identified appropriate target segments for their merchandise and that their stores are positioned to meet the needs of these target segments.

5. *Establish marketing strategies at the store level.* A store's target segments and positioning strategy guides the development of marketing strategy. Strategy development at the store level requires setting prices, determining product assortment, developing an advertising campaign, developing sales promotions, and ensuring adequate service.

6. *Evaluate and control retail performance.* Retail performance should be compared to performance criteria on both the store and corporate level. Control at the store level requires evaluation of advertising, the product mix, inventory, and distribution costs. Control at the corporate level requires the existence of a strategic plan to maintain corporate growth.

The chapter concluded by considering the importance of wholesaling and different types of wholesalers. The main issue facing wholesalers is whether they can increase the efficiency and productivity of the services they offer to avoid being bypassed by company-owned wholesale outlets.

In the next section of the book, we will shift the focus back to manufacturing firms and examine marketing planning at the corporate level.

Questions

1. Why have department stores and general merchandisers found themselves in an increasingly difficult competitive position in recent years? What strategic moves have they made to protect their position? Cite examples.

2. Supermarkets have faced a profit squeeze because of traditionally low margins and increasing costs of store operations. They have reacted by

(a) putting more emphasis on higher-margin nonfood items (scrambled merchandising), and (b) diversifying into other areas. What are the risks of each of these strategies?

3. We noted the prediction by some retail experts that by the end of this century "almost all food and other basic household needs will be acquired through the use of in-home television computer systems, and [that] shopping choices will be made after viewing ... brands on the television screen."[84]

    □ What factors are likely to accelerate the trend to in-home purchasing through interactive cable TV systems?

    □ What factors are likely to inhibit this development?

4. We also noted the prediction that retail sales in the 1980s would be flat or only moderately increasing.

    □ What recent economic and environmental trends suggest stagnant retail sales in the 1980s?

    □ What trends suggest that such a prediction may be overly pessimistic?

5. How did retailers and wholesalers react to stagnant growth in the 1970s and early 1980s? Specifically, what changes occurred in:

    □ marketing planning and management,

    □ corporate strategies, and

    □ new technologies?

6. A supermarket chain decides to establish an environmental scanning unit to assess recent changes in the food retail environment and to determine the implications for marketing strategy. It evaluates (a) demographics and life styles, (b) intratype competition, (c) intertype competition, (d) technology, and (e) legal influences.

    □ What are some of the trends that the unit most likely identified?

    □ What are the implications for strategy in each area?

7. Retailers have chosen a variety of corporate growth strategies in the face of a changing environment. For example, (a) Penney chose to reposition its existing stores, (b) Sears chose to diversify into financial services, and (c) K-Mart chose to expand its stores into new market areas.

    □ What was the nature of each of these strategies as a means of attaining corporate growth?

    □ What are the risks in each case?

8. An executive of a large department store chain, reflecting on the company's strategy of divergent diversification in the 1970s said, "Buying into businesses that had growth potential looked good on paper. But we quickly discovered we are retailers, not drug manufacturers, electri-

cal distributors, or appliance producers. We had to go back into our core markets."

☐ Do you agree with the statement?

☐ Why did retailers follow a policy of divergent diversification?

☐ What prompted many retailers to switch from divergent to convergent diversification?

9. Penney and Sears have been following different strategies regarding product assortment. Penney has been decreasing its diversity of offerings by no longer selling major appliances, paints, hardware, and garden supplies. Sears has maintained, and in some cases expanded, its diversity of offerings.

☐ What is the reason behind each chain's strategy?

☐ What are the risks?

10. An automobile manufacturer is expanding its dealerships in the Sunbelt by 10 percent to account for population growth. It is trying to establish a rational approach to site selection.

☐ What steps should the manufacturer take in selecting sites for its new dealerships?

☐ How can the company use the Huff model described on page 549 to help it in site selection?

11. A drug store chain realizes that it is obtaining information from many different sources with little integration or coordination of this information. It decides to establish a retail information system.

☐ What should be the components of such a system?

☐ What should be the organizational responsibilities of executives administering a retail information system?

12. We distinguished between traditional and progressive wholesalers. The latter have reacted to increasing costs and more intense competition by attempting to increase productivity. In what ways?

Notes

1. "Dayton Hudson Keeps Its Vision," *Advertising Age*, July 9, 1984, pp. 4, 46, 47.
2. "The Synergy Begins to Work for Sears' Financial Supermarket," *Business Week*, June 13, 1983, pp. 116–17.
3. Ibid.
4. "Finally, Woolworth Wields the Ax," *Business Week*, October 11, 1982, pp. 118–19.
5. "Jordan's/Filene's: Department Stores Target the Affluent," *New England Business*, November 1, 1982, pp. 35–37.
6. "Ward's Latest Formula: Hybrid Discounting," *Business Week*, November 2, 1981, p. 77.
7. "Penney's $1 Billion Gamble on Chic," *The New York Times*, July 10, 1983, p. 4F.
8. Ibid.
9. "K-Mart's Squeeze," *Barron's*, October 27, 1980, pp. 37, 44.

10. "A Retailer That's Leading the Way," *The New York Times*, December 12, 1982, Section 3, p. 1.

11. "Inventory of Formats," *Advertising Age*, April 27, 1981, pp. S-4, S-6.

12. *Advertising Age*, April 27, 1981, p. S-4.

13. "Safeway: Selling Nongrocery Items to Cure the Supermarket Blahs," *Business Week*, March 7 1977, p. 54.

14. "Trends in Retailing," *Marketing Communications*, February 1982, pp. 53–57.

15. *Business Week*, March 7, 1977, p. 54.

16. *Advertising Age*, April 27, 1981, p. S-4.

17. Marlcolm P. McNair and Eleanor G. May, "The Newest Revolution of the Retailing Wheel," *Harvard Business Review* 56 (September–October 1978): 81–91.

18. "IBM, CBS and Sears Plan a Joint Venture In At-Home Marketing Through Videotext," *The Wall Street Journal*, February 15, 1984, p. 8; and "The New Sears," *Business Week*, November 16, 1981, p. 146.

19. Robert F. Lusch, *Management of Retail Enterprises* (Boston: Kent, 1982), p. 156.

20. Allan L. Pennington, "Do's and Don'ts of Retail Strategic Plans," *Marketing News*, March 7, 1980, p. 17.

21. Lusch, *Management of Retail Enterprises*, p. 156.

22. "Limited Inc: Expanding Its Position to Serve the Rubenesque Woman," *Business Week*, November 22, 1982, pp. 56, 58.

23. "Limited Puts Lane Bryant on Special Diet," *Advertising Age*, August 30, 1982, p. 4, 18.

24. Robert D. Buzzell and Marci K. Dew, "Strategic Management Helps Retailers Plan for the Future," *Marketing News*, March 7, 1980, p. 16.

25. *Business Week*, March 7, 1977, p. 54.

26. "Retail Trends," *Advertising Age*, November 2, 1981, p. S-6.

27. Ben M. Enis and Gordon W. Paul, "Store Loyalty as a Basis for Market Segmentation," *Journal of Retailing* 46 (Fall 1970): 42–56.

28. *Supermarket Shoppers in a Period of Economic Uncertainty* (New York: Yankelovich, Skelly and White, 1982), p. 16.

29. Roger T. Blackwell, "Successful Retailers of '80s Will Cater to Specific Lifestyle Segments," *Marketing News*, March 7, 1980, p. 3.

30. "Evolution of a Leaner A&P," *The New York Times*, April 27, 1982, pp. D1, D23.

31. *Business Week*, November 2, 1981, p. 80.

32. Bert C. McCammon, Jr., Robert F. Lusch, and Bradley T. Farnsworth, "Contemporary Markets and the Corporate Imperative: A Strategic Analysis for Senior Retailing Executives," presentation at seminar for retailing executives, Harvard University, June 1976, p. 8.

33. *Business Week*, March 7, 1977, p. 53.

34. Buzzell and Dew, "Strategic Management Helps Retailers," p. 16.

35. Pennington, "Do's and Don'ts of Retail Strategic Plans," p. 17.

36. Lusch, *Management of Retail Enterprises*, p. 83.

37. Ibid., p. 84.

38. Ibid., p. 191.

39. "Electronic Shopping Builds a Base," *Business Week*, October 26, 1981, pp. 125, 129, 130.

40. "U.S. Panel Indicts 3 Food Concerns for Price Fixing," *The Wall Street Journal*, October 13, 1980, p. 7.

41. Ray O. Werner (ed.), "Legal Developments in Marketing," *Journal of Marketing* 43 (Fall 1979): 125.

42. "7-Eleven Takes Steps to Move Beyond Image," *Advertising Age*, December 7, 1981, pp. 4, 78.

43. *The New York Times*, July 10, 1983, p. 4F.

44. *Business Week*, November 16, 1981, pp. 140–46.

45. *Business Week*, June 13, 1983, pp. 116–17.

46. "The Walgreen Formula: Digging in for New Growth in Drug Retailing," *Business Week*, March 1, 1982, pp. 84–85.

47. "The Re-Greening of Walgreen," *Sales & Marketing Management*, July 4, 1983, pp. 38–41.

48. Ibid.

49. *Forbes*, April 30, 1979, p. 97.

50. "Reflection of the Age," *Advertising Age*, November 2, 1981, p. S-20.

51. Morris L. Mayer and J. Barry Mason, "Discount Dept. Stores Will Prosper in '80s Despite Intense Competition," *Marketing News*, March 7, 1980, p. 6.

52. *The New York Times,* April 27, 1982, pp. D1, D23.

53. "Zale Sparkles in Strategy Shift," *Advertising Age,* October 5, 1981, pp. 4, 120.

54. "Brush on the Glitter to Lure in the Crowd," *Advertising Age,* November 1, 1982, p. M-10.

55. Ibid.; and *New England Business,* November 1, 1982, pp. 35–37.

56. Lusch, *Management of Retail Enterprises,* p. 505.

57. "Sears' Overdue Retailing Revival," *Fortune,* April 4, 1983, p. 134.

58. Ibid.

59. David T. Kollat and Ronald P. Willett, "Customer Impulse Purchasing Behavior," *Journal of Marketing Research* 4 (February 1967): 21–31.

60. "The Teen Market," *Product Marketing,* Spring, 1982, p. S-26.

61. "Selling, Retailing's Lost Art," *The New York Times,* March 15, 1983, p. D-4.

62. Ibid.

63. Robert F. Dietrich, "37 Things You Can Do to Keep Your Customers — Or Lose Them," *Progressive Grocer,* June 1973, pp. 59–64.

64. "Computer Mapping of Demographic Lifestyle Data Locates 'Pockets' of Potential Customers at Microgeographic Level," *Marketing News,* November 27, 1981, Section 2, p. 16.

65. D. L. Huff, *Determination of Inter-Urban Retail Trade Areas* (Los Angeles: University of California, Real Estate Research Program, 1962); and D. L. Huff, "Defining and Estimating a Trading Area," *Journal of Marketing* 28 (July 1964): 34–38.

66. David A. Gautschi, "Specification of Patronage Models for Retail Center Choice," *Journal of Marketing Research* 18 (May 1981): 162–74.

67. "Charles Tandy Never Stops Selling," *Fortune,* December 1976, pp. 178–85.

68. Lusch, *Management of Retail Enterprises,* p. 59.

69. "Woolworth is Still Rummaging for a Retail Strategy," *Business Week,* June 6, 1983, p. 82.

70. Ibid., p. 83.

71. *The New York Times,* December 12, 1982, Section 3, p. 30.

72. "Foremost-McKesson: The Computer Moves Distribution to Center Stage," *Business Week,* December 7, 1981, p. 115.

73. Ibid.

74. E. Jerome McCarthy, *Basic Marketing* (Homewood, Ill.: Richard D. Irwin, 1981), p. 396.

75. "A Funny Thing Happened on the Way to the Computer Store," *Sales & Marketing Management, Special Report, Managing Costs for More Productive Selling,* December 8, 1980.

76. "Warehouse or Wholesaler — Food Chains Disagree on Best Distribution System," *Supermarketing,* February 1977, pp. 5, 6, 38.

77. *Business Week,* December 7, 1981, pp. 115, 116, 118, 122.

78. Ibid.

79. "One U.S. Industrial Distributor in Seven," *NR, Issue,* January 17, 1981, pp. 1–3.

80. "The Practical Side of Marketing," *Industrial Distributor,* June 1981, p. 39.

81. *Business Week,* December 7, 1981, pp. 115, 116, 118, 122.

82. Ibid.

83. "A Food Supplier's Bigger Bite," *Business Week,* February 22, 1982, p. 136.

84. McNair and May, "The Newest Revolution of the Retailing Wheel," pp. 81–91.

PART IV

Strategic Marketing Planning

In Part III we focused on marketing strategies at the individual product level. However, there is a broader aspect to marketing plans and strategies: a multiproduct level. Planning at this level is called *strategic marketing planning* and occurs for both the corporation and the strategic business units.

Strategic marketing planning consists of matching a company's resources to marketing opportunities to ensure long-term growth. Thus it must include (1) developing a corporate growth strategy for the firm, (2) defining the overall mix or portfolio of product offerings, and (3) controlling marketing expenditures and strategies to guarantee that plans are being implemented. The sequence of marketing planning at this broader level is:

Strategic Marketing Plans		Corporate Growth Strategies		Product Portfolio Strategies		Marketing Control and Evaluation
(Chapter 18)	→	(Chapter 18)	→	(Chapter 19)	→	(Chapter 20)

We will deal with these topics at both the corporate and the strategic business unit level.

Strategic Marketing Planning and Corporate Growth Strategies

FOCUS OF CHAPTER

Much of marketing strategy deals with the firm's total product mix and attempts to ensure future corporate growth. Consider the following:

- Should RCA attempt to be a leader in new video technologies, despite its withdrawal from the videodisc market?

- Should Sears continue its policy of diversification into financial services, should it consider entering other areas such as in-home video technologies, or should it do both?

- Should Procter and Gamble expand its offerings in soft drinks after having acquired Orange Crush?

- Does the merger of Connecticut General and the Insurance Company of North America into a new corporation (CIGNA) mean a consolidation of these companies' existing financial services, or should the new corporate entity consider expansion into new markets and new services?

Answering each question requires strategic planning at the corporate or SBU level. The strategic plan (1) must provide a blueprint for a rational allocation of corporate resources, (2) to ensure corporate growth, (3) while maintaining control over marketing operations.

The first consideration in this chapter is the nature of strategic marketing planning. We will be reminded of the distinction first made in Chapter 4 between the strategic marketing framework in this part of the book and the product marketing framework described in Part III. We will then look at the process of strategic marketing planning at both the corporate and the strategic business unit level. The process in both cases is very similar. The basic difference is the focus on overall growth at the corporate level and the concern with the product mix at the SBU level. The final section describes a major output of strategic marketing planning — corporate growth strategies. We will look at alternative growth strategies by considering the strategic directions of several major American companies.

Purposes of Strategic Marketing Planning

Top management's major responsibility is to develop a sound strategic plan that will guide marketing actions at all levels of the corporation. The strategic marketing plan must fulfill several objectives if it is to provide proper guidance to meet marketing opportunities.

1. *Define the corporate mission.* The strategic plan should define the company's overall mission. Failure to define the company's mission adequately has led some major corporations into far-flung acquisitions that had no basic purpose in promoting long-term corporate growth. Companies such as Schlitz, Olin, Colgate, and Westinghouse have gone through periods of acquisition and diversification unrelated to their corporate mission. For Schlitz the acquisitions proved nearly fatal.

As we noted in Chapter 2, the corporate mission should lead a company to identify marketing opportunity. When RCA defined its mission as ensuring it would be "the technological leader again in [its] core business of electronics and communications," the company betrayed a resource rather than a customer orientation.[1] The result was a willingness to sink $200 million into the development of videodisc technology without adequately assessing the potential competition from videotape players. We might wonder what would have happened had the company stated its mission as "satisfying the in-home entertainment needs of the American public." Perhaps RCA might have recognized the need for in-home recording capabilities and put its money into videocassette recorders.

2. *Set out corporate objectives.* Defining a broad corporate mission is not enough. The strategic marketing plan must set out corporate objectives that provide clear guidelines for marketing action. Kellogg has established strategic objectives in the face of stagnant demand for cereals. Top management has decided to:

- □ seek new domestic markets by introducing adult-oriented cereals,
- □ stimulate the demand for cereals abroad, and
- □ limit diversification in unrelated lines to categories with $500 million or more in yearly sales, a growth rate above 10 percent per year, and high-priced, high-margin entries.[2]

3. *Provide guidelines for developing a product mix.* The development of clear corporate objectives has helped establish Kellogg's overall product

mix: an expanded product line in cereals and limited diversification into high-growth food lines. The company has introduced Nutri Grain cereals to fitness-oriented younger adults and sodium-free Rice Krispies and Corn Flakes to health-oriented senior citizens; and it has diversified by entering the yogurt market with Whitney's, a higher priced product that meets its criteria for sales, growth, and high margins.[3]

Chesebrough-Pond's product mix was based on two objectives: (1) find candidates for acquisition that dominate a market with few competitors, and (2) build on successful brands by rapidly introducing related products in the line.[4] As a result of these strategic criteria, Chesebrough entered the food business for the first time by acquiring Ragu spaghetti sauce because it was the dominant brand in a field with few competitors. It has also successfully capitalized on the Vaseline and Pond's names by introducing Vaseline Intensive Care lotion and Pond's Cream and Cocoa Butter lotion. But some analysts feel that Chesebrough's strategic plan calls for too broad a product mix without an adequate definition of mission to guide it.[5]

4. *Integrate marketing and nonmarketing resources.* The strategic marketing plan requires a consideration of all corporate resources — manufacturing, research and development, finance, management, and marketing. Top management must specify how these resources are to be used and what additional resources must be acquired.

5. *Establish corporatewide performance goals.* The strategic marketing plan establishes standard performance goals for all business units such as return on investment, return on net assets, or discounted cash flow. Business units are then evaluated on these financial goals.

As an example, new management at Courtaulds Ltd., a large British textile producer, now requires a minimum 12 percent return on investment from all major operations.[6] Business units that do not meet this limit are candidates for divestment. Courtaulds's nylon-producing business unit was unable to meet this criterion because of competition from American companies such as DuPont, and folded in 1981. The minimum ROI criterion, although rigid, was made necessary by "the aftereffects of a 10-year acquisition binge."[7] Courtaulds's strategic marketing plan thus calls for retrenchment in the face of declining profitability and a tight adherence to financial performance goals on the SBU level. In fact, SBU managers are being encouraged to shift resources from cash-rich to cash-poor products with growth potential to ensure the 12 percent return rate. In so doing, SBU's are being encouraged to finance their own expansion rather than look to corporate management for resources when they are cash poor.

6. *Provide guidelines for allocating resources.* One of the major purposes of strategic planning at the corporate level is to allocate resources to the various business units. Similarly, strategic planning at the SBU level is designed

to allocate resources to the business unit's product lines. The amount of money to be allocated to each unit will depend on its performance. Top management will assess the SBU's earnings and ROI, its ability to act as a net source rather than a user of cash, and its earnings potential. Allocations to SBUs will be spelled out in the corporate plan. Thus, Courtaulds Ltd. ceased supporting its nylon operation and cut back allocations to its fiber and fabric divisions by one-third to permit it to concentrate on higher growth areas such as paints, plastics, and cellophane.[8]

The strategic marketing plan also deals with allocations between internal development and external acquisitions when seeking new areas of opportunity. Kellogg's strategic plan emphasizes internal development to ensure growth, whereas General Mills emphasizes acquisitions as a hedge against a stagnant cereal market.

Once it has made allocation decisions, top management seeks to control expenditures in the SBUs and to evaluate performance to ensure that operations conform to the strategic plan. Therefore, allocations require subsequent evaluation and control.

7. *Establish a long-term planning horizon.* The strategic marketing plan must include a long-term view because of the need to examine alternative investment opportunities across markets. As we saw in Chapter 3, opportunity identification requires a consideration of the future competitive, technological, and consumer environment. Assessing changes in social trends, cultural forms, economic conditions, political and regulatory trends, and technological capabilities requires forecasting the marketing environment for five to ten years ahead. Exxon Chemical has established such a long-term strategic planning framework. The company is in a high-growth, capital-intensive industry that is subject to rapid technological change. Therefore the company must take a long-term view in assessing opportunities. According to its president,

> In the last several years, we have endeavored to push our vision as strategic planners to the end of the century. A company our size has to look ahead at least twenty years. For part of our long-term planning we have set up quarterly forums ... [to] imagine what it's going to be like in the distant future, where we should go, and what we should do to get there.[9]

8. *Ensure top management responsibility.* The strategic marketing plan is the responsibility of top management at both the corporate and the SBU level. Top management responsibility is essential since the strategic plan guides the allocation of corporate resources and affects the firm's financial welfare. Middle management's support is unlikely without top management's participation.

At IBM top management's participation in strategic planning is ensured through a Corporate Management Committee composed of the chairman of the board, the president, and three senior vice presidents. The committee provides the overall direction to the company, with each member responsible for one area of operations.[10]

Differences Between Strategic and Product Marketing Planning

In Chapter 4 we distinguished between corporate and marketing planning. A good corporate plan is a strategic marketing plan, since it guides company resources to marketing opportunities over the long term. Therefore the distinction between corporate and marketing planning also applies to the differences between the strategic marketing focus in this section of the book and the product marketing focus in the previous section. These differences are summarized in Table 18-1. Thus:

- the strategic plan is concerned with *corporatewide* criteria of performance, whereas the product plan is concerned with *marketing* objectives such as sales and market share;

- the strategic plan is concerned with the company's overall *product mix,* whereas the product plan is concerned with the composition of a *marketing mix* of price, promotion, and distribution strategies;

- the strategic plan integrates all *corporate resources,* whereas the product plan utilizes *marketing resources* to meet customer needs;

- the strategic plan *allocates* resources across SBUs, whereas the product plan *implements* product strategies by specifying how products are to be delivered and customers influenced;

- the strategic plan is a *long-term* document designed to forecast environmental changes, whereas the product plan is a *shorter-term* document designed to forecast more immediate changes in customer demand and competitive reactions; and

- the strategic plan is the responsibility of *top management* and SBU management, whereas the product plan is the responsibility of *middle-line* product managers.

TABLE 18-1
Differences Between the Strategic Marketing Plan and the Product Marketing Plan

THE STRATEGIC MARKETING PLAN IS CONCERNED WITH	THE PRODUCT MARKETING PLAN IS CONCERNED WITH
Corporate objectives	Marketing objectives
The firm's product mix	The product's marketing mix
Integrating corporate resources	Integrating marketing resources
Allocating resources	Implementing plans
The long term (five to ten years)	The short term (one to three years)
Top management's responsibility	Middle management's responsibility

The Strategic Marketing Planning Process

In this section we will describe strategic marketing planning at both the corporate and SBU levels. Since the strategic business unit is essentially a minicorporation with profit responsibility, strategic planning at the SBU level is almost identical with strategic planning at the corporate level.

THE CORPORATE LEVEL

The steps involved in developing a strategic marketing plan are illustrated in Figure 18-1. The strategic marketing plan differs from the product marketing plan in five ways. (1) The strategic marketing plan requires the integration of business activities that include nonmarketing functions. (2) The strategic plan treats alternatives as investment opportunities. (3) Strategies are designed to guide corporate growth and specify the firm's product mix. (4) Resources are allocated to the SBUs based on evaluation of alternative investment opportunities and prospects for growth. (5) Corporate management evaluates the profit performance of the SBUs to control expenditures and activities and to provide for future planning.

Integrating Business Activities

The strategic marketing plan in Figure 18-1 starts out with the development of corporate objectives. In the previous section we saw the need for a set of corporate objectives to provide a framework for evaluating alternative opportunities and allocating corporate resources accordingly.

The next consideration in the strategic marketing plan is the integration of marketing and nonmarketing activities. One of the most important points of interaction is between marketing and *research and development* (R&D). Development of new products requires close communication between R&D and marketing. Marketing research must provide R&D with insight into consumers' needs to help engineers and scientists to formulate new product ideas.[11] In turn, R&D must transmit the physical properties of products and likely benefits and problems to marketing. Without this interaction, R&D could develop a well-engineered, high-quality product that is unrelated to consumer needs.

The importance of coordinating marketing and R&D in the strategic plan is illustrated by the 3M Company. The company instituted a formal strategic marketing planning process in 1981 because of a need to coordinate the efforts of 150 separate business units. The objective of the strategic plan was to "lead 3M away from declining or mature industries such as automotive supplies toward growth markets . . . like electronics and communications."[12] One growth area the company identified was industrial abrasives. R&D devoted its energies to developing a new abrasive designed to grind heavy metal. The result was a new mineral that is said to be 2.3 times stronger than other abrasives. Once developed, the product was successfully marketed to a select niche, heavy users of metal abrasives. The coordination between opportunity identification in the strategic plan and R&D resulted in a successful new product introduction.

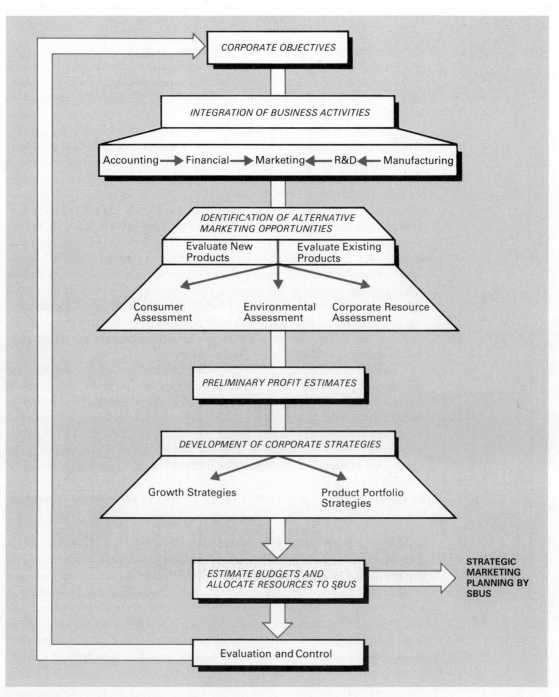

FIGURE 18-1
Strategic marketing planning at the corporate level[a]

[a]This figure also applies to strategic market planning at the SBU level. The only adjustments are that (1) corporate objectives become SBU objectives, (2) corporate strategy becomes SBU strategy, (3) budgets and allocations are made to product lines at the individual product level, and (4) the arrow at the bottom of the figure feeds into marketing planning at the product rather than the SBU level.

Close coordination must also exist between marketing and *manufacturing.* The size of manufacturing facilities for new and existing products must be based on sales forecasts. The effects of sales of one product on other products in the company's mix must also be estimated to determine adjustment in manufacturing schedules.[13]

Marketing activities also interface with *financial* responsibilities in the firm. Determining performance goals requires financial statements and budgets for each business alternative. In addition, investing in new products or expanding markets for existing products may require an assessment of financial markets to evaluate alternative sources of capital.

Accounting is another nonmarketing area requiring integration with marketing activities in the strategic plan. Costs must be estimated for alternative investment opportunities. Further, costs must be allocated to various marketing activities for existing products. For example, when General Electric runs an advertisement for several appliances or sends appliances to dealers in one shipment, costs must be allocated to each individual product to develop a profit and loss estimate. Cost allocations play an important part in evaluation and control. Evaluation of performance is frequently based on costs (for example, selling or advertising costs) as a percentage of sales. Accounting information and procedures will affect such cost allocations.

Inadequate integration between marketing and nonmarketing functions in the strategic plan may lead certain areas in the firm to pursue their vested interests at the expense of corporate profits. For example, manufacturing strives for efficient production requiring long runs and fewer and simpler products. Marketing would prefer shorter production runs to facilitate quick distribution and provide for more models to meet the varying needs of consumers.[14] The orientation of manufacturing would be inefficient in meeting consumer needs, whereas marketing's orientation may be cost inefficient. Top management must ensure that no area is neglecting corporate goals to satisfy its particular interests.

Identifying Alternative Marketing Opportunities

Establishing the role of marketing and nonmarketing activities is a prerequisite for identifying marketing opportunities, since these activities represent the resources of the firm. The steps involved in identifying opportunity — defining markets, evaluating consumer needs, studying the marketing environment, and assessing the fit of corporate resources — were described in Chapter 2. In the strategic marketing plan, opportunities must be identified on a multiproduct basis both for (1) new products and (2) the possible expansion of existing products.

Evaluating new product opportunities

Top management seeks to identify alternative marketing opportunities and to allocate resources to one or more. The strategic marketing plan at 3M identified three primary areas of opportunity: industrial abrasives, industrial tape for computer circuitry, and personal computers.[15] In each area it developed or acquired a new product.

Top management at 3M was responsible for evaluating each product and deciding whether to move ahead. Before making this decision, it most likely delegated to each strategic business unit the task of evaluating customer demand and assessing competitive offerings. For example, for the new industrial abrasive (known as Cubitron) top management probably asked the Industrial Abrasives Division to evaluate the new product. A need for a heavier-duty abrasive was identified among auto, refrigerator, and metal producers. The product was developed and demonstrations took place at the Coated Abrasives Method Center, a 3M research lab.[16] Customer feedback indicated a need existed among the segment. On the basis of this feedback from the SBU, the product was given the green light and resources were allocated for introduction.

The industrial tape entry involves a new technology competing with proven products and has met with limited success. Management at 3M says the product is "relatively untried." It adds, "We're up against a well-established technology that works, with an infrastructure already in place."[17] In this case top management could have asked the SBU to cease production, but it decided to move ahead because the company has "more financial, manufacturing and technical resources, with their knowledge of adhesives and plastic films, than the other companies . . . making this kind of product."[18] In other words management was willing to incur a longer payback period for the product because of the fit between company resources and marketing opportunity.

Evaluating existing products

Figure 18-1 illustrated the dual nature of strategic planning in considering opportunities for *existing* as well as *new* products. For example, in the late 1970s Pillsbury decided to revitalize its line of grocery products.[19] A marketing study pointed to certain products that were candidates for expanding market shares. As a result the company began to market many of its grocery products more aggressively, increasing advertising by two and a half times for some products.

Evaluating existing products does not always lead to market expansion. Frequently the strategic plan will call for selective retrenchment as well as expansion. At Parker Pen a new management team recognized the uncontrolled growth of its product line. There was no strategic planning to define an appropriate corporate mission and product mix. As a result the new management team is emphasizing deletions of existing products over market expansion or new product introductions. The new strategic plan calls for "gutting Parker's product line by 80%, reducing the number of items sold to less than 100 from more than 500."[20] The plan also calls for consolidating manufacturing operations as the line is reduced, with the objective of reaching a 20 percent to 25 percent return on equity compared to 8.9 percent in 1981.

Developing Preliminary Profit Estimates

Strategic planning at the corporate level requires profit estimates for the operations of each business unit. SBUs must develop preliminary profit and loss statements reflecting revenue projections and costs. At Courtaulds Ltd. the SBU's estimated return on investment was the basis for allocating resources. As we noted, a minimum ROI of 12 percent was targeted for each SBU. The nylon operation fell below the minimum and was divested. Paints are well above the 12 percent target. They represent 36 percent of profits with only 9 percent of sales and are therefore targeted for further expansion. Because fabrics are close to the minimum, allocations for them have been cut back by a third.[21]

A key element in profit estimates by the SBUs is a projection of ROI and payback periods for new product entries or for existing products targeted for expansion. A hypothetical profit projection for the three new products that the 3M company had evaluated is shown in Table 18-2. The five-year ROI projection for Cubitron and the Whisper Writer are positive, and payback is well within the acceptable range. Beam Tape is questionable and probably would not fall within the company's limits of acceptable performance. The company decided to move ahead because it felt a five-year average might be short-sighted since it was in a unique position to exploit opportunity. It is the only company in the United States producing tape that can connect micro-electronic circuits well enough to compete with the prevalent technology of bonding.[22]

The decision to introduce Beam Tape illustrates the flexibility of strategic marketing planning. If strict corporate criteria of performance were followed, Beam Tape probably would not have been introduced. But top management based its decision on long-term environmental factors.

Developing Corporate Strategies

The corporate plan should establish company-wide strategies as a blueprint for growth and selection of the firm's product mix. Figure 18-1 shows two

TABLE 18-2
Hypothetical Profit Estimates for Three New Product Entries at 3M

	INVESTMENT OPPORTUNITIES		
Performance Criteria	Cubitron (Industrial Abrasive)	Beam Tape (Industrial Tape)	Whisper Writer (Personal Computer)
Return on Investment (Five-year average)	22%	15%	21%
% Net Revenue of Sales before Taxes	26%	18%	23%
Payback Period	3.6 years	6.3 years	4.0 years

types of strategy (corporate growth and product portfolio) resulting from strategic marketing planning. Although corporate growth and product portfolio strategies are interrelated, they provide different operational guidelines.

Corporate growth strategies provide guidelines for allocating resources to internal development or external acquisition, to the introduction of new products or expansion of markets for existing products, and to an orientation toward risk or stability. These guidelines might lead one firm to rely on external acquisition to exploit new product opportunities, another to diversify into unrelated lines, and a third to develop new products internally for existing markets.

Product portfolio strategies provide guidelines for eliminating, maintaining, or increasing the investment in existing products, for introducing new products in high-growth areas, or for filling "gaps" in the product mix to ensure an adequate cash flow and a balance between well-established products and higher-risk entries with growth potential.

Courtaulds Ltd.'s corporate growth strategy calls for substantial cutbacks in many lines and for using the excess cash generated by these cutbacks for selective acquisitions abroad. The company developed a new operation, Courtaulds U.S. Developments Inc. to investigate acquisitions in American specialty chemicals.[23] There is little emphasis on internal new product development for growth. These guidelines for growth have determined the company's product portfolio strategy: to retrench in fibers and fabrics to finance an entry strategy in specialty chemicals, and to build up existing paint and plastic lines.

Budgeting and Resource Allocation

The culmination of the corporate planning process is the development of a budget for each of the SBUs; this is based on the assessment of investment opportunities and a review of existing operations. The budget is nothing more than a preliminary profit and loss statement for the business unit as a whole. Top management asks business unit managers to submit estimated costs and sales forecasts. These estimates are then combined with the evaluation of new opportunities and assessment of existing operations to provide top management with a basis for allocating resources to each SBU. In some cases a separate budget may be submitted for new ventures to permit top management to trace performance and control expenditures better.

The budget provides an estimate of production, physical distribution, and marketing costs. Budgets are also presented to account for contingencies. For example, a large engineering company requires its business units to prepare a sensitivity analysis to allow for variances in revenues that might be caused by uncontrollable factors. A food processor asks each of its business units to plan for the possibilities of higher fuel costs and reimposition of price controls when developing budget estimates.[24] Contingency budgets give SBU management the flexibility to adjust cost according to competitive reactions.

The allocation of resources to the SBUs in the strategic marketing plan permits SBU management to initiate its own round of strategic planning. This was represented in Figure 18-1 as an arrow from resource allocation to strategic marketing planning at the SBU level.

Evaluation and Control

Once resources have been allocated to the business units, their performance must be evaluated. Establishing the budget provides management with a basis for evaluation and control. Sales performance can be traced and evaluated against budgeted forecasts. Costs can be held within budgeted limits.

Inadequate controls over the operations of its SBUs can cost a company millions of dollars. Westinghouse failed to control its SBUs in the mid-1970s because of a lack of strategic planning at the corporate level. For example, it formed a business unit to build low-cost housing on government contracts. It gave management of the SBU a blank check to achieve growth. Management then used this power to acquire contracts without thought for corporate profits. But many of the contracts had substantial losses built in. The result was a $61 million loss in one year and $85 million in debt that had to be repaid by Westinghouse.[25] (We will consider evaluation and control in more detail in Chapter 20.)

The last step in strategic marketing planning in Figure 18-1 is a feedback loop from evaluation and control to marketing opportunity and corporate objectives. This feedback allows management to use its current experiences in the next strategic planning cycle.

THE SBU LEVEL

The existence of strategic business units as profit centers requires SBU management to undertake a strategic planning process that parallels planning by top management. With minor modifications Figure 18-1 could apply equally well to strategic marketing planning at the SBU level (see note at bottom of Figure 18-1). Whereas the strategic plan at the corporate level guides the operations of each business unit, the SBU's strategic plan guides the operation of the individual product market units (PMUs). Input is required from product managers on profit projections of individual products in the line. The SBU's strategic plan thus guides the development of the marketing plan (product, price, promotion, distribution strategies) by the product managers. The sequence is:

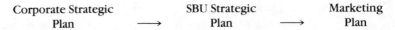

Corporate Strategic   SBU Strategic   Marketing
Plan $\longrightarrow$ Plan $\longrightarrow$ Plan

At 3M strategic plans at the SBU level are five-year plans. Product managers are asked to submit their evaluations and estimates so that the business unit can then develop an overall estimate and submit it to top management. In the Business Communications Product Division, product managers define their industry and their business, asking themselves such questions as, "If I could start all over again, how would I run this business differently?" They then list key success factors and devise a development program and marketing strategy for each item [in the business unit]. The approach helps to provide uniform planning across the corporation.[26]

The importance of strategic planning at the SBU level is illustrated by Beech-Nut, a subdivision of Nestlé. When Nestlé purchased Beech-Nut in 1979, it gave its new SBU financial support in a move to become second only to Gerber in the baby food market. In 1979 Beech-Nut was third behind Heinz. But Beech-Nut management saw potential for capturing market share because both Heinz and Gerber were diversifying away from baby foods as a hedge against a decreasing birth rate. Beech-Nut management developed a plan to market its product line more aggressively. The plan called for:

- introducing new baby food products,
- redesigning their package,
- instituting a direct-mail program offering coupons,
- increasing the ad budget,
- increasing the sales force,
- increasing promotional support to the trade,
- repositioning the line to parents by emphasizing taste appeal, a new benefit not previously emphasized because of the mistaken assumption that infants have undeveloped taste buds.[27]

This well-orchestrated plan succeeded in increasing Beech-Nut's market share so that by 1982 Beech-Nut surpassed Heinz.

INTEGRATING STRATEGIC AND PRODUCT MARKETING PLANNING

One other element of strategic marketing planning should be emphasized: the necessity for close integration between strategic and product planning. Figure 18-2 demonstrates that integration between the strategic and product marketing plan is required at every phase of the planning process. First, corporate (or SBU) objectives provide the basis for marketing objectives. For example, one objective stipulated in 1982 by top management at Helene Curtis, the hair-care company, was to "shed its image as a low-priced imitator of premium products."[28] As a result marketing objectives focused on defining opportunities in the hair conditioner and shampoo markets for new product introductions.

Figure 18-2 shows that the assessment of marketing opportunities in the marketing plan is used in the evaluation of alternative investment opportunities in the strategic plan. The focus on opportunity in the hair conditioner market led Helene Curtis to develop a new conditioner that could be left on the hair for varying amounts of time to offer light or deep conditioning. Top management

FIGURE 18-2
Integration of strategic and product marketing plans

assessed this new product as an investment alternative to supporting lower-priced products such as Suave, an inexpensive line of hair grooming products.

Decisions on investment opportunities in the strategic plan lead to product mix decisions, which then affect marketing mix strategies in the marketing plan. Top management's decision to introduce the new conditioner (called Finesse) meant a basic revision in Helene Curtis's product mix away from lower-priced items. The marketing mix implications were direct. The company was now willing to invest heavy sums on advertising and promotion for the new conditioner.

Sales and cost estimates are developed in the marketing plan. These are then integrated into an overall profit estimate for each business unit in the corporate plan. The positive sales forecasts for Finesse led Helene Curtis to risk $35 million in its introduction, an amount nearly equal to its total stockholders' equity.[29] Obviously, the company felt that the profit potential of the product was high enough to warrant the risk.

The final point of integration in Figure 18-2 is evaluation and control. The strategic plan provides for control of the marketing plan since it specifies procedures for evaluating sales performance and controlling marketing costs at the individual product level. Helene Curtis's management will control expenditures on Finesse to ensure that competitive pressures do not force increases in promotional expenditures that the company may not be able to afford.

RESULTS OF A LACK OF STRATEGIC MARKETING PLANNING

We have described strategic planning as the primary means of defining and exploiting marketing opportunities. But what happens when a large company fails to define guidelines for developing new products, promoting existing products, and acquiring new businesses? A good example is Westinghouse, a company that failed to plan strategically in the mid-1970s and was in deep trouble as a result.

Analysts of Westinghouse found that there was no corporate design for growth and development. "The company . . . got most of its input from middle management sources."[30] As a result individual divisions and business units were running in separate directions with no corporate controls. They entered businesses that appeared profitable in the short run, but without an adequate assessment of long-term risks.

The consequences of this lack of corporate planning and control were a series of disastrous moves. Westinghouse had to sell its appliance business, because the company never developed a strategy to meet competition from mass merchandisers such as Sears or from companies with strong dealer networks such as General Electric.[31] In an effort to build short-term volume for its industrial products it entered into lower-priced contracts for fixed turbines that guaranteed losses through the 1970s. And we have already noted its short-sighted venture into government contracted low-cost housing.

In contrast to Westinghouse, General Electric has developed longer-term marketing strategies at the top, and middle managers are charged with implementing those plans under the guidance of top management.[32] As a result, marketing opportunities in areas such as large appliances, power equipment, and electrical components have been well defined.

The outcome of Westinghouse's failures in the mid-1970s was a new management team that has instituted a strategic planning process to:

- developed specific performance goals,
- hold middle managers accountable to these goals, and
- introduce a value based planning process that requires each SBU to "analyze alternatives ranging from further investment to divestiture."[33]

The strategic planning process caused the company to deemphasize mature industries such as lighting and cooling products in favor of services, cable TV, robotics, and defense electronics.[34]

Corporate Growth Strategies

Figure 18-1 showed that there are two outputs from the strategic marketing plan: corporate growth strategies and product portfolio strategies. In this section we will consider corporate growth strategies. Development of such strategies is the responsibility of top management. In the next chapter we will consider product portfolio strategies in the context of the firm's overall product mix. Product portfolio strategies are developed for the whole corporation and within each SBU.

A company can pursue several alternative growth strategies. We considered some of these strategies in the previous chapter in terms of retail growth. Figure 18-3 categorizes growth strategies in a more general sense based on whether the company seeks growth from (1) existing or new markets and (2) existing or new products. A company emphasizing existing products can (1) *penetrate existing markets* by increasing advertising expenditures or by decreasing price, or (2) attempt to *expand into new markets.* In each case, it will spend less on research and development and product testing, and more on advertising and sales promotion than if it had emphasized new products.

A company emphasizing new products can (1) introduce them into existing markets through a strategy of *product expansion* (expand existing product lines by adding new models, sizes, or styles), or (2) *diversify* by introducing new products into new markets.

The lower portion of Figure 18-3 shows that a strategy of diversification

FIGURE 18-3
Corporate growth strategies

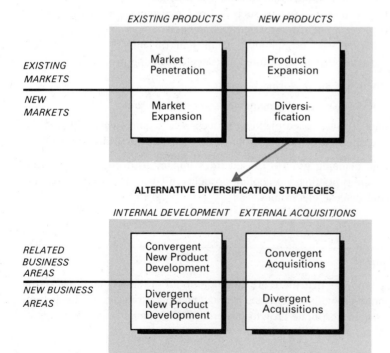

can be achieved by internal development (e.g., Gillette developing new products for women) or by external acquisition (e.g., Philip Morris acquiring Miller and 7-Up to diversify as a hedge against overreliance on cigarettes). Further, new products can be introduced in business areas in which the company currently has offerings or alternately in new areas.

MARKET PENETRATION

Companies use market penetration to ensure the growth of well-established products. Such a strategy is followed when a company believes that market share for one or more of its brands can be increased through more advertising, couponing, price reductions, or other marketing efforts. The most effective means to increase market share is by obtaining a competitive advantage.

A good example of a policy of market penetration is that of Sandvik, a diversified Swedish company. The company feels it has a competitive advantage in one of its product lines, cemented carbides, because of superior research and development and rigorous product controls. It competes with three larger companies including General Electric in this area. As a result of its competitive advantage, the company's goal is to double its market share "in part by encroaching on competitors."[35]

Another means of penetrating a market is by increasing the demand for the brand among current users. This can be achieved by convincing consumers to use more of the brand or by introducing new uses. Arm & Hammer increased the demand for its baking soda by emphasizing the following new uses (as quoted from the Arm & Hammer package):

- as a toothpaste ("pour soda into your hand and brush with wet toothbrush"),
- for indigestion relief ("Half a teaspoon in 1/2 glass of water and feel the burp of relief"),
- as a pot cleaner ("fill sink with solution of 3 tbsps. to quart of water to clean coffee and tea pots, thermos jugs, etc."),
- as an air freshener ("open container and leave in refrigerator or freezer"), and
- as a skin conditioner ("one cupful into bath cleans off oils and perspiration and will leave your skin feeling smooth, clean and fresh").

MARKET EXPANSION

A company relying on existing products for growth may seek to expand into new markets (lower left-hand box in Figure 18-3) in any of these ways: (1) expand geographically; (2) expand into new market segments; and (3) expand primary demand for the product category by convincing nonusers to become users.

Geographic expansion is the simplest route to expanding the markets for existing products because it requires no substantial change in strategy. In expanding its geographic base, the company can use essentially the same advertising and pricing strategies. Media and distribution will have to shift to a broader regional and national base, but the basic product appeal can remain the same. Procter and Gamble's decision to expand Folgers coffee to national distribution did not require changing the distribution channels or type of advertising media used. It required an expanded use of these facilities.

Market expansion can be international. As we noted, Kellogg has looked to international markets to maintain growth in cereals. But the company is confronted with the problem of changing the eating habits in markets where the notion of eating dry cereal is clearly foreign.[36] An extensive promotion and education campaign achieved success in Britain and Australia but has made little progress in France.

A company may also seek to expand markets for existing products by appealing to new segments, either by directing appeals to new demographic groups or by broadening the brand's appeal to new benefit segments. Anheuser-Busch, the leading brewer in the United States, has traditionally appealed to the heavier beer-drinking segment (blue-collar, middle-aged, less affluent). However, the company has not been successful in challenging Miller's dominant position in the light beer market, which contains younger and more affluent drinkers and a larger proportion of women. This segment is likely to grow faster than the heavier beer-drinking segment. Therefore, Anheuser's strategic plan is to expand into the light beer market.[37]

Finally, market expansion can be achieved by influencing nonusers of the product category to become users. At times, producers of staple goods such as orange juice, cranberries, and veal band together to undertake a cooperative industry campaign to increase primary demand. For example, milk producers have joined to advertise milk as "the fresher refresher" and have directed their campaign to adult nonusers.

PRODUCT EXPANSION

A strategy of product expansion directs new products to existing markets. This can be accomplished by modifying existing products or by extending existing product lines to include new brands. A company may seek to improve an existing product to combat inroads by competitive brands. Modifications may involve a change in taste, color, size, or effectiveness of the product. Frequent references are made in advertising to "new, improved" Tide, Crest, Clorox, and so on.

A company may also wish to expand its product line to give existing markets more alternatives. Durable goods manufacturers may expand the range of alternatives for refrigerators, cars, washing machines, and so on by providing more colors, options, and sizes. A company may also introduce new brands to provide a greater range of alternatives to existing users. As we noted in Chapter 10, Ban deodorant capitalized on its strength by introducing seventeen additional products in its deodorant line.

DIVERSIFICATION

A policy of diversification involves introducing new products to new markets (lower right-hand box in Figure 18-3). Diversification can be pursued by development of new products or by acquisition. Moreover, the strategy may involve introducing new products in related business areas or in totally new areas. The advantage of introducing products in related lines is that the company can use existing managerial know-how, raw materials, production facilities, and distribution channels (convergent development). But in some cases growth strategies require the acquisition of new resources to take advantage of market opportunities (divergent development). These approaches to diversification lead to four strategies designed for new products and new markets (see bottom of Figure 18-3):

1. convergent new product development,
2. divergent new product development,
3. convergent acquisitions, and
4. divergent acquisitions.

Convergent New Product Development

Companies frequently develop new products internally to utilize existing resources. Gillette's development of a line of women's personal care products is an example. Gillette can utilize its managerial know-how in marketing toiletries and can use its existing production facilities, sales force, and distributive network to manufacture and market these products. Yet a strategy of convergent product development should not be motivated by company resources; it should be based on consumer needs. Gillette's strategy is to "pick large, growing markets. Its products claim distinctive properties that set them apart from competitors."[38]

Another example of convergent development is Dun and Bradstreet's "new product blitz" in information services. D&B was a conservative, risk-averse company that originally concentrated on "new ways to package and sell information that happened to be on hand." Now the company is focusing on "the changing needs of the marketplace and [is devising] ways to fill those needs."[39] The company is developing new services that will use existing resources by combining the capabilities of previously unrelated divisions. For example, two Dun and Bradstreet business units, NCSS and D&B International of Canada "joined forces to create Keypoint, a service that provides on-line information on 50,000 Canadian businesses."[40]

Divergent New Product Development

Divergent new product development is rare because the company would have to develop a product line internally by acquiring outside manufacturing, managerial, and marketing resources. Such resources are generally obtained by direct acquisition of companies in the desired line.

One example of successful divergent development is the case of Armour-

Dial. Armour, originally a meat producer and packer, sought a use for the natural by-products of meat production. It decided to manufacture soap to utilize these by-products. The company recognized its lack of expertise in marketing personal care products and sought the managerial and marketing resources to do so. The result was the successful introduction of Dial Soap based on a claim of fighting bacteria.

The danger of entering unrelated lines to utilize existing production capacity or raw materials is illustrated by a large paper producer. The company had little experience in marketing consumer goods. Yet because of excess capacity, it decided to introduce a brand of disposable diapers. Unlike Armour it did not acquire the marketing capabilities, and the brand failed.

Convergent Acquisitions

Convergent acquisitions occur when a company acquires a direct competitor or a company in a related line. Dr. Pepper's acquisition of Canada Dry in the early 1980s is an example. Dr. Pepper also acquired the rights to market Welch's carbonated soft drinks. Its strategy is to obtain an increasing share of the soft-drink market by staying outside of the cola market and avoiding a direct challenge to Coke and Pepsi.[41] Revlon is also following a strategy of convergent acquisitions. It originally marketed beauty care products and diversified into health care products in the mid-1970s. Currently the company is pursuing an active acquisition policy restricted to these areas.[42]

A company may also follow a more directly convergent strategy by acquiring a close competitor. Such a policy could be blocked for antitrust reasons, as when the Justice Department restrained Mobil Oil from buying Marathon. But if the companies are not too large, acquisition may be allowed. For example, in 1982 Stroh breweries acquired Schlitz to expand Stroh's regional base and product line.[43]

Divergent Acquisitions

Companies also acquire unrelated firms to broaden their profit base and ensure future growth. Sandvik has sought divergent acquisitions in the American market because "its large market shares in Europe limit growth there. In contrast, the U.S. market represents tremendous potential."[44] Its corporate growth strategy involved acquiring a hand power tool company, several food-processing companies, and a manufacturer of industrial equipment. Pillsbury saw the growth potential in fast foods and acquired Burger King, Steak and Ale houses, and Poppin Fresh Pies restaurants. Today it claims to be the second largest restaurant company in the world.[45]

Companies may also seek divergent acquisitions as a hedge against increasing competition in their industry. Polaroid's position in the camera market weakened substantially in the late 1970s because (1) Eastman-Kodak introduced a competitive instant camera line, (2) demand for instant cameras was dropping, and (3) the company's attempt to market instant home movies failed miserably, requiring a $68.5 million writeoff.[46] As a result the company began to diversify into nonphotographic markets for the first time in its history. It is seeking acquisitions in industrial chemicals, and it has formulated new industrial technologies such as precision optics and chemical curatives. The company also realizes that "hard marketing effort is required to transfer Polaroid's consumer market reputation into industrial market sales."[47]

A third reason for acquiring businesses outside of the company's product mix is as a hedge against declining markets. Philips Industries, the leading producer of mobile homes and recreational vehicles, began diversifying when the market for these products collapsed in the mid-1970s.[48] Some companies have been criticized for failing to provide a hedge against a decline in core markets. Kellogg has been faulted by some marketers for an overreliance on the cereal market and failure to diversify as a hedge against declining cereal demand.[49]

There are significant risks in divergent diversification. In the early 1970s many large companies pursued such a strategy by acquiring high-growth companies. But they soon realized that their managerial and financial know-how did not extend to unrelated businesses. As a result a rash of divestitures began occurring in the late 1970s and were accelerated by the recession in the early 1980s. As we noted in Chapter 17, this trend was as pronounced in retailing as in manufacturing.

DYNAMIC CORPORATE GROWTH STRATEGIES

The classification of corporate growth strategies we have described is an oversimplification in two respects: (1) it does not reflect the changes that occur in corporate strategies over time; and (2) it does not suggest that companies are likely to engage in simultaneous strategies. By definition growth strategies are subject to change with changing economic, competitive, and technological environments. For example, Mennen moved from a strategy of product expansion to convergent internal development. The move was required because of lack of growth, increased competition, and overly conservative past management. One executive described the older strategy as a policy of "line extensions in the men's and baby categories." He added, "They were what you could call lower risk propositions that were not designed to build new businesses."[50] In 1975 a new management team was brought in that emphasized new products, primarily through internal development. The company introduced Millionaire cologne and Hawk fragrance. It strengthened the position of its Speed Stick deodorant to become the number one seller, and it repositioned its Skin Bracer to a broader market segment. As a result, sales increased fourfold from 1976 to 1980 and profits doubled.

Companies can also pursue growth on many strategic fronts. A good example is Procter and Gamble's growth strategy. P&G is pursuing almost all the corporate strategies we have described. It is pursuing market penetration by actively advertising its major brands such as Tide, Ivory, Crisco, and Charmin to increase market share. It has pursued market expansion for some of its brands (e.g., Folgers). It is following a policy of product expansion by extending its product lines in household cleaners, detergents, disposable diapers, and shampoos.[51] It is also actively diversifying on several fronts. Internal new product development has resulted in an artificial cocoa butter, and in a cholesterol-reducing drug that could be manufactured as a noncaloric margarine. The company is also entering the prescription drug business through acquisition because it realizes it does not have the expertise to market drug products. It is therefore seeking to buy its way into the business as it did earlier with coffee, toilet paper, cake mixes, and soft drinks.

The Procter and Gamble example demonstrates the broad front on which companies can pursue corporate growth strategies. A combination of strategies may be most likely to ensure growth.

Corporate Strategies in Low-Growth Industries

Figure 18-3 may leave the impression that companies seek high-growth industries to maximize profits. This is not always the case. At times companies purposely compete in low-growth markets. The paradox is that corporate growth can be achieved in low-growth industries.

Why would companies elect to compete in low-growth industries? Profits may be more easily attained in these industries, since they are less competitive. Frequently small firms see opportunities in low-growth industries as the best means of avoiding confrontation with larger competitors. They may be able to (1) achieve greater productivity, (2) appeal to a particular market niche, or (3) develop a competitive advantage by introducing a better product. In each of these cases there is greater potential for profits than in attempting to compete with larger firms in higher-growth areas.

HIGHER PRODUCTIVITY

Smaller, leaner firms are frequently more productive than larger ones. Unifi, a textile firm, has effectively competed with larger rivals in a low-growth area by increasing productivity fivefold since its founding in 1971, and has halved labor costs per pound of production.[52] Republic Gypsum, a one-plant wallboard producer, competes against billion-dollar National Gypsum and U.S. Gypsum because of greater flexibility. It has only 2 percent of the market, but serves the Sunbelt very effectively. When demand is down, it extends its sales area. As a result it can operate at 94 percent of capacity, compared to 70 percent for the industry, and shows an operating margin three times greater than those of its rivals.[53]

MARKET NICHE

In Chapter 8 we identified one segmentation strategy as a market niche or concentrated segmentation strategy. As we noted, such a strategy is desirable for a firm with limited resources that may not be able to compete head-on with larger rivals. For example, American Motors has substantially scaled back its production of cars and has chosen to concentrate its production and marketing resources in a market niche the bigger manufacturers have largely ignored — jeeps.

Identifying a market niche in a stagnant industry is, in a sense, trying to identify growth in low-growth areas. For example, the number of movie theaters has continuously decreased since World War II because of TV, and now, new in-home technologies. Yet General Cinema identified a growth opportunity in this area, shopping center theaters. Today General Cinema has 700 shopping center theaters (Cinema I, II, . . . theaters) enabling it to increase earnings an average of 20 percent per year over the last ten years.[54]

COMPETITIVE ADVANTAGE

Another strategy in low-growth industries is to develop a unique competitive advantage. Baking soda was not going anywhere until Arm & Hammer advertised new uses. The demand for motorcycles was fairly stagnant until Japanese manufacturers began concentrating on producing smaller motorcycles.[55] Hanes revitalized demand for hosiery by introducing L'Eggs into new distribution outlets. L&M has found a means of expanding sales by making generic cigarettes. In each case the company has identified a competitive advantage in a low-growth situation.

Corporate Retrenchment Strategies

At times companies must go through a painful process of retrenchment before growth and profitability are possible. Retrenchment may be necessary because of lack of planning (e.g., Westinghouse), declining demand in core markets (e.g., Courtaulds's fiber and fabric businesses) or disastrous acquisitions that have drained the company's resources (e.g., Schlitz).

Companies faced with the necessity of retrenchment have generally been taken over by new management teams who better recognize the need for strategic planning. This was true at Westinghouse, Courtaulds Ltd., and 3M. New management realized that retrenchment was a necessary prelude to growth and either (1) cut costs, (2) pruned product lines, or (3) got rid of poor acquisitions.

CUT COSTS

When new management took over at Philips Industries in 1978, the company was close to bankruptcy. The president saw that the only chance of survival was to cut back costs drastically and look for new business opportunities. He consolidated manufacturing operations, shut five plants, laid off 27 percent of the work force and instituted ongoing cost-cutting analyses. Prudent acquisitions with the funds released by these cost-cutting measures began to increase earnings. By 1983 earnings increased by 55 percent despite a 6 percent decrease in sales.[56]

PRUNE PRODUCT LINES

Lack of strategic planning by top management frequently leads to inefficient expansions of product lines. Management at Parker Pen and 3M made reductions in the number of products offered a central feature of the strategic plan. When new management took over at Helena Rubinstein, the cosmetics company, profits were decreasing in the face of constant sales increases. Management realized the company was saddled with inefficient product lines. As a result it sold three of its low-priced lines and its American manufacturing facilities, and destroyed outdated inventory.[57] The result was a smaller, leaner, but more profitable company.

ELIMINATE ACQUISITIONS

Many companies have embarked on an acquisition strategy without a rational long-term plan for growth. Frequently companies are attractive targets for acquisition because of their profitability and production or marketing resources. But management is deflected from the core businesses, and other units in the corporation may suffer. This is what happened at Ralston Purina in the 1970s. Management began an aggressive acquisition strategy to diversify from grocery products. By 1979 the company was running a Colorado resort, breeding shrimps in Panama, growing mushrooms, fishing for tuna, operating its own canneries, and running the St. Louis Blues hockey team. The company could not adequately digest these acquisitions. A new management team began a process of retrenchment in 1983 to get back to its core markets representing the company's area of expertise. As the new chairman said, "Our future growth will come primarily through aggressive new product development in our core businesses [animal feed, grocery products and restaurant operations]."[58] The company thus switched from a strategy of divergent acquisitions to convergent new product development.

Summary

A key responsibility of top management is the development of a strategic marketing plan that will guide corporate growth and the firm's product mix. The strategic plan should:

- establish corporate objectives,
- integrate marketing and nonmarketing activities,
- identify alternative marketing opportunities,
- assess the potential profitability of these opportunities,

- allocate resources to the various business units on the basis of opportunity evaluation, and

- control marketing activities to make sure they conform to the strategic plan.

Strategic planning also takes place at the business unit level. The basic difference between strategic planning at the corporate and the SBU level is that the corporate plan allocates resources to the SBUs, whereas the SBU plan allocates resources to the individual products.

A major output of strategic marketing planning is the development of corporate growth strategies. Firms can devote their resources to revitalizing or expanding existing products, or to introducing new products. New products can be developed internally or acquired externally. Rarely will a company devote its energies to one of these strategies. The key questions in a corporation's growth strategy are, How much of our resources should we devote to existing versus new products? and How much should we emphasize internal development or external acquisition?

At times firms will pursue profitability in low-growth industries. This course is likely to be followed by smaller firms to avoid competition with larger rivals. Profitability can be achieved in stagnant industries by increasing productivity, identifying a market niche, or achieving a competitive advantage in terms of product quality or distribution.

Firms may also use corporate retrenchment as a prelude to growth. Retrenchment may be necessary because of inadequate planning, declining demand, or a poor series of acquisitions. In such cases a new management team frequently takes over and cuts costs, prunes the product mix, and divests the company of prior acquisitions.

In this chapter, we focused on the nature of strategic planning and corporate growth strategies. In the next we will consider the other basic element in strategic marketing planning, the composition of the firm's product mix.

Questions

1. A large Hollywood movie studio establishes a new marketing division with the responsibility of researching, advertising, and distributing its movies. The director of the marketing division feels the company's corporate mission should be customer rather than production oriented, and defines it as "Developing movies to meet changing customer tastes in a dynamic cultural and social environment."

   □ Do you agree with the definition of corporate mission? Why or why not?

    ☐ Does the definition of mission exclude certain corporate growth alternatives?

2. What corporate objectives could be established for the mission in question 1? How would corporate objectives change if a broader statement of corporate mission was developed?

3. We cited the fact that Courtaulds established a minimum 12 percent ROI for all its strategic business units. What are the pros and cons of establishing the same performance goals for all SBUs in a corporation?

4. The head of a newly formed low-calorie SBU of a large food company decides to establish a planning committee responsible for planning for the SBU as a whole and for each of its product lines. The charge to the planning committee says, "You will be responsible for (1) determining future environmental trends, (2) defining opportunities, (3) allocating resources accordingly, (4) developing marketing strategies based on the opportunities identified, and (5) ensuring that these strategies are implemented." Do you agree with the responsibilities assigned to the planning committee? Why or why not?

5. What risks does a company face if it fails to coordinate marketing plans with:

    ☐ research and development,

    ☐ manufacturing,

    ☐ finance, and

    ☐ accounting?

6. Top management at 3M decided to introduce Beam Tape, although the product is relatively untried and is competing with an entrenched technology.

    ☐ Why did management decide to introduce Beam Tape?

    ☐ What are the dangers of management's arguments in introducing Beam Tape?

7. When Mobil purchased Montgomery Ward, Mobil pushed it to take certain actions such as expanding a Montgomery Ward Florida-based discount chain to national status. On the other hand, when Nestlé acquired Beech Nut, it allowed the new SBU's management to develop a plan to challenge Gerber and Heinz. What are the pros and cons of Mobil's more activist position and Nestlé's more laissez-faire attitude?

8. The chapter cited Helene Curtis's introduction of Finesse hair conditioner as an example of integration between the strategic plan and the marketing plan (see Figure 18-2). What might have happened had there been no integration at Helene Curtis between strategic and marketing planning?

9. What are the alternatives for growth when a company relies solely on existing products?

   □ What are the pros and cons of each strategy?

   □ In the long run can a company rely solely on existing products for growth?

10. What are the dangers to a firm acquiring companies outside its area of competency (pursuing a strategy of divergent diversification)? Cite some successes and failures among companies acquiring businesses outside of their core markets.

11. A company with a dynamic process of strategic planning will demonstrate an ability to change its corporate growth strategies in response to a changing competitive or customer environment.

   □ Cite some examples of such changes.

   □ In each case to what environmental conditions did the firm adjust its corporate growth strategies?

12. A president of a small electronics company says, "The problem with strategic planning is that it is biased toward high-growth industries. We do most of our business in markets with stable demand on the basis of our superior productivity and technology, permitting us to provide high-quality products at lower prices."

   □ What is the rationale behind this strategy? What are the risks of relying on low-growth markets?

   □ What strategies other than attempting to establish superiority in productivity and technology are available to small firms in low-growth markets?

Notes

1. "Following a Slow Start, RCA Plans a New Push For Its Videodisc Player," *The Wall Street Journal,* October 13, 1981, p. 35.

2. "Kellogg Looks Beyond Breakfast," *Business Week,* December 6, 1982, pp. 66–69.

3. Ibid. p. 69.

4. "Chesebrough-Pond's Growth via Market Control," *The New York Times,* May 11, 1979, pp. D1, D5.

5. Ibid.

6. "Courtaulds: Survival of the Fittest is the Rule at Britain's Textile Giant," *Business Week,* April 11, 1983, pp. 88, 92, 94, 99.

7. Ibid., p. 88.

8. Ibid., p. 94.

9. "How Exxon Chemical Prepares for the '90s," *Chemical Week,* July 30, 1980, pp. 38–41, at p. 38.

10. "No. 1's Awesome Strategy," *Business Week,* June 8, 1981, pp. 84–90.

11. Yoram Wind, "Marketing and the Other Business Functions," *Research in Marketing* 5 (1981): 237–64.

12. "3M's Search for Strategic Identity," *Industrial Marketing,* February 1983, pp. 80, 82, 86, 88, 89, at p. 80.

13. Wind, "Marketing and the Other Business Functions," p. 242.
14. Ibid., pp. 242–43.
15. *Industrial Marketing,* February 1983, p. 82.
16. Ibid., pp. 82, 86.
17. Ibid., pp. 86, 88.
18. Ibid., p. 86.
19. "Now for the Greening of Pillsbury," *Fortune,* November 5, 1979, pp. 126–36.
20. "New Chief Pens Bold Plan for a Parker Resurgence," *Advertising Age,* July 26, 1982, pp. 4, 56.
21. *Business Week,* April 11, 1983, p. 94.
22. *Industrial Marketing,* February 1983, p. 86.
23. *Business Week,* April 11, 1983, p. 99.
24. David S. Hopkins, "New Emphasis in Product Planning and Strategy Development," *Industrial Marketing Management* 6 (1977): 411.
25. *Business Week,* January 31, 1977, p. 61.
26. *Industrial Marketing,* February 1983, p. 88.
27. "Beech-Nut Reborn," *Sales & Marketing Management,* December 6, 1982, pp. 26–29.
28. "The Big Gamble at Helene Curtis," *Business Week* January 24, 1983, pp. 60 and 62.
29. Ibid., p. 60.
30. *Business Week,* January 31, 1977, p. 61.
31. Ibid., p. 63.
32. Ibid., p. 62.
33. "Operation Turnaround," *Business Week,* December 5, 1983, pp. 124–33.
34. Ibid.
35. "Sandvik Inc.: A U.S. Spearhead for its Parent's Worldwide Expansion," *Business Week,* November 9, 1981, p. 80.
36. "Outlook Brightens for Profitable Kellogg," *The New York Times,* March 25, 1982, pp. D1, D6.
37. "Anheuser Tries Light Beer Again," *Business Week,* June 29, 1981, p. 136.
38. *The Wall Street Journal,* November 5, 1981, p. 31.
39. "How D&B Organizes for a New-Product

Blitz," *Business Week,* November 16, 1981, p. 87.
40. Ibid.
41. "Dr. Pepper's New Bosses Avoid Cola Battles, Push for Gains From Promotion, Expansion," *The Wall Street Journal,* November 16, 1981, p. 29.
42. "Revlon's Health-Care Push," *The New York Times,* October 8, 1981, pp. D1, D4.
43. "U.S. Conditionally Permits Stroh to Buy Schlitz," *The Wall Street Journal,* April 19, 1982, p. 4.
44. *Business Week,* November 9, 1981, p. 80.
45. "Pillsbury Feeds Frozen, Restaurants for Growth," *Advertising Age,* September 21, 1981, p. 4.
46. "Polaroid Needs Brighter Image," *Advertising Age,* May 4, 1981, pp. 4, 92.
47. "Polaroid Seeks Business Focus," *Industrial Marketing,* October 1981, p. 8.
48. "Philips Industries: Cutting Costs to Make the Best of Bad Times," *Business Week,* January 10, 1983, p. 94.
49. *Business Week,* December 6, 1982, pp. 66, 68, 69.
50. "Mennen Hands Reins to Hand-Picked Team," *Advertising Age,* October 19, 1981, p. 56.
51. "P&G's New-Product Onslaught," *Business Week,* October 1, 1979, pp. 76–82.
52. "The Market Share Myth," *Forbes,* March 14, 1983, pp. 109, 110, 114, 115.
53. Ibid.
54. Richard G. Hammermesh and Steven B. Silk, "How to Compete in Stagnant Industries," *Harvard Business Review* (September–October 1979): 163.
55. Ibid., p. 165.
56. *Business Week,* January 10, 1983, p. 94.
57. "New Owners Give Helena Rubinstein a Face Lift," *Ad Forum,* July 1982, p. 42.
58. "Ralston Purina: Dumping Products That Led It Away from Checkerboard Square," *Business Week,* January 31, 1983, pp. 63–64.

CHAPTER 19

Evaluating the Company's Product Mix

FOCUS OF CHAPTER

A firm's success in the marketplace depends on its product offerings. In the last chapter we described how top management develops guidelines for corporate growth. In this chapter we will describe how the firm arrives at a balanced product mix to ensure profitability.

The basis for evaluating the firm's product mix is **product portfolio analysis.** In the first part of the chapter we will describe approaches to product portfolio analysis. Product portfolio analysis is a means of ensuring that firms direct their resources to high-growth markets while maintaining the strength of established products in lower-growth markets. The objective is to maintain an adequate cash flow within the company and direct it to areas of greatest marketing opportunity.

In the second part of the chapter we will look at various product portfolio strategies. Firms can attempt to invest in growth markets, build the market share of existing products that could do better, maintain the position of strong brands, or get rid of unprofitable products or acquisitions. These strategies apply to the mix of products within a strategic business unit and to the firm's overall mix of businesses.

Finally we will consider factors that affect the profitability of the firm's product mix. Factors such as the quality of the products produced by the firm, the growth rate of the industry, and the amount of money spent on advertising and new product development have been found to be related to profitability.

The strategic planning sequence in evaluating the firm's product mix is therefore:

Analyze the Product Portfolio $\longrightarrow$ Develop Product Portfolio Strategies $\longrightarrow$ Evaluate the Profitability of the Product Mix

The evaluation of the profitability of the product mix leads into the question of evaluating and controlling the firm's marketing performance in the next chapter.

Product Portfolio Analysis

Product portfolio analysis is being used widely to analyze corporate product mixes. One study found that at least half of Fortune's largest 1000 corporations use some form of product portfolio analysis in planning.[1] Product portfolio analysis is a key element in strategic marketing planning.

In Chapter 4 we described product portfolio analysis as the application of principles of stock portfolio analysis to changes in the firm's product mix. Investors buying a portfolio of stocks realize that different stocks may be purchased for different objectives (short-term earnings versus long-term growth) and can provide different yields. Similarly, top management develops a portfolio of products to attain a reasonable balance of current earnings and future potential. Products providing current earnings are established products with high market shares. These solid, cash-generating brands may be in lower-growth markets. To ensure future growth, firms will want a proper mix of cash-generating brands and higher-risk entries in growth areas. Thus, Gillette can use a cash-generating brand such as Right Guard in the relatively stable deodorant category to finance entry of brands such as Aapri in the high-growth facial cleanser market.

Figure 19-1 shows that product portfolio analysis relies on two components in evaluating the firm's product mix. First is an assessment of the area of

FIGURE 19-1
The basic product portfolio matrix

MARKETING OPPORTUNITY (Based on Current Growth or Investment Attractiveness)	ABILITY TO EXPLOIT OPPORTUNITY (Based on Current Market Performance or Company's Resources)	
	HIGH	*LOW*
HIGH	1. Exploit Opportunity	3. (a) Enhance Company's Ability to Exploit Opportunity (b) Do Not Consider
LOW	2. Maintain Profitable Position	4. (a) Avoid Markets (b) Divest Existing Products

opportunity in a particular industry or market. Opportunity is generally defined in terms of current industry growth or potential attractiveness as an investment. Second is the company's ability to exploit opportunity, which is based on its current or potential position in the industry. The company's position can be measured in terms of market share if it is currently in the market, or in terms of its resources if it is considering market entry. These two factors, opportunity and the company's ability to exploit it, form the matrix in Figure 19-1. The matrix shows four possibilities:

1. High opportunity and ability to exploit it result in the firm's introducing new products or expanding markets for existing products to ensure future growth.

2. Low opportunity but a strong current market position will generally result in the company's attempting to maintain its position to ensure current profitability.

3. High opportunity but a lack of ability to exploit it results in either (a) attempting to acquire the necessary resources or (b) deciding not to further pursue opportunity in these markets.

4. Low opportunity and a weak market position will result in either (a) avoiding these markets or (b) divesting existing products in them.

Although these alternatives are oversimplified, they do provide a basis for the firm to evaluate new and existing products in an attempt to achieve balance between current yield and future growth.

The two types of analysis to be considered below — the Boston Consulting Group's growth/market share matrix, and General Electric's market attractiveness/business position matrix — both have the same purpose as that shown in Figure 19-1: to evaluate opportunity and the company's ability to exploit it. Thus, when Procter and Gamble first thought of entering the disposable diaper market, it saw the area as an excellent opportunity for growth. P&G felt it had the capability to be successful despite its lack of experience in paper products, because of its general success in marketing consumer packaged goods. As a result the product would be placed in the high-growth/high-company-capability position of the product portfolio matrix. The subsequent introduction of Pampers was one of the most profitable introductions in the company's history.

BOSTON CONSULTING GROUP'S GROWTH/SHARE ANALYSIS

The most widely used approach to product portfolio analysis is that developed by the Boston Consulting Group (BCG).

Criteria for Evaluating Products in the BCG Matrix

The BCG analysis emphasizes two criteria in evaluating the firm's product mix: the market growth rate and the product's relative market share (see Figure

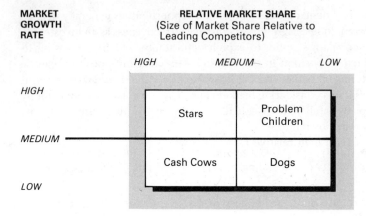

FIGURE 19-2
The BCG product portfolio matrix

19-2). The reason BCG uses these two criteria is the finding that they are closely related to profitability.[2]

The *market growth rate* (corrected for inflation) represents the product category's position in the life cycle. Products in the introductory and growth phases require more investment because of research and development and initial marketing costs for advertising, selling, and distribution. Cellular radiophones (cordless phones with unlimited range) are products that are beginning to be tested and will require substantial investment. The category is also regarded as a high-growth area. Videocassette recorders are passing into a growth stage after having been in an introductory phase for seven or eight years; they require investment for marketing costs.

Relative market share represents the company's competitive strength (or estimated strength for a new entry). Share is compared to that of the leading competitor. Thus Hershey, with a 23 percent share of the chocolate bar market, is in a relatively strong competitive position because the market leader, Mars, has only a 36 percent share. Ford Motors has a higher share of the automobile market, but is in a relatively weaker position because General Motors' share is over 60 percent.

Market growth and market share are used to represent the **BCG portfolio matrix** in Figure 19-2. The BCG matrix is an extension of the matrix in Figure 19-1. Products are positioned according to marketing opportunity (market growth in Figure 19-2) and the company's market position (relative market share in Figure 19-2).

Alternative Product Positions in BCG's Matrix

Figure 19-2 presents four categories of products according to position in the product portfolio matrix: stars, cash cows, problem children, and dogs.

Stars

Products with high growth and market share are known as **stars.** These products have high potential for profitability. They should be given top priority in financing, advertising, product positioning, and distribution. As a result, they need significant amounts of cash to finance rapid growth and frequently show a negative cash flow.

Cash cows

Products with a high relative market share but in a low growth position are **cash cows.** These are profitable products that generate more cash than is required to produce and market them. Excess cash should be used to finance high opportunity areas (stars or problem children). Strategies for cash cows should be designed to sustain current market share rather than to expand it. An expansion strategy would require additional investment, thus decreasing the desirable positive cash flow position of cash cows. An example of a cash cow is P&G's Crest toothpaste. The brand has maintained a high market share in a low-growth market.

Problem children

Problem children have low relative market shares but are in a high-growth situation. They are called problem children because their eventual direction is not yet clear. The firm should invest heavily in those which sales forecasts indicate might have a reasonable chance to become stars. Otherwise divestment is the best course, since problem children may become dogs and thereby candidates for deletion.

Dogs

Products in the bottom right quadrant of Figure 19-2 are clearly candidates for deletion. Such products have low market shares and, unlike problem children, no real prospect for growth. Eliminating a **dog** is not always necessary. There are strategies for dogs that could make them profitable in the short term. These strategies involve "harvesting" these products by eliminating marketing support and selling the product to intensely loyal consumers who will buy in the absence of advertising. But over the longer term, companies will seek to eliminate dogs.

Internal Cash Flow as the Criterion of Evaluation

As can be seen by the description of the four alternatives in the BCG matrix, products are evaluated as producers or users of cash. Products with a positive cash flow will finance high-opportunity products that need cash. The emphasis on cash flow stems from management's belief that it is better to finance new entries and to support existing products with internally produced funds than to increase debt or equity in the company. The emphasis on cash flow increased in the early 1980s, with interest rates hitting historic highs, making external funding to exploit marketing opportunity all the more expensive.

Brands with high relative market shares generally produce more cash than firms wth low relative market shares. As a result the BCG matrix can also be presented as follows:

CASH NEEDS FOR INVESTMENT	CASH GENERATED	
	HIGH	LOW
HIGH	Stars (0)	Problem Children (−)
LOW	Cash Cows (+)	Dogs (0)

Investment Scenarios Based on Cash Flow

On the basis of the preceding figure, the flow of funds should go from cash cows (a) to stars to reinforce their position in the expectation that they will eventually become cash cows and (b) to problem children to build them into stars. These scenarios are represented at the top of Figure 19-3. Scenario 1 calls for investing in a problem child to transform it into a star. Scenario 2 calls for investing in a star to maintain its competitive position so that when industry growth slows, it will become a cash cow. In both cases funding comes from existing cash cows.

As an example of the first scenario, Hershey bought Friendly Ice Cream Corporation, a low-share regional ice cream company, with the intention of investing in the company to transform its ice cream line into a star. Hershey's success in financing the line with its established candy brands helped boost earnings by 25 percent and its return on equity to 19 percent, one of the highest returns among specialty food companies.[3] Similarly, when Philip Morris bought Miller beer, the brand was languishing as a low-share problem child in a growth market. Philip Morris invested heavily with funds from its cigarette brands and transformed Miller High Life into a star (scenario 1) and the second leading brand in the market. The decline in growth of the domestic premium beer market because of competition from imports and from new light beers then transformed Miller High Life into a cash cow (scenario 2), permitting the brand to finance the company's new star Miller Lite.

The bottom of Figure 19-3 shows two loss scenarios: a star becoming a problem child, and a problem child becoming a dog. In both cases cash cows

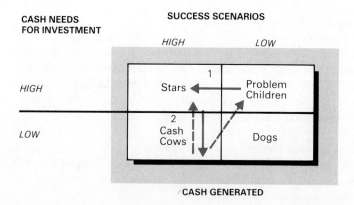

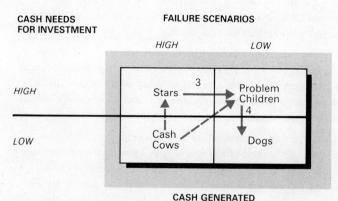

Note:
Solid Line = Product Flow
Dotted Line = Cash Flow

FIGURE 19-3
Success and failure scenarios in product
portfolio analysis

wind up funding losing propositions. When Procter and Gamble introduced Pringles potato chips, it expected the brand to become a star in the high-growth chip-type snack food market. It quickly became apparent the brand would not meet market share expectations, yet the company continued to sink money into it (scenario 3 in Figure 19-3). P&G could afford the expenditure because of an abundance of cash cows, but a lesser company might have gone bankrupt.

A problem child can also quickly become a dog if a company misreads a product's position, seeing it in a growth market. Polaroid introduced instant movies (Polavision) in the firm belief that it was establishing a new film category that would grow rapidly. Sales did not meet expectations, and the category was eventually eliminated (scenario 4). Again the venture was possible because it was funded by a highly successful established product, the instant camera.

Limitations of the BCG Analysis

BCG's growth/share matrix revolutionized strategic marketing planning when it was first introduced in the early 1970s. Companies began to accept the notion of a balanced mix of products and to view product growth in a more dynamic sense. But BCG's product portfolio analysis has been faulted for being too oversimplified. The most serious deficiency is the assumption on which the analysis rests, that market share is related to profitability.

The relation of market share to profitability

Several studies have demonstrated a link between market share and profitability. One found that companies with a high market share have higher profitability because as market share increases:

- there are greater economies of scale in purchasing and in marketing expenditures (i.e., a company with a market share twice as high as its leading competitor does not have to spend twice as much on advertising or distribution to maintain its customers);[4]

- market leaders develop unique competitive strategies and can charge higher prices resulting in higher profits[5] (e.g., Clorox, the market leader in bleach, can charge a few cents more than most of its competitors because it differentiates itself through packaging and promotions, even though all bleaches are standardized); and

- the firm gains experience in production and marketing, resulting in lower average costs over time (BCG found that every time production doubled, per unit costs fell an average of 25 to 30 percent. BCG labeled the relationship between higher market share and lower production costs the **experience curve** because as volume increases, the company learns to manage its resources more efficiently to reduce costs).[6]

No one doubts that there is a relationship between market share and profitability. The problem is that the relationship is not universal. For example, in highly competitive markets the only way to gain share might be through price cuts, which reduce profitability. In the early 1960s Ford was determined to obtain market leadership over Chevrolet. It forced its dealers to cut prices and increase trade-in allowances. The company gained market leadership for a short time but at tremendous expense. Certainly in this case, high market share did not provide cash-generating potential as is assumed in the BCG portfolio analysis.

Small, efficient companies can also be very profitable when they carve a niche in the market and can compete with larger companies. In Chapter 18 we cited Republic Gypsum, a one-plant wallboard company that competes effectively with billion-dollar competitors. The company's products certainly cannot be classified as problem children, despite a low market share and high growth.

The example of Republic Gypsum also casts doubt on the experience curve. Larger companies do not necessarily have lower per unit costs. The relative importance of experience and economies of scale varies by product type and industry. One study found that four of the eight lowest-cost producers analyzed achieved their position without the benefit of high relative market shares.[7]

The evidence suggests that although a large market share may be an important contributor to profitability, it is by no means necessary to success. The marketing implications of this finding are important. A market share strategy might dictate price reductions and excessive advertising to ensure market dominance. But such a strategy could lead to lower profits, especially if (1) the industry is in a low growth phase, (2) it is highly competitive, or (3) technological advances result in the introduction of higher-quality products.

Other shortcomings of BCG's growth/share matrix

Several other factors also limit the usefulness of the BCG approach in evaluating a firm's product mix. First, the growth/share matrix relies on cash flow for making decisions to introduce, build, maintain, or divest products from the mix. But the analysis totally ignores the fact that cash can be borrowed. As one marketer said, "If you have a profit, you can get cash."[8] Therefore, profitability may be a more appropriate criterion for evaluating performance than cash-generating ability.

Second, growth rate is not the only factor that defines marketing opportunity. At times opportunities for profit exist in low-growth markets. As we noted in Chapter 18, Unifi has been making consistent profits in the face of a stagnant polyester market while its bigger competitors, such as Monsanto and Celanese, have gotten out.[9] Unifi's profitability is due to factors such as ineffective competitors, production efficiencies, and technological advances, not to market growth.

Third, the assumption in the BCG analysis that products in high-growth areas need more cash and products with high market shares generate more cash is frequently untrue. Factors such as competitive entry, product innovation, managerial efficiency, and capital intensity may make these assumptions invalid.

GE'S MARKET ATTRACTIVENESS/BUSINESS POSITION MATRIX

The general limitations of the BCG approach motivated several companies to work toward an improvement of portfolio models. General Electric, working with the consulting firm of McKinsey and Company, extended the BCG model to incorporate a much larger range of variables that could affect product performance.[10] Rather than dealing simply with the growth rate of a market, GE also defined its attractiveness. Market attractiveness is defined by many variables such as profit margins, level of competition, market diversity, cyclical nature of the market, and growth rate. Having defined the overall attractiveness of a market, GE then assessed its own business position in it. Whereas BCG just relied on market share to define business position, GE also included the growth of the company's target segments, its overall influence on the market, its position relative to competition, its experience, and its financial and production resources.

The variables that are included in defining these two factors are shown in Table 19-1. Those which define market attractiveness are in the left-hand column; those which constitute the company's business position in the market are on the right. The variables are divided into five major categories: market factors, competition, financial and economic factors, technological factors, and sociopolitical factors.

Products are evaluated on these criteria and placed in a portfolio matrix using the two major dimensions of market attractiveness and business position. The three-by-three matrix in Figure 19-4 suggests three general courses of action. Products with high attractiveness and business position are candidates for further investment and growth. Products in the middle range are candidates for selective investment, depending on their specific situation, and are managed for their short-term earnings. Products low in attractiveness and business position are candidates for harvesting (cut back on expenditures and maintain the product as long as earnings are adequate) and for eventual divestment.

At GE management is asked to evaluate individual offerings on the criteria in Table 19-1 and then place the product in the matrix in Figure 19-4. Offerings can be evaluated by weighting each criterion by importance and then rating it. Using just five of the variables in Table 19-1 for simplicity, assume GE is evaluating its current line of garbage disposal units. Management determines the importance of each of the criteria and then evaluates the market's attractiveness and GE's position in the market. Using the analysis shown in Table 19-2, management finds the market attractive in terms of its size, lack of seasonality, sufficient capacity utilization, and opportunities for technological differentiation from competitive products. The only negative is the high level of competition. GE finds its line very strong on all counts, with only moderate strength in competitive advantage.

The basis for the overall assessment of the product line is a set of norms that the company has developed in analyzing other products in the mix. Thus, any market or product that scores higher than 250 is regarded as a candidate for investment and growth, and any market/product assessment under 125 would lead to a harvest/divest strategy, with intermediate strategies in between these two extremes. Using the analysis in Table 19-2, management places the garbage disposal line in the invest/grow category but maintains a close watch on the competitive intensity in the market.

Standard Brands' Utilization of the GE Portfolio Approach

Portfolio analysis is designed to evaluate not just one line but the firm's overall product mix. In the mid 1970s Standard Brands (now Nabisco Brands) evaluated its product mix using GE's portfolio model. In 1976 the company began to

TABLE 19-1
Factors Contributing to Market Attractiveness and Business Position

ATTRACTIVENESS OF YOUR MARKET	*STATUS/POSITION OF YOUR BUSINESS*
1. MARKET FACTORS	
Size (dollars, units, or both)	Your share (in equivalent terms)
Size of key segments	Your share of key segments
Growth rate per year:	Your annual growth rate:
Total	Total
Segments	Segments
Diversity of market	Diversity of your participation
Sensitivity to price, service features, and external factors	Your influence on the market
Cyclic nature	Lags or leads in your sales
Seasonality	
Bargaining power of suppliers	Bargaining power of your suppliers
Bargaining power of customers	Bargaining power of your customers
2. COMPETITION	
Types of competitors	Where you fit, how you compare in terms of
Concentration	products, marketing capability, service, pro-
Changes in type and mix	duction strength, financial strength, management
Entries and exits	Segments you have entered or left
Changes in share	Your relative share change
Substitution by new technology	Your vulnerability to new technology
Degrees and types of integration	Your own level of integration
3. FINANCIAL AND ECONOMIC FACTORS	
Contribution margins	Your margins
Leveraging factors, such as economies of scale and experience	Your scale and experience
Barriers to entry or exit (both financial and nonfinancial)	Barriers to your entry or exit (both financial and nonfinancial)
Capacity utilization	Your capacity utilization
4. TECHNOLOGICAL FACTORS	
Maturity and volatility	Your ability to cope with change
Complexity	Depths of your skills
Differentiation	Types of your technological skill
Patents and copyrights	Your patent protection
Manufacturing process technology required	Your manufacturing technology
5. SOCIOPOLITICAL FACTORS	
Social attitudes and trends	Your company's responsiveness and flexibility
Laws and government agency regulations	Your company's ability to cope
Influence with pressure groups and government representatives	Your company's aggressiveness
Human factors, such as unionization and community acceptance	Your company's relationships

Source: Adapted from Derek F. Abell and John S. Hammond, *Strategic Market Planning* (Englewood Cliffs, New Jersey: Prentice-Hall, 1979), p. 214.

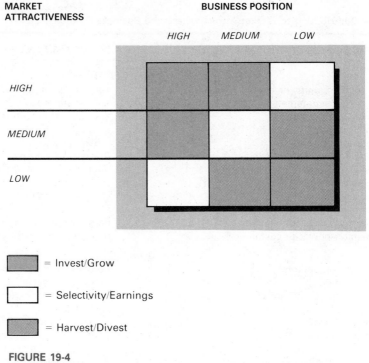

FIGURE 19-4
General Electric's market attractiveness/business position matrix

Source: Adapted by permission from Charles W. Hofer and Dan Schendel, *Strategy Formulation: Analytical Concepts.* Copyright © 1978 by West Publishing Company. All rights reserved.

concentrate more intensively on brand-name consumer goods while reducing its involvement in food ingredients such as sugar substitutes.[11] As a result of this strategy Standard Brands felt it necessary to evaluate its product mix periodically. It now gives its managers a data package with projections of inflation, economic growth, shifts in population, and other environmental changes. It then asks management to evaluate specific markets and the company's position in these markets, using criteria such as those in Table 19-1. The data package helps management assess the market environment. On this basis, products are entered into the portfolio matrix in Figure 19-4.

Figure 19-5 presents results of this analysis.[12] Smooth & Easy, a line of sauce and gravy bars, was in a potentially profitable market and was regarded as a strong entry with a distinct competitive advantage. Pinata Foods and Planters Nuts are specialty and snack food categories that the company acquired because of their growth potential. Walker Crisps, a British subsidiary, was considered by management as a candidate for long-term growth. Fleishman's Corn Oil was a well-established product that was in a strong market position in a growing market. The company was willing to treat the brand as a growth opportunity, even though it was not new.

TABLE 19-2
Evaluating Products by Market Attractiveness and Business Position

MARKET ATTRACTIVENESS					
	Importance Weights (10-point scale)	X	Market Attractiveness Rating (10-point scale)	=	Market Attractiveness Evaluation Score
Size of market	9	X	10	=	90
Seasonality	2	X	9	=	18
Competitive concentration	9	X	3	=	27
Capacity utilization	3	X	10	=	30
Technological differen- tiation	7	X	9	=	63
			Total	=	190
BUSINESS POSITION					
Market share	9	X	10	=	90
Seasonality	2	X	9	=	18
Strength relative to competition	9	X	7	=	63
Company's capacity utilization	3	X	10	=	30
Technological skills	7	X	9	=	63
			Total	=	264

Norms for Evaluation	Decision Criterion
Excellent = 250 +	Invest/grow
Good = 175–249	Invest/grow or selectivity/earnings
Fair = 125–174	Selectivity/earnings
Poor = Under 125	Harvest divest

Several lines were in the selective investment/short-term earnings category. For example, Standard Brands' line of Souverain Wines was not a major factor in the domestic wine industry because of competition from established brands such as Gallo and Taylor. But wine consumption is growing rapidly, making the market attractive. On the other side of the coin Standard Brands was in a strong competitive position with its established candy bars such as Baby Ruth and Butterfingers, but a variety of factors made the candy bar market relatively unattractive. As one executive said, "The industry is growing at a modest rate but, because of our distribution and technological strengths, our own business is doing very well."[13] As a result the company was willing to invest moderately in these lines for the short-term.

Finally, several products were in the harvest/divest category. Chase & Sanborn, once a leading brand in the coffee market, had only a 4 percent market share in 1979. But it had strong brand-name recognition. Management

MARKET
ATTRACTIVENESS

BUSINESS POSITION

	HIGH	MEDIUM	LOW
HIGH	Pinata Foods Smooth & Easy	Fleishman's Corn Oil	Souverain Wines
MEDIUM	Planter's Nuts Walker Crisps, Ltd.	Fleishman's Yeast Royal Gelatin Desserts	Chase & Sanborne Coffee
LOW	Baby Ruth Butterfingers Confectionary Line	Pet Foods	Ufima Coffee

FIGURE 19-5
**Standard Brands' product mix according to the market attractiveness/business
position matrix**

Source: Compiled from "Zero Base Helps Rationalize Product Strategy," *International Management,* February 1979, p. 38; and "Standard Brands: A Blueprint for a New Packaged-Goods Drive," *Business Week,* February 6, 1978, p. 91.

felt the brand could still generate a lot of cash for several years. The brand was kept alive but with no promotional budget. The company did divest itself of its French coffee subsidiary, Ufima, because the return on investing in the brand was less than alternative returns such as that for Pinata Foods.

The result of the portfolio analysis in Figure 19-5 showed management that about half its sales were coming from products in the invest/grow category, 30 percent from those in the selectivity/earnings group, and 20 percent from harvest/divest products. Although the mix represented a sound distribution of products, management realized it had to watch its coffee and pet food lines for possible divestment. This type of portfolio analysis should be carried out each year to track products and account for environmental change.

PRODUCT MIX ADDITIONS AND DELETIONS

Product portfolio analysis is a dynamic planning tool, since it requires considering the addition of new product lines and deletion of existing product lines. Firms are likely to emphasize the addition of new products rather than the deletion of existing products, since new products are more closely linked to profitability. However, product deletion decisions can be as important as new product decisions. Existing products that are not achieving targeted market share and earnings can represent a drain on resources that puts an unnecessary burden on other products in the mix. Yet sometimes unprofitable product lines are retained because of management inertia, lack of an adequate product mix evaluation process, or simply a nostalgic refusal to eliminate a long-standing part of the company's mix. Moreover, organizations rarely reward managers for sound decisions to delete products. Attention goes to those who successfully introduce new products and increase profitability of existing products. As a result product deletion decisions have not received the attention they deserve.

Product portfolio analysis provides a framework for change in the product mix — both additions and deletions. The criteria in Table 19-1 can be used to assess new product opportunities and to identify candidates for product deletion. A new product candidate projected to be in a positive position both from the standpoint of market opportunity and the firm's ability to exploit it deserves further development. Of equal importance, an existing product that is in a poor market and has few growth prospects should be considered for divestment.

Planning for Product Deletions

Management tendency to ignore product deletion decisions warrants a more rigorous planning framework for such decisions. A product deletion planning process based on portfolio analysis is presented in Figure 19-6. The first step is to assess product performance on the criteria in the right-hand column of Table 19-1. If the product meets market share, earnings, resource utilization, and other performance criteria, it will be retained and slated for either growth or selective investment for shorter-term earnings. If it does not meet objectives, then the market will be evaluated for growth potential. If growth potential is adequate, the product will be retained and marketing strategy revised. The product might be modified, it might be repositioned through advertising, prices might be cut, or other changes made to better exploit marketing opportunity.

If the product receives negative ratings on both product performance and market assessment, then it is in the harvest/divest portion of the portfolio matrix (lower right in Figure 19-2). At this point two factors might cause the company to keep the product in the line. First, although the product may not be profitable, deletion may have a negative effect on other product lines. For example, assume GE's black-and-white TV line is unprofitable. Deletion of the line may have a negative effect on the highly profitable color TV line, because dealers may be reluctant to stock GE TV sets unless both alternatives are available. Another possibility is that consumers might be loyal to GE products, and lack of availability of a major line might diminish such company loyalty. If deleting the product has a negative effect on overall profitability, the company would retain the product and change marketing strategy to diminish losses. Finally, if deletion of the product has no negative effect on other products, the company might choose to retain the product if elimination of marketing

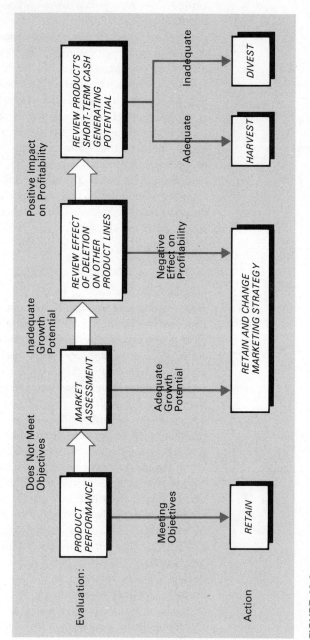

FIGURE 19-6
A product deletion planning model

costs would result in short-term earnings (a harvesting strategy). Barring this option, the product should be deleted from the firm's mix.

Chase & Sanborn's poor product performance and a flat coffee market caused it to be placed in the harvest/divest category. Deletion of the product would have no negative effects on other products in the line, since there was no link in demand to other products and no desire on the part of retailers to retain the product. The product's well-known name led the company to conclude that the brand still had cash-generating potential, and thus to harvest and then possibly divest it.

Product Cannibalism

Figure 19-4 suggests that product mix evaluation can sometimes lead to retention of unprofitable products or lines because of their positive effects on other products in the company's mix. The opposite can also be true. Products that appear to be profitable may have a negative effect on other products or lines in the firm's mix. Such a negative effect is generally due to **product cannibalism** in which one product draws sales from other products offered by the company. For example, when General Foods introduced Maxim freeze-dried coffee, many purchasers of the brand were users of Maxwell House instant. Although Maxim met sales expectations, net earnings for the coffee line were less than projected since the brand attracted fewer users from competitive brands.

Planned cannibalism

Product cannibalism can be planned or unplanned. Planned cannibalism results when technological improvements warrant bringing out additional products that might compete with others in the company's mix.[14] Thus, General Electric had to bring out a color TV line, even though it might have cannibalized sales of its black-and-white line, because if it did not it would have lost customers to competitive makes. Similarly, General Foods had to introduce Maxim freeze-dried instant coffee; otherwise it might have lost Maxwell House customers to Nestlé's Taster's Choice freeze-dried. These examples suggest that product cannibalism is the inevitable consequence of technological advances. As companies introduce improvements, consumers will naturally switch from one company brand to another.

Planned cannibalism is also the result of a desire to provide a fuller range of product alternatives in the marketplace. For example, General Motors encourages competition among its Oldsmobile, Pontiac, and Buick divisions. It recognizes that a customer switching from an Oldsmobile to a Buick does not represent a net gain for the company. But it would prefer to lose a customer to another GM division than to Chrysler or Ford. Product cannibalization is encouraged because a broader product mix will ensure retaining more GM customers.

Alfred P. Sloan, Jr., the person most responsible for building GM, once described planned cannibalism in the company: "We operate a free competitive economy within ourselves. Our competition is one division against another, as well as against firms on the outside."[15] Yet GM could not be content with just switching GM customers in a game of musical chairs. When it introduces a new model, it expects to sell to customers who now own competitive makes. For example, when Ford introduced the Mustang, 70 percent of sales came from buyers who would have purchased another Ford. Yet the introduction was considered a success because 30 percent of the customers were attracted from competitive makes.[16]

Unplanned cannibalism

Unplanned cannibalism can have negative consequences on profitability. The firm introducing a brand that unexpectedly cannibalizes other products in the mix will experience lower net earnings from the introduction than it anticipated. The new product may be achieving its sales goals at the expense of earnings for related products. For example, Diet Coke represented a major new product introduction for Coca-Cola, the first time the Coke name was used on a brand other than the company's major brand. The rationale for introducing the brand was to direct a diet cola toward males, since Tab, the company's long-standing diet cola entry, was purchased primarily by females. Diet Coke was also supposed to be better tasting than Tab. Preliminary sales results in 1982 suggested, in the words of one supermarket manager, that "sales seem to be coming from other Coca-Cola products. It's taking sales away from Tab and Coke. The Pepsi line is holding up."[17]

If that is true, cannibalization by Diet Coke of Tab and Coke could be the result of oversegmentation of the cola market. It is possible that two diet cola brands in a company's product mix is a waste of marketing dollars. Tab could have been reformulated to improve taste and repositioned to appeal more to males. On the other hand, some market analysts project that Diet Coke will be the leading diet brand in the industry. If so, the question is how deeply will it cut into Tab sales?

Other reasons have been cited for unplanned cannibalization in addition to oversegmentation of the market:

- inadequate product positioning,
- insufficient differentiation between company offerings,
- overemphasis on new product introductions without adequate concern about additional benefits,
- attempts to ensure shelf space in supermarkets by flooding the market with additional brands,
- pressure from top management to introduce new products to meet earnings and growth objectives, and
- failure to justify additions to product lines on the basis of consumer needs.[18]

Product Portfolio Strategies

Once the firm has analyzed its portfolio of product offerings, it is in a position to develop strategies to ensure profitability. Product portfolio strategies can be developed on two levels: (1) for individual lines within the mix and (2) for the firm's overall direction in developing its future mix. Portfolio decisions about individual product lines are made at the SBU level. Companywide product mix decisions are made by top management in the corporate strategic plan.

STRATEGIES FOR PRODUCT LINES WITHIN THE MIX

One can use GE's market assessment/business position analysis to expand the three strategies cited in Figure 19-4 to seven options as follows:

Invest/Grow	*Selectivity/Earnings*	*Harvest/Divest*
Establish	Sustain	Harvest
Reinforce	Hold	Divest
Build		

These seven strategies are presented in the market/assessment business position matrix in Figure 19-7.

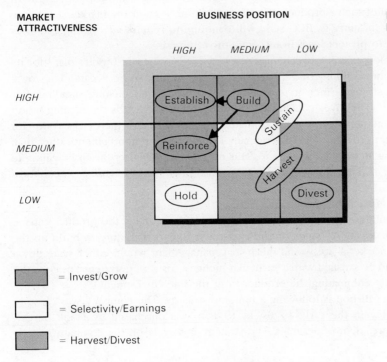

| MARKET ATTRACTIVENESS | BUSINESS POSITION | FIGURE 19-7 Product portfolio strategies |

= Invest/Grow

= Selectivity/Earnings

= Harvest/Divest

Invest/Grow

The invest/grow option may involve establishing a new product in an opportunity area that the company feels it can effectively exploit. An invest/grow strategy could also mean reinforcing an established product in a moderately strong market category. For an existing product that is not very well established but is in an attractive market a building strategy is appropriate, since investment is warranted to position the brand better in the market.

Establishing the product

Establishment is the primary objective for a product just entering an attractive market. The hope is that the product will quickly become a source of profit; in BCG terminology a star rather than a problem child. Xerox is following this strategy in entering the office automation market. The company sees the market as attractive in terms of growth, competition, technology, and lack of seasonality. Funds are available from its cash cows, namely its copier and duplicator lines. These "will remain the main business of Xerox for the foreseeable future," but the company sees the office automation market as the "office of the future."[19]

Reinforcing the product

A strategy of reinforcement is sound for an existing product that has already established itself in a strong market position. The success and continued growth potential of such a product invites competition to enter the market. Therefore a successful entry (a BCG star) will continue to require advertising and sales support to protect itself from competitive inroads.

A good example of a reinforcing strategy is Anheuser-Busch's plans for its leading beer, Budweiser. Budweiser would ordinarily be a candidate for a holding strategy since it is a highly successful brand of long standing. But company executives concluded that although Budweiser is the leading brand in the industry, it "was not a mature brand and that there was room for significant growth."[20] So the company is following a reinforcement rather than a holding strategy for the brand. This means that Anheuser-Busch is willing to consider market expansion strategies requiring increased advertising expenditures.

Building the product

A building strategy is relevant if the company feels the product can be more successful in competing in an attractive market. Failure to build up the brand's market share would mean that management would either scale down effort and be satisfied with a particular niche (a sustaining strategy) or consider eventually eliminating the product from the line (divestment).

Hazel Bishop is following a building strategy. The company was close to bankruptcy in the early 1970s. In 1978 it was purchased by Frank Berger, former president of Seagram. The strategy is to rely on the company's name (more than 80 percent of women twenty-eight and over had heard of it) and advertise for growth. If a building strategy can increase market share, then it might provide the basis for future diversification. Berger "is known to be in the market for a wine and spirits company and a men's grooming line, and admits that Bishop will fuel the growth of future endeavors if his gambit with the company pays off."[21]

Selectivity/Earnings

A company may wish to invest selectively in brands that are faring poorly but are in strong markets (sustaining the brand). A company may also wish to maintain profitable brands in low-growth markets by holding the brand's position through limited support.

Sustaining the Product

A sustaining strategy is reasonable if the brand is in an attractive market and can either (1) improve its position or (2) sustain profitability by appealing to a small niche. Standard Brands' Souverain Wines is not doing well in a growth market because of intense competition from established brands. But the continued increase in wine consumption may cause Standard Brands to support the brand selectively in the hope that earnings will improve.

A company may also sustain a brand if it appeals to a core market in a particular niche. Such products may not require much advertising. Given a core market and low marketing costs, these products could be the source of short-term earnings. For example, Murphy's Oil Soap appeals to a small segment of consumers interested in a high-quality gelatin-type soap. The company is satisfied to sustain rather than to build share. An attempt to build share would require more cash and might invite competition from larger competitors.

Holding the product

A holding strategy is used to maintain the dominant position of an existing brand in a low-growth market (profitable cash cows). Demand is stable and competition is less intense. As a result cash is being generated. Companies should resist the temptation to overinvest in these products since the industry is not an attractive investment and a higher market share is unlikely.

Procter and Gamble is engaged in an active holding strategy for some of its older lines to finance new product development. One P&G executive stated, "The cash-generating base for the new-product drive will be the company's household-product lines [detergents and soap products]."[22] Products such as Ivory Soap, Tide, and Charmin will provide the cash base for expanding in high-growth areas. But a strategy of holding does not involve milking these products dry. Rather, P&G "plans to feed its cash cows, enlarging the stream of investment funds earmarked for diversification by boosting current market share in its established consumer businesses."[23] In other words, P&G is willing to maintain advertising and promotional expenditures for its leading brands to ensure revenues sufficient to finance diversification into fields such as prescription drugs and synthetic foods.

Harvest/Divest

Harvesting represents a conscious cutback of most marketing support because of insufficient earnings in an unattractive market. It frequently leads to divestment if the product represents a continued drain on company resources and the money can be better spent elsewhere.

Harvesting the product

The elimination of marketing expenditures for poor performers in low-growth areas can lead to contributions to earnings in the short term. Some well-known brands have undergone harvesting strategies. For example, when Ipana toothpaste began losing market share to Crest, Bristol-Myers sold the brand rights to two entrepreneurs who continued to market it while stopping all advertising. The brand continued to sell to loyal customers for years, making a good profit for its owners.[24] Lifebuoy soap lost sales when better-smelling and milder soaps began to be introduced into the market. Lever Brothers continues to distribute the brand with little advertising. Again, a hard core of loyal users makes the brand profitable for the company.[25]

Divesting the product

Divestment is frequently required because of an overly aggressive corporate acquisition policy. Large firms have occasionally acquired other companies with no rational growth plan and little thought to the resources and marketing know-how required to profitably introduce these products. In the mid-1970s, Olin had acquired companies producing sleeping bags and propane stoves, and was aggressively marketing products such as polyester chloride. Profits from these lines were slim. By the late 1970s the company had divested itself of these lines to concentrate on products such as brass sheeting and hydrazine chemicals — "products that fit in much better with its established corporate expertise."[26] The purpose of the divestment strategy was to eliminate products that were a cash drain to support products with the best growth potential.

Nestlé has undergone a similar process of divestment. A new president was brought in in 1981 to "set priorities, invest in businesses that hold potential and drop those that won't make money."[27] Nestlé began to divest itself of small businesses that are not profitable. This could mean withdrawal from the instant soup, cheese or bottled water categories. As a result of divestment, Nestlé is expected to become "a leaner, more clearly focused U.S. food company with stronger market shares and better profit contributions."[28]

An important issue in divestment is whether the line is eliminated or sold. A line that is unprofitable for one company may fit into the product mix of another company. Lever Brothers did not view its Glamorene rug cleaner as warranting investment. However, Airwick was looking for several entries into the rug cleaner area, purchased the brand from Lever as a target for investment, and made it profitable.

Dynamic Product Portfolio Strategies

The scenarios for success and failure in Figure 19-3 demonstrate that product portfolio strategies are dynamic. They must change over time, requiring shifts in corporate resources. A successful product introduction would mean moving from a strategy of establishing to reinforcing to holding the brand (scenario 2 in Figure 19-3). Successful products such as Gillette's Right Guard and P&G's Crest toothpaste followed this line of strategies and are now cash cows. Failure of a new product would mean moving from a strategy of establishing a brand to an attempt to sustain it to eventual product divestment (scenarios 3 and 4 in Figure 19-3). This was RCA's course in deciding to withdraw its videodisc entry, SelectaVision, from the market.

Product strategies are also dynamic in that a company must pursue more than one strategy to maintain a balanced portfolio. Figure 19-5 showed that Standard Brands followed a strategy of trying to establish Smooth & Easy, building Fleishman's Corn Oil, and reinforcing Planters Nuts because it saw these brands as investment opportunities. It followed a strategy of sustaining Souverain Wines and holding its confectionery line as a means of obtaining short-term earnings, in some cases to finance the brands in the investment category. It is harvesting Chase & Sanborn coffee and its pet foods line and divesting Ufima Coffee to maintain balance and profitability.

COMPANY-WIDE PRODUCT PORTFOLIO STRATEGIES

The product portfolio strategies we have just cited are generally formulated at the business unit level. Product portfolio strategies are also formulated to meet the company's overall objectives for investment and growth. Three general product-mix strategies can be formulated on a company-wide level: expansion, repositioning, and retrenchment. Product-mix expansion involves an increase in the firm's product lines in the same general areas of operations. Product-mix repositioning requires diversification into unrelated areas, frequently as a hedge against a downturn in the company's basic business. Retrenchment requires cutting back product offerings.

Product Mix Expansion

A policy of product-mix expansion is illustrated by Castle and Cooke, a large processor of fruits and vegetables. Castle and Cooke's management concluded that a decreasing birth rate would mean a leveling off of demand for food products. But unlike other food companies (e.g., Gerber, General Mills) it did not seek to diversify away from foods. Rather, it is expanding its product mix by "branching out within the food business and acquiring companies that produce higher-profit items — especially fresh or frozen fruits, vegetables and seafood."[29] The company's rationale is that these items are becoming increasingly popular among dieters and represent high-growth items. Its acquisitions in these areas have "given C&C a more stable earnings curve by making it less susceptible to the vagaries of weather, consumer tastes, and commodity prices."[30]

Product Mix Repositioning

A company-wide repositioning strategy is frequently motivated by a necessity to reduce the risks of economic downturns and cyclical swings in demand. Borg-Warner reevaluated its product mix of automotive parts right after the 1973 energy crisis. It dropped hundreds of marginally profitable items and supplemented its basic line of automotive components with courier services, detection systems, and heat pumps. By the late 1970s its profit margin had doubled and long-term debt was reduced by almost 50 percent.[31]

Some of the largest corporations have recently repositioned their product mix to ensure greater stability in profits. General Electric has begun to shift away from its traditional dependence on electrical equipment and other businesses tied to the state of the economy and to move toward "a new emphasis on high-growth high-technology businesses such as factory automation and financial and information services."[32] DuPont has sought to exploit its technological know-how in fibers by selling its dye business and withdrawing from acetates while extending its offerings in acrylics, nylons, and polyester fibers. One DuPont executive explained, "We don't retreat from markets, but shift resources when we can emphasize future growth."[33]

Product Mix Retrenchment

Companies have sometimes had to cut back on their product offerings. Levi Strauss & Co., the manufacturer of jeans, diversified aggressively into other apparel in the late 1970s. The company had planned to spend $400 million to build forty new factories for an expanded apparel line.[34] But by 1982 it was apparent the diversification drive was in trouble. The company overestimated the power of the Levi name for apparel other than jeans. As a result, the company is retrenching by eliminating many of these lines and going back to producing and marketing what it knows best — jeans.[35]

Factors Affecting Profitability of the Product Mix

Once the right combination of product-mix strategies has been formulated, management must evaluate performance. General Electric's product portfolio analysis suggests that profitability might be a more relevant criterion than cash flow in evaluating the product's position in the portfolio matrix. This is becaue products with a low cash flow may be highly profitable (for example, a product selling to a select niche of the market), and products with a substantial cash flow may be unprofitable (for example, products achieving a high market share because of unprofitable price cuts or large advertising expenditures).

A large and ongoing study, first initiated by General Electric, attempts to evaluate the effect of the firm's actions on the profitability of the product mix. The study, known as Profit Impact of Marketing Strategy (PIMS), collects data from over 1500 business units in over 200 companies and relates a variety of strategic factors to profitability as measured by return on investment.[36] Many of the factors considered in GE's analysis of market attractiveness and business position (Table 19-1) are related to ROI.

The PIMS study found four major factors related to ROI. Two of them, market growth and market share, form the basis of the BCG product portfolio analysis. With some exceptions that we noted earlier, both factors have a positive effect on profitability. But two other factors also affect profitability — investment intensity (measured by investment as a percentage of sales) and the intensity of marketing effort (measured by marketing expenditures as a percentage of sales). These two factors are negatively related to ROI.[37] However, the PIMS study found that these relationships by themselves are not likely to provide management with much guidance. Carrying the relationships to a logical conclusion, a manager could say, "Let's eliminate all marketing expenses since marketing intensity has a negative effect on profitability." The key question is, Under what circumstances does each of these relationships operate? For example, high market share is more likely to be profitable when investment intensity is high, and marketing intensity is more likely to lead to lower profits when a product market share is low.

Of the four factors that affect profits, management has little control over only one — market growth rate. It directly controls marketing and investment intensity, and influences its own market share through marketing strategies. The marketing manager will be most interested in the effect of marketing expenditures and market share on profitability. In this section we will therefore consider PIMS findings for these two factors.

EFFECT OF MARKETING EXPENDITURES ON ROI

The PIMS data analyze marketing expenditures as a percentage of sales (marketing intensity) because this figure reflects the efficiency of a firm's marketing strategy. A company with an inefficient marketing program could increase marketing expenditures without adequate sales results, thus driving up expenditures as a percentage of sales. But marketing intensity also reflects historic patterns. Consumer packaged goods generally have much higher marketing-to-sales ratios than consumer durables, because packaged goods rely more on advertising, coupons, and price deals for sales. As a result, margins and ROI are generally lower for packaged goods.

The PIMS study found that marketing intensity is particularly likely to produce lower profitability under the following circumstances:[38]

1. *When investment intensity is high.* The combination of high marketing expenditures and large investments in a product drives ROI down. ROI was only 9 percent for business units with high marketing and investment intensity, but it was over 27 percent for business units that were low on marketing and investment intensity.

2. *When market share is low.* Heavy marketing expenditures depress ROI for low-share businesses. Companies with a higher share can better afford to increase marketing expenditures, even though sales results may not be immediate. Campbell's soup drove Heinz's entry, Great American Soups, off the market with heavy advertising and dealing. It could afford to spend heavily to protect its market share.

3. *When product quality is low.* Heavy marketing expenditures are unlikely to increase sales when product quality is not on a par with competition. As a result, marketing expenditures become a greater proportion of sales. This finding merely confirms that you cannot sell a poor product by increasing marketing effort.

EFFECT OF MARKET SHARE ON ROI

The PIMS data have shown a direct relationship between market share and ROI. A company whose market share is 10 percent higher than its competitors' obtains a return on investment that is an average of 5 percent higher.[39] But higher market share does not always produce higher profitability. The PIMS data showed that market share is more likely to produce high profitability under these conditions:[40]

1. *Spending on research and development is high.* High market share is more likely to be profitable when the firm is willing to spend on research and development. For leading companies R&D is likely to result in profitable new product entries. But higher R&D expenditures are not necessarily effective for low-share businesses, possibly because low-share businesses find it harder to follow through with subsequent product development.

2. *Products are standardized rather than made to order.* Firms producing products on order do not require higher market share for profitability since they are selling to a smaller and more select group of customers.

These findings again demonstrate that the profitability of the product mix depends on a variety of factors, not just market share.

Summary

A firm must arrive at a balanced mix of product offerings to ensure profitability. Product portfolio analysis is the basis for evaluating the firm's product mix. Product portfolio analysis attempts to ensure a reasonable balance of products providing current earnings and future yields. Products with current earnings provide the means of funding higher growth products with excellent future earnings potential.

Two types of portfolio analysis were described. The first, the Boston Consulting Group's growth/share analysis, classifies products by their position in the product life cycle (market growth) and their market share relative to competition. Cash flow is the criterion of performance, since the analysis emphasizes the need to finance products with high growth and market share potential with the cash provided by established products. But growth/share analysis is oversimplified because (1) it assumes that growth and share are related to profitability — relationships that do not always hold — and (2) it does not take account of other factors that might affect profitability, such as ease of competitive entry, innovativeness, production efficiencies, and the cyclical nature of the business.

As a result of these weaknesses, General Electric developed a potentially more powerful approach to product portfolio analysis using a much wider range of influences on the product mix. It analyzed products on the bases of their market attractiveness and the company's capability to exploit marketing opportunities. The resultant market attractiveness/business position matrix provides a basis for developing product portfolio strategies.

GE's analysis developed three broad strategy scenarios. The first is invest/grow. The emphasis on growth might involve alternative strategies of *establishing* a new product in an area of opportunity, *reinforcing* an existing product that is in a strong market position, or *building* an existing product in a growth situation into a market leader. A second scenario involves a more selective approach to investing, with the purpose of achieving short-term earnings. A company may wish to invest selectively in brands that are faring poorly but are in strong markets by *sustaining* them so that they can more profitably appeal to a specific segment of the market. A company may also wish to *hold* strong brands in low-growth markets in their current position with limited support. Finally, companies may wish to withdraw marketing support for weak brands in unattractive markets. Companies can withdraw marketing support for a product and *harvest* earnings. They can then *divest* themselves of the product once it begins to lose money.

Developing product portfolio strategies requires continual additions to and deletions from the product mix. An important element of portfolio analysis is therefore establishing criteria for these additions and deletions, particularly the latter. A model for planning product deletions was described to facilitate this process. Adding and deleting products also illustrates the necessity of determining the factors that affect the profitability of the product mix. A major study — Profit Impact of Marketing Strategy (PIMS) — was described. The effects of two important factors influencing the profitability of the product mix — marketing intensity and market share — were considered.

In the next chapter we will consider another key element in strategic marketing planning, the evaluation and control of marketing actions.

Questions

1. The director of marketing planning for a multidivisional electronics company is considering using product portfolio analysis to evaluate (a) the mix of SBUs in the company and (b) the mix of products in each SBU. What is the purpose of product portfolio analysis in each case?

2. The director of planning in question 1 has been hesitant to adopt product portfolio analysis because of a concern that it may be viewed as a definitive tool in establishing the company's SBU/product mix. The director views it more as a planning aid than as a means to determine the company's product mix.

   □ Do you agree?

   □ What are the pros and cons of using product portfolio analysis to evaluate the firm's product mix?

3. Consider the basic portfolio matrix in Figure 19-1. How are (a) the BCG analysis (Figure 19-2) and (b) GE's approach (Figure 19-4) linked to this basic matrix?

4. In the Boston Consulting Group analysis, what are the limitations of:

   □ using market growth as a measure of opportunity?

   □ using relative market share as a measure of (a) current performance or (b) future potential to exploit opportunity?

5. One critic of BCG's portfolio approach faulted it for using internal cash flow as a criterion in evaluating the company's product mix by saying "If you have a profit, you can get cash."

   □ What is meant by this statement?

   □ What is the rationale behind BCG's use of cash flow as a criterion in evaluating the product mix?

   □ What are the limitations of using cash flow?

6. What is the experience curve?

   □ What is the relevance of the experience curve to BCG's portfolio analysis?

   □ What are the limitations of the concept of an experience curve?

7. The director of planning cited in question 1 is trying to determine whether to use the BCG approach to portfolio analysis or the GE approach. What are the relative advantages and disadvantages of each?

8. Select two products in the same category (e.g., 7-Up and Orange Crush). Evaluate them using GE's portfolio approach as illustrated in Ta-

ble 19-2. This will require: (a) selecting the appropriate evaluative criteria from Table 19-1, (b) determining the importance of each criterion, (c) rating the two products on each criterion, (d) computing overall scores for market attractiveness and business position, (e) evaluating these scores against a set of norms based on previous product experiences, and (f) positioning the two products on the portfolio matrix as in Figure 19-4.

☐ Justify the selection of the criteria used to evaluate the products.

☐ What are the strategic implications of the positioning of each product?

9. We noted that Chase & Sanborn, once a leading coffee brand, was being harvested by Standard Brands in the late 1970s.

☐ How could the company have used the product review process in Figure 19-6 to reach this decision?

☐ Why do so few companies have a formal product review process such as that in Figure 19-6?

10. An executive at one of the major auto companies says, "Product cannibalism is an overrated concern among many of our marketing managers. We don't avoid product cannibalism, we plan for it and even encourage it."

☐ Why would a company plan to have some of its product entries cannibalize existing products in the line?

☐ Under what conditions is product cannibalism likely to be of greater concern to product managers?

11. Which of the seven portfolio strategies in Figure 19-7 do you believe represents the greatest potential risk to a company? Why?

12. What is the purpose of the ongoing Profit Impact of Marketing Strategy (PIMS) study?
What are the limitations of the findings as a basis for developing corporate growth and product portfolio strategies?

Notes

1. "Oh Where, Oh Where Has My Little Dog Gone? Or My Cash Cow? Or My Star?" *Fortune,* November 2, 1981, pp. 148–54, at p. 148.

2. Sidney Schoeffler, Robert D. Buzzell, and Donald F. Heany, "Impact of Strategic Planning on Profit Performance," *Harvard Business Review* 52 (March–April 1974): 137–45.

3. "Hershey Steps Out," *Forbes,* March 17, 1980, p. 64.

4. R. D. Buzzell, B. T. Gale, and R. G. M. Sultan, "Market Share — a Key to Profitability," *Harvard Business Review* 53 (January–February 1975): 97–106.

5. Ibid., p. 101.

6. Barry Hedley, "A Fundamental Approach to Strategy Development," *Long Range Planning* 9 (December 1976): 2–11.

7. W. K. Hall, "Survival Strategies in a Hostile

Environment," *Harvard Business Review* 58 (September–October 1980): 75–85.

8. *Fortune,* November 2, 1981, p. 150.

9. "The Market Share Myth," *Forbes,* March 14, 1983, pp. 109, 110, 114, 115.

10. *Corporate Planning Techniques and Applications,* Robert J. Allio and Malcolm W. Pennington, eds. (New York: American Marketing Association, 1979), p. 19; and Peter Lorange, "Divisional Planning: Setting Effective Direction," *Sloan Management Review* 17 (Fall 1975): 77–91.

11. "Zero Base Helps Rationalize Product Strategy," *International Management,* February 1979, p. 38.

12. Ibid., pp. 38–41; and "Standard Brands: A Blueprint for a New Packaged-Goods Drive," *Business Week,* February 6, 1978, p. 91.

13. *International Management,* February 1979, p. 39.

14. Michael G. Harvey and Roger A. Kerin, "Diagnosis and Management of the Product Cannibalism Syndrome," *University of Michigan Business Review* 31 (November 1979): 18.

15. "Private Label? No, it's Now 'Presold' — Wave of Future," *Advertising Age,* September 30, 1974, p. 66.

16. Harvey and Kerin, "Diagnosis and Management of the Product Cannibalism Syndrome," p. 23.

17. "Diet Coke Reflects Changes in Market and the Industry," *The New York Times,* August 23, 1982, p. D4.

18. Harvey and Kerin, "Diagnosis and Management of the Product Cannibalism Syndrome," p. 20.

19. "Trying to Duplicate Success," *Sales and Marketing Management,* February 8, 1982, pp. 24–27.

20. "Budweiser Still No. 1 in Sales," *The New York Times,* February 16, 1982, p. D1.

21. "Hazel Bishop Brand: Resiliency Paying Off," *Advertising Age,* November 16, 1981, pp. 4 and 97.

22. "P&G's New New-Product Onslaught," *Business Week,* October 1, 1979, pp. 76–82, at p. 79.

23. Ibid.

24. Philip Kotler, "Harvesting Strategies for Weak Products," *Business Horizons* (August 1978): 19.

25. Ibid.

26. "Olin's Shift to Strategy Planning," *Business Week,* March 27, 1978, p. 102.

27. "Nestlé Chief's Mission: Pick Winners, Ax Losers," *Advertising Age,* September 7, 1981, p. 4.

28. Ibid., p. 64.

29. "Castle & Cooke: Growth in Food Through Aggressive Acquisition," *Business Week,* April 24, 1978, p. 92.

30. Ibid., p. 93.

31. "Product-Market Planning," *Planning Review,* November 1979, p. 13.

32. "Can GE Shake the GNP Image?" *Financial World,* May 15, 1982, p. 16.

33. *Industry Week,* October 13, 1980, p. 79.

34. "Levi Strauss is Stretching its Wardrobe," *Fortune,* November 19, 1979, pp. 86–89.

35. "It's Back to Basics for Levi's," *Business Week,* March 8, 1982, p. 77.

36. Ben M. Enis, "GE, PIMS, BCG, and the PLC," *Business,* May–June, 1980, pp. 10–18.

37. *PIMS, Profit Impact of Market Strategy* (Boston: The Strategic Planning Institute, 1977), pp. 12–74; and Derek F. Abell and John S. Hammond, *Strategic Market Planning* (Englewood Cliffs, N.J.: Prentice-Hall, 1979), pp. 277–83.

38. *PIMS, Profit Impact of Market Strategy,* p. 35, 42, 55, 59.

39. Buzzell, Gale, and Sultan, "Market Share," p. 97.

40. Schoeffler, Buzzell, and Heany, "Impact of Strategic Planning," pp. 137–45.

CHAPTER 20

Marketing Evaluation and Control

FOCUS OF CHAPTER

Marketing management must evaluate and control marketing plans to ensure that they are effectively implemented. Advertising expenditures cannot be increased arbitrarily to gain market share, nor can prices be cut haphazardly to attract competitors' customers. Marketing strategies must conform to a game plan that establishes profitability objectives and describes how to attain them.

In this chapter we use a five-step model to describe the process of marketing evaluation and control. The steps are:

1. Establish profitability criteria,

2. Develop revenue projections based on sales forecasts,

3. Develop and implement marketing plans if revenue projections meet profitability criteria,

4. Evaluate marketing performance to determine if it is deviating from plans, and

5. Control marketing strategies by modifying the plan or correcting past actions.

We will describe each step except marketing planning, which we described previously. Evaluation and control are carried out at two levels — the product-planning and corporate (strategic) planning level. Product management monitors the product marketing plan by controlling advertising, sales, price, and distribution strategies. Top management monitors the strategic marketing plan by controlling the acquisition of companies and the firm's overall product mix.

Purposes of Marketing Evaluation and Control

Marketing management must control marketing activities and expenditures for both product marketing plans and strategic marketing plans.

PRODUCT MARKETING EVALUATION AND CONTROL

At the product marketing level, evaluation and control translates into controlling the activities involved in the marketing mix, specifically:

- advertising,
- sales promotion,
- personal selling,
- price, and
- distribution.

Measures of performance for each area are developed to evaluate and control particular tasks. For example, advertising effectiveness can be measured by the cost of reaching the target segment, by increases in brand awareness, and by changes in attitudes toward the brand. Effectiveness of sales promotion strategy can be evaluated by determining the percentage of sales represented by deals or coupons. Personal selling can be evaluated by average sales calls per client, revenue per sales calls, and number of new and lost customers per sales period. Distribution can be evaluated by maintenance of inventory levels, transportation costs per order, and coverage in distribution channels. In each case, management is likely to estimate advertising, promotion, selling, and distribution costs as a percentage of sales.

STRATEGIC MARKETING EVALUATION AND CONTROL

At the strategic marketing level corporate and SBU management seek to ensure that the best marketing opportunities are being pursued. This means tracking and controlling marketing expenditures across product lines within each SBU. The product mix will be controlled by utilizing product portfolio analysis. The balance of expenditures between internal product development and external acquisitions will also be tracked and controlled. Acquisition strategy is a particularly important area for strategic marketing control since many companies cited in previous chapters — Olin, Nestlé, Quaker Oats, Colgate, Schlitz — acquired companies haphazardly without thought to capabilities and know-how. Effective control at the top would have ensured that acquisitions met well-defined corporate objectives for growth and profitability. For example, at Lipton, management defines the following criteria for targeting companies for acquisition:

- dominant market position,
- high delivered profits,
- patent protection,

- high growth rate,
- low capital-to-sales ratio, and
- simple management and employment situations.[1]

The importance of marketing control at the strategic planning level is well documented by a comparison between GE and Westinghouse. In Chapter 18 we noted the failure of strategic marketing planning at Westinghouse. This failure was due in large part to the absence of corporate controls over SBU activities. *Business Week* described GE as "growing rapidly as a result of its strong financial controls and marketing strategies." It added, "Managers are under strong corporate control with limits to the directions they may take and the amounts they may spend or commit."[2] In contrast, "Two basic failures [at Westinghouse were] an absence of strategic planning and a dearth of financial controls."[3]

Strategic evaluation and control became particularly important in the early 1980s because of the slowdown in economic growth. Less chance of exploiting marketing opportunity meant increased pressure to cut marketing costs. As a result procedures to monitor and control marketing activities received more attention. Yet firms must be attentive to strategic controls regardless of economic conditions. Without systematic evaluation of marketing activities, unprofitable products can continue to hang on. Such products tend to consume more management time and advertising and sales support than their profit potential warrants.[4]

A Model of Marketing Evaluation and Control

Figure 20-1 presents a model designed to evaluate and control the marketing plan. A sequence of steps is presented on the left of Figure 20-1 leading to three possible action consequences on the right: (1) continuing marketing strategy as planned; (2) modifying the plan because of deviations in cost or revenue; and (3) terminating the plan and considering alternative investment opportunities. In the rest of this chapter we will consider the five components in Figure 20-1 that make up the process of evaluation and control.

Establish Profitability Criteria

Management has taken two approaches in estimating profitability, depending on the treatment of marketing and other costs. In one — the net profit/ROI approach — indirect costs are allocated to the product on the basis of some formula devised by management. In the other — the contribution-to-profit approach — indirect costs are not assigned to the product. As a result the product's net contribution to profits can be determined.

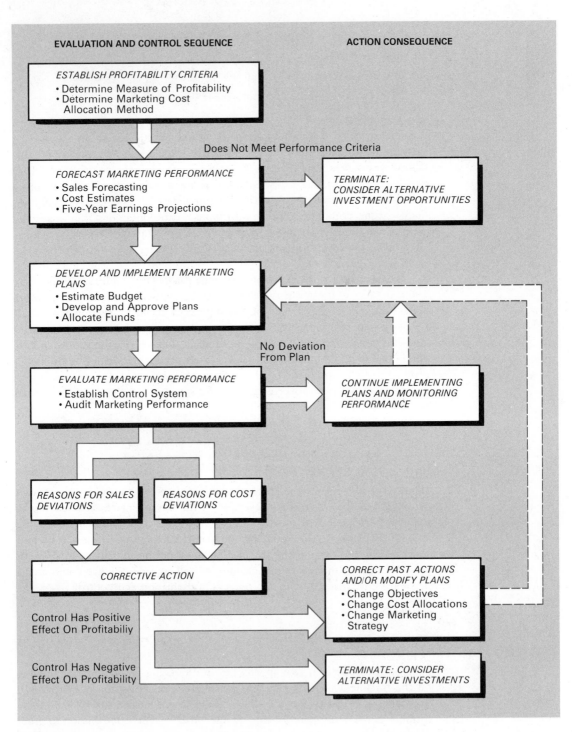

EVALUATION AND CONTROL SEQUENCE

ACTION CONSEQUENCE

ESTABLISH PROFITABILITY CRITERIA
- Determine Measure of Profitability
- Determine Marketing Cost Allocation Method

Does Not Meet Performance Criteria

FORECAST MARKETING PERFORMANCE
- Sales Forecasting
- Cost Estimates
- Five-Year Earnings Projections

TERMINATE: CONSIDER ALTERNATIVE INVESTMENT OPPORTUNITIES

DEVELOP AND IMPLEMENT MARKETING PLANS
- Estimate Budget
- Develop and Approve Plans
- Allocate Funds

No Deviation From Plan

EVALUATE MARKETING PERFORMANCE
- Establish Control System
- Audit Marketing Performance

CONTINUE IMPLEMENTING PLANS AND MONITORING PERFORMANCE

REASONS FOR SALES DEVIATIONS

REASONS FOR COST DEVIATIONS

CORRECTIVE ACTION

CORRECT PAST ACTIONS AND/OR MODIFY PLANS
- Change Objectives
- Change Cost Allocations
- Change Marketing Strategy

Control Has Positive Effect On Profitabiliy

Control Has Negative Effect On Profitabiliy

TERMINATE: CONSIDER ALTERNATIVE INVESTMENTS

FIGURE 20-1
A model of marketing evaluation and control

Marketing management generally favors the latter approach because it provides a cleaner assessment of a product's performance. A net profit rather than contributed profit approach frequently relies on arbitrary methods for allocating overhead costs that often distort true product performance. Both approaches will be briefly considered.

NET PROFIT/ROI APPROACH

Net profits are determined by deducting the following from sales revenues:

1. Costs that vary directly with sales such as labor, materials, manufacturing costs, distribution costs, and commissions on sales.

2. Nonvariable costs that can be directly assigned to the product. These include most marketing costs required to promote and administer the product — personal selling, product advertising, sales promotions, and product management's salary and administrative expenses.

3. Costs that cannot be assigned specifically to the product. These include corporate advertising and joint costs such as general salary and administration and plant overhead.

Example of a Net Profit Approach

Table 20-1 presents a hypothetical profit and loss statement for a hair conditioner in its fifth year after introduction based on a net profit approach.

Product advertising costs are the major assignable expenses for the product in Table 20-1, representing over one-third of net sales. This high advertising-to-sales ratio is typical for toiletries and cosmetics and is frequently even higher. Management has elected to allocate nonassignable costs according to the product's sales as a percentage of company sales. If the product represents 5 percent of company sales, it is assigned one-twentieth of nonassignable costs. For example, if the company spends $4 million yearly on corporate advertising, the product will be assigned 5 percent of the total or $200,000.

The net profit for the product in the fifth year after introduction is $600,000. Based on a total investment of $5.7 million, the return on investment is a rather lackluster 10.5 percent. Management will evaluate the ROI in comparison to the cost of capital. In the case of the hair conditioner, the cost of capital was 15 percent. Therefore, the investment in the product is regarded as unprofitable because it is bringing in a lower rate of return than the cost of capital required to generate the product. This also means that the rate of return is worse than the average return of alternative investments. But limits to using ROI as a measure of profitability have prompted management to use a contribution-to-profit approach.

Limitations of the Net Profit Approach

The drawback in using net profit as the criterion of performance is that it is essentially an accounting convention originally designed to report the aggregate effect of a firm's operations to its stockholders and creditors. The profit com-

TABLE 20-1
Profit and Loss Statement for a Hair Conditioner in its Fifth Year after Introduction (in thousands)

Sales revenue			23,800
Variable costs			9,600
Labor		3,500	
Materials		2,000	
Manufacturing		2,800	
Variable sales commissions		200	
Distribution		1,100	
Assignable nonvariable costs			12,200
Personal selling		500	
Product advertising		9,000	
Sales promotion		2,500	
Salary (product management)		200	
Contribution to profits			2,000
Nonassignable costs			1,400
Corporate advertising		200	
Fixed joint costs			
Manufacturing		700	
General administration		500	
Net profit			600
Investment	5,700		
Plant & equipment	4,200		
Research & development	1,500		
PROFITABILITY CRITERIA:			
Return on investment (600/5,700) = 10.5%			
Contribution as a percentage of			
sales (2,000/23,800) = 8.4%			

putation has little to do with evaluating a product's performance. This is because "There is no way of scientifically allocating production and marketing costs incurred jointly by several products in a line."[5] Management could make some products look better (or worse) than they are by just changing the criteria for allocation. For example, assume that management changed the ground rules for allocation in Table 20-1 and decided to allocate indirect costs on the basis of investment rather than sales, reasoning that investment is a better gauge of use of general administrative and manufacturing resources than sales. Since the product was introduced recently, investment in plant and equipment and research and development are quite high, representing 10 percent of total investment. Now, the product is responsible for 10 percent of all nonassignable costs, whereas before it was responsible for 5 percent. The effect is as follows:

(Data in Thousands)

Sales   23,800

Variable costs   9,600

Assignable non-variable costs	12,200	
Contribution to profit		2,000
Nonassignable costs	2,800	
Net profit (loss)		(800)
ROI	−14.0%	

The net went from a $600,000 profit to an $800,000 loss. Return on investment went from 10.5 percent to −14.0 percent, even though the contribution to profit has remained unchanged.

CONTRIBUTION-TO-PROFIT APPROACH

The alternative to the net profit approach is simply to disregard indirect costs and to account for only those costs which are "specifically incurred in designing, manufacturing and marketing each product."[6] This is known as the contribution approach because the excess revenues over assignable product costs are the contribution of the product to profits and to unassignable costs.[7] Using the contribution approach, one evaluates the sales performance of a product only in conjunction with expenses attributable to producing and marketing it. Thus, in Table 20-1 the contribution of the hair conditioner was $2.0 million.

Contribution to profit is a more realistic assessment of product performance than net profit because it accounts for only the costs that the product incurred. There is a second advantage in using a contribution approach: by eliminating unassignable fixed costs, the manager can better relate changes in marketing expenditures to changes in product performance. Including unassignable costs to obtain net profits would muddy the waters. For example, assume that advertising expenditures in Table 20-1 were increased by $1 million. The incremental profit (or loss) from a change would be reflected in the contribution-to-profits figure. The net profit figure would mask the effects because it includes unassignable costs that do not vary with changes in sales.

RETURN ON STOCKHOLDER'S EQUITY

The previous profitability measures were designed to assess the performance of individual products. Management must also assess the overall performance of the firm. The appropriate measure for corporate performance is the return on stockholder's equity. This is measured as net corporate profits as a percentage of the equity capital in the firm.

Figure 20-2 presents profitability criteria for the three basic marketing planning levels — corporate, SBU, and product market. At the product market level the appropriate measure is contribution to profits because the unit of analysis is the individual product. At the SBU level profitability analysis is for

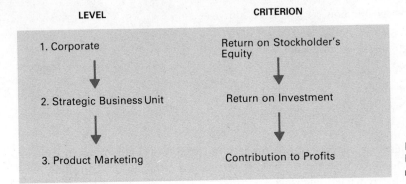

FIGURE 20-2
Profitability criteria at three
marketing planning levels

the unit as a whole across products and product lines. Allocating unassignable costs is easier, since these costs can more easily be attributed to the busines unit as a whole. Therefore net profit and ROI are reasonable criteria of performance. At the corporate level the appropriate criterion is not investment but equity. Therefore the appropriate performance criterion is stockholder's return.

PROFITABILITY CRITERIA FOR FUTURE PERFORMANCE

Having selected profitability criteria for performance, management must establish performance levels. At Courtaulds Ltd. a minimum ROI of 12 percent was established for all products. When new management took over at Westinghouse in 1979, they established an ROI of 15 percent as a reasonable goal for all product lines with a 7 percent ROI as a definite divestment level.[8] Performance goals should be higher than the firm's cost of capital. In the early 1980s this would have meant typical ROI goals of over 18 percent.

Although profitability is most important, it must be remembered that management establishes other performance criteria as well. Sales, market share, the capital-to-investment ratio, and the marketing-expenditure-to-sales ratio are frequently established as criteria to evaluate future performance for new and existing products.

Forecasting Marketing Performance

Having established profitability criteria for a product, management will want to determine if the product is likely to meet these criteria. If not, it should consider alternative investment opportunities. Determining whether the product will meet performance criteria requires forecasting sales and estimating costs. On this basis a profit and loss statement can be developed as in Table 20-1 for at least a five-year period to determine contribution to profits, ROI, and payback period (the amount of time required to recover all of the investment in the product).

SALES FORECASTING

Four types of sales forecasting techniques will be described:

1. judgmental forecasts,
2. forecasts based on consumer responses (generally consumer reactions to new products in product use tests, lab tests, and test markets),
3. forecasts based on historical sales data, and
4. predictive models.

Judgmental Forecasts

Managers frequently rely on their judgment to reinforce quantitative estimates of sales. One study found that 96 percent of the companies interviewed used some form of judgmental method in forecasting sales.[9] Yet few of these companies relied only on managerial judgment. Most used historical analysis or customer surveys in conjunction with judgmental forecasts. Companies relying solely on judgment probably felt they knew the market intimately and did not think it worth the cost to survey customers.

Judgmental forecasts are frequently determined by a *panel of experts* who meet and try to reach consensus on sales forecasts. Yet such techniques are frequently biased by the influence of senior management in group discussions. In one case the head of a panel of experts stated that his forecast represented the legitimate product objective and insisted that others conform to his opinion.[10] An extension of the panel consensus method, the **Delphi technique,** was developed to overcome these biases. Delphi requires experts to make individual forecasts without meeting and to state their reasoning in writing. Forecasts are not influenced by personalities or senior management. Forecasts are pooled and sent to the participants who are then asked to make a second forecast. Generally, a consensus is achieved after three or four rounds with a free exchange of information.

Another judgmental technique, the *expected value approach,* is an offshoot of decision theory. Management is given various scenarios — for example the introduction of new technology, entry into the market by the company's chief competitor within one year, or shortages in raw materials. In each case managers are asked to estimate the probability that the circumstance will occur and to predict the sales results as a consequence. Managers then weight the estimated sales by that probability to arrive at a forecast for the product.

Consumer Responses

Many companies rely on systematic product tests of potential customers to develop sales forecasts. Systematic testing occurs in developing new products or reformulating existing products. Forecasts are developed in the earlier phases of development before test marketing and then in the test market phase.

Forecasts prior to test marketing

In Chapter 9 we described a sequence of tests given before placing a new product in test markets. The sequence was:

- concept tests,
- product use tests,
- sales wave experiments,
- simulated lab tests, and
- controlled market tests.

Each test provides management a basis for estimating trial rate and, in some cases, repeat purchases. Therefore, the tests are a means of estimating sales on the basis of consumer responses. As testing proceeds the forecasts become more reliable, because the tests do a better job of simulating actual market conditions.

Table 20-2 presents results of a forecast for the hair conditioner cited in Table 20-1 before the product was test marketed. The forecast is based on a product use test and a subsequent sales wave experiment. In the product use test consumers were asked to rate the likelihood of purchasing the product (which we will call Hair-Free) on a five-point scale (definitely will buy, probably will buy, might buy, probably will not buy, definitely will not buy). An earlier study of sixteen new product concepts found that these ratings could be translated into an estimated probability of buying the product as follow:[11]

defnitely will buy	99 percent chance of buying
probably will buy	76 percent chance of buying
might buy	40 percent chance of buying

Applying these probabilities to the results of the product use test (i.e., saying that 99 percent of those who said they definitely will buy would then buy when the product becomes available) resulted in an estimate that about 50 percent of the target group (defined as women between thirty and fifty with very oily hair) would buy the product. But this percentage would have to be reduced because (1) not all target consumers would be aware of Hair-Free and (2) the product would not achieve 100 percent distribution. If 60 percent of target consumers would be aware of the product and if it achieved 85 percent distribution, about 25 percent of the target would buy the product for an estimated sales volume of 2.57 million units (25.7 percent times 10 million women in the United States estimated to be in the target group).

The 2.57 million units represent initial trial, but management realized it would also have to account for repeat purchases. The sales wave experiment

TABLE 20-2
Sales Forecast Based on Consumer Responses Prior to Test Market

1. *Trial rate estimation* (based on product use test)
   38% said they would definitely buy in product use
   test. Of this 38%, 99% are likely to buy. 38% × 99%   = 37.5%

   12% said they would probably buy in product use
   test. Of this 12%, 76% are likely to buy. 12% × 76%   = 9.0%

   10% said they might buy in product use test. Of this
   10%, 40% are likely to buy. 10% × 40%   = 4.0%
   Percentage of all women in target group likely to buy = 50.5%

   But
   Only an estimated 60% of all women in target group
     are likely to be aware of product and
   Distribution of product is likely to reach only 85% of
     the target group.

   Estimate of trial: 50.5% of women × 60% awareness ×
                 85% distribution   = 25.7% (trial rate)

   Trial rate in units: 25.7% trial rate × estimated 10
   million women in target group   = 2.57 million units

2. *Repeat purchase rate estimation* (based on sales wave
   test)

   40% of initial triers will repeat; 40% × 25.7% = 10.3% of target group will
     repeat or 1.03 million women (10.3% × 10 million women in target
     group).

   These women buy an average of 3.4 times a year. Number of units based
     on repeat: 3.4 × 1.03 million women = 3.50 million units.

   Total units based on trial and repeat = 2.57 million based on trial
                                           3.50 million based on repeat
                                           6.07 million units

3. *Number of units per purchase* (based on simulated lab test)

   On average, 1.1 units are purchased per shopping trip.
   Total estimated sales are 6.07 million × 1.1 = 6.67 million

   SALES FORECAST IN UNITS   = 6.67 MILLION

   SALES FORECAST IN DOLLAR = 6.67 MILLION UNITS × EXPECTED
   PRICE OF $2.39 PER UNIT   = $15.9 MILLION IN THE FIRST YEAR

gave consumers the opportunity to buy the product repeatedly. Using this data management then estimated that 40 percent of those who first tried would buy again. Further, they would buy an average of 3.4 times in the first year. On this basis, an additional 3.5 million units were estimated (40 percent of the initial triers buying 3.4 times). Total sales were thus estimated at 6.07 million units.

One further modification was required, because many consumers buy more than one unit of a product when purchasing. Using data from a subsequent simulated lab test, management estimated that the average number of units bought per shopping trip would be 1.1. Therefore, the final sales estimate was 6.67 million units (6.07 million times 1.1). At an average sales price of $2.39 per package, the sales estimate for the year would be $15.9 million. This forecast was for the first year of operation. Management also projected sales for the next four years on a judgmental basis, assuming that sales would grow by 20 percent in the second and third years as brand awareness became widespread. Sales would level off in the fourth year as competition intensified and would take a slight dip in the fifth year.

Forecasts based on the test market

Test marketing is the last step before introduction of a new or reformulated product, and its results should be projectable nationally or regionally. Projectability requires that areas selected for test marketing be representative, meaning that the test cities should reflect national or regional parameters on criteria such as distribution facilities, number of TV stations, market size, and market demographics. (See Table 9-2 for criteria used to attain projectability.)

If the test cities are truly representative, a sales projection would simply require multiplying the sales results in test market by a factor equal to the national or regional population. If the market size in the test area is one-twentieth that of the national market then one would multiply sales results by 20 to obtain the sales forecast. But absolute representativeness in test areas is hardly ever achieved. Differences always exist between the test areas and the total area in which the product is to be introduced. Therefore, some adjustments must be made in sale results in test areas to project them.

One simple approach is to weight sales results by differences between the characteristics of the test area and the area of introduction. For example, assume that the market share of the leading hair conditioner is 30 percent nationally. But in the area in which Hair-Free is being tested, the leader's share is only 20 percent. The leading conditioner just happens to have weaker distribution in these test cities and cannot deliver premiums and coupons as effectively. Moreover, test results show that consumers who intend to buy Hair-Free are *less* likely to be loyal to the leading brand. As a result, the sales figures in the test market are inflated because there are fewer users of the leading brand.

The producers of Hair-Free apply a statistical method known as *covariance analysis* to the sales results. The method will weight sales to account for disparities between the sample (the test city) and the universe (the national market). The analysis will weight not only for differences in the market share of the leading brand but for other differences as well — demographic, product use, brand awareness. As a result of applying covariance analysis, the sales results in the test market were weighted downward by almost 15 percent.

Had the company just projected results based on the differences between the size of the test market and the national market, the sales forecast for the first year of operation would have been $15.2 million, a figure close to the forecasts made from the product test and the sales wave experiments in Table 20-2. But as a result of recognizing the differences between test and national characteristics, the forecast was scaled down to $13.2 million, a difference of $2.0 million!

Forecasts Based on Historical Data

Companies also use past sales data to forecast sales. Such a technique is applicable to products that have been on the market long enough to establish a sales trend. The simplest method would be to *extrapolate* a sales trend into the future. Sophisticated statistical methods for extrapolation can be used. But these techniques have one common problem: they assume that past trends apply to the future. As a result, they fail to account for possible changes in the competitive economic, or technological environment as well as changes in actions the company itself might take.

Another historical approach is the use of *historical analogy* to forecast sales of similar products. Past sales results of similar products are used to forecast sales of the new product. This technique is used to forecast sales of new products when the company does not want to spend the money on consumer surveys or does not trust a jury of experts to forecast sales. It is most reliable when the new product is very similar to past products. The danger in using this technique is that it does not account for differences between the new and the old product. Despite the weakness of historical methods of forecasting, the survey of forecasting techniques found that 60 percent of the companies reported using some method of historical forecasting.[12]

Sales Forecasting Models

The weakness of historical forecasts and managerial judgment has led some companies to use quantitative methods of forecasting sales. These methods are based on survey results, test markets, and consumer panel data (periodic data from a panel of consumers reporting purchases). Two types of models have been used for sales forecasting — probabilistic and deterministic. **Probabilistic models** rely on the consumer's past purchasing behavior to estimate the probability of buying a brand. **Deterministic models** use marketing variables such as advertising expenditures, price level, couponing, and so forth to predict sales. Deterministic models are important because they are the only sales forecasting technique to provide diagnostic as well as predictive information to management. For example, a deterministic model might predict that sales will not increase enough to warrant an increase in advertising expenditures. The model is not only predicting sales; it is also telling management not to increase the advertising budget.

Probabilistic models

One simple forecasting model is to estimate the consumer's probability of buying from past purchases. The *linear learning model* is derived from learning theory and postulates a learning curve.[13] As the consumer repurchases a brand, the probability of purchasing again increases. If the consumer remains loyal, the probability of repurchasing levels off close to 100 percent. If the consumer stops buying for several purchase cycles, the probability of buying again will quickly decrease. The linear learning model relies on consumer panel data that provide purchase records over a long enough time to make probability estimates. From these estimates the total number of buyers and total sales can be forecast for a given time period.

The linear learning model can be applied only to existing products, since a long record of past purchases is required to estimate purchase probabilities reliably. Probability models have also been used in forecasting new products from test market results. These models all require an estimate of initial trial and repeat purchases to predict market share. Most estimate market share at some steady state where new triers are no longer as likely and repeat purchases stabilize. At such a point market share is not likely to change much from one period to the next. Market share at the steady state then becomes the basis for predicting sales of the new product. (See pages 283–284 in Chapter 9 for an example of a probabilistic model using test market data to forecast sales.)

Deterministic models

The problem with the probability models we have described is that they do not take account of environmental factors in sales forecasts. They rely solely on the likelihood that the consumer will act in the future as he or she did in the past. These models do not provide for changes in company or competitive strategies that could substantially change trial and repeat rates and therefore market share.

Deterministic models forecast sales on the basis of marketing variables. Associations among advertising, price, distribution, product characteristics, and sales results are developed from consumer responses across a wide range of product categories. One such model, known as TRACKER, is presented in Figure 20-3.[14] The right side of the model presents the outcome variables; the left side presents the input variables (factors that influence the outcome). With the exception of product satisfaction (a consumer variable), each of the input variables is a component of the marketing plan.

Advertising expenditures determine brand awareness. Brand awareness is a prerequisite to being a trier and is therefore directly related to trial. The marketing variables influencing trial are price level, distribution, and couponing. Price does not affect brand awareness, but it does affect trial. Too high or too low a price may discourage trial. Couponing is a strategy designed to get nonusers to try the brand. And distribution will affect trial since it determines availability. Trial is a prerequisite for repeat use. Whether the consumer will

INPUT VARIABLES   **OUTCOME**

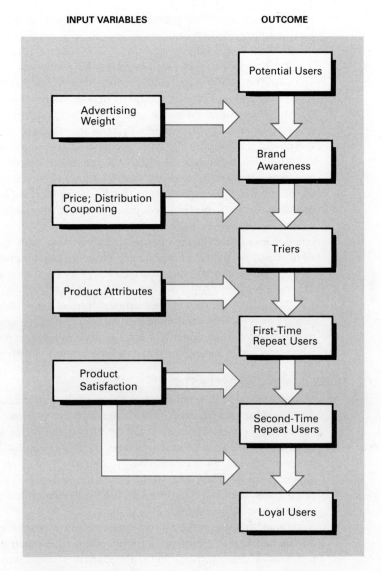

FIGURE 20-3
A model to forecast sales of new products: TRACKER

Source: Adapted from Robert Blattberg and John Golanty, "Tracker: An Early Test Market Forecasting and Diagnostic Model for New Product Planning," *Journal of Marketing Research* 15 (May 1978): 192–202.

buy again is determined by the product's attributes. The key question is whether the consumer will buy repeatedly and become loyal to the brand. Loyalty is determined by the consumer's overall satisfaction with the brand.

The data for the model are determined from consumer surveys and company records. The relationships among advertising weight, brand awareness, price level, trial, and so forth are estimated by a multiple regression program. Here one derives separate estimates for each product category rather than applying one general model to all products. In applications for eleven product categories, the model was found to be fairly accurate.

The main advantage of TRACKER and other deterministic models is in allowing management to play "what if" games. The statistical associations in the model will forecast the results of a 5 percent increase in advertising weight on sales, or a 10 percent reduction in price. Management can also apply sensitivity analysis to sales results by incrementally increasing or decreasing components of the marketing mix and estimating sales results. For example, what would be the effect on revenue of incremental increases of one percent in sales promotional expenditures, or a 5 percent decrease in advertising expenditures?

Of course, sensitivity analysis assumes the model is reliable and can accurately predict sales increments from marketing effort. Such accuracy is highly unlikely from any marketing model. Yet deterministic models do provide management with a tool for evaluating the potential profit impact of their marketing strategies.

PROFIT PROJECTIONS BASED ON FORECASTS

Management will develop projections of product profitability for at least the first five years on the basis of the sales forecast. A profit and loss statement such as the one in Table 20-1 will be formulated for each year. Profitability projections will require cost estimates for each year. Estimates of marketing expenditures are obtained from the product marketing plan. The plan stipulates expenditures for advertising, sales promotion, and distribution as well as expected price levels. Manufacturing, research and development, and administrative costs must also be obtained from management.

Table 20-3 shows the five-year projections for Hair-Free. The sales forecast for the first year is the projection from test market when differences between test market characteristics and national market characteristics are accounted for ($13.2 million). It is *not* the unweighted figure presented in Table 20-2 ($15.9 million). Subsequent sales forecasts are based on the expectation that sales will increase by about 20 percent in year 2 and 30 percent in year 3, will start leveling out in year 4 because of increased competition, and will take a slight dip in year 5 as a result of an expected decrease in price.

The assignable nonvariable costs in row 3 are primarily costs of marketing. Marketing costs are high in the first year to establish brand awareness and encourage trial. Advertising and sales promotion expenditures represent most of the $9.5 million. These costs decrease in years 2 and 3 once brand awareness

TABLE 20-3
Five-Year Revenue Projections for a New Hair Conditioner
(in millions of dollars)

	YEAR 0	YEAR 1	YEAR 2	YEAR 3	YEAR 4	YEAR 5
1. Sales revenue	0	$ 13.2	$ 16.2	$ 21.1	$ 23.9	$ 22.8
2. Variable costs (labor, materials, manufacturing)	0	4.4	5.4	6.5	7.2	6.9
3. Assignable nonvariable costs (marketing)	0	9.5	8.0	7.0	9.0	10.0
4. Investment	5.7	0	0	0	0	0
5. Contribution to profit	−5.7	− .7	2.8	7.6	7.7	5.9
6. Discounted contribution (at 15%)	−5.7	− .6	2.0	5.0	4.4	3.0
7. Nonassignable costs (overhead, administration)	0	.8	1.0	1.3	1.4	1.4
8. Discounted cash flow (at 15%)	−5.7	−1.3	1.2	3.9	3.3	1.9
9. Cumulative discounted cash flow	−5.7	−7.0	−5.8	−1.9	1.4	3.3

is established, but rise again in year 4 as a result of increased competition. The company forecasts that couponing and dealing will increase substantially in year 4 to meet price pressures from competition.

The contribution to profit (row 5) is discounted in row 6 of Table 20-3 to account for the present value of future contributions. It is discounted at 15 percent compounded annually, which is the current cost of capital. Thus, the $5.9 million contribution to profit in year 5 is worth only $3.0 million in current dollars. Row 6 shows that by the second year the product is contributing to profit and overhead.

Management will wish to examine two additional performance criteria — cash flow and payback period. Cash flow is important since it shows the amount of money available to expand the product's future operations or to support potential stars. As we noted in Chapter 19, it is one of the primary criteria in analyzing the firm's product mix. Payback period is the time it takes for the company to recover its initial investment in plant and equipment and research and development. Row 8 shows the discounted cash flow. Nonassignable costs are allocated to the product to compute the discounted cash flow, but depreciation is not included and is added back. Row 9 shows the cumulative cash flow. The payback period is reached by the fourth year since cumulative cash flow is positive at this point. The projection exactly fulfills company criteria of no more than a four-year payback period.

The projections also show that the product just meets company criteria for contribution. Management requires an average contribution of 20 percent of sales (row 5 divided by row 1 in Table 20-3) over the first five years. The product achieves an average contribution of 21 percent of sales. But there is some cause for concern since the product may show marginal performance after the fifth year if competitive pressures continue to dampen sales revenue and force up advertising and sales promotion costs. Despite these cautions, management decides to introduce Hair-Free because it has met the profitability criteria based on the sales forecasts.

Developing and Implementing the Marketing Plan

Having decided to introduce the new conditioner, management must now develop and implement a marketing plan (step 3 in Figure 20-1). The process of planning at the product level was described in Chapter 4 and at the corporate level in Chapter 18. From the standpoint of evaluation and control, the most important planning task is estimating required resources in the form of a marketing budget. The budget is based on the five-year profit and loss estimates in Table 20-3. Assignable costs for the first year would be:

Product advertising	$ 7.0 million
Sales promotion	1.2 million
Personal selling	0.5 million
Distribution	0.6 million
Product management salaries	0.2 million
TOTAL	$ 9.5 million

Management would allocate funds for the marketing costs. The sequence leading up to the allocation of funds is thus:

1. establishing profitability objectives,
2. forecasting sales, and
3. developing marketing plans incorporating planned marketing expenditures.

The process of budgeting at Philip Morris is similar. According to the chief financial officer at Philip Morris:

> We first work up an estimate of what we think we can sell in the marketplace [the sales forecast]. We then evaluate such things as next year's campaigns, new ads, and new products. ... All of these things are then discussed with our advertising firms ahead of time. They give us their estimated cost, and based on that we build our marketing budget. This budget is reviewed first within the operating company where it is related

to a unit volume goal. This unit volume together with operating revenues and operating expenses generates a bottom line [the contribution to profits in Table 20-3].[15]

These estimates are developed within Philip Morris's business units. After the budget is reviewed within the operating companies, it is then evaluated by corporate management. The last step is to present the budget to the chairman of the board.

Evaluating Marketing Performance

Once the marketing plan has been implemented, the next step in the process of control is to monitor performance to determine if actual performance is deviating from planned (step 4 in Figure 20-1). Good marketing control systems must be able to determine the specific area in which performance is deviating and must give management a clue as to why these deviations are occurring.

Pinpointing and analyzing deviations from plans requires (1) a system to identify deviations and (2) a marketing audit to investigate reasons for deviations.

SYSTEMS FOR EVALUATION AND CONTROL

Three types of systems are used to track and evaluate marketing performance:

1. after-the fact-control systems,
2. steering control systems, and
3. adaptive control systems.

After-The-Fact Control Systems

As the name implies, **after-the-fact control systems** apply controls at the end of a planning period. Performance is usually evaluated at the end of the year and action is taken to correct deviations from plans. Management will first compare actual sales to sales forecasts for the product. Then it will analyze any deviations in sales results to discover their causes.

Most important is the ability to distinguish deviations due to environmental factors from deviations due to company actions. Environmentally caused deviations are generally beyond the company's control and include changes in consumer needs, unexpected competitive actions, the development of new technologies, or a change in economic conditions. Deviations due to company actions may involve inefficiencies in allocating sales effort, in selecting advertising media, in establishing profitable price levels, or in positioning the product to meet consumer needs. Corrective action due to unexpected changes in the environment would require *changing marketing objectives.* Corrective action due to company actions would require *changing marketing strategy.*

Management will evaluate costs as well as sales, comparing actual costs to budgeted costs. Deviations due to cost overruns will be examined. Such deviations may be caused by cost increases by suppliers, inadequate estimates of the cost of distribution or manufacturing, or unplanned increases in advertising or promotional effort. Once it has identified the reasons for sales or cost deviations, management will revise budgets for the next planning cycle. Revised sales and cost estimates then become the basis for a new five-year profit and loss statement.

As an example of after-the-fact control, consider the deviations in actual performance for the new hair conditioner in the fifth year after introduction (Table 20-1) from planned performance represented in the profit and loss statement (last column in Table 20-3). Sales revenue was actually $1 million higher than forecast. But the contribution to profit was almost $4 million *lower.* Part of the explanation is inflation, a factor beyond management's control. Variable costs of production were $2.7 million higher than estimated.

But management could not attribute the shortfall in contributions solely to factors beyond their control. Assignable nonvariable costs were $2.2 million higher than budgeted. The increase was due to greater expenditures on sales promotions and advertising. The product manager for Hair-Free could argue that increased competition necessitated deviating from the budget to maintain sales. But there is no evidence that the additional costs were matched by an increase in sales. In fact, much of the increase in promotional costs was caused by greater expenditures for coupons. An analysis of promotional effectiveness showed that coupons were not being redeemed at the expected rate. Therefore, the additional expenditures in advertising and mailing coupons probably did not pay off in increased sales.

As a result of the evaluation of marketing performance, sales promotion expenditures were budgeted at a significantly lower level for year 6. The lower budgeted level then became the performance criterion for the next planning cycle.

Steering Control Systems

Steering control systems attempt to determine deviations from plans during the planning period rather than at the end. Actual performance is projected to the end of the planning period. If performance is predicted to deviate from objectives, corrective action will be taken to bring the plan back into control. In other words, the plan is *steered* to meet its objectives.[16] The advantage of steering control is that corrective action can be taken before deviations occur. Action is more immediate than in after-the-fact systems.

Steering control requires up-to-date monitoring of performance. If an annual product marketing plan is being monitored, the performance reports should occur at least monthly. A useful device for monitoring performance is the *control chart.* The control chart shows the budgeted expenditure level as a mean and variations from the mean as upper and lower limits allowed by the plan. Performance is monitored. If it comes close to the upper or lower limit, a review takes place and corrective action is instituted before expenditures go out of control (beyond the limits set by management).

Control charts for the amount budgeted for advertising and sales promotion for the new hair conditioner in the fifth year are illustrated in Figure 20-4. The budgeted level is the center line in the chart. Management is allowing a 10 percent variance around advertising expenditure levels. A 20 percent variance is allowed for sales promotion because coupons and deals are frequently used to counter competition and must therefore be kept more flexible.

Monthly performance reports show that advertising expenditures did rise, particularly at the end of the year, at a level close to the upper limits. Such a rise was anticipated for the end-of-year holiday period. Management kept a close watch on these expenditures. The sales promotion control chart shows a steady rise at midyear that exceeded the upper limits of the chart. Management decided to investigate these deviations immediately. Sales promotions were divided into their components: coupons, point-of-purchase displays, in-store deals, free samples, and other promotions. Two of the components are in Figure 20-4, coupons and point-of-purchase displays. The deviation in the promotional budget is due almost entirely to excess expenditures on couponing. Management further categorized coupon expenditures by sales region, two of which are presented in Figure 20-4. Expenditures in the Eastern region account for much of the variance and are out of control. On further investigation, management determined that the sales manager for the Eastern region requested a substantial increase in couponing beyond budget because of an increase in coupon activity by the leading hair conditioner in the region. The product manager for Hair-Free supported the request. Management decided to scale back couponing since expenditures were about 30 percent above budget. But management did increase the budget allocation for coupon activity to counter competition. Similar action was taken in one other sales region with excess expenditures on couponing. This steering control system permitted management to take this action in September, four months before the normal end-of-year planning review.

Adaptive Control Systems

Adaptive control systems are similar to steering control systems in encouraging planning adjustments before the end of the reporting period. But whereas steering systems require action based on deviations in performance, adaptive systems require action based on changes in environmental conditions. Steering control systems are *reactive;* they react to deviations from the plan. Adaptive control systems are *proactive;* they anticipate the need to deviate from the plan before actual deviations occur.

For example, rather than wait for sales promotions to go out of control in the East, an adaptive control system would have tracked competitive couponing and increased the budget for couponing as a result. Advanced allocations would have permitted the product manager for Hair-Free to coordinate couponing

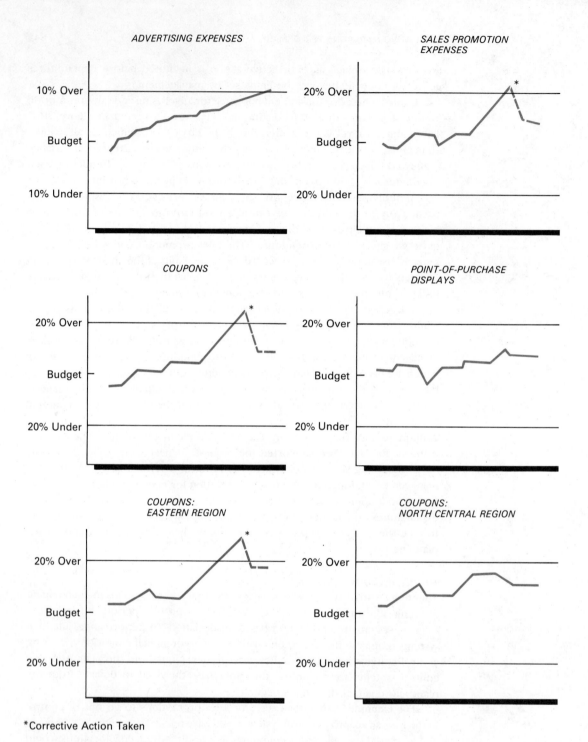

*Corrective Action Taken

FIGURE 20-4
Control charts for advertising and sales promotion expenditures

across regions better rather than taking what amounted to emergency action to counter competition.

The adaptive control system therefore encourages changes in the marketing plan. The objective is "to develop standards that reflect the operating environment during the reporting period, not the hypothetical environment that was used to develop plans before the period."[17] As a result, the adaptive control system changes the "desired levels of performance to reflect the economic, technological and social environment actually experienced during the reporting period."[18] The system is adaptive in that it is changing with conditions during the reporting period. Monitoring changes in competitive activity, technology, or social and economic conditions should be the responsibility of an effective marketing information system. Top management should be involved in administering such a tracking system, since these environmental conditions affect the definition of marketing opportunity for the firm. The competitive information system developed by GTE (see pages 68–69) is an example of an important component of an adaptive control system. GTE systematically collects information on competitive marketing, production, and investment strategies so it can act proactively rather than reactively.

THE MARKETING AUDIT

The **marketing audit** is a periodic and comprehensive review of marketing operations. It deals with the company's total marketing environment cutting across products and business units. The marketing audit is designed to:

1. identify changes in the environment requiring revisions in marketing opportunity assessment,

2. evaluate marketing planning and control procedures, and

3. appraise marketing strategy to determine if actions can be carried out more profitably.

Since results of the audit are likely to suggest changes in strategy and planning, the audit should be part of a control system. An audit should not be reserved for periods when the company is in difficulty but should be conducted periodically on a proactive basis. In after-the-fact control, the marketing audit should be conducted at the end of a planning cycle. In steering and adaptive control systems, the marketing audit is conducted as an ongoing review of strategy and operations.

A marketing audit is conducted at two levels: product marketing and strategic marketing. The *product marketing audit* evaluates components of the firm's overall marketing strategy: product, distribution, price, advertising, sales promotion, and personal selling. Key areas are designated for review, and the auditors then assess operations in each area. For example, in distribution, the auditors might review the types of distributors used, the intensity of distribution to ensure product availability, the adequacy of customer service, and the efficiency of physical distribution functions such as transportation, inventory control, and warehousing. An equally comprehensive list of review criteria would be developed for each of the other functional areas.

The *strategic marketing audit* reviews key areas at the corporate and business unit level, specifically:

1. the corporate mission,

2. definition of marketing opportunity,

3. evaluation of the marketing environment,

4. adequacy of corporate growth strategies,

5. the firm's product mix,

6. validity of profitability criteria and cost allocations, and

7. effectiveness of planning methods and control systems.

Questions for review and evaluation are developed in each of these areas. For example, in assessing the evaluation of the marketing environment, the auditors would identify key changes in the economic, technological, legal, regulatory, social, and cultural environment to determine if they are being adequately tracked by management. If not, then questions would arise as to the adequacy of opportunity identification and the development of growth strategies.

A comprehensive marketing audit might have helped several firms avoid unprofitable actions. For example, a marketing audit might have:

- steered companies such as Quaker Oats, Nestlé, Olin, and Schlitz away from unprofitable acquistions outside their areas of expertise;

- identified the failure to define corporate mission at Parker Pen;[19]

- pointed to a drain on profitability at 3M that was caused by a product line out of control;[20] and

- foreseen the problems that would eventually face Westinghouse because of inadequate strategic planning and control.[21]

Corrective Action

The last step in the evaluation and control model in Figure 20-1 is action to correct deviations from the plan. The model requires an evaluation of the profitability of corrective action. If corrective action proves to be a stopgap measure to minimize losses, the company should terminate the product and seek alternative investment opportunities. Polaroid could have continued to support the market for instant movies by increasing advertising and reducing prices for Polavision, its instant movie camera. But the company recognized the lack of consumer benefits in taking instant movies. It terminated the line and diverted its resources to acquiring high-growth industrial companies as a hedge against Eastman-Kodak's entry into the instant camera market.

If corrective action is indeed corrective and likely to lead to higher profits, the company can: (1) change marketing performance objectives, (2) change cost allocations, or (3) change marketing strategy. For example, General Foods' audit of the pet foods business led it to scale down performance objectives for its Gaines division. The audit found that growth in pet foods slowed in the early 1980s because of several factors: a slowing of new household formations, overcapitalization of some companies, the severe recession during this period, and the growth of generic pet foods.[22] As a result, the president of the Gaines division commented, "We have recognized a changed environment and have faced up to how you have to act."[23] The division is now a "leaner but healthier dog food business at GF," positioned for slower growth. Reducing sales objectives did not mean cutting profitability goals. Parallel with a reduction in sales objectives is a cutback in spending. The division cut advertising spending, consolidated manufacturing to two plants from three, and cut back marketing personnel.[24]

Corrective action does not always mean a cutback in costs or a scaling back of performance objectives. Sometime expenditures must increase above budget. For example, Budweiser had cut back on advertising expenditures in the late 1960s because a study showed that advertising was not having a sufficient effect on sales. But when Philip Morris bought Miller and increased the advertising stakes, Budweiser felt it had to increase expenditures again to avoid losing market share. Today Budweiser is maintaining a high level of advertising expenditures to protect its position as the market leader.

Corrective action could also mean a change in marketing strategy as well as a change in expenditures. When Philip Morris bought 7-Up, the intention was to confront Pepsi and Coca-Cola head-on. But increases in advertising expenditures did not make up for weakness in 7-Up's network of bottlers. Sales results fell far short of goals. The alternatives were (1) to reduce sales expectation and cut back marketing costs for the brand (a mild harvesting strategy), (2) to try to push the product through the bottlers by offering discounts and incentives, or (3) to try to reposition the brand totally, create demand at the consumer level, and pull the product through the bottler network. Philip Morris chose to do the last by positioning the product as a caffeine-free soft drink. Corrective action in this case involved a complete reorientation of marketing strategy.

Summary

Marketing management must evaluate marketing strategies and control them to make sure they conform to plans. Evaluation and control requires:

1. Establishing profitability criteria
2. Developing revenue projections

3. Implementing marketing plans

4. Evaluating marketing performance for deviations from plans

5. Taking corrective action where required.

Profitability criteria can be established using a net profit approach or a contribution-to-margin approach. The former includes nonassignable overhead and administrative costs; the latter includes only costs assignable to marketing and production. Marketing management favors profits measured by contribution since this measure reflects the true cost of product introduction and maintenance.

Having established performance objectives, management will then *project revenues* by forecasting sales. Various forecasting methods were reviewed: judgment, product testing before and during test market, historical data, and models to predict sales of new and existing products. Projections of product profitability are developed over a five-year period on the basis of the sales forecasts. Costs must also be projected to determine the product's contribution to profit and projected payback period.

If profit projections meet goals, management will then *develop and implement a marketing plan.* The plan requires a budget derived from cost and revenue projections. Budgets are allocated to individual products by business unit management, and are allocated to the business units by top management.

Implementing the marketing plan requires *evaluating performance* to determine if actual performance is deviating from plan. A control system is required to measure any such deviations. The system could determine deviations after the end of the planning period. The control system can also determine deviations during the planning period and steer performance toward planned goals. A third type of control system seeks to anticipate the need for changes in performance goals by tracking changes in the environment. Such an adaptive system involves continuous changes in plans. Part of the system of control is a periodic and comprehensive review of marketing operations known as a marketing audit.

Evaluation and control lead to three possibilities: (1) continue operations as planned, (2) take corrective action to conform to plans, and (3) terminate the product and consider alternatives for investment. Frequently *corrective action* is required. Then the company can do one or more of the following: (1) change objectives, (2) change cost allocations, and (3) change marketing strategy.

In Part V we will focus on important strategic areas in marketing that deserve special consideration: international, service, and not-for-profit marketing.

Questions

1. What are the different purposes of evaluation and control in (a) product marketing planning, and (b) strategic marketing planning?

2. Evaluate Lipton's criteria for considering companies for acquisition cited on pages 624–25.

   □ Do you agree with these criteria?

   □ Do they provide sufficient guidelines for considering companies that are not in Lipton's core businesses?

   □ What additional acquisition criteria might you propose?

3. What are the problems in using net profit as a criterion to evaluate product performance? Given these problems, why do managers continue to use net profit as a primary criterion of evaluation?

4. Consider net profit, contribution to profit, and return on stockholder's equity as measures of performance. Which of these three is the most relevant for each of the following cases?

   □ evaluating 3M's performance as a company,

   □ evaluating Cubitron, 3M's new industrial abrasive, and

   □ evaluating the performance of 3M's industrial abrasive SBU as a whole. Why?

5. We suggested that management should set ROI goals higher than the current cost of capital.

   □ Why?

   □ What are the implications of doing so in inflationary periods?

   □ What are the limitations of this policy?

6. What are the pros and cons of the four basic approaches to sales forecasting: managerial judgment, forecasts based on consumer responses, historical data, and use of forecasting models?

7. In each of the cases listed below, a company wants to forecast sales for one or more of its products. Consider the sales forecasting methods cited in the chapter. Which method would you recommend for:

   □ a firm that has experienced a steady rate of sales growth in the last ten years?

   □ a company in a highly volatile industrial market that is controlled by a few large producers?

   □ a consumer goods company that frequently tests new hair care and toiletry items?

   □ a consumer goods company that finds a predictable relationship between its price and promotional activities and sales results?

     □ a company that is introducing a new diet drink similar to one it introduced several years ago?

8. The TRACKER forecasting model in Figure 20-3 is designed to provide diagnostic marketing implications as well as to predict sales for new products.

     □ What types of strategic implications might the model provide for a company that has mapped out a strategy to introduce a new diet soda and now wants to predict sales?

     □ How might the product manager for the new diet soda use the model to make decisions about possible changes in marketing strategy?

9. After-the-fact control has several weaknesses as a control system.

     □ What are they?

     □ Why is after-the-fact control the most commonly used control system?

10. Assume that a company uses a steering control system and finds total advertising expenditures out of control.

     □ How can a company use control charts (as in Figure 20-4) to further identify why advertising expenditures went out of control? (Provide examples of the specific categories of advertising expenditures the company would want to track to determine why total advertising expenditures are out of control.)

     □ What corrective actions might the company take in each case?

11. What is the difference between an adaptive and a steering control system? Why is an adaptive control system considered proactive, whereas a steering control system is considered reactive?

12. Adaptive control systems rely more heavily for control on an integrated MIS than do other control systems.

     □ Why?

     □ What are the informational requirements for adaptive controls?

Notes

1. H. M. Tibbetts, "The Product-Line Audit: An Approach to Profit-Oriented Marketing," *Management Review* 66 (March 1977): 14–17.

2. "The Opposites: GE Grows While Westinghouse Shrinks," *Business Week,* January 31, 1977, p. 60.

3. Ibid., p. 61.

4. Peter Doyle, "Market Planning in the Multiproduct Firm," *Industrial Marketing Management* 4 (1975): 183–92.

5. Ibid., p. 184.

6. Trevor Bentley, "Measuring Product Profitability," *Management Accounting* 61 (July/August 1979): 17–18.

7. Frank H. Mossman, Paul M. Fischer, and W. J. E Crissy, "New Approaches to Analyzing Marketing Profitability," *Journal of Marketing* 38 (April 1974): 43–48.

8. *Business Week,* January 31, 1977, p. 66.

9. James T. Rothe, "Effectiveness of Sales Forecasting Methods," *Industrial Marketing Management* 7 (1978): 116.

10. "12 'Prescriptions' for Better Forecast-Strategy-Goal Link," *Marketing News,* March 18, 1983, Section 1, p. 6.

11. Alin Gruber, "Purchase Intent and Purchase Probability," *Journal of Advertising Research* 10 (February 1970): 26.

12. Rothe, "Effectiveness of Sales Forecasting," p. 116.

13. Alfred A. Kuehn, "Consumer Brand Choice as a Learning Process," *Journal of Advertising Research* 2 (December 1962): 10–17.

14. Robert Blattberg and John Golanty, "Tracker: An Early Test Market Forecasting and Diagnostic Model for New Product Planning," *Journal of Marketing Research* 15 (May 1978): 192–202.

15. "Marketing Strategy at Philip Morris Involves More than Spending Money," *Management Accounting* 7 (January 1980): 12, 14–16.

16. Subhash Sharma and Dale D. Achabel, "STEM-COM: An Analytical Model for Marketing Control," *Journal of Marketing* 46 (Spring 1982): 104–13.

17. William F. Bentz and Robert F. Lusch, "Now You Can Control Your Product's Market Performance," *Management Accounting* 7 (January 1980): 17–25, at p. 18.

18. Ibid.

19. "New Chief Pens Bold Plan for a Parker Resurgence," *Advertising Age,* July 26, 1982, pp. 4, 56.

20. "3M's Search for Strategic Identity," *Industrial Marketing,* February 1983, p. 80.

21. *Business Week,* January 31, 1977, pp. 60–66.

22. "GF Execs: Committed to Lean Pet Foods Unit," *Advertising Age,* November 8, 1982, pp. 4, 100.

23. Ibid., p. 4.

24. Ibid.

PART V

Special Areas of Marketing Management

Until now, we have focused primarily on the marketing of industrial and consumer goods in domestic markets. But we noted in Chapter 1 that marketing principles are applied to several other areas. Specifically, marketing plans and strategies can be developed for:

- international as well as domestic markets,
- services as well as products, and
- not-for-profit as well as profit-making activities.

In the last section of the book we will consider these three areas; international marketing in Chapter 21, service marketing in Chapter 22, and not-for-profit marketing in Chapter 23. The basic marketing principles described in previous chapters generally apply in each of these three areas, but there are enough differences to justify giving them special attention.

The discussion of not-for-profit marketing in Chapter 23 is extended to include a consideration of the broader social responsibilities of the marketing manager in the context of consumer rights.

CHAPTER 21

International Marketing

FOCUS OF CHAPTER

Many of the companies cited in previous chapters operate on a worldwide basis. To firms engaged in international trade, marketing is the evaluation of opportunities and implementation of strategies in other countries. This cross-national focus makes international marketing more complicated and risky, but more potentially lucrative than domestic marketing. International marketers must consider differences between markets in cultural norms, as well as political climates, trade regulations, economic conditions, and competition. As a result of the great complexities in marketing planning, many firms that are fairly astute marketers in their domestic operation have failed to adapt to foreign conditions. Consider the following:

- In 1981 Campbell Soup cut back its three-year-old canned soup business in Brazil, despite a $2 million award-winning ad campaign. The company discovered that Brazilian housewives did not feel adequate if they did not make soup they could call their own. They preferred dehydrated products of competitors such as Knorr, which they could use as a soup starter with their own ingredients.[1]

- In the early 1970s Tokyo-based Shiseido Company, the third largest cosmetic company in the world, pulled out of the United States because of a failure to build brand loyalty for its product line. The company used Japanese models only and featured makeup colors unsuitable to American tastes. Shiseido also discovered that "splashy promotions, frequent gift-with-purchase offers, and expensive in-store cultural festivals did little to build a consistent, everyday business."[2] Successful promotional techniques in Japan did not work in the United States.

- Pepperidge Farm imported the Delacré line of luxury biscuits from England, thinking they could be established as a top-of-the-line product.

The company discovered that the recipes were too rich for American tastes.

■ Kellogg's assumption it could sell Pop Tarts in Europe proved false simply because the product had to be toasted and many European homes did not have toasters.[3]

Each of these examples represented a failure to understand consumer needs and business conditions in foreign markets. But many of these companies learned from their mistakes and attempted to make their international efforts a success. Campbell is considering a modified soup line to suit the needs of Brazilian housewives. Shiseido has introduced a line in the United States that has won the praise of cosmetics buyers. And Pepperidge Farm has shifted the positioning of the Delacré line to a more folksy and traditional American cookie.

These examples illustrate the importance of a careful evaluation of foreign markets by international firms. In this chapter we will focus on the evaluation of opportunities and development of strategies in other countries. First we will consider the environment of international marketing. Then we will describe the process of planning international marketing strategies at two levels: corporate and product market. These two levels reflect the two basic planning levels described in previous chapters: strategic marketing planning and product marketing planning.

Importance of International Marketing

Increased competition from foreign manufacturers has led many American firms to place more importance on international marketing. A reflection of the importance of international trade is the fact that in the late 1970s, 79 percent of all manufacturing jobs created in the United States were linked to exports.[4] But international trade is also concentrated in a few companies. Fewer than 10 percent of American firms engage in exporting, and 250 companies account for 80 percent of all exports, representing about $200 billion in sales.[5] International marketing is clearly big business.

Among American companies that emphasize international trade are Pan American (which earns more than 90 percent of its revenues from overseas operations),[6] Coca-Cola, IBM, Polaroid, Gillette, Johnson & Johnson, and Pfizer (each of which earns more than 50 percent of its revenue abroad).[7] Conversely, many firms that are generally regarded as American operations are foreign owned but have sizable representation in the United States — for example, Nestlé, Lever, Lipton, Howard Johnson, Shell Oil. Nestlé, a Swiss-based company, make only 4 percent of its earnings in domestic (Swiss) operations.[8]

These firms are all known as multinational companies because they directly market their products, and in some cases manufacture them, in foreign markets.

Not all companies that engage in international marketing are multinationals. Some companies export products overseas through third parties (export agents, export trading companies) and divest themselves of responsibility for marketing their product abroad. Others market their products abroad but do not actively pursue global marketing opportunities. They view foreign markets as secondary efforts or extensions of their domestic operations. The true multinational company is one that gives foreign operations top priority in its long-term growth strategy.

The Environment of International Marketing

International marketing operates on the same principles as domestic marketing:

- Target markets must be identified in various countries.
- Products must be developed to meet the needs of these markets.
- A marketing plan must be developed to price, promote, and distribute products in each country.
- A strategic plan must be formulated to ensure that the multinational company
    - develops the right product mix across countries, and
    - implements sound corporate growth strategies on a global basis.

In short, companies must apply the same sound principles of marketing abroad as they do at home. Yet the four examples cited at the beginning of this chapter suggest that many marketers forget these basic principles.

Despite the similarities between international and domestic marketing, one difference stands out: international marketing is much more likely to be affected by differences between countries. Such differences have no parallel in domestic operations. Even in a country as diverse as the United States, a manufacturer aiming at different social and demographic segments does not face the diversity that an international marketer faces when operating in different countries.

In this section we will consider differences between countries in trade regulations, economic conditions, competition, culture, and the political environment that the international marketer must consider.

TRADE REGULATIONS

International marketers must understand various trade regulations and barriers that operate in foreign countries. Since World War II there have been attempts to ease trade barriers and encourage international trade.

Trade Barriers
Countries impose trade barriers to protect domestic industries and to raise money. The most common is the *tariff,* a tax on imported goods. Sometimes

tariffs are so high they effectively prohibit imports. In Mexico the tariff on foreign fabricated auto parts ranges from 60 to 80 percent on the item's value.[9] Some countries also set import *quotas,* a limit on the import value of certain product categories. Until recently the United States set import quotas on Japanese motorcycles to protect domestic manufacturers, principally Harley-Davidson.

Countries can also establish nontariff barriers. One type is *monetary restrictions.* Countries have sometimes blocked foreign currencies to cut off or reduce imports as a means of bringing their balance of payments into line. Some countries also require an exchange permit to export goods. This permits a country to regulate trade through the approval of such permits and to stipulate low or high rates depending on whether it wants to encourage imports or not. Another nontariff barrier is *product standards.* Japan has a variety of product standards that restrict American exports. To sell an American car in Japan one must go through volumes of documents on standards plus local testing of almost every vehicle, adding as much as $500 to the price of the car.[10] In the United States the Food and Drug Administration requires an average of twelve years of testing before a foreign drug product can be licensed.

Easing Trade Barriers

In 1947 the United States and twenty-two other countries signed the General Agreement on Tariffs and Trade (GATT) to reduce tariffs and create a watchdog agency to monitor them. Since 1947 the GATT agreement has reduced tariffs seven times, the most recent being the "Tokyo Round" in 1979. The average tariff today is 8.3 percent in the United States, 9.8 percent in Western Europe, and 10.9 percent in Japan, a marked reduction from pre-World War II levels of 50 to 60 percent.[11] When the Tokyo round of tariff reductions becomes fully effective in 1988, the average tariff will be 4.3 percent in the United States and 2.5 percent in Japan.[12]

Trade barriers have also been reduced through the formation of *economic communities.* The best known is the European Economic Community (better known as the Common Market), formed in 1958. It seeks to eliminate trade barriers between members and to encourage economic union. Other economic communities are the European Free Trade Association (composed of non-Common Market countries), the Latin American Free Trade Association, and the Council for Mutual Economic Assistance (composed of Eastern European countries).

ECONOMIC ENVIRONMENT

International marketers must be aware of the economic environment in foreign markets they are considering for entry. Several economic considerations may govern the decision to enter a particular country. These include the country's economic development, and the purchasing power of its target segments.

Stage of Economic Development

A country's stage of economic development will determine the potential for a wide variety of goods. Pepsi-Cola and Singer sewing machines do not seem affected by level of economic development in identifying their potential; these products are purchased in the least developed countries and the most advanced. But most other products are affected by economic potential. One author asks whether marketing is relevant in less developed countries, because of their lack of purchasing power. He concludes that international marketing is relevant regardless of economic development as long as it is geared to customer needs.[13] Thus the less-developed countries would not be good markets for automobiles, but they might be excellent markets for motorbikes.

Countries can be categorized as (1) less developed, (2) developing, (3) industrialized, and (4) postindustrialized economies. These classifications vary according to gross national product, literacy rates, the evolution from an agricultural to an industrial economy (as in developing countries), the evolution from industrial to service economies (as in postindustrial economies), and the range and quality of products demanded.

Another consideration in economic development is whether the economy is based on free market exchanges or centralized planning. Most countries have elements of both. The United States is regarded as a free market economy but exerts significant control over utilities, telecommunications, and transportation. The USSR and most other Communist countries are based on centralized planning, but private enterprise exists in the exchange of certain items and in selling black market goods. An international marketer must recognize the latitude that exists in setting prices, distributing, and promoting products. Amoco recognized the degree of centralized planning in China and directed its advertising not to final consumers but to decision makers in ministries that oversee petroleum exploration.

Purchasing Power of Target Segments

Level of economic development indicates the general purchasing power of a country. Marketers must evaluate purchasing power of target segments abroad. These are likely to vary across countries. In the postindustrial countries purchasing power is more homogeneous than in other economies because of a higher standard of living. In less developed countries extreme variations in purchasing power are common. It would not be surprising to see Mercedes or Rolls Royce in Peru or Ghana because of the existence of a small and powerful elite. The largest market for Lamborghinis, an automobile costing more than $50,000, is in Portugal, one of the poorest European countries, because of the existence of a wealthy, status-conscious elite.[14]

COMPETITION

Competition also influences market entry. Any company considering entry into the detergent market may be discouraged by the world dominance of Colgate,

Unilever, and Procter and Gamble. The effectiveness of Japanese competition through higher productivity has depressed the U.S. steel industry. Lower-priced Japanese copiers forced Xerox to slash its prices by 47 percent on certain items in 1982.[15]

These examples illustrate the importance of evaluating competition proactively rather than reactively. In most cases American industry has *reacted* to Japanese competition by seeking protection, cutting prices, and offering more consumer-oriented designs only after Japanese companies made inroads. The American automobile industry's reluctance to make smaller, more economical cars opened the market to Japanese imports. The energy crisis did not initiate the trend to smaller cars; it only accelerated it. By the early 1970s Japanese imports were already established.

CULTURAL ENVIRONMENT

The generally accepted norms and values of a country (that is, its culture) will influence marketers in two ways. First, the culture influences the nature of consumer needs and product usage. Second, culture influences the manner in which business is conducted.

Cultural Influences on Consumer Needs and Usage Patterns

Different customs, language, and symbols in foreign countries will affect consumer needs and product usage.

Customs

Consider the following examples of differences in customs affecting product usage:

- Some African and Middle Eastern countries consider shaving a luxury and have restricted imports of products such as Gillette's Trac II razor or have assessed prohibitive tariffs.[16]
- Women in the Cook Islands and in many Latin American countries are accustomed to stooping over their low stoves.[17] Attempts at introducing modern stoves failed because the women found it uncomfortable to have to stand upright and cook.
- The success of Avon salespersons in the United States could not be transferred to Europe because European women regard at-home calls, even by other housewives, as an intrusion of privacy.[18]

Stridsberg cites several other examples of differences in product usage due to local customs:

- Corn on the cob is an hors d'oeuvre in Britain.
- Germans prefer salad dressing in a tube.
- Vicks Vapo-Rub is used as a mosquito repellent in tropical areas.

- Oatmeal is a dessert in northern Holland, northern Germany, and Scandinavia.[19]

Language
Language has also affected marketing strategies, particularly advertising themes and brand names. For example:

- General Motors' Nova did not sell in Latin America because *no va* in Spanish means "won't move."[20]
- Gillette changed the name of its Trac II razor to G II in many foreign markets when research revealed that *trac* in some Romance languages means "fragile."[21]
- Pepsi-Cola's theme "Catch that Pepsi Spirit" translated into Spanish as "Catch that Pepsi Ghost." As a result, the company came up with a successful *"Diga Si a Pepsi"* (Say Yes to Pepsi) campaign in Spanish markets.[22]

Symbols
Culturally derived symbols and imagery also have a direct effect on marketing strategy. For example:

- Two elephants are a symbol of bad luck in Africa, forcing Carlsberg to add a third elephant to its label for Elephant Beer.[23]
- Amoco Oil used red and purple in ads trying to reach decision makers responsible for petroleum exploration in Chinese ministries because red stands for life and purple for quality in Chinese culture. Several ads also had a moon which is a traditional symbol of good luck.[24]
- Japanese consumers are more likely to focus on nonverbal communications than are Americans. The ability to catch visual symbols and cues appears to be culturally induced. Therefore, Japanese advertising is primarily mood oriented.[25]

Cultural Influences of Doing Business Abroad
A second influence of cultural norms and values is the manner in which business is conducted abroad. Consider the following examples:[26]

- A senior American executive was irked when an Asian businessman suggested changing the date of the American's visit ten days before the event. The American thought he was receiving shabby treatment. In fact, the Asian executive considered the meeting so important that he had consulted with a religious advisor who urged a more auspicious date for the talks. Anyone familiar with the local scene would have grasped the significance of the change, which the Asian meant as a compliment.

■ American executives negotiating a contract in the Middle East found that there was no time to have their revised negotiating proposal typed, and submitted a handwritten version, thinking nothing of it. But the Arabs across the bargaining table considered the gesture so bizarre that they began to analyze it intensely, seeking messages. Some concluded the Americans were trying to imply that they considered the whole contract unimportant.

■ A common frustration many Americans feel overseas involves dealing with strikingly different concepts of time. In many Third World countries especially, anywhere from 50 to 80 percent of the time spent talking with businesspeople will be spent discussing anything but business. Although the American often views this personal chitchat as a waste of time, it can be crucial to business.

POLITICAL ENVIRONMENT

Political instability and government interference in international trade frequently inhibit market entry and the maintenance of foreign operations. American companies have lost sizable holdings in Iran, Libya, Cuba, and Chile because of revolutions. Holiday Inn has lost millions of dollars in Lebanon because of its civil war. Oil companies have lost substantial facilities because of the Iran-Iraq War. International companies have also been expropriated by host countries; for example, in 1969 Standard Oil was expropriated by Peru. According to one estimate 12 percent of all foreign investment in 1967 was nationalized by 1976.[27]

Wars, revolutions, and nationalization may be unforeseen events. But companies should be able to assess the potential for events such as these in foreign countries. The recent experience in Iran and the growing potential for political instability has caused some companies to undertake formal political risk assessments. The purpose is to identify high-risk countries and either avoid investment or prepare for future contingencies should a company have holdings in these countries.

Political interference may be more subtle than outright expropriation. In 1977 the Indian government ordered Coca-Cola to disclose its closely guarded formula or to cease operations in India. The company decided to leave India.[28]

On the positive side, some countries are attempting to encourage foreign investment. The Sudan encourages investments in high-priority industry by exempting foreign investors from corporate taxes for five years.[29] Colombia provides similar tax breaks to foreign investors.

International Marketing Planning and Strategies

To succeed in foreign markets, multinational companies must develop a marketing plan that can identify and exploit global marketing opportunities. The international marketing planning process is illustrated in Figure 21-1. It is similar to the marketing planning process described in Chapter 4 (Figure 4-4), with development of objectives, identification of marketing opportunities, establishment of market strategies to exploit opportunities, and evaluation and control of international marketing plans. Figure 21-1 shows that international marketing plans are developed (1) at the corporate level across products and countries (multinational strategic planning), and (2) at a local level for a product in a specific country (product marketing strategies.)

The first step in international marketing planning is establishing marketing objectives. The key question for the firm considering international operations is whether to begin selling in foreign markets. For current international marketers the requirement is to establish profitability and sales goals on a market-by-market basis.

The second step requires identifying marketing opportunities using an analysis of environmental conditions and market demand. The firm might decide to enter new markets or expand its base in existing markets. Third, on the basis of opportunity assessment, the firm develops a multinational growth strategy that guides corporate efforts in adding new markets, expanding investment in existing markets, harvesting low-growth markets, or eliminating operation in unprofitable markets.

Until now, the firm has analyzed marketing strategies on a multinational basis. In the fourth step, the firm begins to evaluate operations on a market-specific basis. The first consideration is how to go about entering new markets — by exporting products, licensing, using joint ventures, or establishing manufacturing and marketing operations abroad. The next requirement (the fifth step in Figure 21-1) is to establish strategies for products. The firm will identify market segments for particular products in specific markets and develop positioning strategies to meet the needs of these segments. Further, it will establish advertising strategies, select distribution channels, and determine price levels.

The final step is to evaluate performance both within specific markets and across markets to determine if sales and profitability goals have been reached, and if longer-term growth objectives are being achieved. In the rest of this chapter we will consider each of the six planning steps in Figure 21-1 in more detail.

Developing International Marketing Objectives

The first step in international marketing planning should be to develop marketing objectives to guide entry into foreign markets and strategies to be used in these markets. Objectives should be of two types: (1) those dealing with market entry and (2) those designed to evaluate performance in international markets. Market entry refers to the entry of a particular product or product line in a specific country (e.g., Campbell Soup's entry into Brazil with condensed soups.)

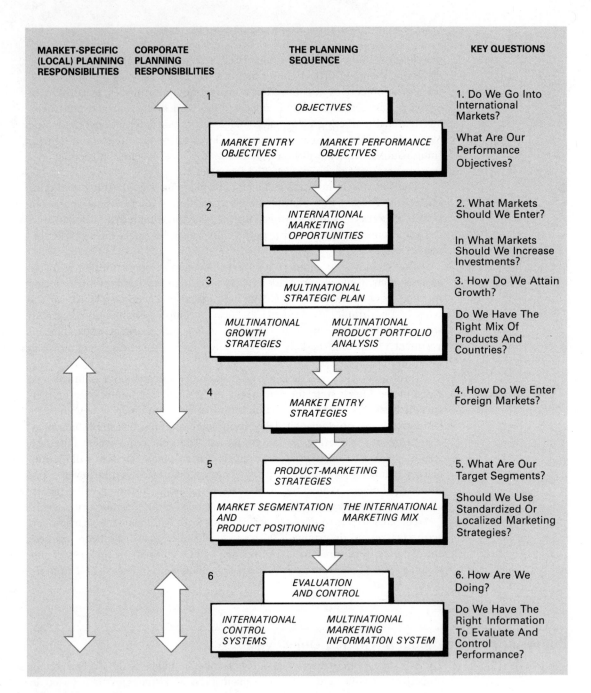

FIGURE 21-1
International marketing planning process

Therefore, by market we mean the market for a particular product in a given country.

MARKET ENTRY OBJECTIVES

The first consideration in establishing market entry objectives is the degree of commitment to foreign operations. The firm that views foreign operations as an integral element of its overall growth plan will establish a very different set of objectives than the firm that considers foreign operations as a mere extension of its domestic goals. One study identified firms that are committed to developing worldwide marketing strategies as *geocentric* (the truly multi-national firm), and firms that view foreign operations as an export of domestic strategies as *ethnocentric*.[30]

Geocentric Objectives

For the **geocentric firm** the primary objective in determining whether to enter a foreign market should be to identify unmet consumer needs and to meet them. But as we indicated, allocating resources to foreign operations is complicated by trade barriers, political regulations, and differences in customs and business practices. The multinational firm must take environmental constraints into account in evaluating foreign opportunities. Objectives to establish market entry should be based on:

- minimum market size,
- market growth potential,
- acceptable tariff levels,
- acceptable price controls,
- attainable product standards,
- political stability.

Management should rate countries on such criteria and determine whether market entry would meet international objectives. A poor rating on any criterion could mean a decision against entry, even if an opportunity exists to meet a defined set of consumer needs.

Ethnocentric Objectives

The **ethnocentric firm** could base its decision for market entry more on domestic than foreign market conditions; it might want to use, for example, excess capacity to drive down unit costs. The following international marketing objectives are motivated primarily by domestic operational considerations:[31]

- *Flee recessions.* During the deep recession in the early 1980s, several international firms increased their efforts in areas with greater economic growth.

■ *Counter demographic trends.* The decrease in the birth rate in the United States caused Gerber baby foods to establish operations in Costa Rica where the birth rate was increasing.

■ *Escape domestic competition.* Squirt, a low-share soft drink brand facing intense competition in the United States, is a leading brand in the less-competitive Central American market.

■ *Lower unit costs.* This objective is particularly important for capital-intensive industries such as steel and autos. Japanese steelmakers rely on their domestic market for only 40 percent of production. Exports allow them to increase production and lower costs. Exports have also helped Japanese steelmakers move along the experience curve, thus increasing their productivity more than American steelmakers.

■ *Revitalize the product life cycle.* When American moviemakers find that domestic sales are declining, they sometimes export films to foreign countries.

■ *Dispose of excess inventories.* Some firms seek to dispose of inventories overseas by **dumping** the products at lower prices. Many countries have antidumping laws that preclude such actions, however.

MARKET PERFORMANCE OBJECTIVES

Performance objectives for each foreign market should be based on the same criteria as in domestic operations, namely:

■ return on investment,

■ contribution to profits,

■ market share,

■ cash flow,

■ sales, and

■ marketing costs.

If the multinational firm subscribes to concepts of strategic planning, it will realize that these criteria do not have to be the same for each country. A product in one country might be a cash cow with a high market share and cash flow used to support the same product in another country that might be a problem child the firm is building up. The market share objective for a firm's product in the first country might be 20 percent but only 5 percent for the same product in the second country. Similarly, ROI goals will differ by product in each country depending on the particular role assigned the product in the multinational's growth plan.

International Marketing Opportunity Analysis

The assessment of international marketing opportunities should be undertaken for specific products on a country-by-country basis. Opportunity should be evaluated on a formal basis by listing key evaluative variables and weighting them by importance. This is done in Table 21-1. Two types of variables are

TABLE 21-1
International Marketing Opportunity Analysis

MARKET VARIABLE	PRODUCT-COUNTRY VALUE	IMPORTANCE WEIGHT	ENVIRONMENTAL VARIABLE	PRODUCT-COUNTRY VALUE	IMPORTANCE WEIGHT
Market Size		8	Barriers to Entry		8
$100 million or more	10		None	10	
$75–99 million	9		*Low	8	
$60–74 million	8		Medium	6	
*$40–59 million	6		High	1	
.	.		Price Controls		6
.	.		*None	10	
$5 million or less	1		Acceptable	8	
Market Growth		10	Moderate	4	
10%/annum or more	10		Unacceptable	1	
* 9%/annum	9		Product Standards		6
8%/annum	8		None	10	
.	.		*Acceptable	8	
.	.		Moderate	4	
.	.		Unacceptable	1	
1% or less	1		Political Stability		4
Level of Competition		9	Stable	10	
None	10		Moderate	6	
*Low	8		*Unstable	1	
Moderate	6				
High	4		Social Attitude Toward		
Intense	1		Foreign Business		5
Cyclicality		5	Excellent	10	
Low	10		Good	8	
*Medium	7		*Fair	6	
High	1		Poor	1	
Norms and Values of		8	Inflation		7
Target Segment			Under 7%	10	
Converge	10		8–15%	8	
Neutral	6		16–40%	4	
*Diverge	1		*Over 40%	1	

*Indicates hypothetical rating for Gerber's baby foods in Central America. Total Market Opportunity Rating = 466. Assume average for other international investment opportunities is 350. Gerber's entry into Central America would then be evaluated positively.

listed, market and environmental. An importance weight is assigned to each variable on the basis of managerial judgment. The firm in this example places greatest value on market growth, minimal competition, market size, and the likelihood the target segment's values and norms conform to the prospective positioning of the product. Notice that the firm considers market variables significantly more important than environmental variables. This could be a mistake where the political and economic climates are uncertain.

Regarding environmental variables, the greatest emphasis is given to trade and political factors that facilitate market entry (lack of tariff barriers, quotas, and so forth). Price controls and product standards are singled out but are given less weight. The firm gives political stability little weight.

Outcomes for each variable are listed in Table 21-1 with a value for each. The most desirable outcome is valued at 10 and the least desirable at 1. A multinational firm is likely to consider more variables and outcomes than those listed in Table 21-1, but the procedure is the same. An overall opportunity score for a product in a country can be computed by multiplying the importance weight by the value of the outcome for each variable and summing the results across variables. Such a score would then be compared to scores for alternative foreign investment opportunities.

Assume Gerber used Table 21-1 to evaluate the opportunity to introduce its baby food line into Central America. Market growth is rapid because of the birth rate, the level of competition is low, and market size is moderate. Trade barriers, price controls, and product standards are low or nonexistent. However, the firm finds that mothers may resist using prepared baby foods (norms and values of target segment) and rates political stability and inflation as negative. The potential resistance to prepared baby foods is sufficiently important to result in a no-go decision. But the overall product-country rating is higher than those of alternative foreign investment opportunities Gerber might have been considering (e.g., baby foods in Africa, frozen foods in Europe). The higher market potential (based on the birth rate) convinces management to enter the market and attempt to overcome cultural resistance through marketing strategies. It considers several strategies — for example, introducing a partially prepared food and allowing mothers to be involved in the preparation; or introducing the prepared line and mounting an educational campaign.

The opportunity analysis in Table 21-1 is very similar to the evaluation of investment attractiveness in the GE portfolio approach (see Table 19-1). There are several limitations to this approach, however. First, it relies on the judgment of managers who may not be fully aware of local conditions. Second, the data required for reliable estimates of market size, growth potential, and competition are sometimes difficult to obtain. Third, the decision to enter a market is not always made on the basis of an overall opportunity score. Management might decide against entry because of one negative factor, despite the existence of several positive ones, if that negative factor is sufficiently compelling (e.g., adverse cultural norms).

The Multinational Strategic Plan

In the multinational firm marketing opportunity analysis should become the primary input into the multinational strategic plan (step 3 in Figure 21-1). The firm can assess a broad range of foreign investment opportunities by analyzing several markets (both new and existing) and array them by investment attractiveness. Thus Gerber might have evaluated baby foods in Africa, the Middle East, and India, as well as in Central America; frozen foods in Europe; and soft foods directed to the geriatric market in the United States. An evaluation of alternative foreign investment opportunities based on the analysis in Table 21-1 will allow management to allocate the multinational firm's resources to opportunity.

The two components of the multinational strategic plan in Figure 21-1 are the same as those described in Chapters 18 and 19 — a multinational growth strategy and a multinational portfolio analysis. The multinational growth strategy develops an overall course of action to exploit opportunities in foreign markets. Multinational portfolio analysis tries to ensure that the company is in the right mix of foreign markets with the right mix of products.

MULTINATIONAL GROWTH STRATEGIES

In Chapter 18 we categorized corporate growth strategies according to whether the firm was relying for growth on existing or new products in existing or new markets. The result was four general approaches to growth. The same framework can be used in examining multinational growth alternatives except that (1) instead of markets we can refer to countries and (2) instead of existing or new products, we can refer to a narrow versus broad international product mix. The resulting matrix in Figure 21-2 presents four general growth strategies for multinational companies:

1. *Market concentration* (a narrow product mix directed to a few countries),

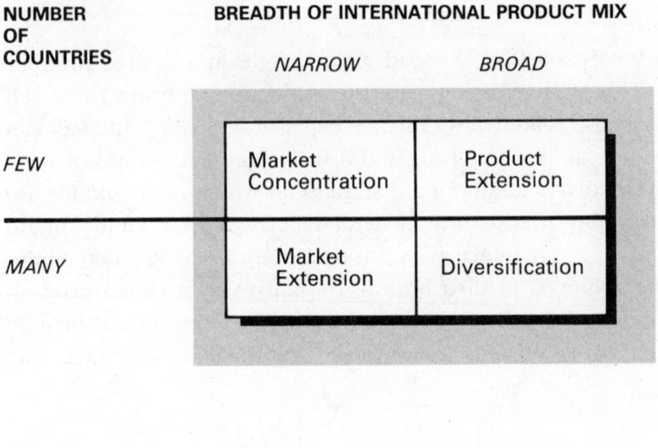

NUMBER OF COUNTRIES	BREADTH OF INTERNATIONAL PRODUCT MIX	
	NARROW	*BROAD*
FEW	Market Concentration	Product Extension
MANY	Market Extension	Diversification

FIGURE 21-2
International growth strategies

2. *Market extension* (a narrow product mix directed to many countries),

3. *Product extension* (a broad product mix directed to a few countries), and

4. *Diversification* (a broad product mix directed to many countries).

Market Concentration

Many companies direct single products to one or a few markets. General Foods sells chewing gum in France, ice cream in Brazil, and pasta in Italy.[32] None of these businesses is large enough to justify sales on a global basis. Therefore, market concentration is a logical strategy if a product can be sold profitably to a limited market.

Another motive for pursuing a strategy of market concentration is the belief that the product appeals to a fairly homogeneous group in a few countries. Playtex is marketing its haircare line in highly industrialized countries where women's haircare needs are relatively homogeneous. The company may feel that extending the line to other markets is too risky.

Market Extension

A strategy of market extension is suitable for firms with a unique product line that can appeal to the needs of different customers in many countries. Such a strategy requires a company to be at a competitive advantage in order to permit it to sell a narrow product line on a global basis. Pepsi-Cola, Coca-Cola, and Singer sewing machines are examples. These companies seek to create a competitive advantage so their product line will be regarded as superior on a worldwide basis. Honda has successfully pursued a strategy of market extension by developing an inexpensive, reliable, and easy-to-use motorcycle. Before Honda established a mass market, motorcycles were regarded as big, expensive machines targeted to a small segment. The combination of a good inexpensive product, a worldwide message, and a superior distributor network permitted Honda to outflank its major competitors, Yamaha and Kawasaki, and rapidly expand into foreign markets.[33]

Product Extension

Product extension involves selling a broad product mix in a limited number of foreign markets. This strategy is logical if the multinational firm (1) is well entrenched in these markets and views further expansion as risky, and (2) can achieve economies of scale in advertising and distribution. Economies of scale in advertising might involve a family brand strategy in which many brands are advertised under the corporate name. General Electric uses a family brand advertising strategy in the international as well as the American market. Economies of scale can also be achieved in distribution. By marketing a broad product mix in a few countries, a company can distribute many of its products through the same intermediaries, achieving economies in transportation, storage, and direct sales.

Diversification

Diversification is an aggressive international growth strategy that involves expansion of both the product mix and foreign markets. Such a strategy can be employed by firms with sufficient resources to accomplish fast entry into many markets on a multiproduct basis. The strategy also requires a broad enough product mix to appeal to many segments in different markets.

A company that is currently pursuing a diversification strategy is S. C. Johnson. The company markets a broad range of household and personal care products in foreign markets. It currently sells in forty-four countries and is expanding its foreign operations at the rate of two countries a year. It derives 60 percent of its $1.8 billion in sales from foreign markets, and by the year 2000 projects 80 percent of its sales will come from abroad.[34]

MULTINATIONAL PRODUCT PORTFOLIO ANALYSIS

The second requirement in multinational strategic planning is developing a product-by-country portfolio. The purpose is to position products in foreign markets by (1) the opportunity for profits and (2) the firm's ability to exploit opportunity. Positioning products/countries on a product portfolio then allows the firm to determine whether products should be candidates for further growth, for selective investment, or for harvesting and eventual divestment. The portfolio will also help management determine the potential sources for investment on the basis of projected cash flows.[35] Thus, the strength in the United States of products such as Maxwell House may be a source of cash for entry of the brand into additional markets. In short, the objectives of product portfolio analysis are the same as those cited in Chapter 19, except that products in the international portfolio are positioned by country or region.

Because of the range of environmental and market factors required to evaluate products in foreign markets, the GE/McKinsey approach should be the basis for multinational portfolio analysis. This approach utilizes a broad range of variables to analyze both market opportunities and the firm's ability to exploit them (the firm's business position).

The Multinational Portfolio

A hypothetical multinational portfolio for Gillette is illustrated in Figure 21-3 using the GE/McKinsey approach. Four product lines are represented in various areas of the world by their market attractiveness (opportunity) and business position (the firm's ability to exploit opportunity). The determination of market opportunity was illustrated in Table 21-1. Each product-country is positioned on the vertical axis by an analysis of the market potential and environmental conditions that is based on variables such as those in Table 21-1. Products in each region should also be positioned by the firm's business position in that particular market. The horizontal axis shows whether the firm has the physical and financial resources and the know-how to exploit opportunity.

Business position can be evaluated in the same manner as marketing opportunity. Management defines several variables that indicate the firm's resources

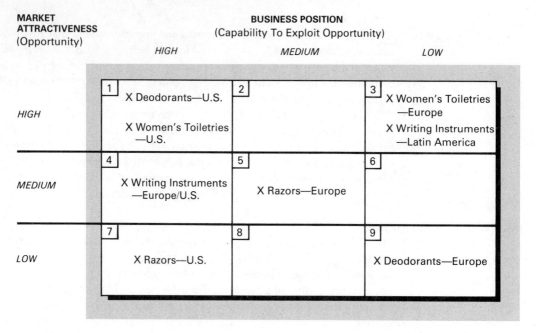

MARKET ATTRACTIVENESS (Opportunity)	BUSINESS POSITION (Capability To Exploit Opportunity)		
	HIGH	MEDIUM	LOW
HIGH	**1** X Deodorants—U.S. X Women's Toiletries —U.S.	**2**	**3** X Women's Toiletries —Europe X Writing Instruments —Latin America
MEDIUM	**4** X Writing Instruments —Europe/U.S.	**5** X Razors—Europe	**6**
LOW	**7** X Razors—U.S.	**8**	**9** X Deodorants—Europe

FIGURE 21-3
Hypothetical multinational product portfolio matrix for Gillette

and the product's position relative to competition. An example is in Table 21-2. Assume Gillette follows the successful introduction of its women's line of toiletries in the United States with an attempt to market them in Europe. After two years it assesses its current business position, using the variables in Table 21-2. The table lists two types of variables, those dealing with the product's market position and those dealing with the firm's resources. Market position is represented by market share, sales, share of the leading competitor, and ROI. Company resources are measured by the strength of the distribution system, local market support (local personnel, use of local ad agency), plant capacity, and current capital requirements.

Because of differences in customs and use of cosmetics in Europe, Gillette's line does not take off as it did in the United States. Further, the company has not yet established strong local representation. As a result, the line receives a low overall rating in business position (right-hand side of the matrix in Figure 21-3). But an analysis of marketing opportunity based on variables such as those in Table 21-1 shows strong potential for women's cosmetics and toiletries in Europe. As a result, the product is in the upper right-hand part of the matrix in Figure 21-3.

Investment Strategies
Once the products have been positioned by country or region, the firm can determine whether various countries warrant investment for growth (boxes

TABLE 21-2
International Marketing Business Position Analysis

MARKET POSITION VARIABLES	PRODUCT-COUNTRY VALUE	IMPORTANCE WEIGHT	COMPANY RESOURCE VARIABLES	PRODUCT-COUNTRY VALUE	IMPORTANCE WEIGHT
Market Share		10	*Channels of Distribution*		8
20% or more	10		Strongest		
15–19%	8		channels in		
10–15%	6		country	10	
.	.		Equal to		
.	.		leading		
*2–4%	2		competitor	8	
1% or less	1		.	.	
Sales		10	.	.	
$75 million or more	10		*Weak Support	2	
$50–74 million	8		No Support	1	
$30–49 million	6		*Local Marketing Support*		8
.	.		Best in	10	
.	.		country		
*$6–10 million	3		Equal to		
$5 million or less	1		leading		
Return on Investment		10	competitor	8	
25% or more	10		.	.	
20–24%	8				
.	.		*Weak Support	2	
.	.		No Support	1	
.	.		*Plant Capacity*		4
*10% or less	1		Excellent	10	
Market Share of		6	*Good	8	
Leading Competitor			Fair	5	
2% or less	10		Poor	2	
3–5%	8		None	1	
6–9%	5		*Capital Requirements*		6
.	.		None	10	
.	.		*Low	8	
.	.		Medium	5	
*20% or more	1		High	1	

*Indicates hypothetical rating for Gillette's deodorant line in Europe. Total Business Position score = 178. Assume average business position scores for other Gillette lines in foreign markets is 350. Therefore, Gillette is rated in poor business position for deodorant line in Europe.

1, 2, and 4 in Figure 21-3), investment to maintain current position (boxes 5 and 7), or a reduction in effort through harvesting and possible divestment (boxes 6, 8, and 9). Box 3 presents a problem, because the firm is not sure whether to move toward divestment because of the poor business position, or to invest for growth because of the opportunity.

In the hypothetical example in Figure 21-3, Gillette could invest in the women's toiletry line by transferring cash from some of its stronger products (razors in the United States). But the weak distribution channels and lack of any strong local support would make this a risky decision. One possibility would be to consider a joint venture with a European firm that has a strong distribution network and strong marketing support. Such a joint venture would provide local facilities. It would also provide local know-how permitting a positioning of the toiletry line to take into account differences in customs and usage.

Market Entry Strategies

Once the multinational firm has evaluated marketing opportunities and alternative foreign investments, it is likely to decide to enter markets of opportunity. A key question is how? Should the company export the product from its domestic base, should it license the manufacturing process to foreign operators, should it enter a joint venture, or should it establish full-fledged operations abroad?

These four options represent different approaches based on the investment required and the control the firm can exert over its international marketing operations (see Figure 21-4). Indirect exporting through a domestic intermediary requires the least investment and provides the least control. Direct ownership requires the greatest investment and provides the most control. The truly multinational (geocentric) firm is likely to be involved in either joint ventures or direct ownership. Firms that view international marketing as an extension of domestic marketing (ethnocentric firms) are more likely to engage in exporting or licensing.

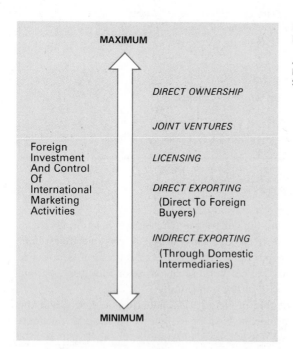

FIGURE 21-4
Market entry strategies

Source: Adapted from Thomas C. Kinnear and Kenneth L. Bernhardt, *Principles of Marketing.* Copyright © 1983 by Scott, Foresman and Company. Reprinted by permission.

EXPORTING

A firm that exports its products does not have to invest in manufacturing facilities abroad. For this reason exporting is a frequently used method of marketing abroad. In 1981, American companies exported $240 billion to foreign countries.[36]

Firms can export indirectly through domestic intermediaries who then sell abroad, or they can export directly by selling to foreign intermediaries. Hershey uses exporting rather than licensing or direct ownership because it realizes that foreign sales will never represent a large part of its $1 billion in annual sales. The company established an international department in 1977 to export directly. In some markets (e.g., Japan) Hershey has granted exclusive distribution rights and sells directly to its exclusive distributors. This gives them more control over the way the product is marketed abroad.

LICENSING

Licensing is a way to shift the risks of production and marketing on to a licensee yet gain the benefits of entry into foreign markets. Weight Watchers International has entered into agreements with thirteen companies to offer licenses for a series of health products. The purpose, as explained by the company's marketing manager, is to "hook up with first-rate, nationally-minded companies that can guarantee quality in their products and appeal to the population at large."[37]

But licensing has its risks. One is that the licensor can lose control. For example, Pepsi-Cola licenses production to government-owned companies in Egypt. There have been complaints that the Egyptian version of Pepsi lacks the flavor of the domestic product.[38] In addition, if the licensee is very successful, it may cancel the license and become a competitor.

JOINT VENTURES

A firm that does not have the required expertise or the financial resources to exploit an opportunity abroad might consider entering into a joint venture with a foreign company. Both companies would invest in the venture and share ownership. In some cases a foreign government might require joint ownership as a means of ensuring local participation in foreign investments.

Two large Japanese computer manufacturers entered into joint ventures with American firms to gain distribution and software skills in the face of IBM's superior position. Fujitsu entered into a joint venture with TRW, and Hitachi with National Semiconductor. Both companies lacked sufficient resources to develop the required distribution and software capabilities in the United States, partly because IBM was so successful in competing with them in Japan. Fujitsu "was eager to expand abroad to increase its economies of scale for the fight with IBM back home."[39]

Mitsubishi had a different set of motives in considering a joint venture to manufacture a car with Chrysler. Such a venture could have avoided import restrictions, reduced shipping costs, and paved the way for Mitsubishi to acquire equity in Chrysler.[40]

DIRECT OWNERSHIP

Direct investment in manufacturing facilities represents the greatest commitment to, and control over, foreign operations. Direct ownership provides the firm with several advantages. First, it is generally cheaper to produce abroad than in the United States. Second, stronger relationships with foreign wholesalers, retailers, and suppliers can be established. Third, the firm avoids trade barriers against American-made goods. Fourth, the firm can follow a more proactive marketing strategy since it retains direct control over product quality, pricing, distribution and advertising. The multinational firm with a growth strategy is more likely to enter foreign markets through direct ownership. This is one reason why in 1982 total American investments abroad were over $200 billion.[41]

Deere and Company, a producer of agricultural equipment, has followed a policy of direct ownership of manufacturing facilities. It owns factories in five countries outside the United States and a share in manufacturing facilities in two others. In addition, it maintains wholly-owned sales branches in thirteen countries.[42]

Product-Marketing Strategies

Having entered into a foreign market, the international marketer must develop specific marketing strategies for each product. The principles in developing marketing strategies for products abroad are generally the same as those we outlined in Part III. In this section we will focus on the one major issue that distinguishes marketing strategy in international versus domestic operations, namely whether strategy should be developed country-by-country (a localized approach) or across countries (a standardized approach).

STANDARDIZED VERSUS LOCALIZED STRATEGIES

The differences in characteristics between countries strongly suggest that marketing strategies must be localized to meet differing customs and political and economic conditions. But the economic rationale for **standardizing marketing strategies** across countries is compelling because of economies of scale. Standardization and localization are not dichotomies. Companies rarely develop the same advertising for each country and distribute the product through the same channels at the same price. They equally rarely shun standardization completely. The strategic question is Where on the continuum from standardization to localization should marketing strategy be placed? To answer this question the international marketer should have an appreciation of the benefits of standardization and localization.

Standardized Marketing Strategies

Companies like Pepsi-Cola, Coca-Cola, Singer, Ford, and Goodyear have followed a fairly standardized marketing approach because they believe their products have universal appeal. Such standardized strategies lower unit marketing costs, permitting a company to reduce prices while maintaining quality and reliability. The Japanese have followed this strategy very effectively and have largely ignored differences in national customs, tastes, and preferences.[43] Another advantage of a standardized marketing strategy is improved control over local marketing operations. Strategies developed locally might not follow a company's global game plan.

However, the marketer using a standardized approach gives up the flexibility to adjust strategy country by country. The constraints of a global strategy would prevent localized adjustments such as changing distribution strategies or targeting a product to new segments. Expansion through standardization is more likely to occur by introducing a new product or strategy in all the company's foreign markets.

Localized Marketing Strategies

A company can run into danger when following a standardized strategy if it is not aware of local customs and practices. Many advertisers are wary of standardized advertising strategies because they are developed in the home market. One advertising executive says, "The single most common misconception of new U.S. international marketers is that creative strategy can be exported. It seldom can, and the more complex it is, the less likely it will travel well."[44] Localization is necessary if there are substantial differences in taste and use between countries. For example, Nestlé recognizes the need to adapt Nescafé to local needs. The product is blended differently in every country it is sold in.[45]

Patterned Standardization

Few multinational companies leave the development of marketing strategies entirely in the hands of their foreign operations. The trend in international marketing has been to move toward a compromise between standardization and localization that has become known as **patterned standardization.** This compromise requires the company to establish an overall marketing strategy but to leave implementation to executives in local markets who are aware of national traits and customs. Headquarters develops the product's overall positioning but not the detail. Foreign operations are responsible for creative execution of the positioning in advertisements, media planning, publicity, and sales promotion. In other words, strategy is developed at the corporate level whereas tactics are developed at the local level.

Schweppes has rejected a standardized approach for its tonic, because uniformity in packaging and label designs would not work. But it has also rejected localization, because the company finds it must maintain a consistent image across national boundaries. Its solution is to follow a strategy of patterned standardization by selecting a common positioning around which local operations could build in fifty-four countries. The marketing director of Schweppes International says, "Once the local people start adding their own creative input to the central core, they become the most committed and enthusiastic of converts."[46]

The remainder of this section considers two basic areas of product-marketing strategies identified in Figure 21-1: (1) market segmentation and product positioning, and (2) the international marketing mix. These areas are considered based on whether strategies should be localized or standardized.

MARKET SEGMENTATION AND PRODUCT POSITIONING

The international marketer must identify a target segment for products introduced into foreign markets. The strategic alternatives are the same as those outlined in Chapter 8 — whether to market a single product or a product line to one or several segments. In international marketing an additional consideration is whether the marketer should identify a segment for a product within a given country, or identify target segments across countries. This question extends the issue of standardization versus localization to market segmentation. If segments are country-specific, a localized marketing strategy must follow, since the segments are based on different sets of needs. If common segments are identified in several countries (e.g., a teenage segment for jeans) a standardized marketing strategy, or at least a strategy of patterned standardization, may be used.

Common segments across countries must share demographic or life style characteristics. Douglas and Dubois present the case for such cross-national segmentation:

> Within different countries, similar sub-culture groups — businessmen, senior citizens, teenagers, working wives — may possess similar consumption patterns because of shared problems and outlooks. In this case, management may prefer to segment to sub-groups across national boundaries. For example, members of the teen cult throughout the world may provide an appropriate target for Coke, college teeshirts and blue jeans, pop records, fan magazines and motorcycle accessories.[47]

The greater mobility of consumers in industrialized nations makes the likelihood of "shared problems and outlooks" greater, increasing the likelihood of cross-national segments.

Several companies have successfully followed a cross-national segmentation strategy. Omega identified an international business elite as its target segment for its quartz digital watches. It then developed two positionings on a worldwide basis: a rational appeal that focused on the mechanism of the watch and an emotional appeal that emphasized the finish and beauty.[48]

Identifying common segments across countries does not always result in a common product positioning, however. Renault was unable to use the same positioning strategy throughout Europe for its Renault 5. For the French market it used a "fun" image based on a little Supercar (see Figure 21-5). In other countries the purchase of a car was perceived more seriously. Therefore, in

Positioning of the Renault 5 in France

Positioning of the Renault 5 in Italy

FIGURE 21-5
Different positionings for the same product category

Source: Susan Douglas and Bernard Dubois, "Looking at the Cultural Environment for International Marketing Opportunities, *Columbia Journal of World Business*, pp. 106, 107. Courtesy Renault USA, Inc.

Germany the campaign focused on modern engineering, in Finland on construction and reliability, in Italy on road performance, in Holland on quality.[49]

THE INTERNATIONAL MARKETING MIX

International marketers must develop an integrated set of product, promotional, distribution, and pricing strategies in foreign markets. Again, the major question is whether these strategies should be standardized across markets or localized. A common strategy does not have to be followed for a particular product. A product's characteristics can be standardized across markets, but different promotional strategies might be used for each market. The Renault 5 was the same car, but it was sold differently in various European markets. Similarly, a company can have a standardized distribution strategy but vary product characteristics and advertising to suit local needs.

One study of senior executives in twenty-seven multinational companies found that standardization was greatest for products.[50] Brand names, physical characteristics, and packaging tend to be standardized across countries because of significant savings in manufacturing costs and simplified trademark protection. Also, the increasing mobility in industrialized areas means that a consumer going from one country to another will recognize the same product. Distribution was also fairly standardized. Where possible, companies use similar channels in each market and sometimes use intermediaries cross-nationally. Such standardization saves in transportation and selling costs.

The study found significantly less standardization in advertising and pricing. The basic advertising message was frequently established by the home office but with significant local variation. Pricing was also fairly localized because, as one executive said, "Manufacturing costs, competitors' price, and taxes all vary from country to country."[51] The least standardized decision was on media allocations because of significant differences in the availability of advertising media from country to country. Let us look at international marketing strategies for each of these components of the marketing mix.

Product Strategy

As we noted, most companies tend to lean more toward standardizing products than toward adapting them to local conditions. But there are dangers in product standardization if the company is exporting a "home-grown" product on the assumption that success in the domestic market will mean success abroad. For example, after a successful introduction of the Swinger instant camera in the United States, Polaroid introduced it into the French market. But the French were not ready for instant photography. Only 5 percent of the French market was familiar with instant photography compared to 85 percent in the United States.[52] Similarly, Kellogg's assumption that it could export Pop Tarts into Europe, Campbell Soup's assumption that it could sell its condensed soups in Brazil, and Gerber's assumption that it could export baby foods into Brazil, all spelled failure because of the mistaken notion that success in the United States could be exported.

Product adaptation

Cultural differences and differences in patterns of use sometimes require adapting products to local needs. Procter and Gamble makes several versions of Ariel (a top-selling concentrated powder detergent), depending on local conditions. The American version is designed for lower water temperatures, greater sudsing, and faster performance. In Germany the washload is soaked longer and at higher temperatures, so Ariel matches these conditions.[53] Corn Products International varies a product as mundane as bouillon cubes to suit local tastes. It is sold in chicken and beef flavors in the United States and

Europe. But in Mexico, tomato and shrimp flavors are added, in Argentina corn flavoring, in Kenya chili, in Ireland mutton, and in Thailand pork.[54] P&G and Corn Products recognize the advantages of product standardization. But they also realize that if they are successfully to market products that vary in taste and use, they must change their product formulations.

Patterned product standardization

Recognizing the limits of product standardization and the greater costs of product adaptation has led some companies to use a patterned product standardization. General Motors is designing new "world cars" that have a standardized body and interchangeable parts. Its X-car was designed on this basis; interchangeable parts and various options allow it to adapt the car to local conditions. American Motors is following a similar approach. It builds the basic jeep design in fourteen nations. But the Chairman of AMC notes, "All are tailored to individual national needs."[55]

New Product Development

Most multinational companies are flexible enough to be able to develop new products to meet the needs of foreign markets rather than just exporting successful domestic products. For example, Procter and Gamble, Quaker Oats, Swift, and Monsanto are researching the nutritional needs of consumers in underdeveloped countries and are formulating new food products to meet these needs. Colgate-Palmolive developed an inexpensive manual washing machine with the tumbling action of an automatic washer for use in homes without electricity.[56] But as one writer notes, in few instances have companies developed new products for the needs of specific foreign markets.[57] Usually a product is developed domestically and exported as is or adapted to local needs.

Promotional Strategy

Promotional standardization is not as common as product standardization. But several firms have attempted to establish standardized campaigns because they believe their products can be sold through global appeals. Most companies have either adapted campaigns to local markets or followed a patterned standardization strategy, developing a basic theme and allowing local variations.

Promotional standardization

The argument has frequently been made that good promotional themes have universal appeal. One American advertising executive provided the rationale for a standardized promotional strategy:

> Different peoples are basically the same. ... An international advertising campaign with a truly universal appeal can be effective in any market. ... The desire to be beautiful is universal. Such appeals as "mother and child," "freedom from pain," "glow of health," know no boundaries.[58]

Another reason to use standardized appeals is the proximity of many foreign countries and the consequent overlap in media outreach. For example, German TV broadcasts are received by 40 percent of Dutch homes with TV sets; 4 million French housewives tune in to Radio Luxembourg; and *Paris Match* magazine has a substantial circulation in most Western European countries.[59] If campaigns for a product are differentiated, media overlap could cause confusion in regional markets. The growth of cable and satellite transmissions will also encourage marketers to "address target markets that stretch across a number of countries rather than market on a country-by-country basis."[60]

Promotional adaptation

Promotional standardization creates the same risks as product standardization — the possibility of ignoring significant differences in local consumer needs. This danger led one advertising executive to comment, "You probably sacrifice a lot in effectiveness in the process [of exporting promotional campaigns]. My recommendation is to challenge the local agency to improve on the U.S. campaign."[61]

As a result of these misgivings many multinationals adapt promotional campaigns to local markets. Until 1981 Levi Strauss used an adaptive strategy to sell jeans around the world. Appeals differed as follows:

- In Europe TV commercials had a super-sexy appeal.
- In England ads advertised Levis as an American brand and used a Wild West setting.
- In Japan the brand was positioned as legendary, with the theme "Heroes Wear Levis."
- In Australia commercials touted product benefits such as tight fit with comfort.[62]

Patterned promotional standardization

The costs and fragmentation of adaptation and the dangers of standardization have caused many companies to move to a patterned promotional standardization strategy. In 1981 Levi changed from a localized approach to one in which "the broad outlines of the campaign are given but the details are not."[63] The company's director of advertising says that the home office develops basic building blocks for a campaign by using core values like honesty, credibility, and social responsibility. The implementation around the core is left to local agencies.

Differences in media availability between countries increases the likelihood of patterned standardization. For example, commercial TV time is available for one hour each evening in Germany and is not available at all in Sweden; magazines are a major medium in Italy but a minor one in Austria; newspapers are national in the United Kingdom but local in Spain.[64] A patterned standardization strategy can adapt to differences in media availability between countries.

Distribution

Good distribution facilities are essential if products are to be marketed successfully abroad. One of the reasons for Budweiser's success in Japan is the distribution clout wielded by its distributor, Suntory Ltd. The company has distributed the brand where Japan's affluent well-traveled youth gather.[65]

However, distribution is made difficult by the diversity of foreign intermediaries. For example, in Japan Procter and Gamble distributes soap through a complex chain. It first sells to general wholesalers, who sell to basic product-specialty wholesalers, who sell to specialty wholesalers, who sell to regional wholesalers and local wholesalers, who finally sell to retailers.[66] Although the distributive chain is not as complicated in other countries, the Japanese system illustrates the variety of channel arrangements available to international marketers.

Distribution structure in international marketing

In Figure 21-6 we attempt to simplify the structure of international channels by showing two broad categories of intermediaries — export intermediaries in the home country, and import intermediaries in foreign countries. A company can distribute indirectly by selling to domestic merchants and agents who then sell abroad, or it can develop channels abroad by selling directly to foreign intermediaries. These intermediaries in turn sell to retailers or direct to foreign consumers.

Figure 21-6 lists two types of intermediary both at home and abroad — merchants and agents. Merchants take title to the goods; agents do not. Among domestic merchants the most important intermediary is the **export trading company (ETC).** An export trading company buys a product and assumes all distribution and marketing tasks abroad. Small companies are likely to use ETCs since they cannot afford marketing or distributing abroad.

Export merchants are domestic wholesalers operating in foreign markets. **Complementary marketers** are companies with marketing facilities or contacts abroad who take on other manufacturers' products for distribution. Expanding their product line permits them to reduce transportation and storage costs. General Electric has been distributing merchandise for other suppliers for years.[67] GE's eventual establishment of its own export trading company was a natural outgrowth of these activities.

Domestic export agents include *manufacturers' agents* and *brokers.* They bring domestic sellers and foreign buyers together on a commission basis. **Export management companies (EMCs)** are similar to export trading companies except that they do not take title to goods. They serve as the export department for domestic manufacturers by marketing their products overseas, and they assume marketing and distributive functions on a commission basis.

Foreign intermediaries are also composed of merchants and agents. *Foreign wholesalers* can sell to other wholesalers or to retailers. *Foreign agents* include manufacturers' agents and brokers who operate in the same way as their

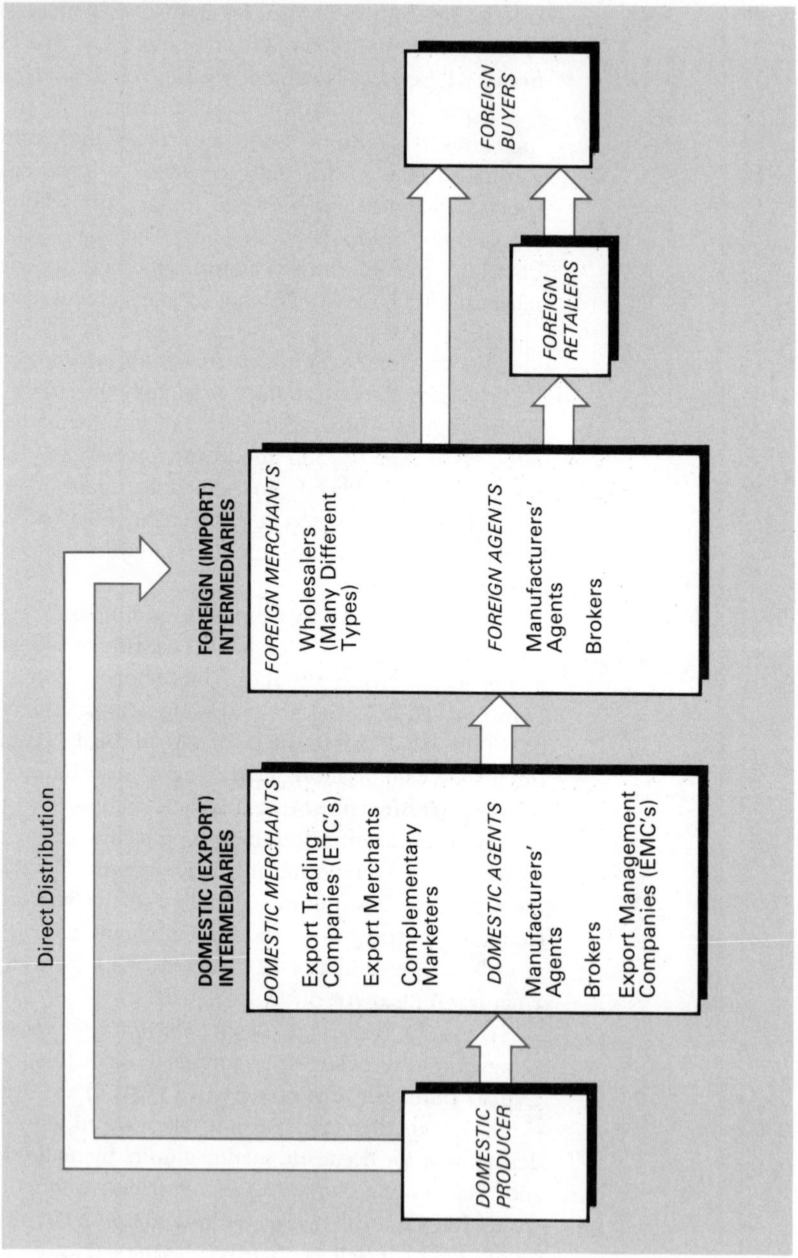

FIGURE 21-6
International distribution channels

Direct Distribution

DOMESTIC (EXPORT) INTERMEDIARIES

DOMESTIC MERCHANTS

Export Trading Companies (ETC's)

Export Merchants

Complementary Marketers

DOMESTIC AGENTS

Manufacturers' Agents

Brokers

Export Management Companies (EMC's)

FOREIGN (IMPORT) INTERMEDIARIES

FOREIGN MERCHANTS

Wholesalers (Many Different Types)

FOREIGN AGENTS

Manufacturers' Agents

Brokers

DOMESTIC PRODUCER

FOREIGN RETAILERS

FOREIGN BUYERS

domestic counterparts, except that they bring domestic seller and foreign buyer together operating from foreign markets.

Characteristics of international distribution

Several factors distinguish the distributive structure in Figure 21-6 from the channel relationships outlined in Chapter 16. First, as we noted, there are more possible channel arrangements. Second, more intermediaries increase the cost of distributing products abroad. The price escalation that results from the required margins of various levels of wholesalers and retailers sometimes increases export prices by three or four times what they would be in the domestic market. Third, poor warehousing and storage facilities abroad also increase the costs of distribution. Fourth, foreign retailers tend to be smaller and less productive. This is yet another factor that drives prices of exports up.

The net effect of all these factors results in an international distribution system that is inefficient by American standards. Multinational companies seeking to improve productivity have begun to establish sales branches abroad to maintain better control over distribution and to keep prices down. Deere and Company has set up sales branches in Latin America with networks of eighty or ninety independent dealers to distribute its agricultural equipment.[68] These branches give the company better control over the way foreign intermediaries handle sales, service the product, and train operators.

Price

Price may or may not be an active ingredient in the international marketing mix, depending on the firm's orientation. The geocentric firm views price as an "active instrument for the accomplishment of marketing objectives."[69] It will use price to try to attain ROI and market share objectives from overseas operations. The ethnocentric firm views price as a vehicle for trying to sell what it can in foreign markets. Since it views international operations as an extension of domestic sales, it is often willing to price at a low level to "dump" excess inventory or to use excess production capacity. The geocentric firm looks with concern to price escalation. It will try to shorten its channels of distribution to hold down costs and stimulate demand in foreign markets. The ethnocentric firm sets the prices of its exports according to conditions in the domestic rather than the international market. As a result it will be more willing to price low to dump its goods.

These differences in pricing objectives lead to differences in price determination. Most international marketers use cost as a starting point in pricing. The two general approaches to cost-plus pricing in international markets are variable-cost and full-cost pricing. Firms that use a variable cost approach are interested in recouping the marginal costs of goods that are to be sold overseas. They are not concerned with the fixed costs of plant or administration. They are domestically oriented and view foreign sales as a bonus, a means of defraying domestic manufacturing costs. As a result these ethnocentric firms will be more likely to use a low price and pay less attention to positioning or communicating product benefits.

Firms that price on a full-cost basis are likely to be multinationals with foreign operations. They do not distinguish between goods slated for domestic or foreign markets. All marketing effort must be profit oriented. They view foreign operations as profit centers rather than as extensions of domestic operations. In pricing they must account for all costs, both fixed and variable. These firms do not always price on a cost-plus basis; they may use the demand-oriented pricing methods described in Chapter 15. They realize that demand for the same product differs in different countries. As a result, prices can vary by elasticity of demand from one country to the next. Prices will be set higher in countries with inelastic demand for a product because demand is more likely to be maintained in the face of higher prices.

Evaluation and Control

The last step in the international marketing planning process in Figure 21-1 is evaluation and control. The multinational firm must track performance in its various markets and determine whether objectives have been met. If not, the firm must consider whether it wants to institute corrective actions to monitor and control foreign operations more closely.

Evaluation and control are more difficult in international marketing for several reasons:

1. *Greater potential instability due to political and economic factors.* A multinational firm may establish objectives and plans only to find them useless because of unforeseen political events or economic factors such as runaway inflation.

2. *Less control over foreign subsidiaries.* Distance, differences in business customs, and an unfamiliar environment make control from the home office more difficult.

3. *Less control over channels of distribution.* It is more difficult to control distribution channels in foreign markets because of the diversity of these channels and the fact that control is frequently attempted at a distance.

4. *Less control over price.* Because of tariffs, trade regulations, and price escalation, the multinational firm frequently finds it must sell at a higher price than anticipated. Also, if it sells the product through foreign merchants or retailers, the multinational firm may find it difficult to stipulate the final sales price.

5. *Inadequacy of data.* International marketing data are frequently incom-

plete and unreliable. Market statistics are not comparative, making cross-national evaluation difficult.

The control system adopted by a multinational firm is likely to depend on the marketing strategy. Companies following a standardized marketing strategy are interested in comparing performance between countries. As a result, they are likely to review performance and initiate controls at the end of the operating period. Firms using product or promotional adaptation will institute an adaptive control system that gives their foreign subsidiaries much more latitude in developing strategies and in deviating from plans during the operating period. These firms must be able to change their promotional budgets and allocations across countries during the operating period to take account of unforeseen contingencies. Failure to adapt to a quickly moving international environment could put them at a serious competitive disadvantage.

Regardless of the emphasis on control, a key requirement in evaluating performance is the establishment of a *multinational marketing information system.* Such a system is essentially the same as the marketing information system described in Chapter 7, except that it covers more than one country. The multinational marketing information system is made up of several subsystems, each representing a foreign market. The multinational company will collect information on sales, track costs, and conduct marketing research cross-nationally. A key consideration here is the comparability of data the firm is collecting. Management will try to ensure that estimates of market potential and sales forecasts based on the information system are comparable and valid. A second difference between a multinational and a domestic information system is that the former will place more emphasis on the environmental scanning part of the information system. Because of the importance of political, economic, and cultural factors, the firm will seek to monitor environmental trends cross-nationally.

Summary

Firms with multinational operations will want to evaluate opportunities and implement strategies in foreign markets. These firms realize that their marketing strategies are likely to be motivated by differences in the cultural, economic, political, and regulatory environment of the markets in which they operate.

A key requirement for the multinational firm is to develop an international marketing plan capable of identifying and exploiting global marketing opportunities. Marketing strategies are developed at two planning levels. The corporate (strategic) plan defines international marketing objectives, identifies opportunity, develops a multinational growth strategy, and analyzes the firm's offerings in various countries by product portfolio analysis.

A key outcome of the multinational strategic plan is the allocation of corporate resources to various products in foreign markets on the basis of opportunity for growth and the firm's ability to exploit these opportunities.

The second planning level in the international marketing plan focuses on particular products in foreign markets. The first requirement is the development of entry strategies. Markets can be entered by exporting the product through domestic intermediaries, by licensing foreign businesses to produce and market the firm's products, by joint ventures with foreign companies, or by direct ownership of manufacturing and marketing facilities. Direct ownership represents the greatest control and investment.

Having developed entry strategies, the international marketer must formulate specific marketing strategies for each product. Product marketing strategies require defining a target segment for the product, positioning it to meet the target segment's needs, and developing a marketing mix to implement the product's positioning strategy. The most important consideration in developing international marketing strategies is whether to standardize marketing strategies across countries or to vary strategies by country to meet differing customer needs and environmental conditions.

The final step in the international marketing plan includes evaluation and control. Control is complicated by the uncertainties of the international environment, distance, and inadequate data. In the next chapter, we consider another area of strategic application — the marketing of services.

Questions

1. Why do many firms follow sound marketing principles in domestic markets but lose sight of these principles when marketing abroad?

2. Assume Kodak is considering introducing its disc camera into South American countries.

   □ What trade, economic, cultural, and political factors will it have to consider?

   □ Which of these factors should be given the most weight in the decision to enter the South American market?

3. Apply the international marketing planning process shown in Figure 21-1 to Kodak's possible introduction of its disc camera into South American markets. Specifically:

   □ develop performance objectives,

   □ list the criteria used to identify marketing opportunity,

   □ suggest a market entry strategy,

   □ identify possible target segments, and

   □ develop a positioning strategy for the disc camera in the South American market.

4. Assume that an American producer of home care products is considering introducing a line of floor cleaners into Western Europe.

   ☐ How might the company approach the decision if it has (a) a geocentric perspective; (b) an ethnocentric perspective?

   ☐ What might be the motivations for entry in each case?

5. Under what circumstances would a firm follow each of the four international growth strategies cited in the chapter (market concentration, market extension, product extension, and diversification)?

   ☐ What are the risks of each strategy?

   ☐ Can a firm follow more than one strategy to achieve growth in international markets? Cite an example.

6. Both the hypothetical multinational product portfolio matrix for Gillette (in Figure 21-3) and the actual domestic product portfolio matrix for Standard Brands (in Figure 19-5) use the GE market attractiveness/business position matrix.

   ☐ What is the difference in the purpose of the two analyses?

   ☐ What are the strategic implications of Figure 21-3 for Gillette?

7. What market entry strategies would you suggest for each of the following companies, and why?

   ☐ An American firm wants to introduce its line of hydraulic lifts in an Asian country that has strict trade regulations. Yet the company wants to maintain close control over the marketing and distribution of the line.

   ☐ A company is seeking to utilize excess production capacity in its American plants and is considering entry into foreign markets as a means of doing so.

   ☐ A company wants to introduce its line of high-quality biscuits into Western Europe, using the same marketing strategy it uses in the United States. Yet it does not have the advertising and distribution facilities in Western Europe to do so.

8. A Pepsi-Cola executive once justified the company's standardized approach to developing international marketing strategies by saying the company wants to establish "one Pepsi-Cola image that is the same throughout the world. ... Management does not believe that each country requires an individual advertising and product approach."[70]

   ☐ Do you agree with the statement?

   ☐ What are the pros and cons of a standardized rather than a localized approach to developing advertising strategy?

9. The risks of a standardized or a localized approach to international marketing strategies has led to the development in recent years of a compromise between the two, known as patterned standardization.

☐ What is patterned standardization?

☐ What are examples of patterned standardization in the development of (a) product strategy? (b) promotional strategy?

10. Why is advertising strategy less standardized than product or distribution strategies in international marketing?

11. What is the difference in the approach to international pricing strategy of a geocentric compared to an ethnocentric firm? Specifically, what are the differences in:

☐ pricing objectives,

☐ methods of setting prices, and

☐ pricing strategies?

12. Why is a multinational firm more likely to require an adaptive control system rather than an "after-the-fact" control system? What are the implications for the development of an international marketing information system?

Notes

1. "Culture Shocks: Pitfalls Lie Waiting for Unwary Marketers," *Advertising Age*, May 17, 1982, p. M-9; and "Campbell Soup Fails to Make it to the Table," *Business Week*, October 12, 1981, p. 66.

2. "Shiseido's New Face in the U.S.," *Business Week*, May 11, 1981, pp. 99, 100.

3. "New Foreign Products Pour into U.S. Market in Increasing Numbers," *The Wall Street Journal*, November 11, 1982, p. 22.

4. "Thinking Big, Thinking Internationally," *Advertising Age*, December 6, 1982, pp. M-4, M-5, M-50.

5. R. Wayne Walvoord, "Foreign Market Entry Strategies," *S.A.M. Advanced Management Journal* 48 (Spring 1983): 14.

6. Philip Kotler, *Principles of Marketing* (Englewood Cliffs, N.J.: Prentice-Hall, 1983), p. 572.

7. Philip R. Cateora, *International Marketing* (Homewood, Ill.: Richard D. Irwin, 1983), p. 6.

8. Pierre Liotard-Vogt, "Nestlé — at Home Abroad," *Harvard Business Review* 76 (November–December 1976): 80–88.

9. Cateora, *International Marketing*, p. 57.

10. Ibid., p. 61.

11. Ibid., pp. 65–66.

12. "Why the Tokyo Round was a U.S. Victory," *Fortune*, May 21, 1979, p. 131.

13. Warren J. Keegan, *Multinational Marketing Management*, (Englewood Cliffs, N.J.: Prentice-Hall, 1980), p. 67.

14. Kotler, *Principles of Marketing*, p. 576.

15. "Xerox Slashes Copier Prices," *The New York Times*, July 1, 1982, p. M-16.

16. "Yankee Goods and Know-How Go Abroad," *Advertising Age*, May 17, 1982, p. M-16.

17. J. Douglas McConnell, "The Economics of Behavioral Factors on the Multi-National Corporation," in Fred C. Allvine (ed.), *Combined Proceedings of the American Marketing Association*, Series No. 33 (1971), p. 264.

18. Susan Douglas and Bernard Dubois, "Looking at the Cultural Environment for International Marketing Opportunities," *Columbia Journal of World Business* 12 (Winter 1977): 102–9.

19. Albert Stridsberg, "Watch that Foreign Market — Everything Changes," *Advertising Age*, April 29, 1974, pp. 60, 62.

20. "Maintaining a Balance of Planning," *Advertising Age*, May 17, 1982, p. M-21.

21. Ibid., p. M-14.

22. "Flavors of Spanish," *Advertising Age,* April 6, 1981, p. S-18.

23. McConnell, "The Economics of Behavioral Factors," p. 264.

24. "Pipelining Image Ads to China," *Advertising Age,* May 17, 1982, p. M-20.

25. George Fields, "The Japanese Communications Base — The Art of Saying it Without Words," *Japan Marketing/Advertising,* 23 (Winter 1983): 67–76.

26. "For a Businessman Headed Abroad Some Basic Lessons," *The Wall Street Journal,* January 16, 1978, p. 2.

27. Joseph V. Miscallef, "Political Risk Assessment," *Columbia Journal of World Business* 16 (January 1981): 47.

28. "Coca-Cola Ordered by India to Disclose Formula for Drink," *The Wall Street Journal,* August 13, 1977, p. 11.

29. Cateora, *International Marketing,* p. 159.

30. Yoram Wind, Susan P. Douglas, and Howard V. Perlmutter, "Guidelines for Developing International Marketing Strategies," *Journal of Marketing,* 37 (April 1973): 14–23.

31. "Eleven Reasons for Firms to 'Go International,' " *Marketing News,* October 17, 1980, pp. 1–2.

32. Keegan, *Multinational Marketing Management,* p. 264.

33. Thomas Hout, Michael E. Porter, and Eileen Rudden, "How Global Companies Win Out," *Harvard Business Review* 60 (September–October 1982): 98–108.

34. "U.S. Fuels World Goal of Johnson," *Advertising Age,* March 9, 1981, pp. 4, 78.

35. Yoram Wind and Susan Douglas, "International Portfolio Analysis and Strategy: The Challenge of the 80s," *Journal of International Business Studies* 12 (Fall 1981): 69–81.

36. Thomas C. Kinnear and Kenneth L. Bernhardt, *Principles of Marketing* (Glenview, Ill.: Scott, Foresman and Company, 1983), p. 740.

37. "WW is Getting Fat on Italy's Diet Craze," *Advertising Age,* November 23, 1981, p. 66.

38. "Egypt an Oasis for Soft Drinks," *The New York Times,* August 1, 1978, p. D1.

39. "TRW: Fujitsu's Key to the U.S.," *Business Week,* May 19, 1980, p. 123.

40. "Mitsubishi Revs Up to Go Solo," *Business Week,* May 3, 1982.

41. "Luring Foreign Money: The Way It's Done," *U.S. News & World Report,* September 14, 1981, pp. 51–52.

42. Marianne Paskowski, "Deere & Co.," *Industrial Marketing,* February 1981, pp. 66–70.

43. Theodore Levitt, "The Globalization of Markets," *Harvard Business Review* 61 (May–June 1983): 92–102.

44. *Advertising Age,* December 6, 1982, pp. M-4–5.

45. Liotard-Vogt, "Nestle — At Home abroad," p. 84.

46. "How Schweppes Used Satellite Broadcasting to Harmonize its International Marketing," *International Management,* March 1983, pp. 78–79.

47. Douglas and Dubois, "Looking at the Cultural Environment," p. 105.

48. Ibid.

49. Ibid., pp. 106–7.

50. Ralph Z. Sorenson and Ulrich E. Weichmann, "How Multinationals View Marketing Standardization," *Harvard Business Review* 53 (May–June 1975): 38–44, 48, 50, 54, 166, 167.

51. Ibid., p. 42.

52. Cateora, *International Marketing,* pp. 412–13.

53. *The Wall Street Journal,* November 11, 1982, p. M-16.

54. Eric D. Haueter, "Organizing for 'International Marketing'," *Vital Speeches of the Day* 49 (August 1983): 620–24.

55. "Detroit Pulls Out Stops to Catch Up With World," *Business Week,* June 22, 1981, pp. S-1, S-44.

56. Kinnear and Bernhardt, *Principles of Marketing,* p. 745.

57. Keegan, *Multinational Marketing Management,* p. 276.

58. Arthur C. Fatt, "The Danger of 'Local' International Advertising," *Journal of Marketing* (January 1967): 60–62.

59. Saul Sands, "Can You Standardize International Marketing Strategy?," *Journal of the Academy of Marketing Science* 7 (Spring 1979): 117–34.

60. Comment by John Ryans in *Advertising Age,* May 17, 1982, p. M-7.

61. *Advertising Age,* December 6, 1982, p. M-5.

62. "Exporting a Legend," *International Advertiser,* November/December 1981, pp. 2–3.

63. "Levi Zipping Up World Image," *Advertising Age,* September 14, 1981, p. 34.

64. Kotler, *Principles of Marketing,* p. 584.

65. "Japan Agrees 'When You Say Bud, You've Said It All,'" *Advertising Age,* March 28, 1983, p. M-23.

66. Kotler, *Principles of Marketing,* p. 586.

67. Cateora, *International Marketing,* p. 593.

68. Paskowski, "Deere & Co.," p. 68.

69. Cateora, *International Marketing,* p. 554.

70. Norman Heller, "How Pepsi-Cola Does It in 110 Countries," in John S. Wright and Jac L. Goldstucker, *New Ideas for Successful Marketing* (Chicago: American Marketing Association, 1966), pp. 694–700.

CHAPTER 22

Service Marketing

FOCUS OF CHAPTER

A chapter devoted to the marketing of services is likely to raise the question, "Is service marketing substantially different from product marketing?" The answer is yes, and these differences are becoming more apparent. Services are intangible; products are tangible. Services are consumed at the time of production, but there is a time lag between the production and consumption of products. Services cannot be stored; products can. Services are highly variable; most products are highly standardized.

These differences produce differences in strategic applications that often stand many product marketing principles on their head. For example, product marketers often emphasize the intangibility of tangible objects (e.g., using a perfume will change one's self-image), whereas service marketers try to emphasize the tangibility of intangible services (e.g., you are more secure buying life insurance from Prudential because it is like the *rock* of Gibraltar).

Recognition that specific marketing principles are applicable to services has led service marketers to become more sensitive to the needs of their customers. Consider the following recent demonstrations of the increasing marketing orientation of service industries:

- Prudential is no longer just a life insurance company. It plans to become "a nationwide financial department store offering a greater range of financial products and services and appealing to a higher income group."[1] Management is now talking in terms familiar to any product manager — positioning services to upscale consumers, expanding the service mix to include health insurance and brokerage services, linking Prudential to the financial security needs of the customer. The company spent over $20 million to advertise its service mix in 1982.[2]

693

- In an attempt to acquire marketing skills, Citibank has begun hiring product managers from packaged goods companies. Eleven of the forty highest-ranking marketing executives at Citibank began their careers at companies such as General Mills, General Foods, PepsiCo, and Lever.[3]

- The Houston Grand Opera is trying to expand its audience base through TV advertising and diversification of its offerings into light opera and musicals. The success of this marketing effort has resulted in a tripling of subscriptions and an operational budget that has expanded almost twentyfold.

In this chapter we will first consider the nature and importance of services. We will cite differences between services and products and describe the implications of these differences for marketing strategy. We will then consider the need for service management responsibility in a service firm in the same context as product management responsibility in a manufacturing operation.

Importance of Services

Services have become an increasingly important part of the American economy. Expenditures for services are almost as great as those for products. Since World War II the proportion of GNP generated by service industries increased from 35 percent to almost 50 percent.[4] (Some sources estimate the proportion spent on services today to be as high as two-thirds of GNP.)[5] Two out of every three workers are now employed in service industries. By the late 1970s consumers were spending 45 cents out of every dollar on services, representing total expenditures of over $600 billion.[6]

Services are likely to become more important in the future. Over thirty years ago economists were predicting that the move from an agrarian to a manufacturing economy would be followed by a move from a manufacturing to a service economy.[7] Economic development involves a shift from primary industries (mining and agriculture) to secondary industries (manufacturing) to tertiary industries (services). This trend has been borne out, leading to predictions that by 1990 expenditures for services will outweigh those for products.

The shift from a manufacturing to a service economy is the result of greater consumer affluence and more leisure time. Consumers have the time and the purchasing power to devote to entertainment, sports, travel, and personal care. The demographic and life-style trends cited in Chapter 3 have also led to increased expenditures for services. Consider the following:

- The increase in single-person households and smaller families means more discretionary income and more time for travel and entertainment.

- One result of the increasing number of senior citizens has been an increase in the demand for health care services, recreational facilities, and entertainment to suit the needs of the elderly.[8]

- As the baby boom generation began entering its years of prime earning capacity in the 1980s, it became a prime target for a variety of services: fast foods, travel, entertainment, personal care.

- The development of a "me" orientation in the 1970s and 1980s led to increasing demand for services that offer a sense of personal achievement (sports, cultural pursuits, education, and physical fitness).[9] The pursuit of immediate gratification will result in continued emphasis on services.

Nature of Services

Marketers must better understand the nature of services because of their increasing importance. In this section, we will:

- classify the various services offered in our economy,

- describe the characteristics of services, and

- determine the implications of service characteristics for marketing strategy.

CLASSIFICATION OF SERVICES

A classification of services is useful because of the great diversity of service institutions. If service marketers are to develop marketing strategies, they must know where their services "fit in" relative to competition and to consumer needs.

Figure 22-1 presents the amount spent on major service categories as a percentage of total expenditures for services. Of each dollar spent on services, 34 percent goes to costs for shelter. These expenses are for apartment or house rentals (services that substitute for physical ownership) or for mortgages (financial services). Medical services are the next most important item, followed by household operations (electricity and telephone). Personal business, the fourth most important category, is made up of personal care services (beauticians, physical fitness facilities) and professional services (lawyers, accountants). Transportation, recreation, education, and foreign travel make up the other major service classifications.

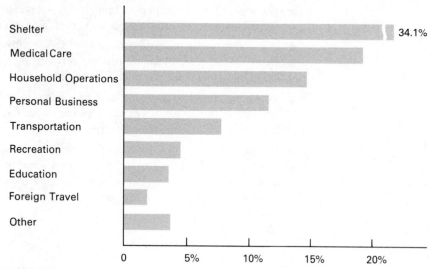

FIGURE 22-1
Expenditures by type of service

Source: U.S. Department of Commerce; and Fabian Linden, "Service Please," *Across the Board*, August 1978, p. 43. © 1978 The Conference Board.

Products and Services

Although Figure 22-1 is useful, it does not provide any major strategic implications. It would be more meaningful to classify services as either facilitating the sale of products or being independent of products. Figure 22-2 presents a four-part classification of products and services depending on (1) whether the product or service is the primary offering and (2) whether a product or service is in a supportive role. A product that is offered with no service support is called a pure product. Soft drinks, toiletries, magazines, and a host of other

SUPPORTING ROLE IS PLAYED AS A	PRIMARY OFFERING IS A	
	PRODUCT	*SERVICE*
PRODUCT	Pure Products	Equipment-Intensive Services
SERVICE	Product-Related Services	Pure Services (labor-intensive)

FIGURE 22-2
A classification of products and services

consumer packaged goods generally do not require service support when sold to the consumer.

Many consumer products require postpurchase service support. These are called product-related services (lower left-hand box in Figure 22-2). Products under warranty, such as automobiles, large appliances, and electronics, must have service support networks. But product-related services include services other than repairs such as information, credit, delivery, and handling. Many industrial products require these services. The greater complexity of industrial goods makes postpurchase maintenance and repairs the norm rather than the exception.

One writer feels that manufacturers will begin placing more emphasis on product-related services in the 1980s because continued differentiation of products will soon become prohibitively expensive for all but the largest firms:

> Customers will not buy a specific brand because of what it does; all brands will be able to do the same thing. Rather they'll buy from a company they feel will support it and give maximum post-sale satisfaction.[10]

As a result, companies will develop a more explicit service support strategy for products — improving product reliability, upgrading parts availability, improving service personnel training, investing in additional service facilities.[11]

When the service rather than the product is the primary offering, a product can play a supportive role (upper right-hand box in Figure 22-2). Automatic teller machines are products that provide bank customers with a service. Airplanes are products that provide a travel service. Telephones are products that are required to convey telecommunications services. These services are called *equipment intensive* in comparison to services that rely only on people. Those are called pure services in Figure 22-2 since they require no product intervention. Services such as education, medical care, legal advice, and appliance repairs are almost totally *labor intensive*.

The distinction between labor-intensive and equipment-intensive services is an important one. Labor-intensive services can vary more in quality because they rely on people rather than machines. As a result, the service marketer must be more concerned with maintaining quality control over services. A bank manager will be more concerned with motivating tellers to provide quality service than with installing and maintaining automatic teller machines, even though both provide similar services.

Although product-related services are important, in the rest of this chapter we will focus on equipment and labor-intensive services as the primary offering. As a result it is important to develop a more detailed classification of primary service offerings, one that relies on the inherent characteristics of services.

A Classification by Service Characteristics

Two of the most important characteristics that distinguish services from products are their intangibility and greater variability in service performance. In Figure 22-3 services are classified by these characteristics.

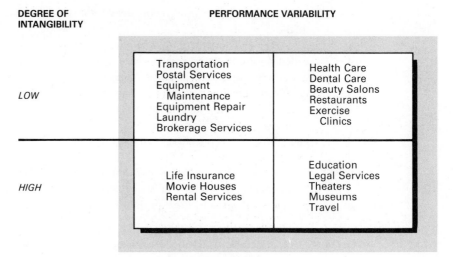

DEGREE OF INTANGIBILITY   **PERFORMANCE VARIABILITY**

LOW	Transportation
	Postal Services
	Equipment
	    Maintenance
	Equipment Repair
	Laundry
	Brokerage Services
		Health Care
		Dental Care
		Beauty Salons
		Restaurants
		Exercise
		    Clinics

HIGH	Life Insurance Movie Houses Rental Services	Education Legal Services Theaters Museums Travel

FIGURE 22-3
A classification by two service characteristics

Services in the upper left-hand box in Figure 22-3 are more tangible and standardized than other services. These include freight transportation, postal services, maintenance and repair of industrial equipment, laundry and dry cleaning, and brokerage services. Services that are more standardized but intangible include life insurance, movie houses, and rental services. Tangible services that vary more in performance (upper right-hand box) are health and dental care, beauty salons, restaurants, and exercise clinics. The last category, highly variable intangible services, is the most difficult to manage. These include education, legal services, theaters, museums, and travel.

The classification is useful because it gives the service marketer some strategic guidelines. The more intangible the product, the harder it is to communicate its benefits. The more variable the product, the harder it is to control performance and ensure postpurchase satisfaction. Service marketers in the lower right-hand box in Figure 22-3 have the difficult task of trying to communicate the benefits of a vague service that they may not be able to guarantee. On the other hand, service marketers in the upper right box may be able to communicate service benefits more easily but run the risk of failing to deliver on their promises. Although ambiguity in promoting the service is less than for intangible services, the possibility of unmet expectations is higher. Thus, patrons of medical, dental, and personal care facilities may be led to have certain expectations that may not be met.

STRATEGIC IMPLICATIONS OF SERVICE CHARACTERISTICS

Services have several characteristics that must be considered when developing service marketing strategies. As we noted earlier, services are (1) intangible and (2) more variable. They are also (3) consumed and evaluated as they are produced, and are (4) perishable.

Intangibility

When a product is purchased, something is acquired that can be seen. When a service such as travel, entertainment, or education is purchased, there is nothing tangible to show for it. As one writer states, "After a day of buying services, the customer still has an empty market basket."[12] What the consumer is buying is a performance provided by the seller.

The intangibility of services makes advertising and promotion more difficult than for products because the marketer must communicate an idea or concept rather than a physical object. Marketers have developed two strategies to facilitate communicating the benefits of a service: (1) developing a tangible representation of the service and (2) focusing on the service provider rather than on the service.

Make services more tangible

One way to make services more tangible is to develop a physical object that represents the service. In a sense a college degree is a physical manifestation of a service since it symbolizes the educational experience. Financial institutions have developed bank credit cards as a physical manifestation of credit. As a result of the credit card, customers can now "store" credit and carry it around with them.[13] The tangibility of the bank credit card has also allowed banks to differentiate their credit service by creating different brand names and images. For example, American Express conveys prestige by offering a gold card, and will soon introduce a platinum card to create an even higher level of status for the most frequent users.

In many cases a tangible representation of the service is not possible. Then service marketers have attempted to associate the service with a tangible object that attempts to convey the benefits of the service. Life insurance companies try to develop a link in the consumer's mind between their services and some tangible object that will create a positive association. For example, consider the following advertising themes:[14]

- Under the Traveler's *umbrella*,
- I've got a piece of the *rock* (Prudential),
- The Nationwide *blanket* of protection,
- You're in good *hands* with Allstate.

Umbrellas, cupped hands, blankets, and rocks are meant to convey protection and security.

Focus on the service provider

The service provider (airline pilot, life insurance agent, doctor) is more tangible than the service itself (e.g., airline travel, life insurance, medical care).

The service provider usually has a level of skill and expertise that represents the service. As a result, advertising often focuses on the skill and technical competence of the service provider. Thus, airline ads frequently show competent pilots and courteous flight attendants, life insurance ads present agents as concerned family counsellors, bank advertising emphasizes the personal attention of its executives. In each case, the service becomes more tangible because of the association with the service provider.

If this approach is to be used, it is important to ensure that the service provider is presented as a credible and knowledgeable source of service. Life insurance agents and bank executives are portrayed as being sensitive to customer needs and having basic facts at their disposal, thus increasing the consumer's confidence in the service company.

Service Variability

Service industries tend to be labor intensive, whereas manufacturing is more capital intensive. As we saw in Figure 22-2, some services (e.g., telecommunications services) are more equipment- than people-based, but in general services are provided by people, not machines.

As a result, services are much less standardized than products. An opera singer, actor, or ballet dancer may be superb in one performance but mediocre in another. A customer going to a restaurant may obtain excellent service on one occasion but be kept waiting on another. A shopper may find that salespeople are helpful and courteous in one trip, but rude in another. On the other hand, consumers purchasing the same toothpaste, cereal, or tennis balls expect the same performance. As James Schorr, executive vice-president of marketing at Holiday Inns, said:

> When you buy a box of Tide, you can reasonably be 99 and 44/100 percent sure that this stuff will work to get your clothes clean. When you buy a Holiday Inn room, you're sure at some lesser percentage that it will work to give you a good night's sleep without ... people banging on the walls and all the bad things that can happen to you in a hotel.[15]

High service variability means the consumer faces greater uncertainty and risk in purchasing services,[16] and the service provider must control quality to ensure adequate service. As in product marketing, profitability in service marketing relies on repeat purchases. The higher the service variability, the less loyal the consumers will be to a particular service company. The service marketer can try to achieve greater standardization in several ways.

Increase control over the service

The service institution has a vested interest in ensuring that the service provider represents the company in a positive manner. Automobile manufacturers want to ensure that the service facilities of their independent dealers are clean, efficient, and prompt, and that service personnel are courteous. Negative service experiences will reduce the chances that a consumer will buy the same car again and may result in negative word-of-mouth about the company. Because of the large investment in equipment and the millions of dollars spent on advertising, it is in the manufacturer's interest to ensure that the service facility conforms to the product image the company is trying to convey.

Quality control can be augmented by carefully screening and training service personnel. Automobile manufacturers establish job specifications for service personnel and run clinic and training programs on repair procedures. Quality control can also be improved by establishing standardized procedures for providing services — for example, specifying repair procedures step-by-step in a manual.

Many service companies have turned to franchising as a means of quality control. Companies like McDonald's and Carvel franchise each outlet and provide the operator with standardized uniforms, food products, and selections to maintain the same quality.

Switch from people to machines

One way to make sure services are standardized is to provide service through machines rather than people. A good example is the growing use of automatic teller machines (ATMs). By transforming the delivery of certain banking services from humans to machines, banks have reduced the variability of their services. In-home shopping also represents a replacement of people by machines. Two-way interactive cable TV systems create greater uniformity of ordering and delivery.

Many people are likely to resist a move to equipment-based services. Consumers tend to like human interaction in the service process. Most prefer to ask questions and obtain advice from a person rather than a machine.

Reduce perceived risk

Another strategy is to accept service variability, but to reduce the consequent risk in the eyes of the consumer. Consider the following strategies to reduce risk:

- a barber offers a money-back guarantee that customers will be satisfied with their haircuts,
- a cultural institution increases the number of single-seat tickets while decreasing subscriptions to reduce the financial risk of a bad season's series, and
- a bank waives the prepayment penalty on home mortgages.

Another risk-reducing strategy is to try to convince customers of a service's reliability by encouraging positive word-of-mouth. E. F. Hutton's campaign, "When E. F. Hutton talks, people listen," attempts to generate word-of-mouth through advertising by communicating positive reactions to the company's brokerage services. By depicting positive word-of-mouth it attempts to assure customers of the service's greater reliability.

Simultaneous Production and Consumption

Products are generally produced, then sold, and then consumed. Services are usually sold first, then produced and consumed at the same time. A consumer buys a plane ticket first. The service is produced as the plane takes off, and consumption occurs because the consumer is on the plane. Similarly, services for health care, hotels, beauty care, entertainment, and education are reserved in advance and then consumed as they are offered. The simultaneous production and consumption of services means that (1) distribution of services must be simple, (2) services must be delivered close to the customer, and (3) the image of the service producer becomes more important.

Simplicity of distribution

Because services are consumed when they are produced, they cannot be stored, transported, or inventoried. As a result, the distribution of services is much simpler than the distribution of goods. Distribution involves the simple transfer of the service from the provider to the consumer, with the occasional use of intermediaries such as real estate brokers, ticket brokers, or travel agents.

Importance of many locations

Because services cannot be stored or transported, the service marketer's job is easier since most intermediaries can be eliminated. But services then must be offered in many locations. Consumers may be willing to travel a distance for certain services (health care, air travel) but service establishments such as banks, movie houses, restaurants, beauty salons, and dry cleaning establishments must be located close to the consumer. As a result, the service is produced in several locations.

Offering services in more than one location increases costs because of duplication of facilities. This is one reason why productivity is lower in the service than in the product sector. Several strategies can permit service marketers to enjoy more centralized production of their services, for example:

- *Reduce the number of outlets by encouraging consumers to travel longer distances for the service.*[17] This can be done through price incentives, better facilities, and more attractive decor. Banks could widen their trading area by offering free advice on estate planning, preferred mortgage rates for customers, and free checking accounts.

- *Combine complementary services into central facilities.*[18] Health maintenance organizations provide many medical services in one location. Service providers (doctors) benefit from the shared costs of the central facility. Similarly, movie houses that offer several movies benefit from centralized refreshment services and one staff.

- *Encourage one-stop service shopping.* By offering a combination of services in one location one is likely to attract consumers from a wider area. Such a strategy represents the "scrambled merchandising" of services. Sears uses scrambled merchandising by selling life insurance, brokerage, and real estate services in many of its locations. Customers are likely to be attracted by the convenience of shopping for products and financial services in the same location.

Image of the service provider

Since service production and consumption occur simultaneously, the consumer is generally present when the service is being provided. As a result, the service provider's impression is one of the most important determinants of a repeat purchase. Consumers may prefer a particular airline, beauty salon, or health care facility because of the way the service provider offers the service.

The importance of image extends to the service facility as well as to the service provider. The decor of a doctor's or lawyer's office is important in conveying an image of competence. That is why many professional firms spend large amounts on furniture and office decor to create the right atmosphere.

Service Perishability

If services are not consumed when offered they go to waste. An empty airline or theater seat represents lost revenue. The hairdresser or barber sitting idly because of lack of customers represents idle capacity. Shifts in demand for products can be accommodated for the most part by taking goods from inventory. But there is no inventory of services. As a result, services have a much more difficult time regulating supply to meet demand, because demand is rarely steady or predictable enough to avoid service perishability. The service marketer can try to overcome the problems of perishability by trying to match supply and demand. Sasser recognized two strategies for doing this:[19] (1) varying supply in accordance with demand (a strategy that we will call **service supply management**); (2) keeping supply fairly constant but trying to smooth out demand to avoid excess capacity (a strategy we will call **service demand management**).

Service supply management

The service manager has several means of varying the supply of services in accord with demand:[20]

- Perform only essential tasks during peak periods and nonessential tasks during slack periods.
- Let consumers perform certain services to take the pressure off supplying services during peak periods (e.g., self-service gas pumps, self-service and waiter-service sections in restaurants).
- Share equipment and staff with other services to reduce periods when

facilities go unused (e.g., several airlines sharing gates, ramps, baggage handling, and ground personnel).

■ Use part-time employees during peak demand periods to increase the level of service.

Service demand management

The second strategy for matching supply and demand is to try to alter demand so it is in line with supply. This strategy tries to influence consumers rather than control facilities. Service managers have several ways to try to smooth out demand:[21]

■ Use differential pricing to try to shift demand from peak to nonpeak periods — for example, weekend and night rates for long-distance telephone calls, matinee prices for moviegoers, lower electric rates in the evening.

■ Stimulate demand during nonpeak periods; for example, urban hotels that cater to businesspeople during the week offer weekend minivacation packages. There is a risk in such a strategy if the service offered in the off-peak period requires different skills and facilities. Weekend vacationers have a different set of needs than weekday businesspeople. If the service establishment's facilities and personnel are not equipped to fill these needs, its reputation might suffer.

■ Presell the service. If services are presold, the manager knows the peak demand periods and can try to shift excess demand to other periods and other facilities. An airline that has a booked flight can try to shift customers to another flight rather than lose them to another carrier.

Many companies do not rely on either service or demand management; they use both, as when telephone companies employ more operators during peak hours and offer off-peak rates.

Service Management

The service characteristics and strategies we have described differ from product characteristics and strategies. Despite these differences, the process of arriving at service marketing strategies is essentially the same as that for products, namely:

■ define marketing opportunities;

■ position services to a target market and segment the market on the basis of service needs;

■ formulate a marketing mix composed of promotional, price, and distribution strategies, and

- in so doing, ensure the capability to:
  - □ develop new services, and
  - □ evaluate and control the mix of existing services.

As a result of these similarities, most of the chapters in this book are as relevant to the service marketer as to the product marketer.

Service marketing strategies require a *service manager* to develop and implement them just as a product manager develops and implements marketing strategies in a manufacturing firm. In this section we will consider the service management function, specifically:

- the nature of service management, particularly the lack of a marketing orientation in service firms;
- the service marketing system; and
- the distinct marketing problems that must be resolved by the service manager.

NATURE OF SERVICE MANAGEMENT

Because services are created and consumed simultaneously, service management involves both operations (managing the support facilities and personnel for the service) and marketing (creating, delivering, and evaluating the service). A service *operations* manager and a service *marketing* manager are required. Historically, the delivery and evaluation of the service have been under the control of operating personnel. There has been no separate marketing management responsibility for these functions. As a result, many service firms have not developed a marketing orientation that requires determining customer service needs, developing services, and delivering them to ensure that customer needs are met.

Lack of a Marketing Orientation in a Service Firm

The lack of a marketing orientation in service firms was documented by George and Barksdale in a study in the mid-1970s.[22] They found that compared to manufacturing firms, service firms were less likely to:

- have marketing mix activities carried out in a marketing department,
- have an overall sales plan,
- develop sales training programs, and
- perform pricing analysis and collect information on competitor's prices.

Moreover, service firms spend significantly less on marketing activities as a percentage of sales than do manufacturing firms. According to one executive:

> In service industries, people aren't oriented to the marketing concept; marketing is not as important in the service industry as in the package goods industry. Most organization charts of the service industry show the head of

marketing is not the equal of the head of operations; he just doesn't have as much horsepower.[23]

Why have service firms been less marketing oriented than product firms? First, until recently most service firms have enjoyed a seller's market. The demand for services tended to exceed the supply. There was no competitive pressure to become more consumer oriented. It was only the rampant inflation of the 1970s with escalating service costs that put a serious damper on service demand for the first time since World War II. Second, the nature of services makes the necessity for a marketing orientation less obvious. In manufacturing firms, similar products are competing head-to-head. The need for product differentiation, unique product positioning, and strong advertising is more apparent. Service offerings are less standardized. Service managers are more likely to view their offerings as unique. Thus the view that "the service will sell itself" is more likely. Third, service delivery is closely related to personal selling. In many cases, the service is created and delivered by a salesperson. Yet as we saw in Chapter 14, salespeople are frequently unmotivated and not attuned to customer needs. Bank tellers, hotel clerks, waiters, and baggage handlers are not always motivated to provide quality service.

But service firms are beginning to adopt a more consumer oriented view of service creation and delivery. Many firms have created the position of a service marketing manager that is separate, yet closely linked to, service operations.

The Service Marketing System

To understand the role of the service marketing manager better, we must understand the nature of service operations and service delivery as part of a **service marketing system.**

The service marketing system is represented in Figure 22-4 as composed of two subsystems: a *delivery system* and a *marketing support system*. A third subsystem, the **service operations system,** is linked to but not part of the marketing system (thus the dotted lines in Figure 22-4). Each of these subsystems is considered below.

The service operations system

Operations is responsible for facilities and personnel management. As an example, the Firestone Tire and Rubber Company is renewing its emphasis on its nationwide network of automobile repair facilities because expenditures on auto repairs are increasing as consumers are keeping cars longer. The company has introduced a computer that is hooked up to the engine and "spits out a printed list of the automobile's problems free of charge."[24] The service operations system at Firestone would be responsible for ensuring that Firestone's repair shops have the facilities for implementing the MasterCare program, including the new diagnostic computer. It would also be responsible for screening and hiring personnel and providing training in the use of facilities such as the diagnostic computer.

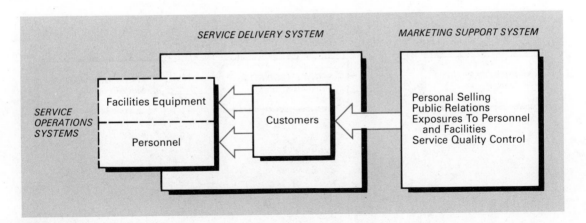

FIGURE 22-4
The service marketing system

Source: Adapted from Christopher H. Lovelock, *Services Marketing,* © 1984, p. 341. Reprinted
by permission of Prentice-Hall, Inc., Englewood Cliffs, New Jersey.

The service delivery system

The delivery system represents the interaction between the customer and
the service provider, and between the customer and the facility. Since services
are consumed when they are offered, the delivery system represents the creation
as well as the delivery of the service. In a bank the delivery system is the
interaction between the bank teller or bank officer and the customer (a customer-
personnel interaction) or between a customer and an ATM (a customer-facility
interaction). At Firestone the delivery system is represented by the interaction
between the customer and service personnel.

The service marketing manager should be responsible for the delivery
system. Just as a product manager tracks sales and evaluates consumer reactions
to the product, the service marketing manager evaluates consumer reactions
to the service and handles inquiries and complaints. An important element in
handling consumer responses is to ensure that service quality is maintained.

The marketing support system

The marketing support system assists the service marketing manager in
marketing the service to customers. It assists in promoting the service through
advertising and public relations, motivating sales personnel to deliver the service
effectively, and evaluating the service through marketing research studies.

Role of the Service Marketing Manager

Figure 22-5 summarizes the responsibilities of the service marketing manager
in the service system. There are three points of contact. The marketing manager
interacts with the operations manager to ensure the quality of the service. The
marketing manager interacts with marketing support services to develop a

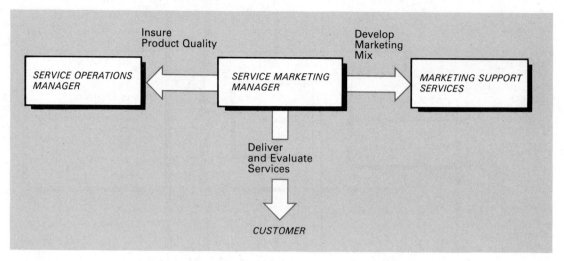

FIGURE 22-5
Responsibilities of the service marketing manager

marketing mix for the service. And most important, the marketing manager interacts with the customer to ensure proper delivery of the service by service providers and to evaluate customer reactions.

PROBLEMS FACED BY THE SERVICE MARKETING MANAGER

The service marketing manager faces a distinct set of problems that are largely a function of the nature of services. These problems focus on the need to manage:

- service quality,
- the customer service encounter,
- demand for services,
- the service mix, and
- service productivity.

Service Quality

Services are variable and frequently of poor quality because they are labor intensive. It is difficult to motivate salespeople when the services they provide are not terribly exciting. As we noted, many service firms are replacing people with machines to try to decrease service variability. Another solution to the problem of service quality is to transfer the service function to the consumer. Self-service minimizes interaction with the service provider, quickens service delivery time, and frequently decreases the cost of the service. Direct dial telephoning, self-service gas pumps, and supermarkets were developed not only to decrease cost, but to increase service quality and efficiency by eliminating a service intermediary.

The Service Encounter

A third solution to the problem of service quality is to motivate the service provider. Only a few services can eliminate the service provider. Most services require what Czepiel has called the "service encounter," that is, the interaction between the service provider and the customer in the creation and delivery of the service.[25]

In Chapter 14 we noted that sales personnel will be motivated if sales goals are viewed as attainable and if the rewards for performance are adequate. In service firms neither of these criteria are likely to be met. First, performance goals for service providers are rarely specified. Bank tellers, flight attendants, reservation clerks, or telephone operators rarely have measurable goals such as sales quotas. Second, as Czepiel notes,

> the people who are most actively involved in delivering services to customers are generally the lowest paid individuals in the service system. The result is "rudeness, insensitivity, or mere inattention to the client on the part of . . . these service providers."[26]

The solution to the low motivational level of many service providers has been to (1) develop a professional customer service division and (2) internally sell the need for high-quality service to the firm's employees.

Customer service division

A customer service division would be responsible for setting service standards, monitoring performance, and evaluating customer satisfaction. American Express's Customer Service Division substantially improved the productivity of service delivery in several areas. The company was dissatisfied with the speed of processing applications for new charge cards and replacing lost or stolen credit cards. The company loses an average of $2.70 for every day a user is without a card.[27]

The service division carefully studied the procedures for processing applications and reports. It developed 180 service performance criteria, from simple courtesy to complex financial approvals. On this basis, it set performance standards for service personnel, but more important it devised guidelines on how to meet them. The result? Replacement of lost cards was reduced from two weeks to two days. Speeding up replacement resulted in $2.4 million of added revenue for the company. The program was successful because service personnel were made aware of (1) performance goals, (2) procedures to achieve these goals, and (3) the importance of their function in satisfying consumers. As a result, the manager of the division believes, "We are becoming a customer-driven service organization."[28]

Internal marketing to employees

Another method to motivate service providers is to view them as customers and sell them on the firm and the importance of the service. In this approach one uses research to determine employee problems with performing services, and advertising and personal selling in order to motivate the employees to improve performance. Instead of directing a marketing mix to customers, one directs it to employees.[29]

Managing the Demand for Services

Another problem faced by the service marketing manager is the difficulty in synchronizing demand for services with supply. We noted this problem earlier as a function of the perishability of services. The service manager is more likely to try to smooth out demand so it matches supply because service facilities are frequently inflexible. If a service firm has fixed capacity, four demand conditions may occur as illustrated in Figure 22-6:[30]

1. demand exceeds maximum available capacity, resulting in lost business;

2. demand exceeds optimum capacity (the point where demand and sup-

FIGURE 22-6
Demand conditions for a service

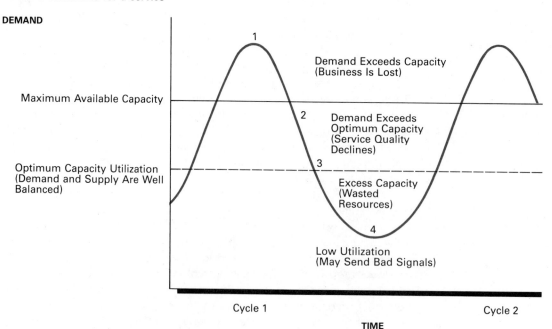

Source: Adapted from Christopher H. Lovelock, *Services Marketing*, © 1984, p. 281. Reprinted by permission of Prentice-Hall, Inc., Englewood Cliffs, New Jersey.

ply are in balance), and customers are accommodated, but may experience a deterioration in service because of crowded facilities;

3. demand and supply are well balanced; or

4. demand is below optimum capacity, resulting in underutilization of resources.

The service manager wishes to avoid lost customers (condition 1), customers who experience inferior service (condition 2), or customers who may doubt the quality of service because of a lack of use (condition 4). If demand exceeds optimum capacity, the service manager may wish to engage in **demarketing,** that is, discouraging the use of the service in peak periods. Utilities will encourage customers to use less electricity in peak periods by informing them of energy conservation measures. Producers of home heating oil and natural gas educate customers on improved insulation in the winter.

Some service firms are reluctant to demarket their services for fear of permanently losing customers. It is unlikely that hotels will discourage travel during peak periods. In such cases, prices are increased to try to smooth out demand and divert consumption into off-peak periods. Similarly, prices are reduced in off-peak periods to increase demand.

The service manager should realize that the various components of the marketing mix can be used to smooth out demand, for example:[31]

- advertising to avoid peak periods (e.g., Mail Early for Christmas),

- varying the service to create demand in off-peak periods (e.g., making a ski slope into an alpine slide in the summer),

- varying distribution by modifying the time and place of service delivery (e.g., stores staying open late for Christmas shopping), and

- pricing to encourage off-peak consumption.

Managing the Service Mix

The service marketing manager must constantly evaluate and control the firm's service mix. A food or cosmetics company can identify its product mix. But since services are intangible and highly variable, a service mix is harder to define. Consider a travel agency. Its service mix might be composed of thousands of packages, some designed for individual customers.

A reasonable basis for evaluating the firm's service mix is by product (service) portfolio analysis. Services can be evaluated as investment alternatives, and the firm's capabilities in delivering services can be objectively evaluated. Weak services can be harvested or eliminated, and established services can be viewed as cash cows that can support services in growth areas. The Public Theater in New York, an off-Broadway nonprofit developmental theater, has produced several successful plays that made Broadway including "A Chorus Line." The Public Theater's service mix includes musicals, cabaret shows, avant garde movies, and experimental productions supported by cash cows such as "A Chorus Line."

A service mix analysis will also allow a company to avoid entering service areas in which it has no expertise. It will provide a reasonable basis for evaluating new services and the possible deletion of existing services. As an example, Bank of America has expanded its service mix in recent years to include Charles Schwab, the country's largest discount broker, Capital Management Corporation, a workers' compensation company, and a large insurance company. Bank of America is also introducing new financial services such as its Cash Maximizer Account to improve its competitive position.[32] The firm's service mix expansion will create earnings pressures in the short run, but the company is willing to accept these pressures to strengthen its service offerings for the long term. A service mix analysis will signal to Bank of America when it is entering service areas in which it has limited facilities or marketing expertise.

Service Productivity

Perhaps the most compelling problem facing the service marketing manager is the need to improve service productivity. Low service productivity is a result of the very nature of services: high variability, perishability, intangibility, and labor intensity.

The problems we have cited (low service quality, poor delivery by service providers, difficulty in matching supply and demand) are indications of low productivity. Moreover, guidelines for improving service productivity are the same as the ones we have cited, namely:

- move from labor-intensive to more capital-intensive operations,
- establish attainable performance goals for service providers,
- synchronize demand and supply,
- reduce the number of service outlets,
- increase control over service delivery, and
- regulate the service mix to avoid introducing services that do not take advantage of the firm's expertise.

Development of Service Marketing Strategies

The central responsibility of the service marketing manager is to develop marketing strategies. This means:

- developing new services to meet consumer needs,
- directing such services to defined market segments,

- positioning new services or repositioning existing services to communicate service benefits,

- developing a marketing mix composed of advertising, price, and distribution strategies to ensure the creation and delivery of services.

NEW SERVICE DEVELOPMENT

The new service development process is similar to new product development described in Chapter 9, since both require determining customer needs, developing offerings to meet these needs, testing these offerings, and developing a marketing plan for introducing them. But the similarity stops there. In product development the description of the product is tested (the concept test), and is then translated into a product that is test marketed. In service marketing, the fact that services are variable and intangible makes them much harder to test. The lack of a physical object means that revenue predictions derived from concept tests and test markets will be much more uncertain.[33] As a result of these difficulties, one bank executive involved with the testing of new financial services concluded that the successful development of a new service is so difficult that "it makes new product development look like child's play."[34]

An outline of the new service development process would be almost identical to that for product development in Figure 9-4. The basic steps are illustrated in Figure 22-7. The first step is the most important: identifying the need for a new service or the redesign of an existing service. For example, in the late 1970s Federal Express identified the need to redesign its customer service operation (taking orders, answering questions, tracing packages).[35] The problem was that these services were handled very defensively by "a bunch of far from dynamic people usually drawn from the secretarial ranks, sitting in a back room trying to make nice-nice."[36] The fact that these services were performed on a local basis throughout the country made quality control difficult. As a result, customers were dissatisfied with followups and the company had difficulty handling any sudden increases in volume.

The proposed solution was a new service concept (second step in Figure 22-7) — customer information services provided through a centralized telephone system located in the company's home base in Memphis to process all orders and complaints. The third step in the development process is a feasibility analysis of the new service. This step may require evaluating competitive services, technology, and company resources and capabilities to deliver the service. Federal Express found that no other air freight company had developed a computerized ordering system. The company studied its current system and compared it to the proposed computer-based order entry system. The savings in processing orders and handling complaints was estimated at $7 million annually.

The company then developed a description of the new service concept and tested it by conducting focused group interviews with customers (the

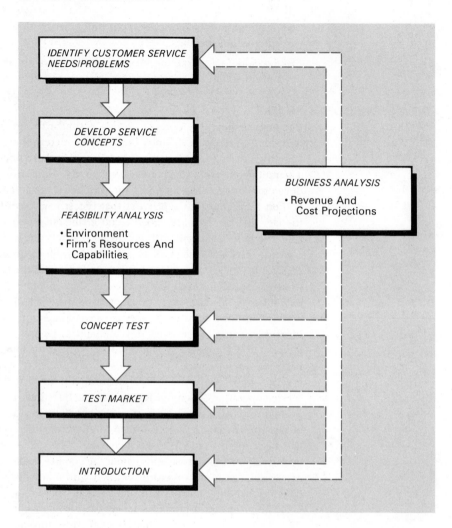

FIGURE 22-7
The new service development process

fourth step in Figure 22-7). These revealed consistent opposition because customers felt it was important to have service available locally. Yet further probing revealed that the most important customer need was responsive answers to their questions about delivery and status of their packages.

Federal Express then test marketed the service in Newark, once twenty-seven new customer service agents had been installed at phone lines in Memphis. Customers reacted favorably to the new service. They "sensed a new aura of professionalism and responded to it."[37] Most customers were not even aware they were talking to service agents outside their area. The company did encounter some difficulty before going national with the service. Cost projections were fairly accurate. But the $7 million forecast in savings could not be substantiated because centralized service agents did not handle many more calls than local agents.[38] The company introduced the system because of the qualitative improvement in service, but the projections demonstrate that uncertainty in testing a new service is greater than that for a new product.

MARKET SEGMENTATION

As in product marketing, service marketing requires identifying the needs and characteristics of a market segment. Only then can the service be positioned to meet the needs of the target segment.

Procedures for identifying market segments and segmentation strategies in service marketing are essentially the same as those described for product marketing in Chapter 8. The initial basis for segmentation should be consumer benefits. Once benefit segments are identified, their life-style and demographic characteristics can be determined. For example, one study of financial services interviewed 1900 bank customers and identified five benefit segments.[39] Table 22-1 lists the benefits each segment desired from bank services as well as the segments' characteristics and behavior.

Segmenting bank customers in this manner gives the service marketer guidance in developing new services and advertising existing services to defined customer groups. It is apparent that a bank can do little to market services to the uninvolved segment. They have no specific needs for financial services, are suspicious of banks, and are insecure in dealing wih bank personnel. But each of the other four segments provides strategic guidelines. Bank marketers could develop investment counseling services to appeal to segment 1 (planners and dealers). Further, they could advertise services that compete with other financial institutions (for example, money market accounts) and cite the advantages of dealing with banks (such as federal insurance on deposits). Advertising to the conservator segment could focus on the safety of dealing with a bank and the convenience of having several bank services for one-stop financial shopping. Advertising to the service seekers could focus on the friendliness of the bank and personal service. One large bank appeals to this group by using the theme "Your personal banker." Segment 5 (the hopefuls) could be a particularly profitable segment because of their high bank loyalty. Advertising to this group should emphasize financial security through the growth of savings deposits.

The benefit segmentation analysis in Table 22-1 permits banks to determine which segments they will appeal to and what required services and promotional strategies they should use to attract the target customers. Some banks will follow a broadly based segmentation strategy and appeal to several segments, whereas others may try to carve out a smaller market niche, appealing to a segment that is not being offered sufficient financial services.

TABLE 22-1
Benefit Segmentation of the Financial Services Market

SEGMENT	PERCENTAGE OF SEGMENT	BENEFITS DESIRED	CHARACTERISTICS	BEHAVIOR
1. Planners and dealers	33	Profits Investment counsel Not convenience	Optimistic Well informed High income Self-confident	Multiple investments Use of nonbank services (e.g., money markets with nonbank institutions) Savings accounts
2. Conservators	20	Privacy One-stop shopping Service	Cautious Older	Savings Accounts
3. Service seekers	16	Service Social interaction	Less educated Lower income Widows	Savings accounts
4. Uninvolved	19	None	Low self-esteem Pessimistic Suspicious of banks	Little use of bank services
5. Hopefuls	12	Financial security Personal attention	Young adults Black Female Less educated Lower income	High bank loyalty

Source: Adapted from "Measuring Markets by Hopes and Fears," *The Wall Street Journal*, June 3, 1982, p. 27. Reprinted by permission of *The Wall Street Journal*, © Dow Jones & Company, Inc. (1982). All rights reserved.

SERVICE POSITIONING

Positioning a service is more difficult than positioning a product because of the need to communicate vague and intangible benefits. Many products can be positioned by their looks, feel, smell, or taste. Services must be positioned by symbols, imagery, and association. For example, Merrill Lynch positions itself as a brokerage house that is optimistic about the future. The implication is that if you invest through the company, you can profit from the growth of the economy. But Merrill Lynch does not try to explain this positioning through words. It has used symbols such as a bull with the slogan "We are bullish on America."

Sometimes a service company must reposition itself to communicate its benefits. Even though Firestone has been in the auto repair business for over fifty years, consumers see it as a tire company. Its greater commitment to its auto repair service means that it must change its image. But this will be difficult. As one auto parts executive said, "Right now their image is tires. It's going to be a long, hard pull for them."[40]

Proper positioning is particularly important in introducing a new service. The marketer must compare the new service to competitive services and determine if it is adequately positioned to meet the needs of the intended target segment. Figure 22-8 presents a hypothetical example of the positioning of a new service, a picturephone, relative to other telecommunications services. Business executives responsible for telecommunications were presented with the concept of a picturephone and were asked to rate it along with communications alternatives. The picturephone was associated with three benefits: nonverbal communication, multiple communication, and multiple use. The example indicates teleconferencing facilities with picturephones could provide a needed alternative to the telephone, the mails, and even airline travel.

THE SERVICE MARKETING MIX

Positioning a service and delivering it to a target segment requires a marketing mix composed of advertising, personal selling, distribution, and pricing strategies.

FIGURE 22-8
Positioning a telecommunications service by customer needs

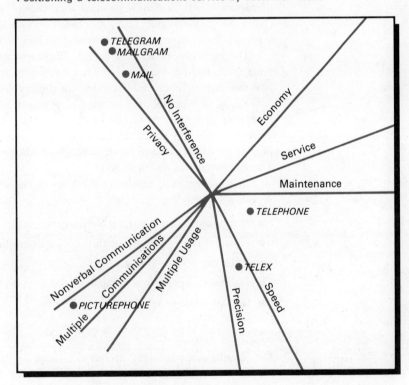

Source: Adapted from Henry Assael, *Consumer Behavior and Marketing Action* (Boston, Mass: Kent Publishing Co., 1984), p. 208.

Advertising

In previous sections we have emphasized the need to make services more tangible by linking them to objects in advertising. Another important objective of service advertising is to reduce the risk of buying a service. This can best be accomplished by establishing the credibility of the service organization and emphasizing the reliability of the service. Using experts and respected individuals in testimonials, linking the service to some objective source such as a government agency, and using two-sided advertising appeals (e.g., Avis's theme, "We're Number 2 but we try harder,") are all means of enhancing the credibility of the service organization.

Service advertising differs from product advertising in several other respects. Since "the service advertiser ... is often left with describing the invisible, articulating the imaginary and defining the indistinct,"[41] it is more important to try to make the service understood to the customer.[42] This means that service advertising is more likely to be informationally oriented. For example, Prudential uses both print media and TV to explain the benefits of its life insurance policies.

The intangibility of service also means that advertising continuity is more important in service than in product advertising.[43] Consumers can more easily remember products than ideas. As a result, service advertisers must continually associate their services to symbols and themes to develop positive images.

The variability of services is more likely to lead to a discrepancy between what the consumer expects and what the service provides. As a result, service advertisers must be careful not to use the puffery that is often typical of product advertising. Holiday Inn once promised "no surprises" in its advertising campaign. Operating personnel were against the campaign because they knew surprises were inevitable in the hotel business.[44] The campaign raised consumer expectations and created more dissatisfaction when expectations were not met. The campaign was discontinued.

In summary, the following guidelines should be followed for effective service advertising:

- Link the campaign to tangible objects,
- Enhance the credibility of the service organization,
- Make the service understood,
- Maintain a continuous campaign, and
- Do not promise what you cannot fulfill.

Personal Selling

The simultaneous production and consumption of services means that "the service employee is a factory worker and salesperson wrapped up in one."[45] The link between personal selling and service delivery means that "personal selling is much more real for the service firm than for the goods firm."[46]

In previous sections we have seen that the service encounter between customer and salesperson is the weakest link in service marketing because of the lack of adequate training and motivation of many service providers. The criteria for an effective sales approach described in Chapter 14 apply to an even greater extent to service marketing. They are:

- Develop an accurate impression of customer needs,
- Formulate a sales message to meet customer needs, and
- Evaluate the effects of the message and adjust the sales approach accordingly.

The following guidelines of particular importance in service marketing might be added:

- Develop customer trust to enhance a perception of reliability,
- Convey a professional impression to enhance trust and credibility, and
- Monitor customer satisfaction after service delivery.

These guidelines are easier to state than to implement. They can be effectively implemented only if customer service departments develop adequate training programs and performance standards.

Distribution

The simultaneous production and consumption of services also means that the channel of distribution is generally limited to a buyer and a seller. Occasionally, an intermediary such as a travel agent or real estate broker may be used. But there are no wholesalers or retailers who take physical possession of a service.

In some cases service distribution is becoming more complex. By introducing credit cards, banks have become intermediaries between retailers and consumers. Companies such as McDonald's that franchise their services have introduced an intermediary between the consumer and the service organization. But such channel relationships are much simpler than channels in manufacturing industries.

The most important issue in the distribution of services is location. Service organizations realize that the service must be brought to the customer to ensure convenience. But increasing the number of locations makes it difficult to control service quality and tends to decrease service productivity.

Pricing

Service pricing decisions are made in a more varied environment than product pricing decisions. Colleges charge *tuition*, insurance companies charge *premiums*, banks charge *interest*, doctors and lawyers charge *fees*, and entertainment facilities charge *admissions*. (Notice that the term *price* is rarely used.)

The labor-intensive nature of services has caused prices of services to increase faster than product prices. During the inflationary 1970s the cost of auto repairs tripled, the cost of lodging went up two and a half times, and laundry services, life insurance, and medical costs doubled.[47] Demand for services tends to be less price elastic than for products, meaning that as prices rise, consumption of services will not decrease as fast as for products. This is one reason why the proportion of expenditures devoted to services is increasing.

Methods of determining prices for services cannot be as scientific as those for products. Demand-oriented methods are difficult to implement because of the uncertainty in projecting service demand. Cost-oriented methods are more common, but these too are difficult to implement because it is hard to determine the cost of people-based services.[48] The method of pricing that is most often used is based on value rather than cost. Value is determined by "what the market will bear" and by cost. Value-based pricing makes price determination much more variable than for products, because it relies on the service organization's judgment of the consumer's perceived value of the service.

The more capital intensive the service, the more likely it is that demand- or cost-oriented pricing methods can be used. This is because it is easier to estimate costs and project revenues when physical objects are involved.

Regardless of the method of price determination, the price of a service usually influences its image. Since services are more ambiguous than products, consumers are likely to associate the price of a service with quality.

Summary

Service marketing is different from product marketing. Services are intangible, perishable, and more variable in quality, and are consumed as they are created. These differences result in important strategic implications for the service marketer. Since services are intangible, attempts should be made to link them to tangible words and objects. Since services are produced and consumed at the same time, they cannot be stored or transported. As a result, they must be offered in many locations. Since services are variable, service marketers should try to improve service productivity by increasing control over the services provided and, where possible, switching from people to machines. Since services are perishable, service marketers should try to match supply and demand by encouraging demand in off-peak periods, discouraging demand in peak periods, or both.

The need to develop distinct marketing strategies in service firms requires a service marketing manager. This individual faces a set of problems that are a function of the nature of services, namely the need to manage:

- service quality,
- the customer service encounter,
- the demand for services,
- the service mix, and
- service productivity.

These management functions take place within a service marketing system that is composed of a delivery system designed to facilitate the interaction between the customer and the service provider, and a marketing support system designed to provide promotional, sales, and informational support.

The central responsibility of the service marketing manager is to develop marketing strategies. This requires:

- developing new services to meet consumer needs,
- directing such services to defined market segments,
- positioning new services or repositioning existing services, and
- developing a marketing mix composed of advertising, personal selling, distribution, and pricing strategies to ensure the creation and delivery of services.

In the next and last chapter, we consider another marketing area not previously discussed, not-for-profit marketing.

Questions

1. If service marketing is different from product marketing, why has Citibank, a leading financial service institution, begun hiring product managers from consumer packaged goods firms?

2. What are the strategic implications of being in each of the product/service categories in Figure 22-2?

3. Assume a life insurance company has developed a new life insurance plan targeted to working women to make benefits more comparable to those for men. It is concerned about the difficulties of communicating intangible benefits such as security, protection, and peace-of-mind. What strategies can the company develop to communicate these intangible benefits?

4. What are the strategic implications of the fact that most services are consumed when they are produced?

   What is likely to happen when the production and consumption of services do not occur simultaneously?

5. A fast-food franchised chain finds significant variability in service in various locations. Customer complaints are frequent at several locations. The company fears if it does not decrease the variability of service, it will begin to lose customers to competition. What strategies can it develop to reduce service variability?

6. A regional airline finds it is overbooked during peak periods and has significant excess capacity during slack periods. It is trying to compete with larger airlines on its routes by offering better service and price. It

recognizes the inherent problem of service perishability in transportation.

☐ What strategies can it develop to try to (a) cope with demand, and (b) manage demand?

☐ What is the difference between an approach that attempts to cope with demand and one that tries to manage demand?

☐ How would these strategies put the company in a better position to compete with the larger airlines?

7. One service industry manager was cited in the chapter as saying, "In service industries, people aren't oriented to the marketing concept; marketing is not as important in the service industry as in the package goods industry." Why have most service firms lagged behind packaged goods manufacturers in developing a marketing orientation?

8. What are the responsibilities of the service operations system, the service delivery system, and the marketing support system in Figure 22-4? What interactions between the three systems does Figure 22-5 suggest?

9. Assume that Sears evaluates its financial service mix (casualty insurance, brokerage services, real estate, and so forth), using a portfolio approach. What types of strategic implications might emerge from such an analysis?

10. In this chapter we stated, "The most compelling problem facing the service marketing manager is the need to improve service productivity."

☐ What are the reasons for low service productivity?

☐ Which of these reasons do you believe to be the most direct cause of low productivity?

☐ How can service managers increase productivity?

11. An executive with experience in both new service development and new product development concluded that trying to develop new services "makes new product development look like child's play." Assume a telecommunications company is testing a new service, teleconferencing, a service that permits visual communications between cities through the use of picturephones.

☐ Why would it be more difficult to test this service than to test a product?

☐ Would you do anything differently in testing this service than in testing a product?

12. A large bank is introducing in-home banking tied to customers' home computers. Should the bank follow the five guidelines for service advertising stated on page 718? How should it implement each of these guidelines?

Notes

1. "More Than a Foot in the Door," *Marketing & Media Decisions,* Spring 1983, Special Edition, p. 94.
2. Ibid.
3. "Marketers Start to Help Banks Recognize Gains from Selling," *The Wall Street Journal,* September 3, 1981, p. 25.
4. U.S. Department of Commerce; and Philip Kotler, *Principles of Marketing* (Englewood Cliffs, N.J.: Prentice-Hall, 1980), p. 623.
5. J. J. Boddewyn, "Advertising Regulation in the 1980s: The Underlying Global Forces," *Journal of Marketing* 46 (Winter 1982): 29.
6. Fabian Linden, "Service Please," *Across the Board,* August 1978, p. 42.
7. See Colin Clark, *The Conditions of Economic Progress* (London: Macmillan, 1951); and Nelson N. Foote and Paul K. Hatt, "Social Mobility and Economic Advancement," *American Economic Review* 43 (May 1953): 364–78.
8. Henry Assael, *Consumer Behavior and Marketing Action* (Boston, Mass: Kent Publishing Co., 1984), p. 235.
9. "DDB Study: More Driving for Success," *Advertising Age,* January 25, 1982, p. 10.
10. Milton M. Lele, "How to Protect Your Unguarded Battlefield," *Business Marketing,* June 1983, p. 69.
11. Ibid., pp. 69–76.
12. William R. George, "The Retailing of Services — A Challenging Future," *Journal of Retailing* 53 (Fall 1977): 86.
13. James H. Donnelly, Jr., "Intangibility and Marketing Strategy for Retail Bank Services," *Journal of Retail Banking* 2 (June 1980): 41.
14. Ibid., p. 42.
15. "Greater Marketing Emphasis by Holiday Inns Breaks Mold," *Advertising Age,* January 15, 1979, p. 47.
16. Dennis S. Guseman, "Risk Perception and Risk Reduction in Consumer Services," in James H. Donnelly and William R. George, eds., *Marketing of Services* (Chicago: American Marketing Association, 1981), pp. 200–4.
17. Gregory D. Upah, "Mass Marketing in Service Retailing: A Review and Synthesis of Major Methods," *Journal of Retailing* 56 (Fall 1980): 63.
18. Ibid., p. 64.
19. W. Earl Sasser, "Match Supply and Demand in Service Industries," *Harvard Business Review* 54 (November–December 1976): 133–40.
20. Ibid.
21. Ibid.
22. William R. George and Hiram C. Barksdale, "Marketing Activities in the Service Industries," *Journal of Marketing* 38 (October 1974): 65–70.
23. *Advertising Age,* January 15, 1979, p. 50.
24. "Firestone Tries the Service Business Again," *Business Week,* June 20, 1983, pp. 70–71.
25. John A. Czepiel, *Managing Customer Satisfaction in Consumer Service Businesses* (Cambridge, Mass: Marketing Science Institute, 1980), Report No. 80–109.
26. Ibid., p. 4.
27. "Boosting Productivity at American Express," *Business Week,* October 5, 1981, pp. 62, 66.
28. Ibid., p. 66.
29. Leonard L. Berry, "The Employee as Customer," in Christopher H. Lovelock, ed., *Service Marketing* (Englewood Cliffs, N.J.: Prentice-Hall, 1984), pp. 272–73.
30. Lovelock, *Service Marketing,* p. 281.
31. Ibid., pp. 284–86.
32. "BofA's Brash Fight to Build Deposits," *Business Week,* January 17, 1983, pp. 98–99.
33. Dan R. Thomas, "Strategy is Different in Service Businesses," *Harvard Business Review* 56 (July–August 1978): 164.
34. G. Lynn Shostack, "Breaking Free From Product Marketing," *Journal of Marketing* 41 (April 1977): 73–80.
35. Penny P. Merliss and Christopher H. Lovelock, "Federal Express: Customer Service Department," in Lovelock, ed., *Service Marketing,* 1984, p. 356.
36. Ibid., p. 360.
37. Ibid., p. 363.
38. Ibid., p. 365.
39. "Measuring Markets by Hopes and Fears," *The Wall Street Journal,* June 3, 1982, p. 27.
40. *Business Week,* June 20, 1983, pp. 70–71.
41. Stephen Unwin, "Customized Communica-

tions: A Concept for Service Advertising," *Advertising Quarterly* (Summer 1975): 28.

42. William R. George and Leonard L. Berry, "Guidelines for the Advertising of Services," in Lovelock, ed., *Services Marketing,* 1984, p. 410.

43. Ibid.

44. Ibid., p. 411.

45. Howard Geltzer and Al Ries, "The Positioning Era: A Marketing Strategy for College Admis-sion in the 1980s," *A Role for Marketing in College Admissions* (New York: College Entrance Examination Board, 1976), p. 77.

46. Philip Kotler, "Strategies for Introducing Marketing Into Nonprofit Organizations," *Journal of Marketing* 43 (January 1979): 37.

47. Thomas C. Kinnear and Kenneth L. Bernhardt, *Principles of Marketing* (Glenview, Ill.: Scott, Foresman, 1983), p. 689.

48. Thomas, "Strategy is Different," p. 163.

CHAPTER 23

Not-For-Profit Marketing

FOCUS OF CHAPTER

Not only profitmaking firms market their goods and services; nonprofit institutions such as museums, charitable organizations, and colleges also market their offerings. The development and application of marketing plans and strategies by these institutions is known as *not-for-profit marketing*. The social nature of the services provided by many of these organizations has also led to the use of the term *social marketing*. Regardless of the designation, however, the nature of these activities clearly differentiates them from activities in which profit maximization is the goal.

Not-for-profit marketing is big business, because the nonprofit sector accounts for over 20 percent of economic activity in the United States. Charitable foundations alone control over $30 billion in revenues and make grants of over $2 billion a year.[1]

Some nonprofit institutions have recognized the importance of developing integrated marketing programs to sell their services and ideas. Consider the following examples:

- As college enrollments declined in the early 1980s, colleges began to compete for students by becoming more customer oriented. They are relying on admissions personnel to recruit students (personal selling), are sending information to prospective applicants (direct-mail advertising), are bringing students on campus (distribution), and are offering more scholarship aid (price).

- The shift to an All Volunteer Army has prompted the military services to become more customer oriented. National advertising campaigns demonstrate the benefits to teenagers of joining the military.

- Charitable organizations such as the Heart Fund and the American Cancer Society use national advertising campaigns to influence people to stop smoking. They have also used sophisticated direct-mail campaigns to try to attract funds from defined donor target segments.

- Government health agencies are beginning to use marketing techniques, for example:[2]
  - ☐ the Cancer Information Office of the National Institute for Health has produced and pilot tested a "Helping Smokers Quit" kit, and
  - ☐ the United States Department of Agriculture is using mass media to improve children's eating habits.

In this chapter we will first consider the nature of not-for-profit marketing. We will focus on the characteristics that differentiate it from other marketing activities, and on the difficulty of using traditional marketing techniques because of these differences. We will next describe the process of developing marketing plans and strategies in the nonprofit sector. In the last section, we will broaden the discussion beyond not-for-profit marketing to consider the responsibilities of the marketing manager to the consumer in both the profit and nonprofit sectors. Since not-for-profit marketing is frequently directed to inducing social change, a discussion of the social and ethical responsibilities of marketing management is a logical conclusion to the chapter.

Increasing Importance of Marketing in the Nonprofit Sector

Applications of marketing techniques to the nonprofit sector are likely to increase for several reasons. First, social problems such as drug abuse, pollution, and energy depletion are perceived as more serious. The Vietnam War, the energy crisis, periods of rampant inflation, and the most serious economic downturn since the Great Depression have increased public and corporate consciousness of social issues.

Second, managers in the nonprofit sector are beginning to realize that marketing has a role in influencing their publics. Marketing techniques can be used to influence people to change their behavior to help both themselves and society in areas such as smoking, energy consumption, family planning, and drug use. Third, the role and importance of the nonprofit sector as a provider of goods and services is increasing. The arts, mass transit, family planning, and environmental agencies have increased their activities in the last ten years.

Nature of Not-For-Profit Marketing

Although not-for-profit marketing activities are increasing, marketing strategies are probably more difficult to apply to the nonprofit than to the profit sector.

To understand the differences between marketing in the nonprofit and profit sectors, we must understand:

- the purposes of not-for-profit marketing,
- the types and characteristics of nonprofit institutions,
- the characteristics of nonprofit services, and
- the inherent difficulties in applying marketing principles to the non-profit sector.

PURPOSES OF NOT-FOR-PROFIT MARKETING

Products and services marketed by nonprofit institutions have been directed to several social goals; specifically:

- *Improving the individual.* Colleges advertise educational services, health maintenance organizations advertise the need for checkups to maintain health, and museums advertise the benefits of art and culture. These services are designed to improve the individual in different ways.

- *Win people over to social ideas.* Some nonprofit organizations represent certain social positions and use marketing to influence people to adopt these positions. For example, the Sierra Club uses direct mail to further the cause of conservation, the United Negro College Fund uses direct mail and national advertising to further the cause of educating black youth with the theme "A mind is a terrible thing to waste." The National Organization of Women (NOW) uses direct mail to reach opinion leaders in an attempt to further women's rights and encourage support for the Equal Rights Amendment. In each case the organization is not only furthering a social cause; it is also attempting to encourage contributions to further its efforts.

- *Disseminate new information and practices.* Nonprofit organizations also attempt to inform people of new information or new practices that will benefit them. For example, in 1969 the United States Department of Agriculture indicated the nutritional needs of the American public were being met and that daily intakes of sugar and sweets was a necessity. By 1979 the Surgeon General's Report criticized the typical American diet, linking sugar and fat to heart disease.[3] Similar shifts in relation to medical findings on the effect of cholesterol and salt have occurred in the past.

- *Change behavior.* Nonprofit organizations frequently attempt to change an individual's behavior to benefit him or her or to benefit society. The American Cancer Society and the American Heart Fund advertise to influence people to stop smoking; the National Heart, Lung and Blood Institute launched a nationwide campaign to get people to have their blood pressure taken periodically because of the dangers of high blood pressure; the National Safety Council has tried to convince people to use seat belts and not to drink when they drive. Attempts to reduce or eliminate the consumption of cigarettes and alcohol are examples of *demarketing,* since nonprofit agencies are using marketing means to decrease demand for these products.

TYPES OF NONPROFIT INSTITUTION

Nonprofit institutions encompass a broad range of organizations that are:

- cultural (museums, operas, symphonies);
- knowledge-oriented (universities, schools, research organizations);
- philanthropic (foundations, private welfare, charities);
- representative of social causes (family planning, environmental, rights, consumerist, and feminist groups)
- religious (churches, church associations); or
- public (United States Post Office, city/state/federal services).

These agencies can be broadly categorized into those which promote social ideas, beliefs, and causes (e.g., environmental groups, philanthropic organizations, and religious organizations); and those which offer specific services (e.g., entertainment services, public services, and educational services). We will be using the term *nonprofit agencies* to refer to the broad spectrum of organizations, but occasionally we will cite *social agencies* in referring more specifically to those organizations concerned with social causes.

CHARACTERISTICS OF NONPROFIT ORGANIZATIONS

The nonprofit agencies we have described differ from profitmaking organizations in several important respects.

Multiple Publics

Profitmaking organizations deal with intermediaries and consumers to sell their goods and services. Nonprofit organizations must frequently deal with donors and other publics (lobbyists, activist groups, government agencies) as well. They undertake marketing activities that *attract* resources from donors and *allocate* resources to clients.[4] Marketing activities designed to attract and to allocate are likely to be very different. For example, the American Cancer Society will use direct mail to solicit contributions from donors, and might then use these funds to prepare antismoking commercials.

Multiple Exchanges

When nonprofit agencies deal with several publics, they must develop multiple exchanges of resources and services with different donor and client groups. Consider the exchange flows between a hospital and its client and donor groups in Figure 23-1. Whereas a consumer marketer is concerned only with exchanges

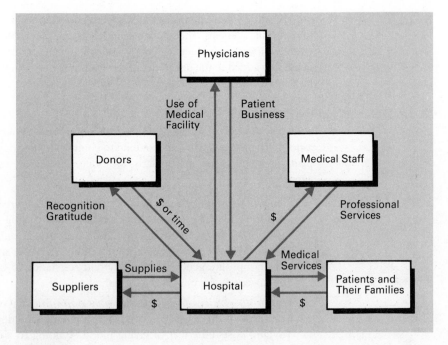

FIGURE 23-1
An example of multiple exchanges in a nonprofit organization

Source: Adapted from M. Wallendorf, "Understanding the Client as a Customer," in G. Zaltman (ed.), *Management Principles for Nonprofit Agencies and Organizations,* AMACOM, 1979,
p. 258.

among the company, its intermediaries, and consumers, the hospital marketer
must be concerned with exchanges among patients, suppliers, donors, physicians,
and the medical staff. The nonprofit agency is receiving services and resources
from donors and from its staff which it then provides to patients and their
families in return for additional resources.

Government and Nonmarket Pressures

Nonprofit agencies are more likely to be subject to governmental influence
because of the quasi-public nature of their operations. Many of them are in
fact government agencies. For example, postal rates and fees for health services
under Medicaid and Medicare are subject to government review. Further,
nonprofit agencies might be required to provide services to uneconomical
segments — for example, the post office maintains rural service and Amtrak
provides service to thinly populated areas.[5]

Service Orientation

For the most part, nonprofit organizations market services rather than physical
goods. The characteristics of services cited in Chapter 22 (intangibility, variability,

perishability, simultaneous production and consumption) apply to the offerings of nonprofit agencies. The difficulties in marketing intangibles and in maintaining effective levels of service also apply. But the particular nature of not-for-profit marketing added to the difficulties of service marketing complicates the marketer's task in nonprofit organizations.

CHARACTERISTICS OF NONPROFIT SERVICES

Services offered by the nonprofit sector differ from other services in several aspects. The following differences tend to complicate the application of marketing plans and strategies;[6] particularly for nonprofit services marketed by social agencies:

1. *Benefits of nonprofit services are not always apparent to the consumer.* Selling the idea of driving more slowly, using mass transit instead of a car, or buying nonpolluting products is difficult because these actions tend to benefit society more than the individual. As a result, nonprofit agencies frequently find resistance to change because of the absence of a perceived individual benefit.

2. *Nonprofit services frequently involve nonmonetary costs* such as time (the cost of driving more slowly), inconvenience (depositing litter), psychic costs (the fear of giving blood or going to a dentist), and social costs (leaving your friends to join the army). The nonmonetary costs are generally more important than monetary costs and make it more difficult to sell social services and ideas.

3. *Since social services are vaguer and less tangible than other services,* the task of influencing consumers is especially difficult. Compare the benefits gained from bank services, air travel, or telecommunications to the benefits of joining a religious organization, smoking less, or contributing to a charitable organization. The benefits to be gained in the latter cases may be more important, but they are broader and less immediate.

4. *We noted that the purpose of nonprofit (particularly social) services is frequently to change behavior* (e.g., stop drug use, stop smoking, conserve energy, use mass transit). Yet as we saw in Chapter 5, marketing strategies are more likely to be effective in reinforcing current behavior than in attempting to change behavior. Therefore, the purpose of social services makes their marketing more difficult.

DIFFICULTIES OF NOT-FOR-PROFIT MARKETING

The characteristics of nonprofit agencies and the services they provide create the following difficulties in applying marketing techniques.

The complexity of the behavior to be influenced and the ideas to be communicated make it difficult to formulate and to position the services being offered.[7] The agency developing a drug therapy program must consider the individual's limited self-discipline, the possible lack of family support, the drug's side effects, and other complicating factors. When an adequate program is developed, how should it be communicated to the doctor and from doctor to patient? Miscommunication and inconsistencies are likely to arise.

Less Control Over Marketing Resources

Nonprofit organizations cannot control the time when their commercials will be aired, since media contribute the time for public service advertising.[8] They cannot control price, since price is represented by the psychic, time, social and convenience costs of the consumer. They cannot control intermediaries such as doctors, clinics, or community centers to pass along services and messages, and they cannot control the message being communicated by these intermediaries.

Difficulty in Segmenting Markets

The broadly based and antidiscriminatory nature of many nonprofit agencies means there is a natural reluctance to target marketing effort to some consumer segments and not to others. For example, a federal effort in the late 1970s to increase awareness of the health risks of asbestos was originally targeted to the highest risk group — shipyard workers in World War II. But then there was pressure to broaden the appeal to related industries, and finally to all workers.[9]

Difficulty in Influencing Target Groups

Nonprofit agencies must often target effort to groups that may show the greatest resistance to change (e.g., drunk drivers, heavy smokers, drivers who avoid using seat belts).[10]

Difficulty in Evaluating Marketing Effectiveness

An educational institution might try to determine the effectiveness of its program by getting feedback from students. But the ultimate criterion of effectiveness, the eventual position of the individual in society and his or her contribution, is difficult to measure. Further, any such evaluation would be difficult to trace to the educational institution because so many diverse factors operate on the individual.

Lack of a Marketing Orientation among Nonprofit Organizations

Compounding the problems of applying marketing techniques to the nonprofit sector is the fact that many nonprofit agencies are not as marketing oriented as they may think. The following reasons have been cited for this lack of a marketing orientation:[11]

- Nonprofit managers tend to overestimate the desirability of their services. Colleges may think they have the best programs, or health care agencies may think they have the best facilities, without regard to the needs of their consumers.

■ Nonprofit agencies tend to ascribe consumers' failure to adopt their services or ideas to ignorance. For a time, the National Cancer Institute thought that many heavy smokers did not believe that smoking was bad for them. A survey found that seven out of eight smokers did believe smoking was bad but did not know how to go about quitting. The institute concluded that part of the marketing mix should be a set of techniques to help smokers kick the habit.

■ Nonprofit agencies put too much emphasis on advertising and personal selling. They tend to ignore other elements of the marketing mix. For example, some consumers are reluctant to go to health care facilities because they are made to feel inadequate by doctors and nurses. This psychic cost can be reduced by training programs to create awareness of patient sensitivities. Improved distribution of medical services can also be a strategy. Health maintenance organizations provide improved delivery by offering many services, thus reducing costs by decreasing the frequency of visits.

■ Nonprofit agencies lose sight of their competition for funds. The American Cancer Society may view the Heart Fund as a competitor for dollars because of the similarity of their objectives. But does it also view the United Way or the March of Dimes as a competitor? All these agencies frequently compete for contributions from the same segments. But they do not formulate differentiated appeals to gain a competitive advantage.

■ Nonprofit agencies are sometimes unresponsive to client needs because their revenues are derived from subsidies, contributions, and endowments. The support they obtain does not depend on improved customer services, better delivery systems, or reduced costs.[12] As a result there is little incentive to be marketing oriented.

Despite these limitations marketing is still an essential activity in nonprofit agencies. In the next section we will consider nonprofit agencies' use of marketing strategies as vehicles for influence and change.

Marketing Strategies for Nonprofit Firms

Management in nonprofit agencies can develop marketing strategies at the two levels cited in previous sections of this book: the corporate (strategic) level and the product (in this case, service) level. At the strategic marketing level, managers in nonprofit firms are concerned with attracting funds, ensuring future corporate development, and defining the appropriate mix of social services.

At the service marketing level, they are concerned with developing services, targeting them to the right segments, and delivering them through promotion, distribution, and pricing strategies. In this section we will consider both strategic marketing planning and service marketing planning in the nonprofit firm.

STRATEGIC MARKETING PLANNING

Few nonprofit agencies engage in strategic marketing planning. Yet in many respects, strategic planning is more important for the nonprofit firm than for other firms. Many nonprofit agencies have a longer planning horizon because objectives of social change (e.g., encouraging energy conservation) take longer to achieve. Therefore, these firms must be concerned with the source and allocation of funds over a longer time.

Like other firms, the nonprofit agency should develop both corporate growth and product (service) portfolio strategies. For nonprofit firms *corporate development* is a better term than corporate growth because the firm is not motivated by profits. Rather, the purpose is to develop the firm's resources to ensure attainment of certain social goals. In some cases the nonprofit agency may actually become smaller or go out of business when the social goal is attained; for example, family planning organizations may not continue to be funded in countries with zero population growth. Service portfolio strategies are designed to develop the right mix of cash-generating and cash-draining services to ensure that sufficient resources are available to attain the agency's objectives.

Corporate Development Strategies

As with corporate growth strategies in profit-making firms, the nonprofit firm can develop new or existing services directed to new or existing markets. Figure 23-2 presents various developmental strategies for a college. It might use a *market penetration strategy* to better cultivate the existing target of students by improving current course offerings, or broadening the set of offerings to evenings and weekends. A *product expansion strategy* would develop new courses, new departments, or even new schools to the same demographic and psychographic student segments that the school is now appealing to. The college could also better appeal to existing student segments through new delivery systems such as courses on videotape or through cable TV.

Developmental strategies can also be directed to new markets. A college could follow a *market expansion strategy* by reformulating existing offerings to meet the specific needs of new markets — for example, developing executive programs for business firms. The college could also begin to use a set of strategies that would *diversify* its activities by developing new courses, departments or schools directed to new markets — for example, establishing special programs for college-age students with learning disabilities.

A college with a well-defined developmental program is likely to follow several of these strategies simultaneously. The purpose is to ensure that the

PRODUCTS

	EXISTING	NEW
EXISTING	Market Penetration Short Courses Evening Program Weekend Program	Product Expansion New Courses New Departments New Schools New Delivery Systems
NEW	Market Expansion Senior Citizens Minorities Business Firms New Areas Of City New Cities Foreign	Diversification New Courses New Departments New Schools

FIGURE 23-2
Corporate development strategies for a college

Source: Adapted from Philip Kotler, *Marketing for Nonprofit Organizations*, 2nd Edition, ©
1982, p. 100. Adapted by permission of Prentice-Hall, Inc., Englewood Cliffs, New Jersey.

services offered by the nonprofit agency will meet the needs of its client segments, and thus attract sufficient resources from clients and donors to maintain service development.

Service Portfolio Strategies

Managers in nonprofit firms must evaluate the mix of services being offered. Portfolio analysis can be used to guide the allocation of the nonprofit agency's limited resources to new and existing services. Well-supported services that attract donations (cash cows) must continue to be maintained to fund new services that might meet important social goals.

Resource allocation in the nonprofit agency is illustrated in the hypothetical example of the YMCA in Figure 23-3. The example suggests that the agency's summer camps are profitable enough to fund other worthy social programs such as classes for the elderly. The hypothetical example shows that hotel service is clearly a candidate for deletion since it is draining cash from other important services. Music concerts rank high in public desirability, but also represent a cash drain. Adult recreation, once a cash cow, now must be subsidized by other programs.

The portfolio matrix guides management in the important decisions of which services to maintain or delete, and suggests the viability of introducing new services.

PUBLIC ATTRACTIVENESS	BUSINESS POSITION		
	HIGH	MEDIUM	LOW
HIGH	Classes for Elderly		Classical Music Concerts
MEDIUM	Recreational Events for Elderly	Classes for General Public	Folk/Rock Concerts
LOW	Summer Camps	Adult Recreation	Hotel Facilities

FIGURE 23-3
Hypothetical service portfolio matrix for YMCA services

SERVICE MARKETING PLANNING

Managers in nonprofit organizations must market individual services. In so doing they must develop services, define the target segments for these services, position them to the target segments, and develop promotional, distribution, and pricing strategies to deliver them.

Service Development

New services must be developed to meet client needs. For example, the National Cancer Institute developed clinics to discourage smoking. The United States Postal Service developed a series of new products: Express Mail to provide overnight delivery, Mailgram to provide quick delivery of messages at a lower price than a telegram; and Controlpak, a high-security system for mailing valuable documents.

Developing new services requires research into the needs of the target segment. For example, if a municipal agency wants to develop mass transit facilities to discourage driving in center-city areas, it must determine travelers' points of origin and destinations, and their attitudes toward the automobile and alternate means of transportation. Too often, nonprofit organizations develop new services with little understanding of client needs. There is not the same motivation to do marketing research as in the profit sector because (1) competition is minimal and (2) funding is not always contingent on the effective delivery of the service.

Market Segmentation

Nonprofit agencies that market social causes and ideas are less likely to segment markets by needs because they feel their messages should be broadly based. Social appeals directed to drug abuse or to automobile safety are likely to be communicated to the public at large. Segmentation is more meaningful for agencies that market specific services (museums, universities, operas), since variations in needs for these services are more easily defined.

Segments can be defined by the needs of donors and by the needs of clients. An example of segmentation by donor needs is a study that identified blood donors by their motivation in giving.[13] Donors included segments who were motivated primarily by:

- money,
- group pressures,
- family responsibilities,
- fringe benefits (e.g., a day off from work),
- altruism, and
- coercion (e.g., a prisoner).

Obviously, appeals must differ to attract each segment. The American Red Cross would probably want to direct its appeals to those motivated by altruism, family responsibilities, and the group. An appeal to altruism might depict the way the blood is used to help those in need of blood, and the dangers if none is available. An appeal to group-oriented individuals might depict peer-group pressures to give blood.

Market segmentation is also relevant for user as well as donor groups. An example is the drive to recruit an all-volunteer army. Market segments for the volunteer army could be described on at least three demographic characteristics: age, residence, and family income (see Figure 23-4). Research by the Department of the Army in 1973 found that the most likely recruits for an all-volunteer army wanted independence, the chance to mature, and the opportunity to travel.[14] These individuals were most likely to be lower-middle-class males aged seventeen to twenty-one who live at home (shaded segment in Figure 23-4). By defining this target segment, the army could better direct its $26.7 million promotional budget to those most likely to join.

These illustrations show that segmentation is relevant to nonprofit services as long as the marketer identifies differences in needs among donor or user groups.

Service Positioning

Nonprofit services must be positioned to meet the needs of clients and donor groups just as products and services in the profit sector are positioned to meet customer needs. Because there is no profit motive, the key question is whether

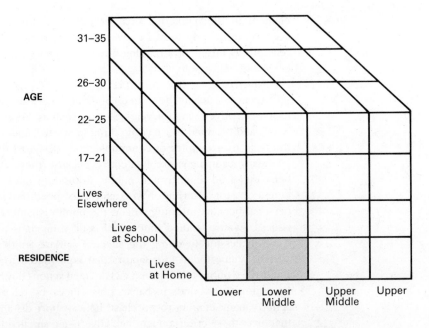

FIGURE 23-4
Market segments for the all-volunteer army

Source: James L. Heskett, *Marketing* (New York: Macmillan, 1976), p. 45; as adapted by William Lazer and James D. Culley, *Marketing Management* (Boston: Houghton Mifflin, 1983), p. 837.

the nonprofit agency is sufficiently motivated to position services to client needs. For example, hospitals and health maintenance organizations are notorious for failing to account for patient sensitivities and are only now beginning to recognize that they might lose patients to other facilities if they ignore their needs.

The Atlanta Ballet Company used concepts of product positioning to change its image from a staid, conservative company to a new and exciting, high-quality art form. It used radio and TV advertising, price discounts, and innovative promotional techniques to convey the message. Its president, commenting on its repositioning strategy, said, "We need an aggressive marketing stance. The years are over when the arts can sell themselves just because they represent culture. I see us competing with the Braves, the Hawks, Saturday night bowling, and even Billy Joel concerts — the whole spectrum of entertainment."[15]

The Promotional Mix
The marketer of social services must develop promotion, distribution, and pricing strategies to deliver these services to user groups. The most important

element in the marketing mix for nonprofit firms is promotion. Nonprofit agencies frequently use (1) advertising, (2) personal selling, and (3) public relations as means of attracting funds and influencing users.

Advertising

Agencies such as the United Fund, the American Cancer Society, and CARE have been advertising for years. Slogans such as "55 mph, a speed we can live with", and "A mind is a terrible thing to waste," and symbols such as Smokey the Bear are examples of communications designed to change behavior.

Many campaigns are ineffective because they are trying to change the behavior of an unmotivated public. Rothschild cites the difficulty of getting people to stop littering or to conform to speed limits because there are few personal benefits in doing so and the public is generally uninvolved in these issues.[16] Wiebe studied four social issue campaigns to determine why some were successful. In citing the success of Kate Smith's bond drive in World War II, Wiebe found four factors that contributed to effective influence: (1) a motivated public (patriotism), (2) directed action (buy bonds), (3) a mechanism for action (buy bonds in banks, post offices, by telephone), and (4) ease of action (many centers to purchase bonds, short distances to travel). Services that meet these criteria might find advertising an effective means of influencing behavioral change.[17]

Advertising is used not only to influence users, but also to influence donors. The most frequently used medium for this purpose is direct mail. CARE uses direct-mail advertising to reach past givers and keeps detailed records of the results.[18] Stanford University divides donors by how much they gave, when they last donated money, and whether this was the first donation. Letters vary by frequency and by content, depending on these factors.[19]

Personal selling

Nonprofit agencies use personal selling to contact the small proportion of donors who contribute the largest portion of funds. Stanford uses personal solicitations to appeal to donors who have the potential to contribute large amounts. The United Fund found that one percent of its contributors donated 10 percent of its funds.[20] When giving is so concentrated, personal selling is a natural means of showing personal attention and gearing the message to the individual donor. When donations come from many minor donors, then advertising or direct mail should be used instead of or in addition to personal selling.

Nonprofit agencies also use personal selling to influence clients. Whereas donors are contacted by fundraisers, direct contacts with clients are made by change agents (outreach workers, family planners, community organizers.)[21]

The problems cited in Chapter 22 in utilizing personal selling to deliver services also apply to nonprofit agencies: frequently they fail to recruit, direct, and motivate their sales personnel adequately. The difficulty is compounded by the fact that nonprofit agencies must often rely on volunteers rather than trained professionals to raise funds or to influence changes in behavior.

Public relations

Public relations frequently is more important for nonprofit organizations than for profit-making ones. As we have noted, nonprofit firms serve many publics and are more subject to government influence. As a result they require public relations to deal with these different constituencies. Nonprofit organizations will use lobbyists, spokespersons in public forums, and news media to express their positions and advertise their services.

Children's Memorial Hospital in Chicago has effectively used public relations. Its director of public relations is responsible for:

- coordinating all dealings with media, either responding to media inquiries or initiating stories;

- promoting special events such as Children's Art Fairs and Community Festivals;

- producing and distributing publications such as the hospital's annual report and *Children's Voice*, a feature-news magazine; and

- maintaining good community relations through events such as open houses and hospital tours.[22]

Distribution

In distributing its services the nonprofit firm faces the problems cited in Chapter 22 for services in general: the simultaneous production and delivery of these services requires that they be easily accessible.

Distribution strategies should be directed to both donors and users. Donations can be stimulated by increasing the number of locations where contributions can be made. An example is the large number of Salvation Army collectors who solicit funds between Thanksgiving and Christmas.

Location can also be a strategy to stimulate use. Some colleges have added branches in suburban areas to increase enrollments. Adelphi College in New York conducted courses on a commuter train at one time, an unusual application of distribution strategy by a nonprofit institution. Some nonprofit agencies use intermediaries; for example, performing arts organizations may use ticket agencies, or charitable organizations may hire professional fundraisers. But in most cases, delivery of services is direct from the agency to the user.

A more complex distribution channel for a nonprofit agency is shown in Figure 23-5. The National Safety Council distributes bulletins, films, and leaflets and conducts training courses on the prevention of drunk driving. Its materials are distributed to 150 local safety councils, which then distribute the materials to business firms, service organizations, schools, police agencies, or directly to drivers.

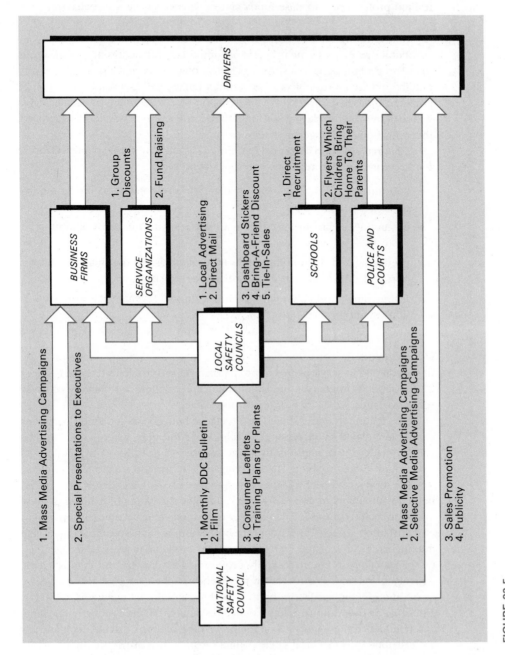

FIGURE 23-5
An example of a complex distribution channel for a nonprofit agency

Source: Philip Kotler and Gerald Zaltman, "Social Marketing: An Approach to Planned Social Change," *Journal of Marketing* 35 (July 1971): 11.

Price

A major difference between profit and nonprofit firms is that the former try to find the price that maximizes profits, whereas the latter try to set a "fair price."[23] Many nonprofit agencies do not expect to recoup expenses through the price charged. They price to recover a reasonable amount of their costs and try to cover the difference through contributions, grants, or subsidies. The postal service, the performing arts, mass transit, and many colleges price in this manner.

However, nonprofit marketers must take account of the nonmonetary as well as the monetary costs of their services. Health care facilities should be aware of the costs of waiting time, inconvenience, discomfort, and insecurity in being under someone else's control.[24] Minimizing these costs would attract more patients to a particular health care facility. Alcoholics Anonymous charges a very high nonmonetary cost for membership — commitment not to drink and public admission of one's problem.[25]

Consumer Rights and Marketing Management's Responsibility to the Consumer

The discussion of not-for-profit marketing illustrates that marketing techniques can be used to further socially responsible causes such as discouraging smoking, eliminating drug abuse, conserving the environment, and saving energy. In each of these cases social agencies have used promotional techniques to influence the public to change its behavior and have attempted to distribute relevant information to further these ends.

Marketing managers in social agencies undoubtedly realize that their purpose is to use marketing techniques to further important social ends. But what of marketing managers in profitmaking enterprises? They too have a broader social responsibility than their day-to-day activities suggest; a responsibility to consumers to ensure that they will be given adequate information to make a sound choice, and that they will be sold safe products. In this section we will consider the responsibilities that marketing management has to the consumer. We will first list some key consumer rights, and then consider three agencies in our society that have a role in ensuring these rights: (1) consumer agencies and individuals, (2) government, and (3) business organizations, particularly marketing management.

CONSUMER RIGHTS

In 1962 President John F. Kennedy sent to Congress a *Special Message on Protecting the Consumer Interest*, the first message ever delivered by a president on this topic. Kennedy spelled out four rights that have come to serve as a basis for consumer protection:

1. *The right to safety* — to be protected against the marketing of goods which are dangerous.

2. *The right to be informed* — to be protected against misleading information, and to be given the facts to make an informed choice.

3. *The right to choose* — to be assured access to a variety of products and services through the workings of a competitive market place.

4. *The right to be heard* — to be assured that consumer interests will receive full consideration in the formulation of government policies.[26]

Since the formulation of these consumer rights, two additional consumer rights have received increasing attention and should be added to the list:

5. *The right to a clean environment* — to be assured that business will act to maintain the integrity of the environment and our resources for future generations.

6. *The right to be a minority consumer without being disadvantaged* — to ensure that minority and low-income consumers will receive the same access to goods, to information, and to lower prices as other consumers.

Three primary institutions in our economy are concerned with ensuring consumer rights as illustrated in Figure 23-6. Consumer agencies and activists operate to provide consumers information to improve their basis for choosing products and services, and to increase consumer consciousness in the marketplace. Government operates through legislation and regulation. Business attempts to ensure consumer rights by self-regulation.

CONSUMER AGENCIES AND ACTIVISTS

Consumer agencies are organizations that are formed to further consumer protection and to ensure consumer rights. Few such organizations have been established on a national basis. Two are Consumers Union and the Better Business Bureau. Both are impartial third parties that attempt objectively to evaluate products and assess consumer complaints.

More attention has been given to individual consumer activists than to these agencies as vehicles for ensuring consumer rights. The best known of these activists, Ralph Nader, became prominent in the 1960s with his exposés of the automobile industry's failures to maintain safety standards. Since then Nader has recruited lawyers and other volunteers into task forces (Nader's Raiders) to protect consumer interests in specific areas and to uncover fraudulent business practices.

Consumerism

The activities of consumer activists and agencies to protect consumer rights have come to be known as **consumerism.** Consumerism is not new. At

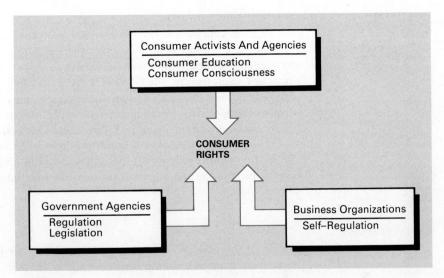

FIGURE 23-6
Agencies involved in ensuring consumer rights

Source: Adapted from Jagdish N. Sheth and Nicholas Mammana, "Why Consumer Protection Efforts Are Likely to Fail," Faculty Working Paper, No. 104, College of Commerce and Business Administration, University of Illinois at Urbana-Champaign, April 11, 1973, p. 3. Reprinted by permission.

intermittent periods consumer protection has been a national issue since the turn of the century. For example:

- Upton Sinclair's exposé of the conditions in Chicago's meat-packing houses in his book, *The Jungle,* was instrumental in the creation of the Food and Drug Administration in 1906.

- Exposés in the 1930s of unsafe medicines, cosmetics, and foods led to an enlargement of the powers of the Federal Trade Commission.

- In the 1960s Rachel Carlson's book *Silent Spring* and Nader's *Unsafe at Any Speed* exposed actions by the chemical and automobile industries that endangered consumers.

- The 1970s saw greater emphasis on providing consumers with information; for example, requirements for unit pricing information, open dating of perishables, and nutritional labeling. The drive to more consumer information was spurred by consumer activists such as Ralph Nader, Esther Peterson, and Betty Furness.

Limits of Consumerism

Despite their activities, consumer activists and agencies have had less effect in promoting consumer rights than government and business. Consumer activists and agencies simply do not have the power to sway government or business when their interests vary. The problem is that consumerism is "a conglomeration of separate groups each with its own particular concerns . . . labor organizations, consumer cooperatives, credit unions, consumer educators, the product-testing and consumer education organizations, state and local consumer organizations."[27]

Furthering the difficulty of consumer interest groups is the Reagan Administration's antiregulatory stance. As we noted in Chapter 3, the result has been a lessening of the emphasis on controls over advertising and resource conservation.

GOVERNMENT

In each of the periods of consumerist activity we cited, government was an active participant in ensuring consumer rights. Specifically:

■ The turn of the century saw the establishment of the Food and Drug Administration to regulate interstate commerce in adulterated foods and drugs, and the Federal Trade Commission to control deceptive and unfair trade practices.

■ In the 1930s the *Robinson Patman Act* was passed to prohibit price discrimination, and the *Wheeler-Lea Amendment* to the Federal Trade Commission Act was passed to control deceptive and misleading advertising.

■ The 1960s saw the passage of the:

☐ *Cigarette Labeling Act* requiring cigarette manufacturers to label cigarettes hazardous to health,

☐ *Fair Packaging and Labeling Act,* which declares the deceptive packaging of certain consumer goods illegal;

☐ *Child Protection Act,* which allows the Food and Drug Administration to remove dangerous children's products from the market; and

☐ the *Truth-in-Lending Act,* which requires full disclosure of all finance charges in consumer credit agreements.

■ In the 1970s new regulatory agencies, namely the Consumer Product Safety Commission and the Environmental Protection Agency, were formed to protect consumer interests. The Federal Trade Commission also took a more activist stand during this period in (1) investigating the effect of television advertising on children, (2) insisting that certain firms engage in advertising to correct deceptive claims, and (3) requiring full disclosure on the package of potentially harmful product features.

MARKETING MANAGEMENT'S RESPONSIBILITY TO THE CONSUMER

The third agency responsible for protecting consumer rights is business. Marketing managers, in particular, have a responsibility to ensure that each of the six consumer rights listed previously will be protected. They must:

- test adequately for product safety,
- provide the consumer with adequate and reliable information,
- give the consumer an adequate choice of products that meet his or her needs,
- provide a means for consumers to register complaints,
- control pollution and be conscious of the use of scarce resources in production and marketing, and
- try to protect the disadvantaged from higher prices, inadequate information, and poor distribution.

The question is whether marketing will accept these responsibilities in the interest of furthering self-regulation, or whether they will abdicate these responsibilities to government in the expectation of further legislation, more controls, and the establishment of more regulatory agencies. The clear preference of businesspeople, from both a pragmatic and an ideological standpoint, is for self-regulation rather than additional government regulation. But business has at times failed to regulate itself adequately — for example, pollution of the waterways by the chemical industry or the failure of some large companies to recall unsafe products immediately. Moreover, the American public has become more mistrustful of business's capability to regulate itself. In a 1968 survey that asked respondents whether business strikes a fair balance between profits and the public interest, 70 percent said yes. When the same question was asked in 1979, only 19 percent said yes.[28]

On the positive side, many marketing organizations have been moving toward more effective self-regulation in the areas of standards for children's advertising, labeling, and product safety. In addition, these organizations have attempted to ensure consumer rights by improving communications with consumers and by developing programs to educate consumers. Over 600 major companies, among them J. C. Penney, Eastman Kodak, Western Union, and the major automobile companies, have established consumer affairs offices headed by a top-level executive.[29] These departments are designed to:

- represent consumer interests in the company,
- receive and resolve consumer complaints, and
- disseminate information to consumers on the purchase and use of company products[30]

Many companies have also begun consumer education programs. There was a growth in the number of these programs in the late 1970s because of inflation and the energy crisis. The purpose of these programs is to "aim to teach people how to seek out, use, and evaluate consumer information so that they can improve their ability to purchase or consume the products and services they deem most likely to enhance their well-being."[31] For example, J. C. Penney employs a staff of home economists who serve consumers by organizing educational programs such as sewing schools through local stores.[32] Such programs represent the positive traditions of marketing in reflecting a desire to further consumer rights and interests.

Summary

The development and application of marketing plans and strategies by nonprofit institutions is known as not-for-profit marketing. Nonprofit institutions include cultural, educational, philanthropic, social, religious, and public agencies. Their products and services are designed to improve individuals, win them over to social ideas, change their behavior, or disseminate information that will benefit them.

Nonprofit agencies offer primarily services. These services differ from those offered by profitmaking organizations in that (1) benefits of nonprofit services are not as apparent to consumers, (2) nonprofit services involve more nonmonetary costs, and (3) the purpose of these services is frequently to change behavior. These characteristics create several difficulties for the marketer of nonprofit services. It is more difficult to:

- formulate and position nonprofit services,
- develop market segments for these services,
- influence target groups,
- evaluate the effectiveness of the marketing effort, and
- control marketing resources used in trying to influence people.

Further complicating the task of marketing managers is that they must market to donors to attract funds and to users to deliver their services.

Despite these difficulties, nonprofit agencies should develop marketing strategies at two levels, the corporate (strategic) level and the individual service level. Strategic planning is rarely performed by nonprofit agencies, but should include the development of corporate growth and product portfolio strategies. Strategies at the individual service level require defining target segments for the agency's services, positioning the services, developing a promotional mix of advertising, personal selling, and public relations directed to both donors and users, pricing the services, and delivering them to user groups.

We concluded by considering consumer rights and the broader responsibilities of marketing management to the consumer in both the profit and the nonprofit sector. Consumer rights to safety, to information, and to a variety of products in the marketplace must be ensured. Three groups have had a role in ensuring these rights — consumer activists and agencies, the government, and business organizations. Marketing management in business organizations must ensure product safety, adequate and reliable product information, and an adequate choice of products to satisfy consumer needs. Marketers prefer to ensure consumer rights through industry self-regulation rather than through government regulation. Recently, marketing organizations have demonstrated greater responsibility to the consumer by establishing consumer affairs departments and developing consumer education programs.

Questions

1. What characteristics of nonprofit services make them more difficult to market than services sold for a profit?

2. An executive of a large philanthropic organization has just finished an executive program on not-for-profit marketing. The course has reinforced the executive's feelings that "Marketing techniques applied to philanthropic organizations are of limited use. I do not see any great increase in expenditures on advertising or direct mail in our industry into the 1990s." Do you agree with the statement? Why or why not?

3. Nonprofit agencies, particularly those which further social ideas and causes, have sometimes been called *change agents.*

   □ What is the relevance of the term?

   □ How can these change agents use *demarketing* techniques to further social causes and ideas? Provide an example.

4. Of the various nonprofit agencies listed on page 728, which do you think have the most difficulty in marketing their services? Which have the least difficulty? Why?

5. Many nonprofit organizations must market to donors as well as to customers (clients). How does marketing to donors differ from marketing to customers in terms of:

   □ the promotional mix,

   □ the types of appeals used,

   □ distribution.

6. A marketing manager who moved from a large consumer packaged goods company to head the marketing effort for a large philanthropic agency said, "My former job was a piece of cake compared to this one.

Not only is marketing more complicated here; it's less controllable." Explain in what ways the development of marketing strategies is more complicated and less controllable in nonprofit agencies.

7. The director of marketing at a large cultural institution has felt frustrated in dealing with top management and trying to influence them to use more constructive pricing and promotional strategies to market musical and theater events. She says, "I am beginning to think that top management feels there is no reason to be marketing oriented because they are used to being in a sellers' market. But that may change, forcing them to take a closer look at marketing techniques."

☐ What factors are likely to cause top management to be more marketing oriented in nonprofit organizations?

☐ Under what conditions are nonprofit organizations more likely to be marketing oriented?

8. Apply the corporate development strategies for a college in Figure 23-2 to another type of nonprofit service such as a philanthropy or a cultural institution.

☐ In so doing specify the alternative strategies cited in Figure 23-2 and the advantages and disadvantages of each.

☐ Why is the term *corporate development* rather than *corporate growth* used in referring to these strategies?

9. Develop a hypothetical service portfolio matrix for a large cultural institution such as the Kennedy Center in Washington, or Lincoln Center in New York. Position various services in the matrix (e.g., a summer rock series in the park for teenagers). Make any assumptions you wish regarding which services are stars, cash cows, problem children, or dogs. (Remember this is a hypothetical example). What are the strategic implications of your matrix?

10. Consider the four factors found by Wiebe to contribute to the success of social issues and campaigns in influencing the public: (1) motivation, (2) directed action, (3) a mechanism for action, and (4) ease of action.[33] How successful would you predict the following campaigns will be based on each of Wiebe's four points:

☐ a campaign by the Department of Transportation to influence people in urban areas to switch from autos to mass transit,

☐ a campaign by the Post Office to mail early for Christmas,

☐ a campaign by the American Cancer Society to influence smokers to quit, and

☐ a campaign by the National Highway Administration to influence drivers and passengers to stop littering the nation's highways?

11. A large, privately endowed college is trying to increase lagging enroll-

ments because it is starting to use its endowment to fund services. It has developed promotional strategies to reach donors through direct mail, and prospective students through direct mail and newspaper advertising. A consultant suggests that the college consider developing new distribution strategies to reach donors, and new service delivery systems to attract students.

☐ How could the college utilize distribution strategies to influence donors?

☐ How could it develop new service delivery systems to attract students?

12. One auto marketing executive commented on marketing management's responsibilities to the consumer as follows: "Consumerism has received more attention than it deserves. Nader's Raiders give the impression that big business is out to take advantage of the consumer at every turn. Self-regulation works pretty well in our industry. We're not out to make unsafe products or to mislead the public."

☐ Do you agree that the public can rely on business to safeguard its rights?

☐ Under what circumstances is marketing management more likely to be concerned about consumers' rights?

Notes

1. Michael S. Joyce, "Grants and Philosophy: The Foundation Perspective," *The 1978 Longwood Program* (Newark, Del.: University of Delaware, 1978), Vol. 10, p. 5.

2. Karen F. A. Fox and Philip Kotler, "The Marketing of Social Causes: The First 10 Years," *Journal of Marketing* 44 (Fall 1980): 29.

3. Ibid., p. 26.

4. Thomas C. Kinnear and Kenneth L. Bernhardt, *Principles of Marketing* (Glenview, Ill.: Scott, Foresman, 1983), p. 701.

5. Ibid., p. 702.

6. Michael L. Rothschild, "Marketing Communications in Nonbusiness Situations or Why It's So Hard to Sell Brotherhood Like Soap," *Journal of Marketing* 43 (Spring 1979): 11–20.

7. Paul N. Bloom and William D. Novelli, "Problems and Challenges in Social Marketing," *Journal of Marketing* 45 (Spring 1981): 82–83.

8. Ibid., pp. 81–86.

9. Ibid., p. 81.

10. Ibid., pp. 81–82.

11. Alan R. Andreasen, "Nonprofits: Check Your Attention to Customers," *Harvard Business Review* 60 (May–June 1982): 105–10.

12. William Lazer and James D. Culley, *Marketing Management* (Boston: Houghton Mifflin, 1983), pp. 829–30.

13. Philip Kotler, *Marketing for Nonprofit Organizations* (Englewood Cliffs, N.J.: Prentice-Hall, 1982), p. 214.

14. Lazer and Culley, *Marketing Management,* p. 836.

15. "Putting a Spotlight on Atlanta's Ballet," *The Atlanta Constitution,* July 2, 1980, p. 5-c.

16. Rothschild, "Marketing Communications in Nonbusiness Situations," p. 16.

17. G. D. Wiebe, "Merchandising Commodities and Citizenship on Television," *Public Opinion Quarterly* 15 (Winter 1951): 679–91.

18. Benson P. Shapiro, "Marketing for Nonprofit Organizations," *Harvard Business Review* 51 (September–October 1973): 123–32.

19. "Stanford University: The Annual Fund," in Christopher Lovelock and Charles Weinberg,

eds., *Cases in Public and Nonprofit Marketing* (Scientific Press, 1977), pp. 73–88.

20. Shapiro, "Marketing for Nonprofit Organizations," p. 128.

21. Kotler, *Marketing for Nonprofit Organizations,* p. 333.

22. Ibid., pp. 377–78.

23. M. Mushkat, "Implementing Public Plans: The Case for Social Marketing," *Long Range Planning* 13 (August 1980): 27.

24. "Health Care," *Marketing News,* July 25, 1980, p. 22.

25. Shapiro, "Marketing for Nonprofit Organizations," p. 130.

26. Executive Office of the President, *Consumer Advisory Council, First Report* (Washington, D.C.: United States Government Printing Office, October 1963), pp. 5–8.

27. Robert O. Hermann, "Consumerism: Its Goals, Organizations and Future," *Journal of Marketing* 34 (October 1970): 56.

28. "The Corporation Haters," *Fortune,* June 16, 1980, p. 126.

29. Richard T. Hise, Peter L. Gillett, and J. Patrick Kelly, "The Corporate Consumers Affairs Effort," *MSU Business Topics* 26 (Summer 1978): 17–26.

30. Leonard L. Berry, James S. Hensel, and Marian C. Burke, "Improving Retailer Capability for Effective Consumerism Response," *Journal of Retailing* 52 (Fall 1976): 5.

31. Paul N. Bloom, and Mark J. Silver, "Consumer Education: Marketers Take Heed," *Harvard Business Review* 54 (January–February 1976): 33.

32. Ibid., p. 40.

33. Wiebe, "Merchandising Commodities and Citizenship," pp. 679–91.

Glossary

Acceptable price range A price range the customer views as realistic. If the product is priced below this range, quality is suspect. If the product is priced above, the consumer refuses to buy.

Adaptive control system A proactive system of identifying and correcting deviations in marketing performance before they occur. If an environmental condition changes (e.g., competitive couponing), the marketer can adjust marketing plans to account for the effects of the environmental change rather than react to the effects of the change after the fact.

Adaptive strategy A marketing approach whereby the needs and attitudes of consumers are determined and products are then developed to meet existing needs, with promotional policy guided by existing attitudes.

Advertising allowances Allowances provided by the manufacturer to the retailer or wholesaler for the purpose of encouraging the reseller to advertise the manufacturer's product.

Advertising wearout As the frequency of advertisements in a particular medium increases, the impact on the target audience of each additional advertisement decreases. This degree of advertising wearout depends upon both the message and the media used.

After-the-fact control systems Compares actual product performance at the end of a planning period to expected performance and determines the causes for any deviations in sales results. On this basis, management can institute changes in both marketing objectives and strategies to increase prof-

itability in the next planning period. One shortcoming of this approach is that it corrects for deviations after they occur rather than before.

Aspiration group A group that a consumer aspires to be associated with, but that he or she is not a member of.

Attention The process of taking note of a marketing communication. Attention is selective since consumers are most likely to note information relevant to their needs and consistent with their beliefs and attitudes.

Attitudes Enduring systems of positive or negative evaluations, emotional feelings, and action tendencies with respect to an object. Consumer's overall liking or preference for an object. A learned predisposition to respond consistently with respect to a given object.

Battle of the brands The fight for retail shelf space and consumer dollars between controlled and national brands. Controlled brands have a price advantage and national brands have an advertising advantage.

Behavioral segmentation Identification of consumer groups by differences in behavior (e.g., users versus nonusers or heavy versus light users).

Benefit segmentation Identification of a group of consumers based on similarity in needs. Often marketing opportunities are discovered by analysis of consumers' benefit preferences. Frequently, one or more segments are identified that are not being adequately served by existing brand alternatives.

Benefit structure analysis This approach to new product development focuses on benefits that consumers consider important to their purchasing decision. The greater the distance between the degree to which a benefit is desired and the degree to which that desire is met, the greater the opportunity for the introduction of a product to meet this need.

Boston Consulting Group (BCG) product portfolio analysis This approach to product portfolio analysis classifies products by their position in the product life cycle and their market share relative to competition. Cash flow is the criterion of performance since the analysis emphasizes the need to finance products with high growth and market share potential with the cash provided by established products.

Brainstorming A group method of generating new product ideas in which discussion is free flowing, and individuals are encouraged to propose any idea, even if it seems remote. No criticism is allowed, and group members are encouraged to improve upon other member's ideas.

Brand image Represents overall perception of the brand, formed from information about the brand and past experience. The set of beliefs that forms a complete picture of the brand.

Brand leveraging Taking advantage of a strong brand image by introducing related items under the well-known brand name.

Brand loyalty Commitment to a certain brand because of prior reinforcement (satisfaction as a result of product usage). Brand loyalty is a result of two components: (1) a favorable attitude toward the brand, (2) repurchase of the brand over time.

Brand management system An organizational system adopted by many leading consumer goods firms in which the responsibility for brand strategy and performance, including profitability, is assigned to one individual, the brand or product manager.

Brokers Intermediaries who do not have continuous relationships with one seller but rather inform various sellers of possible buyers and negotiate deals between buyer and seller on a commission basis.

Buying center The decision-making unit to select products and vendors in an organization.

Cannibalization One product in the line stealing sales from others in the line resulting in lower net revenues than expected. This is most likely to happen if the products are not sufficiently different from one another in the consumer's mind.

Cash cows Low-growth, high-market-share goods, as classified by product portfolio analysis. They generate large amounts of cash that are sometimes used to finance other products, i.e., problem children.

Change strategy A marketing approach in which the firm attempts to change the needs or attitudes of the consumer in order to influence purchasing behavior. Changing consumer needs is usually more difficult than developing products to meet existing needs. Furthermore, changing needs is more difficult than changing attitudes.

Cluster analysis A computer program that groups respondents together by similarity so there is greatest similarity in ratings within groups and greatest difference between groups. (Statistically, the program groups consumers by minimizing within-group variance and maximizing between-group variance.)

Cluster sampling A probability sampling method that identifies geographic areas in the population as sampling units. Geographic units are selected randomly and respondents are then selected within these units in a multistage process. Used when a complete list of the population is unavailable.

Comparative advertising The naming of a competitive product in the marketer's advertisement. Advertisers use comparative advertising to point out weaknesses in and to create a less favorable attitude toward the competitive brand, thus increasing the likelihood of buying the marketer's brand. It has become an important means of competitive positioning.

Comparative influence Influence a membership group exerts in the process of comparing oneself to other members of the group. Provides a basis for comparing one's attitudes and behavior to those of the group.

Competitive parity Setting the promotional budget based on the promotional expenditures of key competitors or on the expenditures of the industry as a whole in order to maintain promotional parity with competitors.

Complementary marketers Companies with marketing facilities or contacts abroad that can use these to market and distribute products of other manufacturers that do not have such facilities or contacts. Expanding their product line permits them to reduce transportation and storage costs.

Complex decision making Decisions in which the buyer is motivated to undertake a process of active search for information. Based on this information, alternative brands are evaluated on specific criteria. The cognitive process of evaluation involves consumer perceptions of brand characteristics and development of favorable or unfavorable attitudes toward a brand. The assumption is that consumer perceptions and attitudes will precede and influence behavior.

Comprehension The organization and evaluation of information so that it can be used to evaluate brands or to be stored in memory for future use.

Concentrated segmentation Also referred to as a *market niche strategy,* this approach targets a single product to a single market segment. Best suited to a firm with limited resources because it avoids conflicts with major competitors in larger market segments.

Conjoint measurement A process that determines the consumer's utility for various product attributes. Consumers are given a limited number of product combinations from the range of all product combinations and are asked to rank order their preferences. Utilities are derived on this basis. Product combinations that were not tested can be evaluated from the derived utilities and the optimum combination of product attributes chosen.

Consumer agencies Organizations, such as the Consumers Union and the Better Business Bureau, formed to further consumer protection and to ensure consumer rights.

Consumer panels A sample of consumers who record their purchases for a wide range of goods over time (brand purchased, store in which bought, price paid, etc.). Such data permit researchers to track brand purchases over time and provides a behavioral measure of brand loyalty based on repeat purchases.

Consumerism The set of activities of independent consumer organizations and consumer activists designed to protect the consumer. Consumerism is concerned primarily with ensuring that the consumer's rights in the process of exchange are protected. A social movement seeking to augment the rights and power of buyers in relation to sellers.

Controlled brands Brands promoted and sold under the label of a wholesaler or retailer rather than of the manufacturer. Distinguished from private brands in that they are promoted.

Controlled market tests A type of preliminary market test in which one or two test cities are selected and the product distributed on a controlled basis to stores. Marketing mix components are varied between stores and sales are measured. In this way, variations in sales can be related to variations in the marketing mix.

Convenience sampling A method whereby sampling units are selected on the basis of convenience (e.g., accessibility). Because it is a nonprobability sampling technique, sampling error cannot be determined and the reliability of the results cannot be estimated.

Cooperative retail advertising A type of product-related advertising in which manufacturers and retailers pool resources to promote both the product and the store. Manufacturers offer retailers allowances to advertise the manufacturer's products, permitting retailers to insert the name of the store and, in some cases, details about the retail establishment.

Corporate growth strategies As an integral part of the corporate mission, these strategies provide a blueprint for the future of the firm by specifying the firm's relative emphasis on (1) market expansion for existing products, (2) internal development of new products, and (3) acquisition of new businesses.

Cost per thousand (CPM) The cost of reaching one thousand members of the general audience or target audience. This criterion tends to be used to evaluate print media and is determined by the following equation: Cost $\times$ 1000/Circulation to general or target audience = CPM

Cost-plus pricing A simple pricing method whereby the firm determines its costs and then adds the desired profit margin. This approach tends to encourage price stability since most competitors will arrive at similar acceptable margins.

Countersegmentation The trend away from segmentation strategies toward aggregation strategies, resulting from the greater price sensitivity of consumers.

Cross-tabulation A method of analyzing data that breaks out the category one variable by another.

Cultural values An especially important class of beliefs shared by the members of a society about what is desirable or undesirable. Beliefs that some general state of existence is personally and socially worth striving for. Cultural values in the United

States include achievement, independence, and youthfulness.

Culture   The implicit beliefs, norms, values, and customs that underlie and govern conduct in a society. The norms, beliefs, and customs learned from society. Culture leads to common patterns of behavior.

Deceptive pricing   A retailer's systematic advertisement of low prices on items that are not available to the consumer or on which hidden charges are added.

Decoding   The sequence of steps in consumer information processing from exposure to attention to comprehension of a message.

Delphi Technique   The Delphi Technique requires experts to make individual forecasts without meeting and to state their reasoning in writing. Forecasts are pooled and sent to participants who are then asked to make a second forecast. A consensus is usually achieved after three or four rounds. This method overcomes some of the problems of panel forecasts, namely strong participant personalities and senior management influence.

Demarketing   Using promotional tools to discourage consumption. A trend that has emerged recently from the realization that the availability of certain goods cannot be taken for granted and that consumption must be limited.

Demographics   Objective characteristics of consumers, such as age, income, or education. This information is characteristically used for media planning.

Depth interview   An unstructured, personal interview in which the interviewer attempts to get subjects to talk freely and to express their true feelings. Can be conducted individually or in groups (focus group interviews). The latter have the advantage of eliciting more information because of group interaction.

Derived demand   Demand for one product may be determined by the demand for the good the product is used to manufacture, i.e., the demand for industrial goods is derived from the demand for consumer goods.

Deterministic model   Predicts a particular course of action based on such input variables as consumer characteristics, brand attitudes, consumer needs, etc. Deterministic models attempt to predict behavior

in exact or nonprobabilistic terms (e.g., purchase versus no purchase).

Differentiated segmentation   A firm using this approach introduces many products within a product category to appeal to a variety of market segments. Separate marketing strategies are needed for each segment. By offering a full line of products, the firm establishes a strong identification with that product category.

Discriminant analysis   A data association technique that determines the degree to which variations in the independent variables explain the variation in the noncontinuous (categorical) dependent variables. Respondents are assigned to one of the groups in the dependent variable (e.g., heavy, medium, or light purchasers of a brand) based on the explanatory power of the independent variables (e.g., demographics or life styles).

Dissonance   A state of tension because information about a brand is not consistent with the consumer's expectations (e.g., negative information about a favored brand).

Distribution centers   Centralized distribution facilities that serve broader markets than warehouses. They maintain full product lines, consolidate large shipments from different production points, and usually have computerized order-handling systems.

Distributors   Wholesalers of industrial products.

Dogs   Products that are identified by product portfolio analysis as having low growth potential and low relative market share. They generate barely enough cash to sustain themselves and are candidates for divestment.

Drop shippers   Limited-service wholesalers who take title to the merchandise they sell but do not take physical possession. They obtain orders from wholesalers and retailers and forward these orders to the manufacturer, who then sends the goods directly to the wholesaler or retailer. Used mostly in the distribution of bulky goods that have high transportation costs (e.g., lumber).

Dumping   The practice of selling merchandise in foreign markets at prices lower than those charged in domestic markets to absorb excess production or inventory.

Encoding   The process of developing the marketing stimulus. The good advertising campaign is one in which the encoding process uses symbols and imagery that successfully communicate the product benefits to the consumer.

Environmental scanning system A system that evaluates information on environmental changes in order to identify future opportunities. Changes that may affect the scope of opportunity include competitive activity, technology, the economy, and social and cultural trends.

Ethnocentric firms International marketing organizations that view foreign operations as an extension of domestic strategies. Their international marketing objectives are motivated primarily by domestic operational conditions (i.e., utilizing excess capacity to drive down unit costs).

Exclusive dealing The contractual requirement by a seller that its customer handle only the company's line of products. If these contracts reduce competition, they violate the Clayton Antitrust Act.

Exclusive distribution A distribution strategy in which manufacturers grant dealers exclusive territorial rights. The retailer gains from a reduction in competition and the manufacturer obtains more direct control over retail operations and a greater sales commitment from the retailer. Exclusive distribution is most likely for high-priced products that are sold based on a quality image (e.g., cars, jewelry).

Exclusive territories Exclusive rights to a geographic area offered by manufacturers to wholesalers and retailers to prevent intermediaries from competing with one another. These contracts are judged on a case-by-case basis to determine whether they restrict competition and violate antitrust rulings.

Experience curve As a manufacturer's cumulative production volume increases over time, so does production experience. The firm learns to more efficiently manage its resources resulting in reduced costs per unit. The experience curve shows the decrease in per-unit production costs over time.

Experimentation Attempting to control extraneous factors to establish a cause and effect relationship between a marketing stimulus (e.g., advertising) and consumer responses (e.g., intention to buy or sales).

Export Management Companies (EMCs) Organizations that are similar to export trading companies except that they do not take title to goods and are paid on a commission basis. They serve as the export department for many domestic manufacturers by marketing and distributing their products overseas.

Export merchants Domestic wholesalers operating in foreign markets.

Export Trading Companies (ETCs) A domestic merchant, the export trading company buys the firm's merchandise and assumes all responsibility for distribution and marketing abroad. Smaller companies are likely to use ETCs because they reduce their costs and avoid the risk of marketing abroad.

Exposure The first step in information processing, exposure requires only that the consumer is present when the marketing stimulus occurs.

Factor analysis A mathematical procedure for determining the intercorrelation between items and reducing the items into independent components or factors to eliminate redundancy. Typically, factor analysis is used to reduce a great amount of data into its more basic structure.

Family brand strategy A strategy of including the firm's total product mix under one family name. Products are identified by the corporate name and the product category, not a brand name.

Flanker brands The introduction of new brands into a product category by an organization that already markets one or more brands in that category.

Focus group interview See Depth interview.

Franchise system A distribution system in which a parent company (usually the manufacturer) grants a wholesaler or retailer the right to sell the company's products exclusively in a certain area. One of the fastest-growing forms of distribution, franchised establishments account for about one-third of all retail sales.

Frequency The average number of times, within a specified time period, that an individual is exposed to the message as a result of the media plan.

Full-line forcing The contractual requirement that an intermediary carry a full line of the manufacturer's products in order to buy from the manufacturer. Such contracts are not illegal unless they are combined with exclusive territory contracts.

Full-service wholesalers Wholesale institutions that perform all the distributive functions required of a middleman—selling, extending credit, storage, and delivery.

General Electric (GE) product portfolio analysis   An approach to product portfolio analysis designed to overcome the weaknesses of the Boston Consulting Group approach, namely the assumption that there is a relationship between growth, share, and profitability. The GE approach considers factors other than growth and share, such as ease of competitive entry and production efficiencies. The General Electric approach analyzes products based on their market attractiveness and the capability of the company to exploit marketing opportunities. It evaluates investment alternatives on their profitability and provides a basis for developing product portfolio strategies.

Generics   Goods sold without brand names and identified only by their contents; "no-frills" goods. They are not advertised or promoted.

Geocentric firms   International marketing organizations that view foreign operations as an integral part of their overall growth plan rather than as a mere extension of domestic operations. They develop marketing strategies on a worldwide basis, taking into account consumer needs and local resources abroad.

Gross Rating Points (GRPs)   Also referred to as the *total number of exposures* produced by the media schedule, this measurement is determined by the reach times the frequency.

Habit   A connection between stimuli and/or responses that has become virtually automatic through experience, usually resulting in the purchase of the same brand. A limitation or absence of (1) information seeking and (2) evaluation of alternative brand choices.

Harvesting strategy   A method used by marketers to reap short-term profits by withdrawing most marketing expenditures and reducing manufacturing costs before pulling the product out of the market.

Heavy half   The fifty percent of a product's users who consume a greater than average amount of the good. A frequently stated principle is that in many categories the heavy half accounts for at least eighty percent of product usage.

Hierarchy of effects   Stipulates the sequence of cognitive stages the consumer goes through in reaching an intention to buy. Needs are formulated, beliefs are formed about the brand, attitudes develop toward the brand, and the consumer then forms an action predisposition.

High-involvement purchases   Purchases that are more important to the consumer, are related to the consumer's self-identity, and involve some risk. It is worth the consumer's time and energies to consider product alternatives more carefully in the high-involvement case. Therefore, a process of complex decision making is more likely to occur when the consumer is involved in the purchase.

Horizontal price fixing   Competitors within an industry agree to maintain a certain price, thus eliminating price competition and limiting consumer choice. This action is prohibited by the Sherman Antitrust Act.

Impulse buying   A tendency to buy on whim with little preplanning.

Industrial marketing   The marketing of goods and services used as inputs in the production processes of other goods. The demand for industrial goods and services is thus derived from the demand for the end products.

Inertia   A passive process of information processing, brand evaluation, and brand choice. The same brand is frequently purchased by inertia to save time and energy.

Informational influence   The influence of experts or experienced friends or relatives on consumer brands evaluations.

Infomercials   Cable television commercials that are longer and more detailed because of lower costs and more specialized interests of the audience. This type of advertising can contain more information than a network commercial; thus the name *infomercial.*

Intensive distribution   Distributing a product through most retail outlets in an area. Most often used for inexpensive, frequently purchased items. These are low-involvement products. If a store does not have a particular brand, the consumer will buy an alternative. Thus intensive distribution is necessary for these goods to avoid losing sales.

International marketing   The development of marketing strategies to sell goods abroad and to integrate these strategies across various countries. Factors that must be taken into account include cultural and linguistic differences and political and foreign exchange risks as well as differences in regulatory structures.

Intertype competition   Competition between different types of firms (e.g., drug stores and supermarkets) selling the same products.

Intratype competition Competition between the same types of retail firms (e.g., supermarkets).

Judgmental sampling A nonprobability sampling method whereby the sample chosen is based solely on the judgment of the researcher with no prior constraints placed upon selection.

Life style An individual's mode of living as identified by his or her activities, interests, and opinions. Life style variables have been measured by identifying a consumer's day-to-day activities and interests.

Limited-service wholesalers Wholesalers that do not perform all the services provided by the full-service wholesaler, offering savings to buyers who do not need these services.

Localized international strategies The development of international marketing objectives and strategies on a market-by-market basis to account for local variation in consumer needs, trade regulations, company resources, and other factors. Planning and implementation of marketing strategies are handled at the local level.

Locational analysis The identification of the best areas in which to locate a store based on the number of potential consumers in the area. Once the area is determined, specific sites should be evaluated based on such factors as size of the site, traffic flow, the number of competitive retailers nearby, and distance.

Loss-leader pricing A strategy used by retailers to increase the traffic in their stores. Popular brands are priced below the retailer's cost to encourage consumers to enter the store and buy other goods.

Low-involvement purchases Purchases that are less important to the consumer. Identity with the product is low. It may not be worth the consumer's time and effort to search for information about brands and to consider a wide range of alternatives. Therefore, low-involvement purchases are associated with a more limited process of decision making.

Macromarketing system All of the elements that constitute the marketing process, including the consumer, the components of the marketing strategy, marketing institutions, and the marketing environment.

Manufacturers' agents Agents that sell a company's product offering in a specific geographic area, often on an exclusive basis. They carry product lines of several noncompeting manufacturers and restrict their activities to selling to wholesalers, retailers, and industrial buyers. They do not take title to the goods they sell and are paid on a commission basis.

Market aggregation strategy A policy of directing a single product (or very few products) to the mass market. This strategy does not attempt to differentiate between market segments. Market aggregation achieves economies of scale in production, marketing efforts, and distribution. It is most profitable when the market consists of consumers with relatively homogeneous needs.

Market expansion The revision of marketing strategies for existing products to increase consumer demand by appealing to new market segments (e.g., through a product repositioning strategy).

Market niche strategy The identification and subsequent targeting of small, homogeneous segments of the market with special needs or characteristics that can be profitably served by firms that do not have the resources to challenge the market leaders in the larger segments of the market.

Market segmentation The process of subdividing a large undefined market into smaller groups of consumers with similar needs, characteristics, or behavior. This enables the marketer to effectively allocate marketing resources to satisfy the needs of a well-defined group of consumers.

Market segmentation strategy Appealing to a market segment with a clearly differentiated product or service offering designed specifically for the target market. Allocating marketing resources to satisfy the needs of a well-defined group of consumers. The identification of market segments enables the manager to develop marketing strategies geared to consumer needs.

Marketing All individual and organizational activities directed to identifying and satisfying customer needs and wants.

Marketing audit A periodic and comprehensive review of marketing operations. The marketing audit is designed to (1) identify changes in the environment requiring reassessment of marketing opportunities, (2) evaluate marketing planning and control procedures, and (3) appraise marketing strategy to determine if any changes would increase profitability.

Marketing concept The philosophy that all marketing strategies must be based on known consumer needs. Marketers must first define the benefits consumers seek from particular products and gear marketing strategies accordingly.

Marketing environment Forces beyond the direct control of the marketing manager (e.g., demographic, cultural, and regulatory trends) that shape demand and influence the resources available to the firm.

Marketing Information System (MIS) The system of people, technology, and procedures designed to acquire and generate information from both the marketing environment and the firm. Such information is integrated, analyzed, and communicated to improve marketing planning, execution, and control.

Marketing mix The marketing variables within the control of the marketing manager that are selected to elicit the desired response from the target market.

Marketing planning A function of the product or brand manager that involves developing the product, defining its target market, and formulating marketing strategies.

Marketing research The systematic collection and analysis of data and the presentation of findings regarding a specific marketing problem or opportunity.

Mark-up pricing A variation of cost-plus pricing in which the profit margin is determined as a percentage of the selling price rather than of the cost.

Membership group A group in which an individual is a member and has face-to-face communications with other members. Groups in which a person is recognized by others as belonging.

Merchandising A primary task of the salesperson of consumer goods, the goal of which is to encourage the use of the manufacturer's promotions (e.g., displays, discounts) by channel intermediaries.

Morphological analysis A structured creative group method in which group members (1) precisely formulate the problem, (2) identify parameters, (3) list all possible combinations of parameters, (4) evaluate the feasibility of all combinations, and (5) choose the best combinations.

Multidimensional scaling A set of computer programs that determine the relative position of brands and concepts in multidimensional space based on consumer similarity or preference ratings of these brands.

Multiple pricing A pricing policy whereby the consumer is offered several items for one price rather than pricing the items singly (e.g., four pieces for $.79 instead of $.20 each).

Narrowcasting A term used to describe the cable television medium. Because cable channels are oriented to more specialized interests than is network television, commercials can be directed to more specific and well-defined audiences.

National brands Brands that are marketed nationally by the manufacturer. Regional and local brands are sometimes lumped together with national brands to distinguish them from private brands and generics.

Need-gap analysis The identification of important consumer needs that are not being met by existing products. Defining such a gap represents an opportunity to the firm to meet these needs by introducing a new product or repositioning an existing one.

Needs Forces directed to specific goals that can be achieved by purchase behavior. The motive force for directing behavior to one brand or another.

Nonprobability sampling Sampling methods, including convenience, judgmental, and quota sampling, in which the probability of selecting a particular element of the universe is unknown, and thus it is not possible to measure the sampling error and reliability of the resulting statistics.

Normative influence The influence exerted on an individual to conform to group norms and expectations.

Norms Rules of behavior in particular circumstances that specify actions that are proper and those that are improper. Beliefs held by a consensus of a group concerning the behavior rules for individual members. Rules and standards of conduct (generally undefined) established by the group. Group members are expected to conform to these norms.

Not-for-profit marketing The marketing of goods and services by not-for-profit organizations (e.g., museums and schools).

Objective-task method This approach develops a promotional budget by specifically defining promotional objectives, determining the tasks required to meet those objectives, and estimating the costs associated with the performance of these tasks.

Odd/even pricing   Sometimes referred to as psychological pricing, odd/even pricing is used by manufacturers and retailers in the belief that consumers are more likely to purchase a product if its price ends with an odd number just under a round number (e.g., a price of $2.99 instead of $3.00).

Opinion leader   An individual who frequently exerts influence on others through word-of-mouth communication. One who exerts a disproportionately large amount of influence on others.

Optimal allocation principle   Allocating expenditures based on the relative impact of each promotional mix component on sales. Management should direct resources to that component of the promotional mix that produces the greatest marginal revenue over marginal cost. This means diverting resources to the component with the highest net contribution to profits.

Organizational buyer   One who buys not for personal use but to satisfy some organizational need. Examples are industrial purchasers who buy products as input into manufacturing processes and institutional purchasers who buy for such organizations as hospitals and schools.

Patterned standardization strategies   A compromise between standardized and localized international marketing strategies. This approach requires that the company establish global marketing strategies but leave the implementation of marketing plans to executives in local markets who are aware of national traits and customs. Strategy is developed at the corporate level, while tactics are developed at the local level.

Penetration strategy   A strategic option establishing a lower price for a new product entry. A mass marketing approach would be followed.

Perception   The process by which people select, organize, and interpret stimuli into a meaningful and coherent picture. The way consumers view an object (e.g., their mental picture of a brand or the traits they attribute to a brand).

Perceptual equilibrium/disequilibrium   Consumers seek to maintain equilibrium by screening out information that does not conform to their predispositions. When consumers choose information consistent with prior beliefs or interpret information to conform to these beliefs, they are processing information to ensure perceptual equilibrium. Acceptance of contradictory information means the consumer is in a state of perceptual disequilibrium.

Perceptual mapping   A group of quantitative techniques that seek to position various brands on a "map" based on the way they are perceived by the consumer. The closer one brand is to another on the map, the more similar it is to the other brand. The basic assumption is that if consumers see two brands as being similar, they behave similarly toward the two brands.

Perceptual organization   The organization of disparate information so that it can be comprehended and retained.

Personality   Personality variables reflect consistent and enduring patterns of behavior. Represents a set of consumer characteristics that have been used to describe target segments.

Physical distribution system   The subsystem of the distribution system that ensures the flow of goods from producer to consumer through the process of ordering, inventory control, warehousing, and transportation.

Portfolio test   A method used to pretest print advertisements. Respondents are shown a dummy magazine or a collection of advertisements and asked to look through them. They are then asked to recall the advertisement and its content.

Post-testing   The evaluation of marketing strategies once they have been implemented. By tracking product performance, this research determines if any adjustments in the strategies are needed so that they are more effective.

Predatory pricing   An attempt to reduce competition by pricing below cost, thus forcing the failure of existing competitors and deterring new entrants into the market. Once competition has decreased, the company can again raise its prices. This action is prohibited by the Sherman Antitrust Act.

Pretesting   Marketing research designed to determine which strategy alternative to implement to exploit a market opportunity.

Price discrimination   Price differences given by sellers to intermediaries or organizational buyers that are not offered equally to the same types of buyers. This action is prohibited by the Clayton Act and the Robinson-Patman Act.

Price elasticity   Measured by the percentage change in quantity purchased resulting from a percentage change in price. When the percentage change in quantity is less than the percentage change in price, consumers are relatively price insensitive and demand is inelastic (price elasticity index less than 1). When the percentage change in quantity is greater than the percentage change in price, consumers are relatively sensitive to price changes (price elasticity index greater than 1). The equation to determine the price elasticity index (PEI) is % change in quantity/% change in price = PEI

Price lining Introducing various brands in a product line at different prices, thus appealing to consumers with different price elasticities (e.g., the quality-conscious consumer, the average consumer, and the economy-minded consumer).

Primary data Data originally collected by the marketing organization for its own immediate well-defined purposes. Methods of collecting primary data include survey research and depth interviews.

Primary demand Total consumer demand for a product category.

Private brands Brands sold under a wholesaler's or retailer's label. Distinguished from controlled brands in that they are not promoted.

Proactive strategies Marketing strategies that attempt to anticipate future competitive actions and environmental trends to exploit the resulting market opportunities.

Probabilistic models Models that treat the response of consumers in the marketplace as the outcome of a probabilistic process over time. They attempt to explain brand loyalty and switching behavior based on past purchases.

Probability sampling Techniques in which every possible sampling unit drawn from a specified population has a known chance of being selected. As a result, the reliability of data from the sample can be estimated (i.e., the sampling error). Probability sampling methods include cluster sampling, simple random sampling, and stratified random sampling.

Problem children Products with low market share in high-growth markets. They require large injections of cash to improve market share. In this situation, management must decide whether to drop the product or continue to invest to support it.

Product The features of the item offered and the benefits, both tangible and intangible, that the consumer receives from it. Includes goods, services, and ideas.

Product cannibalism See Cannibalization.

Product concept A bundle of product benefits that can be directed to the needs of a defined group of consumers through symbolism and imagery. The product concept represents the organization of marketing stimuli into a coordinated product position that can be more easily directed to consumers.

Product-concept fit The degree to which the physical product meets the consumer's expectation based upon the product concept. This measurement can be estimated by comparing the results of the concept test and the product use test.

Production orientation An approach to the marketing process in which management concentrates its efforts on increasing output and reducing manufacturing costs. Selling is considered secondary based on the belief that high-quality products are scarce and can thus "sell themselves." The prevailing view is "we can sell what we produce."

Product Life Cycle (PLC) The phases a product goes through—introduction, growth, maturity, and decline. Changes are required in marketing strategies to meet changing consumer demand and competitive conditions at each phase. A brand's position on the life cycle directly influences positioning, advertising, pricing, and distribution strategies.

Product line consistency Refers to the demand relationship of the items in terms of their end use. If the products are related, the company can take advantage of multiproduct advertising and economies of scale in marketing efforts.

Product line depth A line's depth defines the extent of coverage of the product category by the firm. Some companies seek to provide a full line to satisfy a consumer's desire for a range of alternatives, while other companies may specialize in one or two goods.

Product line length The length of the product line refers to its diversity. An effective means of lengthening the line is through brand leveraging.

Product management system See Brand management system.

Product-market matrix A method of delineating product categories by market type. A matrix is constructed with product categories listed down the side and markets listed across the top. This process is vital to new product development because it identifies market segments whose needs are not being served by the firm and who therefore represent marketing opportunities.

Product Market Units (PMUs) Organizational product groupings, within strategic business units, aimed at broad markets. Individual brands within the PMUs are headed by product or brand managers who are each responsible for developing an effective marketing mix for the product.

Product mix All of the products offered by a particular firm or a strategic business unit within the firm.

Product mix strategies Developed by top and SBU management, these strategies outline which products will be added, supported, maintained, harvested, or deleted by the firm as well as changes in resource allocation among SBUs to improve the firm's overall profits.

Product portfolio analysis The process of classifying products or SBUs baseed on opportunity/ growth and the firm's current or potential ability to exploit opportunity. The firm utilizes this information to identify strong and weak performers and to allocate its resources.

Product portfolio strategies See Product mix strategies.

Product positioning The use of advertising and other marketing mix variables to communicate the benefits of the product.

Product positioning strategies Strategies to communicate product benefits to the consumer so as to achieve a distinctive position in the market.

Projective techniques Techniques used for detecting and measuring wants and attitudes not readily discernable through more direct methods. Consists of the presentation of ambiguous materials (e.g., ink blots, untitled pictures, etc.). In interpreting this material, the viewer "projects" tendencies of which he or she may be unaware or may wish to conceal. Diagnostic devices in which interpretation of ambiguous stimuli are taken to reveal something about the observer, based on previous experience and motives, needs, and interests in play at the time.

Property Fitting Program (PROFIT) A computer program used to associate a brand's position with evaluative attributes. The program identifies the position of each attribute by determining a vector that provides the best fit between the attribute and the brands in a perceptual map.

Pull strategy Promotional strategy (e.g., coupons, premiums, consumer advertising) directed at end users as a means of stimulating demand. This strategy "pulls" the product through the distribution channel.

Push strategy Promotional strategy (e.g., trade discounts, advertising allowances) directed to channel members. This approach is said to "push" the merchandise from the manufacturer through the channels of distribution.

Quota sampling A nonprobability sampling technique whereby the researcher sets quotas of respondents based on criteria determined by the researcher.

Rack jobbers Limited-service wholesalers who supply supermarkets and other retail stores with nonfood items such as housewares and health and beauty aids. The rack jobber owns the goods and the displays (racks) that are supplied and splits the profits with the retailer.

Reach The number of people or households exposed to one or more of the vehicles in the media plan during a specified time period.

Reactive strategies A marketing approach in which the firm responds to competitive actions rather than anticipating and planning for them.

Reference group Any group with which an individual identifies such that he or she tends to use the group as a standard for self-evaluation and as a source of personal values and goals. A group that serves as a reference point for the individual in the formation of beliefs, attitudes, and behavior. Such groups provide consumers with a means of comparing and evaluating their own brand attitudes and purchasing behavior.

Regression analysis A method of analysis that develops an equation that shows the contribution of each independent variable in explaining the variations in a continuous dependent variable.

Response elasticity segmentation Response elasticity measures a consumer's sensitivity to a particular marketing stimulus by associating a percentage change in the stimulus with a percentage change in the quantity purchased. Markets are then segmented by the degree of consumer sensitivity to the marketing stimulus.

Retailer-sponsored cooperatives A type of contractual system that integrates the distributive function among smaller retailers. In an effort to protect themselves against the larger chains with greater purchasing power, groups of smaller retailers acquire and operate their own wholesale facilities.

This permits them to obtain the quantity discounts available to the chains.

Retention The final step in information processing, retention of the advertising message is most likely to occur when the content of the message is relevant to the consumer's needs.

Sales agents Sales agents serve as an extension of the manufacturer's sales force, particularly in industrial marketing. Sales agents have fuller authority to set prices and terms of sales than manufacturer's agents and at times even assume the manufacturer's total marketing effort by specifying promotional and distribution activities for the product line. They specialize in certain lines of trade and are paid on a commission basis.

Sales orientation An approach to marketing a firm's products when management believes that consumers are unlikely to buy unless the company makes a substantial effort to influence them—the "hard sell."

Sales response function An attempt to determine the volume of sales associated with different levels of marketing effort (e.g., advertising expenditure). Such attempts are confounded by the impact on sales of factors other than the marketer's efforts. Sales response functions have been derived by statistical analysis and quantitative models.

Sales wave experiments A preliminary market test in which the new product is placed in the consumer's home for his or her use. Consumers are given the opportunity to repurchase the new product or competitive products up to six times at reduced prices (six sales waves). Researchers can then better estimate the repurchase rate of the new product.

Sample The selection of a subset of respondents from a larger universe.

Scanner system An in-store technology that uses laser beams to read the Universal Product Code (UPC) from packaged goods. The information contained in the UPC is then fed into a computer that tracks sales for inventory purposes and for marketing research.

Scrambled merchandising Occurs when retailers expand their product mix into higher margin items unrelated to their primary business for the purpose of increasing profits.

Secondary data Data collected previous to the current study and not designed specifically to meet the firm's immediate research needs. Sources of secondary data include syndicated research services and the government.

Selective demand Consumer demand for a particular brand within a product category.

Selective distribution Most often used for durable goods like small appliances, stereo equipment, and furniture, selective distribution is a compromise between intense and exclusive distribution. The marketer selects a limited number of intermediaries who can provide the desired sales support and service. Because durable goods have higher prices, consumers are more likely to shop around, enabling manufacturers to limit distribution. Selective distribution allows manufacturers more control over the way their products are sold and also decreases the likelihood of price competition between intermediaries.

Selective perception Consumers perceive marketing stimuli selectively to reinforce their needs, attitudes, past experiences, and personal characteristics. Selective perception means that the identical advertisement, package, or product can be perceived very differently by two consumers.

Service demand management Attempts to overcome the problems of service perishability by keeping service supply fairly constant and trying to smooth out demand (e.g., using differential pricing to shift demand from peak to nonpeak periods).

Services marketing The marketing of intangible services as opposed to tangible products. Because services cannot be stored, generally the service transfer is direct from seller to buyer.

Service marketing system The system responsible for service delivery and designed to facilitate interaction between the customer and the service provider. A marketing support system provides promotional, sales, and information services to support the service marketing system. A service marketing manager is responsible for service quality, the customer-service encounter, the demand for services, the service mix, and service productivity.

Service operations system A system within the service marketing firm that organizes the use of facilities and personnel. It manages the human resources of the service firm.

Service supply management Because it is not possible to maintain inventories of services, strategies must be developed to try to match supply and demand. Service supply management focuses on adjusting supply in accordance with the demand for services (e.g., performing only essential tasks during peak periods and nonessential tasks during slack periods).

Simple random sampling A probability sampling method in which every sampling unit has a known chance of selection, and the sample is selected directly from one universe.

Simulated market tests Experimental supermarket facilities established by research organizations to test new products in a retail environment. Consumers are given money and are invited to shop in the experimental store. Respondents are questioned both before and after shopping to determine whether the introduction of the new products changed their attitudes and purchasing intentions.

Skimming strategy A strategic option establishing a high price for a new product entry and "skimming the cream of the market" by aiming at the most price inelastic consumer. Advertising and sales promotion would be limited to specific targets, and distribution would be selective.

Social class A division of society made up of persons possessing certain common social and economic characteristics resulting in equal-status relations with one another and restricting interaction with members of other social classes.

Social marketing The marketing of social services by nonprofit organizations.

Standardized international strategies This approach to international marketing assumes that some products have universal appeal. It is thus unnecessary to develop individual marketing strategies on a market-by-market basis. Companies such as Pepsi-Cola, Ford, and Goodyear utilize this strategy. Its advantages over localized strategies are lower unit marketing costs and greater control over local marketing operations.

Standard price What consumers regard as a fair price which serves as a basis for judging other prices. There is a range around a standard price that is not likely to produce any change in behavior, such as a change in quantity consumed or a switch to another brand. Outside this range, however, price elasticity is greater, producing significant changes in behavior.

Stars A classification of product portfolio analysis that identifies products with high growth potential and high relative market share. These products require a lot of cash to maintain their growth rate. This rate will eventually slow and the stars may become cash cows.

Steering control systems A method of evaluating marketing performance during the planning period rather than at the end of the period. Performance projected during the period is compared to the performance projected at the beginning of the period. If performance deviates from objectives, corrective action is taken to bring the plan back into control.

Store audits A source of retail sales information for the manufacturer that measures retail sales by subtracting end of period inventory for a product from inventory at the beginning of the period plus shipments. A. C. Nielsen is one organization that conducts audits and supplies information to manufacturers on a syndicated basis.

Strategic Business Units (SBUs) Division level units within the organization that act as autonomous profit centers. SBU management is responsible for establishing strategic marketing plans. The boundaries of SBUs are generally defined by markets based on homogeneous consumer demand.

Strategic leveraging The process of determining the firm's competitive advantage and then committing all necessary resources to this area.

Strategic marketing planning A corporate-level function that (1) defines the corporate mission, (2) establishes guidelines for long-term corporate growth, (3) guides the development of the firm's overall product mix, and (4) allocates available resources to each of the firm's business units.

Strategic window A term used to describe a situation in which the firm's competencies are at an optimum to exploit marketing opportunities.

Stratified random sampling The universe is broken down into mutually exclusive groups (strata). A simple random sample is then chosen independently within each stratum.

Subculture That part of the total culture of a society that is distinct from society in certain respects; for example, an ethnic group, a social class group, a regional group. The ways of behaving that distinguish a particular group from a larger one.

Superstores Very large supermarkets that engage in extensive scrambled merchandising. They are at least twice as large as the average supermarket.

Syndicated research services Sources external to the firm that collect consumer and product information and sell it to subscribing clients. It is not collected for a singular purpose but rather for the multiple needs of various clients and is thus considered secondary data.

G-14 GLOSSARY

Synectics An idea-generation group method based on four concepts: (1) the importance of listening to all participants; (2) the belief that most ideas have some good qualities; (3) a common understanding of a well-defined problem; and (4) the identification of a specific group leader.

Target market A group of consumers with similar needs or characteristics to whom the firm's marketing efforts are directed.

Target return pricing Using a breakeven chart, the firm specifies the desired return on total costs at a certain sales volume and then determines the price that would produce the target return. Price leaders generally use this method to establish market price.

Test market A market in which the new product is tested prior to national introduction. The last step in the process of testing new products, permitting the marketer to evaluate all components of the marketing strategy.

Trade-off analysis A technique that provides a basis for determining the consumer's optimal combination of product characteristics. A limited number of concepts representing combinations of characteristics are presented to consumers. Consumers are asked their preference, and on this basis, an ideal combination of characteristics is identified.

Tying contracts The requirement by a manufacturer that a buyer purchase products not desired in order to obtain the products desired. Most courts have considered these contracts illegal per se.

Unbundled pricing An industrial pricing strategy whereby certain or all elements of the product-service mix are priced separately. Individual charges might be required because costs vary among buyers, all buyers do not need all elements of the product-service mix, or because prices on individual elements are open to negotiation.

Undifferentiated segmentation This approach is a compromise between market aggregation and market segmentation. The firm identifies a wide target market and then directs a single product to this broad segment. By targeting the same product to an aggregation of smaller segments, the firm can achieve economies of scale in both production and marketing efforts.

Universal Product Code (UPC) The set of numbered vertical lines that appear on most packaged goods. The code can be read by scanner systems and contain such information as product type, brand, weight, and expiration date.

Upscale discounting A retail strategy in which national brand name merchandise is sold in no-frill discount stores at lower prices than in department stores and specialty shops.

Vertically integrated channel systems Distribution systems in which institutions at different levels (e.g., manufacturer, wholesaler, and retailer) combine to distribute goods. Integration requires the management of the system so that common objectives (e.g., adequate inventory, quick delivery) are attained and conflicting ones (e.g., level of discounts, use of company's promotional aids) resolved.

Vertical price fixing This type of price fixing involves an agreement between manufacturers and retailers that the manufacturers suggested retail price will actually be charged by the retailer. Once thought of as as means of ensuring manufacturers' profits and legalized by fair trade laws, it is now considered in restraint of trade.

Videotext system Two-way (interactive) cable television systems in which the consumer can select information by requesting it through a home computer terminal and can also order merchandise through the terminal.

Voluntary simplicity A trend toward greater emphasis on a simpler life, self-sufficiency, and a return to the land, as manifested in simpler consumption patterns.

Wholesalers Organizations that buy and resell merchandise to other businesses. They sell to other wholesalers, retailers, and industrial buyers, but not to the final consumer.

Wholesaler-sponsored voluntary chains Groups of retailers organized by a wholesaler into an integrated chain operation. Both wholesaler and retailers benefit; costs are reduced because of increased purchasing power and more efficient wholesale operations.

Name Index

Aaker, David A., 220, 337, 349, 411, 412
Abell, Derek F., 53, 603, 622
Achabel, Dale D., 651
Ackoff, Russell L., 412
Allio, Robert J., 622
Allison, R. I., 349
Allport, Gordon W., 183
Allvine, Fred C., 30, 690
Alpert, J., 480
Alpert, Mark I., 349, 480
Andreasen, Alan R., 749
Ashe, Arthur, 172, 323
Assael, Henry, 146, 184, 220, 243, 245, 249, 348, 350, 520, 521, 522, 717, 723
Assael, Shaun, 480

Baier, Donald, 443
Bailey, Earl L., 480
Ballou, Ronald H., 522
Banting, Peter M., 481
Barksdale, Hiram C., 705, 723
Barry, Thomas E., 443
Basehart, J., 348
Bass, Frank M., 30, 249
Bauer, Raymond A., 184, 185
Beckwith, Neil, 185
Bellenger, Danny N., 184, 214
Bennett, Peter D., 185
Bentley, Trevor, 650
Bentz, William F., 651

Berger, Frank, 612
Bernhardt, Kenneth L., 481, 491, 554, 674, 691, 724, 749
Berry, Leonard L., 723, 724, 750
Blackwell, Roger, T., 560
Blattberg, Robert, 637, 651
Bloom, Paul N., 749, 750
Bobbe, Richard A., 442
Boddewyn, J. J., 723
Bogart, Leo, 350
Bonoma, Thomas V., 381
Borden, Neil H., 350
Boyd, Harper W., Jr., 147
Brehm, J. E., 350
Britt, Steuart Henderson, 412
Brock, Timothy C., 185, 348, 443
Brown, Phillip K., 337, 349
Bubb, Peter Lawrence, 142, 146, 147
Burgoyne, David, 443
Burke, Marian C., 350, 750
Busch, Paul, 348, 443
Buzzell, Robert D., 560, 621, 622

Capon, Neil, 350
Cardozo, Richard, 244, 249
Carlson, Rachel, 743
Carmone, Frank J., 289
Carroad, Connie A., 289
Carroad, Paul A., 289
Carter, Jimmy, 82
Cateora, Philip R., 690, 692

Chestnut, Robert W., 350
Clark, Colin, 723
Claxton, John D., 350
Claycamp, Henry J., 119
Clowes, K., 443
Coaker, James W., 481
Coen, Robert J., 411
Collins, B. J. K., 289
Connolly, Phyllis E., 442
Conran, Frank J., 249
Converse, Paul D., 138, 147
Cooper, R. G., 289
Corstjens, Marcel, 521
Cosby, Bill, 324
Cox, Keith, 184
Craig, C. Samuel, 348
Crane, Lauren E., 349
Cravens, David W., 220, 423
Crissy, W. J. E., 650
Cronkite, Walter, 323
Culley, James D., 737, 750
Cundiff, E. W., 350
Cunningham, Scott, 184, 185
Czepiel, John A., 709, 723

Darmon, Rene Y., 443
Davenport, J. William, Jr., 348
David, H. L., 350, 344
Davis, Harry L., 185
Day, George S., 220
Dean, Joel, 480
DeLozier, M. Wayne, 185

Company Index

Subject Index